PERSPECTIVES

Just Catfishing

For thousands of years before these times, men and women hunted, fished, and gathered. These ancestors lived this way as a matter of survival, though even paintings on cave walls show that they celebrated and surely enjoyed their encounters.

Times have changed, but not so much the basic nature of fishing. The spark to seek, to understand, and to interact with the natural world still burns within us. This is the reason so many of us fish—some to harvest fish for the table, for fish are nutritious and delicious.

We fish for sport, too, for fishing is a challenge. We puzzle over that which we can't easily see or touch through a water barrier. We seek to connect with this puzzle, these fish, with hook and line. So we offer up illusions, tricks—the right bait, the right fly, the right lure, presented in just the right way at the right time.

Fish cannot, we soon find, be bought or bribed. They do not care who we are. They respond best to patience and, finally and primarily, to understanding. For our ancestors, once again, success meant survival. The better they understood the nature of the animals pursued, and the better they became at finding and tricking them, the more successful they were in putting food over the fire.

Today, fishing is a break, a chance to get away from it all. It's a chance for parents and grandparents to connect with children, a chance for adults and children alike to connect with the natural world.

Fishing is a grand game, a sport, part of a lifestyle shared, not just with family and friends but also with millions of other anglers, casual and all consumed, across North America and around the world. Catfishing is, heart and soul, an integral part of this larger world—perhaps the finest proof that simplicity and excitement can at once prevail.

Really, it's just that simple. It's just fishing. It's just catfishing.

Doug Stange

INTRODUCTION

All Along The Road...

Catfish were here and fishing for them was an important part of fishing long before I wet a line for them or thought to write stories about them; and that will be so, long after I depart.

I was, however, lucky to be in the right place at the right time, with a curiosity about and an abiding love for these fish. So, I had a unique chance to live life as a writer and hardcore angler close to the vest through 25 of the most revolutionary years in catfishing.

Part of my approach to fishing and writing has always been to blend the best available science with intense field observation, to offer advice about how to catch fish. Fact remains that most folks don't want to go into the field and not catch anything. I've never been bashful about telling folks how to proceed in their own best interest.

I have also long enjoyed using stories to make points. The classic Me-And-Joe-Went-Fishing Stories from an earlier era seem to have fallen on disfavor during the 1980s and 1990s; but I've always considered my Me & Toad and Me & Toad & Zacker Went Fishing stories to be an integral part of capturing the nature of this fishing, and teaching something along the way.

In this book I chronicle events as they played forth in my neck of the catfishing woods, during a period from the mid 1970s, when I wrote my first articles about catfishing, to about year 2000, a point at which in my estimation catfishing had changed enough to enter a new era—a truly modern era.

All along the way, so much challenge and what fun. The mind tumbles back through all the years, some of the fish, many of the situations, especially living the good life in the field with my buddies Toad Smith and Zacker.

All I wanted to do was teach anglers how to cat more catfish, to change a little bit of how the world looks at catfish and catfishing, and to have fun along the way. So, by hook or crook, design and perhaps divine intervention, part of my lifetime has taken us All Along the Road to the Modern Age of Catfishing.

Take care and good fishing to you.

Doug Stange

In-Fisherman PRESENTS

Life & Times In Catfish Country

ALL ALONG THE ROAD TO THE MODERN AGE OF CATFISHING

IN THE BEGINNING— PRE HISTORY & SETTING THE SCENE

THE TOAD SMITH ERA

21

95

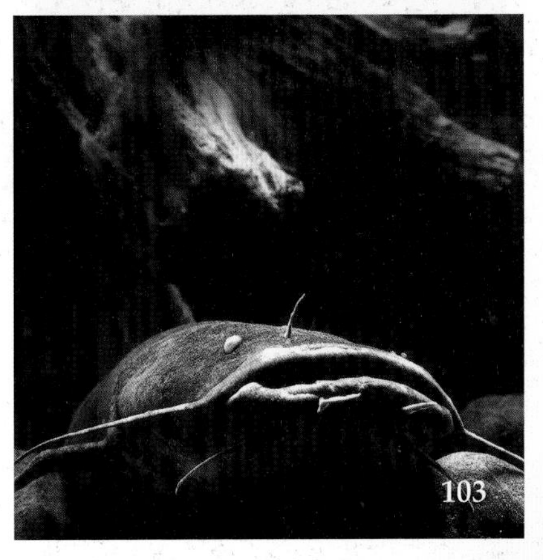

103

TOAD PASSES, THE STORIES CONTINUE

THE ESSENCE OF THE CAT FISHING SCENE

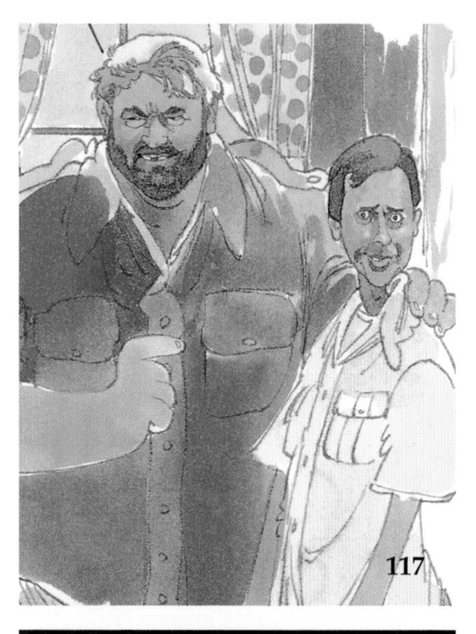
117

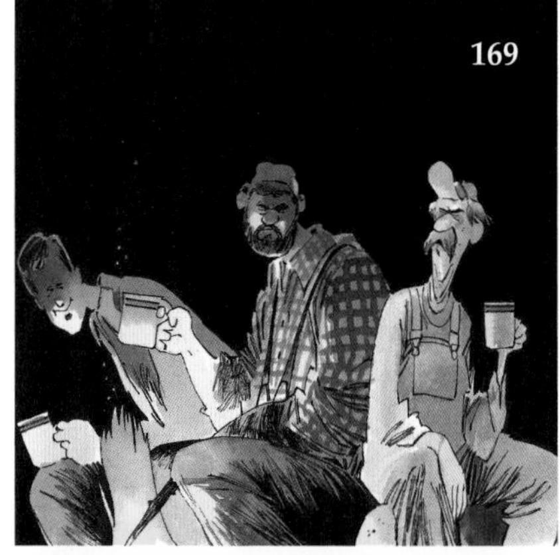
169

183

BIG CHANGE & BREAKTHROUGH TACTICS

207

249

291

GREAT STORIES & PROACTIVE TIMES

THE END IN SIGHT— LET THE GOOD TIMES ROLL

301

349

#383

Catfish Gumbo!

Ingredients

1/2 lb. bacon, diced
1 c. each onion, celery, green pepper, and red pepper, diced
1 tsp. garlic, chopped
1/2 tsp. each white pepper, thyme, and oregano
1/8 tsp. cayenne (or to taste)
8 c. chicken broth
1 lb. smoked sausage, sliced 3/4 inch thick on a bias
1 lb. fish, one-inch cubes

■ *Sauté bacon and reserve. Heat the bacon fat until it just begins to smoke, then add an equal amount of flour. Whisk until the mixture (roux) turns the color of a brown paper bag.*

■ *Add onion, celery, green pepper, red pepper, garlic, cayenne, white pepper, thyme, oregano, the reserved bacon, and chicken broth. Cook gently for 15 minutes.*

■ *Add the smoked sausage and fish. Simmer gently for about seven minutes. Season with salt and pepper and serve garnished with cooked white rice. (By Chef Lucia Watson.)*

SUPER SUMMER SMALLMOUTHS
LEARN HOW FISH REALLY FEED
NEW LARGEMOUTH TACTICS • BROOK TROUT BONANZA
TROLLING FOR PIKE AND MUSKIES • NEW SALMON TRICKS
BIG WATER WALLEYES • STRIP PIT BASS • MONSTER CATFISH
the In-Fisherman
THE JOURNAL OF FRESH WATER FISHING
PRICE $2.75
BOOK #55
A NEW TREND IN TOURNAMENTS

Historic Perspectives

"Crackerjack Cats" is the first of scores of major catfish articles to appear in In-Fisherman magazine. Before joining the In-Fisherman staff in 1981, Doug Stange has in the mid-1970s, written several articles about fishing for stream catfish that appear in Fishing Facts magazine. Stange grows up in Iowa, where catfish are an important sportfish. The other staff members have little experience with catfish and little feeling for how important the fish is to anglers in most parts of the country. So it takes a few years to convince other staff members that catfish should be a natural In-Fisherman topic, right along with everything else that swims. Stange has been a teacher and a coach, dabbling in freelance writing. He is far from a skilled writer and is, indeed, struggling to learn to write. But all the early writing in In-Fisherman is difficult by literary standards. Still, readers wade through, looking for a bit of entertainment and any information to help them understand how to catch more fish. This is the age of rapidly expanding knowledge about fish and fishing—and In-Fisherman is at the forefront of the information boom.

CHAPTER 1

JUNE 1984

Crackerjack Cats

TIGHT ENDS OR TACKLES? Perhaps. But an old-style middle linebacker is more like it. In the mold of Dick "bang-'em-alongside-the-head-and-make-'em-smile" Butkus, I believe.

Picture an all-star football team based on the fish we pursue. Smallmouth bass are the fleet-finned halfbacks, a brown trout the shifty quarterback, king salmon tough tight ends, and you can fill in the other positions yourself. But I do believe ol' CC—the channel catfish—gets my vote for Mr. Mean, the middle linebacker. Smash 'em, bash 'em, run 'em through a brick wall. Nothing flashy, mind you; but if you grab hold, you'd better hang on. They're tough, they're mean, they're feisty, and they're smart to boot. In the game of fishing, you should play with 'em or agin' 'em, but you can't play without 'em.

In short, if your fish roster or fishing schedule doesn't include channel catfish, you're playing with a flat football. Pump up the football, switch your schedule, and make a trade this year.

Along with over 8 million other anglers, I am uncontestably, incurably and unabashedly in love with channel catfishing. Why? Perhaps it's the solitude. You can always find a small river or pond tucked away from the hustle and bustle of the summer fishing crowd. Perhaps it's simply availability? Channel cats are found in every major water environment—ponds, rivers, lakes, and reservoirs—throughout much of North America. Perhaps it's the simple challenge. It's tough to consistently bag big channel cats; and, son, they

Basic Tactics For Channel Catfish In Ponds, Rivers, Lakes, Reservoirs!

do grow big, and wary, feisty, and mean. Perhaps it's the eatin'? Once you land 'em, well, they may just be the best table fish of all.

So let's get catfishing!

CHANNEL CAT CHARACTERISTICS

Actually, whatever fish species you're after, the first step is always the same: know the habits and characteristics of the fish.

It's no secret that channel cats have an extremely sensitive and highly developed sense of smell. While salmon are able to detect odors in a particle-to-volume ratio of 1 to 80 billion, many scientists believe catfish are even more odor sensitive.

Their sense of taste is also highly developed. It's an unusual sense in catfish, because taste organs (buds) aren't found entirely in the mouth. In fact, most of the taste organs are located on eight whiskers (barbels) and their lips. But over 100,000 taste buds are also distributed over the fish's entire body. Channel cats can even taste with their tails!

Obviously, anglers must deal with this tremendous ability to smell and taste. It's both a blessing and a curse. It's a blessing because the right—and what's right to a channel cat may not be particularly right (ripe, yes, but right, no) to you—concoction can attract channel catfish from a long way. It's a curse because catfish also easily detect repulsive human odors. Take care to cover your tracks (in this case, fingerprints) with a live or dead bait, or a commercial scent product such as Fish Formula I for catfish.

Catfish have other highly developed senses anglers must consider. A lateral line system allows them to detect close-ranging, low frequency vibrations such as those given off by a struggling minnow. And they also have an excellent sense of touch.

But the catfish's hearing is exceptional. Catfish are blessed with a set of small bones connecting their air bladder to their inner ear. This set of bones, called Weberian ossides, transmit sounds picked up and resonated (intensified) by the air bladder, to the inner ear. Walk softly along a bank or sit quietly in a boat while pursuing channel cats, because they have an acute sense of hearing.

But can't cats see? Well, of course they can. They're color blind, mind you, but when water is

Quite A Cat

Obviously, this isn't a channel catfish. Although channel cats often approach 20 pounds (the world record is 58 pounds), that's nowhere near the size of this 202-pound 8-foot-long critter.

Wels catfish are only found (unfortunately) in Europe. This one was caught on a spoon by two young anglers and a 73-year-old gent. Imagine trying to drag this brute into a small rowboat as the trio did.

Wels catfish can grow to over 400 pounds; this one was the largest ever taken in Czechoslovakia. The largest North American catfish are blue and flathead cats. Both reach weights around 100 pounds.

clear, vision becomes a primary means of finding food. This is probably why lake and reservoir cats can often be caught on crankbaits and other fairly fast-moving, unscented lures, while river cats seldom are. In murky environments, scent is the key to attracting and focusing a cat's attention. One of the few moving lures that consistently takes channel cats in a murky environment is a leadhead jig. But you'd better move it slowly and tip it with live bait.

Add it up. An acute sense of hearing, smell, taste, and adequate vision. Channel catfish are one of the wariest critters swimming. Basically warier than a walleye or a largemouth bass? Definitely. Channel cats, especially big ones, are formidable opponents.

CHANNEL CATFISH WATERS

Nowadays, channel catfish are critters of small streams as well as large rivers, and, due to stocking, of small ponds as well as large lakes and reservoirs. Channel cats are channel cats wherever they swim. But if channel cats are to survive and thrive in a particular environment, they need to adapt. Channel catfishing in a small river is similar to catfishing in a large river, because you're after the same fish. But the environments are slightly different, and so is the fishing.

For example, a small river catfish angler who's never fished on a larger river, lake, or reservoir might assume that channel catfish are primarily bottom feeders. They often feed on the bottom, but active fish also suspend if it helps them contact food. This is very common in large rivers, lakes, ponds, and reservoirs; however, small rivers are usually so shallow that true suspension isn't an option there. The point is, catfish in different waters have the same basic characteristics, but how these characteristics are expressed is based on environmental options.

It's best to learn to fish for channel catfish in a single type of water, first. When you've mastered one environment, it's easy to move on.

If you're a beginner and have a choice of environments, start small. Fish small rivers first, moving to large rivers, ponds, and reservoirs later. Or, fish small ponds first, moving to small and large rivers and reservoirs later.

BASIC CHANNEL CAT LOCATION

Channel catfish location varies depending on the water type. Still, there are general points that apply to finding ol' CC.

First, channel cats relate to structural elements. Structure is defined by fisheries biologists as "a material or condition which affords fish protection, food, security, or a reference point." Structure may be rocks, logs, standing timber, ledges, points, or

Channel Catfish Range

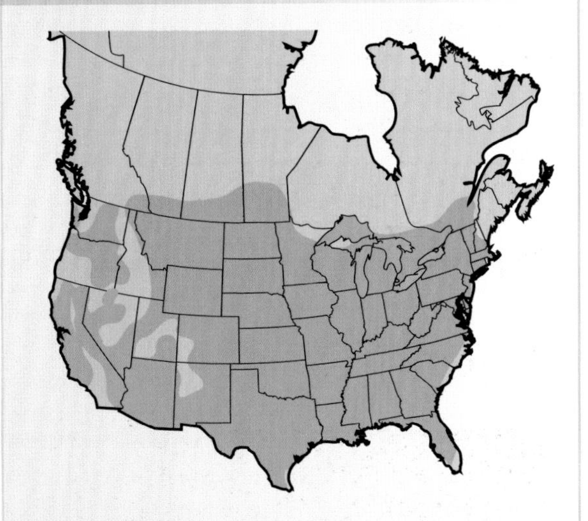

The channel catfish is a favorite with anglers throughout the United States and southern Canada. And why not? Its willingness to bite, wide distribution, fine sporting qualities, and delectability are everything an angler could ask for. Close relatives of the channel catfish, which you can also catch using the basic methods described here, include brown, yellow, and black bullheads; and blue, white, and flathead catfish.

Source: "Freshwater Fishes of Canada," Scott and Crossman, Fisheries Research Board of Canada Bulletin 184.

weedgrowth. It may also be where two different current areas meet, or where light ceases to penetrate the water. In short, structure is a thing or an environmental condition that stands out from the surroundings it's set in. Structural elements tend to attract and concentrate fish.

Look at this concept from a different point of view. "Edges" also attract fish. An edge is an area of change, or where two different areas meet in an environment. For example, an edge is formed by any current-breaking object. Typical current breaks are formed by large rocks, fallen trees, or by natural curves in a river, where fast current is deflected, slows down, and changes direction. Other edges are formed by major changes in river areas, such as from a riffle to a pool or from a pool to a backwash or backwater spot. These areas all attract fish; however, they won't all hold fish all the time. But, whether you're fishing small or large rivers, small ponds or immense reservoirs, the ability to recognize structural elements or "edges" in an environment is a big step toward catching channel catfish.

BASIC ENVIRONMENTS: RIVERS

Let's take a moment to discuss the basic environments you may find channel cats in. First consider rivers.

Channel cats in rivers generally prefer harder bottom and some current; thus, look for structural elements or edges on or near hard bottom, current areas. Current and hard bottom often go hand-in-hand in rivers.

However, if you stop and fish every current break or riffle-to-pool area, you'll be wasting a lot of time. The key is identifying channel cat "home areas" and then concentrating your fishing around adjacent structural elements.

In small rivers, catfish home areas are either (1) timber snags, or (2) relatively deep holes. Walk on past good-looking structural elements that aren't adjacent to possible channel cat home areas.

Fish riffle-to-pool areas, riffle-to-backwash areas, and pools, as well as secondary snags and deeper holes within 100 yards of possible home areas.

Finding channel cats in large rivers is akin to finding them in small rivers, only the scale changes. You can still look for channel catfish "home areas" if you want. However, you're better off picturing "holding areas," because cats in larger rivers do quite a bit of moving.

Typical structural elements that hold fish include timbered snags, riprapped points, wingdams, pilings, and backwater areas immediately adjacent to main current areas. In the case of "backwater areas immediately adjacent to main current areas," simply look for harder bottom areas—sand, gravel, or clay—out of the main current flow, but near it. The farther you're removed from main, or secondary, current areas, the fewer channel catfish you'll find. Of course, there are exceptions.

PONDS

In smaller ponds, certain areas draw fish. For one, an incoming feeder creek is usually important. Channel cats are current fish, and feeder creeks provide the only current in most pond environments.

Another area that consistently concentrates fish is a pond corner. Pond cats wander, and pond corners are perfect, edge-breaking edges. A snag, weedgrowth, a dock, or any structural element in conjunction with a corner usually makes for the best spot in a pond.

LARGER RESERVOIRS

Locating cats in large reservoirs is somewhat like locating them in small ponds. In this case, choose a particular creek arm, or if a reservoir is huge, a secondary arm off a main creek arm, and concentrate on structural items and edges in this relatively small area. Imagine the smaller creek arm as a pond, and proceed to systematically fish the potential areas.

Another popular approach in larger reservoirs is to search for suspended channel cats feeding on shad. You need a depthfinder or, better yet, a graph.

Pick a creek arm or secondary creek arm, and run the open water adjacent to incoming creeks or off points, especially timbered points that

Basic Channel Cat Location

Basic catfish location isn't difficult. Channel cats relate to edges (structural elements) in their environment just as other fish do.

In rivers, concentrate on edges formed by major changes in river areas, such as from a riffle to a pool, or from a pool to a backwash area. Obstructions that break current may also attract fish.

In ponds or small reservoirs, pay particular attention to incoming feeder creeks, natural or manmade debris, or simply corners. In lakes, feeder creeks, points, breakwalls; any sunken islands and major bars are possibilities.

In large reservoirs, it's best to focus on a particular creek arm. Within the individual creek arm, try structural elements such as incoming current and manmade or natural debris, especially when it's found along a creek channel. Cats also roam open water. Be sure to check open water areas near timbered points on deep flats.

We'll detail catfish location in ponds, lakes, and reservoirs just as we do for other fish.

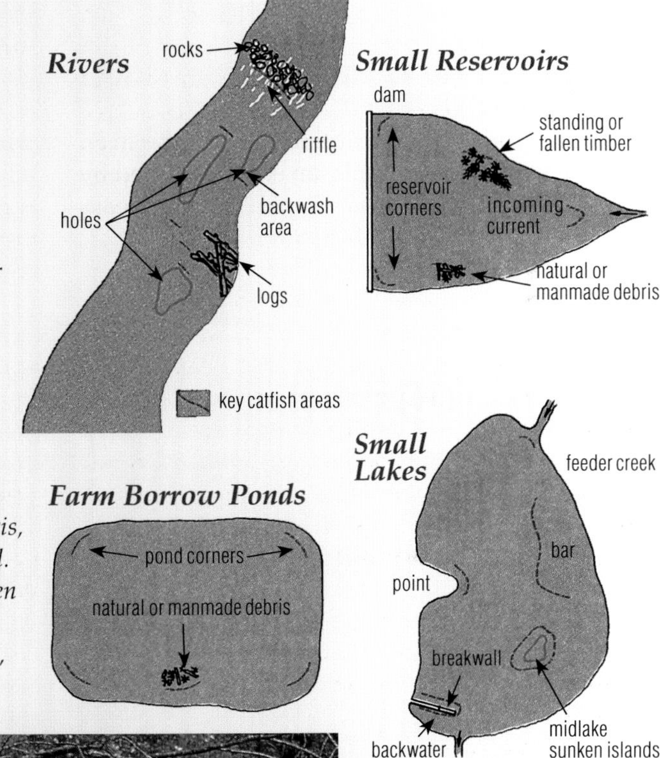

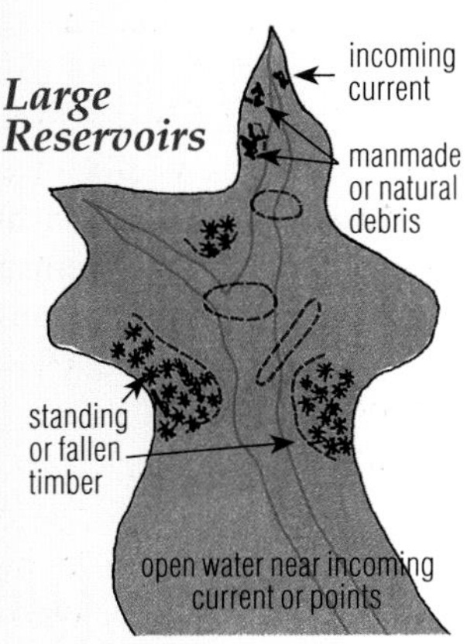

project out quite a way. Find schools of shad with larger fish lying near them, and you may be on channel cats.

LARGER STOCKED LAKES

Large, stocked, natural lakes are one of the toughest environments in which to consistently find channel cats.

Unless a lake is heavily stocked, larger lakes usually offer too many options. Catfishing seems to become a hit-or-miss affair. Still, you can take the same basic approach as in fishing a small pond.

In lakes, pay particular attention to any incoming current. However, the following is probably the best general advice.

On almost every lake, particular catfish patterns develop. Particular riprapped points or breakwalls may be productive during certain yearly periods. Certain bay areas may establish a reputation. In one lake, we discovered channel cats on sunken humps while fishing for walleyes. This soon became an established pattern that anglers take advantage of each year.

The point? When it comes to channel cats and large lakes, ask around. Local scoop will probably provide you with a starting point for your fishing.

BASIC BAIT CHOICES

Live frogs, nightcrawlers, crayfish, salamanders (mudpuppies or waterdogs), grasshoppers, minnow species such as chubs, suckers, or shiners, bluegills, shad, madtoms. Almost anything dead: shrimp, chicken or rabbit liver, smelt, shad, suckers, chubs, frogs. Vile-smelling concoctions made of Limburger cheese, sour fish; stuff that could honestly gag a maggot, indeed throw in the maggots for good measure. And coagulated blood. And at times leadhead jigs and crankbaits. Under the right conditions, channel catfish will eat all these and your dirty socks, to boot.

With so many choices, how do you know which bait to fish?

There are two general approaches to fishing for catfish during any season. Some anglers prefer to "match the hatch" and go with natural baits (either dead or alive) that catfish might normally encounter during a particular season. Other anglers choose to use only attractor (stink or blood) baits.

Obviously, the two categories are related. After all, natural, day-old, dead chubs do have a catfish-attracting odor about them. Logically, though, good anglers use baits from either category depending on the situation. But that brings us back to our original problem: When to use what baits?

Personal preference plays a part in fishing. Here's how I approach the question of which baits to fish. With some experimentation, you can decide on your own approach.

During all seasons, I take both natural and attractor baits with me, but I usually begin fishing with natural baits. Thus, in the spring, I probably start fishing with live chubs or suckers, and proceed to fishing sour chubs or carp, if live chubs don't produce.

As the summer progresses, I continue to use live or freshly killed chubs or sucker minnows; I also take waterdogs along if they're available. Waterdogs are the larval (water) stage of the tiger salamander. This aquatic stage is a superior bait. It seems salamanders take on an unpleasant taste after they change into a land-roving form. Hook a waterdog once through the tail or up through the lips, just as if they were a live chub or sucker.

During early summer, blood becomes one of the deadliest, channel catfish "attractor" baits. Chicken blood seems to be the best catfish attractor, perhaps because it contains certain amino acids that are particularly attractive to catfish.

Bloodbaits generally are my first choice as an attractor bait through the summer and into fall. However, dipbaits (sponge baits dipped into soft goo) and textured baits (doughball-type baits usually packed into spring-encircled treble hooks), both home and commercially made, are great channel catfish attractors and catchers, too.

Crayfish and frogs turn cats on later in the summer, and don't forget grasshoppers if they are abundant. Crayfish can usually be seined in backwater areas, while frogs are best caught with a net. Gather grasshoppers in early morning, when

CATFISH BAITS

Succulent Sour Carp

Ingredients:

A 1-6 pound carp; substitute sucker, mooneye, or any fish with tough skin

A quart jar or two (with lids)

A cup of water

Step 1: *Fillet the carp, but leave the skin on. Scaling is a good idea but isn't absolutely necessary.*

Step 2: *Cut the fillets into sections approximately 1 inch wide, 1 inch thick and 2 to 3 inches long. If the carp's a large fellow, and the fillets are too thick, trim off meat until the chunks are about 1 inch thick.*

Step 3: *Pack the strips loosely into a quart jar and add a cup of water. Screw on the lid and let the jar sit in the sun for several hours. Dig a hole about one foot deep in a spot that the sun hits for most of the day. Bury the jar. Allow the contents to fester inside the jar for several days if the weather is warm, or for several weeks if the weather is cool.*

Result: *Sweet, succulent, sour carp.*

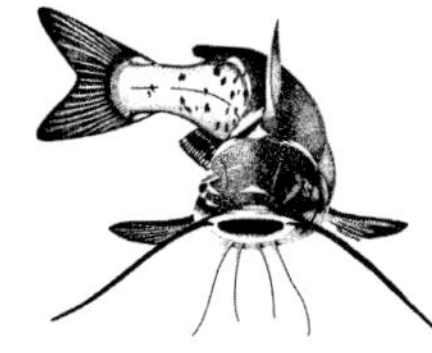

Bait Combos by Season

Bait choice is a matter of personal preference and usually develops from experience with what works in a particular water or region. There are many productive possibilities during different seasons; however, the following combinations represent one approach for spring through fall. Try to keep at least one natural and one attractor (stink or blood) bait with you at all times (at least while you're fishing).

Season	*Natural Bait*		*Attractor Bait*	
	1st choice	**2nd choice**	**1st choice**	**2nd choice**
Spring	live or freshly killed chubs	none	sour fish	none
Early Summer	live or freshly killed chubs	waterdogs	chicken blood	prepared dip baits
Summer	live or freshly killed chubs, or waterdogs	frogs, crayfish or grasshoppers	chicken blood blood baits	prepared dip
Fall	live or freshly killed chubs	frogs or waterdogs	chicken blood	prepared dip baits

Attractor Baits

Attractor baits fall into two categories: bloodbaits and stinkbaits. For unknown reasons probably relating to the chemical content of blood from different animals, chicken blood seems to be most attractive to channel cats. Perhaps it's imagination, so we suggest you conduct your own tests.

To get chicken blood, visit a chicken processing plant. Cut up 1- x 3-inch strips of Band Aid gauze and place the strips in a shallow cake pan, one layer deep. Add about 1/4 inch of blood. Cover the pan with cellophane and refrigerate it. The blood will gel, and you'll have a bait that you can hook onto a single hook and fish for 10-15 minutes. Keep it cool until you fish it.

Chicken kill floors aren't always easy to find; so it's a blessing that Bob's Bait of Nixon, Texas, packages stripped and ready-to-use chicken blood in large, shippable plastic containers. It sure beats holding a pan under a bleeding chicken.

The other jar contains a commercial dipbait. Like fine wine, it only gets better with age.

Any bait that's particularly abundant alongside a stream or pond can be dynamite for catfish. During spring, when frogs are few and far between, they aren't a great bait. But when they're abundant in late summer, they may be a gppd bait. Don't forget to consider grasshoppers, too. When they're thick in late summer, those little tidbits can be a great bait for cats.

Using A Dipbait

Any bait that's particularly abundant alongside a stream or pond can be dynamite for catfish. During spring, when frogs are few and far between, they aren't a great bait. But when they're abundant in late summer, they may be the best possible bait. Don't forget to consider grasshoppers, too. When they're thick in late summer, those little tidbits can even be a great bait for cats.

Various dipworm designs have been on the market since the inception of dipbaits, probably in the 1950s.

1. *Typical dipwormss (like Doc's Catfish Worm or Lindy/Little Joe's Catfish Rig) are made of soft plastic and have plenty of depressions to hold "dip." Dips range from vile concoctions made from limburger cheese, eggs, and cornmeal to mashed fish, eggs, and flour. They all have one thing in common, however; they smell bad. But they're great channel cat attractors, especially during midsummer.*

2. *Drop the dipworm into the festering goo and use a stick to mash it in. (Sure, use your fingers if you dare!) Return the lid to the jar, but don't screw it down tight because expanding gases may cause the jar to explode. If it happens in the back seat of your car, it tends to decrease the resale value.*

3. *The most common method of rigging a dipworm is to use it on a slip-sinker rig. However, because it's seldom necessary to let a cat run with dip, it works great on a three-way swivel rig using a "set" presentation.*

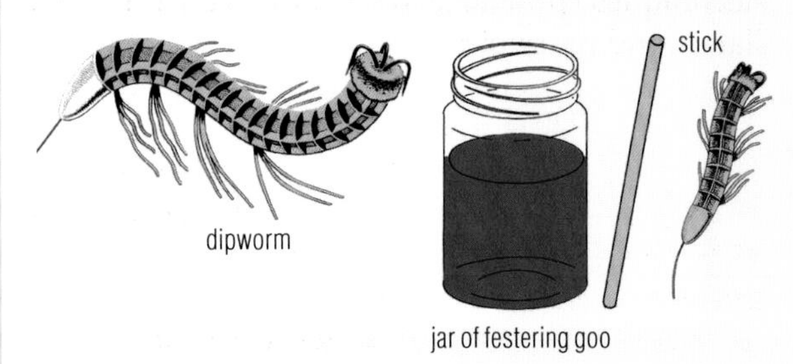

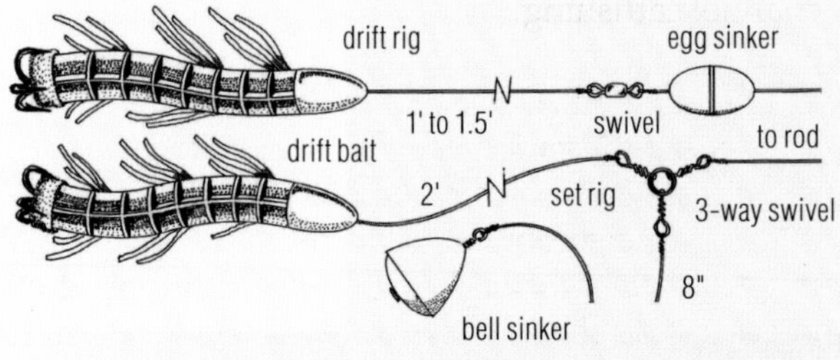

cooler temperatures and dew keep them from jumping around. Nightcrawlers are also a good bait as long as you're not troubled with hordes of small, bait-stealing chubs or bullheads.

Artificial baits such as leadhead jigs and wobbling, minnow or crayfish-imitating crankbaits have their moments, too. However, these moments are limited compared to the consistent catfishing produced by natural or attractor, live and dead baits.

TACKLE

Any angler, regardless of age or social station, can put together a tackle combo that'll bag channel cats. If you prefer fishing with an expensive boron rod, fine, but it's not necessary. A low cost but functional fiberglass rod will do. Actually, functional is a key, no matter if it's rods, bobbers, or hooks.

Match your tackle to the fishing situation. Yet if I had to choose one all-purpose channel-catfishing rod-reel-line combination, it would be a fast-action spinning rod (a quick, responsive tip, tapering quickly into a stiff mid- and butt section) 6 feet long, combined with a spinning reel handling 8- to 14-pound-test line. On most occasions, I'd load the reel with 10- or 12-pound-test line. Armed with this combo, you can fish most environments with confidence.

Granted, of course, that fishing for large cats or cats in heavy cover requires heavier tackle. In such situations, a 7.5 foot flippin' stick or a light muskie or striper rod, combined with a casting reel filled with 25-pound-test line, either Dacron or monofilament, is appropriate. Whether you're a lake, stream, river, or reservoir angler, these two rod-and-reel combos handle 95 percent of your channel catfishing.

OTHER TACKLE ITEMS

Sinkers: A variety of split shot, slipsinkers, and bell sinkers lets you sink baits to a desired depth. Sinkers are an important part of most catfishing rigs.

Hooks: A variety of hook sizes and types is necessary to fish a variety of baits. Plain, single hooks are fine for most fishing situations; however, have spring-encircled treble hooks on hand for doughball-type baits.

Sponges or Dipbaits: Sponges or dipbaits are for pushing into and soaking up gooey, smelly, catfish-attracting concoctions.

Swivels: Straight barrel swivels or three-way swivels are a part of many catfishing rigs.

Strike Detectors: A detector with the ability to sense strikes—a light or alarm that alerts you—is handy while fishing two rods, or at night when you're set up in a known fish-producing area. A simple, effective detector is made by H.T. Enterprises.

Bobbers: Bobbers aid in strike detection and allow you to suspend baits at any depth. Have two types of bobbers, slipbobbers, and plastic bubbles, on hand. Slipbobbers allow long casts, after which the bait slips to a predetermined depth. Plastic bubbles like the A-Just-A-Bubble, filled with water, add extra weight and casting distance. However, in order to cast successfully, the bait must not be positioned too far below the bobber.

These tackle items can easily be carried in a small tackle box. Carry the small box in an old, extra-large lady's handbag, one with a shoulder strap. Another option is a trout creel.

PRESENTATION

Let's examine fishing techniques that consistently produce catfish. While there are many exotic approaches, standard catfishing techniques usually produce fish.

The choice of a particular technique depends on the environment being fished, although the type of bait is also a factor. We'll discuss a basic set of techniques applicable to rivers as well as ponds, lakes, and reservoirs.

SMALL RIVERS

Small-river presentation can easily be applied to large rivers and, in principle, to ponds, lakes, and reservoirs. The first consideration is the two basic types of presentations, "drift" and "set."

A drift presentation uses the natural bait-moving capacity of current. The scheme is a natural: Catfish location is affected by current; thus allow

Basic Rigs

Catfish rigs can be simple or involved, depending on the bait used and where the rigs are fished. We'll focus on simple rigs here, and detail other rigs. Three simple drift rigs are:

1) *Hook and split-shot rig: Add split shot 8-12 inches above bait. Hook size should match the bait being fished.*

2) *Hook and egg-sinker rig: Slip an egg sinker onto your line and pinch a split shot on to hold the egg sinker in place. A swivel can be used in place of split shot.*

3) *Slipbobber rig: Tie a bobber stop onto your line, trim the ends, and slide it up to the depth level you want to fish. Add a small plastic bead and the slipbobber onto your line. Pinch on split shot for weight.*

4) *A simple "set" rig: Starting with a three-way swivel, tie your line to one rung, and dropper lines of about 8 and 24 inches to the other rungs. Add a bell sinker to the short dropline, and a hook and your bait to the other.*

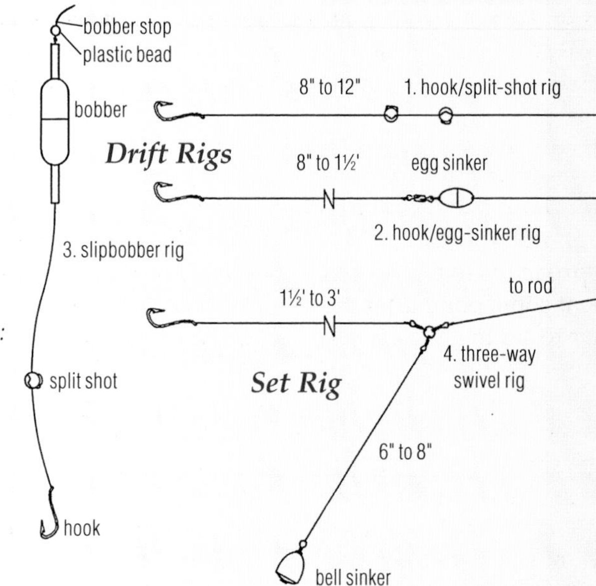

Two rod/reel options will handle 95 percent of your channel catfishing, whether you fish rivers or reservoirs, ponds or lakes. A heavy fast-action spinning rod about 6 feet long, and a reel loaded with 10-, 12- or 14-pound-test line is great for handling small- to moderate-sized cats in relatively open water conditions. Spinning rods allow picky, pinpoint casts to distant areas; it's best to fish smaller baits.

A 7.5-foot flippin' stick and a casting reel loaded with 14- to 25-pound-test line is great in all fishing situations and especially good for fishing obstructed areas. At times, you may even wish to use heavier line: Larger channel cats are unbelievably tough. Actually, a flippin' stick allows the most catfishing options. It's better for controlling drifted baits, "sticking" distant fish, casting heavier baits, controlling bobber movement, reaching or casting over bank-side debris, and a host of other things. Given one all-'round rod/reel choice, choose the flippin' stick.

During summer, wear a pair of tennis shoes and wade right in after cats in smaller rivers. In spring and fall, hip boots or waders are handy.

A large shoulder bag is handy for carrying a limited supply of bait and tackle, plus a small thermos, a knife, mosquito repellent, camera, and anything else you should have with you. Pursuing ol' CC is simple, cheap and plenty of fun.

current to take a bait naturally through current areas where catfish are stationed.

One type of drift presentation consists of using just enough weight to take a bait to the bottom and allow it to drift along naturally. In slow or moderate current, in river stretches generally from 2 to 6 feet deep, this can be accomplished with split shot.

Faster current and/or deeper water calls for a slipsinker shaped like an egg. Slip the egg sinker onto your line and, about 1 to 1.5 feet above the bait (depending on how much you wish the bait to swirl above the bottom), add a split shot or a swivel to hold the egg sinker in place.

The natural-drift, contact-catfish technique is so logical and works so well that it often becomes the only approach for some catfishermen. That's a mistake because a set bait, particularly when you wish to present attractor baits (stink or blood baits) is often as, or more, effective. Channel cats have a tremendous ability to detect and search out food. At times, moving a bait around is counterproductive, because it's more difficult for feeding cats to find.

Although there are many, the most basic set-bait rig is a simple three-way swivel rig. Tie the mainline to one of the swivel rungs and add dropper lines of about 8 and 24 inches in length to the other two rungs. Attach a hook to the longer dropper and a bell sinker to the shorter line. The bell sinker should be heavy enough to hold a bait in the area you intend to fish.

As there are two basic rigs, there are also two basic approaches to hook setting. One approach is to set the hook when a cat mouths the bait just after finding it. You don't allow the catfish to run with the bait. Another approach is to let the fish run, and then set the hook at some point after the run has ended. It's popular to set the hook when the cat makes a second move after the initial run.

Neither method is perfect. Setting the hook shortly after a fish is detected may mean missing it because it doesn't have the bait in its mouth. Waiting until after the cat makes a run often results in slack line that makes it difficult to set the hook when the time comes, or too much line bowed in current may create resistance and alarm a catfish.

With a set presentation, the fish is not allowed to run. Let the fish mouth the bait for a moment—obvious by pinching the line with your fingers—and then engage the reel and set the hook. Many anglers believe set baits should be smaller than driftbaits

River Holding Areas

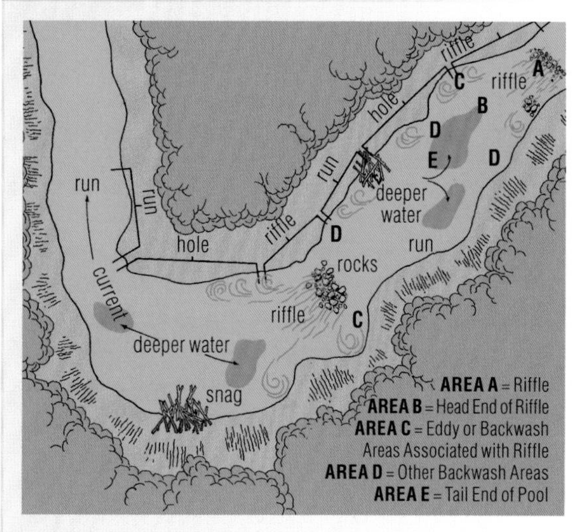

Snags or deep holes are catfish home or holding areas in smaller rivers. The catfish in these areas usually aren't actively feeding, so it makes sense to fish other areas first. Still, make sure you're fishing in the vicinity of a good catfish holding area.

Once you've found a catfish holding area, generally walk upstream to a steeper-gradient riffle area (A). Drift a bait through the area and into the pool (B) immediately below. Continue fishing by checking backwash areas associated with the riffle (C). Make sure to fish other backwash areas (D) and the tail end of the pool (E). The last places to check are the deepest part of holes or the water in front of, or behind, snags.

Repeat this procedure in a riffle area immediately below a catfish holding area. The same basic procedure applies to fishing large rivers, only the scale changes.

because small baits are more easily taken into a catfish's mouth.

A bobber (suspended) presentation can be either a drifting or set presentation depending on where it's fished. Usually a bait suspended on a bobber is drifted naturally into areas with the current.

Bobber rigs are especially helpful in suspending baits over soft bottoms near hard-bottom current areas. Catfish feed in such areas, but weighted baits often sink into the bottom, making them difficult for cats to find.

Here's how you might use these techniques on a small or medium-sized river.

Snags or deep holes are catfish home areas and, generally, the catfish there are not active fish. That doesn't mean they can't be caught, but these areas are usually the last places you should fish. Active fish are usually associated with shallower current areas, especially steeper-gradient riffle areas. Fast-flowing riffles are the first place to check once you've identified a general area that should hold channel cats.

First, drift a bait through the riffle and into the pool below. The next few drifts should take a bait through the riffle and into backwash or back-current areas near the end of the pool. The last place to check is the deepest part of a hole, or the front-end or tail-end of a snag area.

If you systematically approach fishing different areas in small rivers, it doesn't take long to detect fishing patterns that usually apply to other river areas. In other words, if the fish are using one riffle area, expect them to use others, too. It's pattern fishing.

If the cats aren't on drifted baits, try a set bait and fish it in some of the same areas. Another option is to set a bait in one area, while you drift-fish others. Make the set rod a casting or spincasting outfit and leave the reel on free spool. Engage the clicker so you'll be sure to hear when a cat hits and runs. Otherwise, leave the reel on free spool and attach your line to a strike detector. Once the trap's set, a light or buzzer indicates when the bait's been taken.

LARGE RIVERS

In principle, fishing large rivers is the same as fishing small rivers. First, generally look for channel catfish holding areas near current-breaking areas in, or near, main or secondary current (current once or twice removed from main current or the main channel). Productive current-breaking areas generally have hard bottom.

Major current-breaking areas that usually attract cats are submerged islands or humps, breakwalls or wingdams, major river bends, and bridge abutments. The best current breakers are associated with deeper holes. Dams also obstruct catfish movement, and cats often gather in tailwater areas below dam outlets. View all these areas as potentially major holding areas.

Pick any general holding area, and your fishing approach is much the same as for small rivers. Choose between drift, set, or suspended presentations, or combinations thereof. Drift or set presentations are good in any potential feeding or holding area; suspended presentations are best in backwater areas slightly removed from main current.

As in small-river catfishing, fish likely spots upriver from holding areas first. Thus, when fishing a bridge abutment holding area, first look for obstructions and (or) hard bottom upriver from the bridge abutments. Spots should generally be within several hundred yards of major holding areas.

Some large river areas can be fished efficiently from shore, but a boat lets you cover all the potential spots.

SMALL PONDS

Because current is not usually a factor in small-pond fishing, your choice is usually between set and suspended presentations. An efficient approach makes use of both presentations along or near specific catfish-attracting edges such as a pond corner, a projection (point) in the pond, or a manmade or natural cover area. Toss out a suspended bait on one rod and a bottom-set bait on the other.

Suspended presentations are often the most successful pond technique. A good approach is to start fishing with a bait suspended 2/3 of the way down beneath the surface. Thus, in water 15 feet deep, position the bait about 10 feet down.

When you first check out a pond, spend about 20 minutes in each potential area. On return trips you should be able to eliminate some spots. Once you know an area is a catfish attractor, you may wish to spend all of your time in that area.

LAKES AND RESERVOIRS

Basically, approaches to fishing lakes and reservoirs should be based on prior information about where channel cats are caught. If an incoming feeder creek or current area created by water exchange between two lakes or lake areas attracts fish, use basic river-fishing approaches. If the fishing area was a breakwall extending into the lake, use a basic pondfishing approach.

Once suspended catfish are located in a reservoir, it's usually best to present baits slightly above them. Also, if the fish are grouped below schooling shad, it's best to present baits slightly away from, and below, the shad.

UNTIL NEXT TIME

Whether it's a thermos of coffee and a sandwich, or enough mosquito repellent to last through an evening, extra items often help make a catfishing trip a success instead of a nightmare. If it's midsummer, a cooler full of ice not only keeps beverages cool, but also keeps catfish fresh for the table. Of course, on most trips a stringer keeps fish in good shape. A sturdy rope stringer is tough to beat.

Will you be fishing after dark? What about a flashlight or lantern? Do you have matches for a small spirit-lifting fire?

If you're onto big cats in a particular area but have been unable to catch them consistently, try spending an entire night (especially two or three days either side of new and full moons) fishing for them. Crawl into a sleeping bag on a fold-out lawn chair. Your set lines should be on either side of you with the bails open and the line attached to a strike detector. Sleep lightly: You'll be fresh enough to fish the next day and alert enough to immediately respond to strikes throughout the night.

Hip boots are usually handy, although if you're river fishing during the summer, a pair of old sneakers and cutoffs allows you to wade most areas. Don't forget a hat to keep the sun out of your eyes, and polarized sunglasses may help you distinguish river holes.

Crackerjack Cats?

Crackerjack cats? The term "crackerjack" once was popular. Crackerjack is a descriptive word tacked onto anything held to be "really something" or a "humdinger."

"Crackerjack cats" is appropriate in several ways. First, as the term has fallen into disuse, so too have many modern, fancy-pants anglers turned from catfishing. Some of today's anglers only fish for designated, so-called glamour fish like bass, brook trout, or walleyes. Sweating while you're fishing isn't "in." And if you aren't wearing a shirt with an alligator or a fishing insignia on it, forget it. And don't get your hands dirty; use only artificials. Livebait, or worse yet, deadbait? Yecch! The message is that bass (and certain other fish) are in, and cats are out. It's the old two-sides-to-the-tracks baloney with cats on the wrong side. What a shame. Each species has attributes that make it worth pursuing. Great fighter, wary disposition, fine eating. Catfish is glamour on the fin!

Historic Perspectives

Two years go by after the first catfish article is published before Stange convinces the rest of the staff there's a market for another article—that catfishermen want information just like the rest of the fishing world. As you see at the tail end of this article, Stange is asking in 1986 for catfishermen to drop Publisher Ron Lindner a note about getting more catfish info into the magazine.

Some of the information offered here is a little primitive by today's standards but cutting edge for the time. Stange and Otis (Toad) Smith are two of the first to experiment extensively with using blood as bait in rivers. Other anglers go on to find other environments where blood works even better. But it's still hard to get and no commercial sources are available today. You only see mention of channel catfish, as Stange believes it best to keep infrequent chances to write about catfish targeted at the most popular catfish species. Stange's early judgement about the overall productivity of fresh cutbait as an option during almost every season, in most environments stands today.

CHAPTER 2

JUNE 1986

Talkin' Catfish

TALKIN' CATS IS LIKE TALKIN' ADVERTISING OR TALKIN' TURKEY. You need to use a special lingo to get a message across to a special audience. For the ad man it means sales, and for the turkey hunter a Thanksgiving turkey. For the catfisherman, it means consistent catches of what is for millions of Americans their number one sportfish. Catfish around the world speak the same language. Food. Say it right and you catch catfish consistently. Say it wrong and you won't. Catfishing is that simple.

What We Have Here Is A Failure To Communicate!

If this article were about bass, we'd be talkin' vision, for bass are primarily sight feeders. Catfish, however, are famous for their smell and taste senses; almost any type of odiforous and strong-tasting concoction attracts them. Too many fishermen get carried away with this information, though, and assume that the only way to catch cats is by using foul-smelling baits that look and smell like limburger cheese laced with month-old toe jam.

Stinkbaits have a place, but frankly, you can catch catfish, specifically channel catfish, on almost anything if you try hard enough. That's how "best-bait syndrome" gets started. Two novice catmen have limited fishing time. They grab whatever bait is handy—chicken livers are a good example—and they go fishing. They catch some cats, of course, and chicken livers become the world's best bait. Across the river, the ol' boys fishin' cut shad catch twice as many cats in half the time. But our chicken-liver men will keep fishing chicken livers until the Rio Grande (a good catfish river, by the way) freezes over.

If you want to catch catfish on wieners soaked in one of the "new and exciting" scent formulas, you will. If you want to catch 'em on plain weenies, pork rind, pork belly, or pork chops, you can do that, too. That doesn't make them "best baits," for channel catfish eat almost anything. To have a real clue about the best baits given the situation, you must consistently fish many different baits against one another at the same time.

Another problem is that too many catfishermen believe that catfish catches increase proportionally with increases in bait odor. But baits with subtle odors work much better at times. Set your favorite baits aside for a moment as we take a look at the business of baiting up for cats.

SAY IT RIGHT

Although there are many great commercial baits on the market, the basis for baiting up for catfish should rest with natural catfish baits—in other words, baits, dead or alive, festering or fresh, that cats might normally encounter in their environment.

Natural baits can be the only baits that you need, because in one form or another, they can cover all the bases from frisky-fresh to festering-foul. Again, commercial or homemade stinkbait concoctions have a place, but except for their use as a chumming agent, we won't discuss them within this article. Let's battle with the basics this round.

Depending on where you reside in North America, you've probably dabbled with these natural baits: fish, small and large, whole and cut up; frogs and tadpoles; grasshoppers; waterdogs (salamanders); crayfish; nightcrawlers; leeches; clams; and less obvious baits such as dragonflies and hellgrammites. I think coagulated blood can also be considered a natural bait, but used in conjunction with natural baits, it might just work best as a chumming agent. Using commercial stinkbaits and blood as regular bait is a story for another time.

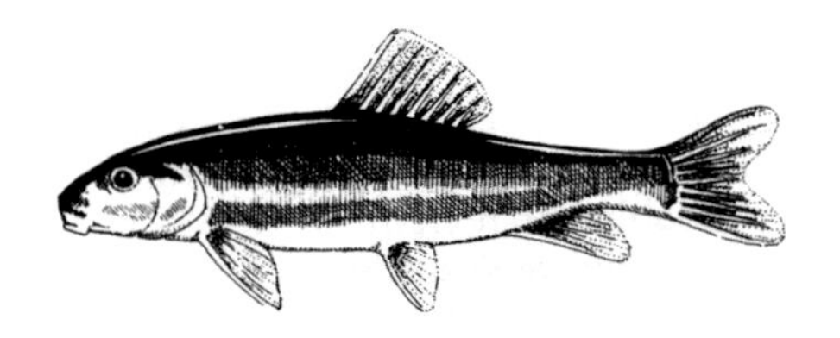

Fish—This category includes fish, small and large, alive or freshly killed, or festeringly dead. It also includes cutbaits or portions of cut-up fish. For the obvious reason that channel catfish are so likely to encounter fish in their environment, this is my choice as the best possible bait category for all seasons.

To be more specific, I'd choose freshly killed minnows or chubs, or cutbait of an appropriate size for the catfish sought. Experience shows that these baits work consistently from ice-out until freeze-up, and at times, during first ice. They are also easily available, cheap, and easy to care for and use.

Cutbait takes many forms. The object is to present a bait with its natural juices flowing freely. Cut the head off an 8-inch sucker or leave the head on and score the sucker's side. That's cutbait.

A portion of fillet is also a popular cutbait. Fillet the sides off a 12-inch sucker and cut the fillets into sections. If you use coarse-scaled fish like carp or mooneyes, scale the fish before filleting them.

I use minnows up to 5 inches long or chunks of about 1 x 3 x 1/2-inch cutbait in environments where I don't expect many catfish to be above 6 pounds. The baits get proportionally larger as the cats get bigger. Fishing the Red River below the Lockport Dam north of Winnipeg, Manitoba, where 15- to 20-pound cats are more common than 6-pounders, calls for 6- to 8-inch minnowbaits and 1 x 5 x 1/2-inch cutbait.

Most of the time, freshly killed, or at least killed and cooled (but firm) baits work well. If you want slightly ripened baits, let them sit in the sun for a while. Storing portions of firm cutbaits, such as carp fillets, in glass jars at room temperature for several days is a good approach when ice-out catfish are feeding on winter-killed fish.

Live minnows like fatheads and various chub, shiner, or sucker species are also a great all-season bait, but they aren't handy to carry around in warm weather. They often are a fine bait during cold-water portions of the season: For several weeks after ice-out or until the water temperature reaches about 50°F, and especially during fall after the leaves fall. Colder water dictates using smaller (3- to 4-inch) baits.

Some of my best catfish catches from heavily fished streams and rivers have been in September and October, when low water and decreasing water temperature herd cats into river holes. Confined fish often mean easy fishing. But the key to triggering those cats often is a lively minnow about 3 inches long. For most of the season, however, the size of the minnow (baitfish) depends on the size of the catfish you seek.

Frogs—Many fishermen think frogs are magic. The problem is that too many fishermen fail to fish frogs versus anything else. In season after season of fishing frogs versus other baits, I have rarely seen frog catches overwhelm those made on other baits. Frogs can be terrific during the last portion of summer when they're particularly abundant. But even then, fresh cutbait or freshly killed baitfish often work as well, or better, and are easier to fish.

The most common type of bait frog is the leopard frog, the same critter that you probably dissected in high school biology. Frogs can be used dead or alive, but a freshly killed and partially squashed frog probably is the most popular bait. Large frogs that are dead for long and stiffen up tend not to produce well. Frog size should match the size of the cats sought.

Tadpoles work, but tend to fall apart once they die (which is quickly). They look like succulent morsels no catfish could resist, but they haven't been a good bait for me.

Waterdogs (salamanders)—A waterdog is the larval or water stage of the tiger salamander. They can be a good but certainly not magic bait. I generally haven't found them to be as produc-

Food For Most Catfish

PHOTO 1

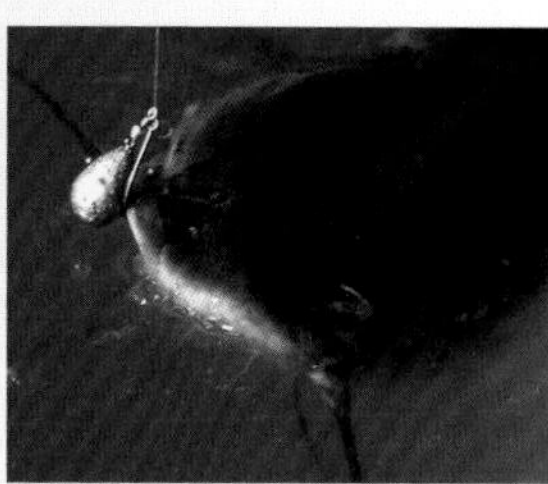

PHOTO 2

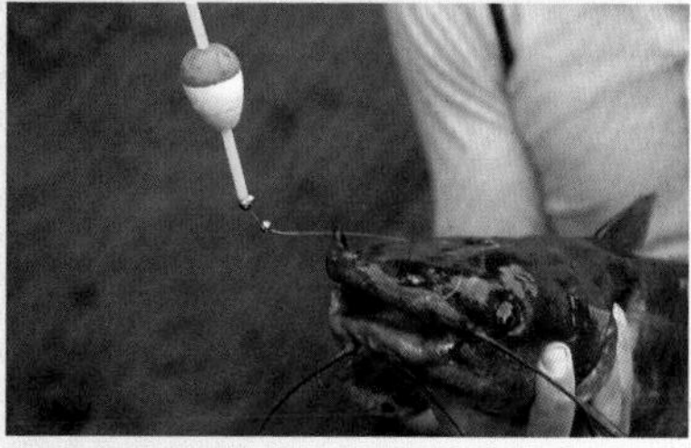

PHOTO 3

Baitfish are the most common food for most catfish, and cutbait or whole baitfish are probably the best catfish baits during most seasons. Such baits are cheap, easily obtained, and easy to use—and also productive.

To prepare one form of cutbait, fillet the side from a baitfish such as a sucker (PHOTO 1). Leave the skin on to help hold the fillet together. The size of the cutbait depends on the size of the catfish pursued.

Rigging for cats can be simple. One popular bottom rig consists of a single sturdy 1/0 or 2/0 short-shank hook tied below a slipsinker and (sometimes) held above the bait by a small split shot (PHOTO 2).

For drifting baits in shallow rivers, try a slipbobber rig. After tying a stop knot on your line, slide on a bead and then the slipbobber. Tie a single hook onto the end of your line and add split shot about 8 inches above the bait (PHOTO 3). Slide the bobber stop up so the bait drags over the bottom in shallow areas, and just above it in slightly deeper areas.

tive as freshly killed minnows or cutbait. I have done well fishing live 4- to 6-inch dogs in stocked ponds. On the other hand, I have done poorly fishing with dead dogs, at any time. If you can get waterdogs, give them a try. Unfortunately, they are rarely readily available and often high-priced.

Grasshoppers—If frogs and waterdogs are good but slightly overrated, then grasshoppers are good and very underrated. When big hoppers are abundant during late summer, they often form the main portion of the channel cat's diet in smaller streams and rivers. They should not be considered a big-fish bait in larger rivers, even when they are abundant, although they often trigger the biggest catfish available in smaller streams and rivers.

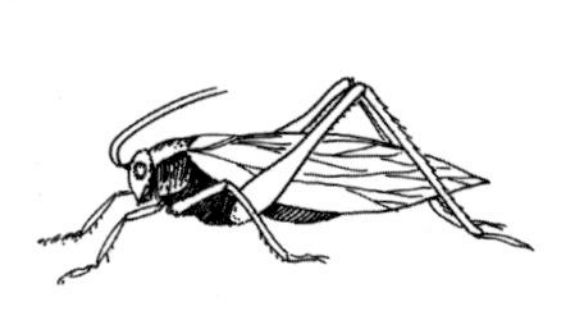

Catfish take grasshoppers off the surface as daintily as trout, but you're better off fishing a hopper, or several on the same hook, near the bottom. Riffle areas wash the flowing hoppers to the bottom. Drift them through these areas to catch cats. Floating hoppers also settle in slackwater spots, become waterlogged and sink to the bottom. The best slackwater areas are immediately adjacent to riffle areas.

Nightcrawlers—Crawlers probably aren't easily available to catfish in some environments, yet they must have a naturally attractive aroma and taste, for catfish that do encounter them usually readily eat them. They can be a fine bait in bodies of water where other small, pesky fish such as bullheads aren't a problem. They're one of my favorite baits immediately after ice-out in natural lakes and some streams.

Several crawlers can be threaded on the same hook. In spring usually just use one crawler on a small hook. As with other baits, freshly hooked crawlers are most appealing to catfish. After fishing a crawler for 10 minutes, rehook the crawler to get more juices flowing or use a new crawler.

Leeches—Leeches are a good bait, but often attract so many small fish that they can be a problem to fish. Still, there's little doubt that they can be productive during late spring and throughout summer. They often work to trigger the most reluctant catfish to bite. Again, though, although they can be productive just about anytime, I've done best on them during late spring and early summer.

Crayfish—Like many baits, the productivity of crayfish probably depends on how common they are. In rivers with many smaller incoming streams, or in rivers with a bottom substrate of rock, gravel, sand, and muck, crayfish often form an important part of the channel cat's diet, especially during late spring, when the craws breed, and particularly throughout summer, when they sometimes molt.

Try crushing the head and part of the hard shell, and then hook them in the tail. If you fish them alive, remove their pinchers and keep them moving constantly to discourage them from crawling under debris. A bobber is an immense help to keep craws drifting along naturally. At times in small streams, just use the meat from a peeled tail.

Clams—Clam meat is a likely looking meal, but I haven't found it to be particularly productive, especially versus easily obtainable baits like fresh cutbait. Does that sound familiar? By now you should see that various kinds and sizes of baitfish, both dead and alive, and cutbaits, are the most readily available, most easily used, and most economical baits available. And they trigger channel cats as well as, usually better than, most other baits.

Fish-type baits, or natural baits in general, aren't the last word in communicating with channel catfish. But understanding and learning to fish with natural baits, especially fish-type baits, is the best basis to start from. Truth be known, you need to go no farther to catch channel cats for the rest of your life.

THE REST OF THE STORY

Finally, coagulated blood is a good bait. I mostly use it in conjunction with natural baits such as chum to stimulate channel cats to start searching for food.

Say you're above a snag (catfish holding area) on a river, but there are no active channel cats working the area. If it's a particularly good snag, it's worth tossing in a handful of coagulated blood. I've seen catfish that couldn't be coaxed from the snag with other natural baits turn on within five minutes after the introduction of blood.

Once the cats turn on, they seem to strike natural baits like cutbaits as well or better than the blood itself. I have seen this happen so often that it's worth mentioning.

Fresh chicken blood is getting to be difficult to find. So are other bloods. You have to visit kill floors to get the stuff. One option is to order coagulated chicken blood from Bob's Bait, Star Route 2, Box 14, Nixon, Texas 78140. Ol' Bob puts together a good blood bait.

By the way, if you'd like to see more than one catfish article a year, or catfish articles that are more detailed than this one, drop that ol' cat man Ron Lindner a line and tell him so. Ron thinks catfishermen don't read and don't appreciate catfish information. Tell 'im he's wrong. You deliver, and I guarantee that we can tell you a ton more about catfishing. Millions of Americans can't be wrong!

Write: Many More Monstrous Cats, to Ron Lindner, In-Fisherman, P.O. Box 999, Brainerd, MN 56401. No need to get longwinded. Ron thinks most catfishermen can't read or write so just jot down something like, "Me like catfish." or "Me more catfeeesh." Misspelling a word or two would be a nice touch. A postcard will do fine.

Blood Basics

PHOTO 1

PHOTO 2

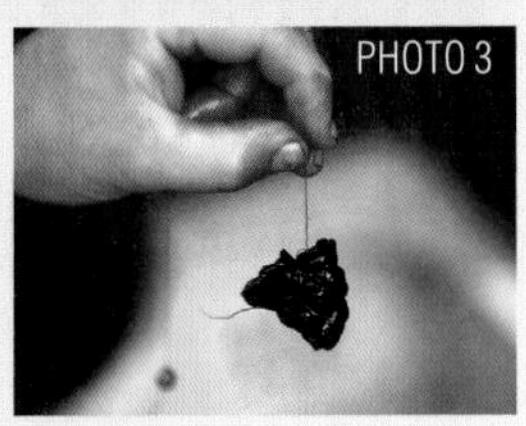

PHOTO 3

Coagulated blood is a fine catfish bait, so if chicken, turkey, hog, or beef-kill plants are nearby, arrange for a visit. Fill the bottom of a shallow cake pan about 3/8-inch deep with blood. Cover the pan and refrigerate to let it jell. Cut the jelled blood in 1- x 4-inch strips. Many fishermen add a layer of Band Aid gauze to the bottom of the pan before adding the blood. The gauze helps when hooking the blood onto a single hook.

Otis (Toad) Smith of Sibley, Iowa, ties a #6 or #8 treble hook to his line and leaves a 4-inch tag end. He wraps a strip of blood around the treble (PHOTO 1) and then wraps the line around the blood to hold it in place (PHOTO 2). Tie off the line with a half hitch (PHOTO 3), and the blood won't come off your hook easily. This also works for rigging clam meat.

Blood is a good chumming agent. Say you're fishing a river. Anchor above a likely looking tangle of wood debris (snag) and fish it with your choice of natural baits. After catching several cats, the bite may slow or stop. Throw in a handful of blood, wait several minutes, and the cats may get active again.

FISH CANADA ON POCKET CHANGE
SMALLMOUTH ACTION ATLAS • MONSTERS!
BIG CATS • ICE PERCH • LIGHT-BITE PIKE
WINDY WALLEYES • BIG-BASS LURES
the In-Fisherman
THE JOURNAL OF FRESHWATER FISHING
Book #71
GIGANTIC, 300-PAGE
SPRING FISHING SPECIAL
MUST READING
CATCH AND RELEASE
HOW MANY SURVIVE?

Historic Perspectives

This story might seem unsophisticated given our present knowledge of catfish and the current level of writing in In-Fisherman; but it is cutting edge for its time and, based on letters to the editor, probably the most popular article of all time in In-Fisherman magazine.

Here we have for the first time Stange creating a storyline featuring a salty old character (Zacker) in an article that also presents solid how-to-fish information. The reader can get involved in the story and be entertained while learning more about catching fish.

The “story” in all this is important at the time, because the trend caused by over a decade of writing in Fishing Facts magazine and in In-Fisherman is away from stories (the classic Me & Joe Went Fishing stories as they are referred to at the time) toward what has become a classic no-nonsense textbook approach to presenting information.

But here’s Stange turning it all around again, getting back to storytelling. He often continues to offer this sort of storyline in his writing about catfish, using Zacker and, later, another character, Otis (Toad) Smith, to make his points—which are always to capture the camaraderie around the many campfires, as well as all the shenanigans that go with a trip into the field. And all along the way, the stories always offer a bit of hardcore information about catching fish. It makes for memorable reading. This is where it all begins.

CHAPTER 3

FEBRUARY 1987

Zacker Bring a Bigger Cat!

FOR SEVERAL SUMMERS, I have used an unusual source to get information to confirm theories about catching big catfish. When you want information about big catfish you go to people who have caught not just a few, not dozens—but hundreds and hundreds—in their lifetime. Problem. You can count on four hands the number of fishermen who have done that, and the number of those who are still alive, on one. And if you insist on talking only to fishermen who have done it totally legally, well, you're not going to be doing much talking.

My source remains a secret, for most of the "old standard" bigcat men are self-described as some of the shadiest old polecats you could ever meet. Illegal trotline sets. Snagging. Netting. Anything to catch a cat. Beat the fish. Win. Income and family depend on it. High water, low water, good weather or bad. No matter. Catch fish. Catch catfish.

Yet they tempered the catching with their brand of conservation. Never take every big cat from a hole; never waste a fish, the rules went. And when the market for cats was bad, they went fishing anyway and kept only enough for the family: Trotline catch-and-release. They lived many a man's dream.

Most of them have reformed, more due to old age and changing times, I suspect, than guilt. But then "guilt" can be a paradox, for guilty by today's standards wasn't necessarily so by yesterday's. The

Christmas Just Past, Catfish Soon Coming. So Long Santa, Bring On Zacker, Bestower Of Gifts—Catfish Knowledge!

Blue Catfish

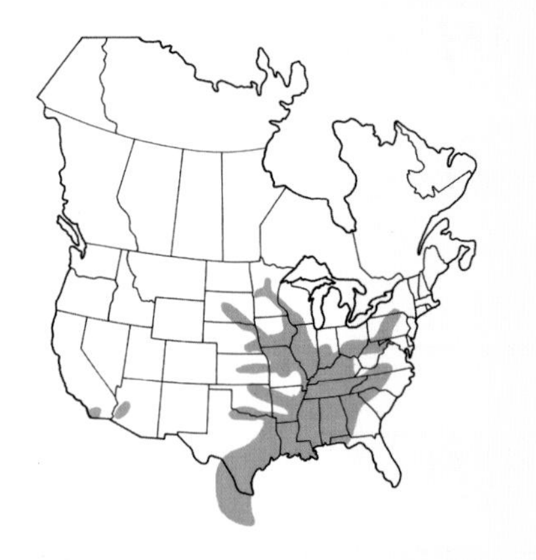

The blue catfish, probably the biggest catfish in North America, is one of the largest freshwater fish. Many fish over 100 pounds have been reported, although seldom verified. Likewise, there are many reports of super-giant blues, fish weighing almost 200 pounds, captured during the 19th Century. Apparently no photographs exist, but there's little question that huge fish used to hang like sides of beef in fish markets along the Mississippi River, during Mark Twain's time.

The blue catfish inhabits the Mississippi drainage and rivers of the Gulf Coast states and is sometimes stocked in reservoirs. Blues generally are huskier than channel or flathead catfish, but their slate-blue color is similar to the color of big male channel catfish. Distinguish it from other catfish by its very long anal fin with a straight bottom margin.

letter of the law and the spirit of it changes with the times, the people, and the part of the country.

Semantics. Give us reality. We need to talk to the ol' polecats before they pass on; too many already have.

Catching a bigger catfish, something many of you dream about, is as wretchedly simple in practice as on paper. I use a simple rule to increase the size of my catch, no matter the environment. Follow the rule and you'll catch some of the biggest cats in any water.

The rules work for me, but could I be certain, knowing that my catches and your catches combined don't equal what once was the yearly catch of some old-timers? So I had to ask: Does this—the approach—make sense?

THE RULE

To catch a bigger cat, the rule goes, *fish big-cat spots on big-cat water using big-cat bait at big-cat times.*

So the story flows.

Zacker, arthritic and 80, a short, thin, frail man, gnarled as an old oak limb, speaks with a voice like rusty barbed wire. Remember Dustin Hoffman playing the mule skinner, Little Big Man (in the movie by the same name), an Indian-raised white man and the sole survivor of the Battle of the Little Big Horn? Remember the cigarette-harsh, hesitating voice and the sentences constantly accented with jabs from a gnarly hand?

"You go down there," Little Big Man goaded Custer at one point before the famous battle, "and there'll be nothing left but a little grease spot." Little Big Man knows but still Custer goes.

Zacker could be Little Big Man. Someday, Dustin Hoffman should play Zacker. Millions of catfishermen would see the movie. For Zacker knows where big cats go.

"Crap," Zacker growls occasionally as he sits smoking a Camel on a bench on a porch overlooking a tiny creek and cows in a meadow behind his home. Mostly he misses the way things were, or dislikes the way things are.

"Crap!" Mostly he hates being 80 and not being on the river.

"Times ain't good," he'll say. "Damn 'em for changin' the river. No sand bars to hunt geese. No holes to corner big cats. Rivers run like plumbing."

"No big cats left?" I asked.

"Course there are," he scowled as he turned toward me. He wanted to be heard. "Maybe more. But 'less you got a free runnin' river—not like these flowing reservoirs today—they're tougher to find and catch. Course you can still catch 'em, but I'd as soon fish a small river now. You can see the holes, you know."

"When you say 'fish,'" I began to ask. "Do you mean—"

"I mean fish," he interrupted, rising up on the bench. "Fish! Course it varied just how we caught those fish—sometimes with a hook and pole line—but more often with lines (trotlines), nets, or come winter, with snagging lines.

Flathead Catfish

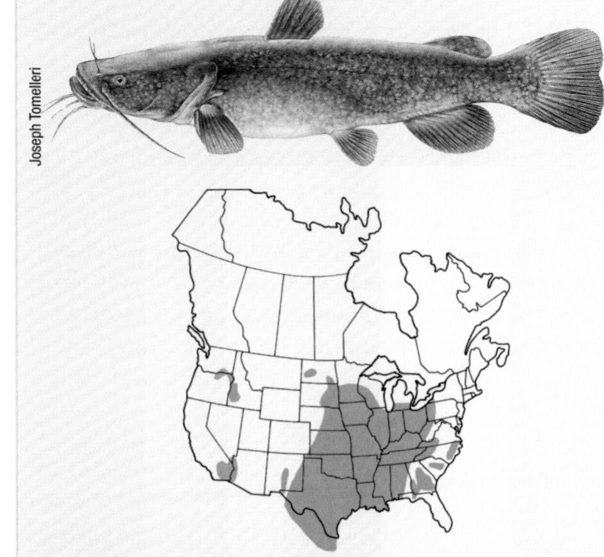

Joseph Tomelleri

The flathead catfish probably is the second largest North American catfish, occasionally reaching a weight surpassing 100 pounds. A solitary fish and a ferocious predator, it does much of its feeding at night.

Flatheads are easy to distinguish because of their brown color and distinctly flattened head. The anal fin is short and round, and the tail is rounded, not forked.

Channel Catfish

Joseph Tomelleri

The channel catfish is the third largest North American catfish, occasionally reaching a weight of 50 to 60 pounds. Though it prefers stream and river habitat, it's adaptable and is successfully stocked in reservoirs and ponds.

Channel catfish have deeply forked tails and a rounded anal fin with 24 to 30 rays. Small fish usually have spots along their silvery or olive-drab sides, but adults usually become steely blue (white belly). Male channel catfish, with their characteristic broad head and slate-blue color, are often mistaken for blue catfish.

"We caught terrible fish in my day: big mud cats (flathead catfish), plenty of forks (channel catfish), and blues (blue catfish). Like one day we worked the run (a circuit of baited setlines). Me and Little Lester and Grunt, the fellas I'd worked with. Great fellas, those two. Lester was 6 foot 4 and could lift a 75-pound cat in each hand, easy. Grunt looked like a grunt (sheepshead) and was 'bout as smart. I could tell you stories.

"They had set clothesline—cord lines tied up with 10/0 O'Shaughnessy, I 'spect—early one evening. We baited with live carp or big river suckers (2- to 3-pound carp and suckers he later told me) when we wanted mud cat—or smaller fish, sometimes dead, sometimes alive, sometimes cut, when we expected forks or blues. Lots of times we mixed baits on each line.

"Tell you one thing about setlines," he continued as he looked into the distance. "Cats are like deer or 'most any wild animal. They have order. Some of 'em—the little turds—have to feed whenever they can and others, usually the biggest, feed whenever they want. And it ain't for long.

"To catch 'em you've got to be there then," he emphasized by turning back toward me and poking at me with his skinny hand. "That's why setlines work. They're always there. Danged right."

ABOUT HOLES

"Tell you somethin' else," he continued. "Don't mean squat where you set a baited line in a hole if there are fish there that aren't feeding when you set the bait. But you got to be patient and you got to have the right bait. A big cat knows what he wants to eat and he knows the hole he lives in like you know your kitchen.

"I've watched them big ones on a moonlit night when the water's clear in June. They lay up in the deepest part of the hole or maybe under a snag. You can fish 'em till hell freezes over and never even make 'em move—until they want to.

"When they start movin' they go 'round the hole a time or two, sort of to warm up before they ever eat somethin'. By that time the healthy fish, including smaller cats, have scattered and only the injured ones or the stupid ones are left. Big cats eat those fish that need eatin'. But if there ain't no injured fish—like on a baited line—they set up in a proper place and then everything's fair game."

"But what if you were specifically pole fishing—you know, sportfishing?" I asked. "Seems to me that the head end of a hole, where a shallow riffle or glide flows into the hole, is consistently the best possible spot."

"Sportfishing!" he laughed. "Tunes sure change. Now some folks say our fishing with lines wasn't right. Now, you gotta race around in a fast boat and catch fish no bigger 'an we used for bait and win money. That's sport. That don't make sense. But that's fine. Seems to me that folks should just let other folks be—long as there's fish and game.

"But far as where you fish, you're doin' real good thinkin'," he said. "The place a big feedin' cat checks most often is the head of a hole. That's where they find a bait the quickest. Just remember that's where they set up when everything's fair game. Tell you what: I think those big cats can smell what's in the water 3 or 4 holes up from where they're at—and they been around long enough to know. Anything that enters the hole from the top side, they know it's there. And once they're set up, they rarely feed back."

"Back?" I asked.

"Yes, back," he said. "That's what I was tryin' to say. Once they're set up proper toward the front of a hole, they don't much bother with baits anywhere else. Once they start feeding, the head of the hole—where the current comes from—is the key.

"But be quiet," he continued, turning toward me again to emphasize the point. "That's another reason setlines work. Because some dink fisherman isn't standing around pawing the ground like some dumb jackass, or tossing his bait in 50 times an hour like some TV fisherman in women's pants.

"You don't wear those pants, do you?" he asked as he squinted at me.

"You mean shorts—cut offs?" I asked. "Me?"

"Good!" he said. "Toss the dang bait in and let 'er set. A big cat hears a bait tossed in the water and it may be 30 minutes before he feels comfortable enough to feed."

"About holes," I said as he eased back on his bench.

"Holes is the home of those big evil-tempered cats," he said as he raised himself on the bench again. "Mud cats live there and so do big forks. But those blues like to move more. You kin catch 'em in holes, but you can't always predict they're there."

"Prediction," I said, "That's another thing. Lots of fishermen think old-timer big-cat guys had an aura about them: Like you had the ability to feel the presence of big cats like a well digger with a witching stick feels water?"

"Aw, crap! You just want to make me mad." He coughed and wheezed, took a "proper" spit, and proceeded.

"Any idiot can figure out where big cats are. They live in those holes. But not every hole: the biggest ones; the deepest ones; sometimes the one with the most cover like fallen trees.

"Pole fishermen are so dang stupid—and lazy. They walk or float a couple miles of river and then they set their butt down and rest. Resting's fine, but only when I know where a big cat is."

"What you're suggesting," I said, "is that a fisherman should take say a 10-mile section of river and walk it or drift it in a boat, looking—surveying—the habitat. Instead of fishing each hole, just check it out. How big is it? How deep? How much cover is there?

"How many other holes are nearby?" I went on. "What are those other holes like? How do they compare with this one? Once a guy has taken an inventory of a pretty good-size section of river, he can make a prediction about where the biggest cats are. Once he draws a map, he can make some logical guesses—"

"No real guessin' involved," he interrupted. "No danged guessin' t'all. Ya darn right I had a map in my head. If I knew how every hole in a 10-mile section of river stacked up, I'd know exactly where the biggest cats were. Big cats are easier than little cats—way more predictable."

"So," I said, "a fisherman might want to pass by 15 consecutive good-looking holes to get to the one hole that's by far the biggest and deepest hole in say a 5-mile river section?"

"Now you got it. Only some city slicker thinks he's gonna catch a big cat without knowing his river. Course those guys think a big cat is 15 pounds. Humph!

"People who used to live on the river knew maybe 50 miles of it. I did. In those 50 miles they'd know there were really only 10 terrible (great) holes. That's where you fish. That's where you catch terrible fish. City slicker knows one mile of river and 4 holes and thinks he's what you writers call a 'river rat.'

"And don't make no difference what size the river is, either, I'll tell you that—only the biggest size of the catfish change. Show me a creek and the idea for finding the biggest cats is the same."

"But bigger rivers have bigger fish?" I said.

"Danged right! That's what I'm saying! There are more big fish in a hole, too. Bigger river like what the Missouri used to be before they crapped it up with dams, well, a good hole might have 15 big cats. You'd catch 5 or 8 of 'em and then fishin' would turn tough. You wait 'til the water came up again. Cats—but not always the biggest ones—move when the water comes up. Holes get restocked. When the water's down and the cats can't move, I can catch every fish in a hole. Though I never did. We always left some. But catching a big cat is the simplest thing ever.

"Coffee?" he asked. "Too much talk."

"Black. I like mine good and black. But I have more questions," I reminded him.

"Too many questions. Coffee time. Proper coffee—boiled. Cookies?"

"Sure, cookies, too," I said. "Need help?"

He turned and squinted at me. "Jest set your butt down there and shut up."

I sat looking over the meadow as Zacker made coffee. I thought of questions we'd covered in an earlier conversation.

"How big were the fish in those days?" I'd asked.

"Didn't weigh 'em much. Got paid by bulk—back of a wagon full," he'd answered. "Big cats

The Home of Big Cats!

Rivers, large and small, usually consist of a series of shallower and deeper spots. Shallows create more current as a volume of water is compressed and pushed forward. Fast-flowing shallow stretches usually have cleaner, harder bottom and are called riffles.

A riffle is followed by a deeper pool or a hole. These are the homes of catfish. The fish hole up in the deepest water and usually feed in the shallows at night.

But some riffle-hole areas are better than others. And some are the very best in a given section of river. Generally speaking, the biggest catfish reside in the biggest and deepest, or at times the most cover-ridden holes in an area.

Knowing the quality of the holes in a large section of river is vital to catching a bigger catfish. Sure, there are cats in every hole. But the biggest fish? They know a section of river like you know your home block. The biggest cats live in the very best holes.

Most fishermen don't catch big cats because they don't know where big-cat holes are. You must survey a large section of river to find the biggest, deepest, most cover-laden holes. If you've surveyed 5 miles of river, you should have done 10. And if you've done 10, why not 15? That's what it takes.

Then it's a matter of fishing with the right bait, at the right time, and with tackle that handles the fish you're after, whether it's a 6-pound cat in a small creek, a 15 in a small river, a 20 in a medium river, a 30 in a bigger river, or a world record in rivers like the Mississippi, Ohio, and Missouri or their major tributaries.

are big cats. But we had a lot of fish that weighed 75 pounds. Some maybe 100."

"Mostly flatheads?" I'd asked.

"Mostly," he'd answered. "But plenty of forks weighed 40 pounds and blues, too."

I'd told him that the world-record channel catfish was a 58-pounder. He'd shrugged. "So what? We've caught hook-and-line forks that easy weighed 60. Records ain't worth much on the river. The fish ain't impressed 'till you catch 'em."

And I'd asked him about the moon—"Do you fish by it?"—and I knew I'd struck upon an important topic by the pause he took before answering.

"The moon—the full moon," he said, "works powerful on big cats. The best days are those before the full moon; maybe starting five days before.

"You know, folks think that all a catfish can do is smell and taste things. But they see darn good and they like to feed at night in light. But there's somethin' about the full moon that makes them active, too.

"Never cared much for the dark moon, 'cause I think the fish might bite best during the day then; but I never fished much then because it was too easy to be seen."

"You mean you didn't want someone to see you fishing—or fishing legally with a pole line?" I'd asked.

"No use ruinin' your reputation," he'd chuckled.

Mostly he was joking, though. Mostly he didn't want anyone seeing his spots. Mostly he fished at night to keep his secrets. The boys would set baits just after dark and pick them up just before daylight, for when big cats first get hooked they make a terrible noise before settling down and sulking on the bottom. Sure. Leave the lines in for 24 hours on smaller-fish water. But not on big-fish water.

And then he'd said something important, something that reinforced an important observation of my own.

"Too often big cats bite during the early daylight hours," he'd said. "You couldn't afford to leave a line in and make a commotion then. Other fishermen wouldn't turn you in, but they'd sure steal your lines and your fish.

"For my money," he'd continued, "the best time for big cats runs from 'bout 4 to 8 in the morning. Big cats feed at night, but they need to see, feel, and smell things to be most successful. They need light, but not too much light. That's one reason the full moon's so good. But most of the time, big cats that don't feed successfully at night get fed full quick in early morning. That's the best bite. As morning progresses, the bite gets worse and worse as more and more cats feed themselves full."

Zacker shuffled back, splashing coffee from each large mug as he came. The cookies were stuffed in a very soiled shirt pocket.

"To the girl who lives on the hill," he chuckled as he gave me my coffee. "Know her?"

"Yeah, I know her," I responded.

"You do?"

"Well, no I don't mean that. I mean I know how the rest of that thing goes."

"Gotcher self into that one, didn't ya?" he laughed. "Here, have a cookie."

"How do you do that?" I asked as I watched him gum a cookie with his five remaining teeth. Crumbs flew as he told me to "Shut up and talk," a difficult assignment.

"About baits," I continued. "Do you use stinkbaits?"

"Tell you somethin' about baits," he answered. "Little cats eat anything, anything at all. Big cats is selective. For my money, the bigger the cat, the more he likes fresh bait. I ain't sayin' smelly baits ain't good and they won't take 'em; I'm sayin' that they just flat like fresh stuff better.

"Take a big mud cat. He's a mean sucker, the meanest fish swimmin', for my money. Danged right! He's the toughest, orneriest, meanest customer that swims in any natural (fresh) water. At times he won't ever pick up a dead bait, much less a ball of stinky crap. He wants somethin' live and big, like a big sucker, or better yet a big carp. Mud cats eat carp like peanuts: crack and a headshake and then the carp's gone. Only time a big mud cat takes dead bait real good is late spring. They take cut (filleted slabs) carp or sucker then.

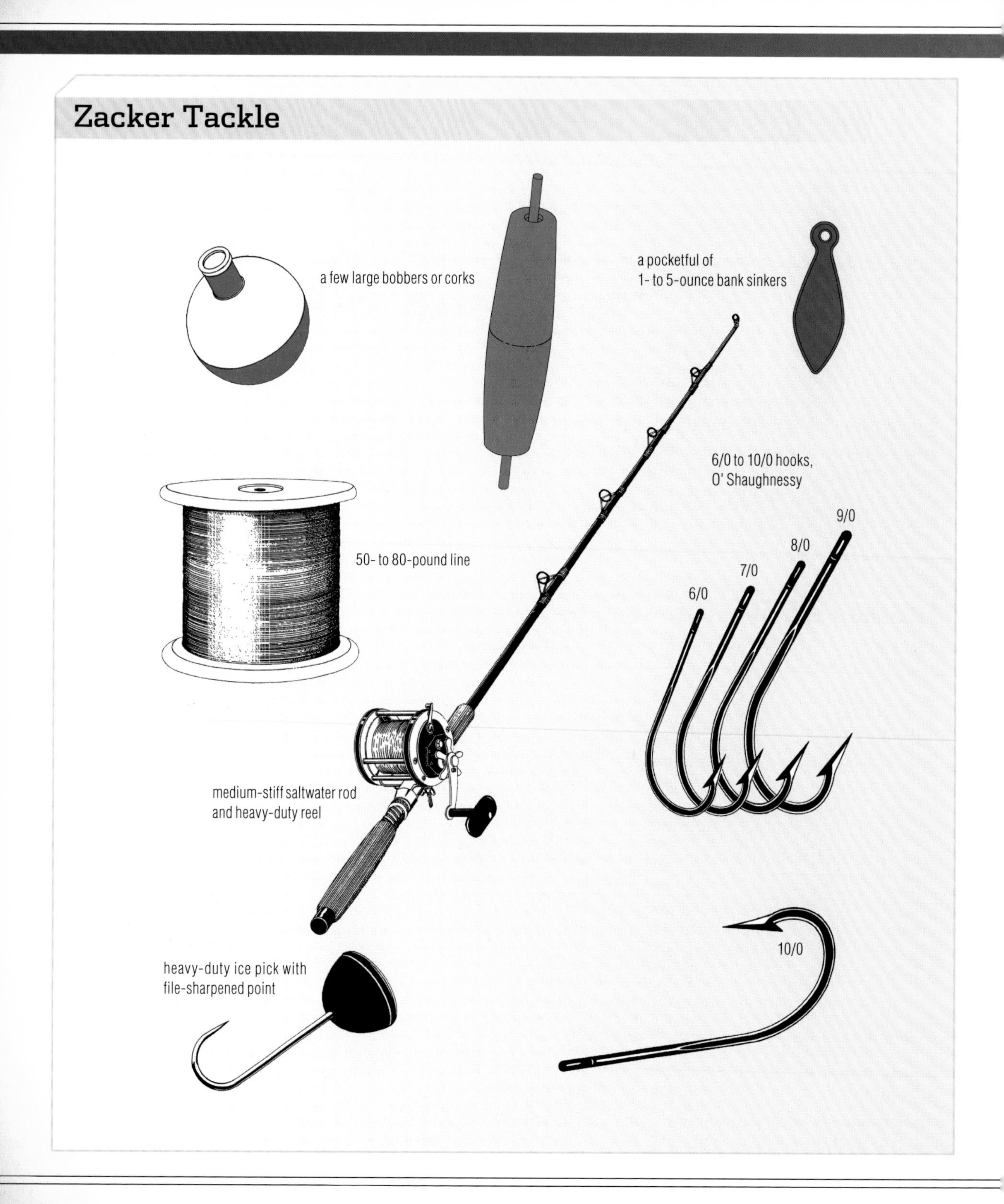
Zacker Tackle
a few large bobbers or corks
a pocketful of
1- to 5-ounce bank sinkers
6/0 to 10/0 hooks,
O' Shaughnessy
9/0
8/0
7/0
6/0
50- to 80-pound line
medium-stiff saltwater rod
and heavy-duty reel
heavy-duty ice pick with
file-sharpened point
10/0

Favored Baits

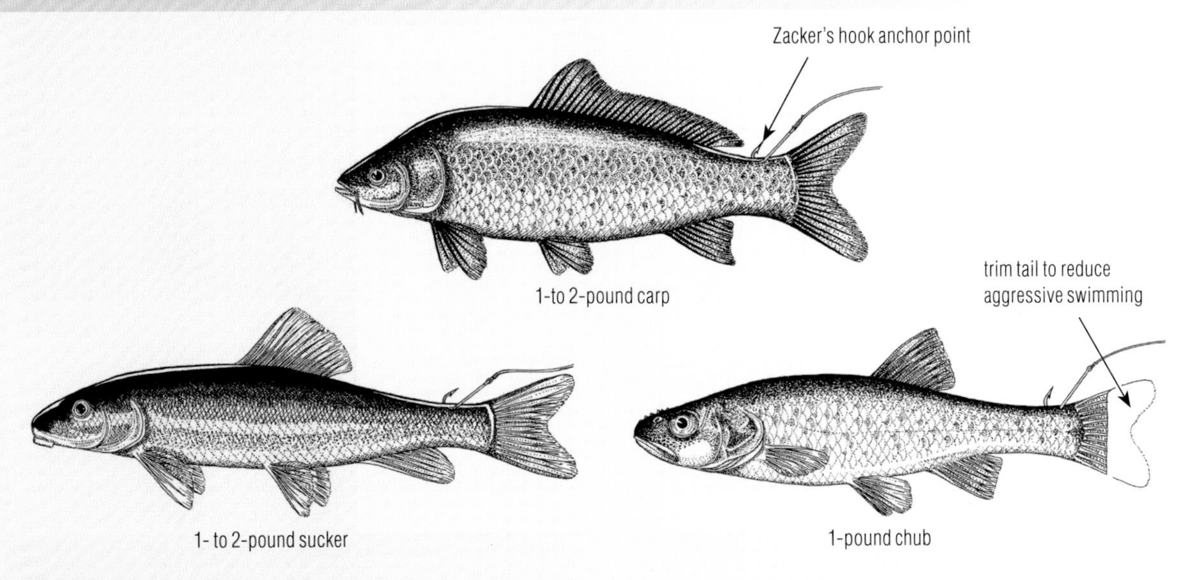

Zacker's Pole Rig

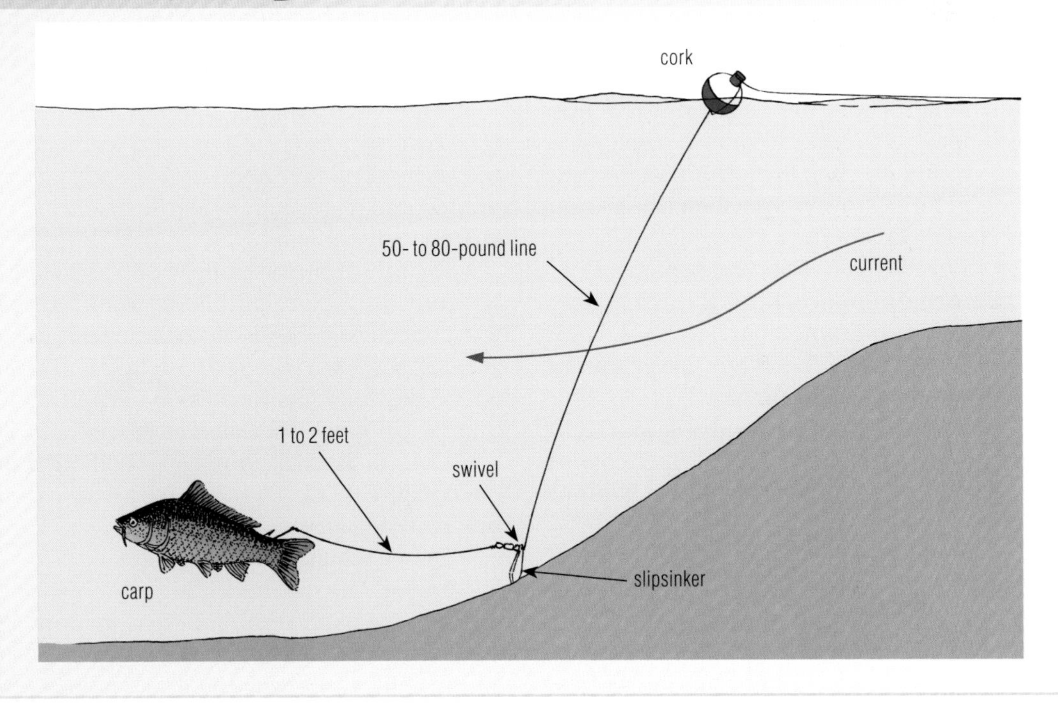

"Big forks is kinda the same; I mean they ain't gonna go out of their way to take smelly baits when they're used to havin' the rule of their roost and eatin' live stuff or stuff that ain't been dead long. One-pound suckers or creek chubs—live ones—are good. Or big chunks of fresh-cut sucker or chub. Just cut the side (fillet) off a big sucker and hook it through once with a 5/0 hook. Don't ball the dang thing up or you can't get hooks.

"There's one time big forks like smelly baits, though. In spring you get those ripe carp—the floaters that died in winter. There's no smell so bad. Cut the side off those fish, chunk it up, and you got a good bait for forks of all sizes.

"Don't claim to be an expert about big blues because we never used to catch that many. But they're killers, too. They like live baits and fresh-killed stuff, stuff that smells fresh. And it's just like the other cats, they don't go pickin' 'round with tidbits lookin' for cookie crumbs. They want a meal."

"Where do you hook your live baits?" I asked.

"Never hook one near the head even when your bait's settin' in current," he said. "Big cat'll crush that bait and swallow it before you know it, and chances are 50-50 when you set the hook or he swims away from your setline that the hook'll dig back into the bait. Had it happen a hundred times before I it out.

"You gotta hook a bait in his thinnest part and that's the part furthest away from their head—right near the clanged tail."

"Top side or bottom side?" I asked.

"Not much difference, but I always hooked mine in the top. And remember," he said, "only hook it once. Keep the barb of your hook exposed, 'specially with a big slab of cut bait."

"So say we're parked at a good hole and we're going to try catch a good fork. No little fish, now—a 20-pounder. How would you fish with a pole and line?" I asked.

"It's simple—easiest thing in the world," he said. "First, get yourself a good rod and reel, like saltwater stuff, and fill the reel with at least 50-pound line. The reel's got to have a clicker on it so you can set it in free spool, but when the fish takes the line out against the clicker, it makes a noise and gives constant resistance. Hook your bait on with a good hook, say a 5/0 O'Shaughnessy. Then toss it in at the head of the hole and wait. Start fishing at dark. If you can't fish all night you wanna get up early and start about 4 and fish 'till 'bout 8."

"You fish with a lantern?" I asked.

"Scared of the dark?" he asked.

"You freelining the bait?" I said, changing the subject.

"You gotta weight the bait so it struggles. It don't have to struggle all the time, but when a big cat gets close, it does. I usually used a big cork and a slipsinker setup.

"Say it's about 4 feet deep in an eddy area near the head of a hole. 'Bout 2 feet up your line (from your hook) you put a big swivel. Tie good knots. Then add a big egg sinker, like a 2-ouncer if you're using a 1-pound bait. If the live bait's too lively you can trim his tail (cut off a portion of the tail fin).

"Then another 4 feet up your line add a big cork. This cork ain't to keep your bait off bottom. The cork gets blown around in the current and keeps prodding your bait; makes it move and struggle. A big cat sometimes will crunch your bait just for the sport of it."

"And when a big cat takes?" I asked.

"You'll know, you'll danged well know," he said as he scratched the stubble on his chin. He nodded and a smile crept across his face. "You'll danged well know!

"Big cat'll grab the baitfish with a vice grip and crush him dead. He might give a mean headshake or two. Your clicker'll go zizzzzzz, zizzzzzz. And then zizzzzzzzzzzzzzz when the fish takes off steadily. Not proper manners for a cat to kill and eat in the same place, 'cause they always move."

"Doesn't the clicker resistance bother?" I asked.

"Small-cat talk," he answered. "Big cats don't care 'bout no pressure as long as it's constant."

"Do we wait to set?" I asked.

"Never!" he shot back. "Big cats crush and kill and have the bait in their mouth right now. When he moves he's got the bait 9 times out of 10. When you get to the rod, engage it, set and hold on. Once I set, I never give an inch; never let the cat run. Hold him. Turn him over. Make him roll and thrash 20 feet away from you, but never give him his head. You win or lose. And if you start losing you use heavier line. Cats don't care about whether the line is 70 or 80 pounds. Maybe in a reservoir or big river these days you can let a fish go a bit. But we never had such good drags, and my method works. Danged right!

"And use a pick (ice pick) to land fish. Nets ain't worth crap! Or a big gaff. And don't never put your finger in a cat's mouth like you do in those pictures you showed me (of 20-pound channel cats); they'll crush your finger, sure. Get your hand in there and they'll break every bone. They're the most terrible thing in the water.

"Danged wonderful, powerful fish," he said as he eased back down on the bench. "Say, Mr. Scientist, you know how old those fish are?"

"Experts say the biggest ones may live 50 years, maybe more," I said.

"Eighty years. Now that's a lot of livin'," he said, pondering his life and the lives of big cats. "Times is rough and times is good, but fishin' times is good times. Love that danged river. Love them danged cats."

"They're still there?" I asked.

"They are. Danged right. But there's sure fewer big blues and mud cats. Too many dams. Too much river crap (pollution). But there's still plenty fish, 'specially forks."

"So I've got time yet to catch a 30-pound channel cat?" I asked.

"Catch a 40 if you want," he said. "Big cats is easy; simplest thing in the world. Course the size of the fish changes with the water. But you find big-fish water, fish it the right time with good bait 'n you'll catch terrible fish. Danged right!"

Fifteen pounds of channel catfish: A small "fork" by Zacker's standards.

Historic Perspectives

So far as we know, this is the longest article ever published about fishing for bullheads. It is written at a time before wide-scale consolidation in the fishing industry—lots of manufacturing companies meant lots of advertising, which mean lots of editorial pages. The April 1987 issue is one of the largest in In-Fisherman history, at 308 pages—plenty of space for material that won't normally make it into smaller magazines. Thus, room for bullheads.

It is here that Stange first introduces Otis "Toad" Smith to readers. Longtime casual acquaintances, Stange and Smith begin to fish extensively together after Smith's heart attack in 1986. Doctors at the time say that Smith will never hunt or fish again, but he endeavors to prove otherwise and does so with a flourish, until his death in 1991. Smith says Stange is the only one who will take him on an overnight trip after the attack, "Because everyone is scared they'll wake up with a 'stiff' in the next bed."

The article doesn't get a lot of notice, however—bullheads aren't exactly high-interest fare for most In-Fishermen—so subsequent introductions to The Toadmonster in hardcore catfishing articles in the magazine are probably the first time most readers hear of the man who will become famous (or infamous) in the minds of a huge number of In-Fisherman readers.

This article is edited to show the flavor of the piece without getting into many of the side issues addressed in the original, which remains what must be the most thorough article ever published on how to catch these panfish.

Toad Smith

CHAPTER 4

APRIL 1987

Peace, Justice, Bullheads, and the American Way

LIFE. FISHING LIVES. WE BEGIN INNOCENTLY, unconcerned with heady stuff like fishing tourneys, graphite rods, and big-fish awards. Grandpa, Grandma, Dad, Mom, please take me fishing. Steal away to panfish—bullheads—and a simplicity that holds life at bay. No sticks stand in the way of fulfillment, for at age 5, 7, or 10, fulfillment is a bullhead. And fulfillment is easy. Life is grand as we store up memories of grandparents, parents, and friends—cherished memories.

More And Bigger Bullheads Or Your Money Back!

The dam breaks. Adolescence. Conformity. Competition. High school. College, perhaps. "Life is complex," a teacher says. Yes. Jobs. Competition. Adulthood. Scratch, bite, kick, scream, stab if you must to get ahead. Nuclear proliferation. Win. A coach, 7 and 2, is fired. Fishing. "Disposable rods and reels and faster boats," an outdoor writer says. Yes. Competition. Keep up with the Joneses, and especially the Martins. Conform. Pressure. We age. We wonder. "Younger women, older whiskey, faster horses," a song says. And bigger bass and more of them? Yes? Bullheads? Bluegills? Not now. Fulfillment is something bigger—always a step away.

Times change, sometimes people. Age 30, 50, 70. There is no old age, only age. Sometimes maturity. Eventually, wrinkles, failing eyesight, gray hair. Sometimes realization. Today or tomorrow may be the day. Only big fish; only certain species? Fish snobbery? Newer tackle; more gadgets? Tackle snobbery? "Fish smarter, not harder," a magazine says. "Live smarter, not harder?" you begin to wonder. We are by grace and our own free choice. Unmerited gifts. Family. Friends. Bullheads. Bluegills. Each bass. Each walleye. Burbot, carp, and redhorse suckers, too. Each day on the water, win or lose—nay, always win, big fish or small, few fish or many. Black coffee. A sunrise. A sunset. Patience.

In less life to live, more time for living?

"Teach a kid to fish," a writer says. Yes! Love of fishing. Of the life that springs from an exuberant youngster sitting quietly, patiently on a bank. A worm, a cast, a tappa-nibble, a hook-set. A smile. This is life.

Bullheads? "Kid's fish," says a passing fisherman. "Kid'll grow up." But in knowing no better, perhaps knowing better? Life ends a little like it begins, so, often there is a sensible kinship among young and old fishermen.

Toad with a very big bullhead.

TOAD

My friend Toad, like me, started fishing for bullheads. His name is Otis Smith, but "Toad's my name, and fishin' and huntin's my game," he'll tell you. I call him "Toadsie." Better you call him Toad.

Toad is a fine cut of a feller, 6 foot 2, 260, 80 or what difference does it make, a man born out of time, the closest thing you'll find to a mountain man in today's world. He wears a beard well and has lived in the wilds of Alaska and the mountains of Montana as well as the plains of Iowa, the Dakotas, and Canada. He is missing part of a tooth and a bit of his tongue sticks out when he laughs, which is often.

These days Toad is a guide; maybe the best there is; maybe the best there ever was. He has caught, trapped, shot, or arrowed—mostly arrowed—everything and will guide for anything. About now he will be guiding bear hunters and fishermen in unknown parts of North America.

To trip with Toad is to travel way back in time. A society-frazzled big-city hunter and fisherman with 8 cups of coffee under his belt will try to hustle Toad along on their first morning together. Toad will look at him and say, "Gimmee that watch." Out comes his bow and to the horror of the hunter, his watch goes on the end of an arrow, and the arrow—Sheewunk!—50 feet high up in the trunk of a tree. "There!" Toad'll say. No one argues because he could kill a bear with his bare hands and once did wrestle a gorilla to the death—honest. Besides, he'll shoot the watch down at the end of the trip. Indiana Toad.

The first time I met Toad I was trudging through mile-high nettles trying to get to the next catfish hole along an Iowa river so small that no one fishes it. Suddenly he was sitting there with his feet propped on a log, hacking away with a Bowie knife on a chunk of deer sausage. His pole was propped in a forked stick and a cool shade fell over the spot. Within reach to his right was blood bait, to his left stinkbait, and the sandwich makings rested on his belly.

"Sometimes it don't pay to move," he said as he stabbed a chunk of sausage. And then, honest (you say that a lot when you tell Toad stories), he kerchunked his knife neatly into a cottonwood two feet to my right. "Sausage?" he asked. Visions of *Deliverance* danced in my head.

What I think I liked most about Toad, besides the fact that he likes a good sandwich while out fishing, is that he is unpresumptuous about fish. Fish are fish, no matter the species; they are to be caught and appreciated. In his spare time, of which there is some, Toad fishes for prairie-lake walleyes. Then he goes carp fishing or maybe after snapping turtles. Maybe he'll head north for Manitoba pike, or south for White River trout. Maybe he'll fish for chubs in a tiny creek near his house.

Toad isn't bashful. He has been known to walk into a restaurant and announce in a perfect bass voice that any TV commentator would cherish, "Well, hello theyyaar. (Pause, while everyone in the world looks up.) My name is Doug Styangahy. I'm no fisherman, but ah plays one on TayVay." Funny Toad.

Classic Toad? We're nearing the end of a trip in the Montana backcountry, and he's going into town; so I give him my credit card to reserve a motel room for me for the night before I fly home at the end of the trip. He returns with a credit card bill for $1,760, and later at midnight, I am greeted in my motel room by Benny's all-girl chorus line. "Out!" I tell the girls. "There's been a mistake!"

"But Toadsie told us to come up," they coo. "We have a credit card billing!"

"Out!" I repeat. "O-U-T! Out!" Funny Toad. (The $1700 bill was fake.)

Toad also has done at least one thing that most folks haven't. Several years ago, he had a serious heart attack. Bypass surgery reduced his heart in actual if not figurative size. He has portions of his heart in a glass jar. Toad, being Toad, used a piece to catch a catfish. "Hey!" he'll say. "Let's not take this life business so seriously."

Toad stories have plenty to do with bullheading, for bullheading isn't so much a picky-picky how-to kind of deal as it is a life philosophy. Bullheads are. Bullheads also are what they are not, which is muskies, pike, and certainly bass.

What bullheads are is the basis of an industry. Bullheads and other panfish are of huge consequence. Millions of fishermen are what they are because of bullheads. Bullheads are why they started fishing and they are why many of them continue to fish. Subtract bullheads (catfish) and panfishermen from the angling force in America and you subtract millions of fishermen—maybe over half. Yet for such importance, bullheads and bullheading remain totally simple.

Take it easy. Boil some eggs and make some liver-sausage sandwiches. Put a big ol' slice of onion on there. Lots of pepper, too. That's livin'. You gotta take your time, just like we're doing with this story. But eventually, it is time to go bullheading.

A Bullhead's Revenge

Bullheads are famous for their sharp dorsal and pectoral spines, spikes, horns, or whatever you prefer to call them. The spines become somewhat blunted as fish age. Bullheads and catfish do not have venom or poison glands associated with their spines. Some very close relatives, madtoms and stone cats, do. A bullhead spining causes infection and that means redness, swelling, and pain. Shallow puncture wounds heal quickly if they are kept clean and exposed to air. No Band-Aids please. Deeper puncture wounds require a doctor's consultation if infection sets in.

BULLHEAD SPECIES

"First thing I'd tell fishermen," Toad would say, "is that they should know what they're catching. Bullheads aren't just bullheads; there are different kinds. And 'yellow belly' ain't one of them.

"There are three basic kinds of bullheads in North America," he would continue. "The most commonly caught bullhead is the black bullhead. There also are yellow and brown bullheads, and most folks think they catch yellow bullheads because their bullheads have yellow bellies and they assume yellow bullheads naturally have yellow bellies, which they often do, but black and brown bullheads can also have yellow bellies, while the yellow bullhead may have either a yellow or a white belly."

"What?"

And then he'd explain. "Folks, what that means is this: Yellow-bellied bullheads may be yellow bullheads, black bullheads, or brown bullheads, but they most likely are black bullheads because they're the most commonly caught bullheads in most lakes; although if you fish big water, your yellow bellies may be brown bullheads, although brown bullheads often sport white tummies, and if you fish deeper water and weeds in real big lakes during midsummer, perhaps your yellow-bellied bullheads really are yellow bullheads, because that's where they live then."

LOCATION

At some point I might ask Toad to tell you about bullhead location during spring. "Look for backwater areas," he'd say, and then I'd ask him to go on.

"Well, backwaters are backwaters, but first you gotta have the right kind of lake, reservoir, or river. Bullheads do well in moderately fertile, fertile, or very fertile waters. In In-Fisherman terms that means late mesotrophic and eutrophic waters. The best bullhead waters are relatively shallow. Most states and provinces have bullhead waters and that's the reason they're so popular.

"Fertile waters also grow lots of bullheads fast. The best bullhead bag limit is the sheer thought of having to clean too many when you get home. I fillet the ones I catch and, ahh, they are fine eating in spring."

"As I was saying, backwaters are backwaters. Look for shallow water connected to a main body of water—something that warms quickly. Sloughs are good. So are feeder creeks. Bullheads love to run up feeder creeks and gather below barriers like dams or small waterfalls. Canals are hotspots, too, and so are dug-out boat marinas; anything connected to a main body of water that warms quickly."

"O.K., hotshot," I'd say. "What if none of the above are available?"

"Well, there goes the neighborhood"

"Aw, here we go. Nine times out of ten, they are available, and if they aren't you're probably dealing with a pond. Look for the shallowest end of the pond, just like you look for the shallowest end of a lake."

"The best waters for trophy bullheads—2-pounders?" I'd ask.

"In the North, the best big-fish waters are moderately fertile waters that also grow big walleyes or bass. This is brown bullhead water. Browns consistently get bigger than blacks or even yellows. These lakes usually don't grow so many bullheads, but the bullheads live longer and get bigger. Moderately fertile southern reservoirs and rivers also grow some hawg 'heads, and so do some ponds."

"So bullheads like soft mucky marshes in spring, huh?" I'd ask.

YAHOO! BULLHEAD STEW

***Bullheads**: Horned pout, pout, chucidehead, butterball, yellow belly, wogger, paper skin, polly, wally, woolly. A bullhead by any other name is still a bullhead. But while you'll certainly know a bullhead when you catch one, you may have trouble distinguishing the basic types: brown, black, or yellow. The reasons? Their ranges overlap, there may be several stocks or genetic variations of each basic kind, and they produce hybrids. In short, brown bullheads may look like blacks or yellows, and so on. Never mind. In spring and early summer they all taste fine.*

"Mister Carp to you..."

*The following range maps were drawn from information from W.B. Scott's and E.J. Grossman's **Freshwater Fishes of Canada,** and Milton Trautman's **The Fishes of Ohio.** These indicate basic ranges that have been extended by stocking.*

Black Bullhead

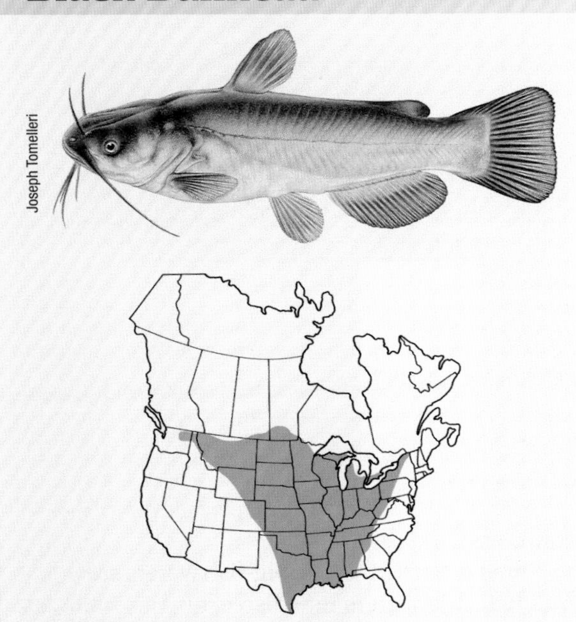

The black bullhead, called "brown" bullhead by many fishermen because its coloration often is more olive green, brown, or yellow than black, is the most commonly caught bullhead. True brown bullheads, however, often are distinctly mottled, the only bullhead to be so marked.

Scientific sources often use the pectoral spine to distinguish the bullhead species. Blacks have a smooth back edge on the pectoral spine, although hybrids (brown + black) may have a slight serration that catches the finger.

Sources confirm that the black is the smallest average bullhead, yet both the International Game Fish Association and the National Freshwater Fishing Hall of Fame list a mammoth 8-pound black caught in 1951 from Lake Waccabuc in New York as the all-tackle world record. Of thousands of Iowa specimens sampled, the largest black was a 15 incher that weighed almost 2 pounds. Of thousands of Ohio specimens, the largest black was a 16.8 incher that weighed 2 pounds 12 ounces. We haven't talked with those New York officials, but we wonder if the fish really was a black bullhead. Black bullheads generally prefer shallower, softer, bottom areas than yellow or brown bullheads, although in spring their habitats may overlap. Black bullheads may live 8 or 9 years, although 3 or 4 years is more typical. Blacks usually are 8 to 11 inches long and weigh less than a pound. World Record: 8 pounds—Kani Evans, Lake Waccabuc, New York, 8/1/1951.

Brown Bullhead

Joseph Tomelleri

The brown bullhead has distinctly diferent habitat requirements than the black bullhead, although during spring the two species often inhabit the same backwater areas. Brown bullheads dominate in bigger, deeper, clearer bodies of water with harder bottom. Blacks dominate in shallower, more turbid waters with soft bottom. Hybrids (black + brown) bullheads are common and, indeed, populations may be almost entirely composed of hybrids.

Pure-strain brown bullheads are easy to distinguish when they're distinctly mottled. They average slightly larger than black bullheads and, sources agree, reach larger maximum size. Of thousands of specimens sampled in Ohio, the largest was 18.8 inches long and weighed 3 pounds 14 ounces. Twenty-one-inch blacks have been reported from Florida, and 6- to 8-pound fish occasionally are reported by anglers.

Like the black bullhead, the typical brown bullhead lives 3 or 4 years, measures 8 to 11 inches, and weighs less than a pound. That 8-pound world-record black bullhead in New York was probably a brown bullhead or a hybrid.

World Record: 5 pounds 8 ounces—Jimmy Andrews, Veal Pond, Georgia, 5/22/1975.

Yellow Bullhead

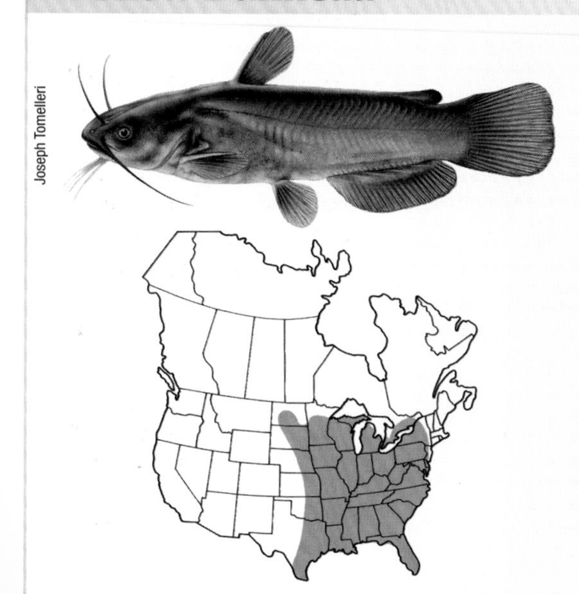
Joseph Tomelleri

The yellow bullhead is less common than either brown or black bullheads and appears to do well only where it does not compete with them. Yellow bullheads prefer clearer water than black bullheads and more vegetated water than browns.

Yellow bullheads are distinguished by a long anal fin and chin whiskers that are yellow or white but never spotted or pigmented. Their coloration is much like the black bullhead, but generally more yellow.

Yellow bullheads average slightly larger than blacks and slightly smaller than browns. The largest Ohio specimen was 18.3 inches long and 3 pounds 10 ounces.

World Record: 4 pounds 4 ounces—Emily Williams, Mormon Lake, Arizona, 5/11/1984.

"In spring, bullheads like to be warm. And once they're warm, they like to eat and make love. But bullheads got class; first they eat. The best food conditions are in the warmest areas and bullheads do feed on or over mucky bottoms. But they prefer to feed over harder bottoms.

"So, harder bottom is what you're looking for in a generally soft-bottomed backwater. Bullheads can find food better on firm bottom. They are more likely to suspend and feed over the bottom when it's muck. Now about bullheads in love."

"I'll handle that," I'd interrupt, fearing the consequence of letting Toad proceed. "Ah, springtime, birds, bees, and bullheads. Bullheads aren't picky about mates, but they are picky about where and when. The 'where' is the 'why for' the softer bottom. Male or female bullheads find an undercut bank, a muskrat tunnel, or any old hole for a spawning site, or they sort of wallow out a depression in the bottom. They need softer bottom.

"When the time comes, usually when the water temperature reaches a sustained 70°F, Mrs. Bullhead finds Mr. Bullhead, or vice versa, and they make fertile weebully eggs. Apparently in some cases, a male or female bullhead may guard the nest until the eggs hatch and also guard the fry for a bit after they hatch. Parental care ensures bullhead success. Finally, however, the little bullies are on their own and travel in dense schools that consist of hundreds of small bullheads. They are forage for pike, other

Backwater Bullheads

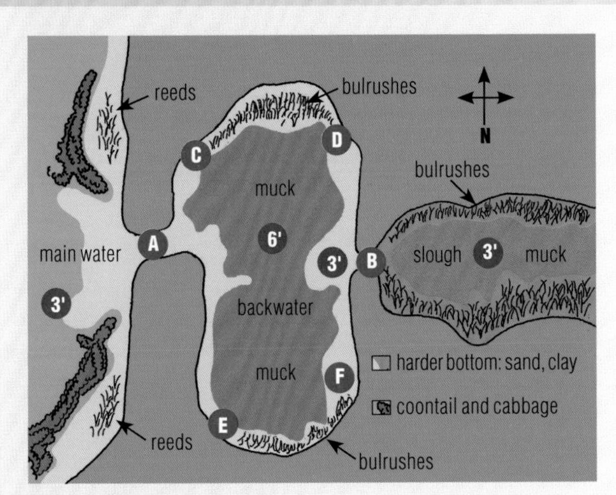

In spring, bullheads are drawn to the warmer water and more abundant food in backwater areas. Bullheads from the main body of water move through the connecting canal into the backwater. Once bullheads are in the backwater, some of them move into the slough. Sloughs are primarily black bullhead territory, however; yellow and brown bullheads would remain in the backwater.

A reverse migration occurs after bullheads spawn. Some black bullheads, though, would stay in the backwater if running water keeps it from stagnating too badly.

The best general fishing areas tend to concentrate bullheads. Look for:

(1) *Funnel areas like* ***Canals A*** *and* ***B****. Bullheads must move through them, and current also tends to concentrate washed-in food that attracts and holds them.*

(2) *Harder bottom, such as along the east and west shorelines of the backwater. Bullheads, especially blacks, feed in, on, or over muck, but even they find food or baits better on harder bottom like the sandy clay that's often found in a backwater.*

(3) *Vegetation breaks like the bulrushes along the north and south shorelines of the backwater. Bullheads travel the front face of these spots but tend to concentrate where vegetation stops* **(C, D, E, F)** *and where it forms points.*

Main-water areas immediately outside of ***Canal A*** *would attract bullheads after they spawn (many bullheads spawn in the main water, by the way). Fish the front face of the reeds and the cabbage, fish the coontail flats, and the outside edge of the deeper weeds.*

bullheads and catfish, and walleyes."

Then Toad would interrupt.

"Forgot something. Besides concentrating on harder bottom, to find prespawn bullheads in a backwater, look for edges. The two most important edges are (1) the shoreline or shoreline drop-off, and (2) the front face of emergent weeds.

"A shoreline is good only if it's lipped. Good shorelines drop off immediately into 1 or 2 feet of water. Also check for a distinct shoreline-related drop-off. Perhaps the shoreline depth tapers gradually out for 20 feet and then drops off distinctly into 2, 3, or 4 feet of water. Anything distinct near shore may gather bullheads.

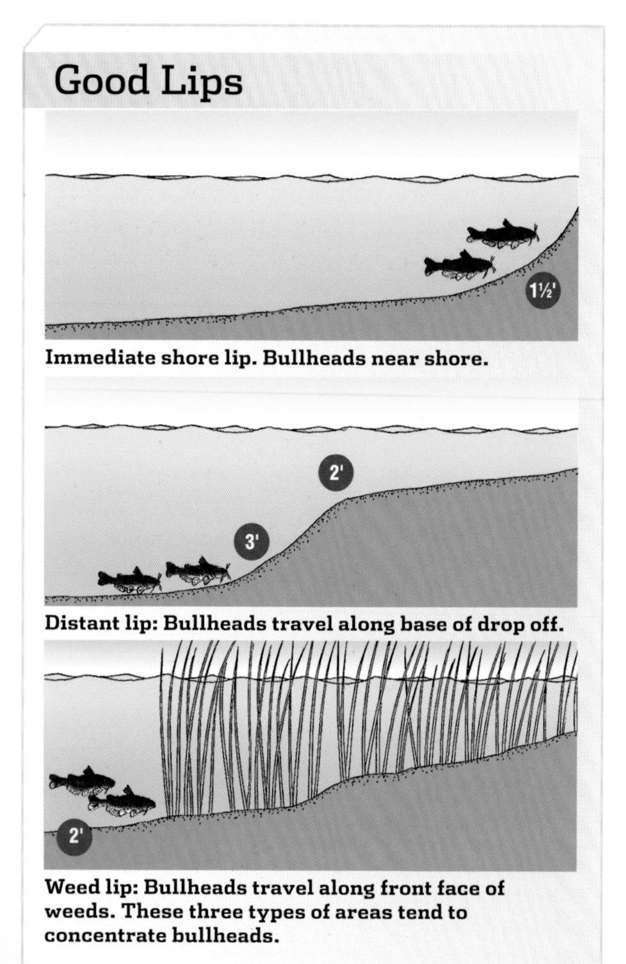

Immediate shore lip. Bullheads near shore.

Distant lip: Bullheads travel along base of drop off.

Weed lip: Bullheads travel along front face of weeds. These three types of areas tend to concentrate bullheads.

"Too few anglers give bullheads credit for being wary. Bullheads, like catfish and carp, have their air bladder connected to their inner ear by a small set of bones. This system intensifies sound. You won't catch many bullheads traveling along a good shoreline if you make too much commotion on the bank.

"About emergent vegetation like bulrushes or reeds. The face of them naturally creates the kind of lip situation that attracts bullheads. Key your fishing where emergent vegetation forms a point that projects into a body of water. A vegetation point is like a long arm that catches and gathers bullheads and pushes them past a specific spot at the tip of the point.

"Don't forget funnels, either. Say you have a necked-down area that leads from the main lake into a slough. The necked-down area is a natural funnel that lots of bullheads travel through."

MORE LOCATION

"Once bullheads spawn," I'd continue, "black bullheads may stay in a backwater area if it doesn't get too warm and stagnant. The best early summer backwater spots have water flowing in to keep them fresh.

"In waters where bullheads filter back into the main body of water, early summer fishing can get tough for awhile. Some bullheads seem to enter a 'sucking' stage where they group in tight schools and collectively dabble at the surface with their mouths slightly out of the water. These fish aren't biters, and exactly what purpose this activity serves beats me.

"Eventually, however, most bullheads in main-lake, reservoir, and river areas gather in weedgrowth. Reedbeds, in particular, are an attractive site in the first part of summer. Later, deeper submergent weedgrowth like pondweed (cabbage) and coontail beds become more important. Bullheads are notoriously nocturnal, although they certainly can be caught during the day, too."

RIGGIN' AND GIGGIN'

Zillions of bullheads have been caught with a cane pole, cord, hook, and worm. Zillions more will be. Yet there are days when fine-tuned rigging information may help.

Hooks—Big hooks often are used because at times bullheads bite so well that they swallow smaller hooks. That's a pain. Toad knows. I can see it now. He'll hold his massive paw in my face for me to see his bleeding trigger finger. "If these kids land another gut-hooked bullhead, I'll cry," he'll snivel.

It's Toad's semi-annual once-a-year neighborhood bullhead bash. Only kids are invited. And me and Toad. Bullheads are hitting the beach compliments of screaming Zebco 202s, the mainstay of a million fishermen. Toad's finger is raw from wrenching hooks from the raspy mouths of bullheads. I'm busy taking pictures.

As the afternoon progresses, the hooks get progressively larger. "Trust me," Toad says as a kid questions the 8/0 hook Toad's tying to his line. "You've caught the little ones; now we're after a trophy."

"But do they make bullheads that big?" the kid asks.

"Trust me," he says. (It takes 42 worms to cover the hook.)

Before the afternoon is finished, Toad will unhook 100 bullheads. "That's a limit!" he'll announce. Happy kids. I take a picture of Toad's finger.

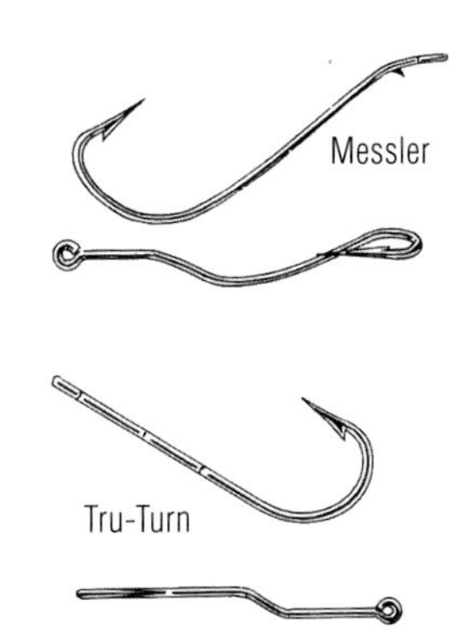

Turn-type hooks increase looking percentages.

To maximize catches yet minimize swallowed hooks, tailor hook size to the size of the bullheads. Generally, choose a 2, 1, 1/0 or 2/0 single hook. I believe that "turn-type" hooks like the Tru-Turn increase hooking percentage. If you fish paste baits, try a #4 or #6 treble.

Leadhead jigs also work. Pick a jig with a 1/0 or 2/0 hook. Add a worm or two. Bullheads eat down to the leadhead and then have a difficult time

Leadhead Jigheads

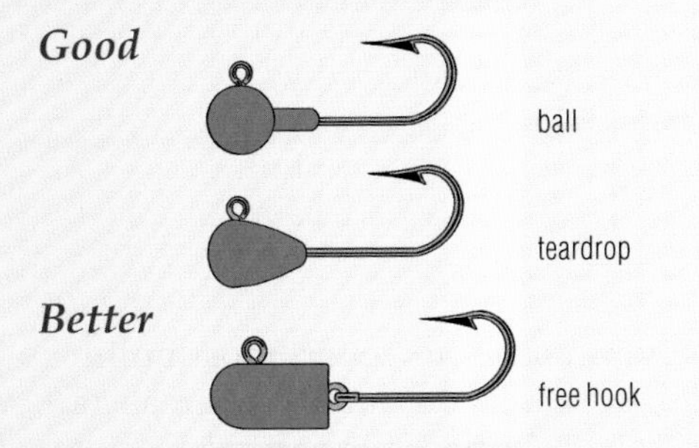

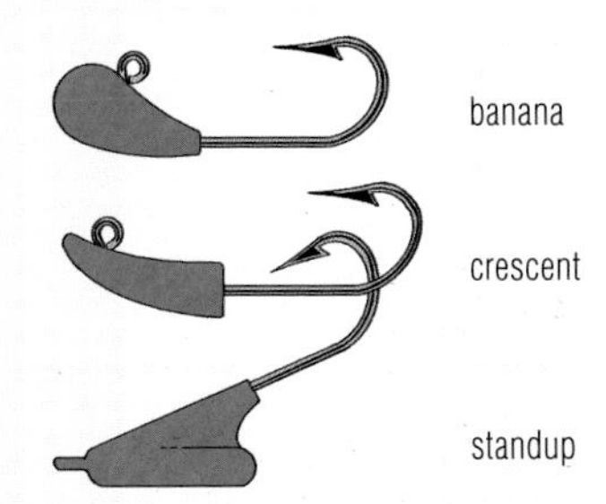

Surprise! Leadhead jigs filled with worms and fished stationary on the bottom are great for bullheads.

Line—Use the heaviest line you can get away with. Monofilament's fine but catfish or bullheads rarely care about line, so it doesn't matter whether it's clear, black, or white. What does matter is how limp it is. The limpness of Dacron makes a hook easier to pick up and less objectionable to eat than when it's tied on with the same test monofilament. Twelve- to 27-pound-test Cortland or Gudebrod Dacron has a place in catfishing and bullheading. Sometimes we use a short section of Dacron leader to tip the end of the monofilament.

swallowing it. By then you should have 'em. The head of the jig makes a handy handle for unhooking, too. Stand-up jigs with wedge heads work best.

Weights—Keep it simple. Stock up on bell sinkers weighing 3/8 to 1 ounce to make bottom-fishing rigs—and BB, 3/0, and 4/0 split shot for weighting float rigs.

Rigs—One standard bottom rig is a "sliprig." Slide a bell sinker onto your mainline and tie the line to a swivel. Make a terminal-hook rig by tying a hook to a 12- to 18-inch piece of Dacron. Tie this to the free end of the swivel.

The "set rig" is another bottom rig. Tie a bell sinker to the end of your line; make a loop knot 6 or 12 inches above the sinker, and tie a snelled hook onto the loop knot. Several loop knots and several hooks may be used.

Both rigs work well, but when the bullheading gets tough, a sliprig is best. If you prefer a set rig, make a "slip-set" sliprig.

Tie a bell sinker to one end of a 6-inch piece of line and a swivel to the other. Slide your mainline through the open end of the swivel and tie it to the swivel end of a terminal-hook rig made from 12 inches of line, a hook and a swivel.

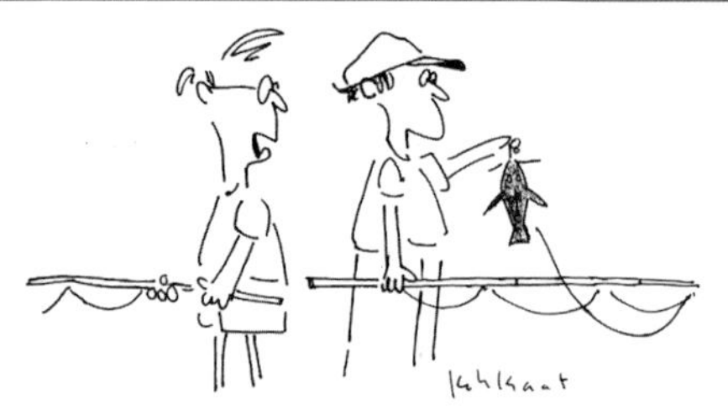

"Some people eat 'em... but then some people eat brussel sprouts."

Lee Nelson of Dickman's Bait Shop in Mormon Lake, Arizona, home of the world-record yellow bullhead, fishes a variation of this rig that works great in water where you also might catch catfish or northern pike. Add a second terminal-hook rig to the free-running swivel. Use a worm on one hook and a dead smelt or other fish bait on the other.

One other rig is a "bottom float rig," which works as an alternative for fishing over soft bottom. It's a sliprig with a 4- to 6-inch terminal line section. Add a small piece of Styrofoam to your hook to keep it off the bottom, or use a large floating jighead.

Bullheading Essentials

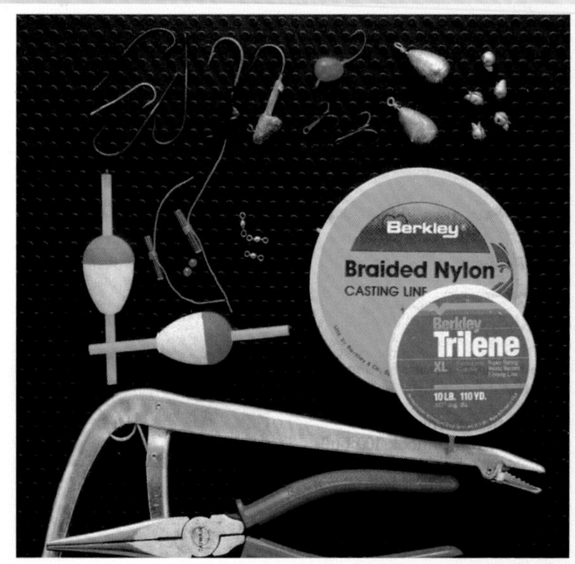

Bullheading is a simple sport, but certain items can make fishing more successful. We recommend (left to right, top to bottom): #2, #1, 1/0, and 2/0 hooks; stand-up leadhead jigs; floating jigheads; #8, #6, and #4 treble hooks; 3/8- to 1-ounce bell sinkers; BB, 3/0, and 4/0 split shot; slipfloats; swivels; and Dacron and monofilament line.

Product comments:

- Turn-type hooks increase hooking success.
- Stand-up leadhead jigs are for bottom-fishing with a worm.
- Floating jigheads are for suspending baits slightly off bottom.
- Bell sinkers are for bottom rig weights.
- Split shot are for weighting floatrigs.
- Slipfloat—for suspending bait.
- Swivels are handy for making rigs.
- Dacron line is limper than monofilament and less offensive to bullheads.

Although there are many float rigs, our favorite is a "slipfloat rig." You need a bead, slipfloat, split shot, and hook rig. Tie a stop knot to your mainline, slide a bead on the line and then your slipfloat. Add enough split shot to settle the float low in the water. Add a terminal-hook rig. Slide the stop knot on your line to adjust the depth of your bait. Usually, fish in the bottom half of the water: If the water is 6 feet deep, fish in the bottom 3 feet.

Baits—Another thing I like about Toad is that he's a Star Trek fan. There was an episode when Captain Kirk, Spock, and the crew were attacked by a huge space ship that Spock verified with his nifty scanning device, as one huge living cell: That's sort of like bullheads, which are the closest thing there is to one big taste bud. Not only do bullheads have taste buds on their lips and whiskers, but also scattered over their body. A bullhead can taste with its tail as well as its stomach.

It's no secret that bullheads like the taste of many things but often prefer nightcrawlers. If you're using single hooks, keep your 'crawler oozing succulent natural juices. To do that, the 'crawler must remain wrigglingly alive. (Say that five times.) Don't stick a hook in his head or heart. Any biology student that listened in class can tell you that a 'crawler's brain and heart are located in about the first dozen worm segments. Start at the tail and slip the hook through the 'crawler several times before making the last slip just ahead of the ring.

A bullhead doesn't know a hook point from a hog's tail. It isn't necessary to hide the point of a hook. Indeed, don't, for covering it hinders getting the hook barb into the bullhead on the hook-set.

Which brings up another point. I'm convinced that the main reason bullheads twist from a hook as they wriggle, twist and thrash on their way in is that the hook isn't set beyond the huge barb that most 'head hooks sport. File the barb almost away or better yet go barbless. A barbless hook sinks in to the max on the hook-set. With a medium-action rod, it's easy to keep the line tight when the fish is coming in. Barbless means more bullheads—and less trouble unhooking them, too.

Bullheads will never be the stuff of bass tournaments, big bucks, or brazen gadgetry. It's like Toad says: Fish are fish and each one's meant to be caught and appreciated. Fish and fishermen stand equal before the Master Caster and each fish species has individual merits that make it unique and worthy of pursuit. Equal rights for fish and man. That's the American way.

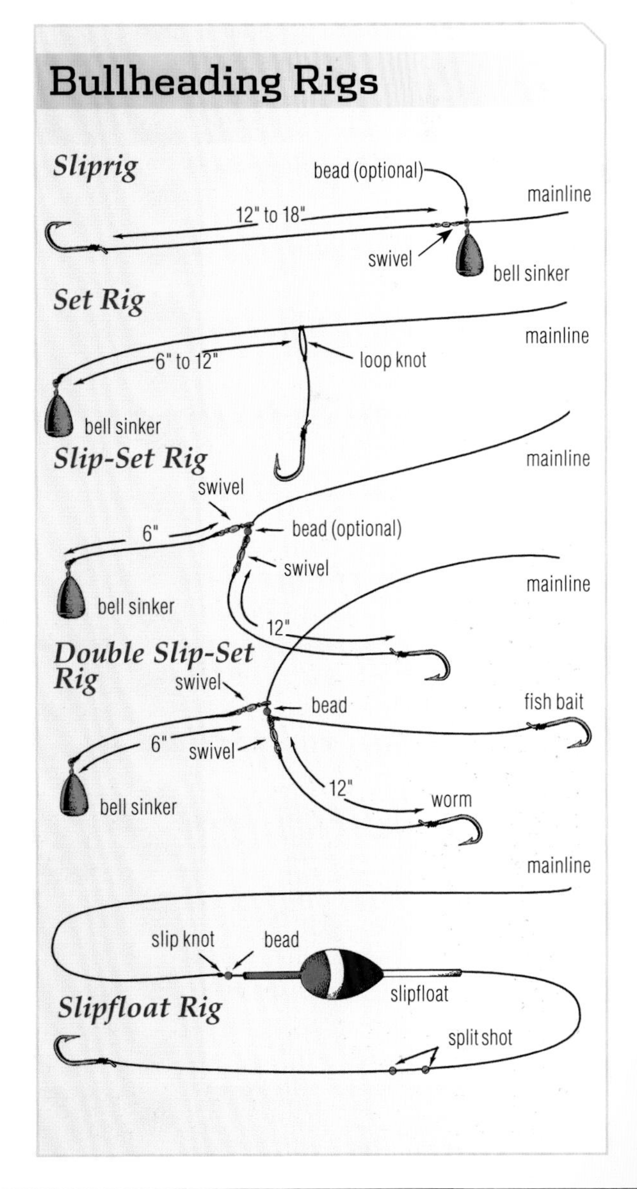

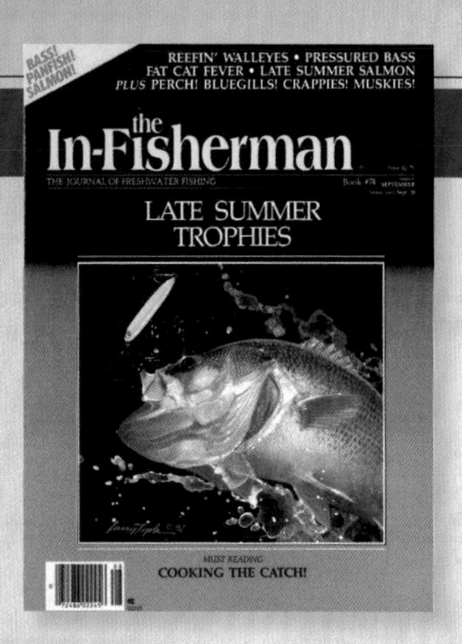

Historic Perspectives

In-Fisherman magazine issues are larger in spring and early summer than in late summer, fall and early winter, because fishing manufacturers have budget money available and do most of their advertising then—the main sales season for fishing tackle. This means more editorial pages in spring and early summer.

August issues are always tight, which in this case means the availability of a meager three pages for catfish. Still, the presentation concept presented here, although simple-sounding today, is a new one for most catfish anglers of the time.

Stange is a pioneer in facilitating the exchange of information between European anglers and North American anglers. Beginning in 1983, many Euro anglers—particularly Dutch angler Jan Eggers, who for a time is In-Fisherman's International Correspondent—visits Stange to fish for carp, pike, catfish, and other fish. Duncan Kay (holding the catfish) at the time is a famous English carp-bait manufacturer and fisherman. Ted Jowett (on the opposing page) is a Manitoba guide Stange often fishes and hunts with. Stange convinces Jowett to guide for catfish on the Red River at Lockport, Manitoba, the first catfish guide in the area. Stange first visits the banks of the Red at Lockport in the mid 1980s, a story for another "historic perspective" as this book moves on.

CHAPTER 5

AUGUST 1987

Increasing Catfish Catches–Instantly

AFTER FOUR DAYS OF CATFISHING up and down 200 miles of the Red River, Englishman Duncan Kay and I were about "catted out." Duncan alone had landed and released five channel cats over 20 pounds and dozens over 10. OK, twist our arms. We'd fish one more day.

There was no hurry, however, to start fishing a good-looking bank spot below the Lockport Dam near Selkirk, Manitoba. We'd drink coffee while we watched the sunrise and other fishermen.

Before we'd cracked the thermos, a nearby catfisherman had a run and missed it. He set hard, had the fish momentarily—then nothing. Disgusted and frustrated after a night of, apparently, constantly losing fish, he tossed his pole to the ground. We couldn't hear what he mumbled, but the thrust of it was, "I can't hook 'em—I just can't hook 'em!"

Yeah, well, it happens. You lose fish. But if you're missing many cats on the hook set, you're doing something really wrong. You can catch almost every decent cat that hits. Most good catmen do.

The secret is fishing with an exposed hook. Unfortunately, many catfishermen, including the frustrated guy on the bank that morning, believe that covering the point of a hook—hiding the darn thing from a fish that doesn't know or care what a hook is—means more cats. It means the opposite. Try the missed tonnage of 16 million catmen, 9 or 10 of whom habitually hide their hooks in their bait. Try a conservative estimate of 10 missed sets per catman per year, times 5 pounds a miss. Heavy stats.

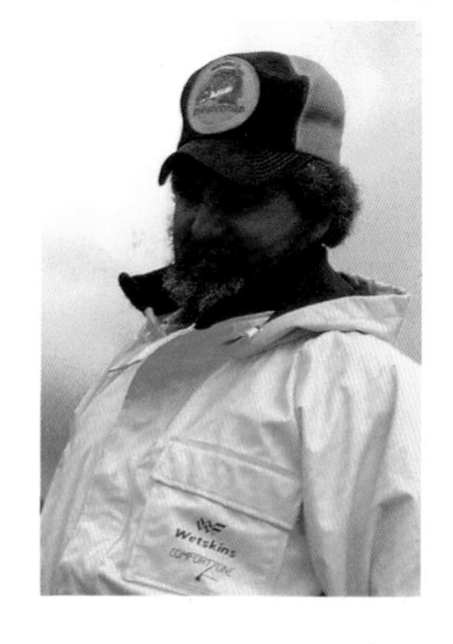

Get To The "Point" Of A Common Problem. There's No Need To Miss Good Cats On A Hook-Set!

Consider the hair rig, a popular English bait-rigging method that places an exposed hook near to, but separated from, a bait attached by an inch-long portion of light monofilament. Not only is a bait easier for wary fish (they have a lot of those in heavily fished English waters) to pick up, but the exposed hook means instant hook penetration on a set.

Of course, many catfishermen do their best to hide hooks but unknowingly fish them exposed anyway. Hooks packed into many dough baits are quickly exposed as the dough washes away.

Take time to try fishing with an exposed hook. If you use a whole minnow or chub, don't push the hook point back into the fish. Slip it once through the head or tail and leave the point exposed.

If you fish a strip of sucker meat or a frog, crayfish, or waterdog, slip the hook through only once. Leave the sharp point exposed and glistening in the September sun.

Dough baits? Pack them on the hook shank. Chicken livers or blood? Leave 5 inches of extra line dangling beyond the knot on your hook. Use it to wrap the blood or liver on the hook shank. If you use mesh to hold your livers, barely slide the hook through the mesh. Leave the point and barb exposed.

You lose more baits to snags. But hooks and baits are cheap, compared to time. And how much is frustration a pound? You never want to miss one of those fat ol' barrel-bellied cats, be they blues, flatheads, or channels. You don't have to. That's the point.

Favored Rigs

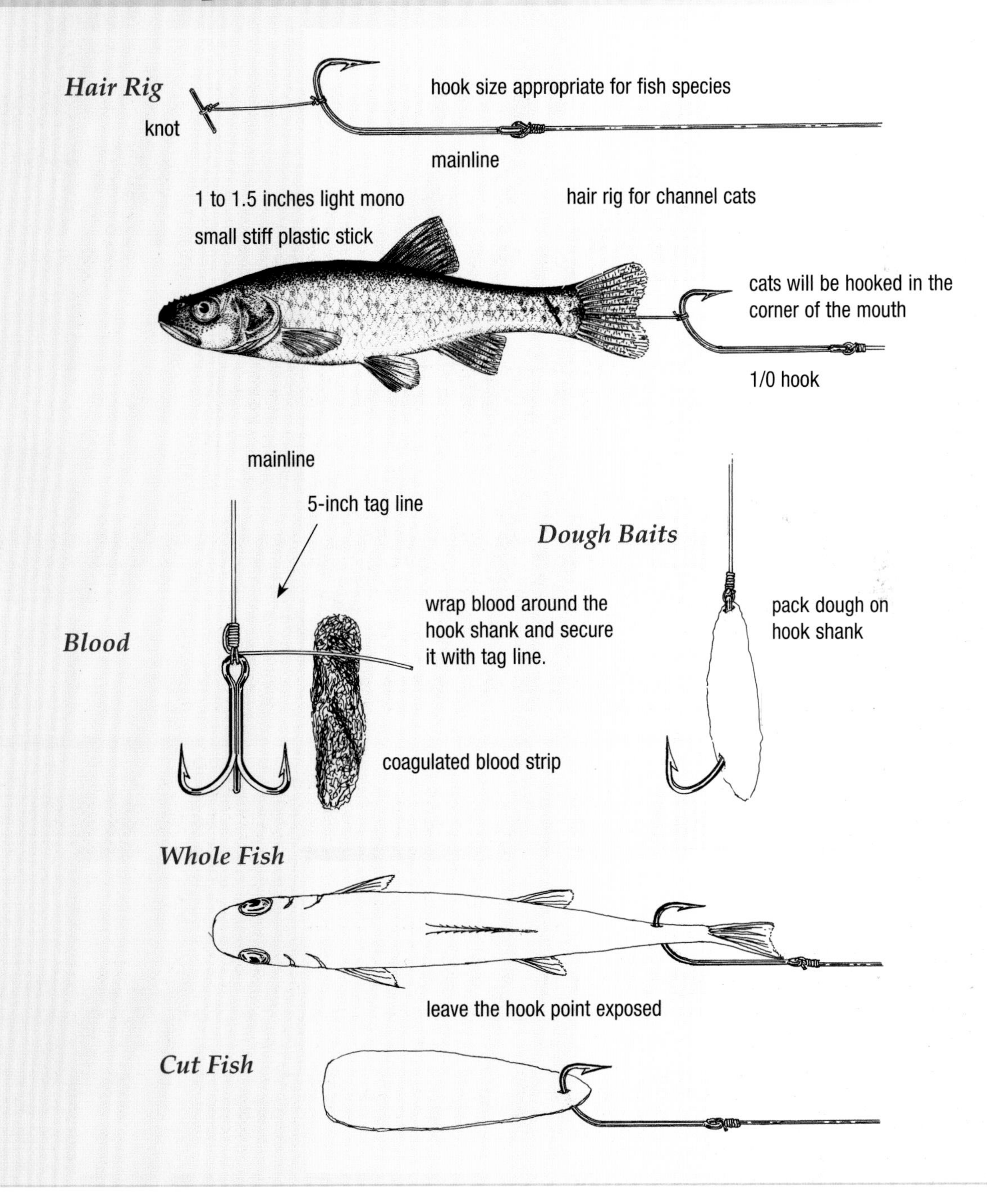

Hair Rig
knot
hook size appropriate for fish species
mainline
1 to 1.5 inches light mono
small stiff plastic stick
hair rig for channel cats
cats will be hooked in the corner of the mouth
1/0 hook
mainline
5-inch tag line
Dough Baits
Blood
wrap blood around the hook shank and secure it with tag line.
pack dough on hook shank
coagulated blood strip
Whole Fish
leave the hook point exposed
Cut Fish

276 PAGES! HOT FISHING!
BASS EXCLUSIVES•AMAZING WALLEYE LURE
HUGE PIKE/MUSKIES•RECORD SMALLMOUTHS
PLUS: CRAPPIES•CATS•WHITE BASS•BLUEGILLS
the In-Fisherman
THE JOURNAL OF FRESHWATER FISHING
Book #78
SPRING
ACTION ATLAS

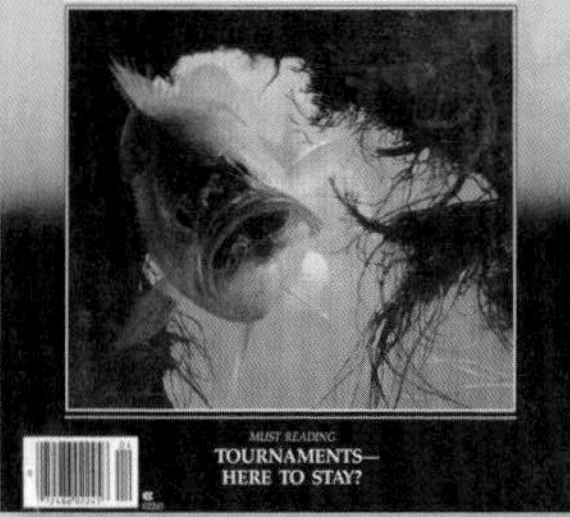

Historic Perspectives

Stange is the reason for In-Fisherman's longstanding commitment to topics concerning fish harvest for the table, including cleaning and caring for the fish and cooking the catch. By February 1988, he is the primary editor (executive editor) of In-Fisherman, responsible for all aspects of the magazine. Thus, In-Fisherman, as is the case with all good magazines with a sturdy primary editor at the helm, becomes in all ways a reflection of his convictions and interests. It is at this point that In-Fisherman begins consistent publication of catfish articles. Eventually, In-Fisherman promises a catfish article in every issue. Eventually, there's an annual Catfish Guide and a revolutionary instructional book, Catfish Fever. Eventually, there's a quarterly Catfish In-Sider magazine. Eventually, catfish become a consistent focus of In-Fisherman Television segments. Eventually, the first-ever catfishing instructional video appears, also titled Catfish Fever. It remains one of the largest if not the largest-selling fishing video title ever produced. On another front, given his interest in conservation and fish-harvest issues, during the next years Stange also integrates into the magazine what he terms "a philosophy of selective harvest." In-Fisherman promotes catch and release of bigger fish to sustain good fishing, but also promotes continuing a tradition of harvesting some fish for the table. In this regard, Stange seeks to include articles that address cooking the catch. Eventually, there is a Taste Tempters column featuring fish recipes. This article is the earliest example of Stange writing about a harvest issue.

CHAPTER 6

APRIL 1988

Fungi Gold!

I BELIEVE GOD HAS ENOUGH of a sense of good humor to tempt us to heaven with small earthly glimpses of it. I have had those visions and like what I see.

Pickin' And Grinnin' And Gathering Gold!

This spring, among friends on a respite from work, we will rise at 4 a.m. to make coffee, black and aromatic. A sweet roll later, for we are in a pleasant rush, we will mosey into a turkey woods to search for a sunrise and gobblers roosted in towering oaks on ancient limestone ridges.

It is the beginning of a day of harvest, a day of life in a woods alive with life and death, a woods where a stream has chiseled its way, where sweet, tangy watercress grows, and small catfish hide along timber blow-downs. Along the bank there is fresh mint, and along the hillside, where a once-green canopy became forest edge littered with bodies of elms, there are morel mushrooms—fungi gold!

By late day, exhausted, there will be a campfire and a sunset as a watercress salad gives way to a first course of panfried catfish or trout and morels sautéed in butter with a touch of garlic and lemon. A sprig of mint graces the edge of the plate. Nibble away as you poke the coals and the minds of your friends.

On a very good day, there will be turkey scallops, too, sautéed in butter and simmered in a white sauce alive with slivers of green and red bell peppers. More morels!

Sometimes, a bit philosophical, I think about this. I wonder about people who cannot harvest with, as I see it, good sense. I do not mind them but enjoy that they make me think. What a shame that they must miss the harvest. Life is this circle of life and death,

and I no more hate the organisms that will some day prosper on me, than I believe these organisms feel dismay at my harvest.

But no matter, for I know who I am: I love the harvest like General Patton loved war. But I cannot decide whether it is the harvest, my love of it, or the realization of self, that is the glimpse of heaven.

In a different time, there's a cabin on a hill in a woods near a lake a good way from the city. This is a cabin the city would hate, for it's like an old, gnarled oak that has lived here for a hundred years: It is part of the hill and the woods, and they do not object to each other.

In the city, there is objection: Only certain trees may grow in certain places in manicured lawns, where certain grasses object to weeds, which object to weedkiller, and homes protest the landscape like acne on the face of an adolescent. No morels, here. No catfish.

The inside of the shack feels good. The people who come here do not mind the woodstove or the years of dust that gather in places not to be bothered by a dust mop. Let the dust grow where it will, like the trees and the morels.

Old lures, battle-scarred, retired now to cabin rafters, feel good, too. So does the rusted lantern above the woodstove. So does the wood floor, worn slick a half-inch deep where friends have gathered to celebrate this place and their escape.

This is where John Ratzloff and Jerry Petermeier came to create *Roon,* a comfortable book about man's love affair with morel mushrooms. Their laboratory: The hills surrounding the cabin, a place where morels grow where they will, without objection, and the cabin kitchen, a spirited place where old pans rattle in anticipation of Petermeier, a professional chef and fishing guide.

Stuffed Morels, Baked or Broiled

Break the stems off the morels. Chop them finely and reserve. Broiling: Leave mushroom caps whole. Baking: Cut the caps in half.

Melt the butter in a skillet over medium heat, add shallots, morel stems, and salt and pepper. Sauté 3 or 4 minutes until moisture evaporates. Add more pepper, parsley, garlic, prosciutto, breadcrumbs, wine, and lemon juice. Combine and cook until the mixture holds together. Add cheese, remove from heat, stir to combine.

Baking: Spoon filling into morel caps and place in buttered baking dish. Bake at 350°F until browned, about 15 minutes.

Broiling: Fill pastry bag with filling and pipe into morel caps. Place on skewers. Broil over coals, 10 to 15 minutes. Brush with butter and turn frequently.

Variations: Wrap stuffed morels with blanched bacon, and alternate onion and tomato wedges on skewers with morels. Try substituting crabmeat for prosciutto. Stuffed onions are nice, too.—Jerry Petermeier

20 large morels
1/4 stick butter
1/2 c. Parmesan cheese, grated
2 tbsp. shallots, chopped
1 tbsp. garlic, minced
1/2 c. prosciutto ham or pepperoni, minced
1/2 c. breadcrumbs
1/4 c. white wine
1 tbsp. parsley, minced
1 tbsp. lemon juice
salt and pepper to taste

Scallops Morel

1 handful fresh morels, or dried morels reconstituted in brandy

Scallops are 3/4-inch-thick portions of turkey tenderloin sliced across the grain and pounded until they are 1/8-inch thick. If using catfish, make sure the fillets are from small fish—or use smaller portions of larger fillets.

Season scallops with salt and pepper. Dredge in flour and shake off excess. Heat a large skillet at medium high. Add half the butter until the foam subsides. Brown cutlets in batches, about one minute each side, and transfer to a warm platter. Cover to keep warm.

Add the remaining butter. Sauté the garlic, peppers, and morels over medium-low heat, about 4 minutes.

If using fresh morels, add the brandy. If using brandy-soaked dried morels, add the mixture. Bring to a boil. Stir and scrape to deglaze the pan. Flame the brandy if you want. Add the cream and reduce the sauce until it easily coats the back of a spoon. Salt and pepper to taste. Return the scallops to the pan. Heat thoroughly, garnish with parsley, and serve—Jerry Petermeier.

1 lb. turkey scallops
(or substitute small catfish fillets)
Flour for dredging
1/2 stick butter
1/2 c. red and green bell peppers, diced
2 cloves garlic, minced
1 tbsp. fresh parsley, minced
1/2 c. brandy
1½ c. heavy cream

Catfish and Morels

Sauté all but the fish in butter, 5 minutes. Place fish fillets on top of mixture, cover and simmer over low heat for 10 minutes. Remove fillets to a heated platter and cover to keep warm. Increase heat under mushroom and vegetable mixture. Boil down liquid by half. Pour sauce over fish, garnish with sautéed whole morels, and serve. Salivate and bark at the moon—Jerry Petermeier.

1 lb. catfish (or other fish)
1/2 stick butter
1 onion, finely chopped
1 tsp. shallots, chopped
1 clove garlic, minced
2 tbsp. tarragon wine vinegar
1/2 tsp. thyme
3 tomatoes, chopped
1 handful morels, chopped
large morels for garnish

276 PAGES! HOT FISHING!
BASS EXCLUSIVES•AMAZING WALLEYE LURE
HUGE PIKE/MUSKIES•RECORD SMALLMOUTHS
PLUS: CRAPPIES•CATS•WHITE BASS•BLUEGILLS
the In-Fisherman
THE JOURNAL OF FRESHWATER FISHING
Book #78
SPRING
ACTION ATLAS
MUST READING
TOURNAMENTS—
HERE TO STAY?

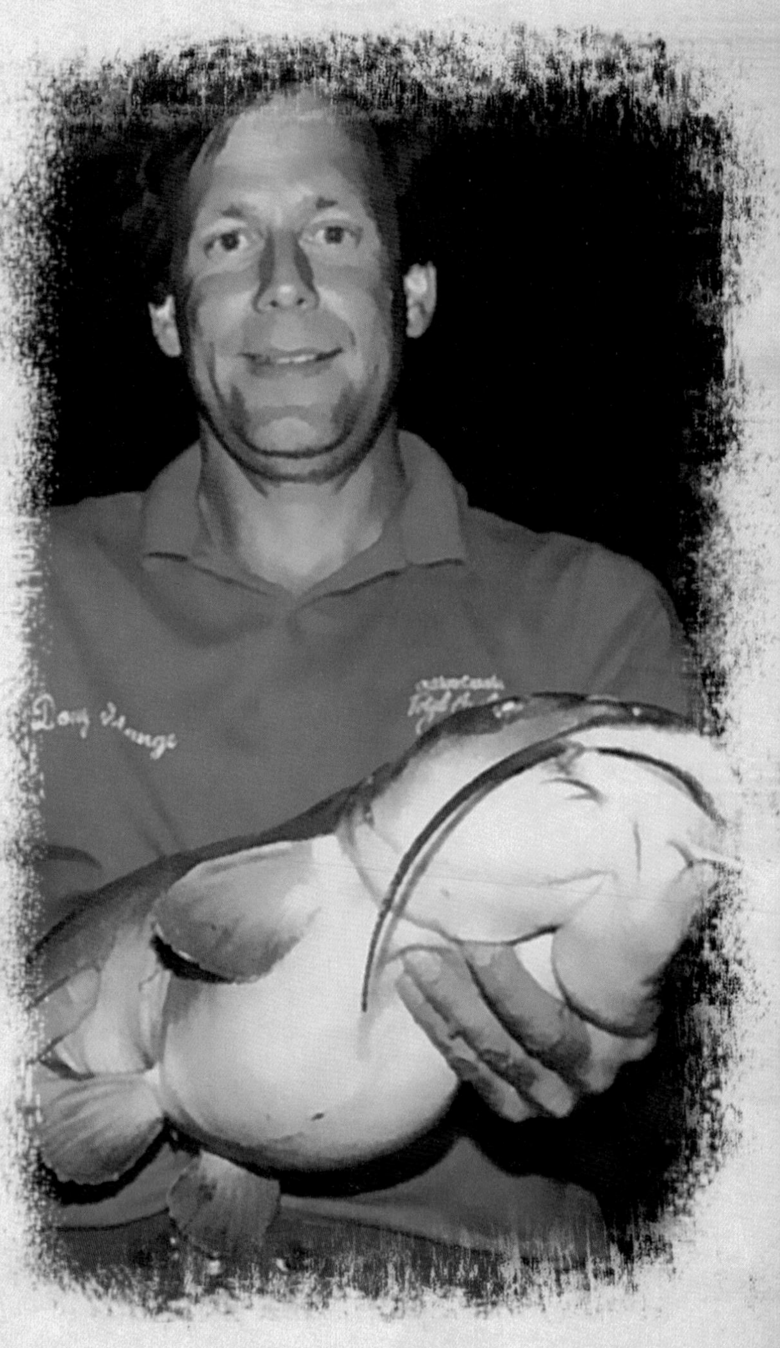

Historic Perspectives

This article appears in the same April issue as the "harvest item" in Chapter 6. Again, from early 1988 on, catfish articles appear consistently in almost every issue of In-Fisherman.

Stange here further relies on Otis "Toad" Smith to add storyline to what is otherwise a hardcore instructional article. The storyline is a primitive attempt, one might note today, but it works at the time. The catfish stories have a different flavor than most of the other articles. Some In-Fisherman readers are beginning to look forward to the catfish articles. A reader survey at this point suggests about 25 percent of readers are catfish anglers.

The river concepts herein are mostly a review of material presented in "Crackerjack Cats," the first catfish article to appear in In-Fisherman. Other instructional notes appear for the first time in print: The advantage of using long rods; specific snag tactics—where to set up and where the fish will be, and when; the use of slipfloats to present baits; the idea that leader length determines bait action and that leaders should be shorter rather than longer most of the time; the idea that a catfish shouldn't be allowed to run before setting the hook. These and more are all revolutionary concepts presented in this article for the first time.

CHAPTER 7

APRIL 1988

Snaggledtoothed Cats!

MY FRIEND TOAD is a typical catfisherman, a guy with so little worldly class that he falls into a class by himself. Now, I'm not saying that Toad isn't a classy, spiffy guy. He's a fine lookin' feller in a neatly pressed shirt, dress slacks, and cowboy boots, ready to go on a hoot and howl. But he looks just a bit out of place, like Davy Crockett in the halls of Congress.

Primary Principles In Action!

Toad looks most comfortable in basic blue jeans. Add a few holes just above the knees, please; make them sag a bit around the butt; it's the first thing that goes when you get older, Toad tells you; make them a day or two dirty—catfish dirty—real dirty. Add a shirt—any old shirt—comfy boots and an NRA (National Rifle Association) hat. Toad's a life member.

Like most good catmen, Toad is oblivious to certain elements that make fishermen from other stations in the fishing world cringe. No self-respecting tournament bass fisherman, for example, would dream of walking along a stream bank packed with itchy-bitchy burning nettles, carrying a backpack filled with stinkbait, flies to the left and flies to the right, much less willingly reach into a blood bucket and grope for just the right chunk.

"I've seen grown men lose their cookies," Toad will chuckle. "Good bait!"

Toad's in tune. In late fall, after a day of hunting or fishing, he parks his 260-pound carcass in a lawn chair in the middle of his backyard, pause to consider the quality of the day, and then promptly fall asleep. Trusty old Gus, the black lab (nark! nark!), is at his feet. It snows. An hour and two inches of snow later, the dinner bell rings and Toad and Gus both snort a time or two, stretch, dust themselves off and head inside. Some things matter; some things don't. Dinner matters.

Catfishing matters, too. Toad and I have tackled many a tangled snag together, looked those snaggletoothed ol' cats straight in the eye, and demanded they come out with their fins up.

Friends. Friends matter, too, which reminds me that there is a common bond between catfishermen, quite unlike anything else in the angling world.

Catfishing is different like Toad is different, and that's why the common bond—friendship—between catfishermen. How to explain? I can't. Don't need to. Catmen know. Catfishing is catfishing. It matters.

SNAGS

Snags matter, too, if you want to catch channel cats consistently from most rivers. Snags are the home of cats in small and medium-size rivers with distinct rifflepool areas.

The best homes hold the most catfish. There are small apartments for one, single family dwellings for 5, small motels for 20, and huge hotels for 50. Spend the most time fishing larger motels and hotels, home of lots of fat cats.

I once caught 49 channel cats from a particularly good snag in two days. Not surprisingly, the fishing slowed. Yet over the course of the season, each time the river rose, cats would move around in the river and the snag would get restocked. That snag lasted two years until a spring flood washed part of it away and silted in the rest.

River snags. Tree tangles. Blow downs. Call'em what you want, they often are the home of river catfish.

Snag Principles

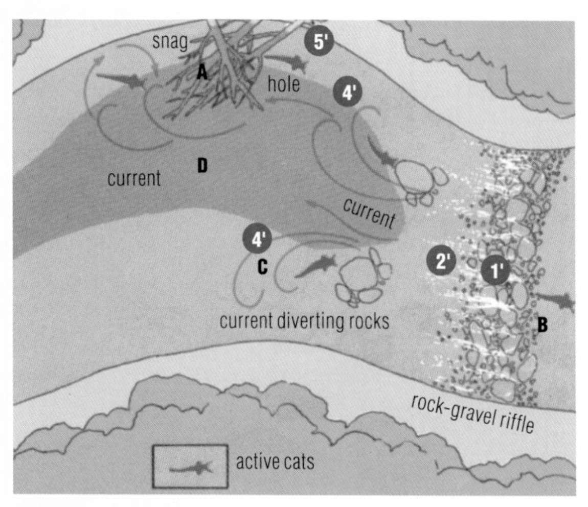

By noting certain principles, you can predict the catfish-holding potential of a snag. But it takes fishing to know for sure.

Some river snags attract catfish, others won't. When evaluating a snag, ask these questions: Is it thick? Is it large? Is it associated with relatively deep water—a deeper hole? Is it associated with an expansive hole?

If the answers are yes, there are bound to be channel catfish relating to the snag, unless the area is fished down.

When a river level is down, cats usually don't move a long distance. Fishing pressure may remove many of the cats from a snag. It takes a big rise in water level to get cats moving. When that happens, you can bet that a good snag will again gather a good group of cats.

Active Cat-Holding Areas in a Typical Hole

Inactive cats ***(A)*** *usually hold in the snag or in the deeper water in a hole. Active cats feed near the snag, but they are just as likely to leave the snag and* ***(B)*** *move ahead of the riffle to feed in the fast, slick water,* ***(C)*** *find a spot to hold and wait for food below the riffle, or* ***(D)*** *roam the hole searching for food.*

The best snags often are the thickest snags, but they must be associated with relatively deeper water. It depends on the stream or river. If 3 feet is deep in the stream you fish during summer, then the best snags are bound to be associated with about 3 feet of water. If a thick snag rests in only a foot of water, it probably won't attract cats.

The size of the snag and the size of the hole associated with it help to determine the number of catfish holding there. The best big snags usually are associated with the most expansive holes.

Lastly, where a snag is located in relation to other snags makes a difference. If it's the only good snag in a one-mile section, then we're talking good fishing; most of the good cats in the mile stretch gather in the snag. If there are many successive good snags, catfish are likely to be more evenly divided among the snags. There also will likely be more total catfish.

The best advice I can give you, and Toad

seconds this, is that you only have so much time in life; walk or float past marginal snags and concentrate on good ones. That may mean walking or floating an extra quarter mile before you fish.

Catfish feed in snags or they feed near them; it depends on the area. Say there's a riffle (shallow, fast-dropping, hard-bottom area where water is constricted and flows swiftly) followed by a deeper pool or hole with a good snag at the end of the hole. Active cats feed near the snag, but they are just as likely to leave the snag and move ahead of the riffle to feed in the fast, slick water, find a spot to hold and wait for food below the riffle, or roam the hole searching for food.

Inactive or partially active cats are likely to hold under the snag. This is the situation most of the time, the situation we concentrate on here. But don't forget to fish other areas, too.

Long rods make catfishing more efficient and fun.

LONGER RODS

Longer rods are the future of catfishing, just as they are the future of many other types of fishing in North America. You don't need a fancy boat, a jump suit, polka-dot undies, or a 50-pound box of lures to go catfishing. It's a low-cost sport. But I think you need a longer rod. At a minimum, switch from your short tackle to a 7.5- or 8-foot-long flippin' stick.

But I recommend going one step further. Consider buying the type of 11-foot-long rods so popular in Europe. They cost $50 to $100. Take care of one, though, and it should last for years.

The advantages? You can cast farther (up to 100 yards) if you need to in, say, a pond, reservoir, or lake situation. You can set hooks at long range, for the long rod lets you sweep your line to remove stretch from monofilament. You lose fewer fish, too. Longer rods keep your line tight constantly. No slack; no lost fish.

The primary advantage in river fishing, however, is in the ability to manipulate a drifted bait around a snag. You can reach farther out from a bank, or left or right from a boat, to make your bait drift where you want to. And when you're using a float, which you often must to fish snags efficiently, you can hold your rod tip high, lift your line off the water, and thus let the float continue drifting as it should and where it should. Last, but hardly least, long rods make fighting catfish fun, and they do it well.

SNAG TACTICS

Be quiet. Catfish are mighty spooky unless they're on a feeding rampage. Walk up to the spot or drift up and drop anchor quietly.

If you're walking or wading, decide which side of the river to fish first. In smaller rivers, I prefer to fish most snags from the opposite bank, and then cross the river downstream and walk back upriver to fish the snag from that side. Fishing from the opposite bank gives you a better chance to probe the outside or current edge of the snag. If catfish are active or interested in feeding, that's where they'll be.

If you're walking the bank of a bigger river, you may not be able to wade across. Use the long rod to hold the rod tip out from the bank. Usually you can fish around a snag by casting from both the front and back sides.

Fishing from a boat is a good idea. Park about 40 feet upriver from the snag and just a bit out into the river from it. Fish the front of the snag, and then drift downriver until you're even with it. Park about 20 feet out from the snag. Fish the front again from a different drift angle. Fish the back of the snag, too. Move on.

SET-RIGGING

Set-rigging means casting a bait into a set position (sometimes it drifts before it gets there) where it stays until a catfish finds it. Set rigs usually are sliprigs. The most typical sliprig consists of an egg sinker slipped on your mainline and about a 1/0 hook tied on the end. Add a BB or 3/0 shot about a foot up your line to hold the egg sinker in place.

There are more complicated sliprigs that work more efficiently, but they also take more time to tie and are more costly. You will be losing rigs on most days. I recommend these changes in basic sliprigging, however.

First, use something other than an egg sinker, for it's the worst possible slipsinker for set rigs. They roll and drag easily in current. Roll anything along a typical catfish river bottom for long and you're snagged.

Much to his credit, I have never heard Toad say an ill word about becoming snagged. He holds a grudge, though. I have seen him calmly remove his shoes and pants, wade navel deep into the water, pick up half a snag, remove his rig, place it daintily in a good spot, and tiptoe back out with a take-that, darn-it smile. Then he'll sit bare-assed in the boat until he dries.

A bell sinker or a walking slipsinker like the Lindy is a better sinker option. Bell sinkers hold best. On the other hand, if I'm quartering a bait with the current and want it to move along just a bit, the Lindy is the choice. It slides but won't snag so easily as an egg sinker.

Your slipsinkers should range from 3/8 ounce to 2 ounces.

A swivel-set rig is more complicated but works very well. Tie a bell sinker on one end of a 6-inch-long portion of monofilament and tie a swivel on the other. Now slip your line through the end of the swivel and tie on a hook. About a foot up your mainline, add a shot to hold the swivel in place.

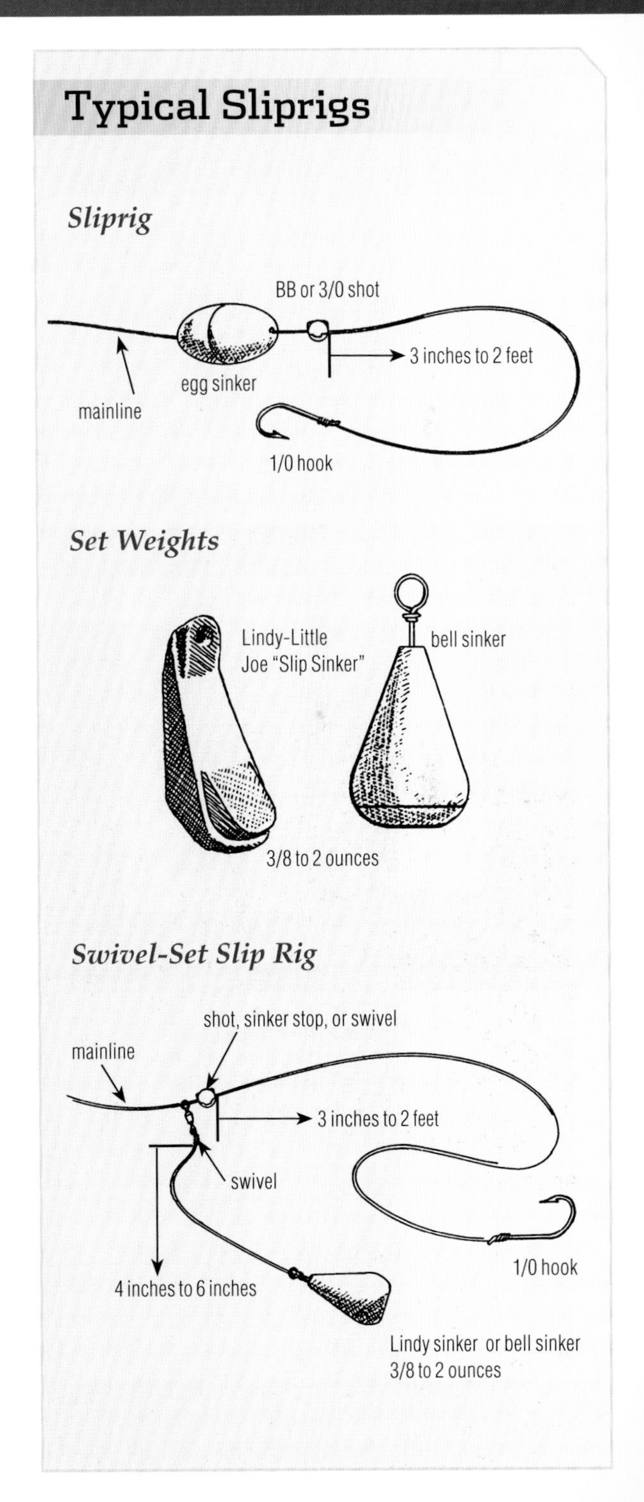

Where you set a shot on your line determines how much action your bait has. The closer you set your shot (and therefore your main weight) to the bait, the less the bait moves in current.

In strong current, set your shot 3 to 6 inches away from the bait, or the bait waves wildly, making it difficult for a cat to grab. The more a bait moves, the more likely it is to get snagged, too.

In reduced current, however, it may help to attract catfish if the bait moves a bit. In slight current, anchor your shot 2 feet above your bait. The average shot setting is about one foot above the bait.

SET-RIG HOOK-SETS

The hook-set. The moment of truth. A cat has grabbed your bait and is moving away. Your heart's pounding and your palms are sweating. Most of the time, you can catch most of the cats that take your set bait. The key is to eliminate rigging problems.

The problem with an egg-sinker sliprig is that you must let your line go as the cat moves away, or else he feels "odd" tension. If you don't let your line go, the cat has to move the sinker in order to move. If the sinker momentarily hangs on the bottom, the cat may get stuck by the hook point and drop the bait.

Constant, sustained tension rarely bothers a catfish; intermittent tension-slack, tension-slack does. With a slip-set rig you have at least one foot of sustained give to let a cat move before you must let your line go or set the hook. I suggest setting the hook.

Picture the 6-inch section of line anchored with the bell sinker as a pendulum. By pulling your rod tip toward you, you can move the bait one foot against the current. Hold there until a cat takes the bait.

When the cat leaves, keep constant tension on him by dropping the rod tip back. When you've dropped back about a foot, the cat usually is turned. Set the hook. If you've matched your bait and hook size to the size of the catfish in the river or stream, the cat has the bait in his mouth, and you catch him, usually in the corner of the mouth.

Letting a cat run causes nothing but problems. So often a cat starts to run and a fisherman lets go

Shot Placement Determines Bait Action

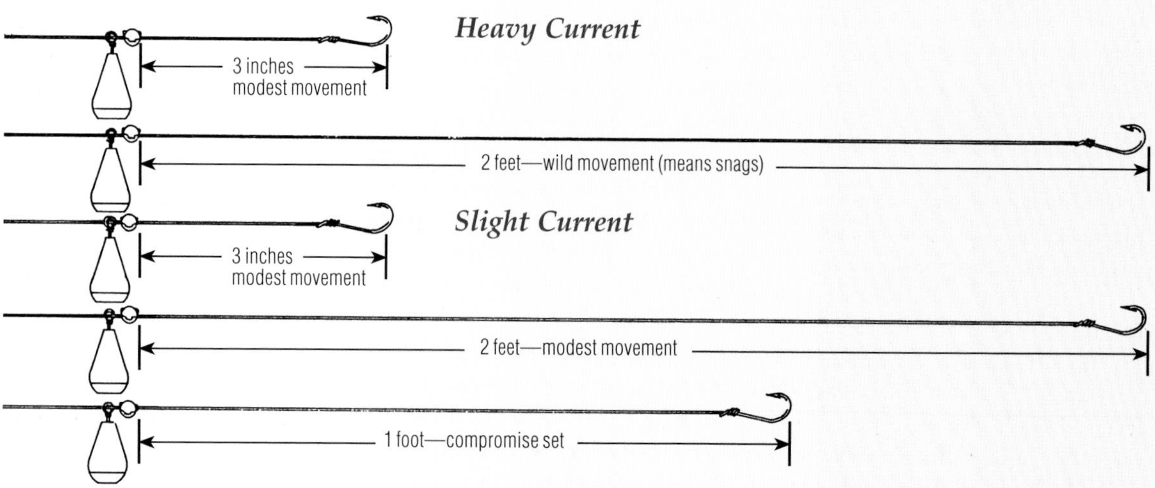

Set-Rig Drift

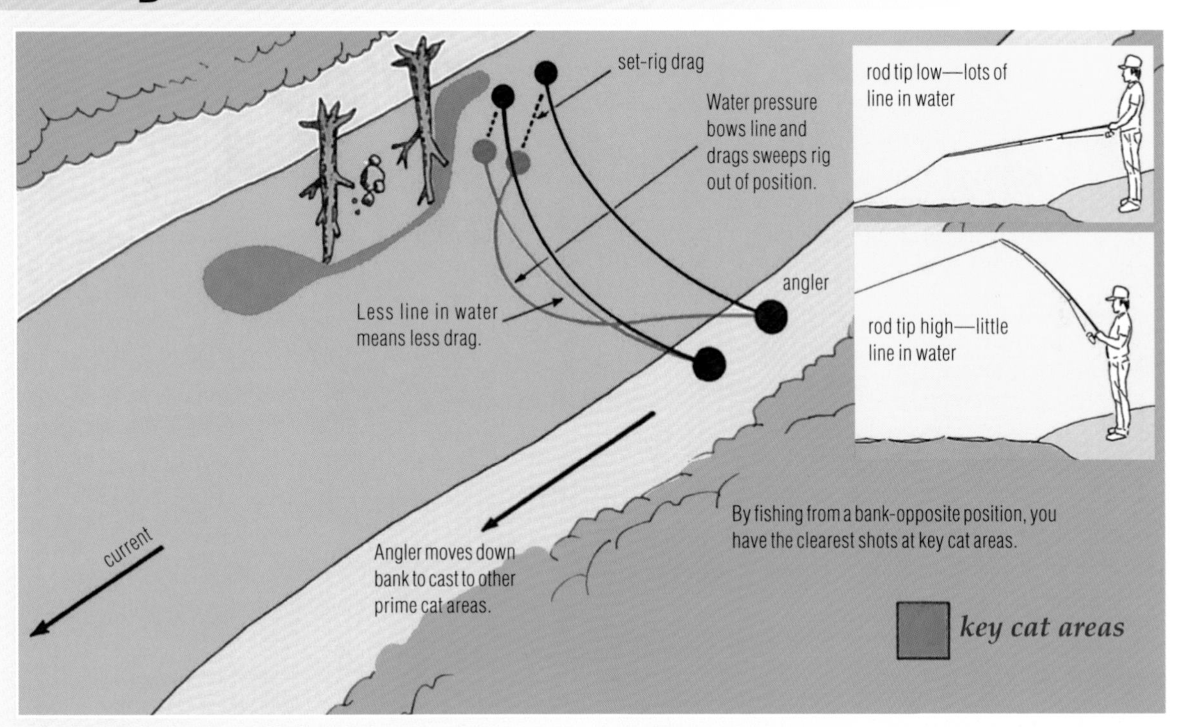
set-rig drag
Water pressure bows line and drags sweeps rig out of position.
rod tip low—lots of line in water
angler
Less line in water means less drag.
rod tip high—little line in water
By fishing from a bank-opposite position, you have the clearest shots at key cat areas.
current
Angler moves down bank to cast to other prime cat areas.
key cat areas

Deal with set-rig drift. Use it to your advantage.

Minimize drift in two ways. Use a very heavy sinker and a rig won't drift. In snaggy areas, this may be the best approach, for a dragging rig means a snagged rig. But too much sinker also means you can't drift a bait when you want to.

The key to controlling rig drift is a longer rod and a sinker that just holds in current. Keep as much line as possible out of water, thus minimizing water pressure on your line, and you minimize drift.

To minimize drift, cast your rig out and hold your rod tip high to cut the amount of line that's subjected to current.

Now you can use set-rig drift to your advantage. Cast the rig into position above, alongside, or below a snag. Raise or lower your rod tip to decrease or increase the water pressure on your line. Use water pressure to drift your rig into proper position or to drift it along a proper position line.

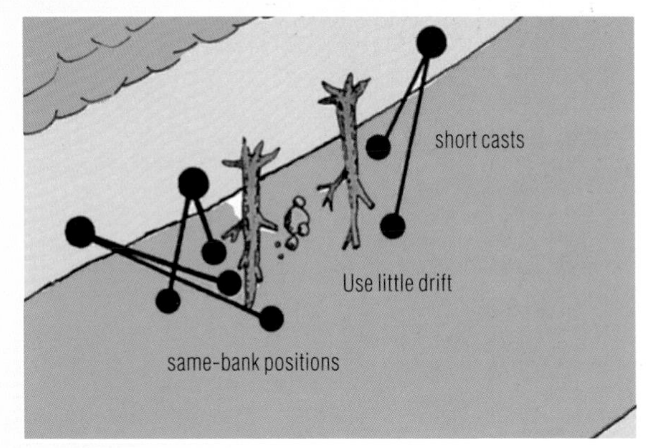
short casts
Use little drift
same-bank positions

Lindy-Little Joe slipsinkers or bell-type sinkers tend to be more controllable than egg sinkers.

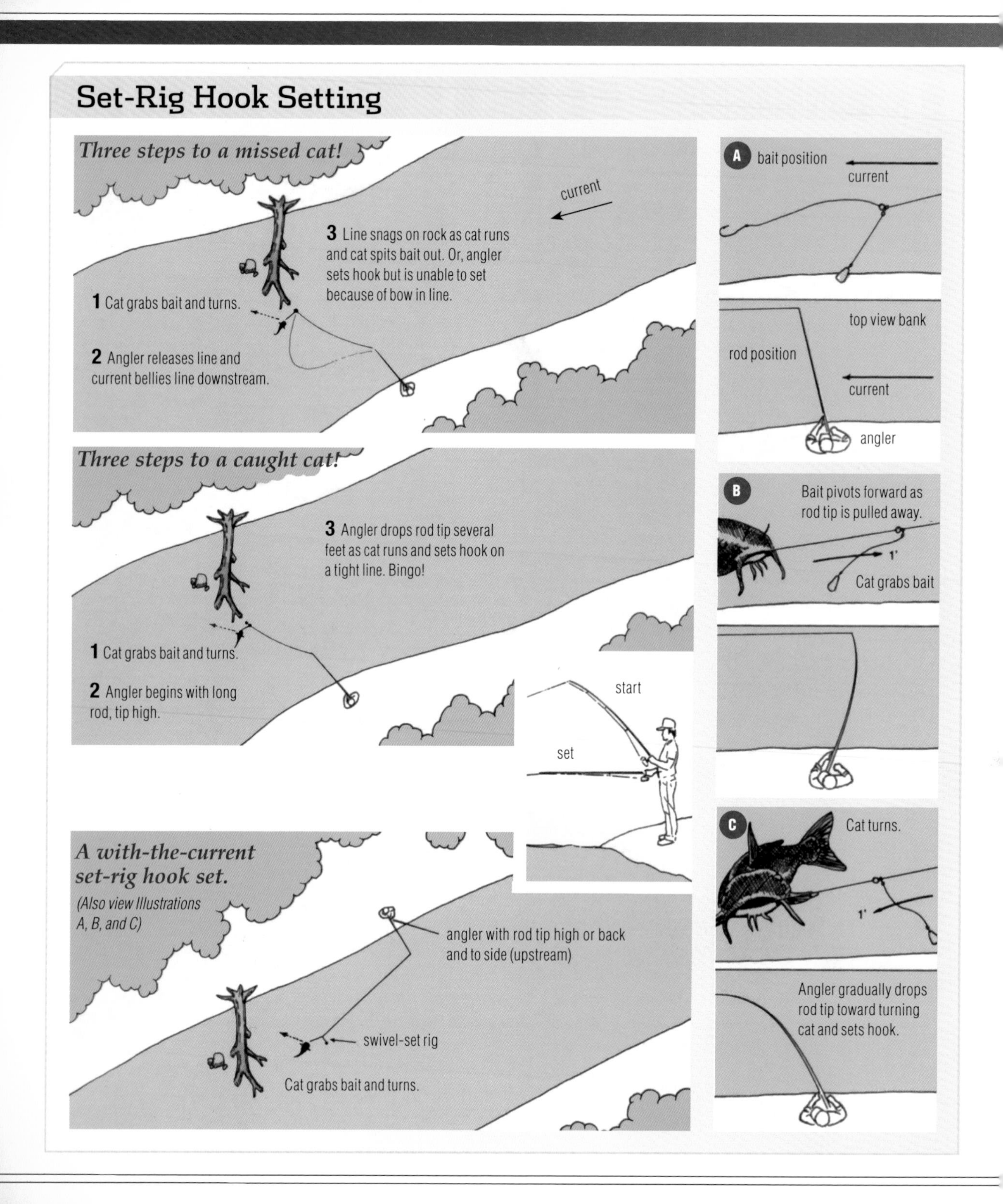
Set-Rig Hook Setting
Three steps to a missed cat!
current
3 Line snags on rock as cat runs and cat spits bait out. Or, angler sets hook but is unable to set because of bow in line.
1 Cat grabs bait and turns.
2 Angler releases line and current bellies line downstream.
Three steps to a caught cat!
3 Angler drops rod tip several feet as cat runs and sets hook on a tight line. Bingo!
1 Cat grabs bait and turns.
2 Angler begins with long rod, tip high.
start
set
A with-the-current set-rig hook set.
(Also view Illustrations A, B, and C)
angler with rod tip high or back and to side (upstream)
swivel-set rig
Cat grabs bait and turns.
A
bait position
current
top view bank
rod position
current
angler
B
Bait pivots forward as rod tip is pulled away.
1'
Cat grabs bait
C
Cat turns.
1'
Angler gradually drops rod tip toward turning cat and sets hook.

of his line. The cat seems like he continues running, but usually it's the current that's dragging your line downriver. By the time you try to set the hook, you have a huge bow in your line. You are lucky to get a good set.

Another problem is that the line may snag on something and make the cat drop the bait. The cat may retreat with your bait into the snag and make it impossible to haul him out, too.

When a cat grabs a set rig in current, give a little and then take a lot—make a good hook set. You miss a few, usually smaller cats, but increase your total hooking percentage.

SLIPFLOAT RIGGING

Slipfloat rigging is the most overlooked option for effectively fishing snags. A properly rigged slipfloat rig keeps a bait poking along the bottom with the current pushing it into pockets and corners where cats lie.

Can you accomplish the same thing with a bait and several shot? Yes, but it's a matter of efficiency. When you cast a shot rig into current, the current is working on your line, as well as your bait. Once the bait and shot are on the bottom, the current bows your line and drags the bait toward you, as well as downriver with the current. That means snags.

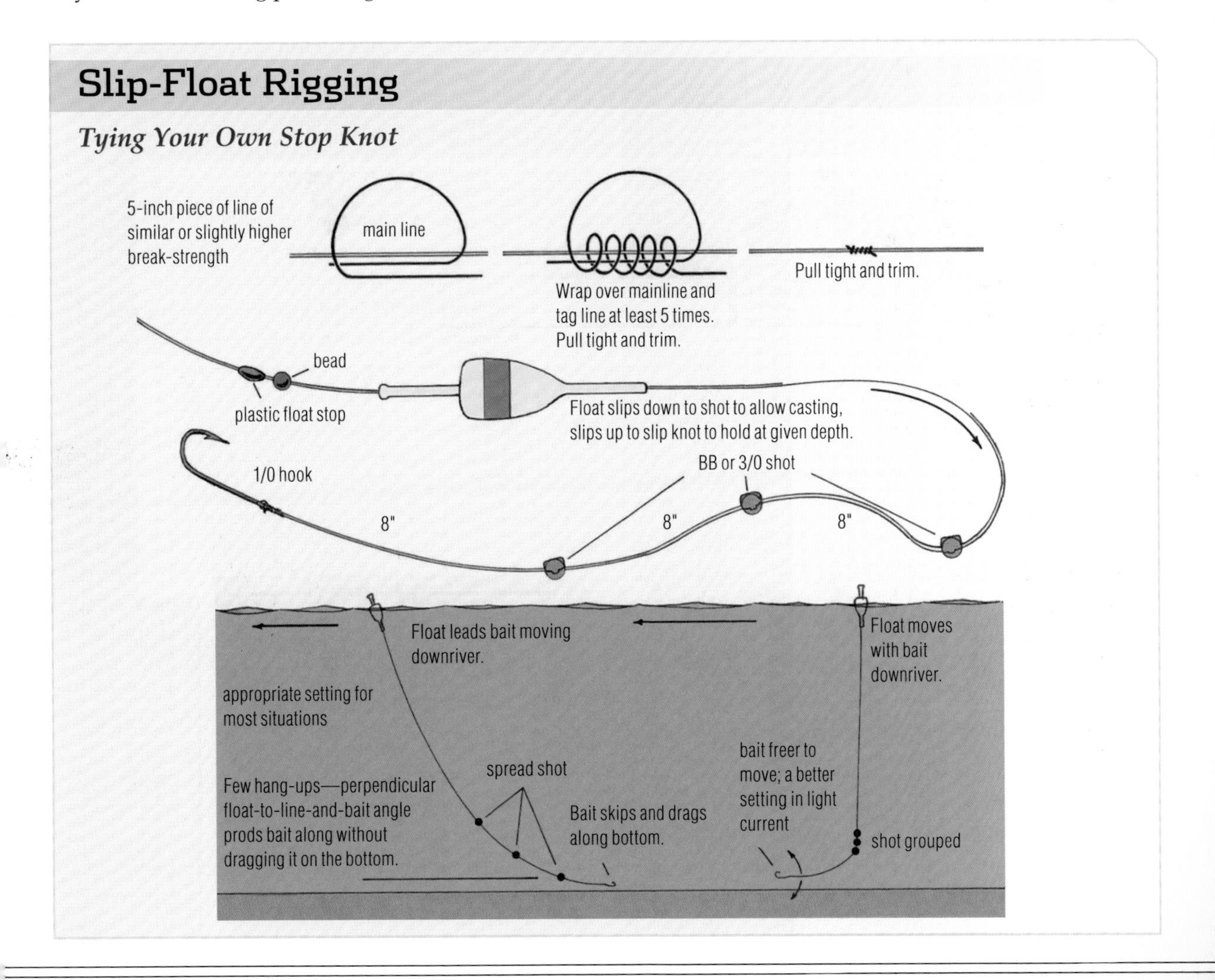

Slip-Float Rigging
Tying Your Own Stop Knot
5-inch piece of line of similar or slightly higher break-strength
main line
Wrap over mainline and tag line at least 5 times. Pull tight and trim.
Pull tight and trim.
bead
plastic float stop
Float slips down to shot to allow casting, slips up to slip knot to hold at given depth.
BB or 3/0 shot
1/0 hook
8"
8"
8"
Float leads bait moving downriver.
Float moves with bait downriver.
appropriate setting for most situations
spread shot
Few hang-ups—perpendicular float-to-line-and-bait angle prods bait along without dragging it on the bottom.
Bait skips and drags along bottom.
bait freer to move; a better setting in light current
shot grouped

Big snags mean heap big fish.

And rarely do you know exactly where your bait is.

A float keeps your bait skipping along the bottom, because the float is above the bait. You aren't so likely to get snagged, and you know right where your bait is.

Watch the float and you learn about current conditions around a snag, too. There's only so much you can tell by looking at the surface. The movement of a bait and float will help you pinpoint your fishing.

A slipfloat slides up your line until it's stopped by a stop knot. You can fish at any depth that you want. When you want to cast, it slides down your line and stays out of the way.

The size slipfloat to choose depends on the total weight of your terminal rig. Say that you've filleted the side off a one-pound sucker and have cut one fillet into three chunks. That portion of fillet will weigh about an ounce out of water and less in water. You need two or three 3/0 shot to get the fish portion near bottom. The combination of shot and bait requires that you have a larger float.

You want the bait weighted so that it skips along the bottom with your float preceding your bait as they move together with the current. Place your shot about 8 inches apart, starting about 8 inches above your bait. A float that sails downriver and never hesitates as the bait hits bottom isn't set deep enough.

With a long rod you can direct a float where you want it. Say you want to fish a snag 30 feet away from you on the other side of the river. Cast the float rig across the river and 20 feet above the snag. Don't engage your reel, but do hold the line with your trigger finger. Hold your rod tip high. At first the current will carry the float and your line straight downriver at the same speed. But as the bait occasionally hangs on the bottom, as it should, your line will begin to bow in the current and tend to pull the float toward you and away from its intended course. To correct this, first let out a bit more line. Second, mend your line: Lift your rod tip and your line off the water and flip it back upstream.

On the first drift past a snag, keep your float and bait moving at least a foot or two outside the snag. Active cats charge out to get the bait.

If that doesn't work, let the float and bait drift up against the snag, and then immediately pull them back a bit and nudge them downriver so they tumble along the snag. To keep them moving, you have to give line. When the bait reaches the end of the snag, it twirls for a moment in the backwash below the snag and then be pulled downriver with the current. You've worked past prime catfish-holding areas.

When a cat grabs a bait, the float stops, is pulled under slightly, and begins to move. Your reaction depends on where the float moves.

If the fish moves into the snag, apply constant but not superheavy tension as you drop your rod tip toward the fish for a foot or two. Then set the hook, for if you let the cat enter the snag, you aren't likely to drag him out.

My experience is that cats that head back into the snag usually are solitary cats. You may only catch a fish or two from such snags.

Slippin' the Float

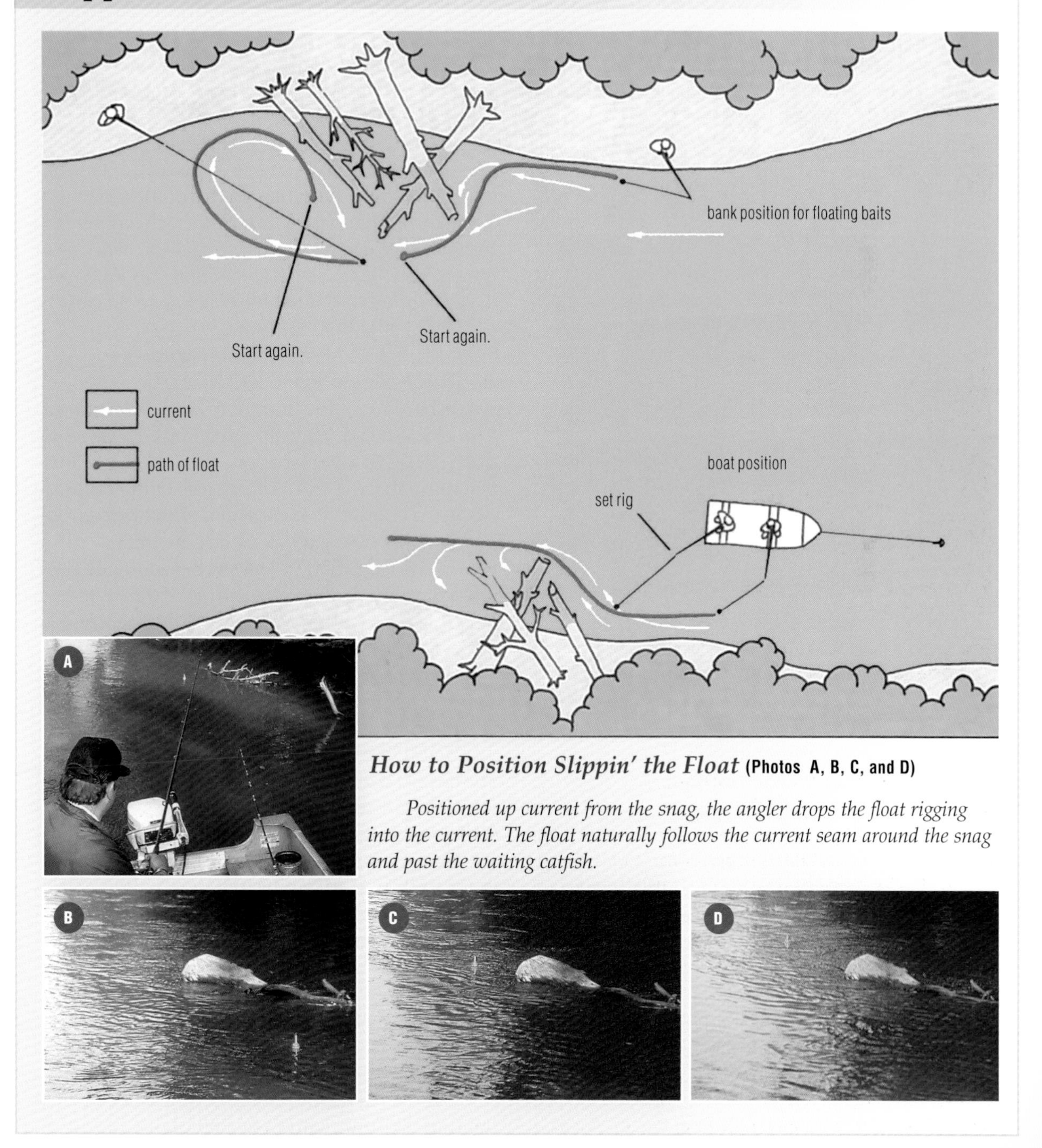

How to Position Slippin' the Float (Photos A, B, C, and D)

Positioned up current from the snag, the angler drops the float rigging into the current. The float naturally follows the current seam around the snag and past the waiting catfish.

Cats that immediately move away from the snag usually are moving away from other cats. You usually find more cats working the snag.

If the float moves away from the snag and away from you, the catfish has turned and you can set the hook anytime; the quicker the better if you want to hook 'em in the mouth.

Cutbait's Good Stuff

Hey Toad! Smile when you slice them suckers!

While the debate about "best baits" continues, use fresh cutbait and you'll catch cats all season. Cutbait can be a freshly killed chub or sucker 4 to 6 inches long, or it can be a portion of a fillet cut from the side of a 1- to 2-pound chub or sucker.

Be sure to keep your hook point exposed to get a good hook-set. Never try to hide your hook point in a bait.

It's interesting to see where the cat goes, though. I've had cats run two pools downriver before they stopped, and I've had cats run over to me so that I could see them lying in the current under my feet.

If a cat runs toward you or upstream, wait until you have an angle on the fish before you set the hook. Having the catfish turned away from you increases the chance that you'll get a good set.

By the way, always be sure that you leave your hook point exposed. Channel cats don't know what a hook point is, and to some degree they're used to crunching down on hard stuff like fish heads or crawfish bodies. Hide the hook point, in say a piece of cut fish, and too often the point never leaves the cut fish to get into a cat's jaw.

A TWO-MAN APPROACH

When Toad and I are working a river in his 14-foot boat, we anchor above good snags. He might use a set rig to fish just above the snag while I use a float rig to drift around the edge of the snag. He sits in the rear of the boat while I stand in the front.

Baiting often works; that is, catfish often respond to an influx of food by beginning to feed. Therefore, in conjunction with our baits, we often toss in free offerings. We only do this above the best-looking snags.

If we know a snag is a good one, we may go a step further, if we aren't catching fish. We may toss in a handful of coagulated blood.

Blood is a powerful catfish stimulant during summer. Toad probably uses a portion of blood while I continue to fish a cut portion of filleted sucker or chub.

Blood seems to turn cats on, but not necessarily only to the blood. Cutbait usually takes as many fish as blood. You might try this and see if it works for you.

There's always more to tell about any catfish topic. I know we haven't said much about baits, but we covered that in a previous article. I said then that my favorite bait was fresh cut fish. It usually works year long. Blood can also be good, and at times, so can crayfish, frogs, or prepared stinkbaits. Most of the time, though, you can catch plenty of cats on

Catch and release big fish to sustain good fishing.

easy-to-obtain cutbait.

One other topic to touch on is the time of day to fish snags. During most of June, river cats are active during the day. As water levels recede, early morning and night-fishing usually are better. One of the best things about catfishing is that you can go after work, paste yourself full of mosquito repellent, and sit quietly near a good snag and catch cats.

Which reminds me of Toad. I'm doing a story on cutbait, right? Toad and I are fishing at night, and I want to take a shot or two of how to cut the bait. So I say, "Toadsie, cut up a few of those slimy dead suckers while I shoot a few rolls of film."

Toad, always willing to help, soon has dead sucker flesh flying; the cooler top is a bloody, slimy battlefield; his hands look like he's been digging in garbage; and the boat looks like a chain-saw massacre has taken place.

"But Toad," I say, "I can't focus. Gimme some light." Naturally, slimy hands and all, Toad grabs the flashlight—and then poke it into his mouth so he can cut and shine at the same time.

Yuck!

"Do you realize what you just did?" I ask.

"Thwupth?" he mumbos wiph a mouph pho o phwaswhite.

Between snaggletoothed cats and sucker-breathed friends, this catfishing is quite a deal.

Toad Smith

How 'bout them cats?

FISHING! FISHING! FISHING!
GUARANTEED BASS•OVERLOOKED WALLEYES
CRAPPIE RIGGING•DOWNRIGGED PIKE/MUSKIE
PLUS: 'GILLS•CATS•WHITE BASS•TROUT/SALMON
the In-Fisherman
THE JOURNAL OF FRESHWATER FISHING
SENSATIONAL
SUMMER ACTION!
SECRETS: HOW LIGHT
DETERMINES SUCCESS

Historic Perspectives

Summer in the deep South begins as early as May, while in the North it usually sets in by July. This short article fits neatly into a summer magazine and presents a simple and timely concept that's as important today as it was in 1988.

On another front, Stange is by this time on the seminar trail, traveling during winter to parts of North America, one of the first in history to discuss catfishing in live forums. Pittsburg, Cleveland, Chicago, Minneapolis. Buffalo, Davenport, Cedar Falls, Omaha, and Lincoln. Stange shares field expiences and science insights with enthusiast audiences, who can spend an afternoon or evening learning about their favorite fish, just the same as those bass boys and walleye boys down the hall. Crowds vary from relatively small affairs in places like Buffalo, where local folks are just beginning to realize opportunities, to standing-room-only gatherings in places like Moline and Kansas City. It isn't unusual for some seminars to end with a standing ovation. Amen brother! And Right On!

One of Stange's favorite topics is "The Best Told Mistakes of Every Catfishing Man," which addresses fundamental problems. This seminar topic eventually becomes a magazine topic. You're invited to sit in on the seminar as you read Chapter 45.

CHAPTER 8

JUNE 1988

Sunrise Cats

NO QUESTION CATFISH, especially some of the biggest ones, tend to feed after dark during summer. For most cat fishermen, however, fishing at night means procedural problems.

Cover of darkness does not erase location and presentation problems so much as intensifies them. If anything can go wrong, it will. If anything can't go wrong, it still will. Wrong is wronger at night. But right can be righter, too, because it's when the big fellas prowl in many bodies of water.

Often there's an alternative. Catfishermen tend to overlook one of the hottest of all potential daily fishing periods, the morning period from about 4 a.m. to 8 a.m. The actual length of the period isn't so important as knowing it often exists, and that it may focus catfish activity so you can take advantage of it.

I'm not saying the period is magic, just very good in most catfish waters, so good that I would almost guarantee that you can increase your catch by fishing then. I offer my own fishing experience and the fishing experience of friends as proof.

Never written about? What else is new? Little of intelligent consequence has been written about catfishing in the last 50 years. Yet, there's so much to say.

On The Prowl For Catfish, 4 To 8—Don't Be Late!

Twenty-two pounds of early morning sunshine!

A CATCH-UP FEEDING PERIOD

Perhaps early morning is a catch-up period for catfish feeding activity. The cats have all night to feed, but apparently they don't always get the job done. Or perhaps they just prefer feeding during the morning. When the sun cracks the horizon, it's like the big boys realize it's "now or never 'till tonight." Who wants to sit pouting in a deep hole or snag with a partially filled belly all day? That's no way to grow to 30 pounds.

Cats are misunderstood, too. Catfishermen dwell on the cat's tremendous combined senses of smell and taste. Cats are unique in that regard. But other senses get overlooked. Rarely do one or two senses key an effective lifestyle. It's the coordination of all the senses that keys effective feeding.

Cats also are extremely sound-sensitive. But that's another story. Here we should consider that cats also have good vision that helps to explain the potential intensity of this catch-up feeding period during the early morning.

The Morning Peek

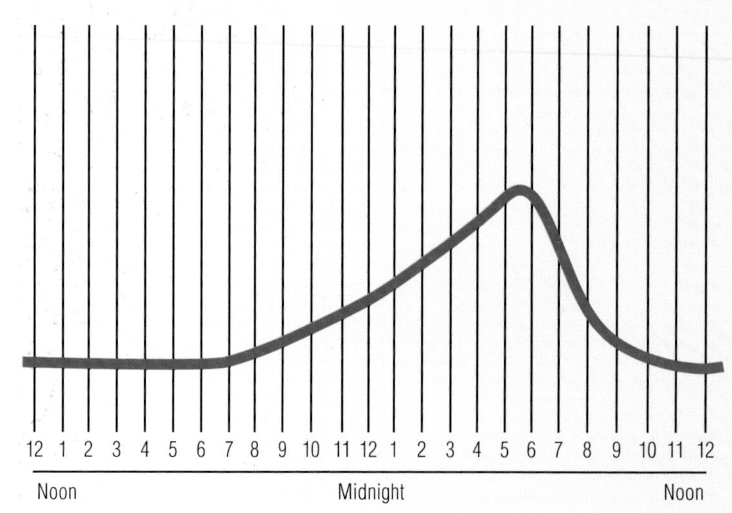

No chart can accurately illustrate catfish activity for each catfish species in every type of water during each season. This one illustrates a general trend in catfish activity on many bodies of water, after catfish settle into a summer pattern.

Catfish may feed during the day or night—24 hours a day or, more likely, portions thereof—depending on the type of water, the water conditions, and the weather conditions. Often, however, bigger catfish become more active after dark during summer. Activity often peaks in an intense early morning feeding period which most fishermen miss.

Most people think catfish are blind, that they don't need or use vision because of their unique smell-taste senses. Other fishermen know that catfish see, but maintain that they rarely use their vision because they live in murky water.

Catfish are splendidly adapted. They can operate in dingy water, using their senses of smell, taste, and feeling. But when the water clears even slightly, they rely heavily on vision, too.

I once kept a small (10 pounds) flathead in our giant office aquarium. He would lie on the bottom during the day, only his gills and eyeballs moving. I could stand 10 feet from the tank, and if I moved, his eyes would follow. Once I had his attention, if I moved my arm slowly to the right, he would follow that too.

Catfish probably have a vision advantage over many prey species at night, but they probably see even better with a bit of light, and continue to have a vision advantage over prey during the morning twilight period. The big boys, the fish that have been in the environment for 10 or 15 years, know the morning period is prime-time feeding, a catch-up bite, or a hurry-up-and-feed bite, given the approaching intense daylight.

Often the bite starts immediately at dawn. Sometimes it lasts an hour, sometimes 2 or 3 hours. I think the length of the feeding period is determined by how effective the cats are in finding prey. Usually the bite becomes erratically— not progressively and predictably—less intense as it gets later. The length of the bite is a matter of effective feeding—the fish quit when they're full rather than it being a matter of how late it is. Often, however, catfish feeding slows by about 10 a.m. during midsummer.

Cats may bite fine during midday and afternoon in many bodies of water, especially during prespawn, spawn, and postspawn. Where I have fished, the sundown bite just usually isn't that good. Apparently it takes awhile for the night environment to get cranked up—often until twilight settles into dark-dark, as I call it.

The midnight shift can be good, but it gets old when you have to work the next day. Fish smarter, not harder. Time it right and you often catch more catfish in 3 or 4 hours at dawn than you would all night. Give it a try during summer and early fall.

That's the thing about catfishing. They say that after you've fished for them long enough and have caught enough of them, you begin to look like them.

Historic Perspectives

Blood is in certain small circles around the country in 1988, known to be a good bait for channel catfish and blues. Stange first mentions the option in Chapter 2, but, so far as we know, it has never otherewise been talked about in print in a national magazine until this extensive article appears, generating a lot of mail and changing the way some anglers approach catfishing during late summer. Other pioneering anglers go on after this article appears to find other strategies for using blood in a variety of situations across catfish country.

Bob Fincher of Texas is an early proponent of bloodbait and sells it for many years in plastic vats that can be shipped. We know of no readily available commercial source of blood today, although in some parts of the country it can perhaps still be procured from butcher kill floors or factories, although that too is becoming a thing of the past. Because it's difficult to get, blood has never become a popular bait choice on a national scale. It probably never will.

CHAPTER 9

AUGUST 1988

Those Bloody Cats!

WOULD THAT YOU COULD SPEND A DAY or two on a river with Toad and me. There would be plenty of catfish, a shorelunch, an evening campfire, and lots of stories and crazy times, and none of this rush that typifies too much fishing today. The only time we move way too often is when it gets too warm and the flies get too bad around the blood bucket.

Blood Draws Flies. Holy Cow Does It Draw Flies!

Flies, with a finely tuned sensory system that lets them identify (smell) different varieties of festering goodies, must qualify as the catfish of the insect world. Some things draw flies more powerfully than others, a fact I never fail to bring to my friend Toad Smith's attention, for he, in my estimation, tends to draw flies more powerfully than I do.

On a scale, cow biscuits draw flies. The worst stinkbait draws more flies. The worst soured fish draws more and more flies. But blood draws more and more and more and more and more flies, and draws them more and more quickly. Blood has an immensely and intensely powerful enzymatic draw for flies—and also for catfish.

Blood certainly isn't magic but it can be so good during late summer that you can't afford not to fish it if you want to catch catfish on a logarithmic scale that exceeds human comprehension.

Channel catfish in particular are strongly drawn to blood.

At times, baits like freshly cut fish or freshly killed crawdads or frogs fish side by side with blood, probably because they have blood in them. Early and very late in the season, these and other baits often outfish blood.

But when summer rolls on, especially by late summer you should consider blood, if for no other purpose than to chum with, especially if you're in a really tough catfishing situation—the kind where there just aren't many cats, or they're getting pounded all the time by your catfishing competition. Toad says you either set bear traps along the bank to reduce competition, or you fish blood to outfish competition. Take your choice.

To get blood, well, something has to bleed, a thought not likely to bother a hardcore catman. Catmen, if I do say so, tend to be earthy folks who know the facts of life. Catmen may live in the city or on the farm, but tend to be country boys at heart; and like ol' Hank Jr. says, "country boys can survive" and get by and know the score, and no number of designer clothes or $50 cologne is going to erase the fact that someday everything's time comes, and that means for chickens, too.

I have caught cats on beef blood and pork blood, but chicken blood seems to be the finest blood of all. Toad knows the location of every kill floor in the states of Minnesota, Iowa, and South Dakota. But it only takes one—hopefully it's a chicken kill factory.

Toad: "Ask permission to get blood. I've never been turned down. Most kill foremen have never been asked before, so they haven't practiced saying 'No,' so it's easy to say 'Yes.' Either that or they think you're so incredibly sick that they'd better say 'Yes' while they call the sheriff in the meantime. Never mind, because you don't need much blood, and you'll be long gone before the sheriff gets there.

"The blood will be lying there all lumpy and congealed, having slid down a shoot of sorts. Dig right in there with your bucket. If you lose your cookies at this point, well, you might as well resign yourself to city-slicker status and baits like nightcrawlers.

"At home in your back yard, near your neighbors if you dislike them, and vice versa, dump the blood out on an old window screen. The runny, juicy stuff sifts right through, leaving the good stuff, the cakes.

"Take a cake and cut chunks—3/4-inch wide and 8 to 12 inches long. Strip the blood chunks into 1/4-inch-thick sections by lifting and peeling strips off the chunk. Place them in a 1-pound coffee can. When you get enough for a meal, thinking in terms of how many cats you want to catch per can, just place the lid on the can and freeze the blood.

"Freezing toughens the blood so it's easier to use. I call once-frozen blood new blood. There are times when it works better than old blood, or blood that's been thawed a time or two and refrozen. Refreezing, however, tends to toughen the blood and make it even easier to work with, unless you get it too warm."

Inevitably there are questions about other bloodbaits, principally paste baits with blood in them. Paste baits are pastebaits and blood is blood. We're talking blood here, not pastebaits. Pastebaits come in many different flavors, and

Stripping Blood

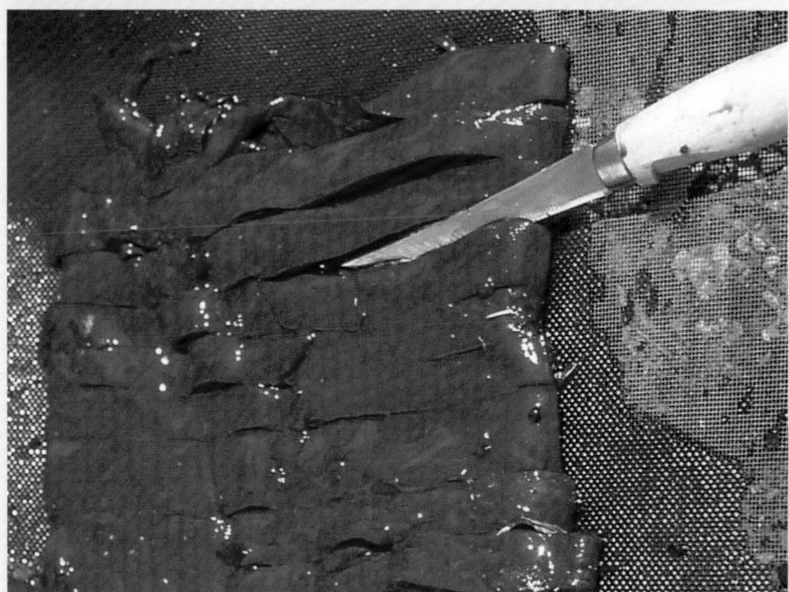

Home from the kill floor with a fresh bucket of congealed blood. Drain the blood on an old window screen.

Separate the individual cakes of blood. Cut each cake into chunks 3/4-inch wide and 8- to 12-inches long. Strip the blood into 1/4-inch-thick sections by making cuts at 1/4-inch intervals along the side of the chunks. Peel the strips off the chunks, lay the strips in a sealable container, and freeze them to toughen them.

sometimes one flavor works better than others. Sometimes blood flavor works well. But blood paste is much different than new blood. Fresh blood usually works better.

RIGGING

Congealed blood does not cast well or fish well in current without being properly rigged. One option is a two-hook method. Slide two 1/0 hooks on your line, leaving an 8-inch tag end. Use the tag end to double the end of your line, leaving the two hooks dangling together at the bottom of the loop. Tie a 3-wrap surgeon's knot, using the doubled end. Tighten the knot just above the two hooks. Slip each hook through a doubled-up portion of stripped blood and cast away.

Toad has another method. Tie a #4 or #6 treble hook to your line. Leave a 10-inch tag end beyond the knot. Wrap a strip of blood around the treble. Wrap the tag end around the blood. Tie it off with a half hitch to hold it in place.

Another method is to substitute a 10-inch

Blood Rigging

Rig blood by wrapping a strip of it around a #6 treble hook ***(1)*** *tied to your line, leaving a 10-inch tag end beyond the knot. Wrap the tag line around the blood* ***(2)*** *to hold it in place. Secure the tag end with a half hitch* ***(3)****. This method works for rigging clams and fresh chicken liver, too.*

section of 10- or 12-pound-test Dacron for the tag-end monofilament. Tie a good knot and trim it. Then tie a 10-inch section of Dacron on the hook eye, and use it to wrap the blood.

A portion of nylon mesh stocking can also be used to hold a wad of blood. Slip a single hook through a bit of mesh and cast away.

CHUMMING

Blood is worth a try in almost any situation, especially for channel cats.

Chumming is the introduction of free offerings, in this case blood, into the area in which you are fishing in order to stimulate feeding or get feeding fish to feed on the baits you've introduced. Too few catfishermen chum and catch too few catfish because of it. Too many catfishermen are too concerned that they are feeding fish full and therefore won't get any bites.

I've never seen it work that way. Feeding fish usually keep feeding until the easy offerings are gone, even if it means continuing to pick up offerings when they have no room in their stomachs. Try chumming, whether you're fishing with cutbait, pastebaits, or blood. Blood just happens to be a powerful feeding stimulant during late summer.

Say you're at the head of a good hole, a hole where you know there are cats. Say the water runs along one side of the hole and swirls around (current changes direction) a large boulder or tree snag. Drift a bait, let's say a cutbait, through the area. Feeding cats likely are just ahead of the boulder, just behind it, or in the tail-out hole farther back. You usually catch aggressive cats on the first few drifts.

If you get no takes and you're certain fish should be in the area, introduce a handful of blood 10 feet ahead of the current break. Often the blood will get cats moving and probing the area. Fish with blood, although often any bait triggers cats once they're motivated to start looking.

Blood works for cats in reservoirs and lakes as well as rivers. The only way to fish it wrong is not to fish it at all, or to fish it like it's a magic bait that makes up for location and presentation problems. You have to be in good cat territory, and you have to present baits properly.

Blood's one powerful draw, a full step above Toad on the fly-draw scale and often several steps above everything else when it comes to attracting cats during late summer.

Bad blood! Big cats! Lots of them!

Historic Perspectives

It's known in small areas of North America that sour fish (rotting fish) is a powerful catfish bait during early spring. On a national scale, most anglers have never heard of the concept, which is presented in timely fashion in this magazine. The prime period for fishing with sourbaits runs from about February in the South into April and May in the North.

It's in this In-Fisherman issue that the first ad for "Catfish Fever" appears. The book is written in 1988 by In-Fisherman Editor Steve Quinn and Doug Stange, with Steve Grooms helping. For his help on many subjects, Toad Smith is added as an author just before the book goes to press. The book quickly becomes the largest-selling catfish book of all time—and that probably remains the case today. This article is likely the first in which Stange hits his stride in capturing the truly unusual character of his friend Toad Smith, using it to add spice to an otherwise straightforward topic.

Through Stange's characterizations of Toad's behavior and character, In-Fisherman readers soon think of him as a lovable long-lost friend, the perfect catfishing companion.

This article is one of the first to use an underwater "tank shot" of a catfish as a lead photo. In-Fisherman's 1400-gallon aquarium is big enough that it can be drained, underwater structure created, then the tank is refilled and fish added to be photographed in a setting like the real world—another pioneering feat for In-Fisherman.

CHAPTER 10

MARCH 1989

Roadkill Cats

TOAD SMITH, MY BEST CATFISHING BUDDY, is a guy so charitable of spirit that he would gladly give up two days of catfishing to help you finish your work so you could go too, and so much the practical joker that he just can't help himself, given a chance to spread a fine film of stinkbait under the lettuce on your sandwich.

The Sour Cats Of Spring Are The Finest Cats Of All!

Then there's the Toad family dog, Gus, a black lab 'bout 90 pounds. Gus is loved ("The *smart* son I never had," Toad likes to say of Gus in the presence of his sons, John and Elliot), yet the subject of constant goodnatured abuse.

Toad's favorite is the meat trick. Gus certainly is better behaved than Toad in most respects. But Gus is a pathetic, slobbering piece of jelly in the presence of baloney on white, rye, the floor, anything. Knowing this, Toad torments Gus.

A baloney sandwich appears: The world stops. Gus does not blink, does not move except to follow the path of the sandwich. Salivary glands gone wild, drool flows, yet Gus' attention and expression are so set that the loveliest female poodle at the peak of estrus could not distract him from his beloved baloney. Don't pet him, don't scratch his ears, just give him a chew, a taste, a succulent, aromatic morsel.

Backwash (eddy) areas consolidate drifting sours and attract cats.

goes on the bridge of Gus' nose.

Geez, Toad. Gus sits there slobbering pathetically, looking cross-eyed at the meat 3 inches from his eyeballs, an inch from his lips, a 1/2 inch from his nostrils. Force a huge smile across your face, grimace and moan, "Woo, woo, woo," without moving your lips. That's Gus: "Woo, woo, woo," he moans, two octaves higher than normal.

"Geez, Toad," we all say, our mouths watering along with Gus'. Toad purposely turns to look out the window—Gus' signal. The meat stands momentarily motionless in midair as Gus' head moves in one barely visible snap. "Woof!" he bellows in a resonant bass voice, telling Toad that he, the wily Gus dog, has outsmarted him, the dreadful Toadmaster.

Cats after ice-out are like Gus and baloney. Obsession. Long winter. Torpid metabolism. Finally, warmer water and metabolic movement. Food please. Food!

The obsession is for winterkill, Ma Nature's roadkill—dead-something fish: shad in reservoirs; bullheads, bluegills, and so on in lakes and ponds; and carp, suckers, carpsuckers, quillback, and such stuff in rivers.

Fish gotta go sometime and the going is better during winter for fish aged, starving, or in other ways not up to Mother's standards. Ice-cold water delays decomposition. Warming water brings decomposition, which brings gas, which makes the winterkilled bloat like a blimp.

Floaters. Prevailing wind or current moves these pale, limp, deadfish chips, until in lakes they stack in necked-down lake areas or bays; in ponds they stack in the corners of the ponds, or in rivers they find their way to backwashes (eddies).

Decomposition continues, the warmer the faster. After a few days in the warm sun, bloated gas

But Toad has time. The sandwich rises and falls, a bite disappearing each time as Toad monitors Gus' agony.

One bite left, Gus crazy with desire, Toad, the sick fellow, raises the last bite to his lips. Surely this moment in a dog's life is comparable to seeing your best friend about to go over a cliff. Toad stops suddenly, pretending he has just remembered Gus. "Gussy wanna bite?" he taunts. "No-no-no-no," he tut-tuts through a sly smile. And then the morsel bladders burst. By this time, some firm floaters have become flaccid, torn sinkers. Certain bays, backwaters, necked-down areas, and eddies are full of them. In rivers, sinkers are washed from eddy to eddy.

Pike, spawners at ice-out, are the first to feed on the winter destruction. Pike love dead (and this is becoming very dead) bait. By the time water temperature reaches 45°F, however, the first cats are wherever, too.

Cats in cold water? Well, now, these are North Country cats. I can't tell you where North Country cats become South Country cats, only that just as there are Florida-strain and northern-strain bass, I know there are North Country cats and South Country cats (Nashville cats?), and that North Country cats feed in colder water in spring and fall. South Country cats don't have to contend with frigid water, so they can feed all season long.

Ninety percent of the cat world seems to think cats stop feeding in September and don't start until May or June. Even in Minnesota and Manitoba, cats feed into November and can sometimes be caught through the ice. And in spring, it doesn't take long to get them going.

Englishman Duncan Kay, a carp bait manufacturer, fished with Doug Stange in the 1980s, working on baits for catfish.

Forty-five degrees? OK, maybe that's not the exact temperature. You know what I mean. You kind of feel it in spring after 20 years of fishing; you kind of feel it's time a week or two after ice-out, and two or three days into warm, stable weather and it's overcast and you know a thunderstorm's coming on and the crawlers might be out for the first time and that the cats, like Gus, will turn into pathetic slobbering fools in the presence of the right food.

There's no helping themselves. The cats will be there where they *must* be. The longer they've lived and the longer they've been programmed, the bigger they probably are and all the more likely to be there, in these spots filled with roadkill.

About roadkill. I have always kept cats and dogs, and lately, kids, and know of puke on rugs and car seats and dog-shucks on Vibram-soled shoes. I have spent 20 years experimenting with stinkbaits. I have spent 7 days in elk camp with Toad without a bath. I have spent hundreds of days toting blood and guts and tolerating flies while catfishing in 100°F heat. I have gutted a hundred

The catfish bait was out all night, Dad, and the raccoons didn't go near it. I guess it's ready!

deer and thousands of fish and arrow-killed bears. I have worked on the kill floor of meat-packing plants. I do not have a weak stomach.

There is, however, nothing so pathetic, so sadly sour as properly soured fish—*sours*, we call them. Good wines take time. Well, there is something in the aging of these roadkilled carci. It's not that it smells so bad, really; it's the pervasiveness of it.

You are at the dentist. "Open wide," you hear as hands approach your face. It hits you. Your stomach turns, your esophagus wretches; you are moments from passing out or at least hoping you do, for the hands of any man are beyond hope for weeks having once handled sours.

Doctors, dentists, preachers, teachers, and priests—folks 'round folks—must wear rubber gloves to handle sours. (One recent study showed baptisms down 50 percent in Illinois and Indiana areas where priests and preachers fish for ice-out cats.) A million dollars says there is no no-scent soap that can handle this wound.

Which is why it works, I suppose.

The best bait is natural—that is, bank-bought with effort. Find your own kill, a carp perhaps if you're fishing a river—and, if it has aged ripely, wearing seven layers of rubber gloves you scale it and fillet it as you wretch and segment it, wrapping it in 7,000 layers of plastic.

Sour shad, suckers, and such are just fine, mind you, except they don't hold together as well as portions of fish with big scales, like carp. Carp's tough. A 7-pounder worth of cut sour will often last the spring in rivers, where they're easiest to find because carp float forever—used to whack 'em with .22 caliber hollow points in the days when kids ran free with rifles. It's the other, smaller roadkill specimens the cats must be feeding on, of course, although festering carp or sheepshead portions are the best bait going.

Making it is never quite the same, but suffices. Times were when I froze several sides of carp in fall, jarred them after portioning them in spring, and buried the jars 6 inches down in the black dirt in a sunny spot in the garden. Soil maintains temperature at night, and in a week or so—or next year or so if you forgot a jar and dug it up with the taters in fall—it was ready, but never quite so ready as it should have been, never quite so ready as a *real* roadkill.

Better to leave the jar sit in the sun by day, I found, bury it at night. Too much work, though.

Better still to sack the fish in say four plastic bags and hang it on the clothesline. Even wrapped, it draws catfish. The ripening process and the quality of the festered mess depends on the sun—sorta like fine wine—Catfish Chablis.

Best of all, I suppose, would be to let the sides soak in a bucket in the basement for a month at about 60°F before you go fishing, but then who except Gus, who relishes rolling in such stuff (Can you explain that?), could stand the odor? An answer is academic really, the idea being almost beyond comprehension, although catmen know no "cat-chum" idea is beyond comprehension, which is why it's mentioned here.

Do not be embarrassed if your mouth starts to water when you handle sours. There you are holding the bait at arm's length to put it on the hook—just nick the hook through a corner of the bait and for heaven sakes don't bury the hook; just leave the hook point exposed so it doesn't set back into the bait on the set. There you are with the bait at arm's length and your mouth's watering—a latent recessive response, I suppose, a Pavlovian response, a genetic trait passed down from our cave heritage.

Although this is about death in the name of spring cats, it's appropriate to interject that the second-best bait going certainly may be more agreeable. No winterkill purist would stoop so low, but live minnows, small chubs, or in a pinch, small suckers work. In the case of minnows, use 3 or 4 impaled through the base of the tail. Chubs: Use one 4-incher hooked the same way. Fish the livebait in the same spots that you would fish the sours.

Cats are as programmed to eat recently injured, still-struggling bait in spring as they are to eat roadkill, although certainly for about a month, the latter with its bloated bladder is a more compelling bait.

This is not about rigs. For now, any of your favorite slip rigs or set rigs will get you fish. The secret is in knowing where the roadkills are and in fishing sours there.

During spring, the best catfishing usually is from midday on. A beautiful, bright, warm, calm spring day that slides gracefully into a warm evening means good fishing; the more days like that in a row the better. In those conditions you may even get an evening bite. If there's a nasty chill to the evening air as the sun sets, however, the bite won't last long.

As the spring rambles on toward summer, fresh cutbait begins to outfish sours, although sours account for cats all season long, especially during late summer (yet another story).

Speaking of stories and bites, the ultimate humiliation for Gus is being bitten—by Toad. Reach across your chest and grab a tiny portion of skin—a pinch—just back of your armpit. Tender territory.

Gus and Toad will be roughhousing, an appropriate nomer, considering Gus' 90 pounds and Toad's 280 or so can be pretty rough on a house. Eventually, Toad pins Gus. Suddenly, realizing his plight, Gus lies perfectly still, desperately hoping that what he knows is going to happen won't.

"Grrrrrr," Toad growls as he ducks down and nips Gus in the tender skin behind his front leg.

"Woo, wooo," Gus moans in a near falsetto. "Woo, wooo, woooo."

Life is many things—politics and war and taxes and bills and plumbing problems. But when you realize it's also a grown man with a mouthful of dog hair and a dog moaning pitifully for mercy, well, I just have to sit there and chuckle. Kind of puts things in perspective, don't you think?

Cats. Pathetic slobbering fools in the presence of road kill.

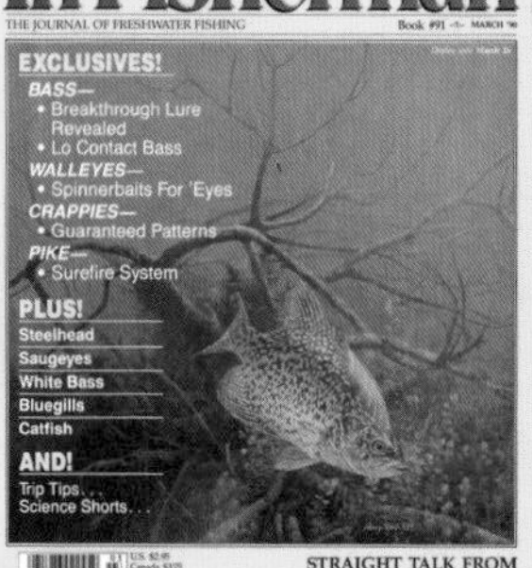

MARCH TIPS & TRICKS
SPRING FISHING TACTICS!
the In-Fisherman
THE JOURNAL OF FRESHWATER FISHING
EXCLUSIVES!
BASS—
• Breakthrough Lure Revealed
• Lo Contact Bass
WALLEYES—
• Spinnerbaits For 'Eyes
CRAPPIES—
• Guaranteed Patterns
PIKE—
• Surefire System
PLUS!
Steelhead
Saugeyes
White Bass
Bluegills
Catfish
AND!
Trip Tips...
Science Shorts...
STRAIGHT TALK FROM PEOPLE WHO REALLY FISH

Historic Perspectives

A lot happens in the years intervening from Roadkill Cats (Chapter 10, March 1989) to this date in 1990. Stange becomes Editor In Chief of all In-Fisherman publications, a position that continues with book publication—20+ years and counting. He begins to enlist the help of other anglers to write catfish articles for In-Fisherman. In June 1989, Steve Quinn contributes his first article, written with Stange. Ned Kehde, later to become an In-Fisherman field editor, and Guido Hibdon (of professional bass-fishing fame) write about trotline tactics. Kehde and Steve Hoffman, now In-Fisherman Publisher but initially hired as the editor of Catfish In-Sider magazine, eventually write many catfish articles for In-Fisherman, Catfish Guide, and Catfish In-Sider.

1990 also is a big year for catfish on TV, with Stange and Toad Smith contributing 4 segments for In-Fisherman Television, including the first show ever shot on night-fishing for flatheads. But every show segment is a first, because only In-Fisherman is covering catfishing. A segment titled "Beyond Forked Sticks" illustrates on TV Stange's fundamental approach to finding catfish in rivers. It soon is the foundation for the first catfish video ever produced, Catfish Fever, available in 1991.

Nels Neilsen is the author of this article, but Neilsen is in reality Stange writing under a pen name, the only time he does so. This isn't the first explanation of Stange's vision of how to find catfish in smaller rivers, but it's perhaps the best.

Illustration by Larry Tople

CHAPTER 11

MARCH 1990

Beyond Forked Sticks

CULTURAL SHOCK. Seems like yesterday I was fishing for salmon with a gentrified bunch from Scotland—moors and kilts and kippers and a misty little private river I shan't name. We toasted each caught fish with a thimble-sized libation poured from a silver flask. Tea and biscuits were properly served at 5 bells and, if I do say, I was treated with utmost dignity—first cast was mine, last cast was mine, and all casts in between, if I preferred.

The Good Book On Channel Catfish Location!

In Scotland we fished with flies. During my day on a southern Minnesota river with Toad Smith, Doug Stange, and Steve Quinn, we fished with flies—literally, that is. They were everywhere and then some, especially around the almighty blood bucket, where occasionally the likes of 250 pounds of grizzled Toad Smith groping in that crimson soup for just the right portion of chicken entrails would have gagged my Scottish gillie (guide).

Stange, Smith, and Quinn wrote "The Good Book" on channel catfish: In-Fisherman's *Channel Catfish Fever—A Handbook of Strategies.* I've known Mr. Stange for a few years because of our mutual love for catfish and because he's reviewed a few of my more important journalistic endeavors—a tolerable sort he is, but a nasty man with a red pen. I've known Toad for only days, but it seems a lifetime, for he's a simple man but one you can never forget. Quinn is, well, Quinn, which we'll get to in a moment.

Was I treated with dignity? Say this, I survived—and after realizing I would never be given first cast, let alone last cast, I fought my way forward and even caught a fish or two.

Stange, Smith, and Quinn. Sounds like a law firm. An odd firm it would be. The threesome is a study in contrasts. Toad, as I've mentioned, is a large fellow who takes life as it comes, slow and easy, a man who gets by in the race to catfish through guile. Mr. Stange usually is two steps ahead of Toad, until Mr. Stange's bait supply suddenly disappears. Guile, you see.

T'wer football at stake, Stange would QB this outfit. "Toad, downriver, out, and into that cornfield," I can hear him say. His life, by comparison, is ever passing at twice the speed of light. Even as you discuss a complicated point of catfishing with him, there's the feeling that he's calculating magazine budgets, writing an article, and doing a grocery list at the same time.

Quinn's a fishery scientist, a completely agreeable sort always seemingly simmering in a scientific stew, the type to pick around a bit and notice this and that while he's fishing. Before he knows it Toad and Stange are 3 miles downstream, or Toad's likely to have grabbed the interesting little creature Quinn was busy contemplating and squashed it for bait.

Which isn't the least bit disconcerting for Steve, who views life with a sort of scientific detachment—he's as likely to stand and watch grizzled old Mr. Toad in awe and contemplation, perhaps wondering back to a college course that discussed the ascendance of man on the evolutionary scale—or he's as likely to stand and watch Mr. Stange in awe and contemplation, perhaps wondering how a laidback South Georgia community would fare with the hyperactive Mr. Stange as mayor.

Enough, though. We're here to discuss catfish with these three who, I must tell you, can catch more whiskered nuzzlers faster than any folks I've met in five decades of fishing. 'Twas their locational handle on channel cats that so impressed me, so inspired me, so convinced me that catfishermen willing to listen could double their catch in a season.

"The easiest way to understand catfish location in rivers is to look at small streams," Stange said during our day on the river. "Small streams are easier to get to know because the catfish's world is compressed into a small area. In a large river,

Toad Smith and Doug Stange planning (conniving) how to take the ever-inquisitive science man Steve Quinn out of competition for catfish on this run downriver. "We'll plant bones from that roadkilled deer with these old bones from a cow along his path downriver. 'Strange,' he'll say, then spend a half hour contemplating this animal. By that time, we'll be 2 miles downriver and 20 catfish ahead, tee-hee, yuk, yuk."

major holes may be half a mile apart. On a small stream, half a mile might contain 10 holes. You can move and see lots of water. More importantly, the continuing combination of riffles, holes, and runs, and the cover elements that may exist in them, are obvious. Small rivers offer the easiest and quickest education in river makeup and how catfish react to it.

Small rivers offer the easiest and quickest education in river makeup and how catfish react to it. The more you see and fish, the better you become at judging the water—true of rivers of all sizes.

"Catfishing on small streams," he continued, "translates directly to catfishing on larger rivers. Yet the anatomy of larger rivers is more subtle and confusing. If larger rivers are all that's readily available, learning to catch cats effectively will take longer."

For your information, the typical small river is about 15 to 50 feet across. You can easily cast across it and move along the banks on foot, crossing without difficulty—easy to see the continuous series of riffles, holes, and runs that make up all rivers. You must judge according to the merits of each series of riffle-hole-run elements in deciding where to concentrate your fishing.

RIFFLE-HOLE-RUN

"As water meanders through a streambed it flows over bottoms of varying hardness," Steve Quinn said. "Riffles form over hard-bottomed areas and are shallower, because current doesn't wash away hard bottom. Riffles form natural dams that obstruct moving water. A pool of water builds at the head of a riffle and eventually flows over the riffle, quickening over the constricted area like water forced through a hose nozzle.

"Riffles in rocky trout streams may be over a quarter-mile long before rocky substrate meets softer substrate and the fast-flowing water begins to scour a hole," Quinn continued. "But hard substrate isn't common in most areas where catfish rivers are located, so riffles usually are comparatively short. In most catfish streams in farm country, riffles rarely run for 30 yards, more likely 20 feet.

"The turbulence of constricted water running over a rock-gravel riffle oxygenates water. Crevices in rock and gravel provide habitat for invertebrates like larval insects that serve as forage for fish."

I considered Quinn's observations. The force of current flowing against the softer substrate at the end of a riffle scours a hole. So, a riffle ends in a hole. A riffle has a ruffled surface. Look for fast, busy water. A hole forms just below it. Toad discussed holes. "Holes (also called pools) are the home of catfish. They're wider and deeper river sections. Depth varies according to current patterns and the size of the river.

"In a small stream, a typical hole during a stable summer period might be 30 feet long, 20 feet wide, and 4 feet deep. The biggest and deepest holes might be only twice those dimensions. Comparisons in size, depth, and available cover in holes are important, however. Well talk about it," he said.

Finding The Riffle-Hole-Run

An obvious (A) riffle, (B) hole, and (C) run.

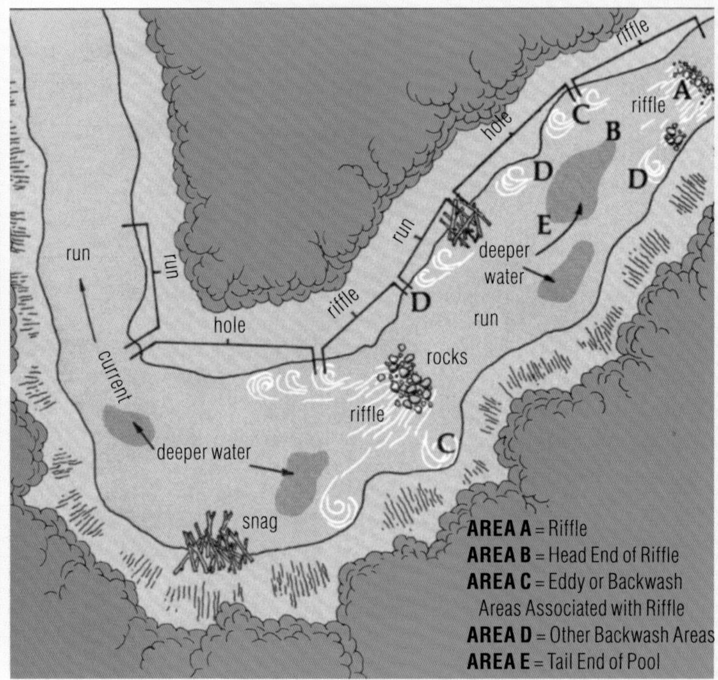

Most rivers consist of a continuous series: riffle-hole-run, riffle-hole-run.

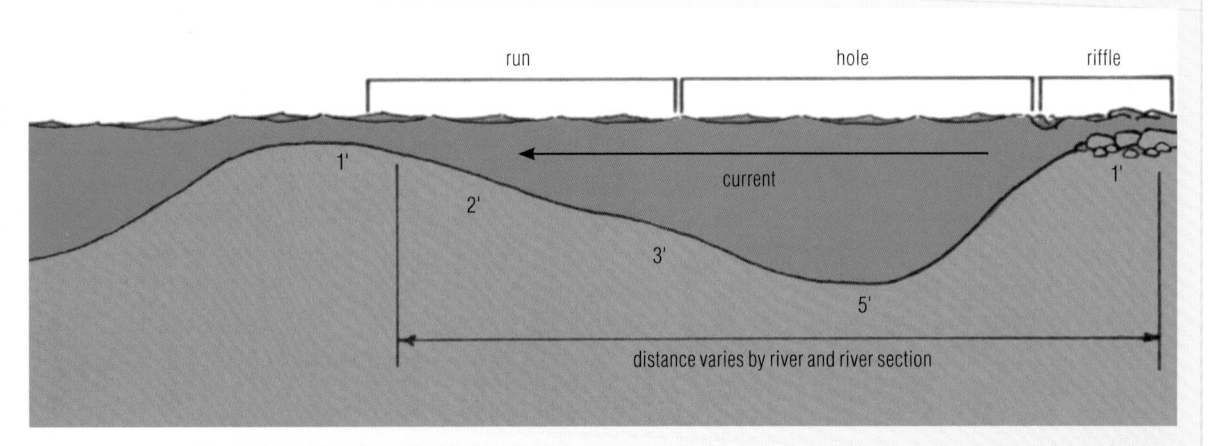

A side-sectional look at a classic riffle-hole-run layout in a small river.

"Holes gradually become shallower at their downstream end as suspended materials sink when water slows. The tail end of a hole becomes a run."

Runs, according to the threesome, are river flats—stretches with no significant depth changes. The bottom usually is sand and silt or gravel, plus debris—wood, tires, brush. In some regions, though, runs may be entirely composed of sand or rock. Catfish move through runs as they travel, but rarely hold for long unless abundant overhead cover offers protection to give resting security. Flats are generally too shallow for cats to hold there unless cover is present.

Catfish make forays onto flats to feed, especially the deeper section of a flat at the rear of a hole and the shallow portion of a flat immediately above a riffle. These shallow flats serve as nursery areas for fish fry and holding areas for minnows, chubs, suckers, and small catfish. Carp often feed on these flats and gar roam there, too. But adult catfish prefer the more immediate confines of a hole area.

Like riffles, runs vary in length depending on bottom composition and river size. In a typical small river with a hole 4 feet deep and 20 feet long, the hole might be followed by a 30-yard run, before the river curves or runs over another area of hard bottom—a riffle—and the cycle repeats.

Stange interrupted. "Holes," he said, pointing to the one we had just walked up to, "specific holes like this one during summer and fall are the center of the catfish world. Holes must be deep enough to provide security, and the surrounding area must offer food. The hole collects living and dead food, drifting or moving downriver.

"See how this hole is laid out?" he asked. "This is a classic—one of the best holes we've seen today. Channel cats tend to move forward into current when they become active and feed. The upper end of a hole—right there," he pointed, "is a key feeding area. There's a definite edge there, a dramatic change in current and depth. The tail end of a hole often tapers so gradually that it fades into the run. The upper end of a hole where a riffle spills water into the hole rarely tapers that gradually.

"See there," he continued. "The scouring force of current at the upper end of holes often exposes rocks or boulders that break current and serve as catfish holding stations. Debris may also wash into this area of the hole and divert current. Cats sometimes rest there when they're inactive, but more often they move deeper into the core of holes or into cover in holes.

"But listen," he said. "Active cats use slackwater behind boulders or debris at the head of a hole as feeding and holding spots. Generally, the area from the bottom of the riffle to shortly downstream of the deepest part of the hole—*the forward section of the hole*—is the best feeding area."

Doug took two cats from the head of the hole, and I caught one before Toad and Steve walked up. They noted that the deepest part of the hole usually follows the tail (downstream end) of the riffle. Again, a hole's width and depth depend mainly on current and bottom. The core of the hole may also offer rocks or boulders for cats to hold near. Usually, though, current slows enough in the core of holes to let catfish lie anywhere.

Then the discussion got serious. "Two major features of holes determine how good a hole is," Stange said as Toad and Quinn considered his explanation. "Cover objects break current. Cover is always a potential attractor, but cover near distinct current has more potential than cover on, say, a flat. Cover near the top of a hole where current has force is especially attractive.

"Channel cats use current to bring food to them. Yet they can't expend all their energy swimming against strong current. They use cover objects to break the force of current and funnel food into specific spots—percentage feeding areas for cats and percentage fishing areas for fishermen."

"Right," Quinn said. "Cover may be a boulder. In the tail of the pool, boulders may be partially silted over, but near a riffle, current sweeps away debris and scours depressions in front of and behind boulders. An old tire may be cover, or logs, or tree roots. Even a sandbar is cover if it deflects current and creates an eddy or backwash area, where current swirls in a circle or bends back upriver."

"The way I look at it," Toad said, "cover serves as a feeding station or rest area, attractive in part because it's different from the rest of the river. Mainly, though, cover helps gather food and lets catfish lie comfortably near current.

"But cover objects aren't equally important," he went on. "Catfish may occasionally use a large boulder near the end of a hole where current slows, but not as often as a boulder at the head of the hole."

"Don't forget though," Stange added, "that with increasing current, the rear boulder might be better."

"Right, right," Toad said. "And if current flows heavily against one side of a hole, identical boulders on the opposite side would receive different use by catfish. Unless current increased drastically, the boulder on the slack side wouldn't attract cats as often as the boulder in faster water. Fish both boulders, however, and you can judge which areas are best, based on present current conditions."

Snags are the other important feature of a catfish hole. I can verify that, because they were the key to our success on the river that day. I haven't told you much about what we were catching or how, because it's another story. Location is so critical for most catmen that I want to concentrate on it here.

The river was low and catfish had pulled into the core of the holes. We'd catch an occasional cat at the tail end of a riffle, but only if it coincided with a snag. The fish were in holes, but mostly in holes with snags. After a bit we didn't even stop to fish good-looking holes unless they had a good-looking snag in them.

Snags may occur anywhere, but usually result from current washing against a bank, exposing tree roots, which causes the tree to topple and gather debris. This usually happens on a flat only during the spring flood stage. The best snags lie near or just rear of the core of a hole, where current slows. Snags on flats may also attract catfish if the flat's deep enough. But cats on flats usually run small.

Holding Areas in a Typical Hole

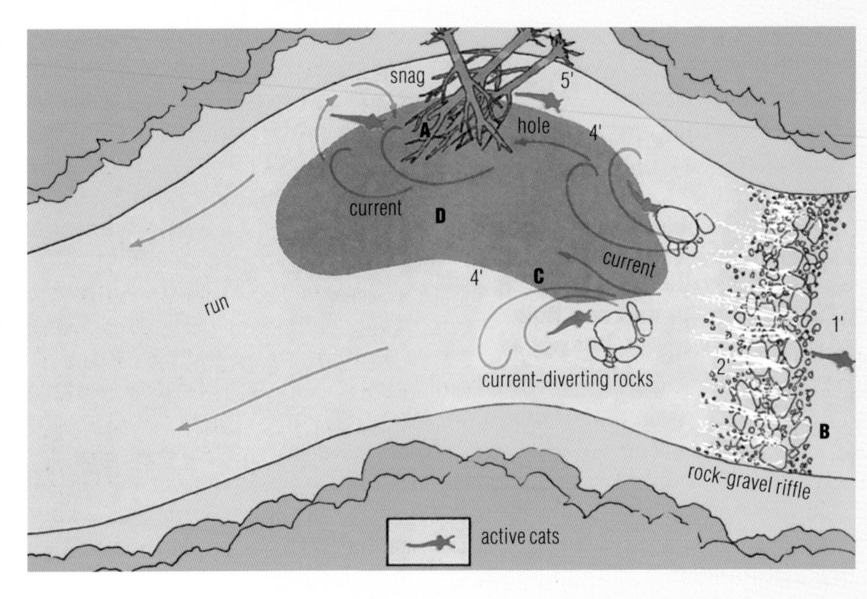

*Inactive cats **(A)** usually hold in the snag or in deeper water in a hole. Active cats feed near the snag, but are as likely to leave the snag and **(B)** move ahead of the riffle to feed in the fast, slick water, **(C)** find a spot to hold and wait for food below the riffle, or **(D)** roam the hole searching for food.*

The threesome emphasized again that snags and cover aren't as important for their physical characteristics as for their location in a hole. Location determines how catfish use them. Cover in fast current near the top of a hole is primarily feeding territory. A snag in quiet water at the lower half of a hole is primarily a holding or resting area. Snags near the core are resting and feeding areas. A snag in fast water right below a riffle would likely be important only as a feeding area.

This isn't to say cats won't rest in the core of a hole when a snag isn't present. They also rest in reduced current behind cover objects. It's a matter of priorities. The biggest cats are likely to use the best feeding and resting areas. Snags in key areas key catfish location.

"Some snags are better than others," Stange said at one point. "A snag in deep water probably is better than one in the shallower part of a hole. Complex snags consisting of dozens of branches are better than simple snags. A snag lying in current is better than one in slackwater.

"Catfish prefer snags offering depth and overhead protection, depth being by far the more important. Cats use simple snags in deep water more than complex snags in shallow water, although during higher water in spring it can happen quite often."

Streams, then, are composed of riffles, holes, and runs. Key elements of a hole are its depth and cover, the most important cover being a snag. The hole is the home of the catfish, especially if there's a complimentary snag to go with it.

The problem is that most catfishermen fish the first convenient hole, usually near a bridge. Or they might drive down a road that ends at the river and fish the first good-looking water nearby. Often they open a lawn chair and crack a cold one. And they probably prop their rod on a forked stick left behind by other anglers.

Feeding Moods And Current

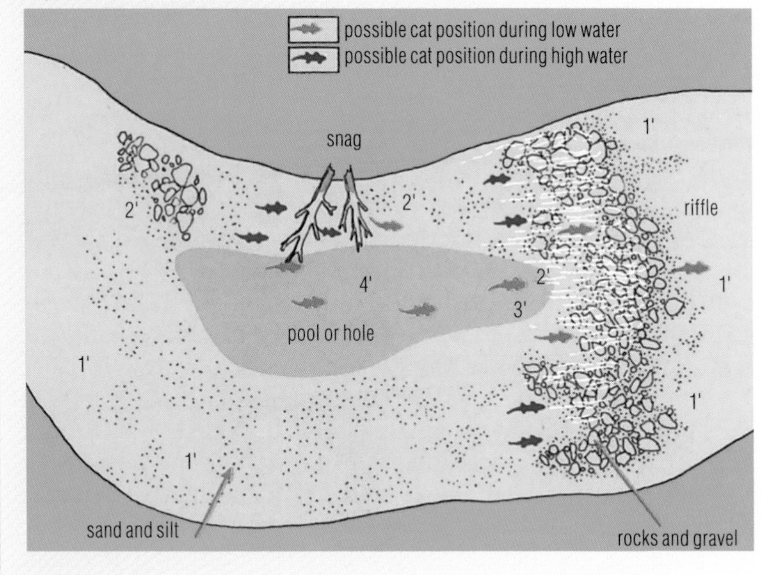

Catfish location changes, depending on feeding mood and current. Active cats tend to stay at the head of the hole, although they also swim around the entire hole to check it out. Inactive or neutral fish hold in the hole's core, or in or behind cover.

Heavy current forces catfish behind cover objects usually found along shore. Low flow draws cats to deeper water away from the bank.

Drift a bait through each possible spot. Usually patterns emerge quickly. If you catch cats at the head of one hole, they probably be at the head of the next one, too.

I dun know, Andrew...yo sho we gots to talk like this here to catch us some of them thar catfeshes?

"Find such a hole and you find catfish, especially if there aren't comparable holes nearby. With similar holes nearby, catfish may distribute among them. Usually, though, a river stretch with more good holes also attracts the most catfish."

"Learn to recognize prime holes by experience—seeing and fishing them," Quinn said. "That, again, is easiest done on a small river. Move. Look and compare. The more river you see, the better you can judge where the fish most likely are.

"Most rivers have prime stretches with better habitat, thus better holes. In a 10-mile stretch of river, there might be a 1-mile prime stretch with more good holes holding more and bigger catfish than all the other miles.

"The other miles might contain sandy runs, marginal holes, and a good hole here and there. Find a good hole in that stretch, and it might produce as well as some of the holes in the prime stretch. The prime stretch, though, holds more cats. Spend your time on prime holes in prime stretches, fishing other prime holes only occasionally."

PRIME HOLES AND RIVER SECTIONS

"They're fishing the same spot fished by most anglers," Toad said. "Holes get fished down—burned out. Don't spend your time on the holes that have had most of the catfish removed.

"You're looking for prime holes in prime stretches. Some holes and some stretches of river are much better than others. Eventually the biggest and the most cats find the best holes.

"Every hole in a river might hold a few cats, but better holes attract more cats. Those are the holes to concentrate your fishing on, but they're the ones most catfishermen don't find because they don't walk or float far enough to compare river stretches and holes."

Toad continued: "A prime hole is going to be larger and deeper with long adjacent runs to produce lots of food, plus cover objects, especially near the top end, and perhaps a big snag in the core of the hole. Everything comes together in one spot to give catfish security, food, and a resting spot. When cats travel by, this hole holds them.

SCOUTING HOLES

By the time we finished the day, we caught and released at least 40 catfish—the biggest about 8 pounds. Amazing? Not for these guys. Not for you, either, once you learn to evaluate holes.

To do that you must fish lots of them. Move—walk or float with a purpose. Compare, compare, compare. Analyze each hole. How big is it? Does it have good cover? A snag? Are there other good holes nearby? Are there tributaries to help restock this hole during changing water conditions?

Start with a map, a topographical map if possible. Look for stretches where the river meanders. Straight stretches won't contain as many riffles and holes as meandering stretches.

Walk or float a 3-mile stretch, but don't spend

too much time at any one hole. Look for deeper holes with more cover than others. Soon you know the best holes in that stretch. Then look at other stretches and compare, compare.

When you're fishing quickly—scouting—fish only for actively feeding cats. Drift a bait above the riffle, then through the riffle once or twice, then into the head of the hole around a cover object or two. If you catch a fish, you've learned a little about the quality of the fish in the area. You also know that at least some cats are active because they're at the head of the hole.

In most rivers, snags key catfishing during summer when water levels drop. No fish on those first drifts? Then move down a bit and drift a bait through the core of the hole. Then move to the snag, if there is one. Drift a bait along the front of it. Move to the rear of the snag. Try a drift or two. Time to move, even if you're sure fish are present but not active.

Off again, moving downstream. Check the next hole. There's always new and intriguing water around each bend.

Scouting works best when the water's low, particularly during prespawn and early fall when cats also are likely to be active. Low, clear water's an asset; high, dirty water obscures cover and snags.

Most catfish anglers are going to be amazed by how many more catfish they catch if they fish quickly, moving, moving again, fishing only for active cats. It's the biggest step to better catches. And it's a strategy that with a bit of practice is simple to employ.

Sure, there are times to sit and outwait catfish—but only after you've seen lots of river and can judge where the best holes are located. Only when you're absolutely sure, do you want to spend an entire morning or evening fishing just one or two holes, probably trying to catch big fish.

In the end, it's hard to believe things can be so simple. Yet most anglers are wasting their lives using ineffective strategies to find fish.

In Scotland, a gillie puts you on fish. Catmen have to find their own. You need to travel where too many catmen haven't traveled before—beyond forked-stick country.

(A) In most rivers, snags key catfishing during summer when water levels drop. (B) Name's Toad. System works for flatheads, too. Tell you 'bout it sometime. (C) On the move!

Historic Perspectives

This one speaks for itself with distinction, in favor of one of Stange's favorite fish. Many readers have noted it as the greatest flathead article of all time—especially as one of the first (probably the first) in-depth articles ever published about this fish and how to catch it. See what you think. The article also is the first to speak passionately in favor of conservation of a fish that at the time was being routinely targeted for slaughter instead of release. This article is the beginning of slow but steady change in the way anglers and fishery departments view the flathead.

CHAPTER 12

JUNE 1990

The Golden Age of Flathead Catfish

Piscator 1: *Catfish, say you? Flathead catfish? But what of my beloved bass, walleyes, muskies, and trout? Surely, you jest my good man, for these I cannot do without.*

Piscator 2: *I jest not, nor would I that you give up walleyes or other such habits. Nay sir, say not "instead of," but "besides."*

Piscator 1: *But why besides? This flathead fellow doesn't play well, I think. I see him not touted on pious pages of outdoor magazines. I see no fishermen dressed in nifty wear sporting odd patches, casting quickly for this flathead fellow.*

Piscator 2: *Ignorance, my friend. Ignorance. Most editors sell bear attacks and recycled bass baloney better than blessed truth. And there's no bounty on this fish, no fame in the catching. Who would wear odd patches and fish like they pursue a heart attack t'wer not a fleeting sense of fame and fortune involved. Then too, heaven help us, fishermen tend to fish for that which other fishermen fish for. Alas, I fear men are like lemmings in some respects.*

Piscator 1: *But I must ask again, why? What, or should I say who, is this flathead fellow?*

Piscator 2: *Say this, my friend, he is a fish of character. Powerful, he is, and tenacious as a pit bull. Flippin' stick and 6 pounds of bass in brush, you say? Difficult? My good man, why not just tap dance with Pee Wee Herman? But a toe-to-tush tussle with a flathead? Sir, one could as well bark at Hulk Hogan's girlfriend.*

A mean sort he is, too, predator to the core. Flathead catfish kill things. The carp that disappear in a crush of jaws may weigh 5 pounds

A Case For Catching The Biggest, Toughest Fish Of Your Life!

Piscator Toad posing with two friends at midnight.

or more. Could as well be drum, gar, or shad. Bluegills. Bullheads. Bass pass, too. Even, I'm afraid, smaller channel cats and flatheads—crushed one and all like so many walnuts. One should bring a large and living sacrifice or bring nothing at all.

And there's more. 'Tis not mockery for fishermen to gush over 10-pound bass and walleyes; 20-pound pike; 30-pound muskies and king salmon. But should we not therefore worship Pylodictis olivaris?

Size, man. Size. He's a monster. Twenties, said in today's lingo, are small change. Try 30s, 40s, even 80s and 90s. I swear it. Question not that 100s are out there, moving somewhere through the deeps. Even a 120 or, heaven help us, a 140 is within reason.

Piscator 1: *But why then such paltry information on how to catch this fine fellow?*

Piscator 2: *Say it, said before—ignorance. But say it thought elusive, too. He's thought a sly fellow. True. He trades in darkness, a Dracula of sorts, given his lust for blood. Catch him, though. Ah, catch him, man, and you stand apart. And 'tis easy, I swear it, although you will pay with sleep.*

Stars, damp darkness surrounding a small fire. The river moves somehow slower at night, heavier, with more character. Silence prevails except for carp sucking the surface film along a far bank lined with downed timber.

Suddenly, "Swaaboosh!" A carp meets his maker in a gruesome crush of jaws and a left-right headshake that rips flesh.

Flathead catfish test prey and fishermen alike, for Toad Smith, faintly lit by firelight, rod and reel and tattered 50-pound-test line in hand, is up to his knees in water flowing through a river hole.

"Manno-manno man," he says as he looks off into the blackness surrounding us. "*Donald* for sure—40 or 50 pounds—or the meanest 30 ever."

"Couldn't stop him, huh," I said, offering something, anything, the obvious.

"Naw. Gone!"

"Fifty-pound test?"

"Yeah. Fifty." He snaps the frazzled line dripping from the tip of his rod.

"Heavier?"

"Naw. Don't need more. Just gotta turn 'em right now. Keep his head pointed right at you all the time. Never give an inch in cover. Won't happen again."

Two days of scouting river and two nights of fishing all night. Fifty channel catfish and 10 pretty good flatheads had hit the bank. But not the illustrious Donald, Toad's name for, well—

We'd narrowed our search for huge flathead catfish to one particular hole in a 10-mile-long section of river.

Problem. While the hole was deep and wide, indeed the deepest and widest hole in this section of river, it was filled with drift timber.

"Trump Towers," Toad said when we'd found this hole of holes. "Donald lives here for sure. Maybe Ivana, too. Maybe even Ms. Maples."

"A Donald" is Toad lingo for the biggest flathead cat in a body of water. Might be an 80 in an Ohio reservoir. Might be a 100 in a Texas tailwater. Might be a 20 in a tiny Iowa creek. Could be a 150 in any state bordering the Mississippi, Missouri, or Ohio rivers. Toad guessed a 45 in the small Minnesota river we were fishing.

Big flathead catfish are something. The only North American freshwater predators that grow larger are alligator gar and sturgeons. Maybe the blue catfish. But they don't equal the flathead as a predator. Nor do other freshwater fish, for that matter. We would have to enter the saltwater league to find a tougher customer.

At the beginning of summer, once the water settles in a river and flatheads settle into the biggest, deepest, most cover-laden holes, lots of carp will be working along cutbanks at night. A month later, if the water stays down, the hole will be silent. The carp are gone. Eaten. Along with bullheads and most other sizable prey in the hole. Won't catch many channel cats under 5 pounds in there either. Dead and gone except for a few smiling flatheads.

And they may be very big and definitely hungry. Get a bait in there at night and you'll catch them—most of them, I believe. A problem of paradoxical proportions. Four 20s, a 30, and a 40 from one hole in one night on a small river seems like a dream come true. But then you realize that if you've done your homework and this is the best hole in a long stretch of river, these fish may be the majority of what's available for many miles. And if you keep them?

But first a bit about how to catch a big one this summer. You already know that big fish in rivers shuffle naturally into the biggest, deepest, most cover-laden holes. Finding those holes is a first and vital step.

You must make comparative judgments about the quality of the holes in a section of river. To do that you must survey large sections of river. You won't know that you're fishing the best hole if you haven't seen the hole around the next bend.

Toad and I survey rivers while fishing for channel catfish during the day. We fish quickly, rarely staying for more than 10 minutes at even the best-looking spots. We catch the active fish and move on.

Occasionally we catch a flathead, too, but it's usually a jolly little small fish, may be a 4 or 5, sometimes a 12 or 14. But it won't be Donald. You might also be surprised how many channel cats we catch by using such tactics. The methods are discussed in *Channel Catfish Fever*, an In-Fisherman Handbook of Strategies.

One of the best holes we found last season was a big river turn following about four miles of relatively straight river. Lots of timber had washed into the turn area from the straight section above. The first night we fished this hole, we caught and released 15 flatheads over 20 pounds. The next night we caught 5 fish. And thereafter, fishing was difficult, which shows that flatheads smarten up. Let those fish rest for several weeks and some will bite again. But if we'd killed them all?

Muskie tackle works. Saltwater tackle is overkill except in unusual situations. Go with a rod 6 to 7 feet long, something with give in the top half and power in the butt. Better to cast with. Better to fight fish with.

The Abu Garcia 7000 is a wonderful big-cat reel. Holds plenty of 30- to 50-pound-test line. Has a "clicker" setting when the reel's on freespool. The clicker lets you know when a fish is taking line, plus keeps constant tension on the fish as it moves. A Garcia 6500 also sports a clicker and holds enough line to battle all but the biggest boys in the biggest rivers.

I usually use Dacron (Gudebrod or Cortland) line, which offers lower stretch and higher abrasion-resistance than monofilament—36-pound test in smaller rivers. Fifty for bigger fish in heavier cover.

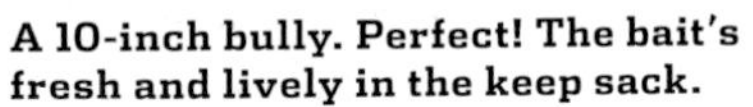

A 10-inch bully. Perfect! The bait's fresh and lively in the keep sack.

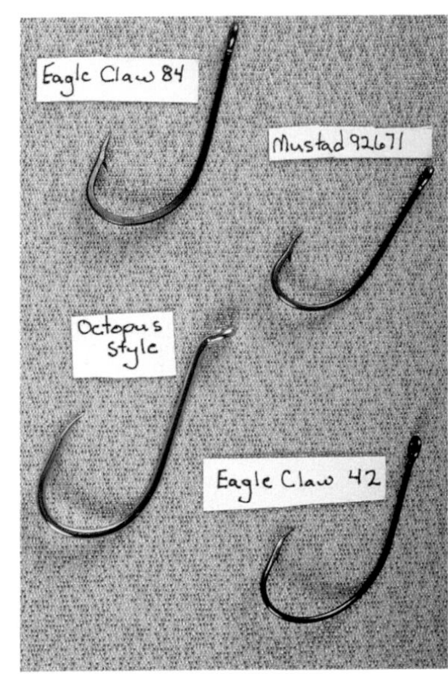

Classic hooks for flatheads!

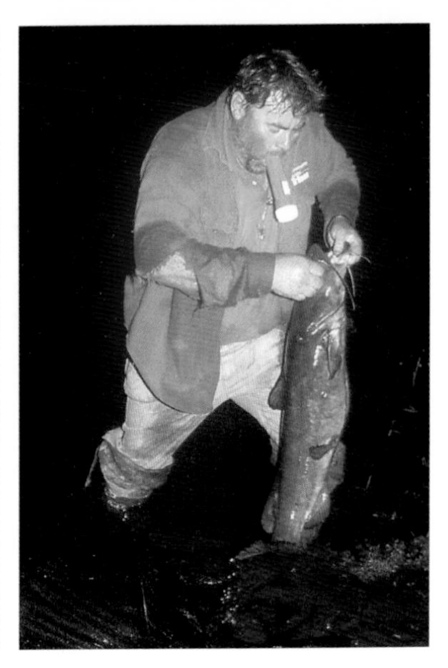

Nighttime's the right time for flatheads!

Of course, monofilament works. Go for something tough. Toad and I used Berkley XT Solar (lime green) a lot last season. Easy to see. Tough. Good stuff. Stren Magnum is a good bet, too.

A 5/0 to 7/0 Eagle Claw 84 or Mustad 92671 is a good standard hook. Slipweights, preferably bell sinkers with swivel tops, should range in size from 1 to 6 ounces. Sharpen the hook and slip it through flesh just below and behind the dorsal fin of a baitfish.

Big, wild, lively bait is vital. Suckers raised in bait ponds don't last long and don't attract as many fish as wild 10- to 15-inch suckers. Green sunfish are wonderful bait. Drum work. Bullheads. Carp. Your neighbor's poodle.

Get set before dark. Set up on an inside riverbend, the low-bank side of the river, and set baits at the head of a hole, in the hole, along a snag, or near a cutbank along the opposite shore. Each rod goes in a rod holder, freespool on and clicker set.

Build a small fire, break out a tub of Kentucky Fried Chicken and wait (you need a big tub if you invite Toad). It will happen. It has to. Flatheads can't help themselves.

If it's a fresh hole that hasn't been fished before, the action will probably start just after dark and continue throughout the night. If the hole has been pressured, it could happen anytime.

When a fish takes, wait just long enough to know the fish has the bait, has turned, and is moving away from you. Don't wait for the fish to swallow the bait. He could move into a snag by that time, and deeply hooked fish may be more difficult to release.

As the fish moves away, set hard, rod tip high, and hold on. Don't give unless you have to. Keep the fish right there. The left-right head rips are like body punches from Mike Tyson. Hold on.

Finding flatheads in a big reservoir is more difficult—more water—but still a sure thing. The next world-record flathead will come from a reservoir. It will weigh around 110. The present all-tackle angling record is a 98.

Plenty of baitfish in creek arms. During early summer, flatheads move into creek arms; set baits on flats along the creek channel. The water on the flat may be only 8 feet deep, while the channel runs 20. Bring friends so you can spread baits along the channel as well as over the flat. If the channel is too far to cast to, fish from a boat, or use a boat to carry baits out, drop them, and row back to a shore position. If you have lively baits and time, flatheads will happen.

Later in summer, if fishing slows inside creek arms, move to flats at the head of the creek arm where it meets the main reservoir.

That's all there is to it, except for specific patterns and details we'll hold for another day. You can certainly break 20 this summer. And once you break 20, you'll break 40. Get a bait in the right place at night and you'll catch them. Perhaps most of them. Which, as I said earlier, is a problem of paradoxical proportions. Four 20s, a 30, and a 40 from one hole in one night—dream come true!

But big flatheads are *vulnerable*, based on hard statistics. May take 25 years to grow a 40-inch 35-pound flathead. And with eating habits like a Sumo wrestler, they just aren't hard to catch once you find them.

Fifteen + 15 + 15 + 15 + 20 + 30 = 110 years. There, strung on a rope draped over a board fence, are 110 years of fish history. Better save that photo, for the time soon approaches when you won't see those fish again in your lifetime. Your sons and daughters won't either.

But there are always more flatheads in the next hole, in the next river, in the next state. Today, perhaps. A handful of flathead catmen find good populations of big flatheads today because few fishermen know how to find and catch them—or, more the case, won't spend the time it takes to do it.

Keep the secret? There are no secrets. Men must tell. And then men must choose, in this case, hopefully, conservation.

This is but a step toward a new age in fishing for flatheads, an age where more fishermen do it. Fishermen must recognize how unique is this amazing predator, which grows so big and bold. With this realization hopefully will come widespread suggestions for regulations to sustain those populations, before we do to them what we did to big bass, walleyes, muskies, and the like before we knew better.

Traditions must change. Noodling, for example. Flathead catfish spend daylight hours in bank holes and crevices. Crazy men wading rivers reach into those holes, probing for catfish.

After finding a cat, noodlers block the hole with a leg. They must then corner the cat in the hole, get a grip on his lower jaw, run a rope stringer through the jaw, and finally drag a green and mighty mean fish from the hole.

But a big flathead will often nip a hand and hold on, and such fish can break an arm with a headshake. What of snakes and snapping turtles? And what of the once-in-a-lifetime (literally) 80 that can drown you?

Change this tradition? Never. Except the ending.

Poly Ball Rig

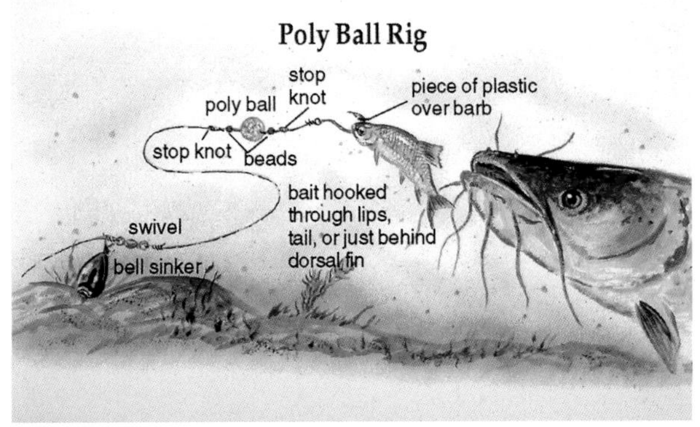

Float-Paternoster Rig

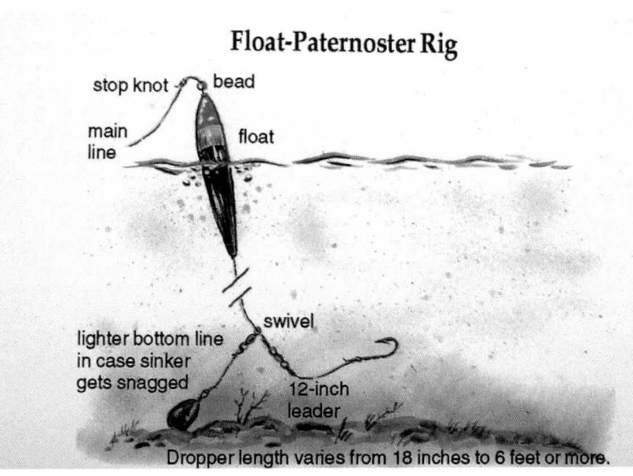

Today, many noodlers don't wrestle flatheads solely to eat or sell them. They like the challenge, the thrill, the idea of being a down-home cat man.

Selective harvest applies to noodling and other traditional forms of fishing like limblining, spearing, snagging, can fishing, and jug fishing. Keep a few smaller fish to eat, enough for a meal or two, and release the hundreds of years of growth represented by what would be a stringer of 30s, a catch not uncommon for noodlers when rivers are down during summer.

Traditions must change. Setlining (trotlining) for example. Setliners are like trappers. To be a successful trapper you must know the habits of your quarry. You must live the life, be outdoors, gather experience, think, and learn. Making skillful sets, tending them, and wrestling big fish in by hand is challenging and can be as exciting as catching a fish on hook and line.

But setlining is by nature more deadly than fishing with hook and line. Setlining during summer when holes are obvious is like setting a land mine along a deer trail. If it's a good trail and you've made a good set you will score. And because you don't have to be there when it happens, it's more likely to happen.

Flatheads can't help themselves. Find a good hole, make a good set with good lively bait, and you'll catch almost every fish that lives there. And the hours are attractive: Set the trap at sunset, pick it up next morning. No lost sleep. Big fish caught.

Successful hook-and-line fishermen pay for flatheads with sleep. The fact limits the catch. I love to set lines; it's the harvest part of setlining

The Big Picture

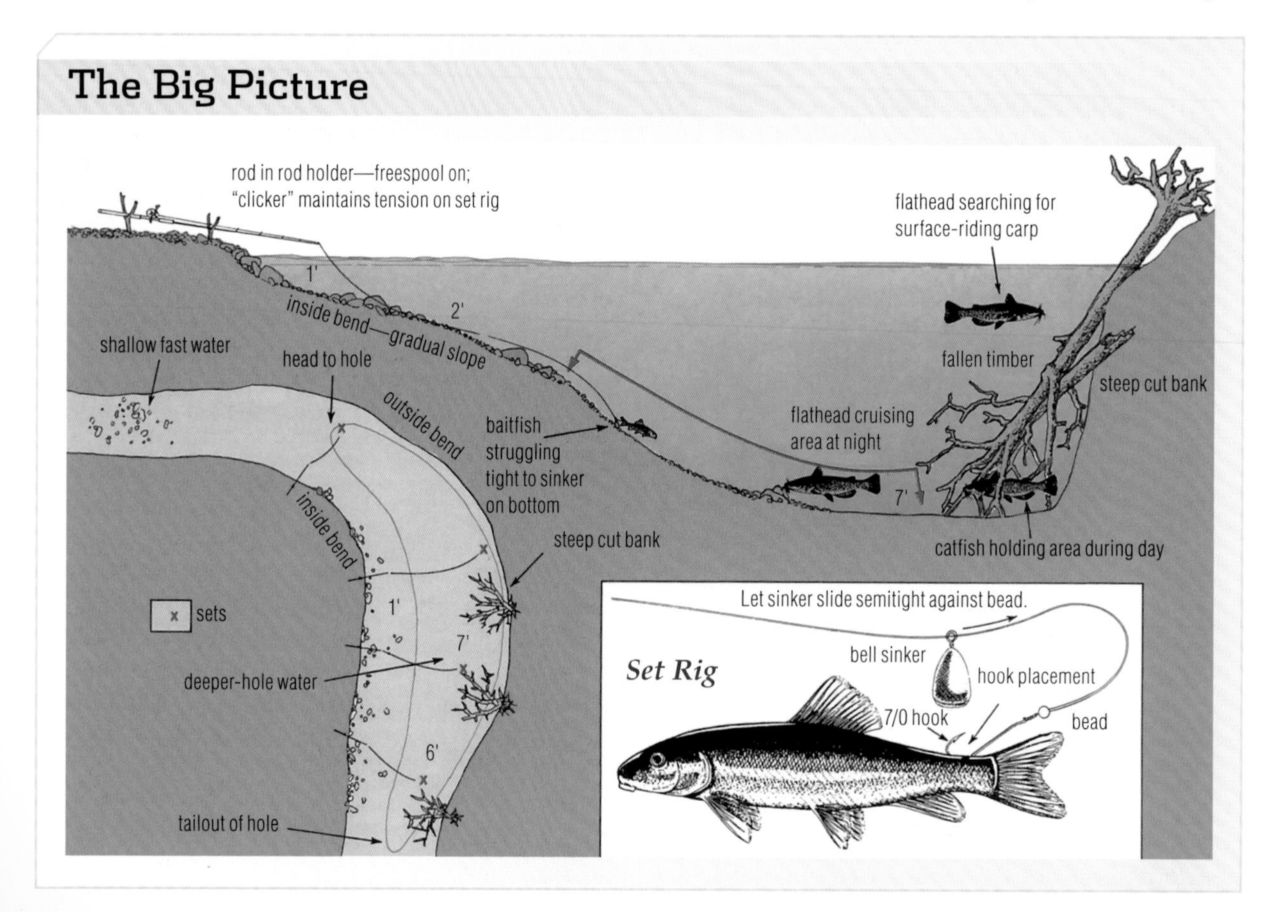

that needs rethinking. Harvest selectively. Time to push for regulations that dictate it.

Commercial fishing is a long tradition in most major rivers that hold flatheads. Fishermen seek them because of their high market value relative to drum, buffalo, and carp. Sportfishing for flatheads has increased in popularity, and catfish anglers are becoming more vocal about their favorite species. They'll make sure resource agencies don't slight cats in their population studies and management plans.

No longer appropriate. Selective harvest, please! Our chance to " do for" flatheads before we "do to" them, and then have to try to undo what we've done.

Conflict between commercial fishermen and anglers is inevitable, as it was for walleyes in the Great Lakes and elsewhere. In Oklahoma, blessed with probably the largest flathead population, fishery managers are pondering difficult allocation problems. The trend's clear. The social and economic importance of recreational fishing means inland commercial fisheries for gamefish are dwindling. And commercial fishermen are content to pursue more predictable and lucrative occupations.

And if big fish eventually die of old age instead of harvest, where's the waste? The payment is in the 40 years of being a big flathead, of being there to thrill men, not in the $2 a pound the flesh is worth at the market.

We raise chickens and turkeys, dumb as a stump, for food. We can even take smaller, more plentiful catfish for occasional meals. If we protect catfish habitat, smaller fish remain readily renewable.

Seeking fame and fortune? Win a bowling tournament. Don't try to ride the backs of a bunch of big dead fish. Stringer shots of big cats prove stupidity, not prowess. Shoot a photo or 10 before you release big boy to continue to spark our existence with his own.

OK, so there probably were more and bigger flatheads a hundred years ago. By comparison to other populations of big fish, however, this is the golden age for flathead cats.

Fish of a lifetime on hook and line? Muskie, you say? Come on, man. You can fish a lifetime today to catch a 35. Muskies got popular first; we did it to them and then we learned. Now it's a very slow and perhaps impossible march to regulate impressive size back.

Flathead cats aren't widely popular even though they should be. Opportunity! I know how overused the word "unique" is today. But today we have the unique opportunity to "do for" a huge predator, instead of "doing to" them and then having to undo what we've done.

Historic Perspectives

This article is the first ever published on tailwater fishing for flatheads with light line in the tailout immediately below dams, explaining where the fish hold and how to catch them. By now, Stange often uses a lively narrative storyline and a conversational tone to make how-to fishing more interesting than the standard instructional written fare of the day. Meanwhile, as noted in passing in this article, catfish continue to play a role on In-Fisherman Television. The segments on flathead catfish that air during the late 1980s and continue to play in the 1990s are the first in the history of TV programming and help to make In-Fisherman one of the most noted programs of its time, then and now. Like bass, trout, and salmon before them—whose champions were James Henshall and Jason Lucas, Joe Brooks, and Lee Wulff—catfish finally have an advocate who speaks for them with knowledge, conviction, and distinction.

CHAPTER 13

FEBRUARY 1991

Mean Mother Monster Flatheads on Thin Line

FLATHEAD CATFISH are arguably the most bodacious fish in North America. A freshwater Sasquatch of sorts, flatheads grow to over 100 pounds. They're mean suckers, too, predators to the core. They'll crack the bones of an unsuspecting carp as easily as a semi truck smashes an acorn on a highway, and enjoy every moment of it. Elusive, too. Few fishermen regularly catch big flatheads.

In Pursuit Of Sasquatch Swimming!

Those fishermen who catch lots of them do it just like I do, with heavy tackle befitting the mean mother of a monster this fish is. That is, before I got light-line religion.

Enter the Reverend (not really) Mike Kohler and catches of 20-pound-plus flatheads on 8-pound-test line. With regularity. Catches of 2, 4, even 10 big fish a trip. From areas within reach of most of you, areas that fishermen don't associate with flathead cats.

The pattern probably plays across North America. Dams. Tailwater areas. Vertical jigging. Walleye tactics and tackle. But for fish that unceremoniously reduce the average walleye to an *Erp!* and a bony bowel movement.

August 1990. It's Kohler on the phone. Bring TV cameras, he's saying. They're baaaack!

It'll be like this, he says, doing his best to paint a picture of a segment for the 1991 In-Fisherman TV Specials:

"Two fishermen, good-looking fellas, star material—that's you and me, he chuckles, and then begins almost to whisper as he continues his story in a delivery sounding a lot like Howard Cosell. Two fishermen slowly motor into position below the gates of a lock and dam. As they move across the turbulent water spinning through the washout hole, they notice large "hooks" on their LCD. Sasqui! (Plural for Sasquatch, he tells me.)

"The stars lower their bowmount electric and begin to 'slip' . . . "

"Make that *deftly* slip," I say, interrupting him. "Implies prowess. Remember, these guys are stars. Besides, I've always wanted to use deftly in print."

"'K right," he says, making the necessary correction, as in: "They lower their bowmount and begin to *deftly* slip with the current as they drop 1/2- or 3/4-ounce leadhead jigs tipped with 3- to 4-inch minnows into 40 feet of water. The jigs ride perfectly vertical on 8-pound-test line below the boat through the 'slacker' water along the bottom of the washout hole, near the back edge of the hole—the tailout area—where it breaks quickly from 35 feet deep up onto the channel shelf in 25 feet.

"They carefully slip along the deep breakline, lifting and dropping their jigs a foot at a time on a tight line. Hooks register along the lip of the washout hole in 32, then 31, 30, 29, 28 feet of water, the tailout lip of the washout hole. Their jigs begin to sweep up the lip—Whomp! 'Son, good fish. Big fish. A won't-move fish,' they say in their best TV fishing-show lingo.

"But it's a won't-move fish for only a moment, "he says. "Then (he pauses) . . . Then (he pauses again, to add suspense to the scenario). Then after several trips following the fish 50 yards upriver, then downriver; after twenty minutes of wondering, Will the hook hold? Will that thin line frazzle or fray? The fish moves the scales to 27 pounds.

"Will we be heroes, or what?"

Who could resist? So crack cameraman and In-Fisherman TV Director James Lindner and I are riding upriver with Mike Kohler in route to a typical tailwater area to shoot a show segment.

"First time when?" I ask as we moved along.

"Nineteen eighty-seven. Late summer. On the Mississippi," he says. "Me and another fella are looking for sauger and white bass—just a quick afternoon outing. Boats are drifting all through the tailwater area, with most staying in typical spots where current reverses itself along the edge of the washout hole.

"Couple hours pass and we're approaching our billionth small whitey and zillionth small sauger. Ho-hum. And, well, I notice a guy drifting way out there over turbulent water where there are supposedly no fish. He has a big fish on. I mean a big fish. Fifteen minutes later, he lands a 'nasty old ugly catfish.' Hey, what do I know about cats, you know? It's not like I grew up in Iowa like you—I don't have cats in my genes. I didn't even know it was a flathead, at the time.

"But I know it's big. So big it demolishes this guy's net. And it's the second 'accident' that day. And whatever 'that' is has gotta be better than another 5-ounce whitey."

"To shorten a long story," I prod.

"A 20, first drift. Honest. First drift. I think it's the bottom, but it isn't and pretty soon this thing is wallowing on the surface and my buddy looks at my new net and I say, Oh no! And then, Aw, geez! And pretty soon I have a pig of a catfish and no net.

"A 16, several drifts later. And finally, one over 30. Biggest fish I've ever caught. Bet the house you know where I was next day and many a day thereafter."

"And you take fish over 20 almost every trip," I say, repeating what he's told me on the phone.

"Nope. Get one over 20 every trip. And there won't be another boat up here after these fish. The fishery's completely overlooked. Yet the handful of fishermen using this pattern have used it successfully on rivers large and small across the Midwest; so I'm betting it works in many, maybe

The Washout Hole And Tailout Area

Most flatheads congregate along the lip in the tailout area of the washout hole. They tend to hold close to the bottom, but can usually be seen on a sonar, graph, or liquid crystal display unit.

The object is to get a jig down to them and keep it riding in the current as vertically as possible below the boat as it's swept down river. Most of the fish are caught within a foot or two of bottom—that's where the slackest water is.

Mike Kohler's best fishing has always been in August, but he thinks the fish might already be in tailwaters by the end of June. Fishing slows in fall.

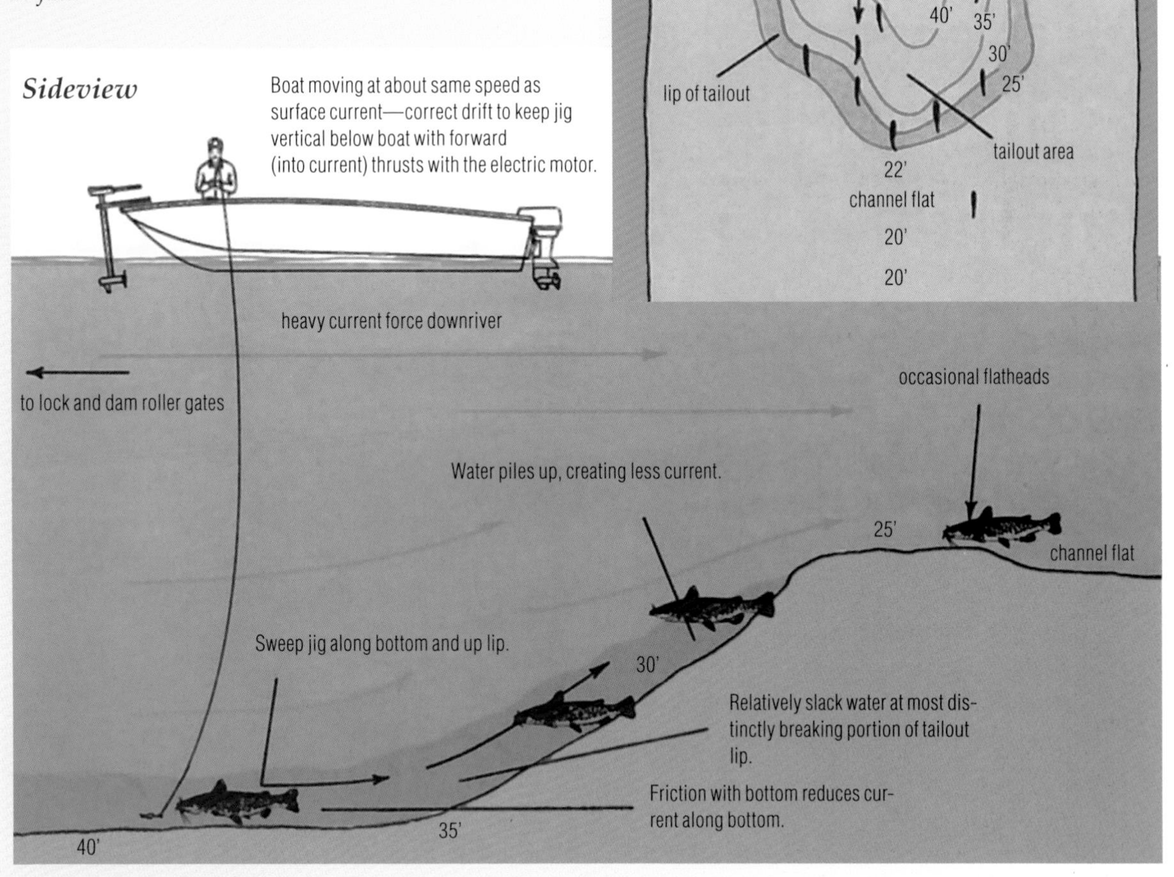

most tailwater areas nationwide."

We pulled into the tailwater with the camera running. "Produce!" Jim Lindner demands as he screws his eye to the lens of his Sony.

"Perfect," Kohlers says, as I stop the boat with the bow facing upriver. We drift stern-first downriver using the bowmount electric to correct our drift. "Gotta stay a safe distance below the dam. Dangerous to get too close. But we also have to get the boat moving downriver about the same speed the turbulence is moving before we drop these jigs. The jigs gotta be in position before we reach the critical tailout lip."

"Flatheads hold in the relatively slack water along the lip of the washout hole. They tend to hold close to the bottom, but can usually be seen on a sonar, graph, or liquid crystal display unit."

"Been awhile since I've fished a washout hole," I tell him. "Once we're drifting back the same speed as the current, we drop the jigs to the bottom as quickly as possible."

"Right," he says. "The water along the bottom's moving slower than the surface water—slower, too, than the water in the middle of the water column.

"Once the jigs are down in position, it's a matter of correcting our drift with forward thrusts of the electric to keep the jigs riding directly below us. The more they swing away from vertical, the less control we have. The jigs gotta be within a foot or so of the bottom most of the time. That's the reason for thin line—less water resistance for better control.

"Right here—most critical area," he says, as we approached the beginning of the break—the lip—at the tailout of the washout hole. "Water builds in the washout hole, then gets forced downriver. But the steep lip at the back of the hole creates a kind of slackwater area—a rim along the lip—for the cats and bait to hold in. We catch cats on the flat downriver from the tailout, too, but only occasionally."

"Time of year?" I ask.

"Well, here the fish seem to appear in August and stay until early October," he says. "Fishing slows during fall as the water cools into the 50°F range. I've only caught small fish then.

"Can't say for sure how early fish appear in tailwaters, though. Maybe as early as June. Depends, I suppose, on the area of the country."

Jig Rigging

Make sure the hook of the jig is sharp. Kill a 3- to 4-inch minnow. Run the jig hook into the minnow's mouth and up through its back just behind the head.

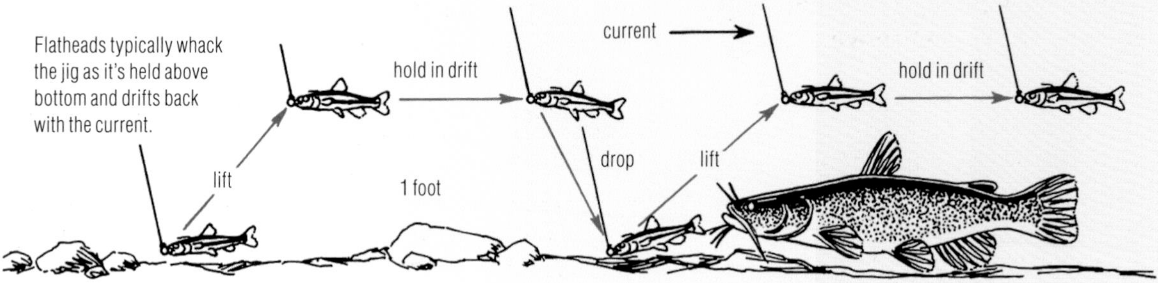

Flatheads typically whack the jig as it's held above bottom and drifts back with the current.

lift

hold in drift

1 foot

drop

current

lift

hold in drift

We finished our drift and begin to motor back toward the dam.

"Try a drift along the far edge of the tailout hole," he instructs. "Let's follow the break as closely as we can until we reach the tailout. Try to stay in 28 to 35 feet of water. It might take us 10 drifts to cover most of this side of the tailout hole. Never know for sure where the fish are going to pile up—and sometimes they're just spread out all over."

I chose a fresh minnow and impaled it on the 1/2-ounce jig. As mentioned previously, we're fishing with 8-pound line, about as thin as it gets for flatheads that might weight as much as 50 pounds.

"About baits?" I ask. "These 4-inch minnows are considered tiny offerings for flatsies."

"Yes, I know," he says. "I've seen you and Toad Smith fishing for huge fish at night with huge baits. All I know is, these jigs work. Bigger baits just get blown out of position too easily in current. But maybe—*Fish on! Big fish! Get the electric! Good fish!"* he shouts, as Jim focuses on him holding a rod arched from butt to tip.

"Gotta keep lots of pressure on these fish!" he shout at me and the camera over the roar of the dam. "Flatheads have such powerful jaws they whack down on the bait and you can't move it. They don't even know you're up above half the time. But eventually they know something's up and they open that big mouth and spit the bait. That's when the jig moves and you have to get a hook—and that could be 5 minutes into the—*No! No! No!"* he shouts.

"Lost him," he says to no one in particular.

"But look there," I say as he reels in. "Slime de line (for two feet above the jig), as we say. Flatsie for sure."

"That's just so typical," he moans. "Man, but with the camera running—fish pulled my bait down sharply just after I lifted it a foot off the bottom and held it there a moment. Whomp! And then I lose him! Man!"

"I like that," cameraman Lindner says. "Good scene, the way the rod bent. The look on your face when you lost him."

"You're not using *that,"* Kohler says through a weak smile.

"For sure! But now we need a star. One big flatsie will do. Fish. Produce. Or do you want me to do it for you?"

Time passed quickly that afternoon. Fishing is slow compared to most outings for Kohler. That happens a lot when a camera's in the boat. I loose a flathead—slime de line. Then Kohler misses a fish on a hook set. Never did feel the fish. Finally, in the evening I set into . . .

"A stump," I say. "Either that or a crankshaft from a 1950 Buick."

Of course I land the fish. Sure, the camera is running. I even let Kohler hold the fish before we release it. "There, you're famous," I tell him. "Fan mail will pour in."

"So ugly they're beautiful," he says as we head back toward the ramp. "I wonder, though, about the TV show and an article telling people how to catch those cats and about people keeping those big fish, now that they know how to do it?"

"We're into teaching people to catch fish and have fun," I tell him. "I had fun. Lots of other folks will, too. But we're also into ensuring a future for fishing. That's why we teach selective harvest.

"You know the story. We want to continue a tradition of eating some fish, because, darn it, they're great table fare. But not big flatheads. We need to release these fish to help sustain good fishing.

"Aren't enough big fish to go around these days," I continue. "Big flatsies are old. May seem like there's a lot of them because few folks are fishing for them, but the supply isn't endless. In a typical outing, you also get a small flathead or two, enough for a couple great meals. Release the big guys; keep a few small fish. That's one aspect of selective harvest.

"Aren't many breakthroughs left in fishing," I tell the Reverend Kohler. "Twenty-pound flatsies on thin line is one of the best. Amazing grace!"

MARCH TIPS AND TRICKS

FISHING! SPRING TACTICS!

the In-Fisherman

THE JOURNAL OF FRESHWATER FISHING

RIVER WALLEYE BREAKTHROUGH

WORLD RECORD PIKE

200 POUND GAR

EXCLUSIVES!

- Tackle Wars Today—Line
- Pressured Bass
- Transition Smallmouth
- Brush Catfish

PLUS!

Pike Files
Bluegill Tactics
Funding Fisheries
Grilling Secrets

AND!

Trip Tips . . .
Science Shorts . . .

STRAIGHT TALK FROM PEOPLE WHO REALLY FISH

Historic Perspectives

The Order of the Sacrificial Oreo. Even today, 20 years after this article is written, an occasional angler references via letter, phonecall, or email his or her own kindred membership in this not-so-secret society. For all the Toad Smith fans out there, the photos taken in this article (from the summer of 1990) help to capture the laidback nature of the man, totally at home and at peace, as he goes in search of catfish with his best catfishing buddy, Doug Stange. This is a down-to-earth story in favor of using a consistently productive bait at the right time and place, and a fishing system that relies on moving to find active fish instead of parking in one spot and taking a snooze. Captured here is the essence of a fishing approach that turns catfishing into an exercise in catching fish instead of an exercise in frustration. Read here and you recognize that the author has lived the life and is sharing without reservation what he knows, so that others can catch more fish and have fun. Vast first-hand experience and a gifted interpretation of that experience always is the basis for the finest how-to writing.

CHAPTER 14

MARCH 1991

Brush Cats—Let' Em Eat Oreos

THE MARCH I KNOW MEANS TOUGH TIMES FOR CATMEN who can't dream in shades of summer catfish. We'll be there soon. Bankside. Digging into a bucket of KFC, lines faintly lit by firelight, waiting for a reel to tell secrets of a flathead, a channel cat, or a blue moving silently through a river hole.

"Geez—you always do that," Toad Smith, a man of prodigious size and character will whine as he forages in the chicken bucket.

"Now what?" I'll ask.

"You ate all the white meat. All of it. Every last piece. You always do that. What kind of guy would do that?"

"Correction, chicken breath," I object. "We started with a Jumbo Meal Deal, right? Twenty pieces of chicken. Beans, 'slaw, mashed 'taters, and biscuits. You ate two pieces before we got out of the chicken factory. You ate four more on the way to the river. And all I know is that by the time I was done setting my lines and had a chance to have my first, I say my first piece of chicken, only 6 pieces were left in the bucket, one of which was a piece of white meat. Which I admit I ate. Heaven knows where the beans and 'slaw went, although I have a feeling I'll find out if I stay on the same bank with you all night."

Snags, Blowdowns, Brush. The Center Of A River Cat's Life!

Just looking—surveying for major snags.

Or it's hours after an early morning start, floating a portion of river. We've been moving, moving, moving, fishing quickly through hole after hole, searching for active cats, trying to see lots of river in order to surmise where big cats might be holding. Ten o'clock. Time for a serious cup of coffee.

"Oreos!" Toad demands.

"Oreos?" I say.

"Yes, Oreos. Magnum bag. Stuffed 'em in the cooler. Oreos. O-r-e-o-s. Oreos!"

"Noreos!"

"Noreos?"

"Noreos."

"No O-r-e-o-s?"

"Yes, no O-r-e-o-s—as in left the cooler in the truck," I tell him.

You'd have to be there to see Toad's face to appreciate the moment. Seeing there is no cooler in the boat, which indeed means no O-r-e-o-s; realizing the truck is miles away, which means no O-r-e-o-s for a minimum of hours, Toad pauses, momentarily speechless as the gravity of the moment careens and crashes within the most basal area of his brain. Brain spinning in retrograde, devastated and beginning to sweat, eyes closed and face contorted in a tight pained smile making him look for all the world like a puppy who has lost Mummy, he begins to swing his head from side-to-side in despair. "No!" he blubbers. *"No!* No-no, no-no, no-no, noooooo—"

Just before his brain kicks into primal defense mode and his body contorts into a large obtuse vegetative state, I reach for a bag stashed safely under my seat. "Oh, Toadsie. Yoo-hoo," I say, swinging the sack of cookies back and forth. "See cookies? Dougie just kidding. See O-r-e-o-s? Yummy yummy."

If cats were as easy as he was, I always tell Toad, fishing would be easy. Toss a handful of cookies on the freeway, you got a Toad. Catfish, on the other hand?

The relative equivalent of a bag of Oreos exists, for channel cats at least, in the form of a bag of freshly killed cutbait—fillet of chub, sucker, carp, and the like. But you just can't toss it any old place on the riverway; you have to present it in the right spot.

The right spot in most rivers is near snags. Call 'em blowdowns, brushpiles, whatever you want; they attract cats, especially if the snag coincides with a hole. Holes, you see, are the home of catfish in rivers. A snag—cover—in conjunction with a hole makes the very best home. The better the home, the more likely catfish will be present—lots of them and perhaps a monster or two or more.

I've experienced the *"or more"* part a time or two. One of the best snags in the whole universe lies on the Minnesota River between Granite Falls, Minnesota, and Minneapolis-St.Paul. That's a river stretch about 200 miles long, in case you go looking. You should find this secret spot in oh, say, 20 years if you search hard. If you get past

A major snag holding area that's likely to attract many cats.

the pit bulls, watch out for the minefield. Sorry, but that's the way it is with cat spots these day. It should be enough that I mention that this wonderful river is one of the world's best catfisheries. The pit bulls really are there, by the way. The river takes an impressive jog after running relatively straight for several miles. The corner hole created by the jog runs for about two city blocks and offers a maximum depth of about 10 feet throughout much of its length.

That's not particularly deep. The draw is the downed timber that lines almost the entire hole. Each spring when high water washes trees and brush downriver, this bend loses a little timber but always seems to gather more. It's like Mother River deals a new hand from a fresh deck each spring—fresh timber arrangements and new spots for cats to hold. It's as exciting to motor upriver to see the hole for the first time each year as it is to fish it.

And that's pretty exciting considering that during prespawn in June, it isn't unusual to crack two or three hundred pounds of flatheads and channel cats from that hole in a good night of fishing. We don't keep a one except a small fish or two that's properly dispatched, cleaned, cared for, and eventually becomes the focal point for a fine meal.

Channel cats are great, but I doubt any other fish is so fine as a fat little flathead freshly filleted and rolled in flour seasoned with salt, pepper, and a touch of cayenne, then fried quickly in snapping-hot bacon grease—yes, yes, oil will do, but you really have to do the bacon grease, the better with some chopped garlic.

Now, I wonder about having to go through this riffle-hole-run business that's so important to finding catfish in rivers. I wonder how many of you are first-time readers who haven't read about reading catfish rivers, either in *In-Fisherman* or our book *Channel Catfish Fever*.

And what would you do if you were me? Would you take time to review, given that the key to finding the best snags rests with understanding basic river layout? If you fish every snag you come to, you will catch plenty of cats, you see.

But if you skip marginal snags to concentrate on the good ones, you'll total an extra ton of cats in just a year or two. Better to review.

Ultimately, the best snags are in the best holes, and therefore you have to know that as water meanders through a streambed it flows over substrates of varying hardness. Riffles form over hard-bottomed areas and are shallower because current doesn't wash away hard bottom. Riffles form natural dams that obstruct flow over the

Just fishing—firsthand surveying for catfish.

riffle, quickening over the constricted area like water forced through the nozzle of a hose.

The force of current flowing against the softer substrate at the end of a riffle scours a hole. So, a riffle ends in a hole.

Holes, also called pools, are the home of catfish. They're wider and deeper sections of rivers. Depth varies according to local geology and current patterns, as well as the size of the river.

In a small river, a typical hole during a stable summer period might be 30 feet long, 20 feet wide, and 4 feet deep. The biggest and deepest holes might be only twice those dimensions.

Holes gradually become shallower at their downstream end as suspended materials sinks when water slows. The tail end of a hole becomes a run.

Runs are river flats—stretches with no significant depth changes. The bottom usually is sand and silt with occasional rocks and patches of gravel plus debris, including snags. Catfish move through runs as they travel, but rarely hold for long unless a snag offers protection. But snags on flats rarely attract many catfish or big catfish. Don't spend much time there. Absolutely don't park near a "flat" snag for a night of fishing—wasted life.

About cover—snags—in conjunction with holes. Cover serves as a feeding station or rest area, attractive in part because cover is different from the rest of the river. Mainly, though, cover helps gather food and lets catfish lie comfortably near current, the supplier of food.

The best snags are near or just downstream from the core of a hole, where current slows. The location of the snag in a hole influences how cats use the snag. Cover in fast current near the top of a hole is primarily feeding territory. A snag in quiet water at the lower half of a hole is primarily a holding or resting area. Snags near the core of the hole are resting *and* feeding areas.

Rivers, then, are composed of a continuous series of riffles, holes, and runs. The hole is the home of catfish, a big one-room home. In that home, the snag or the core of the hole usually is the bedroom, the top of the hole the kitchen. Catfish usually rest around or under the snag or in the core of the hole, but may occasionally snack there, especially when it's near the kitchen. Active cats move around the hole, checking areas that gather food.

Unfortunately, even snags that lie in perfect position in good-looking holes don't always have lots of cats using them. Just as certain snags often gather more cats than others, certain river sections sometimes attract more cats during certain periods. A good snag in a section with lots of cats using it has a better chance of attracting a lot of cats. This is one reason for fishing quickly from hole to hole, looking for active cats, on your first trips to a river you haven't fished in a while or haven't fished before.

Occasionally, though, you also find situations where almost every snag, no matter how small and poorly placed, has a cat or two using it. This most often occurs during prespawn, when cats are actively feeding and roaming. Or it occurs

Toad with the boat loaded for a night on a river sandbar. Tent, in case it rains. Sleeping bags not mandatory, but nice in a pinch—the boys often just sleep on the sand. Might cook over an open fire. Might pack a Coleman stove. Midnight jambalaya a tradition.

in river sections that have a huge catfish population. Yes, such river sections still exist in many parts of the country.

PRESENTATION

If catfish were trout I'd say it makes a difference whether you move upstream or downstream in your search for fish. Trout, like most fish, face forward into current when the water's clear. Walk or drift downstream and they're more likely to see you than if you move upstream.

Drifting a portion of cutbait with a Euro-style long rod and slip float. Seventeen-pound-test line works for most situations for cats up to about 20 pounds. Toad's body by Oreo.

Cats in clear water? It happens. When rain doesn't come for quite a spell and the water's low and cool during early summer, even cat water can become clear. Watch out. Cats can hear and feel a ton times better than trout. Tip-toe or paddle quietly into position, particularly when the water's clear and they can see you after being forewarned by the noise.

When I walk, I usually move downriver. From a boat, if I have time and it won't ruin fishing and I have to motor back to the point of origin to go home, I motor upriver past the holes I'll be fishing on the way back down. This gives me a chance to visually survey holes along the way.

Say you're fishing from a small boat (a handy way to fish a small river), and say you're moving downstream through a river section you haven't fished for several years. Snag ahoy!—about 100 yards ahead. Survey the river in front of the snag to see what precedes it.

Say you immediately move through a shallow riffle followed by a small hole about 4 feet deep (no snag in this hole), followed by a run 1½ to 2½

Drift And Set Rigs

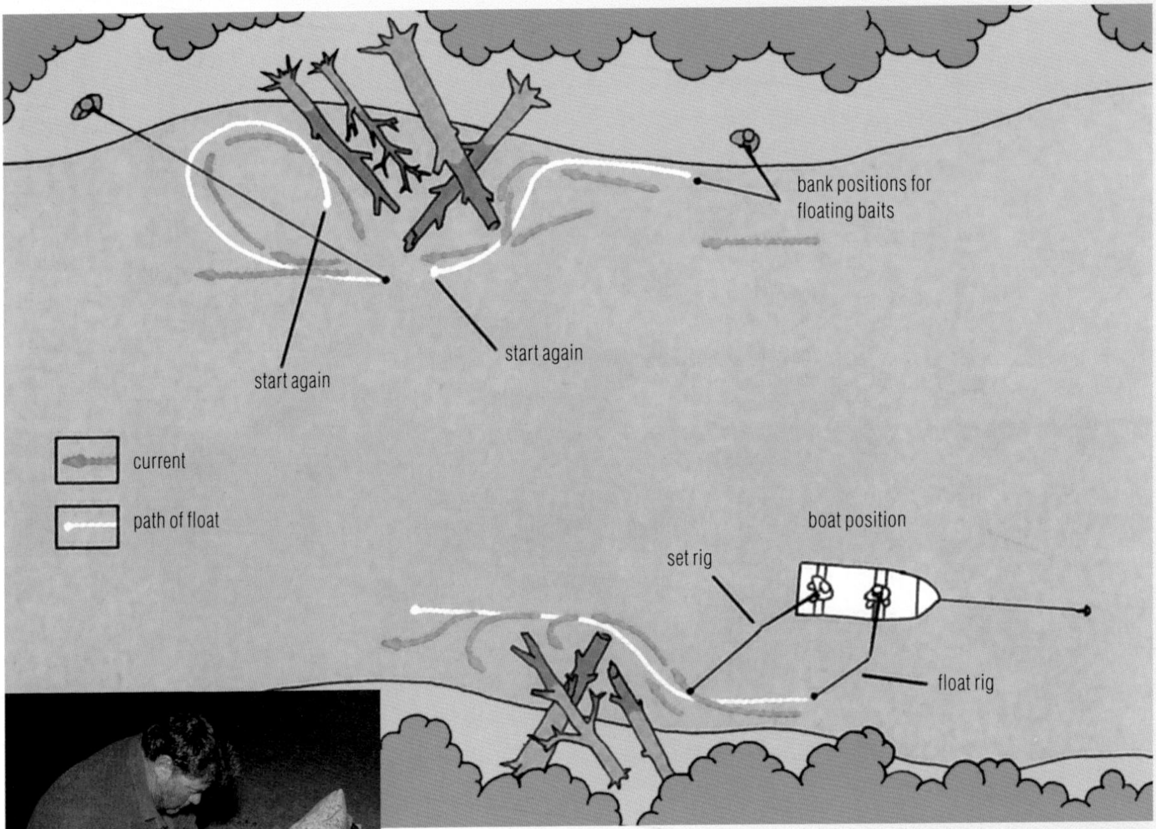

bank positions for floating baits
start again
start again
current
path of float
boat position
set rig
float rig

stop knot
bead
slipfloat
Drift Rig
6 to 12 inches
shot
from shore
from a boat
Sinker slips on line.
Set Rig
6 inches
lead shot
bell sinker
1/0 to 5/0 Eagle Claw 84 or Mustad 92671

Toad rigging for big cats at night after discovering a major hole during a daytime excursion. Heavier tackle required: Muskie tackle heavy-action 7-foot rods, 36- to 50-pounds-test line (depending on the size of the fish in the river) on Garcia 6500 or 7000 reels.

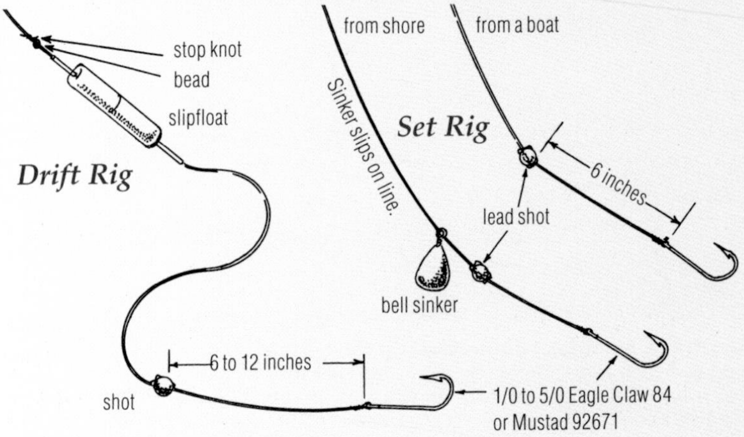

feet deep and then bango, there 20 yards above the snag is a prominent riffle that runs quickly into the hole that has, hip-hip-hooray, the major snag you could see from upriver.

Stop immediately, before you get to the riffle in front of the snag, and toss out an anchor on a short rope. Good. You want to drift a bait or two through the riffle just in case fish are really cracking and they're up in the riffle. Happens. One of you should drift a cutbait below a float, the other should set-line with cutbait.

Set-rigging is easy. Cast the bait to the area you want to fish, let it sink on a tight line, and hold it there. Don't let the bait drift. The aroma and taste molecules from the bait wash downriver and alertscats to move upriver to grab it.

While fishing a set rig, keep your rod tip up at about 10 o'clock. This leaves room to give line by dropping the rod tip toward the cat when he moves away after taking the bait. When he's moved 2 or 3 feet, stick him. Big cats almost always have the bait on the first chomp. Small cats you often miss no matter what you do. Just don't give much line by feeding it from a free spool. Yo miss more cats than you catch.

To fish a float, cast the rig just upriver from the spot you want the bait to bounce through. With your rod tip at about 10 o'clock, feed line from a free spool as the float drifts along. As soon as a fish takes, engage, drop your tip toward the fish as he moves away, and set when your rod tip reaches almost horizontal.

After fishing quickly through the riffle, fish the head of the hole, then the head of the snag and around it. Might take several anchor positions. But rarely are you in the same anchor position for more than 15 minutes. Absolutely don't stay that long if you're not catching fish. One of the most important steps to catching more cats during daytime excursions is to cover more water.

You're looking for a pattern. Some days, often early in the morning and late in the evening, cats are active at the head of the hole. Other times, especially when the water's down and you're fishing during the day, cats only move around the core of a hole or around a snag. After fishing for a mile, this pattern often is so obvious that you can move immediately from hole snag to hole snag, ignoring flat snags, riffles, and everything else.

Toad—just checking for his Sacrificial Oreo.

Once you survey large sections of river you'll find a few holes that you just know huge fish are using. We take some pretty nice cats during the day, but we rarely get into huge channels, blues, and particularly flatheads. That's when you break out heavier tackle, big livebaits, and set lines, and settle in beside a campfire with a bucket of chicken, a bag of Oreos, and a six-pack of cheap diet soda—the good life indeed.

Toad and I, by the way, are members of the *Order of the Sacrificial Oreo;* and I can't be sure that membership isn't the reason we catch so many catfish.

You may join by practicing just one tradition: First Oreo from the bag, the one you want the worst, goes into the river, a token gesture to the cats, the river, and catfishing. If you prefer Fig Newtons, I suppose you could substitute.

Historic Perspectives

Of the many articles that Stange pens with Toad Smith in tow, this one perhaps better than any other captures the simple essence of his friendship with Smith as the two spend time together outdoors. It is the first catfish article Stange writes after Smith's death in November 1991.

The "Addendum" explains a bit about the circumstances.

Even these many years after Smith's death, rarely a month passes without a phone call or an email from someone wanting to talk with Smith or write him a letter—they've stumbled across a book or video, or perhaps an old article, in which he seems just as alive and real today as he was in life.

Illustrations by Larry Tople

More Historic Perspectives

The significance of these pheasants hits home in the Addendum at the end of this chapter.

The Toadmonster and Stange "trolling" a local coffee shop for fishing intell and just generally having a fine time. Mmm, fries and a shake.

CHAPTER 15

APRIL 1992

Mischief Afoot with the Toadmonster—and Flatheads Before the Crowd

AN ICY NORTH WIND swept through the oaks on the ridge above the reservoir, down a limestone bluff, along our bank, whipping our little fire and sending a shower of sparks over the water. It was midnight damp and April cold and lonely along a remote portion of reservoir in a far corner of Missouri. Tomorrow we'd hike a hill and call and kill a turkey on that ridge above us. In the meantime, we were hoping for a flathead catfish—and I was hoping I wouldn't freeze.

Flatheads—A Matter Of Pace & Attitude!

"Can see the headlines now," I mumbled to Toad as I shuffled my sleeping bag closer to the fire. "FAMOUS FISHERMAN FREEZES TO DEATH IN WILDERNESS. WORLD MOURNS HIS PASSING." I pulled my camo stocking-hat down, hunched up the collar on my coat, and dug my body so deep into my down bag that only the 4 square inches of skin surrounding my eyes were exposed to the elements.

"I work hard for 20 years," I continued in mock despair, muffled by the bag. "I become the editor of a big-time fishing magazine. I have a budget for a nice warm motel room—a steak even, after a hard day of fishing. I could be fishing anywhere in the world, probably at no cost, probably some place warm, and here I am freezing to death in the backwoods, about to share a magnum can of beans with someone who looks like an escapee from a penal colony."

"Lucky man," Toad growled. "Keeps you in touch with the real world."

"Now don't do that," I pleaded as he reached for the beans. "At least use a stick."

But he did, that is, he stirred the beans with his index finger. In the flickering firelight, a bean balanced on his finger before he popped it into his mouth and then slurped the syrup from his hand.

"Gacckk," I choked.

"Nummy," he said, through a syrupy grin, and—"So what is it you wanna be, the editor of one of those fancy-pants outdoor magazines in the big city, wear a tie to work, write bogus articles about bears eating people, and drink strawberry margaritas after work? Got news for you, too. Famous fisherman? Nobody'd even know you were gone. Now, me they'd miss."

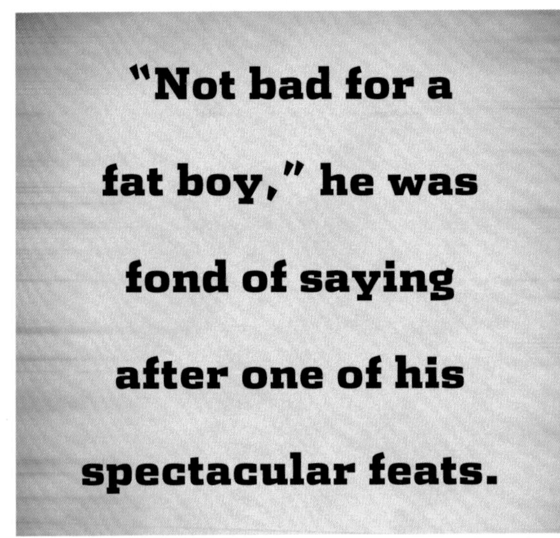
"Not bad for a fat boy," he was fond of saying after one of his spectacular feats.

"Right," I said. "There but for campfires like this one and a companion like you go I, led astray by the big city and the gleam of writing bull about bears and beautiful babes in bikinis fishing for bonefish on the flats."

"There you have it," Toad said. "Watch yourself. Next thing you know you'll be following tournament fishermen around, hoping they'll throw you a bone and thinking it means something. Oh, pwees pwees pwees Mr. Fwamous Toyneyment Fwishermun," he said, paws bent like a puppy dog on his haunches begging for a bone, "tell dis poor witto outdoor writer how you cwaughts all dose twelve-inch bass, woo, woo, woo, woo."

"Think they'll bite?" I asked, peeking out of my bag, down toward our rods set along the bank.

"What, the flatheads? Naw, too early. Maybe in a month. And then maybe only during daytime."

"Then why are we doing this?"

"Well, you never know, you know. They might bite. But I doubt it. Besides, we're camping out, having fun."

I shook my head. Typical trip with the Toadmonster. I'd be at my desk and Toad would call. "Meet me at such and such," he'd say.

I learned not to ask why or what, much less details such as line test or how much food or how much money. "Enough," he'd always say. So I took fishing tackle, enough to cover the bases from cats to crappies. In hunting season, I took fishing tackle plus camo gear and my bow—and bread, lots of bread, whole wheat of course, and onions, bacon, margarine, beans, assorted fresh veggies, and black pepper, lots and lots of black pepper, fresh-cracked of course, and a frying pan.

I am a fair cook, mind you. I can do fancy cuisine. But I've learned my lesson. That flies only so far in the woods, particularly with Toad, who would just as soon do a bacon-and-bean sandwich. Besides, a man can live for weeks, albeit quite rankly, on bread and onions and beans and whatever decides to sacrifice itself to hunting and fishing skills. No packing of course, just stuff things in the back of the truck and go, a fresh Van Halen tape pulsing West Coast decadence through my midwestern veins. (Frank Zappa, by the way, is alive and doing fine by L.A. We had intended to invite him along catfishing this year. We did invite Eddy Van Halen. Just thought you'd like to know.)

And I would get to somewhere—wherever—and Toad would be standing beside his three-quarter-ton red Chevy suburban, a stripped-down barebones job, the better to carry deer and bear and turkeys and catfish, grinning that big tooth-gapped grin of his through a burly beard. Toad was a big man. "Not bad for a fat boy," he was fond of saying after one of his spectacular feats.

"Not bad for a fat boy," I'd say. And there he'd stand by his truck, looking like a chubby cherub, a fat Friar Tuck, mischief dancing in his eyes and in that smile. And I'd look at him and just have to smile.

The ritual was that I would walk up and put my hand in that big paw of his and he would try to crush it. Haw, haw. *"Good to see you again—missed you,"* we'd both say without saying it. And I always knew we were going to have a good time, although a good time at what was hard to say and sometimes I'm not sure we figured it out ourselves, by the end of the trip. But we were always prepared by not being too prepared except to hang loose.

One time in fall we were floating a river catching catfish when we happened upon what Toad referred to as the mother of all squirrel kingdoms—hundreds of big fat fox squirrels running up and down the bank and around in trees and so on. "That's really something," Toad usually would say in a situation like that. "Sure is," I'd usually answer.

So we parked the boat and wandered around pursuing squirrels for the day. That was always one of the things I liked best about Toad, the squirrel thing—not squirrels really but the fact that it was OK with Toad—perfectly natural—to spend an entire day after something like squirrels—two 40-year-old men who have been around the block a time or two both in and out of the woods, out in the woods trying to outsmart a bunch of furry damn rodents, when both of us had the connections to be in Alaska hunting moose or in Montana hunting elk. So there we'd be, totally absorbed, totally oblivious to the rest of the "really important" things in the world, sneaking around trees, crawling around trees, to get a clean shot. "Office sissy," he'd say to me when we spooked one. "No woods sense anymore." "Maybe saw your big butt," I'd say matter of factly. "Humph!" he'd grunt indignantly. And then we'd go after another squirrel.

Yes, the squirrel thing. Squirrels aren't exactly big game, but neither are bullheads or carp or green sunfish or stonecats. And yes, we once spent a day fishing for stonecats below the dam in Crookston, Minnesota. The channel cats just weren't going and I happened to catch a stonecat. And somehow instead of frantically running up or downriver forcing the channel-cat issue, we just sort of drifted into trying to catch stonecats. And before we knew it the sun was setting and we'd been fishing all day for a little tiny catfish that rarely grows to 10 inches. Near as I can recollect, Toad caught 4 and I caught 2. And if I were to tell you more about it you would realize that it was one of the best days I have ever spent fishing—the wonder of it all, one of those "first-time" things, finding the best spots for stonecats and what they would bite on best.

But as I was saying, there we were wandering the hills in this mother kingdom of squirrels. We didn't have to be anywhere in the world in particular, doing anything in particular, so late in the afternoon I walked back to the boat for the sleeping bags and a frying pan and we camped on a hill somewhere near the river and ate catfish and squirrel and wild onions—at least we thought they were wild onions. The next day we were sure they were wild onions, funny how your intestines can verify what you can't find in a field guide. And Toad's intestines were better at such verification than almost anyone I've ever met—Chief Wildflower, the Brule Indians called him with a good bit of straightfaced sarcasm on one of his trips out West to hunt and fish on reservation land.

And next morning we wandered down to this old farm place to borrow some coffee for breakfast. "Hell, no," this old farmer said, "you can't have any coffee but you can sure as hell come in and fix yourselves and me some breakfast." And so there I stood cooking pancakes and bacon on an old kerosene stove and drinking boiled coffee, stuff with a razor edge on it, chasing cats off the counter and listening to this salty old rooster who hadn't been to town in a year and who probably hadn't had a visitor in months, talking about "those old times."

"Hellava cook," they both chortled as I set down plates of cakes. "You'd make someone a good wife." Haw, haw.

Pretty soon Toad and the old farmer were busy poking around what was left of the farm, the old farmer hobbling on a cane and Toad trying to keep up, the farmer talking nonstop about farming with mules and this old tractor and that old pile of assorted junk that lay rusting in the open. Made Toad's day.

Next to hunting and fishing and picking wild things like asparagus and wild onions, Toad liked poking through old junk. Junk. Not antiques or artifacts. It was junk and Toad knew it, just like he knew that he liked it, that it made him think about those old times.

Made me smile. We'd be walking a riverbank, catching cats from brushpiles as we went. And Toad would find a bone sticking up from a gravel bar. "Buff [buffalo]," he'd grunt two octaves below middle C, and his eyes would glaze over and his nose would naturally shift into the wind and he'd stand there like some aborigine envisioning an unending parade of buffalo steaks moving over the next ridge. Toad wanted desperately to be there, you see, for those more than these would have been his times.

It was something we'd talk about around a campfire—those times. "Should've been there," he'd say.

"Would've been a bad deal for buff," I'd say. And I suppose I could take a moment to explain. Toad's catfishing prowess is well known. He was that good with stick, string, and arrow, too. If he could have been there, the Indian tribe that adopted him would have had meat for winter and spring beyond. I do not believe, however, that he would have been popular around the council fire in an enclosed teepee—Chief Wildflower.

People like old farmers could tell that Toad was in no hurry, that he really cared and would gladly stay a week if they needed help, particularly if the hunting and fishing were good. People like insurance salesmen, on the other hand, always sensed that they should be in a real hurry if they happened to strike a Dale Carnegie chord and were wasting even a moment of Toad's hunting and fishing time. Toad was going to live forever—or at least, long enough. And beyond that, what the heck.

We spent two days in those parts, poking around with that old farmer, some 20 miles short of the destination on our float, as near as I could tell. "Could of sworn we were going to float for catfish," I said back at our trucks, as each of us was about to head for our separate worlds.

"You mean we didn't?" he asked, and shrugged.

Typical. And so there we sat on another hot spot. Another adventure, heaven help us.

"Gotta tell you something," Toad said as he passed a plate of beans. "We're after flathead catfish, right?"

"That is correct," I said. "And turkeys."

"Well, we will kill a turkey tomorrow, but tonight, well, about the catfishing. As far as I know there's never been a flathead catfish caught in this reservoir."

I didn't answer at first. Ah, I thought to myself. Now this is beginning to make sense. I have driven 8 hours to a destination I know nothing about without asking any questions. And now I am some place in the wilderness in the middle of the night freezing to death, fishing for flathead catfish a month before they should bite in a reservoir where they don't exist and sharing a plate of beans with a backwoods philosopher whose logic would have stumped Plato.

"But you never know, you know," he said. "They might just bite. And besides, we are having fun camping out."

"Yes," I answered, adopting his logic as best I could. "We are having fun—and they just might bite—assuming of course that we aren't a month early, which we are, and further assuming that they should be here, even if they aren't, because this spot is so good that they should, like their cousins the walking catfish, have hiked from the nearest river so they could be here, so we won't catch them tonight because we're a month early."

"There you have it," he said. "You are a smart man, for an editor."

So far, I realize that this probably seems to have little to do with catching flathead catfish early in the season. But not so fast. Catching flathead catfish—any catfish, really, but particularly flatheads—can be taught via formula other than the typical how-to formula you might find in say a bass article we might feature. Bass fishing has become a complicated and in many cases quite a frenzied and serious affair. Toad would have verified that. "Very serious business," he would have said, trying to keep a straight face. Fishing for flatheads is, or I'm suggesting should be, the antithesis thereof.

This flathead deal really isn't very complicated, you see, and I have no reason to try to make it so—much less try to get you to hurry to make it so. Trust me, you will catch flatheads if you want to. The process is easy, and I will show you how, only a little in this article but certainly in others as the years continue. Trust this too, though: It takes time—there aren't many big flatheads. And I am suggesting that because it's easy but takes time, and because catfishing generally hasn't been the type of high-profile sport that bassing has been—thank God!—that capturing the spirit of this flathead affair is as important as the final act of catching the fish.

Catfishing, particularly fishing for flatheads, is a matter of pace and attitude, things that become part of a lifestyle.

I am saying that catfishing, particularly fishing for flatheads, is a matter of pace and attitude, things that become part of a lifestyle— something you settle into easily as you learn about life and begin to live it and love it, even the bumpy parts, even the big bumps like the passing of a close friend, a Toad. And I guess I'm wondering in print if the spirit of the thing can't best be felt by looking at someone who did it right. Toad did it right a lot of the time, and I'm thankful I was along for some of the ride.

But about catching big flatheads. About being a flathead catfisherman. About flathead catfishing being a lifestyle as much as something you occasionally do. About any of this having anything to do with catching flathead catfish early in the season.

It has occurred to me that all the great catmen I have known are, like Toad, men of a certain distinction. They certainly aren't the only people of distinction in the fishing world, but they are distinctively different.

Al Lindner, whom I dearly love and respect, is a fisherman of distinction. But although we have taken Al catfishing, and he is quite good at it, he is not and I suspect never will be a catman. "Go there. Do this. Try that. You mean I just let the bait sit there?" There is a certain rush to Al's life that doesn't quite fit catfishing. It is like trying to stick Pierre Cardin (don't worry—Toad wouldn't have known who he was either) in a flannel shirt. Even when Al is catching catfish he is really catching bass or walleyes, and that will never change.

That doesn't mean Al doesn't enjoy an occasional bout with cats. But what Al does even when he is catfishing is not catfishing—just as the man who catches a 35-pound flathead on a crankbait while casting for bass has not really caught a flathead. I know the fish looks like a flathead, but the fish is not a flathead, only a small token of desperate good fortune—outright luck, nothing more. There is nothing desperate about becoming consistently good at catching flatheads. If it is difficult, it is only because it's time-consuming and you often end up having to fish at night, which disrupts the rhythm of most lives. But that's another story.

Three Different Early Rendezvous

Early Season Rendezvous—Ponds

Find the shallowest end of the pond. Look for the transition from deeper to shallower water. This is the feeding ground for flatheads during early season.

Early Season Rendezvous—Reservoirs

***Point A**—A cat travel-by area as flatheads move from the main reservoir. Not a feeding area during early season.*

***Point B**—Another travel-by area during early season. The water's too cold near the main reservoir.*

***Corners C**—Top spots during early season. Find these transitions from deep to shallow water.*

***Flat D**—This is where they feed during early season—sometimes all season long.*

Early Season Rendezvous—Small Reservoirs

Divide the reservoir into thirds. Look for a transition area where the water shallows to about 10 feet close to the division between the middle and source of the reservoir. Flatheads roam flats in this area during early season.

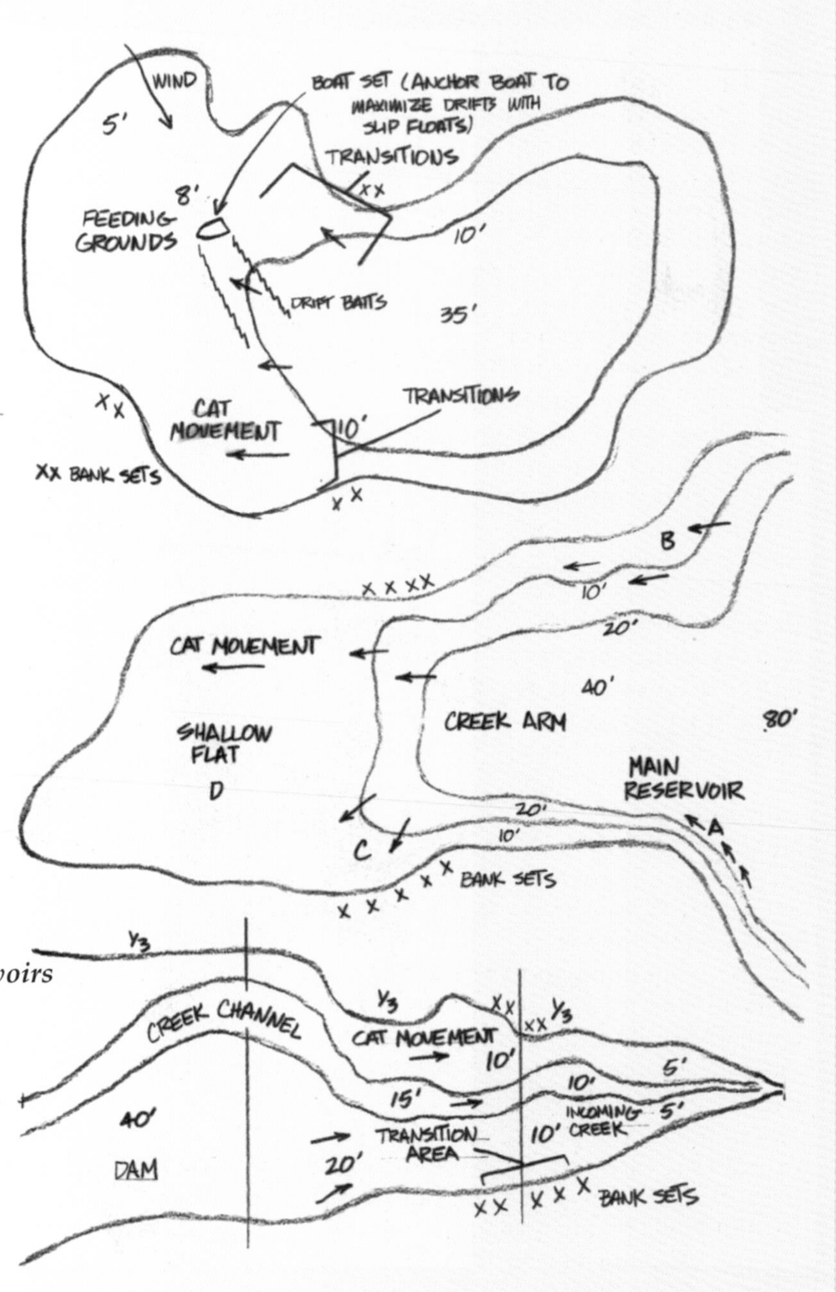

Fishermen with their underwear snugged up too tight, those fishermen who seek no more than one of these desperate acts—one or two old flatheads for no more than the thrill or the fame of it—won't understand. Indeed, the preceding pages may even be seen as a desperate and singular waste of time. Get to it, they will insist. Tell us where, when, and how. Forget campfires and old farmers and fishing for fish where they don't exist. These men and women should take up tournament bass-fishing—or bowling—the sooner the better.

If, however, you really are interested in flatheads, I understand the rush to catch that first big one. But along the way, as you're working on number 5 or 50, consider that the rush isn't the thing. Consider too that even if you go on with the rush and become singularly successful, even if you eventually pose with tons of catfish hanging crucified on fenceposts, a sacrifice to something—ego perhaps—that for what it's worth, from where Toad and I used to sit together on the bank, that you are not a flathead catfisherman, and that you have not really been catfishing, and that you have wasted part of your life only on a scale different from men like The Donald (as in) Trump may be wasting theirs, gathering trophies, accomplishing many singularly outstanding (but desperate?) acts, being noticed by many, but still somehow missing the point.

Toad's trip to Bolivia produced many happy recollections and major stories, often retold around the campfire.

And the point is? Well, it feels right to say that if you don't understand by now, you have missed it. But that's not true, because the truth is I don't know exactly what the point is either.

So far, you have learned that you probably should fish in waters where flathead catfish exist. And that April is too early almost everywhere, even throughout most of the South. May's the month—sometime in May. And you'd best be home by the fire with a bowl of popcorn reading this now in April, dreaming and getting ready for May.

Maybe you are learning trust, too. I'm telling you about craziness because we have been there. We have fished for flatheads. And we have fished for them too early. Call it research. You never know, you know. If they would have bitten in April, we'd be here telling you about it. As it is, I can tell you that you will catch them in May or June if the water's right and you're in the right place at the right time fishing with the right bait. Because we have done that too. Of course, you must fish with the right tackle if you expect to land fish. But all that's easy.

And it will not take long—it's that easy.

For now—homework. Toad would tell you that you need to know which bodies of water hold flatheads, the population level, and the size range of the fish. Then you can decide where you want to fish. Plan your campaign now.

April's the time to be out there just poking around. Time to drive to one of those reservoirs where you think the big guys live, to get the feel of the place. Check the best places to fish from shore. Stop for a cup of coffee at one of those little

Stock-Still For Bass! Page 24
AUGUST I SEPTEMBER 2007
In-Fisherman
THE WORLD'S FOREMOST AUTHORITY ON FRESHWATER FISHING
CATFISH
On A Summer Breeze
Slash The Ripper PIKE
PLUS!
GIANT CRAPPIES—LESSONS LEARNED
BAIT-SET TROLLING SECRETS
LEADCORE WRINKLES FOR WALLEYES
Turbo-Trolling Walleyes!

Besides illustrating many of Stange's stories about Toad and Zacker, In-Fisherman Cover Artist Larry Tople also painted "catfish covers" over the years.

old coffee shops off the beaten trail. "Coffee's on this guy," Toad used to announce, pointing to me when we'd walk for the first time into a little place. Of course every head would turn. "Geez," they must have thought, "would you look at those two."

The bait set, we'd sit there drinking coffee and munching a major order of fries, not saying a word, while the locals eyed us curiously. Finally one of them would have to walk over and say something, if nothing more than "You really buying the coffee?" And before long, Toad would have invitations to birthday parties and chicken dinners and church socials—and catfishing spots no man had ever fished before.

Divide the reservoir into thirds. Look for a transition area where the water shallows to about 10 feet close to the division between the middle and source of the reservoir. Flatheads roam flats in this area during early season.

Oh heck no, it doesn't hurt to wet a line way too early—in April. Toad would, even when it was beyond hope, even if no catfish were present.

"Good practice," he'd maintain, because you won't be catching much and that gives you plenty of time to think and to dream and to figure out what the point is. And if you figure it out, well, good.

I know part of the point for Toad and me was friendship shared during what suddenly became "those times." And I guess that more than anything is what this is about. This, you see, is my first article about cats since Toad's death. And it has not been easy because I didn't know exactly where I was going until just now.

Addendum: In the months since Toad Smith's death, hundreds of you have written to express your sympathy. Toad was a regular feature with me on TV and in articles for *In-Fisherman*. Through those adventures, many of you knew Toad as family.

In 1984, at age 43, Toad had a massive heart attack. Heart surgery left him with a lot less heart. Doctors didn't give him much chance of hunting and fishing again, much less crawling up into bow stands or walking along riverbanks looking for channel cats.

The next 7 years were a story of courage and determination to live right—lots of hunting and fishing and a good bit of writing and talking about it, telling others the fine points of being successful outdoors so they could have fun. I don't believe Toad envisioned becoming a celebrity recognized by fishermen from coast to coast. That part of the deal made him smile. And besides, he liked talking with people, telling stories.

Toad was a world-class bowhunter besides being a great fisherman. On the first weekend in November, a huge snowstorm hit northern Iowa—no hunting. Locked up that weekend, he had a chance to call almost everyone who meant a lot to him. I talked with him the night before he died. I was to meet him to hunt later in the week.

Monday dawned bright and clear. Toad headed for his deer camp in the hills bordering South Dakota. Just short of camp he saw three pheasants. "Camp meat," I know he said to himself. He shot all three birds and retrieved them through deep snow. The heart attack took him quickly as he reached the side of the road.

And he would have said about that: "There! Ha! Do I know how to die, or what?"

FISHING SECRETS!
EXCLUSIVE TACTICS
the In-Fisherman
THE JOURNAL OF FRESHWATER FISHING
MAY '92
CATCH & RELEASE CONTROVERSY
Soft Sticking Bass
Exclusive:
Patterns For Goliath Gills
PLUS!
•Reservoir Flatheads
•Fly-Rod Muskies
•Bait Raft Salmon
Tough Time
AND! Trip Tips•Science Shorts
Taste Tempters•Beyond Tomorrow•And More!
THE CUTTING EDGE OF FISHING FUN

{ Historic Perspectives

This is just Stange having fun with a topic, adding a bit of flavor to his instruction about fishing for flatheads during early season, with a story or two to set the scene, add perspective, and make the discourse flow. As is true in many of the early articles in this book, some of these products are no longer available (most of the floats herein, for example). This article also shows how preferred techniques often change over the years, given even more field experience. The quick-strike rigging mentioned here eventually falls almost completely out of favor in Stange's arsenal of tactics. It's effective but not as good in most situations as a properly placed and appropriately sized single hook. Traditions like preparation of the Midnight Jambalaya go well with catfishing. It's still a pretty darn good recipe, in the field or at home. It goes just as well over a big bowl of grits as on rice.

CHAPTER 16

MAY 1992

Flathead Catfish Before the Crowd–Looking for Poo-Poo

"DON'T TELL ME WHERE. I KNOW WHERE. Just show me the map and I'll show you where to fish—never mind where you caught 'em last night," I told Toad Smith with a wink and a grin. "Someone has to lead this patrol," I continued. "And I'm just the guy to do it."

Toad just scratched his beard and shook his head. In-Fisherman TV director Jim Lindner and I had driven five hours to meet Toad, who had spent the night before checking a new hot spot for flathead catfish. In three hours it would be dark and Jim would be filming the two of us as we fished.

Now the three of us were shuffling into the only little restaurant in a little town in some little corner of rural U.S.A. Never mind where—Minnesota, Missouri, Kentucky, Texas. This little restaurant is wherever you are and is as predictable as the flathead catfish. In the North Country, order a hot beef sandwich—or a cheeseburger and fries. In the Southland, order chicken-fried steak—or a cheeseburger and fries.

Do that and you will recognize your meal when it hits the table. Order pasta and salmon sauce or some other thing or another

Targeting Early Season Flatheads!

in this little chow-down spot and you'll spend your meal wondering how they did whatever it is they set in front of you. But hot beef is hot beef, and chicken-fried steak is chicken-fried steak (well almost), and cheeseburger is cheeseburger wherever they fry or stew or whatever they do to hot beef.

Just like flatheads are flatheads wherever they swim in lakes, ponds, or reservoirs. Flatheads can't help themselves. After a winter and early spring of semi-dormancy, they're on the prowl by May, an uncouth lot, poking through shallow water, intent on sampling anything that moves—carp, bluegills, bullhead, bream.

That limit of 12-inch bass that made some tournament fisherman jump and go ga-ga and hug Ray Scott? Breakfast for one big flathead—*erp, burp*! Is nothing sacred? And, well, excuse me, Ray. That some flatheads end up with muskrat or duck breath should be no surprise. And this water, wherever it lies, is not water to send Poo-Poo, the toy poodle, into for a swim on a dark night.

Poo-Poo should not swim particularly in the transition areas that connect the deeper areas of these bodies of water to large shallow sections. These areas are easy to recognize, which was my point to Toad as we entered the restaurant.

"Lay the map on the table," I tell Toad as Myrtle, our waitress, takes our order. Myrtle, by the way, sings alto in her church choir, recently married Ted the barber—her second marriage, his first—and the two of them love to go to movies and are thinking of getting a dog (a Poo-Poo). Which is all fine and dandy until Myrtle informs Toad that heavens no, she and Ted would never think of actually going ooh-ish fishing and "hurting" those poor little ooh-ish fish and in fact they are dead set against it. At which point Toad kindly informs Myrtle that (1), anytime she and Ted ever want to learn to actually ooh-ish fish, that he, Toad, will gladly help them get started, but (2), in the meantime she has just lost any chance she had for a tip.

The only mean bone in Toad's body was reserved for anti-hunters or anti-fishermen. We never did get a second cup of coffee. "Bet she goobered under your chicken-fried steak," I whispered to Toad as he got his plate.

"Bet I know where you fished last night," I said while this was going on. "Right there (I pointed). Or there or there."

"You got it," Toad said. "I set up right here. Caught a 20 about midnight. Had another couple runs—fish dropped the bait—about 2 o'clock. Caught a small fish at sunrise. Other guys fishing right there caught a fish or two—could see the commotion in their lantern light."

Flathead catfish like the security of deeper water. But when food beckons from shallow water during May and June, they compromise by following deeper water as far as possible into creek arms or bays. They lie there waiting for the sun to set. Then, like a pack of murdering Huns, they mosey shallow, looking for Poo-Poo.

Amend that. Not the Poo-Poo part, but— During early and mid-May, flatheads are almost as likely to bite during the day as they are after dark. Makes fishing difficult. Twelve hours of darkness is tough enough to cover, much less worrying about when fish might bite 24 hours a day.

During early May, I'm partial to fishing the two hours of daylight before dark and 3 or 4 hours after dark. By late May when the fish really get cranking, I like to begin at sunset and fish all night, snoozing off and on, waiting for something to happen by. The morning twilight, never a good producer during early May, is a top time during late May, throughout June, and for the rest of summer.

BAIT

Next to knowing where to fish, the right bait's just about as important as a proper catfish jambalaya cooked bankside at midnight. The jambalaya's a tradition. The bait's absolutely necessary. Can't do the jambalaya without the right bait, which almost guarantees at least a little action. Some nights about midnight, though, when things have been slow, the right bait begins to look mighty tempting, given that the best of it will be big enough to eat.

Forget pond-raised suckers and shiners. Not only do they taste terrible, but I swear they're like a bunch of turkeys raised in confinement, too dumb to know when to come in out of the rain or to be scared. You need bait that's been around the block a time or two in the real world where something's always looking to chew. You need bait that knows when to be scared (and also tastes good in a pinch).

Suckers or creek chubs, 8 to 12 inches long, freshly seined from a creek or river, make great bait because they're active. The bait's your fish call: Flip, flip, flop. Wiggle, wiggle, waggle. Calling all flatheads, ho-dee ho-dee ho, catch and kill me if you can.

A flathead can feel a struggling bait a ways away. I don't know exactly how far. They may be

Doug and Toadie's Hot and Sassy Easier-Than-It-Sounds Catfish Jambalaya

Assignments:

***Toad**—In charge of rice, usually Uncle Ben's Converted ("unconstitutional rice," Toad used to say), which takes about 15 minutes to cook, a little less time than the jambalaya. Takes about 1 cup of rice per 2 cups of water, although you might try something novel like reading the directions on the box.*

***Doug**—In charge of a quickie version of the New Orleans classic jambalaya:*

Ingredients

1 catfish, about 5 pounds, filleted and cut into 1- by 2-inch strips
2 tbsp. prepared chopped garlic (in 5-ounce jars at the store)
2 tomatoes, chopped
1 med. onion, chopped (optional)
2 or 3 jars (12-ounce) medium or hot salsa
dry white wine (optional)
1/2 tsp. cayenne, or to taste (optional)
salt and black pepper, to taste
chopped scallions (optional as garnish)

- *In an 8-inch cast-iron skillet, add the chopped onion and a bit of white wine. Cook the onion over medium heat, stirring for about 3 minutes. Add the chopped tomatoes and reduce them to pulp by cooking about 5 minutes.*
- *Add the salsa and a little more wine (and everything else except the chopped scallions). Cook on high to reduce the liquid by half, about 5 minutes. Reduce the heat to a slow simmer. Add the strips of catfish, cover, and simmer 8 more minutes.*
- *Stir once gently. Garnish with chopped scallions. Serve over rice.*

Soc Clay

We stop by this farmhouse and ask to fish. "Well, heavens yes if I can go along," the farmer says. "We're not listening to some crotchety old farmer complain all day about his corn crop," Toad tells him. "Then you can't fish," he replies. So now we're experts on corn and beans and cattle and hogs, as well as catfish.

able to taste it 30 feet away. And if they're lucky, they can see it at night in clear water at 10 feet.

Pond-raised suckers just lie there when a big cat shuffles by. Active bait's the whole point, nothing but the point, so help me. If you're in a good spot, if you're rigged right, and if flatheads are on the prowl, bait determines success.

Creek chubs are big-time predators themselves, so they're also fun to catch on hook and line. So are green sunfish (and bluegills) 4 to 6 inches long and bullheads 8 to 10 inches long. In a pinch, bluegills and bullheads also do well in a jambalaya.

RIGGING

Next to bait, rigging's the thing. Hooks need be stout and worthy of the fish you seek. Hundred-pound fish are present in some of the reservoirs some of you fish. Some of you might just catch a 100 pounder in the next 5 or 10 years.

But bait and rigging and just generally tackling fish of those proportions is another story. I'll tell you sometime, maybe with a good bit of recollection about those times when our buddy Zacker, that gnarly old poacher (88 now, he thinks, but can't remember for sure) used to rule the river.

Some of you remember Zacker. Toad and I were going to get him out fishing "one last time" this summer. Now Toad's gone and Zacker's still kicking. He'll probably outlive me, too. We'll see about this summer.

For fish up to 40 or 50 or so and bait about the size I've described, 5/0, 6/0, or 7/0 hooks work well. I use 5/0s with smaller bluegills and bullheads. Go with a 7/0 for big suckers—unless you use a quick-strike rig. The Mustad 92671 is a fine hook. Simple. Sturdy. So's the Eagle Claw 84.

File most of the barb off these hooks and make sure they're very sharp. Not much of a barb's needed to hold fish once you hook them. And you don't need a needle-sharp hook to sink into the soft tissue of a flathead. Sometimes, though, when a flathead takes the bait it gets doubled up in its mouth. When you set, the hook sets back into the baitfish instead of into the catfish. Needle-sharp barb-reduced hooks break away and slide through better, substantially increasing your hooking potential.

Quick-strike rigging consists of two hooks—a 5/0 forward and a 7/0 up the line slightly for big bait—rigged in tandem about 3 inches apart. Nick the 5/0 under the skin of the bait at about the dorsal fin. Insert the big hook through the meat at the top of the tail.

I prefer quick-strike rigging for active bait; the extra hook likely won't bother their activity. Use single hooks if snags are a problem. I rarely miss fish that take a bait rigged with tandem hooks. And you don't have to wait long to set.

A flathead likes to crunch a baitfish a good one and immediately worry it like a bulldog with a shoe—back'n forth, back'n forth. After the bait's crushed and ripped, the catfish lets go momentarily and takes the bait deeper into its mouth.

You'll feel the bait being worried. Don't set then. Wait until the fish has a firm grip and begins to move. But it doesn't have to move far.

After experimenting with monofilament and Dacron line for the past five years, I'm convinced that today's tough monos (Trilene XT, Stren Super Tough, Maxima, Bagley Black Label) are best. Thirty-pound test's good when cover isn't a problem. If you have to muscle big fish, go with 40 or 50.

I double the business end of my line by tying a Bimini twist. Toad never did bother to tie that knot, though, and he rarely lost fish because of rasped line. But then Toad rarely fished with anything but 40- or 50-pound line. The Bimini's a heck of a knot—a pleasant sucker just to look at when you've finished tying.

I use Abu Garcia 6500 and 7000 reels. Both reels have clickers, and the 7000 holds enough 50-pound line and you can retrieve it fast enough to put a choke hold on the biggest cat, even with a 100 yards of line out.

Strap those reels to sturdy muskie rods—something 6 to 7 feet long—or to surf rods, something 9 to 12 feet long. Extra length helps you make longer casts. Shorter rods allow more leverage for muscling fish.

A big flathead will tear up a flippin' stick pretty good. Don't go lighter if you can't get a sturdy muskie stick, or a surf rod made for stripers or redfish. Penn makes good composite surf rods. They have a sturdy line of reels with clickers, too. You need a reel the size of the 320 Level Wind.

TERMINAL RIGGING

"Simplest rigging known to man," I can still hear Toad saying to the camera that last night we filmed together: "Slide a slipweight—egg sinker or a bell sinker—on your line and pinch on a lead shot 6 inches to a foot above your hook. Cast the bait out and let it sit on the bottom. The fish is free to grab the bait and run without feeling resistance."

Toad was right and still is. But other rigs work as well or better. Slipfloat rigging's deadly in

One of Toad's biggest, at about 50 pounds, from the Minnesota River.

One of Stange's biggest at just over 50 pounds, also from the Minnesota River.

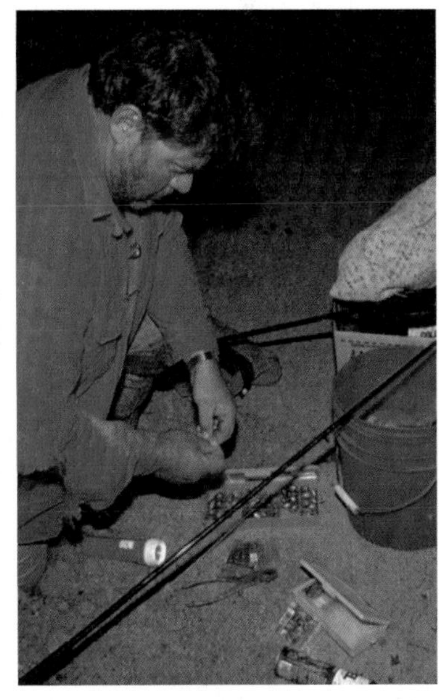

Rerigging on a secret sandbar spot in flathead country.

Strategies And Rigs

Standard Sliprig

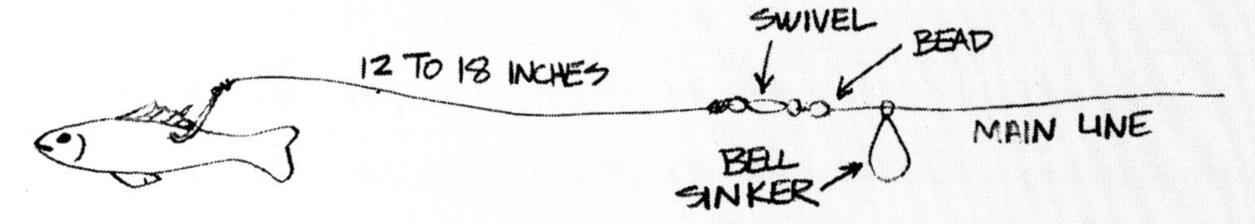

Float Paternoster Rig

Standard Slipfloat Rig

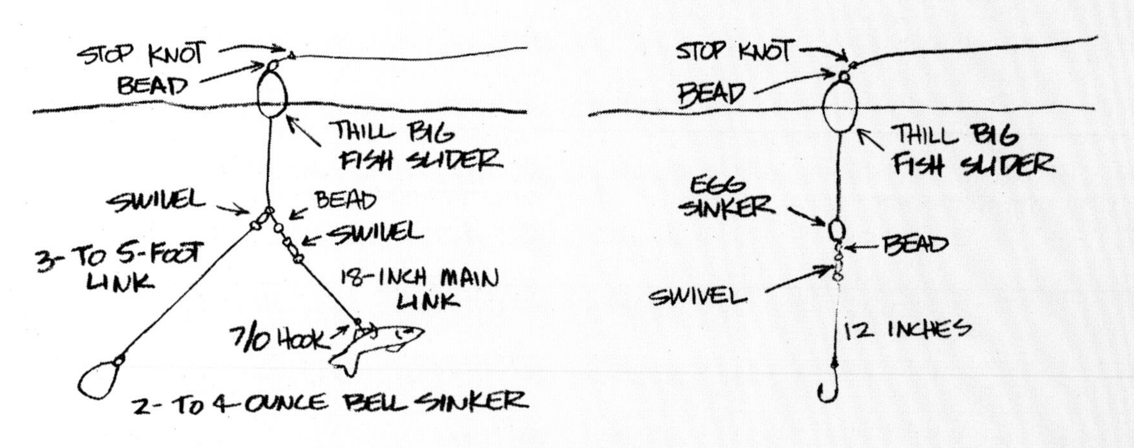

Sunken Float

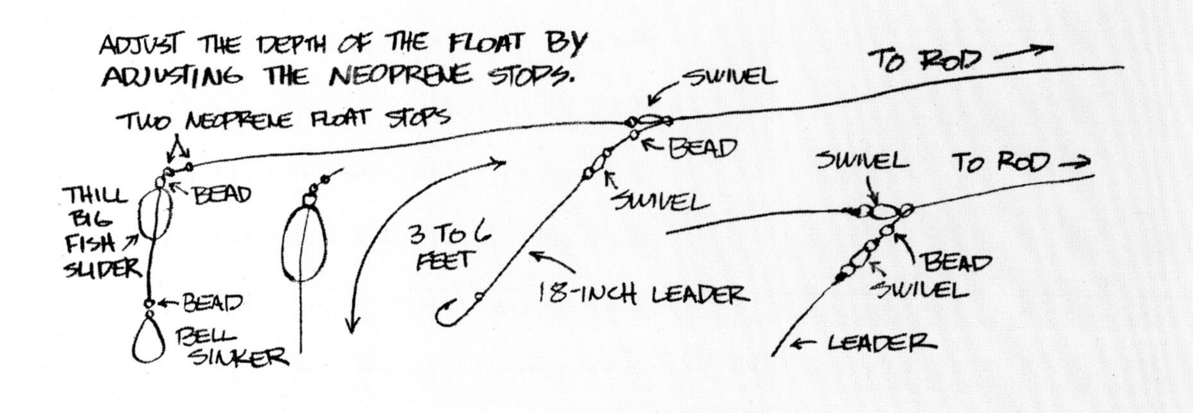

OK, Toad got carried away with the fire. The flathead's a 20 or so, released to snuggle back into the logjam from which it came.

some situations. Flatheads don't always travel the bottom. Even when they do, they can easily sense struggling baits suspended say 8 feet down in 12 feet of water. And suspended baits tend to stay more active than baits on the bottom. Every so often Toad would be sure to pick up each setline and give it a jiggle-jaggle to keep the baits moving. "Just giving them a little tickle," he'd say.

"Good idea," I'd say.

An English-style Paternoster rig's deadly too—one of those all-purpose rigs every North American bait fisherman should know about. It's difficult to describe, easy to picture, and easy to use.

STRATEGIES

Most flathead fishermen prefer to fish from shore, and I'm no exception. Set the baits out, do a small campfire, and stretch out on your sleeping bag. A boat, though, allows you to fish areas where a bank set's out of the question because of private property.

Toad had the perfect strategy for that last night of filming. "Here's what we'll do," I can still hear him say. "The lake's already thermoclined at 15 feet—no use fishing below the thermocline. We'll motor onto that transition zone from deep to shallow water—the spot you pointed out on the map—right where that deep water tucks into the bay. That's the spot."

Toad double-anchored the boat, parallel to the wind, up on the shallow shelf where the cats would roam after dark. Then we rigged baits below slipfloats (Thill Big Fish Sliders or Class Tackle Gazzets) and drifted them about 8 feet down in 12 feet of water, using the wind to take the baits over the flat and along the breakline and over deeper water.

It was a slow night of fishing, but we managed a 25 and a couple smaller cats. I released the big cat while Jim filmed the action. One of the smaller cats became our traditional midnight jambalaya—our last one. Jim got that on film, too. (My only regret is that we took no photos. The photos of Toad and me are from a river trip in 1990.) We talked about selective harvest of flatheads—the need to carry on a tradition of eating some fish—the more numerous smaller fish—and releasing the big fish, those unique individuals that had surmounted huge odds to get so large. The big guys are too unique to go 'round just once.

The problem with "from shore" is the difficulty in placing baits where you want them way out there somewhere. You can't cast big baits very far without tearing them off or injuring them. And lively bait's critical.

Car-top a canoe that you can use to paddle out to drop baits where you want them. Or, as I've done the past few years, slip on a pair of neoprene waders, don swim flippers, and slip into a float tube. The tube's particularly helpful when placing the float Paternoster rig, because you can drop the sinker to the bottom and set the float at exactly the right depth.

The good fishing lasts through prespawn—into early July in most parts of the country. Good times, indeed.

Toad's idea of a good time, by the way, was to turn a 20-pound flathead loose in the local little borrow pit near the golf course in his hometown of Sibley, Iowa. This is where kids come to fish when they get sick of the artificial world of

Rendezvous With Flatheads

Ponds & Lakes

Find the shallowest end of the pond. Look for the transition from deeper to shallower water. This is the feeding ground for flatheads during early season—May, June, and early July.

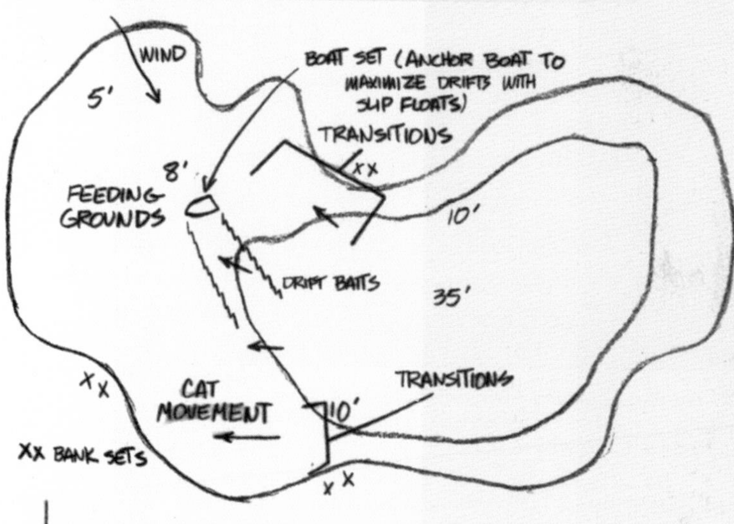

Small Reservoirs

Divide the reservoir into thirds. Look for a transition area where the water shallows to about 10 feet, close to the division between the middle and headwater of the reservoir. Flatheads roam flats in this area during early season.

Big Reservoirs

Point A—*A cat travel-by area. Flatheads move from the main reservoir. Not a feeding area during early season.*

Point B—*Another travel-by area during early season. The water's too cold near the main reservoir.*

Corners C—*Top spots during early season. Find these transitions from deep to shallow water.*

Flat D—*This is where they feed during early season—sometimes all season.*

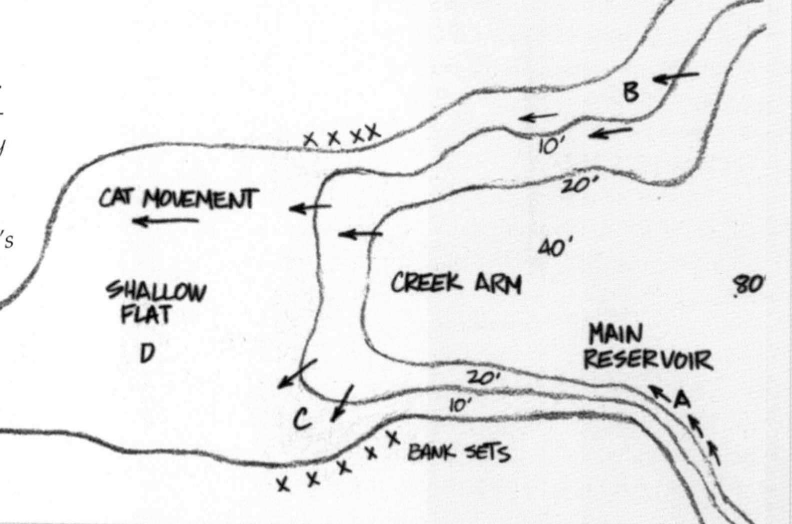

Nintendo, or tire of searching for golf balls lost by guys who wear yellow pants and fuchsia shirts with penguins on them.

Before long, many a Zebco 202 (one of the best reels ever made) had been stripped of line, glass rods had been bent and broken, and stories of monsters with teeth inches long were circulating among kids at the local swimming pool. No kid passed the pit without wondering, and although none would admit it, no kid ventured near the pit after dark.

"No kid ventured near the pit after dark."

Eventually, 11-year-old Jimmy and 12-year-old Johnny would get lucky and land the thing after an epic struggle. And there they'd stand, slimy, soaked, and frazzled after beaching the monster, posing for the local paper, as hooked on fishing as they are on life.

Toad and I often talked about terrible things, like sneaking a 40 into Ray Scott's private pond on his ranch or plantation or whatever they call massive chunks of property in Alabama—you know, the place where he takes President and Barbara Bush bass fishing when they visit. "Whoo-waah!" that soon-to-be-very-fat old flathead would drool. Talk about bass-breath and bony bowel movements. And pretty soon ol' Ray would wonder where all his 10s had gone—woe is us! Great trial and tribulation on the Scott ranch.

And if by chance the President should visit and hook Ol' Bassbreath, there'd be one more 202 stripped of line, one more glass rod bent and broken. And stories of monsters with teeth inches long would soon be circulating among the White House staff. The Pentagon would no doubt be notified and no Pentagon official would pass the pond without wondering whether conspiracy was afoot. We would no doubt spend millions on researching the problem. And although none would admit it, no Republican except Pat Buchanan would dare venture near the pond after dark.

A flathead in cover by day, waiting to go on the prowl after dark.

Poo-Poo on point for catfish!

WIN! FISHING PRIZES!
SUMMER STRATEGIES
the In-Fisherman
THE JOURNAL OF FRESHWATER FISHING
Of Wind & Walleyes
RADIO TRACKING GIANT BASS
EXCLUSIVE STRATEGIES
•Bass In Cover•Classic Pike Tactics
•Giant Salmon & Trout•White Bass At Night
Crude Bait Cats
Trip Tips • Science Features • Taste Tempters
THE CUTTING EDGE OF FISHING FUN

Historic Perspectives

Truth is that Stange didn't like this article as a finished product after writing it and killed it, hoping to rewrite portions of it at another time. The magazine, though, at the last minute needed more editorial pages to make up for a drop in advertising pages, and so the piece was pulled back into duty. Exactly what didn't Stange like about his effort?

"It was a subjective thing," he says today. "I guess it just didn't seem like it measured up to some of the other writing I'd been doing about catfish."

The article worked better than he expected, spurring intense discussion in catfishing circles about dipbaits—just when and where they worked, and especially whether or not they should be considered an option for big catfish. By the time Stange addresses the subject again (Chapters 22 and 31), he and the rest of the catfish world have spent a lot more time working with the baits in all seasons and many more situations. In the interim, catfish stinkbait entrepreneur Sonny Hootman, who along with his sons manufactures Sonny's Super Sticky dipbait in Farmington, Iowa, becomes a Stange confidante, teaching him even more details about dipbaits.

One observation from this article remains: The catfishing world is still waiting for a factory-made catfish nugget that works well enough to outfish other options.

CHAPTER 17

JUNE 1992

Crude Bait Cats

OH WHAT A TANGLED LIFE I LEAD. For when I think of stinkbait, I think of cow chips, hog chips, sheep chips—lots and lots of chips, moist ones, firm ones, and dry ones you can toss like a Frisbee. They are a thing of beauty and as taken for granted by folks in farm country as I suppose smog is by folks in big cities.

All About Baits That Go Stink By Night And Day!

Farm lots smell like farm lots, of course, but pigs smell different from cows and sheep and especially turkeys and chickens. People in farm country take pride in their discriminating noses. When the wind is right, a sage old farmer can tell whether his neighbor a mile away has switched from cattle to hogs or even from cattle to cattle, hogs, and chickens.

You get used to such aromas and in some cases even grow to like them. Good thing, because feedlots were everywhere and still are today. Even our little church in the country had a cattle yard immediately across the gravel road. And on Sunday morning in summer, as verses of "Onward Christian Soldiers" rose toward heaven, a north breeze would carry the powerful smell of prosperity through open windows. Grandma might lean over and observe, "That must be one rich farmer across the road." But aside from a comment or two from grandmas and aunts, only those who visited from afar seemed appalled.

Chips lead me in tangled fashion to channel catfish, because one of the crusty old catfishing characters I knew as a youngster

Big cats usually prefer fresh cutbait to dipbaits and paste baits.

used chips to bait catfish holes in early summer. I can picture him dancing across a pasture—a chip fairy of sorts—searching for just the right chips, cackling hysterically with each find, piling them in a burlap feedsack. He'd slip a big rock into the sack, tie the neck of the sack shut with bailing twine, and toss the sack into a hole in a nearby river.

This "chip fairy" was the first to teach me that catfish move upriver during early summer. "Searching for just the right holes, they are," he'd say with a wink and a grin. According to him, a well-baited hole made them stay long enough so he could catch them. "And in a pinch," he'd add with furrowed brow, hushed voice, and lips pressed tight, "when the worms run out you can always pinch off a piece of prosperity and catch those old cats."

Maybe. Certainly though, channel cats can be tempted by some pitiful concoctions, stuff that smells very prosperous, stuff that sends the faint-hearted retching and staggering teary-eyed. For those of us who grew up in the presence of prosperity, however, stinkbait offers no more than the sweet smell of success. I draw the line, though, at having it spread as a surprise below the cheese on my sandwich—or having it smeared in a skid mark down the rear of my clean underwear. (Always shower in the presence of your clean underwear on a catfishing trip when pranksters accompany you.)

Too many catfishermen, however, get carried away with the supposed solid connection between channel cats and baits that go "gaggola." Cats eat many things in almost any season, but some baits are always better than others. Baits that smell to high heaven often are not a ticket to fried cat fillets.

Indeed, as I have so often stated, fresh cutbait is one of the finest things for most catfishing situations in most seasons. That is, bonk a fresh 5- to 7-inch sucker or chub on the head, remove the head and tail, and place a single 1/0 hook neatly through the body (leave the hook point exposed) about an inch up from the tail of the bait. That's cutbait. Or fillet the side from a larger baitfish like a big sucker or small carp and cut the side into strips about 2 inches long and 1/2 inch wide. Keep your baitfish-in-waiting on ice.

Catfish get programmed to eat what's abundant. That might change by season, but fresh kill as represented by cutbait is almost always present. Crayfish, grasshoppers, worms, and other things turn up during some seasons, too. Aromatic baits like sour carp or shad are most abundant right after ice-out. Baits like dips and pastes and those nifty little briquet-like kiblets so common in bait

Freshly killed cutbait. Be sure to leave the hook point exposed to ensure maximum success on the hookset.

shops are almost never present, except indirectly as stand-ins for real soured baits. I'm afraid I've yet to find a place where the kiblets work.

One of the best places to use dips and pastes is where lots of fishermen are using them. Catfish in heavily fished areas get used to whatever odd concoctions fishermen present to them, be it chicken livers or wieners or french fries or dips or pastes. Channel cats in remote river sections, though, usually are more receptive to "natural" baits—although there are exceptions, particularly after the fish spawn (June, in most parts of North America). I always carry some pungent concoctions during every season.

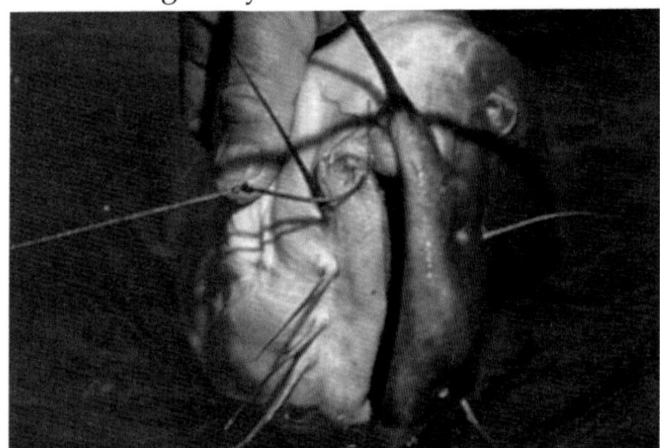

Cats are one big swimming tongue with taste buds distributed over their bodies. The most dense concentrations of taste buds are packed on the barbels and the lips.

SOMETHING YOU SHOULD KNOW

Bad baits smell terrible, but that smell isn't what a channel cat senses. A channel cat's sense of smell is a social sense—for finding spawning areas and identifying other catfish—not a feeding sense.

A channel cat tastes a bad bait with the thousands of taste buds in its skin, spread over its entire body but concentrated mostly around its mouth and on its barbels. A chemical aura oozes from each bait, whether it's fresh-cut, sour, or dipped. This aura is borne by water to the catfish, which recognizes and responds to the aura based on past experience.

Cats don't have to touch a bait to do a preliminary taste test. They find baits that seem interesting from a distance by following the aura. Then they do a close-up check by circling 3 or 4 inches above the bait with their barbels extended down. By this time, without ever touching the bait, most big channel cats (those with experience) have decided if they want the bait. If they do, they grab it in one accurate chomp and leave. Set the hook. No need to wait.

Little fish (those without experience) usually peck or mouth baits, drop them, and then finally pick them up and run. You learn to distinguish these "peckers" from big cats. Big cats rarely peck-peck unless you fish with baits they aren't familiar with—occasionally the case with dips and especially pastes. That's why I often try fresh cut bait before switching to an aromatic bait.

SOURBAITS

I divide crude baits into three categories: sourbaits, dipbaits, and pastes (which include manufactured nugget-type morsels). Sourbaits are natural baits turned rotten and rancid. Sour carp is a classic, although it could be any kind of fish. Carp is abundant, firm-fleshed, and tough-skinned, making it easier to use than shad, which tends to fall apart during the souring process.

Take a small carp and scale and fillet it. Cut the fillets into 1- by 2-inch strips and stuff the strips loosely into a glass jar. Add oh, say, 2

The King of Crude

Who's the king of crude (baits)? With few exceptions, commercial catfish companies mostly in the Midwestare presently small operations that market their products regionally. While Stange isn't recommending any one company's products, he thinks these companies as worth a look-see.

Catfish Charlie Bait Company *(Oskaloosa, IA)—Pastes and dips in many different flavors; also soft plastic tubes for presenting dips.*

Rusty's Channel Cat Baits *(Anthony, KS)—Pastes, dips, and sours in many different flavors; also sponge and other flavor receptacles for presenting dips.*

Doc's Catfish Baits *(Parkersburg, IA,)—Pastes and dips in many different flavors; also soft-plastic ringed worms for presenting dips.*

Doc's Champion Baits *(Wellsville, KS)—Pastes and dips in many different flavors.*

Uncle Josh Bait Company *(Fort Atkinson, WI)—Pastes in several flavors, and plastic dip worms.*

Berkley *(Spirit Lake, IA)—Pastes and bait nuggets.*

Little Stinker/Johnson Fishing *(Mankato, MN)—Pastes, dips, nuggets, and a plastic dip holder.*

Slip a single #1 hook once through a 1 inch x 1.5 inch piece of sponge, drop the sponge into the dip, and use a stick to push the sponge in. Do the same with the worms, which usually rest on the end of a piece of monofilament that has a small treble hook at the end.

While sponges and plastic baits work, neither holds much dip for long, especially in current. I prefer to make "dip bombs" by relying on an egg-sack tying kit steelheaders use. They use a square of fine cloth netting (spawn wrap) to wrap eggs in a tiny ball. Then they tie off this little package with a neat spider thread that requires only a wrap, no knot.

The key, though, is to add a piece of plastic wrap inside the netting to hold the dip. Drop a tiny piece of sponge (for bulk) into the middle of the plastic wrap, then add about a teaspoon of dip. Fold over the corners of the wrap and tie it into a ball. Use a #6 treble or a #4 single hook to poke a few holes in the plastic wrap just before sliding one tine of the treble or the single hook through the plastic wrap and the netting.

This spawn netting also is an excellent way to fish chicken livers (if you insist). As an alternative to spawn netting, try a nylon stocking.

tablespoons of water (or beer or wine plus whatever else you want to experiment with), and screw the lid on the jar, but not too tight—gaaaas, you know. Bury the jar about 6 inches in a garden or where the sun hits the soil for about 10 hours a day (direct sunlight breaks the bait down too much). In 5 or 6 days or weeks or a year or two, it's ripe and ready.

Sourbait is serious stuff. I have been skunked. Skunk mostly comes off with a dousing of tomato juice. Real sourbait does not come off, except in due course as your hide wears off. A dozen scourings with Lava soap speeds the process along, but the smell will still be there.

Other catmen understand, but should you be a doctor, lawyer, grocer, preacher, priest, rabbi, or teacher—better use rubber gloves. And always carry a jar of soured bait ("sours," individual sourbaits are called) in a bucket or leak-proof bag for secondary protection in case of an accident in the trunk of your car.

Just a "chip" off the ol' block.

The bait bagger, spider thread, squares of cellophane and spawn wrap, tiny pieces of sponge, pebbles, and dipbait.

DIPBAITS

Dipbaits are semi-soupy concoctions. Add enough "filler" agent to a dipbait and it can almost pass for a paste. Pastes, though, rely on bonding agents to take them a step beyond goo.

One of my favorite homemade dips begins as month-in-the-sun-aged sour shad or minnows. Shake the jar (check the lid first) until the body parts are suspended in juice, then unscrew the lid and set the jar back in the sun. The sun reduces the liquid to almost a gel. Add a couple raw eggs and stir. Then add just enough filler, such as fine-ground oatmeal, so the stuff is firm enough that you can just write your name on the surface (not with your finger, dum-dum) and have it stay there. Still too thin? Add flour. Too thick? Add another egg or a bit of water.

That's a basic recipe. At the egg stage you can add almost anything. Limburger cheese. Milk solids. Whey. Ground chicken liver. Ground rotten oysters. Chicken blood fresh from a kill floor. Soybean meal. And the stuff only gets better with age. I've had a jar of Bowker's since I was a kid. I don't use it anymore—just open it once a year to remind me how the real thing should smell.

The square of spawn wrap should rest outside the cellophane. Add a piece of sponge (optional), a pebble (optional), and a teaspoon of dip.

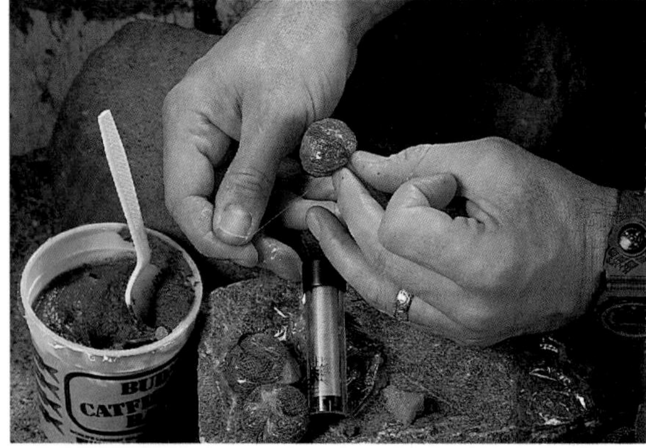

Wrap the package and tie off with spider thread. Bombs away.

Dips usually are fished on a sponge or a "ringed" or a "tubed" plastic worm.

PASTES

Pastes are so firm that you can freeform them into bait balls. Or the pastes are factory-formed into little briquet-like options that come neatly packaged, ready to build a castle with (or fish with). Because pastes mostly are filler material, they're less aromatic than most dips. Most pastes are fished on "ringed" treble hooks, although the briquets require a single #2 or # 4 hook.

European fishermen are leaps ahead of us in creating pastebaits, because pastes are basic to carp fishing, and carp are the most popular fish in Europe. I once spent several years experimenting with European pastes created to my specifications for American catfish. The results were good, but the materials necessary for creating your own pastes aren't available in North America.

I can't be enthusiastic about the pastes I've fished with, not that I've fished them all. I just haven't caught many fish on them, especially versus natural baits or dipbaits.

WHERE AND WHEN

I usually begin fishing with natural baits, then experiment with sours and dips. Present sours and dips on traditional set rigs—a lead shot ahead of a single hook when you're anchored upcurrent of a riffle. Hold the bait in the current and the cats will find it if they're active enough to be working a riffle. If they're not in a riffle, set the bait in the hole below it, particularly ahead of a snag.

Sours can also be drifted along the bottom, using a slipfloat to keep them moving. I don't do well with dipbaits below floats unless they're presented in a slackwater area. Cats often need more time to decide to eat a dip, even when it's neatly presented as a dip bomb, or rigged on a plastic dipworm.

Natural baits and sourbaits work from ice-out through summer. Natural baits also work during fall until freeze-up and through the ice in ice fishing country. Dips work well from just before cats spawn, throughout summer, and into early fall. A good potent paste might work during the same period.

My experience suggests that big catfish prefer natural baits and that you won't catch many 10-pound or larger channel cats on dips and pastes. Sours are good for cats of all sizes during periods when cats are programmed to eat them. Dips are particularly deadly during late spring and summer on cats up to about 5 pounds.

After dark? That's big-fish time. I go with natural baits unless I'm after a bunch of smaller fish.

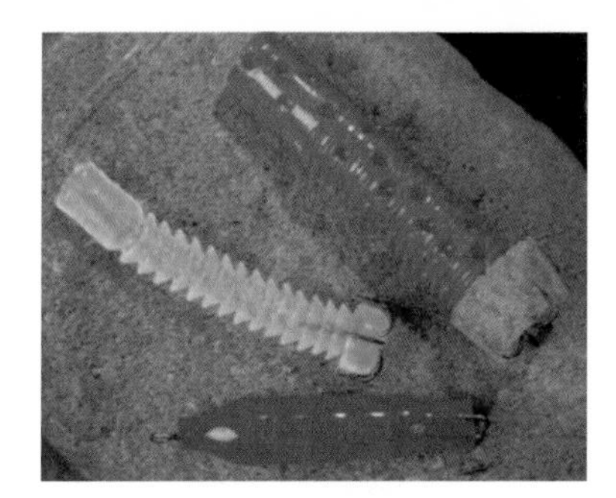

Alternatives
Typical plastic dip holders.

The racing stripe of fresh dipbait down the back of a fresh pair of clean underwear was—you guessed it—a Toad Smith trick. But there was reprisal in the air on that trip to Selkirk, Manitoba (and that portion of the Red River that remains the greatest fishery in the world for 20-pound channel cats). While Toad showered on the last morning of the trip, I ran his underwear, limp and pathetic, up the flagpole in the front of the motel. 'Twas Toad's only pair for the trip, so he was hanging loose and grumbling as we checked out.

The desk clerk that day was a short, stocky good-natured old Slovak fellow with a heavy accent. Just as I was about to sign the bill, the man's wife rushed in. "Husband," she said shaking her head, "you got to see it—underwear up the flag pole."

Hobbling to the window for a peek, he turned— "Cripes, voman," he said, rolling the R for effect and then clutching his heart and doing a perfect Slovak version of Fred Sanford having the big one. "And der vigger dan da Maneetoba flag!"

Jim Olive

Crude baits—pastes, sours, and dips—are a poor option for flathead catfish, which usually prefer livebaits. Blue catfish occasionally are caught on sours, but prefer fresh cutbait and livebaits. Only channel catfish, particularly fish weighing less than 10 pounds, consistently go for pastes and dips. Sours score bigger channel cats during some seasons. But most big channel cats are caught on fresh cutbait. Blues, flatheads, and channels are at times also caught on lures, as was the case with this flathead.

RECORD FISH 1992
FISHING RIP-OFF! See p. 46!
the In-Fisherman
THE JOURNAL OF FRESHWATER FISHING
THINKING BASS INTO THE BOAT
WHICH RIGGING WALLEYES
TIMELY TACTICS!
Radio Tracking Crappies
Alternative Tactic Trout
Changing Times Smallmouth
Cat Bagging Big Time
Spoon Spectrum Pike
PLUS! Master Anglers 1992 • Atlantic Salmon
Coppino • Science Features • Trip Tips . . .
STRAIGHT TALK FROM PEOPLE WHO REALLY FISH

Historic Perspectives

The premise of this modest article is that every catfish angler needs his or her own special "possibilities" bag, constantly packed and ready for action.

Stange writes this article from the perspective of In-Fisherman Editor Steve Quinn. So, Quinn has the main byline on the item, but Stange is the author—this allowing Stange to write from the perspective of someone fishing with him. It's a tactical writing approach used just once in more than 25 years.

The original catbag featured here was retired in 1995, replaced by a bigger model in a large duffel style. Fifteen years later, that one's still going strong and is almost certain to outlast Stange.

CHAPTER 18

APRIL 1993

Cats in the Bag

THE FIRST TIME I WENT CATFISHING with Doug Stange, he brought along a duckboat, a small motor, a cooler, a rod, and a catbag. The boat was to explore upstream or downstream for productive cat water. The cooler held livebait on the way to our destination *(see how all those 10-inch suckers swim?)*, deadbait once we got there *(bang, bang, Stange's silver hammer came down upon their heads)*, and a few iced-down cats on the way home *(we will make a catfish chowder so powerful it will cauterize wounds, drink Zinfandel, eat smoked sausage, and life will be good)*.

What Was, Still Is, And Ever Will Be In The Catbag!

What are we talking about and why are we talking about it? you ask yourself as you stand in the stream near Stange, waiting for a bite. It is because the world according to Castro, Ted Nugent, curried raisins, and dozens of other puzzling topics is but a step from catfishing, for him. We suddenly stand surveying water so low that obviously even the duckboat is out of the question.

I don a trout vest and begin stuffing it with sinkers, hooks, and whatnot. I strap a knife and pliers to my belt and grab a small tackle box. I slip into hip boots, adjust my sunglasses, and bend down the brim of my hat. I'm ready. Then I glance downstream.

Stange and his original catbag in action, this in about 1985.

Stange, jeans wet and muddy, is already a hundred yards away on a prime hole, hauling on a cat. He's stuffed a couple dead suckers into his catbag, which is slung over his shoulder, and has strode off into the wilderness. Publish or perish, he keeps telling me that day—his way of saying get a move on or be sucking hind catfish all day.

I learn that his catbag contains nearly limitless supplies of hooks, bell sinkers, lead shot, and floats—I mooch as the day wears on. Other items lie hidden in the dank recesses of the bag. But what other items?

On the bank, this dingy canvas bag sits upright with an air of belonging, never tipping to reveal its contents. Dogs bark and poop and steal your sandwiches, Stange tells me—catbags just sit there. Catbags are faithful. And they are fine company. He has never had a disagreement with a catbag.

But you have had only one catbag in your lifetime, I say. "That is true, "he says. "This bag has been with me for 20 years. It's much older and more polite than my children and more tolerant and less costly than my wife. I have slept many nights on a riverbank, my head resting on the bag as I considered stars and night sounds and why things are the way they seem to be. Catbags are faithful. They are fine company."

What is it with this bag? you wonder. Is it that as the years have passed, the catbag has become famous through appearances on the pages of *In-Fisherman* magazine and on national television? Viewers call and write, What's in the bag? Furthermore, What's the model number and price, and where can we get one? So I snitch the bag from the back of Stange's vehicle and, holding it hostage, convince him to talk about this catbag of such distinctive character.

IN THE BAG

There's an aroma here. My nose isn't prepared for the odd combination of liquefied nightcrawlers, aged carp intestines, and sweet vanilla-like extracts. Surely, too, somewhere within lie portions of those same two suckers that bit the bullet that first day I fished with Stange. As I dig deeper, he asks about the status of my tetanus immunization.

The core products in the bag never vary, according to him. I suggest, though, that he has no idea what's in the bottom one-third of the bag—and I'm not about to look. It is a mummified mess.

The contents of the rest of the bag seldom vary. Stange switches some items depending on his destination. A trip for flatheads on a reservoir in Ohio requires additional boxes of bigger hooks and additional large bell sinkers. And a day of walking along the 20-foot-wide Little Rock River in Northwest Iowa requires extra small floats. But for 90 percent of his fishing, he just picks up the bag and goes.

My life is complicated, he says. A suitcase is always packed. Stick a pine bough in the suitcase and leave those dirty clothes sit for a week, and

The Unpacking

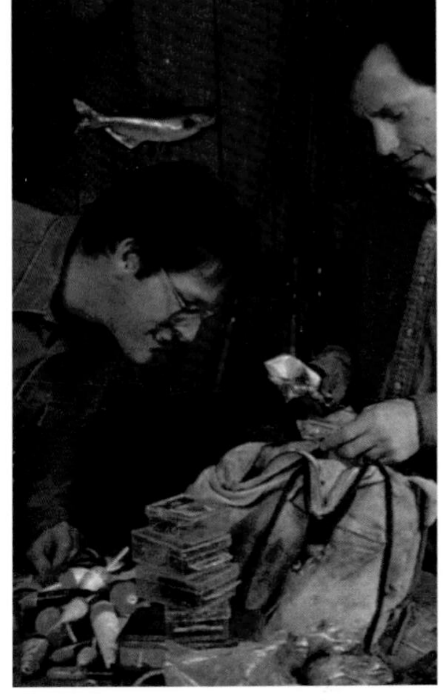

The light of day hasn't seen the bottom of the bag since 1972. Wouldn't get that close—just sayin'.

you're ready to go again. Wrinkled? Hey, the unkempt doctor look is always in. Grab my catbag and go. Life is simple. Life is good. This is the way fishing was meant to be.

The major contents of the bag are no surprise. Hooks, hooks, and more hooks. Floats. And sinkers ranging from small lead shot to giant bells.

HOOKS

Small Plano boxes serve to organize smaller hooks by size. One box holds several dozen #6 and #8 hooks for catching bait—suckers and chubs. The same boxes hold #4 to 1/0 hooks for early-¬season fishing when cats want smaller baits, or for times when cats run small. He stores his three-way swivels (#4s, #6s, and #8s) and swivels (same sizes) here, too.

He stores bigger hooks in their original plastic boxes, usually in quantities of 100. Sizes range from 2/0 to 10/0. He mostly uses 2/0 and 3/0 hooks for channel cats, 5/0, 6/0, and 7/0 hooks for bigger blues and flatheads.

Most of the hooks are Mustad 92671s and Eagle Claw 84s. What fine simple hooks they are. Easy to find—always competitively priced so you can buy them by the hundred. Sharpen them with a file before you use them.

Stange is fascinated with hooks. He experiments. Eagle Claw 9262s are deadly on smaller

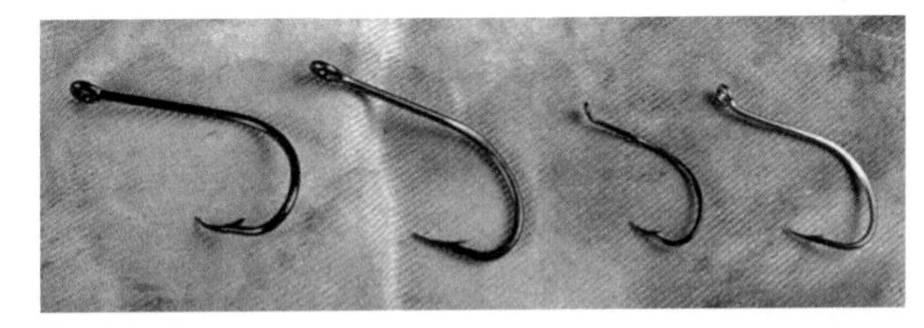

Hook Stuff: Mustad 92671, Eagle Claw 84, Mustad 9262, VMC 7299.

The Right Stuff

Floats.

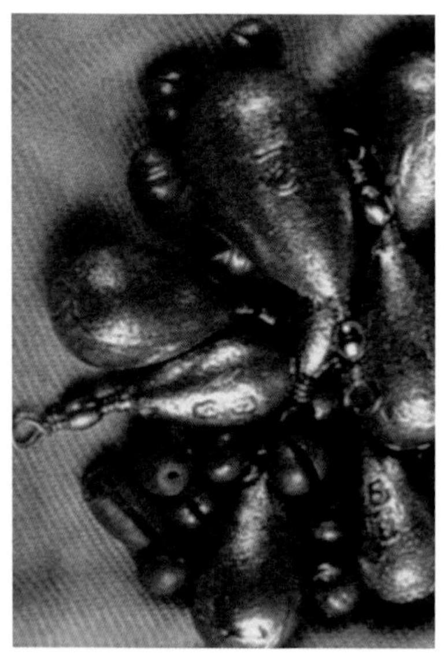

Lead.

Other stuff.

fish. And for several seasons he also has been using hooks like the VMC 7299 SS Octopus (6/0 through 9/0) for big flatheads. The 9262s and 7299s have a turned-up eye that requires a snell knot.

Where are the ringed treble hooks? "I don't fish pastebaits like that anymore," he says. "I use natural baits, usually freshly killed baits, most often portions of sucker or some other fish. Instead of pastes, I use dipbaits, which are more concentrated and more attractive to catfish. I fish the dips with plastic dip holders.

"I pack the plastic baits in Ziploc bags. Always have extra Ziplocs—carry my deadbaits in them, too. And floats."

FLOATS

To find active cats during late spring, summer, and early fall, Stange uses floats to drift baits through riffles and into holes. And he uses floats to suspend baits for catfish that prowl ponds and reservoirs.

His river floats fall into two categories: The stemmed-pear slipfloat design so popular among walleye fishermen makes a fine float for presenting inch-long portions of cutbait. The stem on this sensitive design helps you track the float on a long drift.

Thill Center Sliders and small Thill Big Fish Sliders also handle smaller portions of cutbait or livebait. For bigger baits use a float like the Thill Big Fish Sliders or the Pole Floats.

All told, I counted 24 floats of different sizes scrunched into the catbag. "Running low," Stange says. "Always need to carry plenty of smaller floats. The big floats take up lots of room. Always carry a few, but when you know you're going after flatheads, slip a few more into the bag."

LEAD

Lead's essential for most forms of cat rigs, from float-rigging to the most common kinds of slip-rigging. The catbag probably weighs 20 pounds, three-quarters of which is sinkers. The BB shot's used with the small hooks to catch bait. You need lots of 3/0 shot to couple with most other riggings. Use 3/0 shot to anchor slipfloats. Stange prefers round shot, but the eared variety is handy to work with to get a float drifting along just right.

The problem with egg sinkers, according to Stange, is that they just don't sit well on the bottom. They tend to roll and snag. He prefers the swivel-topped bell design, often termed a "bass-casting" sinker. He orders heavier sinkers in bulk from Memphis Net and Twine (Memphis, Tennessee).

Most of these sinkers in the bag are 1-ouncers for standard sliprigging for channel cats in smaller rivers. But you need 2-, 3-, and 4-ounce sinkers to anchor baits in strong current. And for specific trips, you need 5- to 8-ouncers, though these are best stored in the garage. Stange packs his bell sinkers by size in Ziploc bags.

Not to be overlooked in the lead category is at least a fistful of standup-style leadhead jigs (plain, without dressing). They're great for presenting cutbait on the bottom. Slip the hook through one corner of the bait, always leaving the hook point exposed.

Jig size depends on the river and the size of the bait. For smaller rivers and smaller cats, try 1/4- and 3/8-ounce jigs. Use bigger pieces of bait for bigger cats (particularly in larger rivers)—1/2-, 3/4-, and 1-ounce jigs work well.

OTHER STUFF

Line: Stange uses mostly 14-pound test in small rivers and 17- or 20-pound test in bigger rivers. For big flatheads and blues, it's 30-, 40-, or 50-pound test, depending on how many snags are present and the potential size of the fish. During early season, limper lines like Berkley Trilene XL work fine. The tougher stuff comes later—Trilene XT, Stren, or Ande Premium.

Tools: A Baker Hookout Tool, a pair of pliers, a wirecutter, and an ancient Rapala fillet knife in its sheath are tucked into a pocket on the outside of the bag. I dig deeper into the pocket. So that's where the files are. And a pair of cotton gloves to save your hands when you're into lots of cats.

Accessories: Matches, stringers, a scale, a few electronic bite indicators, a flashlight, several bottles of old sunscreen, and 4 or 5 bottles of various insect repellents. Another Ziploc holds a few Band-Aids, a tube of Neosporin, and a guide to the poisonous reptiles of Iowa. It's a short book.

Oh, sure, there's other stuff in the bag—even a bobber shaped like Snoopy. Was saving that for the next time Toad Smith and I did a TV show together, he says. He was going to do a tongue-in-cheek deal about the need for sophistication in catfishing, and in the background Toad would be doing one of his "Uh-huh-yah-right" bits. Then he'd pull out the Snoopy bobber and offer to fish with it versus my fancy floats.

Of course Toad would have caught fish. Didn't he always? Now that he's gone and we didn't get to do the show, I just carry the bobber as a memento.

The bag, by the way, is an early 1970s-style woman's overnight bag. She's a beaut, for sure, for sure.

"Uh-huh-ya-right!"

RECORD FISH Close To Home
WHERE AND HOW—NOW
the In-Fisherman
THE JOURNAL OF FRESHWATER FISHING
Book #114
Super Slick Spinnerbait Tactics For...
BASS
PIKE
MUSKIES
AMAZING WALLEYE RODS & REELS
TIMELY TACTICS!
CANOE CONNECTION SMALLMOUTHS
POND PANFISH, BASS, AND CATS
TAILWATER CATS
PLUS!
• American Shad • Mexican Bass
• Tackle Technology • Science Features
• Angling Adventures
STRAIGHT TALK FROM PEOPLE WHO REALLY FISH

{ Historic Perspectives

This might be the finest instructional article ever written about this topic central to catfishing. It's easy to read, with the instruction and explanation flowing logically and compellingly from sentence to sentence, paragraph to paragraph, and section to section. The best how-to writing is a work of revelation for those who wait for secrets on understanding a puzzling fishing situation. In this case, once the environmental scene is set, one need only grasp the concept of the "current tunnel" to be in command of the fishing in tailwater areas. In the end, the best how-to writing delivers a gift via skillful manipulation of storyline and explanation based on expert field observation.

CHAPTER 19

MAY 1993

Love is a Many-Splendored Tailwater Catfish Thing

Score Big In This Select Situation!

IT'S NO MYSTERY WHY THE BEST channel catfishing of the year usually takes place in a tailwater area beginning about in May and lasting well into June. It's gluttony. And it's love. Appropriately placed in order. For a fat cat's penchant for chow is hardly affected by the lusty advances of even the loveliest catfish of the opposite persuasion. At least not until the very end, when nature cannot be ignored. Even then, even when a bully big male cat is guarding his brood in a hole in a cutbank, food is welcomed with a bite and a burp when it rolls closely by.

For fishermen, the call is clear and so is the direction to head for good fishing. Tailwaters may be large or small, turbulent or gently flowing, shallow or deep, and dangerous or safe, depending on the river and the subsequent site, construction, and purpose of the dam.

All tailwaters are dangerous in high water. The water immediately below the turbines of large hydro stations, though, where water boils like cauldrons from hell, holds a special terror. Lowhead dams, too, are always dangerous, particularly so because many of them don't look as if they are. But get sucked into the turbulence below and you can kiss it goodbye, even if you're wearing the best life jacket made.

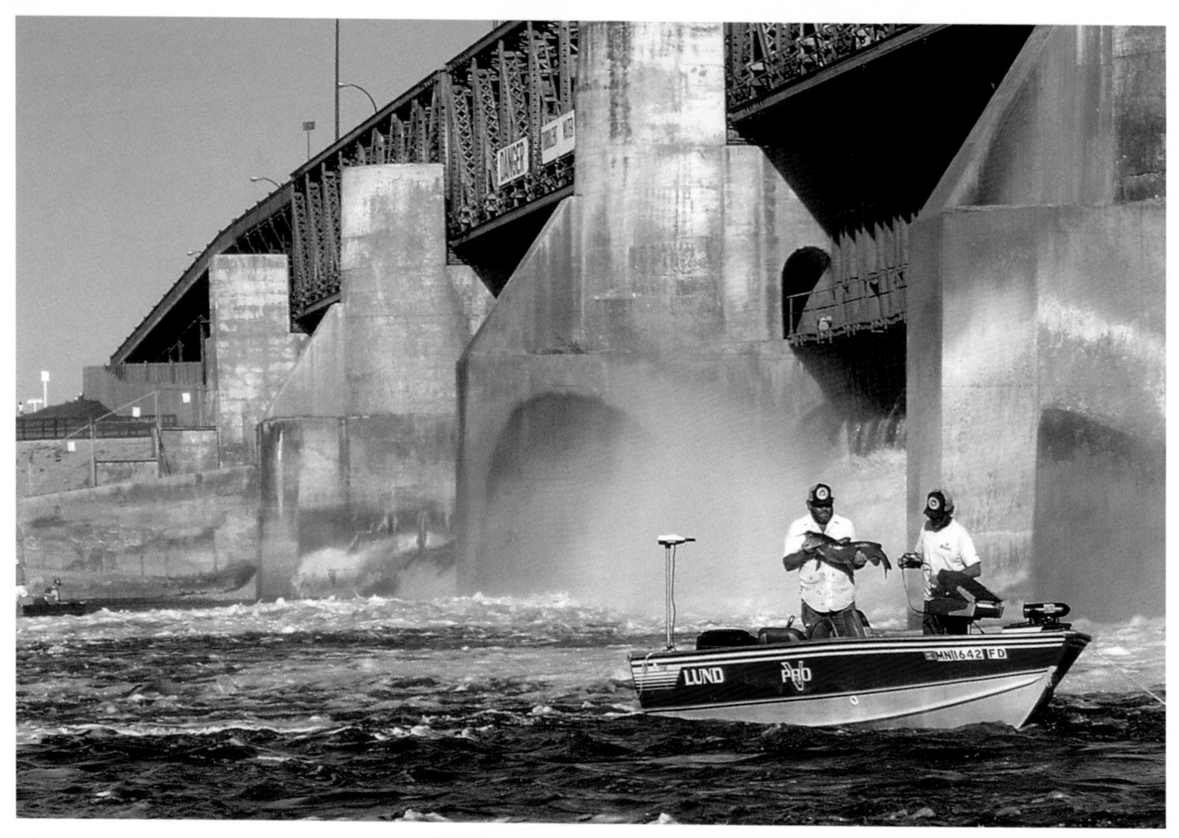

The tailwater area below the Lockport Dam near Selkirk in the late 1980s. Toad Smith showed Al Lindner the ropes while Doug Stange shot a TV segment in another boat.

Cats move upriver during high-water periods in spring. Say a river's free of ice by March. By April the water temperature is poking into the 50°F range, and cats are on the move. Hole by hole, run by run, shallow section by shallow section, they move until they hit barriers. A barrier might be no more than a particularly shallow portion of river. It may be a tremendous buildup of fallen timber stretching across a river. Eventually, it usually is a dam.

A cat consolidation of sorts is going on, the opposite of what happens by late summer. Say a river's 50 miles long. By late summer, catfish are relating to the deepest holes in the river; but those holes usually are evenly spread throughout all 50 miles of river. By late spring, once cats have a chance to move, most of those fish are somewhere in the upper third of the river.

Cats don't all group in tailwaters. But a lot of them at least make it there and stay for a while to feed before gradually moving back downriver to spawning areas, probably the same areas where they've spawned before.

At any one time, once plenty of water is moving during spring, the catfish population in a tailwater area is constantly being replenished by catfish arriving from downriver. And again, because of the supreme feeding conditions in most tailwaters, most cats stay for a while.

The amount of intelligent fishing pressure makes a difference in the number of available fish. Once cats reach a tailwater, the consolidation continues as they move by current into prime feeding areas. Only a few areas might exist in smaller tailwaters, a dozen areas in larger tailwaters. Rarely are there many prime areas. Those are the ones you need to recognize. We'll get to that.

Once the fish stationed in prime areas are caught, it takes awhile for the spots to be replenished. During peak prespawn movements, this may mean several days. During low-water periods in summer, it takes a major rain and increasing water levels to replenish spots. Periods between good fishing may last more than a month in summer.

Toad Smith and I once spent five days fishing the tailwater area below the Lockport dam on the Red River near Selkirk, Manitoba. It's a world-class fishery, the finest channel cat fishery I've ever seen. Toad and I were there during the peak of the prespawn season in early June.

Once you learn to read current, you know exactly where fish should be. Then you need to probe those spots to see what kind of structure lies below. That usually determines how many cats may be there. Once you're anchored right, you can catch most of the cats feeding there, which during June is most of the cats most of the time.

We motored around the tailwater a time or two. "'Bout five spots," Toad said.

"Six," I said.

"We'll see."

I don't remember exact numbers anymore, but it was lots—at least a dozen big fish from the first major current break behind a particular pillar in the dam. Then it was another 3 fish here and another 4 fish there, most of them in the 22-pound class. "Told you it was six spots," I said.

Eventually we headed back to our original hotspot. Once anchored properly, we caught 2 more fish but couldn't scratch another. The next day wasn't much different. We'd anchor on each spot and catch a fish or two, a few of which we suspected we'd caught before, and that's it. It wasn't time of day; we checked that variable thoroughly. There just weren't many fish left in those spots after we'd caught and released the ones that were there. We had to head downriver to get back to good fishing.

On day three and day four we fished exclusively downriver, finding fish at the heads of deeper holes as well as along shoreline breaks. Of course, the fish weren't as concentrated as at the dam.

"What do you think?" I asked Toad as the sun rose on day five.

"Bet those spots will be hot again—new fish ready to rock and roll," Toad said. Indeed. We didn't duplicate the first day's catch, but fishing was good; and again, the best area held more fish.

"Same fish or new fish?" Toad wondered.

"We'll never know for sure," I said. "Could be a few of the same fish we released. Could also be fish that were in a nonfeeding mode, lying somewhere in the tailwater that first day. But I'm betting mostly new fish."

Over the years, I've fished the same type of situation enough to conclude that it's waves of fresh fish. Cats hit the tailwater and stay for a week or so, then casually keep moving the only direction they can when the procreational urge can't be dismissed.

Toad and I had little competition during those early days on the Red River. People were parked all around the tailwater, and people lined the banks, but few folks were close to the current breaks that concentrated fish. Almost everyone was catching a few fish. Few people were catching many. Even when you're on a world-class fishery, you have to be on the right spots.

What were the fish eating? Anything they could get their faces on. Particularly baitfish. In many situations, baitfish ground to fine palatable slabs by turbines. In others, it's baitfish disoriented by their ride through turbulent waters. Also dead baitfish or parts of larger deteriorated fish like carp washed from above, as well as baitfish drawn to the tailwater for the same reason the cats were there.

During spring, therefore, it's rarely necessary to use anything but chunks of cutbait of a size appropriate to the cats being pursued. In small rivers, the best bait may be as simple as a freshly killed 4-inch baitfish. Cut off the tail so current doesn't catch the tail and spin the bait. Slash the sides of the baitfish a time or two to get those succulent juices flowing. Slip the hook through once near the tail of the bait, leaving the hook point exposed, to ensure a good hook-set. Use a #4 or #2 hook like the Eagle Claw 84 or the Mustad 92671. Simple, affordable, sturdy hooks. Lots of snags here, so buying boxes of a hundred saves money.

Cats up to about 10 pounds will take a cut slab of baitfish (suckers and shad work great, but almost anything will do), something about 1 inch x 1 inch x 1/2 inch thick. Increase those dimensions by half an inch at most for bigger fish. Too big doesn't attract bigger fish holding in current. The cats eat almost any piece of fish that comes by, but too big gets more difficult to present properly in current.

Again, leave the hook point exposed by slipping it once through the corner of the skin of the cutbait. A 2/0 hook's just right for fish from 6 to 10 pounds or so. For bigger fish, go with a 3/0 hook. Sharpen hooks with a file and reduce the barb to make sure they set easily.

Weight your bait with a bell sinker, preferably the kind called a bass-casting sinker, which has a swivel on top. Egg sinkers don't work well because they don't hold bottom; you end up with many more snags. Since there's no way to completely eliminate snags, make your own sinkers or at least buy in bulk. One source for bulk bass-casting sinkers is Memphis Net and Twine. Order sinkers weighing 1 ounce for small waters, 2 ounces through 5 ounces for most waters, and 8 ounces for turbulent deeper waters.

This is classic rigging for fishing in current tunnels. No leader. Let the sinker slide right up to the hook. Prevents snags and lets you fish precisely through tunnels until you find key slack-water areas on the bottom where the cats feed.

One of the biggest mistakes catfish anglers make is worrying about the length of leader between the hook and sinker. This is needless worry because no leader is necessary in this situation. Let the sinker slide right up against the hook. The resulting rig looks, casts, and fishes almost like a leadhead jig—exactly what you want. Too much leader causes a loss of feel, lack of control, and snags. If the swivel eye on top of the sinker is so big that the eye of your hook sticks, add a bead to cushion this connection.

Use current to move this rig along the bottom. If your rig's just heavy enough and you hold your line just tight enough to stay in constant contact with current, your rig moves through prime current spots so you can feel everything down there. Lift the rig over rocks and slide it through sand and gravel pockets. Snags are minimized, presentation maximized.

The most important part of this process is acquiring the ability to judge more than bottom content. Bottom content is secondary to current in determining where fish are. Current's the key, and you can use this rig to judge current conditions. Specifically, you are looking for and then feeling for *current tunnels.*

CURRENT TUNNELS

Current edges are formed 1) where current flows moving in opposing directions meet, and 2) where current flows moving at different speeds and consisting of different water volumes meet.

Current tunnels are formed near bottom along current edges or at the rear or tailout of holes gouged by the turbulence of the tailwater. The combination of different currents opposing each other in one respect or another where they meet the bottom—which further tends to reduce current—creates an area of relative calm in otherwise turbulent water. Catfish move easily through these tunnels. Food that washes into these areas moves gradually through them, easily accessible to the catfish holding there.

The way I look at these tunnels, they may be either flat or relatively indistinct in shape, or they are oval and much like a tunnel. The flat tunnels usually form along current breaklines where currents moving in opposite directions meet. The circular tunnels form where currents are moving the same direction at different speeds and with different volumes of water. Most current areas usually have both kinds of tunnels in the same area. The most attractive tunnels are circular.

The most obvious spot for circular tunnels is immediately below the dam. If a pillar separates one lock from another, and if one lock is running water and the adjacent lock isn't, the pillar creates a current edge where a large volume of water crushes and runs over a lesser volume of water moving the same direction.

Again, be careful here. In most major dam areas, so much water is running or it's so deep that the area's impossible to safely fish. Lowhead dams usually don't have pillars. Stay away from lowhead dams. And stay away from areas of massive turbulence. It's dangerous to anchor in some situations, too. Ask folks who should know about local conditions. When in doubt, don't fish there.

To fish through these current tunnels, anchor in the slower water on one side of the turbulent water, as close as possible to the head of the current edge. Cast your bait to the head of the current edge, usually just behind a pillar, and tighten your line to the bait. The objective is to locate the head of the current tunnel and to keep your bait anchored there, or at least move your bait through the current tunnel as slowly as possible. Get your bait in a tunnel and you are going to catch catfish.

Identifying the exact location and length of a current tunnel is dependent on your ability to feel the tunnel with your rig. Cast to the crease at the head of the current break. As your rig falls to the bottom, it's buffeted by current. As your bait hits bottom, it's surrounded by slower-moving water. All the water along the bottom is moving more slowly than the water above. You can do better, though. Probe for the tunnel, the area of relative calm in the storm.

Holding your rod tip at about 2 o'clock, tighten the line to your rig lying on the bottom. The sinker needs to be just heavy enough so turbulent water sweeping against most of your line drags your bait slowly along the bottom. Hit a current tunnel and the bait stops, at least momentarily. The tunnel feels different. Sometimes the bait anchors itself right where it first hits the tunnel. Other times, the boat isn't anchored in perfect position and is dragged along the edge of the tunnel or out of it. With experience, you can judge what's happening.

Hit the head of the tunnel, keep your bait there for two minutes, and you are going to feel the solid *cawonk!* of a channel cat taking the bait. Drop your rod tip a foot or two toward the cat as it begins to move away, and then set. Big cats don't miss when a bait is in a tunnel. And little cats don't dare fin where monsters tread.

Chances are, several cats are working each tunnel. They move forward through the tunnel until they hit the head of the tunnel, then sweep back to the area near the end of the tunnel and work forward again. I picture the tail of a tunnel waggling around like the skinny end of a tornado. Most tunnels are no more than 15 to 20 feet long. The farther back in a tunnel your bait is, the more turbulent the water and the more difficult for cats to find your bait.

Pancake tunnels are most common. They lie along current breaks where currents moving in opposite directions meet. These can be fished from a boat or from shore, using the same anchored bait

Many of the old photos from this article were lost, so the remaining shots in this chapter are from a 2008 trip by Doug Stange and his friend Dr. Edward Dykstra, who here overlooks the tailwater current edges depicted on the adjoining page. His rod tip is point at a current tunnel.

described before. A float also may be helpful in moving a bait along or through these flatter and longer tunnels. Catfish aren't as likely to always lie at the head of the tunnels, so it takes longer for fish to find your bait. Shouldn't take longer than 10 minutes in a spot, though. Fish along areas and move on—or at least try a different portion of a current area.

When using a float, use shot grouped about 6 inches above the bait to get it down quickly in current and dragging along the bottom. Thill Big Fish Sliders work well for holding up a good-sized chunk of meat and enough shot to hold the meat down where the fish are.

Additional weight is necessary from shore. Often you must deal with the disadvantage of a long cast to a current break and, subsequently, lots of current billowing your line and dragging the sinker rig out of position. A long rod helps, at least a 7½-foot-long flippin' stick, but better something even longer. Use the lightest line you can get away with, usually 12-pound test on small waters, 14 or 17 on most waters, and 20 for heavy-duty work.

Hold the rod tip high to minimize the amount of line in the water. Again, don't ever keep your bait in the same spot for long. Let it settle, let it drag, get it to hold. Wait no more than 5 minutes. Move the bait again to be sure you're searching for channel cats, and to be sure your bait hasn't tumbled into a crevice where cats can't find it. Yes, you'll lose rigs. This is the most expensive part of catfishing.

In large and turbulent tailwaters like those found behind TVA dams, and behind the locks

Current Edges

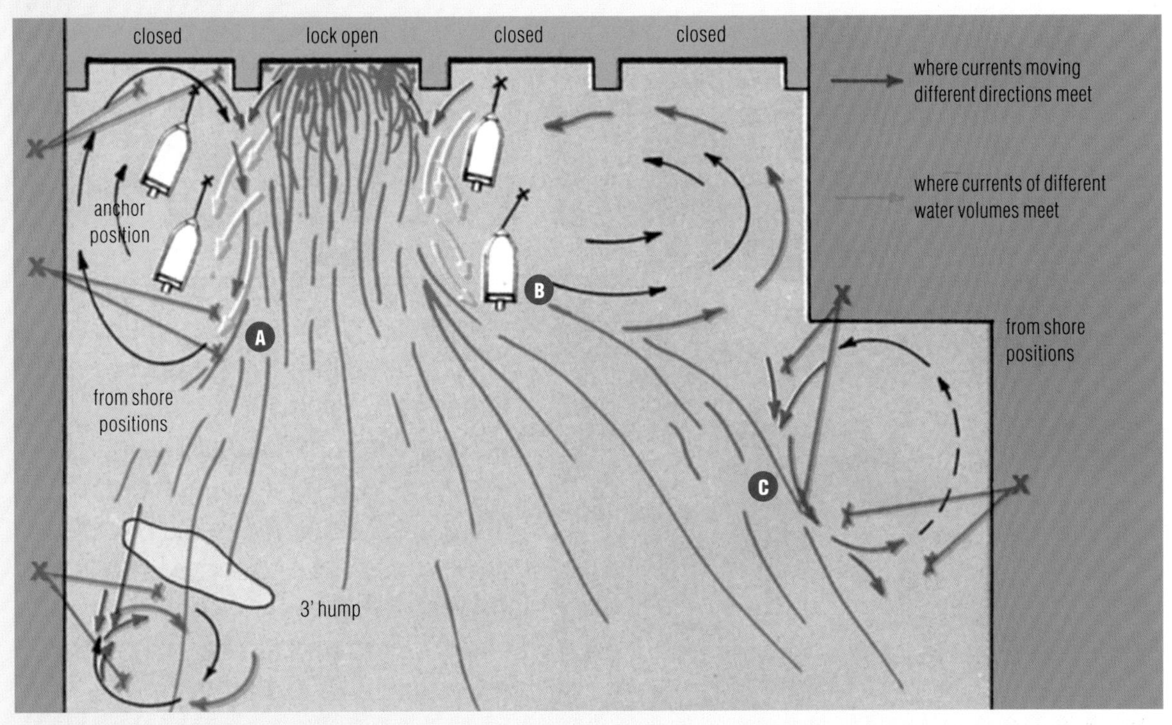
closed
lock open
closed
closed
where currents moving different directions meet
where currents of different water volumes meet
anchor position
B
A
from shore positions
from shore positions
C
3' hump

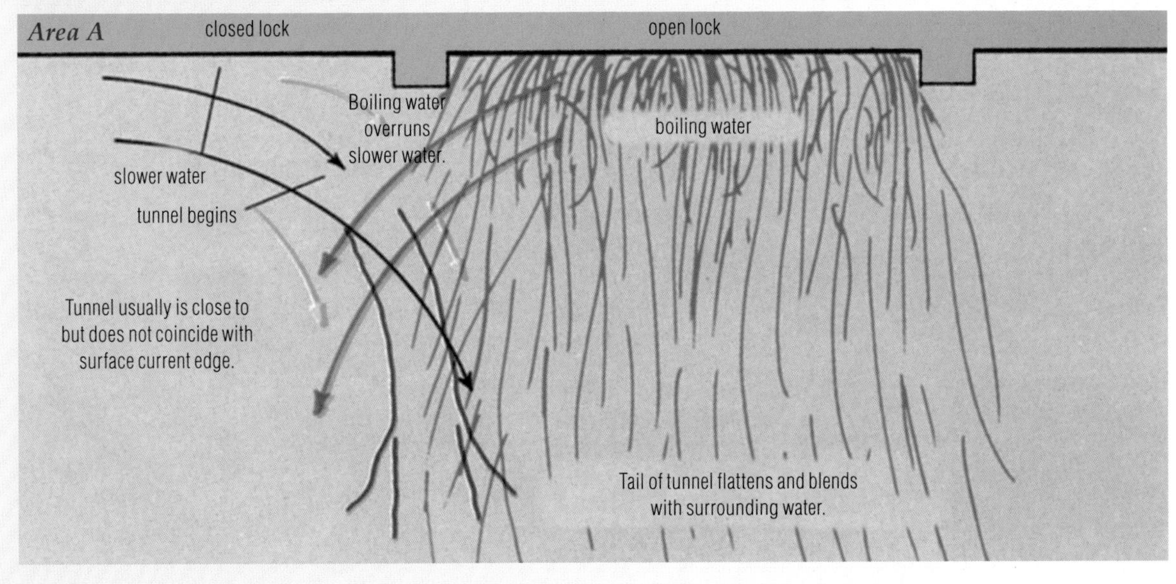
Area A
closed lock
open lock
Boiling water overruns slower water.
boiling water
slower water
tunnel begins
Tunnel usually is close to but does not coincide with surface current edge.
Tail of tunnel flattens and blends with surrounding water.

Dykstra battles a big channel cat with classic tackle, a bass flippin' stick and 20-pound Berkley Big Game line.

The average fish today is even bigger than when Stange first began fishing at Lockport in the early 1980s—25-pound fish common.

Stange hadn't fished at Lockpot since 1988. On his first drop into a current tunnel right below the dam he caught this fish weighing about 25 pounds.

on the Ohio and Mississippi rivers, often no bait holds bottom unless it's fished in slackwater. That's a different story.

One approach is to use a boat to run up into the fast water. Stop the boat along a current crease and let the current get the boat moving at the same speed as the current before dropping your bait vertically to the bottom. Use your motor to keep moving just fast enough to keep your bait vertical below the boat. Again, you're moving the bait along in the slower water on the bottom.

Some of the hottest territory in the tailwater is at the tailout of the hole gouged immediately below the dam. When your bait hits this area, it slows even more as it enters the tunnel that runs along the drop-off lip coming up from the deep water in the hole. This tunnel runs the length of the rear of the hole. But there's no way to fish it perpendicular to current. You can only drag baits through the area on your way while drifting downriver. Once your bait's swept up onto the flat at the end of the tailout hole, reel up, motor back to the end of the turbulence, and begin again.

Someone asked Toad how many cats we'd caught on that trip to the Lockport tailwater. Toad was into keeping track. He saved the antlers from every deer, large and small, that he ever shot. The bone pile filled his basement, spilled over into his living room, his truck, his garage, and into our hunting shack. "Eighty-two," he pronounced proudly.

It was the beginning of his initiation into the realm of disbelief experienced by fishermen who don't understand. The fellow who'd asked had fished for a week to catch 6 fish, and no way would he believe Toad's 82. Pretty soon, Toad learned not to spread disappointment and disbelief. He'd just reply, "Enough."

The ability to find current tunnels and present baits in them is the difference between a few cats and massive catches of bigger catfish. It's easy with practice, once you know what to look for.

DOG DAYS ACTION!
the In-Fisherman
THE JOURNAL OF FRESHWATER FISHING
HIGH SPEED WALLEYES
CLASSIC ROD-REEL COMBOS FOR BASS
TOP PATTERNS FOR PERCH, BLUEGILLS & CRAPPIES
PIKE TACTICS FOR TOUGH TIMES
FOCUS ON CATFISH
BLUES • FLATHEADS • CHANNELS
PLUS! Trip Tips • Science Features • Long Rods • Scales & Weigh Slings • Food Feature
THE SCOOP FROM PEOPLE WHO REALLY FISH

Historic Perspectives

This is a story never before shared with readers about the end of the Toad Smith era: In the aftermath of the surprise at Smith's death in November 1991, Stange is to deliver part of the eulogy at Smith's funeral. Present is a large contingent of hunting and fishing friends, as well as family and friends that don't know him well from being in the field with him—although they all know of his love of hunting and fishing and of his enormous personality. How should Stange speak of his friend on behalf of all of Smith's friends and family in the funeral setting? Smith, it bears noting, has been cremated and his ashes are to be spread on a favorite ridge where he spent treasured years hunting with bow and arrow.

Knowing that Toad wouldn't view kindly a lot of teary sentimentality, Stange walks to the pulpit that afternoon and looks out over the big crowd in the church. Waiting a moment for suspense to build, all eyes looking up at him, Stange begins by turning and taking two steps toward a curtain in the front of the church. "Toad," Stange says, looking at the curtain. The crowd sits in stunned silence, all eyes on the curtain. Stange waits another moment, still looking at the curtain.

"Toad, you can come out now. They're all here."

Such was the enormousness and totality of Smith's ongoing trail of practical joking in real life, that even in real death, given the circumstantial surprise of Stange's delivery, every person in the church momentarily sits dumbfounded at the absolute possibility—the total plausibility—that Smith is behind the curtain about to appear, having faked his death to play "gotcha" with the crowd.

So began Stange's recap of some of the rambunctious life and times of Toad Smith.

Illustration by Larry Tople

CHAPTER 20

JULY 1993

Big Mo Cats

LOOKING BACK NOW ON ALL THOSE DAYS of catfishing with the late Toad Smith, just the two of us on some secluded river, both of us happy to be in what for each of us was good company, and satisfied that there was nowhere else we'd rather be than right there right then, well, it's almost not right to sit here now and tell the truth, that sometimes fishing with Toad was exasperating.

Bodacious Cats From Deep-Lying Structure In River-Run Reservoirs!

Know how those TV sports commentators are always talking Big Mo (Mo being Momentum)? As in this team or that team for no apparent reason suddenly gets everything going its way—base hits just seem to drop, pitches just seem to pop—and Eureka! Big Mo's picked a side. Well, I'm here to tell you, as ol' Diz used to say, that Toad and Big Mo were bosom buddies, best friends, permanent partners.

Big Mo. I'd be drawn into a minor-league cat contest, a pleasant little friendly one-on-one with Toad. Suddenly it was as if all the wind would be sucked from the world, while all the good vibes from heaven above would gather on Toad's behalf and he'd go on a 10-cat run, while I stood there all puckered up and pathetic.

And after setting the hook—I can hear it so clearly now—Toad would pronounce his success with a *"Waaaaaual, nowthere'sanotherone!"* He had this way of really squealing through

A big channel cat in an early-day cradle.

his mischievous gap-toothed Toad Smith smile, really hanging on the *Waaaaaaaaal,* for about 10 minutes, and then finishing the *"nowthere'sanotherone!"* in a millisecond. *"Woaaaaaaaaal,"* he'd say, *"nowthere'sanotherone!"*

Toad wasn't just good, he was lucky. Or maybe it was angels. Toad and I used to talk about angels as we sat next to a fire on some riverbank, darkness focusing thoughts, night sounds bolstering wonder, stars above pronouncing peace, while mosquitoes added a realistic measure of frustration into even this portion of the best of life. I always seemed to end up on the left side of the fire, Toad on the right—political pronouncement for each of us.

Angels remind me that many of you have asked where Toad stood on religion. Toad could be a downright religious sort, even a fair (but unorthodox) biblical scholar; but always out of earshot of everyone—even the two sons and daughter he loved—because when it came down to it, he had big-time trouble rectifying his behavior with biblical standards. Many of us have the same problem. With Toad, though, it was always like heaven and hell were implementing their latest and greatest battle plans right then and there, using Toad as the battlefield; and as Toad often observed, the winner of the ultimate battle may have been predetermined, but often as not when it came to hour-by-hour reckonings, well, hell could get on a real win streak where Toad was concerned.

I'm not glorifying that Toad occasionally wandered the corner of 5th street and hell—just the facts, Ma'am. Many of you—and me too—have wandered there a time or two ourselves. Yet I believe firmly that love has conquered all, and Toad knew it and lived his own daily sacrifice, bore his own cross, lived that love in his way. Perhaps that's the reason he could gather legions of angels to sit on his side when it came to cat contests. And for those of you who don't understand the reason for any of this right here right now, maybe someday grace will call for no reason at all and a tear roll down your cheek for the pain and the joy that others share with you wherever they may be, in Bosnia or in your own backyard.

I have met many great catmen in my travels. Toad was dean of them all because in part he had reached that stage in his life when he understood who he was and what catfishing meant. On a practical level, it didn't take Toad weeks on a body of water to understand. He'd seen so much, done so much, experienced so many catfishing situations that what took others years to figure seemed obvious in a trip or two.

Toad was pretty much a small-river man. But cats are cats are cats, and pretty soon big rivers look like small rivers look like ponds look like small reservoirs look like flowing reservoirs look like natural lakes. So it was that Toad and I knew in a half-dozen trips to "flowing reservoirs" where channel cats and the occasional big flathead held during summer.

I don't think that in his life Toad ever caught a blue cat. Never fear, though, because according to Glen Stubblefield, a Toadlike figure of sorts in his part of Kentucky, blue cats act a good bit like channels and big flatheads. Don Wirth, who gathered the information from Stubblefield, likes to tell the story of a guy pulling up a '66 Oldsmobile from deep water in a reservoir in Oklahoma, opening the trunk and pulling out two 75-pound flatheads. "Cats like cover," Stubblefield says. That the Olds came from deep water in current during summer further illustrates important connections. Cats, structure, current, and deep water go together in river-run reservoirs.

River-run reservoirs are impounded bodies of water with noticeable current. Stubblefield fishes Kentucky Lake and reservoirs like Guntersville and Pickwick on the Tennessee River system. Toad and I fished parts of the upper and middle Mississippi and middle Missouri. Could just as well have been parts of the Ohio and its tributaries.

Toad would tell you that the quality of the current was the chief factor affecting cat location. Stubblefield harps on deeper water, water as deep as 45 feet, where he has tangled with cats big enough to pull his boat upstream. Indeed, he's hung some that, as he puts it, pulled harder than the Midnight Express to Paducah.

The Mississippi and Missouri, and reservoirs like them, are more riverlike than the reservoirs Stubblefield fishes; but the connection remains constant between current and deeper-lying, ¬channel-related structure and current. Sometimes though, channel cats and flatheads move shallow too, so long as it's shallow relative to deeper-lying areas where cats spend most of their time.

When cats drop deeper, they tend to consolidate. During summer, fishing actually may be better during the day and into early evening because the fish are grouped. 'Course you have to find the fish in deeper water. As I've said, for Stubblefield, deep is 45 feet. For us, deep is 25 feet.

WHERE

Stubblefield: "The old riverbank keys catching big blues in a river-run reservoir like Kentucky Lake. Check the banks of a river near you. See the rockpiles? See the small creeks cutting into the river? See the ditches, rockslides, and trees lining the bank? Now flood that area, put it 20, 30, or 40 feet down, and you have prime blue-cat territory

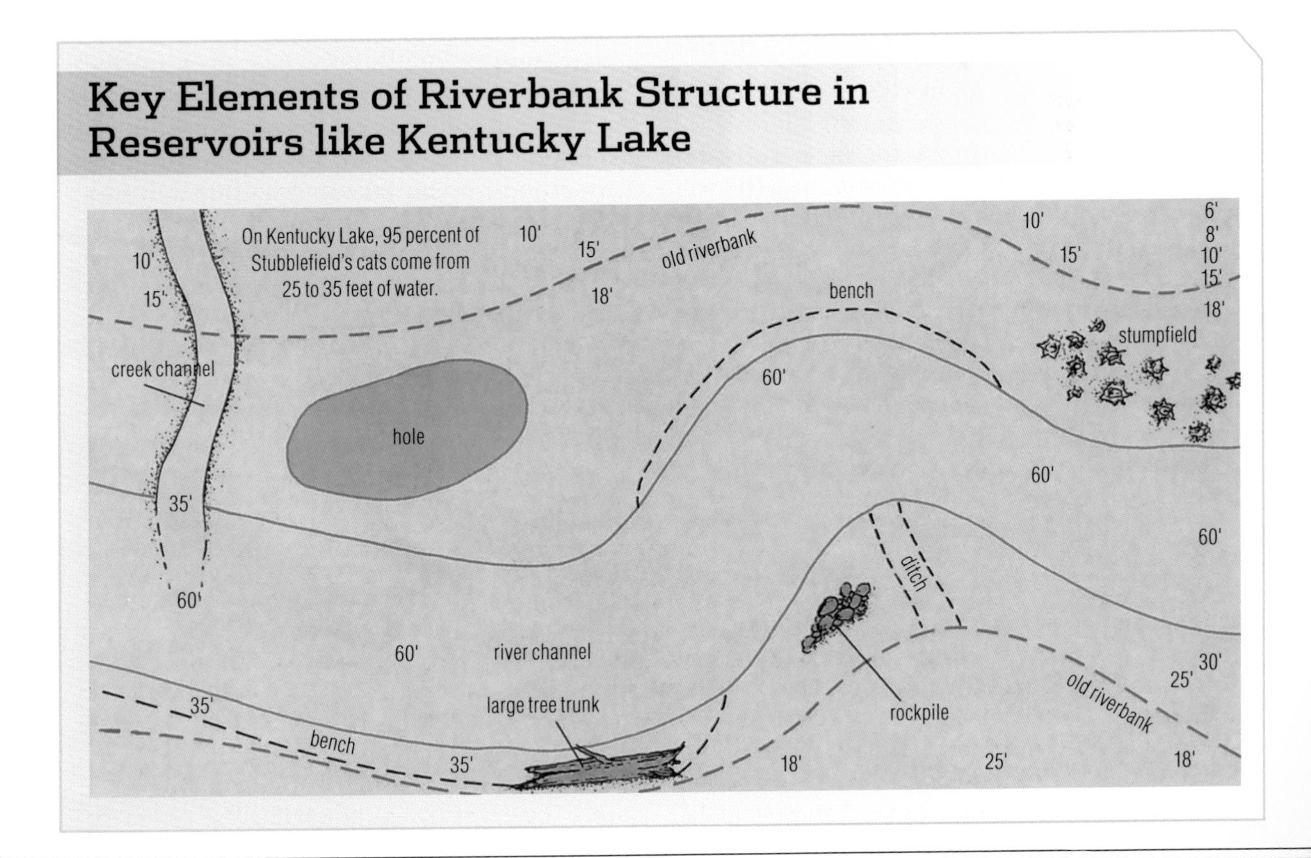

Cutbait works anywhere in the country, shallow or deep.

during summer—as long as you also add current. The best spots aren't in dead water."

Toad would tell you that for channel cats and flatheads, it's only slightly different. The channel remains the key. In this case, picture yourself at the base of the channel drop-off, being carried along downriver by current. Whoosh, current washes you into a depression in the channel. Whoosh, current washes you against a bank with sunken logs.

Whoosh, current washes you past the deep edge of the tip of a wing dam and then behind the wing dam. Whoosh, current washes you past a secondary channel cut coming from a backwater area or an area closed off by a closing dam. Whoosh, current washes you along a riprapped bank. As long as the channel moves distinct current past structural elements, all these locations mean catfish.

Current's the key. The best bite occurs when water is coming from upstream. Generation usually begins mid-morning and continues into sunset. Again, this is a daytime pattern. Want to fish 24 hours a day? Well, cats also move shallow after dark, another story. The daytime story is consolidation. Find the fish and fishing often is better during the day than at midnight.

The best bank structure for Stubblefield is what he calls a "bench." A secondary bank, he explains. "Say the original bank ran from 15 to 18 feet, then dropped down to 25 or 30 feet before dropping into the river," he says. "A bench like this may only be a few feet wide, but cats really stack up here, sometimes."

Stubblefield says these areas hold cats moving from the deepest parts of the channel where it's difficult to fish, to the deep-lying bank structure where they feed some of the time during the day.

Toad, though, would rather have spent time probing another type of cat territory. Of all the other possibilities, channels running from backwaters or creek arms into the main river may be best. Benches aside, Stubblefield agrees.

Stubblefield: "The trick is to fish these cats at the right depth and follow them out until they form a V where they intersect with the old river channel. Sometimes all the cats are on the creek side of the V. Sometimes they're all on the riverside. Most of the action comes in the 30-foot zone where the two areas connect."

The main channels in Toad's waters are shallower than in Stubblefield's waters. Toad usually reversed Stubblefield's procedure, starting in the channel and working his way back into the creek arm. He looked for a lip, a benchlike structural element at the junction of the channel and the feeder cut.

PRESENTATION

For the most part, this is not an anchor-up deal. Move to find consolidated cats, the way walleye fishermen move to find walleyes. Sit comfortably in the bow of the boat, bowmount motor in the water. You're looking for catfish with electronics as you probe vertically below the front of the boat. Before dropping the bowmount, motor around the area and thoroughly search with electronics as you get a sense of the layout.

The cats are on the bottom. Stubblefield uses a modified swivel rig with a small livebait. He prefers a stout 6-foot casting rod and a Garcia 5500 reel loaded with 17-pound-test line. The mainline connects to a barrel swivel with an 18-inch dropline of 25-pound test and a 1-ounce bell sinker on the end.

Another dropline, his baitline, consists of an 18-inch section of 17-pound-test line also tied to the

The Toadmonster, beard free for a change, with a channel cat of about 25 pounds.

Faster-Flowing Reservoir Catfish Structure

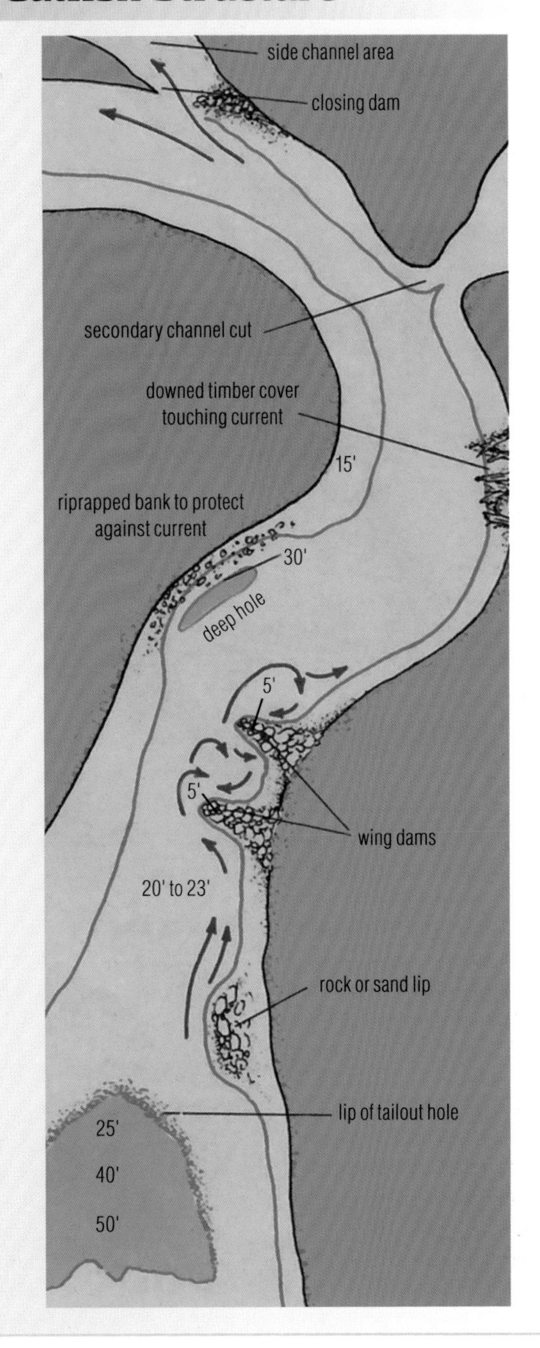

swivel. This section has a #1 or 1/0 hook threaded into a 2- or 3-inch minnow. Pinch the head of the minnow to kill it, thread the minnow on the hook, leaving the point inside the tail to discourage white bass from stealing the bait. Freshly killed minnows are vital; blue cats prefer them.

The surprising part of this advice is minnow size. Toad would have agreed with Stubblefield. "These fish eat bigger stuff when they forage shallow," Toad observed. "But during the day, they pick on smaller stuff."

Toad, however, opted for a slightly larger fresh minnow, usually a freshly killed sucker about 4 inches long. He fished the same rigging he would have used for walleyes; that is, a medium-weight fast-action spinning rod, an old Garcia Cardinal 4 reel and 12-pound-test line, usually Berkley Solar. My favorite combo, by comparison, was a flippin'

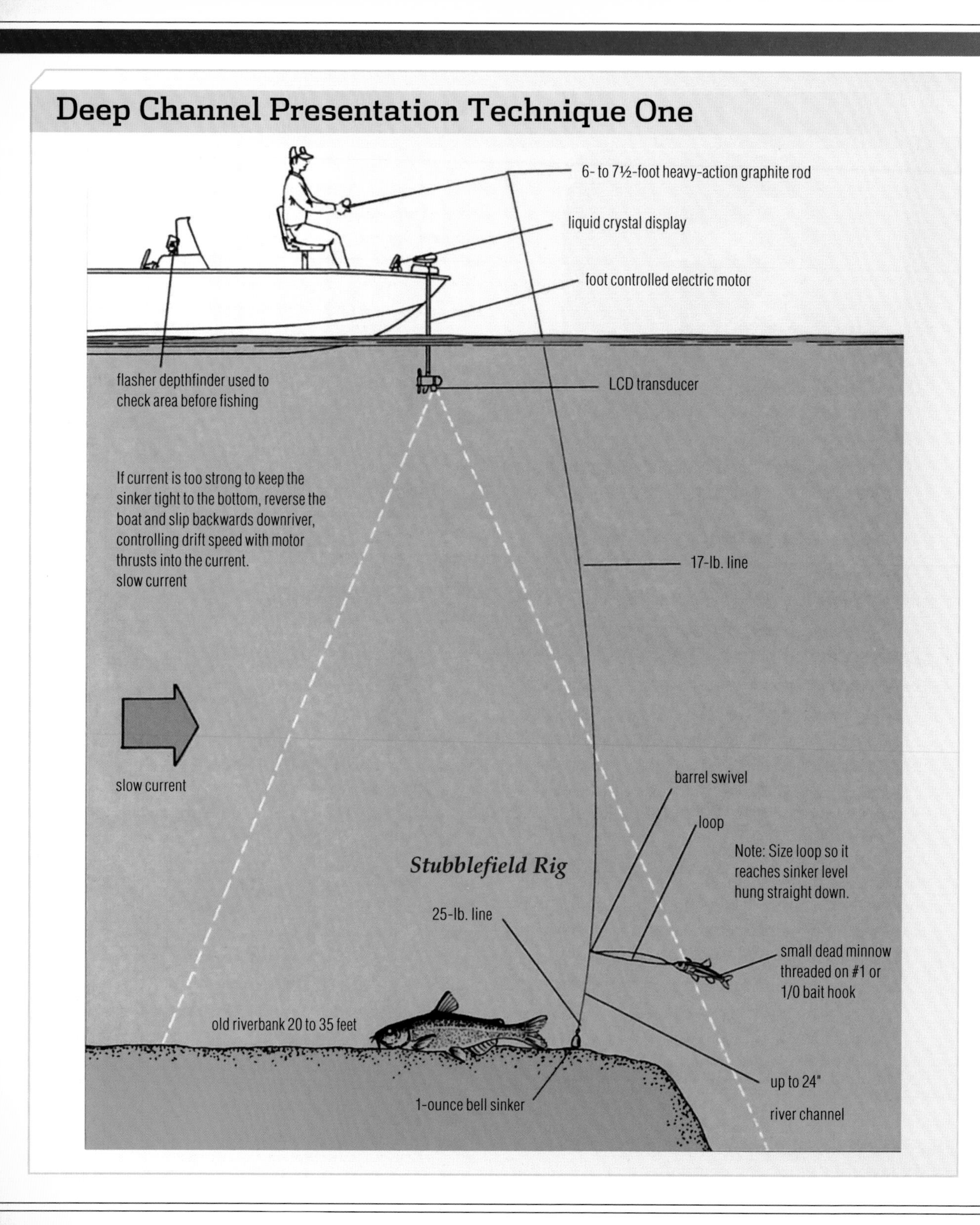
Deep Channel Presentation Technique One
6- to 7½-foot heavy-action graphite rod
liquid crystal display
foot controlled electric motor
flasher depthfinder used to check area before fishing
LCD transducer
If current is too strong to keep the sinker tight to the bottom, reverse the boat and slip backwards downriver, controlling drift speed with motor thrusts into the current.
slow current
17-lb. line
slow current
barrel swivel
loop
Note: Size loop so it reaches sinker level hung straight down.
Stubblefield Rig
25-lb. line
small dead minnow threaded on #1 or 1/0 bait hook
old riverbank 20 to 35 feet
up to 24"
1-ounce bell sinker
river channel

stick, Zebco Quantum reel, and 14-pound-test line.

Toad used un-painted and untied leadhead jigs weighing 1/2 to 1 ounce. His favorite weight was 5/8 ounce. He'd tap the minnow on the head and slip the hook into its mouth and out just behind the head.

Stay in touch with the bottom. Stubblefield keeps his rig bumping along the bottom, which means the bait is always within 18 inches of it. Toad fished the jig as vertically as possible. He'd drop the jig so it just touched bottom, then he'd lift it slightly so the current would sweep it along. Toad's jig was always within 12 inches of the bottom.

That's about it. Sleep in, eat a leisurely breakfast, and get after those cats when the sun's high in the sky. Fish hard and you're more likely to get Big Mo moving your way.

Toad never fished too hard. Often as not, about noon I'd be up front running the boat, sitting there talking to myself—didn't matter if we were into catfish big-time—and I'd turn around and Toad would be flat on the floor, snoozing and snorting like an old Kentucky racehorse. So, dutifully, I'd reel up my bait, swivel around in my seat, and dangle the minnow on his lips. *"Uhrrluup!"* he'd grunt. And then, because his big hairy bellybutton was always poking from between his shirt and pants, well, I'd dangle the minnow there for a moment too. Tickle, tickle. *"Uhrrluup!"* he'd grunt.

Toad was a great catman, not because he could catch so many fish, but because he symbolized for a generation of anglers the great glory found in the simplicity of the pursuit of catfish.

Deep Channel Presentation Technique Two

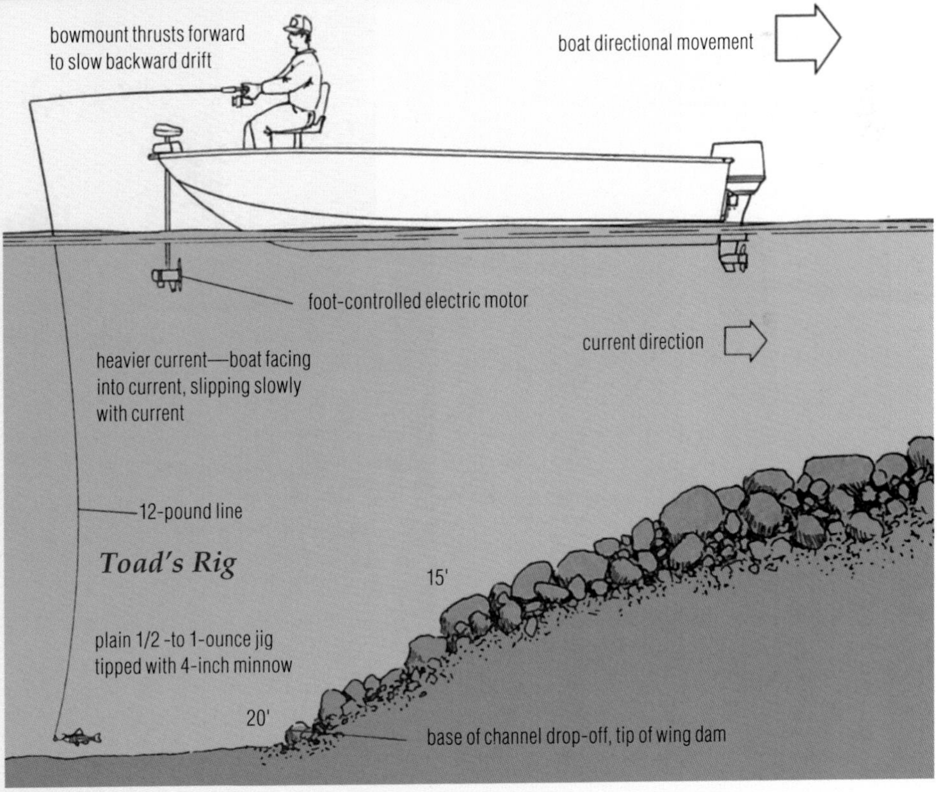

Historic Perspectives

Of the several hundred articles and essays Stange writes about catfish over the course of more than 30 years, this one remains perhaps his favorite, capturing as it does so well the simple essence of life and times in catfish country. Noteworthy too is that In-Fisherman cover artist Larry Tople's contribution to Stange's catfishing stories by aptly illustrating in a memorable cartoon style the adventures of Stange, Smith, and Zacker. Tople illustrates these and other adventures for more than 20 years and continues today.

Illustrations by Larry Tople

CHAPTER 21

MAY 1994

Camp Catfish

SOMEONE ONCE SAID that there are three things no man can do to the entire satisfaction of anyone else—make love, poke the fire, and run a newspaper. I'm not sure about running a newspaper. My list would delete the newspaper part of the deal in favor of running a tight Camp Catfish with the likes of Toad Smith and Zacker in tow. Revise, then, to: make love, poke the fire, and run a tight Camp Catfish with the likes of Toad Smith and Zacker in tow.

The Best That Life Can Offer, At A Price We Can All Afford!

Lord knows Toad used to poke the fire. Lord knows too that Zacker used to pretend he hated it. "Quit with the fire already," Zacker, eighty-something, one of the few remaining real old-school commercial catmen, would cackle as he squinted at Toad. Through a mostly toothless smile he'd then immediately continue, "Hot diggittity dang, but you always was and still is a pain in the arse."

All part of the ritual, Toad would always begin to reply, "Well now, listen you arthritic old bird—" At which point Zacker, timing it just so, would always interrupt, "Arthritis, shmitus. If I weren't 10 years older I'd whup your no good big butt." Toad

Call 'em fast chickens if you want. But not fast enough.

Kansas river minutes from downtown Kansas City, particularly after dark, and you're absolutely alone although almost a million people surround you. That's as good as the wilderness gets for lots of people on short notice, and it isn't too bad when you factor in enough channel cats to feed a portion of the neighborhood, plus a chance at flatheads and blues big enough to chew the leg off a Rottweiler.

Costwise, Camp Catfish isn't exactly a trip to Alaska. Cheap? Well, go figure. Ok, you gotta eat. But then how much do homegrown vegetables—green beans and peas and beets and carrots and new potatoes—cost? Add plenty of butter, of course, and cayenne pepper, which always brings out the best in fresh buttered veggies.

Oh, Toad was a fast one, but always fair. He'd trade a few catfish fillets or a deer roast from the freezer for the veggies and maybe a couple young farm chickens, birds with flesh that looked like flesh instead of those pasty-pale birds that pass for chickens on most meat counters these days. Those "free range" chickens, as folks in the big city call 'em today, led the good life until their time was up with Toad.

"Fast chickens," Toad called 'em. But not fast enough. A few of the chickens, as I came to expect over the years, would have a .22-caliber bullet hole placed just so. "No time to be chasin' chickens," Toad would say. What he meant, of course, was that he'd slowed some over the years. "You double ding-dang betcha," Zacker would have agreed, cackling like the old rooster he was. Add to this larder of fresh veggies and fast chickens a few of the small cats we'd catch from the river. Call 'em fast cats if you want. But not fast enough.

Camp Catfish? Cheap? Well, go figure bait. Even the bait's free if you have time to catch it. Or do as I did and, using a shiny crankbait or two, negotiate a deal with the kids who hang around down by the river park in every little town upriver and down. "Deal," you say, climbing slowly from your pickup

then would also, timing it just so and just as predictably, threaten, "Yeah, I suppose maybe after I dump your skinny little carcass in the river."

"Lard butt."

"Prune lips."

And more.

That was them. But the two of them loved each other every bit as much as I loved them, and we all loved Camp Catfish.

Camp Catfish. In a world full of gizmos and gadgets, high-ticket this and thats, and enough advertising schmaltz to stunt one's intellect, Camp Catfish remained a nifty get-away-from-it-all, get-back-to-the-wilderness-on-the-nearest-river retreat. Forget which river. It was the one nearest us, just as it is the one nearest you. That's whether you live in what's left of small-town rural America or in big-city Cincinnati or Kansas City or even Ottawa, Ontario.

Kansas City for example. Wilderness retreat on a river? Kansas City? The home of fine barbecue and some of the best deep-fried catfish in the universe? Well, yes. Park yourself on the Missouri or on the truck, dark glasses propped just so. "These crawlers (two dozen—hand them over) are free. Whatever you catch goes in here (hand over the 5-gallon buckets). You get these (flash the baits). I'm up at the coffee parlor drinking coffee and trying out a few blond jokes on Mary Lou. Be back in an hour." An hour later, collecting the bait—small carp and sheepshead, plus bullheads, sunfish, suckers, chubs, and more—and be sure to announce, "Here's a couple extra big ones—and the ice cream's paid for and waiting up at the coffee parlor."

Then, too, it's pretty much anything that'll float, if you want to float, to answer that question. We usually took Old Sorta Red, Toad's craft, a 25-year-old 14-foot Lund with a Toad-built livewell and a Toad-built front deck. A tribute to Lunds everywhere, you could still tell it was a Lund, even though the telltale red paint had been eroded by dents and dings, each and every one a story-worthy badge of catfishing courage—telltale accounts of rocks and rapids and logs and boat loadings on backwoods sandbars.

Toad ran Old Sorta Red with a 10 hp sorta Johnson with no skeg and a prop ground to midget dimensions by river gravel and sand, while I directed traffic from the center. Sort of. I'd point to one snag or another indicating my presumption of a hot spot, or wave "Pass on by, pass on by," meaning kiss this spot goodbye. Toad would calmly nod and we'd stop and I'd slip in the anchor or we'd keep on truckin' downriver. Zacker, on the other hand, quit listening to folks and started doing what he pleased somewhere back in the 1920s or thereabouts. He was, as they still say, contrary. Contrary. Zacker used to say that when you're two steps ahead of everyone else you can't always be looking back and listening to those you're leading. I've always pretty much thought he was right about that. So there was no real directing Zacker, although sometimes he could be channeled in one direction or another with sleight of mind. But that's one hellava 'nother story.

Toad ran Old Sorta Red with a 10 hp sorta Johnson with no skeg and a prop ground to midget dimensions by river gravel an sand, while I directed traffic from the center.

The deck was Zacker's domain. Sitting on a boat cushion up front, sometimes he'd fish, often he'd snooze, sometimes come September he'd whack away with a .22 at squirrels in the trees along the bank as Toad and I fished. Even with a touch of cataracts, he was a crack shot. Whack! Whack! Whack! And then his old Remington would jam. "Ding-dang new-fangled ammo," he'd cuss.

By then, though, given that three shots meant at least a squirrel, he'd always look at the two of us in the back of the boat, pause, letting the moment build, squint for a second or two, swirl his lips around once, twice to get the spit to the back of his mouth, and then cackle a squeaky, wheezing "Fetch boys!" And a "Hot diggity-dang!"

Now if this was by perchance unlawful—shooting from the boat, that is—well, all I can offer in our defense is that A) you didn't argue with Zacker when he was armed, and B) shooting furry rodents from a boat didn't seem like anything too serious given some of the more serious parts of Zacker's past, which were rarely worth bringing up. And if any of you think you might want to turn him in, well, pretty soon I'll be glad

Caught in a doublecross somewhere in the Dakotas, Zacker was shot point blank.

to tell you where to look him up. No need these days to take with you a large contingency of the local constabulary.

So it would go, along about midnight on some riverbank, Toad sitting there with a green willow stick shaved just so, poking the fire, and Zacker making important points (weren't they all) by jabbing the air with his gnarled old left hand, a Camel cigarette forever propped between bent fingers. A younger Zacker could have been the Marlboro Man, except for the Camels. The stories would flow, interrupted only by long pauses to consider stars and night sounds and the way things would be if catfishermen ran the world instead of, as Zacker always contended, a bunch of lily-livered lying money-grabbin' jackals with feathers in their shorts. I always pretended he was talking about fat-cat commentators like Rush Limbaugh, even though Zacker was pretty much an equal opportunity haranguer.

By this time, Toad would be telling "bone stories" as the fire cracked and sent sparks drifting into the night. Bone stories. We usually set camp on a likely gravel bar with a deep hole on the outside bend of the river, the deep hole preferably filled with downed timber, the better to harbor mambo flatheads. We would have whiled away the afternoon, stopping here and there to anchor upstream from river snags for channel cats. Night was for flatheads.

So, 'long about when the sun was oh say six fingers from the horizon, we'd let the channel cats be. Sure, we could have caught another 10 fish in the meanwhile, but what the heck. We'd all caught our share of channel cats before, especially Zacker, who maybe caught more cats in one net pull in the old days than most of us catch in ten years. We'd motor for a mile or two or three or even five, back to a prime piece of flathead real estate. Pulling the boat up on to a sand- or gravel bar, it was time.

Chores. We set a tent only if rain threatened or it was early June and the mosquitoes were intolerable. I am and Toad was a fair camp cook, so we'd take turns. I'd gather driftwood for the fire, while Toad set a cook site. At times, we'd wait to eat a midnight chowder or do a midnight chicken or fish fry with sautéed veggies. Best set up before the sun goes down, though.

Over the years we worked out a chicken recipe we all agreed was double-durn good, if not the best Sunday-go-to-catfishin' chicken recipe ever invented. Simple, too. In a 10-inch cast-iron skillet, heat almost an inch of oil over the medium heat from a coal-glowing fire. Meanwhile, dust the pieces from a couple chickens in about two cups of flour with two teaspoons each of salt and black pepper added. Then dip the dusted chicken parts in evaporated milk and dust them again in the flour. Fry the pieces, turning them occasionally for about 30 minutes. Don't be getting the oil too hot, now. Fast chickens deserve only golden brown and crispy moist. Watching Zacker mumble an ear of fresh sweet corn was not appetizing, but you have to humor a man with three teeth. Yes, sir, we all agreed, beans and sweet corn and God's own fast chicken enjoyed bankside under the midnight stars was just about as close to heaven as any of us were going to get before our time.

I didn't meet Zacker until he was about 80, long past his wild times. A story captures the flavor of the man. Seems that in his younger years, probably the late 1920s between his first bouts of serious commercial river running, Zacker fell in with one of the many bands of bootleggers who in big black sedans ran liquor from the way-back parts of Canada into the U. S. by way of the Dakotas.

This was serious business. Caught in a doublecross somewhere in the Dakota backcountry, Zacker was shot point blank several times, his body stuffed into a car trunk. Several days later, the car and Zacker turned up in the biggest city in the Dakotas at that time. Somehow still alive, he wandered from a hospital before the constabulary arrived. He holed up for over a month in the back of a shut-down saloon, before making his way back to his home on the river. The other stories—and there are many—are mostly of his days on the river, which he never again left. "You're bound to draw bad cards when you're young and get a touch of the greed," he used to say.

For all I know, Zacker may have been born with arthritis. Maybe it was from bullet wounds. Whatever, he couldn't walk much, heck, he could barely crawl out of a boat. So Toad would always want to help him lift his skinny behind out of the boat, which I'm sure Zacker really appreciated, but the rule of the game was not to show it, so it would always set off a round of barking and bickering: "Get away, get away, get your hands off me. I know about your kind. Just stay away. When the day comes I can't get out of a boat by myself, well, I'll just curl up and die."

"We'll all starve to death if we have to wait for you to get out of the boat," Toad would finally say as he'd grab all 120 pounds of Zacker by the britches and with one hand set him next to the spot where the driftwood pile would form. Zacker, sitting there and picking at the pile, could build a heck of a fire. The fire line at the point of his blaze would always point just a bit into the wind, even if that wind was only a tiny breeze. And then he'd tell you about it. "Absolutely," we'd say, nodding but not paying much attention. But then Zacker wasn't paying much attention either. We were all sort of lost in our own thing.

About then, camp set, Toad would set a line or two and promptly wander off into the distance down the gravel bar and along the river. On a bone run. Often I would wander along. I have told you before, that next to hunting and fishing and picking wild things like asparagus and wild onions, Toad liked poking along river banks and river ridges, looking for artifacts and such. Pretty soon he'd find a bone sticking up from a gravel bar. "Buff (buffalo)," he'd grunt. And his eyes would glaze over and his nose would naturally shift into the wind and he'd stand there like some aborigine envisioning an unending parade of buffalo steaks moving over the next ridge. Toad wanted desperately to be there, you see, for those more than these would have been his times. He would have killed some of those animals justly with bow and arrow, said his thank yous to Mother Earth, and then gladly relished the honor of the first bite of still warm animal heart.

The bone and sundry-other-item pile, then, stacked neatly by Toad's side alongside the fire as we waited for catfish on those dark nights, was his and our way of rubbing elbows with those who had come and gone before, inhabitants of some past Camp Catfish. There he'd sit, juggling a particularly ancient bottle in his hand, the old bottle barely visible in the firelight. It would take him awhile to get the feel of the thing, trying to conjure up a vision of those times and those people past who were responsible for the bottle being there with us, so many years fast-forward.

"An old river rat," he'd say. "Little log shack yonder, up on some river ridge. Yup. One of those old Dakota boys. Name was something like, well, maybe like Jess Johnson. Fished the river during good times and bad—mostly bad. Hard times. Did

Zacker would squint over Toad's way and interrupt, "Buffalo bone? Hells bells, that's just a rib from some old Hereford, you dimwit."

some clamming too, to sell for button-making in those old days. No real family to speak of. Yup, this old 96 proof rheumatic bottle was his friend on the river that night in 19 and 10." Toad would continue long into the night.

The best stories were about Indians and buffalo, of cunning maneuvers to get within range and of quick kills with bow and arrow, followed by celebrations of harvest—feasting and dancing into the night. And we'd all raise a piece of chicken to toast the past and the present and whatever was to come. Mostly Zacker and I would sit quietly and listen as the fire cracked, occasionally nodding, "Fine, fine," in agreement with Toad's stories. Just often enough, though, after Toad would start one of his bone stories, Zacker would squint over Toad's way and interrupt, "Buffalo bone? Hell's bells, that's just a rib from some old Hereford, you dimwit." "Longhorn steer," Toad would bargain. "Hell's bells, might even have been a milk cow," Zacker would suggest with noticeable disgust. And then the bickering and barking would intensify and things would have to settle before the mood was right for more bone stories.

Toasting times past and present and whatever was to come. Zacker died two springs ago. Most of you know, too, that Toad passed on several years ago just before the peak of the deer rut in November. I note his death before the peak of the rut because Toad would expect me to note and duly and very verbally protest on his behalf such an untimely demise. Toad to Lord I can only imagine during those last seconds: "Um, uh, Lord, I know I don't have much room to negotiate, but You don't suppose, do You, that we could squeeze another two weeks and just one more big buck out of this deal?" Lord to Toad: "No. But if it helps, just wait till you see the size of the bucks up here."

Toad was 51. Zacker was just about 90, as best anyone could figure. Found him in the afternoon sun in a rocking chair on his back porch 'bout a mile from the big river he loved. They built him a new house about five miles away from the old river when they built the Dakota dams in the '60s, flooding the river bottoms that used to run Zacker wild. The two of them—Toad and Zacker—would stand there looking at all the miles of water. "Don't wind much, does it," Zacker would say.

"Covered a lotta good bones," Toad would note. "Geese don't stop much these days, either." Zacker:

"If arseholes were airplanes, the place those damn fellers came from would be an airport." Zacker's day was a good spring day to die. Toad for his part died with a pheasant gun in his hands, his boots on, and a smile in his heart. Zacker just lived too long to go with a fishing pole in his hands, but I'm sure the smile was there just the same.

I know because of Camp Catfish. It's pretty hard to spend such serious time with someone around so many campfires and not know from whence his spirit flows. It occurs to me just now that a man really can poke the fire to the complete satisfaction of everyone else when the everyone elses are Camp Catfish friends.

It might be easy by this time for you to think that perhaps over the years the catfish became almost beside the point. At times, I suppose, but for the most part, no. Those old cats were one basis upon which those friendships were built. They were one passion that fueled dreams and many a scheme. They were the reason an old poacher like Zacker and a character like Toad Smith gladly shared the same fire with a contrary fishing editor like me. Behind every story, through every bite of fast chicken, around every riverbend was the hope that the clicker on a reel would crack the night as a catfish—flathead, channel cat, or blue—signaled its presence.

So you see, this article is how-to Camp Catfish. It's easy if the passion for those old cats burns bright.

Some time late into the night, so long as the cats weren't biting, we'd all drift off as the fire burned low and the early morning light sneaked over us, along with a morning chill and a bit of fog. Usually a big fish would have run all the line off one of our reels. Toad would reset the lines and then, as the sun cracked the horizon, I'd poke the fire and set coffee brewing.

Sitting there with first coffee was the quietest part of the day. No one said much until the caffeine got coursing just right. What would this day bring? And another night? Big fish? We always hoped for such a fish or two. Lots of fish? That was always nice. Whatever the new day brought, though, Camp Catfish was always the best that life could offer at a price we could all afford.

Addendum: These days, with Zacker and Toad gone, a new Camp Catfish brews. My son has become a good friend. Somehow he seems to understand—has some of the same passion for the catfish in the same raw form that was once Zacker's and Toad's and mine. I don't know if it will last, but I think so. And if it doesn't, well, I'll enjoy it while it does. He's naturally pyrotechnic, so I don't have to worry about maintaining the fire. He's a real talker, too, like his mother, so once again I can just sit back and listen. But I worry about his being this-generation soft—or is it this-generation smarter? He tends to like a tent over his head. And last time out he sneaked along his portable Nintendo. Toad would have had to master Nintendo. Zacker, with little fanfare, would have dropped the funny little machine into the river.

You're right, by the way. The measure of a Camp Catfish isn't ours or anyone else's Camp, for each Camp Catfish is unique, the sum total of those who share it.

Finally, through it all, I find it curious that somehow deep inside these past few years, "I know" that rivers will prevail. Water is life. But like life it needs direction—it needs to go somewhere, do something, not just sit there. Recent generations seem somehow bent on changing that, somehow convinced that we rule rivers. Dams are a monument to it all, a shallow and temporary attempt to tame the untameable. Rivers really do run through it and always will. Rivers are inevitable. And so long as man survives, Camps Catfish will always reside riverside, no matter the millennia and the ever-changing fish species. Camp Catfish and the friendships based on fishing are as inevitable as rivers, one of the surest things that ever was and ever will bind at least some men past, present, and future.

ANTI FISHING AGENDAS! PAGE 11
AMERICA'S BEST ANGLERS GATHER HERE
the In-Fisherman
THE JOURNAL OF FRESHWATER FISHING
Vol. 19 No. 5
RATTLEBASSIN'
PAGE 65
Secret Sanctuary Pike
Radio Tracking Walleyes
Peak Pattern Panfish
The Frugal Catman
PLUS!
Oddball Trout • Scent Baits • Moon Times
• Top Trip Tips • Science Reviews . . . And More!
ENCOURAGING SELECTIVE HARVEST

Historic Perspectives

So far as we know, this is the only detailed article ever written about making your own dip-bait—a truly bad-ass concoction tough enough to give even a racoon a belly ache and serious case of the cramps. Good luck if you live in the city and have neighbors within 500 yards. Good luck if you live in the country for that matter.

Stange: Over the years, working with several different dip manufacturers and experimenting a bit on my own with blends like the one touted here, I find it hard to keep from gagging at times. Then one day I'm fishing with the late Gregg Meyer, who for many years worked as a police detective. "Just do what we do when we have to deal with bodies that have gone bad," he says. "Wear a painting mask with a little Vicks Vapor Rub on it." Works.

This recipe is great, but, as Stange says, it's a lot easier and likely more effective to buy a tub of Sonny's Super Sticky.

Illustrations by Peter Kohlsaat

CHAPTER 22

JULY 1994

The Frugal Catman Does Gourmet Goo

IN TWENTY YEARS OF WRITING about fishing for catfish, I've said in print a dozen times that cats on occasion eat almost anything—wieners, french fries, jelly beans, chicken gizzards. I have used cow chips bagged in burlap to bait cat holes—that is, draw cats to a hole and hold them there. And I could go on, from half-inch portions of tampon used to dip chicken blood, to teriyaki roadkill concoctions that would make even the most jaded catman sing, *Ah So*!

A Bad-Ass Blend For Channel Cats!

My approach for channel cats usually includes fresh strips of fish flesh (cutbait), along with a smelly option or two during summer and early fall. I almost always catch bigger cats on the cutbaits. Frogs and craws can be good for big channels, too. Bigger chubs or other live fish also can be a key at times. Sometimes, though, when rivers are running soupy warm, fish go crazy for the smelly stuff, particularly juicy, runny dipbaits. To the tune of 10 to 1, dips outfish fresh baits—sometimes.

To understand why dipbaits can be so good for channel cats, consider the potent potential of sourbaits. Classic sourbaits are strips of flesh cut from winterkilled carp, suckers, or shad that wash up on shore just after ice-out. As you might imagine, sourbaits work fine just after ice-out, but also from time to time during the rest of the season. And yes, sourbaits are easy to make: Just mix fish portions and water and let them sour in jars in the warm afternoon sun.

Sourbaits are the basis for most dipbaits. That is, many dipbaits have sour fish as a basic ingredient. Dipbaits are semi-runny concoctions into which portions of sponge or ringed plastic worms are dipped to hold the dip so it can be delivered to the cat area.

Fishermen smell the potent potential of these baits; cats taste them. A cat's sense of smell is a social sense (finding and relating to other cats), apparently not used to find food. Catfish, though, have taste buds spread across their bodies and concentrated on their barbels (whiskers) and lips and tongue. So they taste things long before they see them or touch them with their barbels. As I've said, smaller cats are particularly enthralled with smelly options.

Some fine commercial products are available, but you want to know how to mix your own, like, say, Bruce Yager, river rat and galloping gourmet of the dipbait scene. Being a frugal sort, he brews his own. Powerful stuff. I talked with Yager about his home brew. According to him, you need:

2 gallons of small fish
flour
1 to 2 oz. pure anise oil
1 to 2 c. syrup
dry catfood
vegetable oil
chicken livers
To this list add:

An old blender, cheesecloth or old sheet, two 5-gallon pails with lids, a drill and paint mixer, and plastic jars with lids.

The Base—Yager: "Minnows and creek chubs make an excellent base, as do small bluegills or crappies. Local baitshops usually give me all the dead baitfish I need. Sometimes I head to a local creek with a minnow net. Other times we make a family outing of catching stunted panfish from nearby ponds. Freeze small amounts of bait if you can't get enough in a day. Remember that these fish must be under about six inches long.

Dip Delivery System

Paste baits are firm enough to free-form into bait balls. If you don't wish to brew your own, consider commercial baits of a semisoupy consistency that must be delivered into catfish holding areas via a plastic holder or sponge.

Present dips with only enough weight to keep them in the area you wish to fish. Add a lead shot 6 inches above the hook. In slightly heavier current, use a small bass-casting sinker blocked by a tiny lead shot or swivel 6 inches above the bait. Don't wait to let a cat swallow the bait. Anytime you feel a bump followed by movement, set the hook

Sour The Fish—Rotten fish is the basis for this attractant. It's the way to put the stink in stinkbait. Yager: "Drill holes in the lid of one of the five-gallon buckets—enough so the gasses can escape. Add the two gallons of fish plus just enough water to cover the fish. Seal the lid and secure a piece of cheesecloth or sheet over the top. If the top isn't covered, every fly in your home state will lay eggs in the vent holes. A maggot farm isn't what we're shooting for, here.

"Now place the bucket in the hot sun where the contents can cook and fester. Just stay upwind and let nature take her course for at least two days. A week's better. If you can get within 10 feet of the bucket without gagging, it's not done yet."

Making Mush—When the fish is ripe, remove the cheesecloth and turn over the bucket, draining off the liquids through the vent holes. Yager: "Serious business going on here. This really stirs up the odor. If you just can't stand it at this point, better quit now, because it gets worse, believe me."

Blender time! Yager: "Make it an old blender, because this is the only thing it will ever again be used for. You need a blender with variable speeds—one that can chop, grind, and puree. Need I say wear old clothes, gloves, and maybe a towel over your nose and mouth? I also place a fan at my back to blow away the smell.

"Fill the blender about halfway with rotten fish. Heads, innards, bones and all pulverize into a smooth mush, thus the reason for using only small fish. Pour this special blend into the other five-gallon pail and continue mixing until all the fish are reduced to a gray goo. "

If the neighbors haven't called the police by now, Yager says it's time to add his "secret" ingredients.

First Secret Ingredient—Yager: "Most catfish baits use a flour or cornmeal base for bulk and flavor. My recipe, however, calls for finely ground dry catfood. (They're catfish, aren't they?) Catfood contains corn and soybean meal and everything else a hungry catfish loves—animal fats, fishmeal, bonemeal.

And it's vitamin-fortified.

"For two gallons of whole fish, use one gallon of catfood. Grind the catfood into powder in the blender and add it to the fish-mush in the mixing bucket. A little vegetable oil added to the blender facilitates grinding.

"If you don't use about 12 to 14 ounces of vegetable oil for grinding the catfood, then add the rest to the mixture. Mixing works best with an electric drill, a paint mixer attachment, and some elbow grease. If the mush is too dry, add more oil. Too thin? Add flour."

Second Secret Ingredient—Many baits contain pure anise oil. Yager adds one or two ounces to the bait. Get the pure extract, a highly concentrated licorice, not just anise flavoring. Check your grocery store or pharmacy.

Third Secret Ingredient—"Chicken livers," Yager says. "Nothing lays a scent trail like blood. Livers are proven favorites, so blend them to liquid in their own blood and add this puree to the basic blend. Use as much as you like or none at all. I add about a half gallon containing plenty of blood. Get this at a grocery store or from a processing plant."

Again, adjust the consistency of the bait either by adding flour or vegetable oil. The dip should be thick enough to hold its shape, yet thin enough to stir easily with a stick—like thick oatmeal.

Bonding Agent—A bonding agent makes the dipbait sticky and gives it substance. Without it, the bait washes away much too quickly in current. Although many formulas use molasses or Karo syrup, Yager prefers baker's syrup, a corn syrup in five-gallon buckets sold at bakeries. "You need a cup or two mixed in with your bait to make it nice and sticky," he says. "This syrup is similar to Karo corn syrup but doesn't break down as readily and is much thicker. The stuff pours like STP motor oil additive. If you can't find it, substitute Karo or thick molasses."

Dip Delivery System

Commercial-grade plastic dip holders are popular delivery systems for dipbaits.

AGING THE BAIT

The best containers for your gourmet goo are large plastic jars with screw-on lids, so Yager suggests you consume lots of peanut butter and instant coffee.

Fill them little more than halfway, according to Yager. "Fermentation causes the bait to expand," he says. "You don't want this stuff blowing up on your basement shelves. Store the jars out of sunlight, but check them occasionally to make sure none are about to burst. If they expand too much, open the lids and stir the contents to release excess gas and restore the bait to its original volume."

There. Ready to go. But like many fine red wines, this stuff improves with age. Yager suggests it's "real good in 3 weeks, even better after 3 months."

Using the Bait—Like other dipbaits, this one needs adjustments for consistency before using. The bait gets softer as it warms, thicker as it cools. Add flour or vegetable oil to get the right consistency. Yager carries a small bottle of oil and little flour in a Ziploc bag.

Plastic ring-style worms are available from most stores that sell catfish baits. Most are prerigged with a small treble hook on a short leader.

Just dip the worm into the jar and work it in with a stick. I rebait about every five minutes in swift current.

Yager says his gourmet goo works in hollow soft plastic lures too. Mix the recipe on the thin side and fill a plastic mustard or catsup bottle. Walla! See you on the river. If you're fishing downwind, you'll know I'm there long before you see me.

Dip Bombs

Make dip bombs by using the egg-sack tying kit steelheaders use. They wrap spawn into a tiny ball in a square of fine cloth netting. Then they tie the package with a neat "spider thread" that requires only a wrap, no knot. The key is to add a piece of plastic wrap inside the netting to hold the dip. Drop a tiny piece of sponge (for bulk) into the middle of the plastic wrap, then add about a teaspoon of dip. Fold over the corners of the wrap and tie it into a ball. Use a #6 or #4 single hook to poke a few holes into the plastic wrap just before casting the bait.

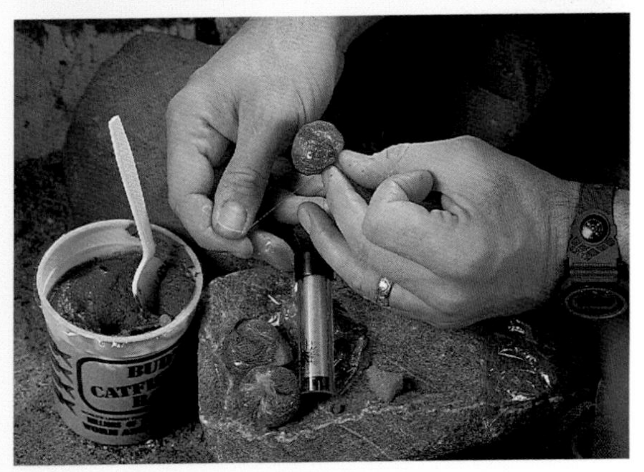

BASS & WALLEYE NOW!
WHO'S WHO & WHAT'S NEW ON ICE
the In-Fisherman
THE JOURNAL OF FRESHWATER FISHING
BASS BONANZAS
PERSPECTIVES: BASS IN COLD WATER
SMALLMOUTHS ON THE EDGE
Cats When It's Cold
Four Baits For Pike & Muskie
Rendezvous With River Crappies
PREDICTING HOT WALLEYE BITES
PLUS! • THE TRUTH ABOUT BAG LIMITS
• TRIP TIPS • MOON TIMES • KOKANEE SALMON • SCIENCE REVIEWS
AMERICA'S BEST ANGLERS GATHER HERE

Historic Perspectives

Stange previously mentions the consolidation of catfish in river holes during fall and winter, but this is the most thorough look at the topic at the time this article is printed in 1994.

A year later, working with Cumberland River Guide Jim Moyer, winter strategies for blue cats are brought forward for the first time, forever changing the way anglers fish during winter. In subsequent years, strategies for winter flatheads also are explored and explained, although once winter sets in, many flatheads are snagged or occasionally can only be "bothered" into biting. In-Fisherman also runs articles about ice fishing for channel cats—and we also fish for them on ice on TV for the first time.

Anglers begin to realize that catfish in many environments can be caught 365 days a year.

CHAPTER 23

OCTOBER 1994

When Cold Cats Ride a Warm Southwest Breeze

Cold Water Cats Are Catchable Right Now!

MOST FOLKS QUIT TOO SOON. "Watch the wind," Zacker, that dean of old-school river catmen, used to say. "Wait for those gusty southwest breezes. When the wind stays south-southwest for two—better three—days in a row, you'll be catching cats!"

Zacker spent 80 years on the river. When it came to catfish, he was rarely wrong. Subsequently, some of my most pleasant days of fishing have occurred on sunny October and early November afternoons when gusty southwest breezes whisked leaves across the water as I watched lines set in key spots along a deep river hole.

Fresh from a morning hunt, a brace of mallards or wood ducks and maybe a squirrel or two are ready to be picked or skinned clean as the cat lines do their work. Eventually, I'll build a little fire bankside, brew fresh coffee, and sit there in the afternoon sun, resting against a fat old log. Hope I don't snooze long, because sooner, not later, when the spot is right, it will happen—often quite often and quite often big.

Indeed. It was October 4, 1991, at about 6 in the evening when one of my biggest flatheads ever came calling. It wasn't a 50, but a very big fish for a small North Country river. The fish and I both sat bankside, huffing and puffing, me almost wetter than the fish, after wading in up to my knees to grab her by the lower jaw, and then being thoroughly thrashed. I sat with my wet butt on the sandbar, rubbing the rasped-raw knuckles of my left hand. The wind was, as Zacker had foretold, stiff from the southwest. The light was soft and setting fast. I remember it all as the fish lay there with her big fat flat head resting on sand, lower jaw protruding in a characteristic pout, her tail curled just so.

"Aw, don't get shook," I said aloud as I rolled forward on the sand and pushed her so her head was back in the water. She wallowed forward, I pushed a little more, and she was gone. I hope she lives another 25 years. Maybe we'll meet again this fall when she weighs 50.

Of course, it's possible to catch those old cats when the weather gets cold, which is right about now in the North Country and coming soon for those of you who eat your barbecue from rib shacks that advertise Lone Star beer. Cold is all about perspective. Last February, having left Minneapolis at a nifty 10 below zero, I arrived in Miami—on route to film in the Florida Keys—on a fine balmy 70°F morning. Over a cup of espresso, one of the baggagemen on break told me that come January, when the water temperature in all those Miami canals drops into the 60s, cats just sort of seem to go on strike.

By comparison, I've caught channel cats in the North Country at first-ice and beyond, but the fishing slows by mid-October in Minnesota and late October in Iowa. For that matter, the cats aren't really cracking in the great states of Kansas and Missouri 'long about the peak of the deer rut, either. And I'm told that hardcore folks in Arkansas and most parts of Texas pretty much hang it up by December. North Country cats tolerate cold better than southern cats, so the fishing across North America slows just about the same time even with a 20- or 30-degree disparity in water temperature, North versus South.

In comparison to summer quests, when it's

Ten River Miles

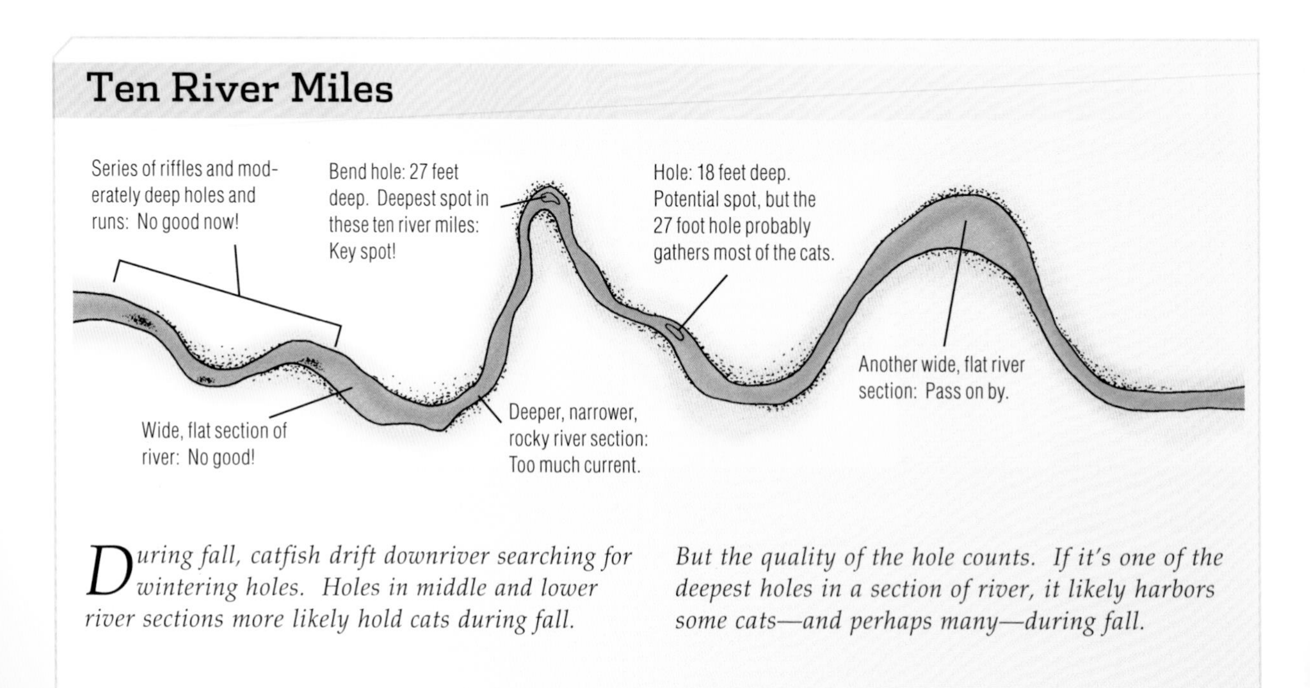
Series of riffles and moderately deep holes and runs: No good now!
Bend hole: 27 feet deep. Deepest spot in these ten river miles: Key spot!
Hole: 18 feet deep. Potential spot, but the 27 foot hole probably gathers most of the cats.
Wide, flat section of river: No good!
Deeper, narrower, rocky river section: Too much current.
Another wide, flat river section: Pass on by.

During fall, catfish drift downriver searching for wintering holes. Holes in middle and lower river sections more likely hold cats during fall.

But the quality of the hole counts. If it's one of the deepest holes in a section of river, it likely harbors some cats—and perhaps many—during fall.

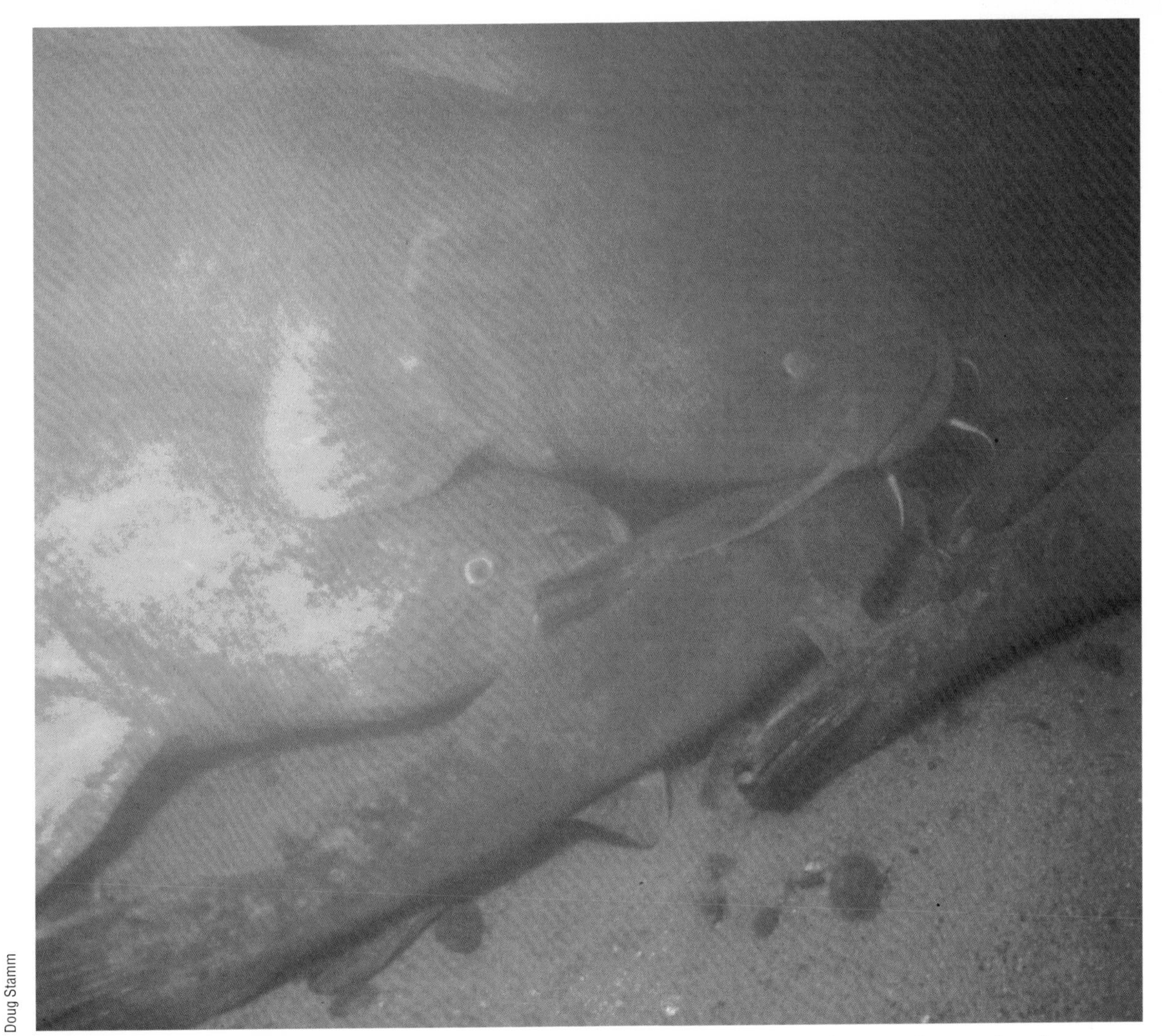

Doug Stamm

Pioneering underwater photographer Doug Stamm was the first to photograph wintering stocks of consolidated flatheads.

unwise to sit too long in any spot except a big-fish hole after dark, fishing during fall often is a waiting game at a good deep hole. Cats are beginning to move to spots where they spend the winter. Eventually, some of the best river holes, those with plenty of depth and enough current, hold tremendous populations of cats. Consolidated cats. And, so long as the hole isn't filled in by changing river patterns, cats gather there year after year.

Kevin Stauffer and Brad Koenen, fishery research biologists with the Minnesota Department of Natural Resources, verified this pattern. Last year during October and November, they sampled (via electroshocking) the resident catfish populations in one of Minnesota's best cat rivers, the Minnesota. "We'd sample a pretty goodlooking deeper hole without bringing up a catfish," Stauffer said. "Then we'd sample another hole and bring up hundreds of fish. Depth was the primary variable. Almost 97 percent of the cats sampled came from holes deeper than about 22 feet."

All told, in 7.7 hours of electroshocking, they counted 15 flatheads and 2,670 channel cats, a tremendous number of fish for the time spent. Interesting, I said. Why so few flatheads? I told them that I could usually catch flatheads in early October but not in November, when I could still catch a few channel cats.

"Perhaps flatheads more likely winter in shallower holes with timber cover," Stauffer theorized. "Perhaps the fish just didn't respond to the type of electric current we were using." But I fish those kinds of spots, I said. I just don't catch flatheads once the water starts to get real cold.

"Then perhaps the fish just aren't there," he said. "Perhaps they've migrated farther downriver. Perhaps, too, their metabolism slows quicker than that of the channel cat. We'll know more in another year."

Their research illustrates that if you find the right hole—and there probably aren't many of them—you'll be on top of a bunch of fish. You should be able to catch some of them if the water's not too high and dirty and so long as you do a few things just so. I can tell you what to do to enjoy yourself on a fine fall day. But you must find the right holes. I know the location of potential holes by having surveyed a large section of river during summer.

Bait—Livebait or fresh cutbait's the key. Cutbait works just as well for channel cats and blues. (Flatheads usually prefer live fish, although they occasionally take other baits.) I use strips of sucker fillet about an inch square and a half-inch thick. Keep the hook point exposed for a good hook-set. Just run the hook point once through the skin on one corner of the bait.

As the water continues to cool and indeed gets just nasty cold for your area of the country, you need live fish, sized appropriately for the cats you're after. I prefer creek chubs for channel cats. My experience with blue cats is limited during the beginning of winter. Later, they prefer cutbait.

Rigging

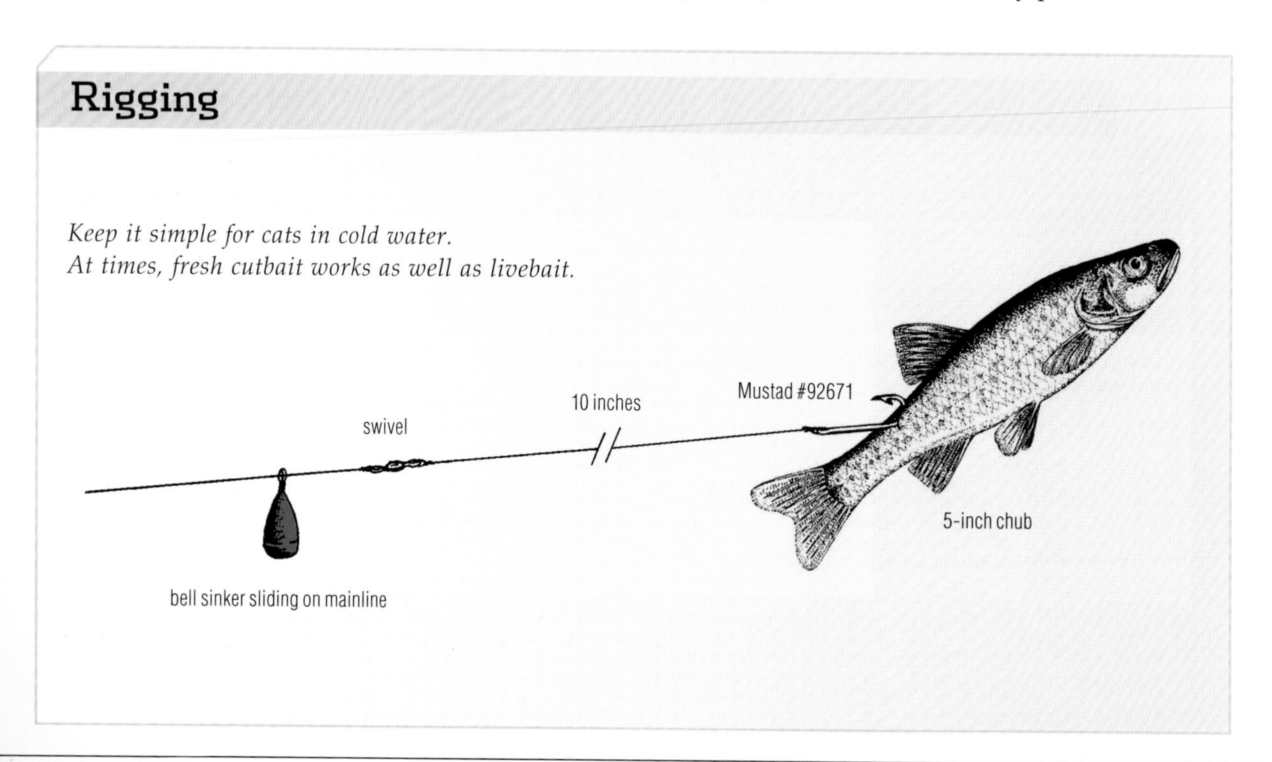

Keep it simple for cats in cold water. At times, fresh cutbait works as well as livebait.

Flatheads like chubs, too, but for flatheads I prefer bullheads about 5 inches long. Make the chubs about 5 inches long, 4 inches in smaller rivers with smaller channel cats. It's critical that the baits be lively. Hook live fish just through the skin on the back between the dorsal fin and tail.

Note again, that while I've caught channel cats even in very cold water, that's not the case with blues and flatheads. Again, though, most of the waters where I fish don't contain good populations of blue cats.

On the other hand, many of the waters I fish contain good populations of flatheads. We've mentioned a few possible reasons why they may become more difficult to catch when the water cools. Perhaps, too, the channel cats might be just so much more numerous that flatheads can't get at a bait. During summer, though, flatheads are so mean and nasty and aggressive that even a couple of them move channel cats right out of a hole. It must be the metabolic thing—flatheads get lethargic faster than channel cats—perhaps in combination with the fact that they've migrated downriver.

Almost forgot. At the beginning of this period, I've caught channel cats on lively ribbon leeches so popular for walleyes during summer. I haven't fished with leeches in extra-cold water. Rig a large leech on a black Northland Tackle Phelps Floater and a leader about 6 inches long. The rest of the rig is standard livebait rigging.

Rigging—Standard livebait sliprigging works. For flatheads, I slide a 2-ounce slipsinker onto my mainline. The leader consists of a swivel and 10 to 12 inches of mono, the same test as the mainline, rigged with about a 3/0 hook like the Mustad 92671. The farther your bait is from your sinker, the more snags you have to contend with. Use the same rigging for channel cats, but go with about a 1-ounce weight for smaller baits and reduce the hook size appropriately.

Tackle—Go with lighter tackle than you used during summer. So long as snags aren't a problem, for flatheads I use muskie-grade bucktail rods and casting reels loaded with 20-pound mono. For bigger channel cats, I go lighter with bass flippin' rods and casting reels loaded with 14-pound-test mono. Lighter line allows livebait to swim more actively.

Bait Placement—Active cats move to the head of a deep hole to feed, but during late fall they usually don't swim up into heavy current or move shallow enough to enter a riffle. Set at least one bait at the head of the hole in deeper water just away from current. Set another bait in the middle of the deepest part of the hole. Set other baits in deep slackwater alongside the hole.

Winter—Channel cats can be caught at first-ice and beyond from wintering holes, but it's another story. Catfish in wintering holes occasionally are caught by a walleye angler who snags one or, sometimes, even gets one to bite. For most of those anglers, it's the biggest deal they've ever hooked into. But it rarely says on the back of the photo that here moments before lay a sleeping cat, patiently waiting the winds of spring.

Then, too, there are those few who think the world is theirs alone and as a matter of greed cast snagging hooks or use electricity or nets or gig sticks to rob the world of these "banks" of catfish. This is like walking into our national treasury and removing the gold. These consolidated catfish are the very fish that eventually spread up and down the river during other seasons to provide our fishing. No one should take more than a harvestable share, a renewable share, so that cats will be there for future generations.

Warming Trends—For those of you looking for a winter break in latitudes on a line with and south of about southern Iowa, big-time warming trends for weeks in a row may melt thin ice and warm the water enough for cats to suddenly believe spring is upon them. In those moments in December, January, or February, cats become active. The baits of choice seem to be livebait or the same sourbaits that work well at ice-out during a normal spring. As Zacker said, we're looking for cold cats riding a warm southwest breeze.

HOT WALLEYE LURE REDISCOVERED! Page 73
MAY/JUNE 1995
the In-Fisherman
INCREDIBLE BAIT
SUPER BASS
Page 42
OUTBOARD MOTOR
GIVEAWAY!
FAB-FOUR
FLOATS
FOR CRAPPIES
Page 62
HOT
TRIP TIPS
page 32
PLUS:
• Tracking Smallmouths
• Secret Bass Perspective
• Targeting Tiger Muskies

Historic Perspectives

A story about Zacker gets the discussion started about a fishing system that has now been found workable for giant fish in most areas of the country where big flathead catfish swim, although it's just a vision in Stange's mind when this article is written in 1995.

Part of Stange's vision is brought better into focus after he fishes with ace limb line, log line, and pole line experts Red Rheums and Gary Van Pielt to get a better idea of how they make their near-surface sets. Rheums and Van Pielt may be the first such anglers to fish primarily for the sport of it, releasing most of the fish they catch on their set lines. That's "Uncle Red" with a 62-pound fish caught during a trip with Stange.

CHAPTER 24

MAY 1995

A Secret Near-Surface System for Giant Catfish

I WISH AT THE BEGINNING of this article that I was standing just about right over there in a spectacular photo, wet from head to toe from wrestling bankside with and then finally straining to hold up just an awful whopper of a flathead catfish. OK, so the fish would have to weigh 70 pounds to impress you folks from Oklahoma, maybe be a blue cat near 80 to get the attention of them that's old-school blue-cat boys from Kansas, Missouri, or Nebraskie. OK too, and so much the better if the photo were of you, to heck with me, I'd just as soon see you hang Old Hawg Lips anyway. Honest. Which is why I want to run this system by you. You're some of the best friends I have. Might just as well be all of us together doing the exploring and having all the fun.

In The Ring With Smokin' Joe!

The truth is that what I consider potentially the most productive part of this secret near-surface system exists only in my mind, has never been tried, has never lassoed even one giant flathead or big blue or channel cat. That's how come it's such a secret. I know, though, that it works because I've been round the block almost too many times by now, had the good fortune to fish with some of North America's best catmen, from old-school commercial boys and recreational poachers like Zacker, to gifted hook-and-line cat catchers like Toad Smith, and phenomenal limbline and trotline folks like Uncle Red Rheums. Shared a boat with Catfish Corner Bill Marsh, too. And many more. I've seen things and been told things that most hook-and-line anglers find hard to believe—I found them hard to believe at first too, but given time, well, hot-diggity, but there surely are some crazy things going on out there in the wild woods.

Some of the most interesting things have to do with that interface where the domain of big cats meets ours, at or near the surface of the water. I don't intend to get into all kinds of gollygee stories here, just enough to make the point that the biggest cats, particularly flatheads, but also blues and channels, feed big-time at or near the surface. Indeed, huge cats often eat big livebaits right off the surface over deeper water near shore. But these big cats also move shallow to push prey against the surface and the shore.

It was Zacker, truth be told, who first mentioned a pattern for flatheads moving into very shallow water in Missouri River sloughs (before the dams, in the '30s, '40s, and '50s) at a time that coincided with the first litters of bank-dwelling muskrat offspring reaching the ripe age when they first take to water. "Big flatheads moved so shallow their eyes were above water," Zacker used to say. "There they'd lie like alleygators."

Zacker used to block the entrance of a slough with a net. You know the rest of the story. Trapping was no sure thing, though. Saw a picture of Zacker once with a big sling on his arm. Seems he'd grabbed a pretty green 60-pound-class flathead by the lips just as it was about to escape into the darkness. Apparently, the cat wouldn't let go and neither would Zacker—there was a whole lotta twistin' and turnin' goin' on. "Sombritches broke my arm," Zacker said. "Hurt, too."

In more recent times, working those midnight hours on the river, I've seen flatheads wallowing shallow enough to see their eyeballs as they

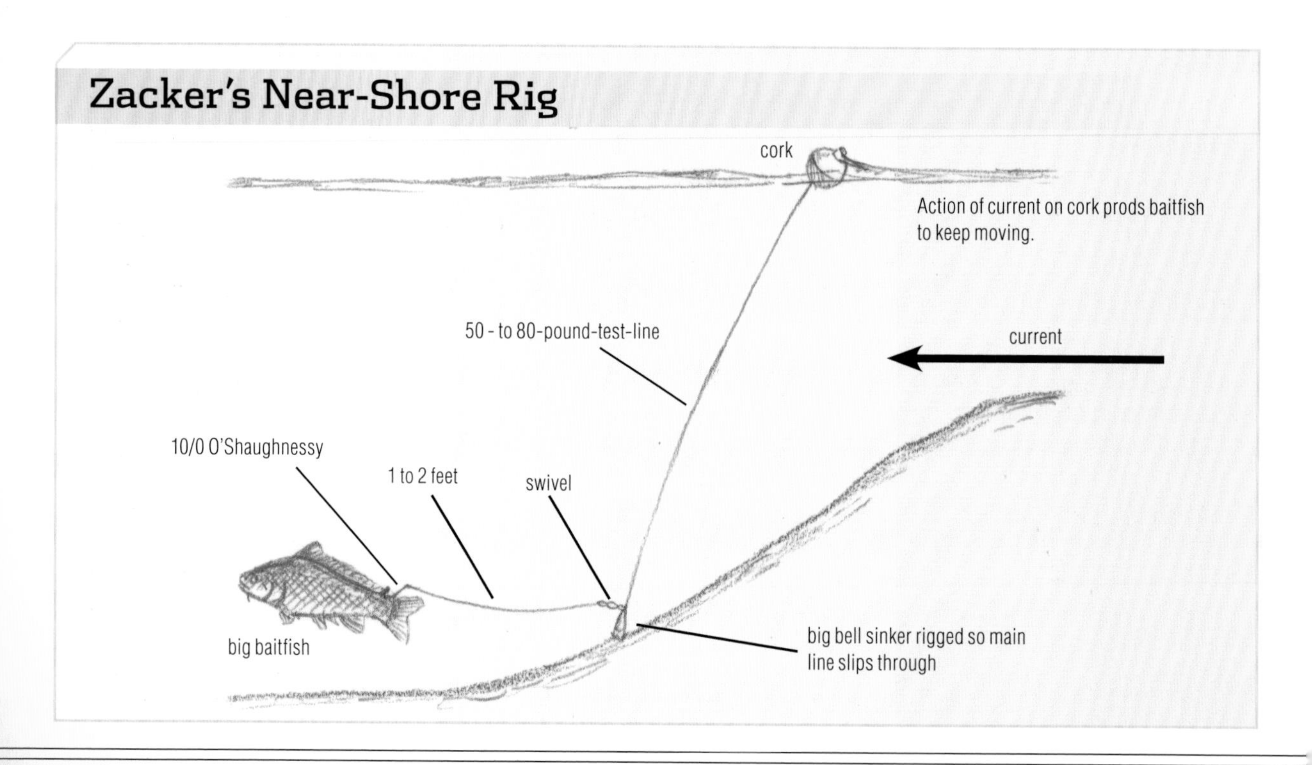

cornered carp and bullheads in shallow pools. I've seen big channel cats do the same thing to get frogs. Of course, too, it's common for folks who have spent serious time at night on a good river to hear flatheads gullup (Zacker's word) unsuspecting carp as the carp suck surface film in logjams. "Crush 'em like a bag o' bones," Zacker'd say. Then he'd cackle and wheeze. He liked the thought. Blue cats, too, often pin big shad and suckers right up against riverbanks, catching their prey as it rebounds off the bank.

Giant cats sure enough are freshwater sharks of the most serious and vicious sort. Problem these days is that most of the folks who experience this shark activity usually aren't rod-and-reel catmen but setliners—limbliners, logliners, dittystickers, trotliners. Good folks. Hardcore, lots of them. I hope those states that still allow these traditional forms of catfishing (noodlin' included) continue to do so. Agreed, though, the boys need the clamps put on 'em when it comes to harvesting big fish. This generation of setliners and grabbers needs to fish for sport and harvest selectively.

I was about to observe that rod-and-reel anglers generally get in a rut thinking that baits have to be set near bottom for cats, often as not in or at least near deep water. Setliners naturally think bottom, top, and everywhere in between. They know that the right bait will call a big cat in so long as it's set right. They also know catching the big boys is a nighttime affair, and that at night cats, often as not, feed up, not down.

Certainly, nearby deep water often is a key to big cats. The big boys aren't going to work inches of water during the day. Sometimes it's necessary to fish deep. But after dark, especially during the prime-time prespawn season in May and June, the big boys feed near the surface and beyond, often pushing into very shallow water.

The first time I fished rod-and-reel tactics with Zacker, we caught a pair of 30-pound flatheads that took baits we placed in a shallow eddy next to a big riffle area adjacent to a deep hole. He fished the baits not more than 10 feet offshore, while we sat by a small fire about 15 feet up the bank from where the rods were set. Each wild creek chub about 10 inches long spent half its time on or near the surface, struggling to get away. A slipsinker on the bottom and a big-old 2-inch-wide red-and-white cork above kept those baits working from top to bottom in that shallow water right near shore. English anglers would recognize this as a crude but effective paternoster rig.

"Big old bobber won't bother fish?" I asked.

"Cats don't know bobbers from sin," Zacker-said. "Might as well be a big stick for all they care. Just so a big cat don't eat the bobber. Happens."

"But when you fish a big chub under a big bobber, don't the fish ever reject the bait when they feel the resistance from the float?" I asked.

"Never," Zacker said. "When big cats is feeling just mean and nasty, sure enough sometimes they just kill the bait—crush it flat and say, 'There. Take that!' and leave it. But that's nothing to do with the float, just bad cat temperament. When they want something, resistance just makes 'em madder. Tie a line to a tree stump and if a big cat wants the bait, he'll struggle with it until he hooks himself. Smokin' Joe catfish, yes sirree. That's how setlining works."

Smokin' Joe catfish. I heard Zacker say it so often over the years that at one point I asked. Zacker was a boxing fan. He didn't have a TV in the house, but he'd hobble a mile down the road to a little backcountry bar to see a good fight on the tube. Told me he always packed a shotgun in case the boys at the bar was a-wantin' to watch *I Love Lucy* or some such rerun. (Actually, I think, as was sometimes the case, he exaggerated just a bit about the shotgun.) The boys used to tell me that on fight night he'd always come hobbling in with a big bag of catfish or paddlefish fillets. "Cook 'em up, boys," he'd howl. "And a yahoo!" Then he'd sit there and drink one Hamms—never more—and root for his man.

In later years, Joe Frazier was his man. Smokin' Joe. Might take Smokin' Joe a round or two to get into the swing of things, but once he'd been batted and butted good a time or two by a few Ali jabs or a Foreman hook, he got focused, his

A General Overview of Prespawn Catfish Location

May and June encompass the Prespawn Period for cats across much of North America. Cats are moving, looking, searching—hungry.

In ***large reservoirs,*** *cats use flats at the back one-third of large creek arms off the main reservoir. After the spawn, try points or flats nearer the mouth of the creek arm where it meets the main reservoir. The best creek arms usually are in the middle or lower portions of the reservoir nearer the dam. In dams without many creek arms, cats may move to the upper third of the reservoir—the shallowest portion, farthest from the dam.*

In ***smaller reservoirs,*** *try flats or points at the mouths of small creek cuts. Cats, particularly flatheads, also run riprap areas near bridges or causeways. Riprap along the face of the dam also attracts some cats.*

In ***ponds,*** *try just off structural elements like reed or bulrush points, places that roaming catfish funnel past. Cats also funnel into distinct pond corners, as well as up the proverbial creek that provides the water that sustains the pond.*

In ***lakes,*** *look for running water, first from feeder creeks or pouring in over dams in rivers that connect lakes. If feeder creeks or rivers are deep enough, cats feed in them. Otherwise they gather on the flats formed where current flows into the lake. Also check current caused by necked areas between portions of the lake. Bridges and adjoining causeways signal potential spots. Finally, in some lakes, cats also wander the flats at the mouth of marshy backwaters.*

Meanwhile,in ***large-pool rivers*** *like the Mississippi and Ohio, cats usually move upriver to the immediate tailwater. This is the best time of year for fishing along current breaks right below a dam. Cats, though, also use wing dams and closing dams, generally in the upper third of the reservoir. And channel cats, in particular, move into side-channel areas that often can be viewed as small rivers. They usually gather along current breaks caused by protruding structural elements. Check riprap shoreline stretches too.*

In ***small rivers,*** *look for barriers to cat movement upstream, the most obvious being a dam. Large, shallow, rocky riffles also stop cats in holes below the riffles, and so much the better if the hole offers cover in the form of fallen timber and brush. The biggest concentrations of catfish often are in the 3- to 5-mile stretch below a dam, or in the mile or so stretch of smaller river where it enters a larger river, lake, or reservoir.*

mind set. Once set on target, he was as relentless and tenacious as a pit bull and strong as a team of oxen in pursuit. Smokin' Joe didn't need to see an opponent. He was always close enough to feel him, to touch him, to crush him with one punch, just like a big cat in pursuit of prey. Smokin' Joe cats. It was a term of endearment and respect.

Eventually that night we could hear big cats working the surface along the deep bank across from us. "Don't suppose we should flip a bait over there?" I suggested. "Nope," he said. "Gotta keep the bait where fish can feel it thrashing about. We could set up over there if there was someplace to sit. Nope. Cats'll get here. Just give 'em . . . " Bawhoosh! zzzzzzzzzz—the clicker on the reel tracked line. "When big cats prowl, nothin's safe," Zacker said as he horsed the fish. "Everything hides. Nothin' moves. If it does, big cats can feel it. They track it down and kill it. They're lookin' to pin stuff shallow."

In recent times, one of the more impressive cat-be-goings-on I've seen have been the exploits of modern-day Kansas limb-, log-, and poleliners, Uncle Red Rhuems and Gary Van Pielt. Definitions: **Limbline and logline**—about a 10-foot piece of 500-pound waxed braided nylon line with a 12/0 Mustad or Eagle Claw Circle C hook or a 10/0 O'Shaughnessy, weighted down with an 8-ounce egg sinker. At about 4 feet from the top of each line, a 2-inch-wide by 12-inch-long section of rubber inner tubing is tied in as a shock absorber. Limblines are tied to tree limbs overhanging bankside cat-prowling areas. Loglines are tied to a heavy-duty spike driven into a log in a logjam over a cat hole. Prime baits for big-boy flatheads include 1-pound carp and other big baitfish. Big goldfish do in a pinch. Bullheads are good, too.

Polelines—The same braided nylon line and hook arrangement—without the rubber tubing—tied to the end of a 2-inch-diameter (tapering to 1-inch) 15-foot-long ash pole, run at a 30-degree angle into the bank to dangle a bait in a bankside cat hole. Have a lookie at my illustrations on the following pages, which explain the system as it exists in my

Possible Sets

Area A, *the mouth of a feeder creek, is a top spot all season, but it's the best of all spots when the water's high during early season. When the water's up, set inside the creek. When the water's down, set near the point where the creek meets the main river. This is a good spot to set one bait on a bank stick while working another bait below a float or a paternoster rig.*

Area B *is a bank spot just downstream from fallen timber cover. During early season when cats are moving and hungry, they tend to follow the bank when the water's up. The cover stops prey, and cats roam slack-water spots looking for food at or after dark.*

Area C, *an eddy area, is a top spot for cats after dark all season.* ***Area D,*** *the backside of an island, is a lot like* ***Area C*** *only tends to be even more productive during early season when cats are roaming. A better set spot inside the island can't be reached from our home base across the river.*

Obviously, you need a boat to make the sets from your home-base position. The farther away you set, the heavier the sinker on the dropline must be.

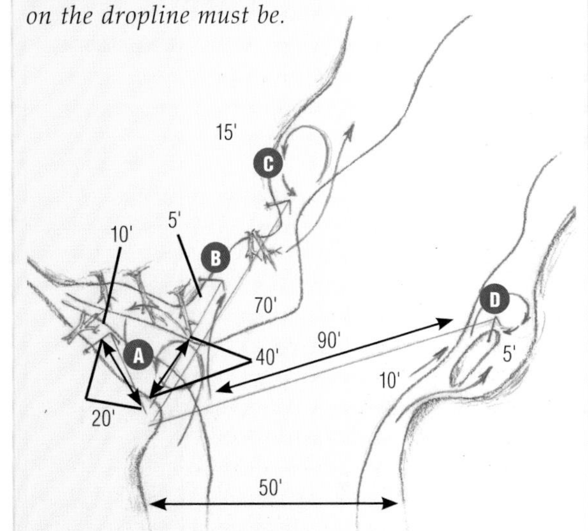

Near-Shore Options

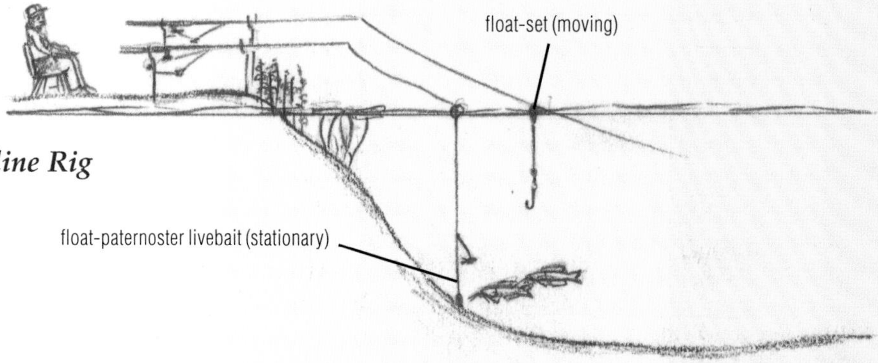

float-set (moving)

Need Headline Rig

float-paternoster livebait (stationary)

Float-Paternoster Rig

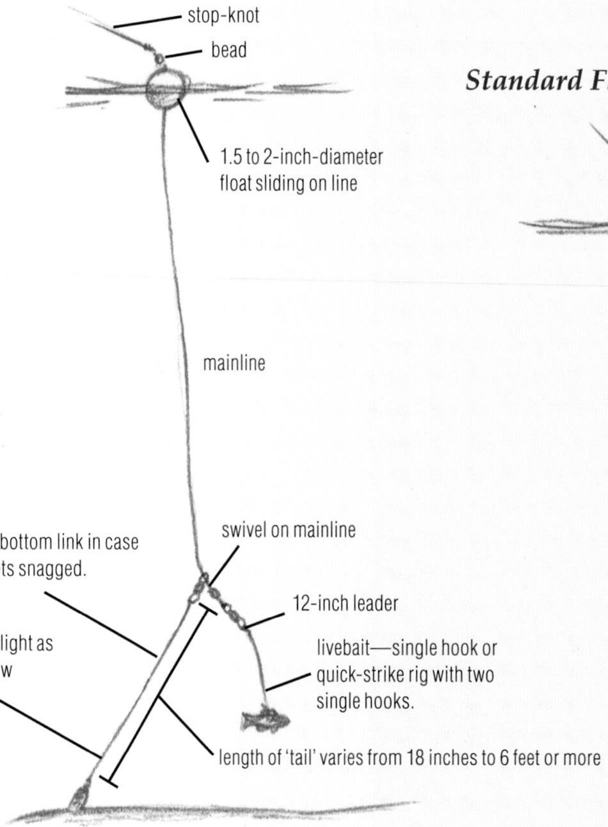

stop-knot

bead

1.5 to 2-inch-diameter float sliding on line

mainline

swivel on mainline

lighter bottom link in case lead gets snagged.

12-inch leader

lead weight as light as conditions allow

livebait—single hook or quick-strike rig with two single hooks.

length of 'tail' varies from 18 inches to 6 feet or more

Standard Float Set

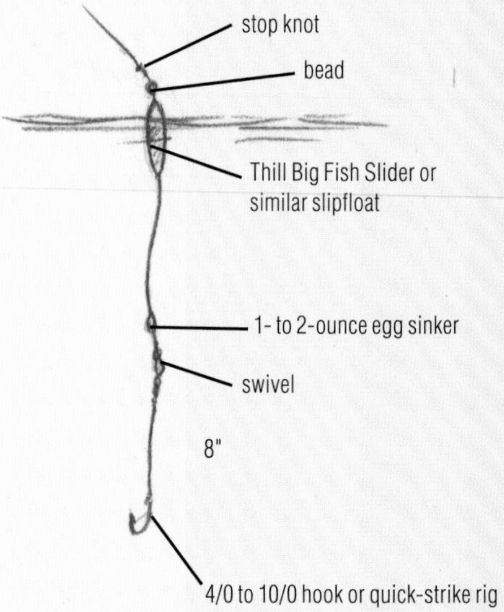

stop knot

bead

Thill Big Fish Slider or similar slipfloat

1- to 2-ounce egg sinker

swivel

8"

4/0 to 10/0 hook or quick-strike rig

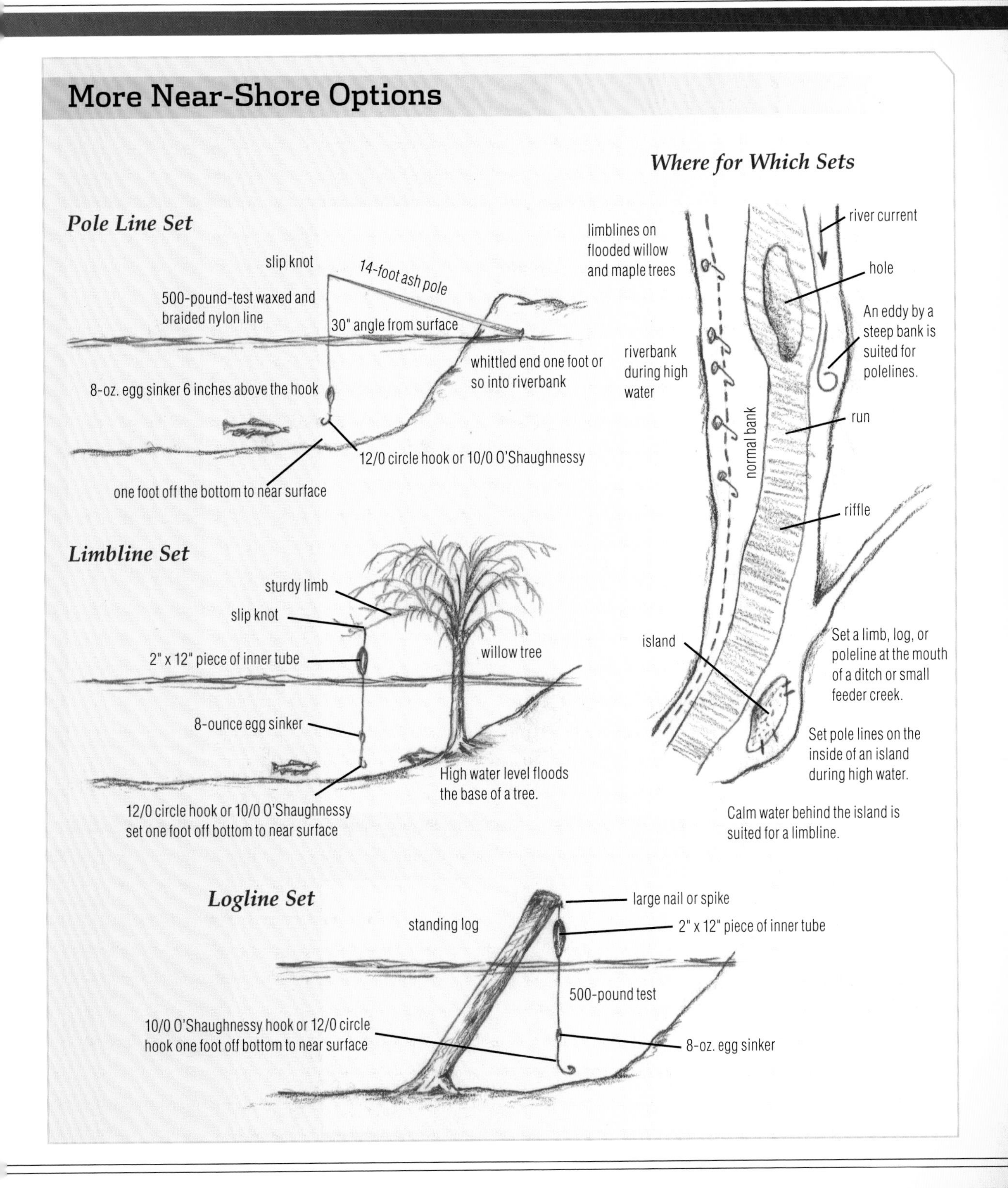
More Near-Shore Options
Pole Line Set
slip knot
14-foot ash pole
500-pound-test waxed and braided nylon line
30" angle from surface
whittled end one foot or so into riverbank
8-oz. egg sinker 6 inches above the hook
12/0 circle hook or 10/0 O'Shaughnessy
one foot off the bottom to near surface
Limbline Set
sturdy limb
slip knot
2" x 12" piece of inner tube
willow tree
8-ounce egg sinker
High water level floods the base of a tree.
12/0 circle hook or 10/0 O'Shaughnessy set one foot off bottom to near surface
Where for Which Sets
limblines on flooded willow and maple trees
river current
hole
An eddy by a steep bank is suited for polelines.
riverbank during high water
normal bank
run
riffle
island
Set a limb, log, or poleline at the mouth of a ditch or small feeder creek.
Set pole lines on the inside of an island during high water.
Calm water behind the island is suited for a limbline.
Logline Set
large nail or spike
standing log
2" x 12" piece of inner tube
500-pound test
10/0 O'Shaughnessy hook or 12/0 circle hook one foot off bottom to near surface
8-oz. egg sinker

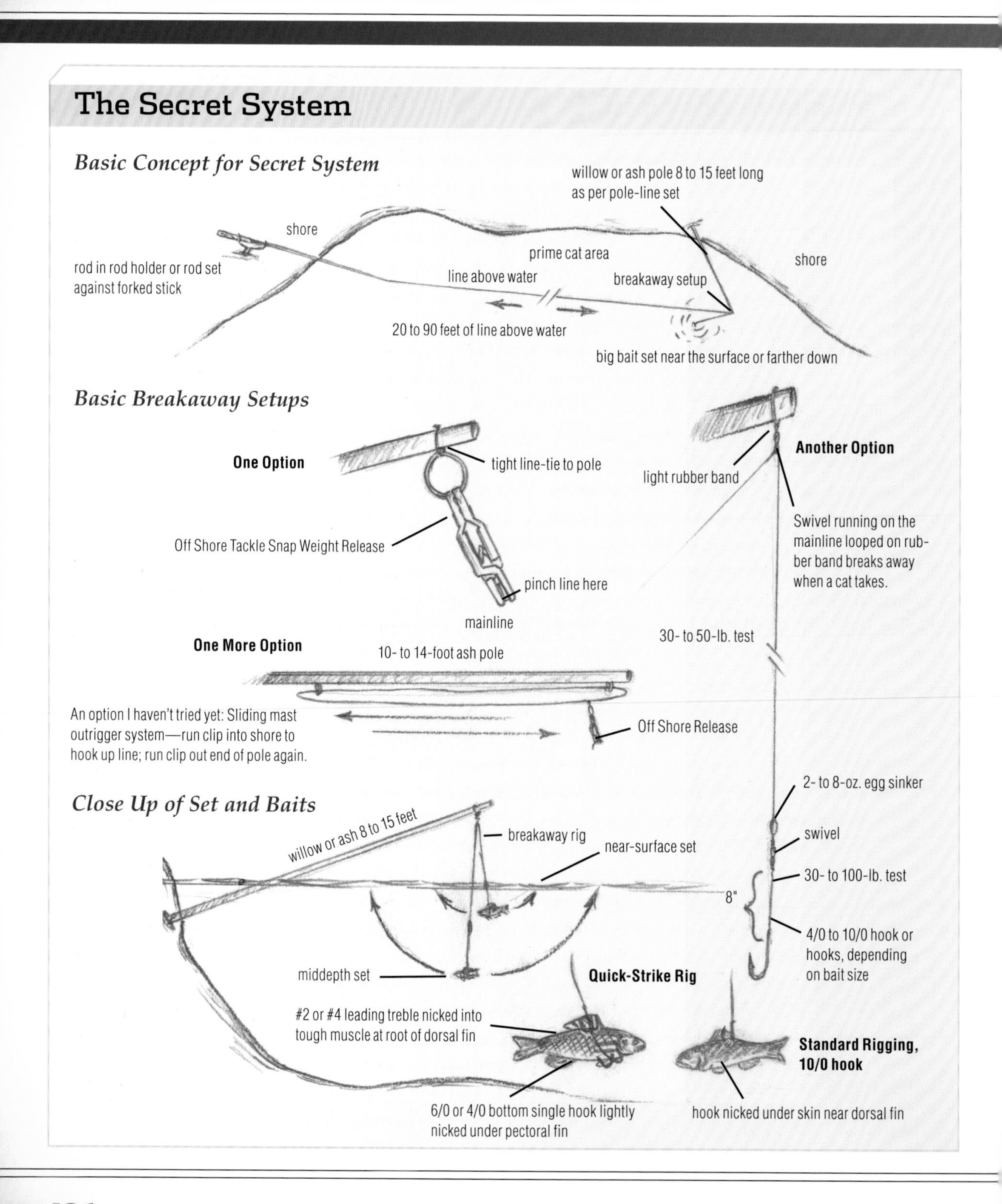

The Secret System
Basic Concept for Secret System
willow or ash pole 8 to 15 feet long
as per pole-line set
shore
rod in rod holder or rod set
against forked stick
prime cat area
shore
line above water
breakaway setup
20 to 90 feet of line above water
big bait set near the surface or farther down
Basic Breakaway Setups
One Option
tight line-tie to pole
Another Option
light rubber band
Off Shore Tackle Snap Weight Release
Swivel running on the
mainline looped on rub-
ber band breaks away
when a cat takes.
pinch line here
mainline
One More Option
10- to 14-foot ash pole
30- to 50-lb. test
An option I haven't tried yet: Sliding mast
outrigger system—run clip into shore to
hook up line; run clip out end of pole again.
Off Shore Release
Close Up of Set and Baits
2- to 8-oz. egg sinker
willow or ash 8 to 15 feet
breakaway rig
near-surface set
swivel
30- to 100-lb. test
8"
4/0 to 10/0 hook or
hooks, depending
on bait size
middepth set
Quick-Strike Rig
#2 or #4 leading treble nicked into
tough muscle at root of dorsal fin
Standard Rigging,
10/0 hook
6/0 or 4/0 bottom single hook lightly
nicked under pectoral fin
hook nicked under skin near dorsal fin

mind right now. I've included a few other more standard riggings for near-shore rod-and-reel sets. I want to know how you do, including what you do to modify the system. Let's get together to report our findings from this season for an article in early 1996. Send photos, you bet. If you catch old Smokin' Joe, release him, though, because he's probably older than you and smarter than me.

THE SECRET SYSTEM

May and June encompasses the Prespawn Period across most of cat country. Cats are moving and hungry. One drawback to this period is that rainfall often fills rivers right up to the banks. Actually, this can be a blessing. During this period of intense activity, cats are forced to seek feeding grounds. Many catfish move into the mouths of what were small feeder creeks or rivers, places that at normal water levels wouldn't attract many catfish. Usually, too, not many of these places exist, so plenty of competition arises among the catfish that use these areas.

This is prime time for the big boys. In rivers with channel cats, blues, and flatheads, big flatheads and blues dominate prime feeding areas. Small cats move or get chewed on. Only the biggest channel cats hold their own in this competitive environment. Much of the feeding still takes place at night or during twilight, even though the water's dingy.

In spots, say no more than 6 feet deep, just set the bait about halfway down. The bait naturally spends plenty of time wallowing near the surface. It's the surface or near-surface frolicking that calls big cats. In deeper areas, just get the bait down a foot or so.

Big cats, particularly big blues and flatheads, come to the siren call of a big baitfish struggling shallow. So effective is this system we outlined in *In-Fisherman* in February 1994 that Minnesota fishery scientists, faced with high water and the task of catching enough cats to conduct a tagging study, abandoned nets and electrofishing in favor of Rheums' and Van Pielt's setline system.

I believe we can use the best information and rigging methods from the setline boys, modify their rigging, and make similar rod-and-reel sets for big cats. You might note, of course, that successful setlining relies on dozens of sets, while at best we're allowed a couple of rod-and-reel sets apiece. Yeah, well? Success still is a matter of setting the right bait in the right place at the right time. I've had nights where I scored a dozen big cats. Over the course of a season, though, a good night with rod and reel is one big fish a night. This system is potentially a way to increase your odds that some of those big fish are huge.

Blue cats also bite specialized near-surface livebait sets, as shown by Gary Van Pielt.

{ Historic Perspectives

Many of the tackle recommendations noted herein are by now dated, but this is for its time the most exceptional information ever offered about doing battle with heavy-duty catfish. Stange sets the scene with stories about the hallowed waters where Ed Elliot caught the former world-record blue catfish—an area Stange later fishes—and talks with some of the big-cat boys fishing that stretch of the Missouri River during an era for giant fish (interesting historic perspective). On target too is Stange's prediction that catfishing is poised in 1995 for a renaissance in fishing for giant blue cats. If you want to take the step from average catfish angler to big-cat man, this article is fundamental to success.

Illustration by Ron Finger

CHAPTER 25

JULY 1995

Heavy-Duty Cats

Tackling Up For Big Mama!

MAYBE YOU WON'T MIND A STORY about a special time and place and the unusual circumstances that caused them back in the late 1950s. I wasn't old enough to fish the Big Mo (Missouri River) back then, but that old-timer Zacker was there, and I've talked to several other old buzzards who could still cackle up a story or two about fishing for some of the biggest blue cats in the history of the rod-and-reel scene.

Blue cats were originally fish of big rivers. Today, they also reside in reservoirs, particularly reservoirs fed by big rivers. Blues range farther and at times work heavier current than channel cats and flatheads. They're also probably the biggest of the cat clan, even more likely than flatheads to surpass 100 pounds.

In the old days, blues ranged up the Missouri as far as Pierre, South Dakota. Then, with construction of the Gavin's Point dam at Yankton, South Dakota, about 150 miles southeast of Pierre, the fish were stopped short. Cats that would have spread upriver congregated in the 20- to 30-mile-or-so section below Gavin's Point.

Zacker always used to say that big cats grouped in the same territory are like a bunch of roosters stuffed into a hen house. Don't work. After the "peck-ordering" gets done all good cat holes have

Ed Elliot's blue cat record stood for 30 years.

a big boy or two or three, while small cats—10s, 20s, and 30s—are pushed into lesser terrain. A handful of old-time cat-sackers like Zacker soon discovered this unique opportunity for big fish.

One of the best spots was at the mouth of the James River where it entered the Missouri below Yankton. This was a big eddy hole away from the main river flow, however, and the boys mostly considered it a spot for flatheads which, as I've said, generally prefer less current than blues. The big blues apparently pushed up to the dam and then dropped back into the series of sandbar holes some 25 to 30 feet deep.

This, by the way, is how it still works today in river sections below dams on big rivers where big blues roam. Always some big cats in the tailwater, but most of the biggest boys don't hold there for long after May and June. Those old cat-sackers knew those just-a-little-bit-downriver holes were the ticket at night in July and August.

Some of the boys anchored in heavy current and fished the head of holes in the main river flow. Others set up along the edge, where the bank flat dropped off into a hole. Sometimes, too, when the river was really ripping, the boys fished holes behind bridge abutments.

The 97-pound blue caught by Ed Elliot in 1959, which was the world record for more than 30 years, came from a big sandbar hole in this area. I was lucky at age 10, a fledgling cat kid, to see the frozen fish on display in the Lewis Drug Store in Sioux Falls, South Dakota. I remember running the line—still in the fish's mouth—through my fingers, marveling at how heavy it was.

Later I learned that many of those old boys tackled up pretty much the same way—with Dacron "squidding" line (cord, almost) testing up to 120 pounds, spooled on a Penn 209 or 309, coupled with a heavy-action 6- or 7-foot Penn saltwater rod of one model or another. The baits were big and freshly killed, usually suckers or redhorse with the head squashed, the tail and other fins removed, and slashes cut down the sides of the bait to ooze juices. Big sections of fresh cutbait, usually part of a side off a 1- to 2-pound baitfish, were popular, too.

A big bait like that was fished on a 10/0 O'Shaughnessy—Mustad or Eagle Claw—held down with about an 8-ounce bell sinker. The rod was then set tip up at a 30-degree angle over the gunnel, the butt secured with a sandbag or some such thing, and the freespool mechanism on the reel tightened so the reel would just click steadily when a fish took in the heavy current.

The heavy line was necessary because the fish were mostly fought from anchor—too dangerous to up anchor and run down the Big Mo in pitch darkness after monster catfish. Lines in those days also weren't of such consistent quality as they are today. Twenty pounds or so margin of error was a blessing on many a night, given the things that could go wrong in the dark with a huge fish on.

A RENAISSANCE

We're ready for a renaissance in fishing for monster blue cats. For that matter, plenty of huge flatheads roam big rivers and reservoirs, too. Even plenty of smaller waters hold flatheads heavy enough to tear the average angler a new bean barker.

The monsters are here now, perhaps not quite so large as in the 1800s but seemingly bigger than a generation ago. Perhaps it's because today blues in particular have the opportunity to feed and sulk in huge reservoirs during some seasons—territory unknown to cats two generations ago. Then they can pick right up and run a stretch of big river above or below the reservoir.

Taming such fish takes time. You have to find the fish and get them to bite, and you must have the talent to handle the big boys once they're hooked. You need good tackle. Doesn't have to be that expensive. A few well-planned purchases stand a lifetime of duty for big cats.

Exactly what you need depends on the situation. Takes sturdier tackle to bully a 20-pound flathead to the bank from a snag area in a small river, than to waylay a 50-pound blue from a boat hovering in open water over a reservoir channel—unless that channel bank is lined with stumps.

The thing about big cats, whether they be monster blues, flatheads, or record-class channel cats, is that often you really don't dare give much quarter once you've stuck a fish. As I've noted, many environments are snag-infested—most environments have at least some snags and debris. Many battles with big cats are an attempted no-give, take-all contest with a cat using every muscle to turn away from pressure so it can take line into a snag. Every time you give much ground, chances increase that the catfish might be lost to a miscalculation.

In a lot of cases the cat angler after record-class fish sports tackle heavy enough to waylay a 700-pound bluefin tuna. Toby Cat, though, usually lives near a terrible tangle, while Charlie Tuna swims the deep blue waters of the open sea. Give an inch and Toby's gone.

Get geared up right and often even the largest cat won't take much line. Every head rip from the cat, however, snaps your rod tip down and punches the rod butt into your midsection. You need to be knees bent, back straight, in the best athletic position possible. Tug-of-war time. Tough duty. You win or you lose right now. It's the closest thing in freshwater fishing to putting a half-nelson on Hulk Hogan and just holding on.

Medicine for Big Cats 1995

Left to right: The 7-foot Shimano Titanos TA-70M and Shimano TLD 20/40S spooled with 30-pound Stren High Impact; the 6.5-foot Zebco Blue Runner BRGC66MT and Penn GTi330 spooled with 50-pound Ande Classic; the 6-foot Zebco Blue Runner BRGC60M and Garcia 7000 spooled with 50-pound Silver Thread AN40; and the 10.5-foot Shimano Titanos TA-106MH and TLD20 loaded with 40-pound Berkley Big Game.

I've landed 500-pound sharks. The pressure from a 30-pound flathead or a 50-pound blue is shortlived by comparison, but momentarily as intense in tight quarters. Too, a horsed catfish is still green at net. You can give a little line once the fish is away from trouble, but you still must control the fish at net. You're going to get bruised and wet.

RODS

Shorter rods provide more leverage with less torque and are therefore better for horsing fish, with less strain on you. Little-bit-longer rods make it easier to cast baits, but mean more torque on you when you fight fish. In theory, the best rod for an intense battle in close quarters is either a medium-fast or fast-action heavy-power casting rod measuring 5.5 feet. On the other hand, the best rod for a long-distance cast into a tailrace area, or from shore in a reservoir creek arm, is something on the order of a 10- to 12-foot medium-fast-action and medium-power surf-style casting or spinning rod.

This tackle is pretty much saltwater or muskie variety. Given that few of you have access to tackle shops with saltwater tackle, you might try a Bass Pro Shops Offshore catalogue or call directly to companies to get catalogues and the name of a dealer nearest you.

Casting rods—We work with Zebco Blue Runner tackle when we film saltwater shows for the In-Fisherman Television Specials. Two saltwater casting sticks that transfer perfectly to freshwater duty for big cats are the 6-foot BRGC60M, a medium-action medium-power stick rated for lines testing 15 to 40 pounds and lures weighing 1 to 4 ounces; and the 6.5-foot BRGC66MH, a medium-heavy-action and medium-heavy-power stick rated for lines testing up to 50 pounds and lures up to 5 ounces.

Line recommendations for company rods and reels are just that, by the way, not the 11th commandment lost by Moses on his way down the mountain. Load up with heavier line if the situation calls for it.

The lighter stick has a pleasant action that works for flatheads in smaller rivers. Backed by 50-pound test, the rod works with you to drag big fish from snaggy water. I'm pretty sure you could drag a 50 out on his ear, although I've yet to catch one that big from smaller water. The rod also works well for short-range fishing in open water from a boat or a bank position. Casts up to about 100 feet are possible with this rod.

The heavier (and a little longer) stick allows easier casts with heavier baits. Coupled with about 80-pound line, a stick like this one would be my choice to whip a world record in a tight corner. In open water, you can drop to 40- or 50-pound line.

Each company that makes saltwater casting rods offers rods comparable to the Blue Runners. Consider the same categories of rods in slightly longer models—say a maximum of 6.5 to 7 feet—if you think you can bully a fish with them. Again, rods a little bit longer cast and handle baits more easily.

For water without snags, saltwater spinning gear is an option, albeit on the light end of the scale. You can't bully fish with spinning tackle like you can with casting tackle, but you certainly can beat big fish in unobstructed water. I've used Shimano Sojourn SJ-70M rods (7-foot medium-action medium-power, rated for 30-pound line and lures up to 2 ounces) to beat a dozen tarpon over 100 pounds and sharks to 200 pounds. Coupled with 30- or 40-pound line, you can cast a big bait a fur piece and beat any cat in freshwater, so long as snags aren't a problem.

Surf rods—On the need-for-distance end of the scale, step up to heavy surf rods. The physics doesn't change, folks. Longer rods allow less control, less ability to bully. Casting tackle bullies better than spinning tackle. Use the shortest surf rods you can get away with—7-footers, if possible.

In the casting category, a rod like the Shimano Titanos TA-70MH is a mighty mean stick—a 7-footer that handles line to 40 pounds and baits to 6 ounces. For casting farther, step up to a Titanos TA-106MH—a 10.5 -footer that handles line to about 40 pounds and baits to 10 ounces.

Learn to use a shock leader for surf-style casting. Knot books from Berkley, Stren, Ande, and other companies show how to tie the Uni-Jam, Albright Special, and other knots for connecting heavy tippet to lighter backing.

In the spinning category are surf rods like the Zebco 8-foot Blue Runner BRGS80 and 10-foot BRGS10, medium-heavy-action, medium-heavy-power rods. The 8-foot rod handles line testing 30 pounds and lures to 8 ounces. The longer rod handles line to 40 or 50 pounds and lures up to about 10 ounces. Heavier surf tackle in the spinning category includes Shimano Sojourn rods, the 7-foot SJ-70MH (40-pound line and 5-ounce baits) and the 11-foot SJ-10M (40-pound line and 10-ounce baits).

I've mentioned rods I've had my hands on, out in cat terrain. Other companies offer comparable rods you might prefer.

REELS

Casting reels—For short-distance work, you can load a reel with heavier line than recommended and still get good performance. The Garcia 7000, for example, holds about 225 yards of 20-pound test. I load it with 50 for heavy-duty work in close quarters. The Shimano TR-200G is another fine reel in this category. Distance casting, though, requires a drop in the recommended line category.

To fish heavier at long distance, try a reel like the Penn 500M, which handles 300 yards of 30, or on the top end still casts well with about 240 yards of 40. The 500M isn't a level wind, however. Initially, freshwater anglers sometimes find it puzzling to have to spool line with a finger, but if I can do it, you can. If you insist on a level wind, try a Penn GTi 330, which costs only a little more. The Shimano TLD 20/40S is another top reel in this category—not a level wind.

The main danger in "over-lining" is that the reel spindle will bend in a no-give contest. The Garcia 7000 is on the light end of the spectrum for super-heavy work. To deal in tight quarters with fish that might weigh more than 60 pounds, I'd load a reel like the Penn 500M with 80 and hold on. Hundred-pound test on the 500M is stretching it, but I wouldn't rule it out in the right situation.

The next step up for you folks who are strictly searching for a world record in snag-infested water is just a guess on my part. I've used the Shimano TLD25, which holds 350 yards of 50-pound line, coupled with the Zebco Blue Runner BRCG66MH, to handle substantial sharks and tuna in saltwater. For big cats, you can easily load with 80- or 100-pound test for battle at short range.

Spinning reels—No spinning reels offer the cranking power to make them feasible for record-class cats in tight quarters. In open water, however, you can certainly whip a big boy with 20- or 30-pound line. Many anglers also prefer spinning reels coupled with a surf-casting rod. To make do, a reel must have a large diameter spool and hold enough line.

Penn 7500SS and 8500SS reels are noted for their dependability over dozens of years of heavy-duty work in saltwater. The reels hold 250 and 325 yards of 20-pound line, respectively, although you can hike up to 30-pound line on the 8500SS. The Shimano BTR6500 BaitRunner Plus is another strong option—185 yards of 30-pound. Also check the Daiwa Black Gold BG90 (225 yards of 30), Mitchell Orca OR90 (325 yards of 25), and the Zebco Great White GW80 (350 yards of 20).

LINE

The rule still holds: Use the lightest break-strength line you can get away with, not because catfish are wary of heavy line, but because lighter line is more manageable and allows longer casts. I use monofilament lines that have proven tough and strong in saltwater—Ande Premium or Ande Classic, PRADCO Silver Thread AN40, Berkley Big Game, and Stren High Impact.

I'm most familiar with the Ande lines and the Silver Thread AN40, having used both extensively in saltwater and for four years in freshwater for big cats. Ande Classic is the tough guy in this crowd—a little thicker, with a slick, tough skin. I've landed tarpon with 20-pound Ande Classic frayed almost in half on bridge abutments. It's an amazingly tough line.

I haven't had that much experience with the superbraids, the so-called superlines that hit the market two years ago. Superbraids (Spiderwire, Stren Kevlar, Fenwick Iron Thread, Berkley Ultra Max, to name a few) don't stretch and therefore are super-sensitive. They should work fine, particularly for manhandling big cats. But we might have to reconfigure fish-fighting tactics and perhaps use rods with more give.

Superbraids, by the way, while very thin and strong, aren't particularly abrasion resistant because they're so thin. Around cover, lines testing at least 80 pounds probably are required to offer the thickness to be sufficiently abrasion resistant.

HOOKS

With all this talk of 10/0 hooks, an angler might get the idea that big hooks are required to land big cats. Actually, use the smallest hook you can get away with. Cats have a mouth with plenty of soft flesh. Small hooks bite more quickly than big hooks. Big cats also have tremendous jaw muscles. When a cat clamps down, a smaller hook moves more easily on a hook-set.

Hook Positions
Below a float, the hook should be horizontal with, not perpendicular to, the alignment of the dorsal fin.
on a bottom rig in slow to moderate current or slackwater
for very heavy current
The traditional O'Shaughnessy design remains a top choice for big cats.
10/0
7/0
5/0
2 to 3 inches
tandem-rigging below a float
The 7/0 Kahle-style hook is a good choice in heavy current when threaded with smaller chunks of baitfish.
7/0
Cut or chunked baitfish threaded on a Kahle or wide-gap hook, a good presentation for blue cats and channel cats in heavy current. Skipjack herring filleted and chunked are the favored bait in the South. Shad, suckers, goldeyes, and other oily baits work, too.
The Eagle Claw 84 (top) and Mustad 92671 are fine, simple designs for all but the toughest duty.

Of course, hook size and style must be tailored to the situation. Any hook, large or small, must be sturdy enough to match your rod, reel, and line. The light-wire Aberdeen, so popular among crappie anglers (to use an extreme example), bends straight in an instant when coupled with no-give cat tackle. But then in tight quarters with no-give heavy-duty cat tackle, other popular hook designs

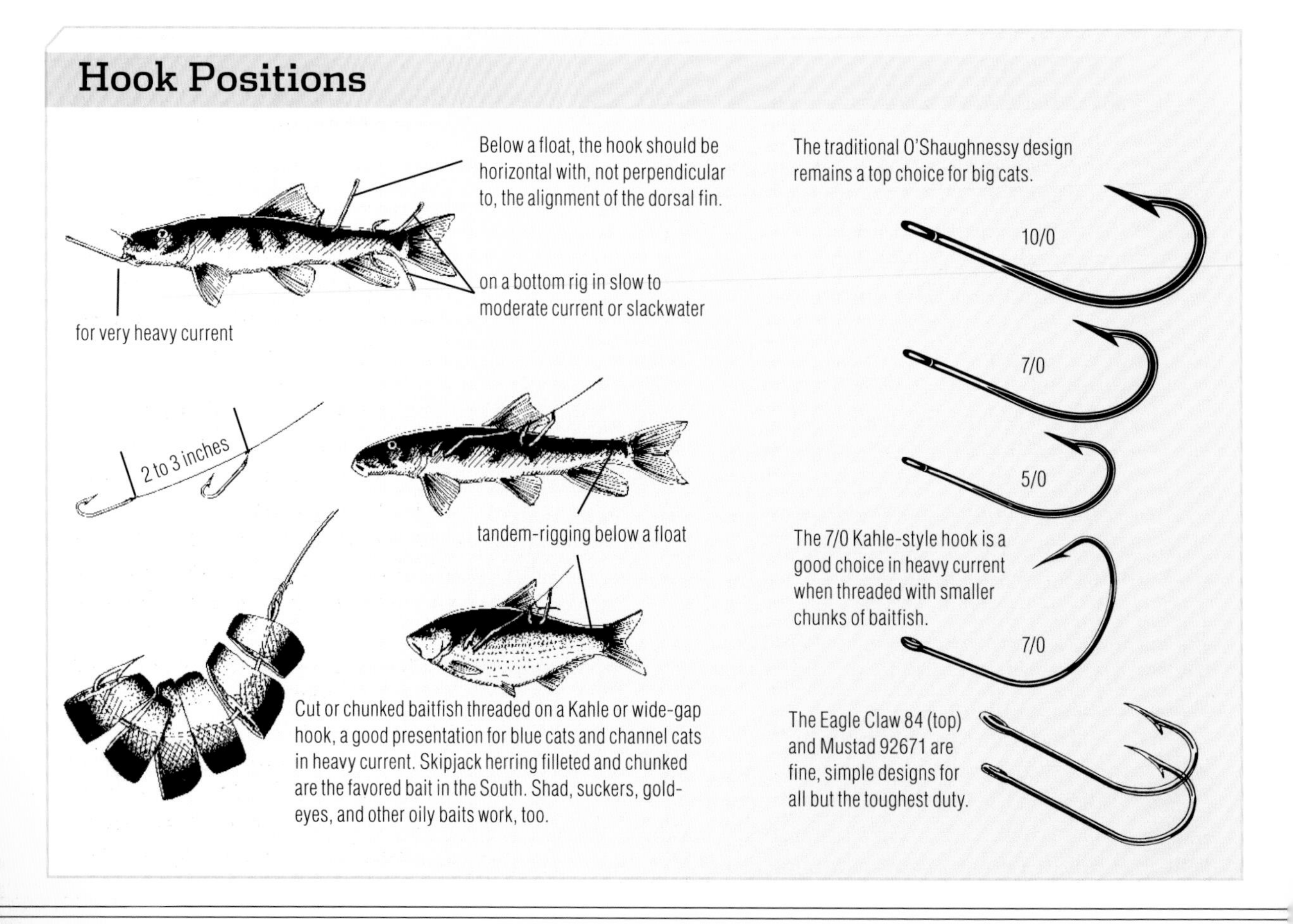

for cats—I'll mention them in a moment—also straighten out. First, another thought.

Once you've chosen a sturdy hook design, match the size of the hook to the type and size of the bait. Big blue cats and channel cats often go for a single strip of cutbait with a hook slipped once through the skin so the hook point remains exposed. This doesn't require a huge hook. On the other hand, big flatheads are best tempted with big livebaits, perhaps suckers, carp, or goldfish weighing a pound or more. A small hook is too likely to set back into the bait, not break free and find catfish flesh. Big baits generally require a bigger hook, one with a gap sufficient to prevent the hook from setting into the bait.

Perhaps the sturdiest and most versatile hook design for big cats is one of the oldest, the same hook used by catmen generations ago. I've fished for almost 40 years with the nickel Eagle Claw 254N and bronze Mustad 3406 O'Shaughnessy designs. Should you break off on a fish, the hook will rust away. Sizes range from less than 1/0 up to 10/0, plus a 12/0 and a 14/0. A 5/0 is a good choice for a strip of cutbait; a 7/0 is for bluegills and other livebaits measuring up to about 7 inches. Switch to a 10/0 for bait in the pound class.

The Mustad 92671 and Eagle Claw 84, both a modified sproat design with a shorter shank than the O'Shaughnessy and a beaked point, are other simple sturdy hooks I often recommend. Both hooks are available in sizes to 10/0. The 92671 and 84 are sufficient for all but the most brutal situations—neither design is quite so sturdy as the 3406 and 254.

Hooks are an engineering marvel. The subtleties in performance between one design and another, once understood, often mean better fishing. The hooks I've mentioned are affordable top performers. Explore similar options from VMC, Gamakatsu, Owner, and other companies, as well as different hook styles.

The Kahle design, for example, is a top performer for blue cats and channel cats when you need to pack small chunks of baitfish on a hook to make a big package from small offerings. The Kahle fishes well in current, but likely bends out when coupled with the heaviest tackle. A 7/0 Kahle, however, may be a fine option in the relatively open water frequented by blue cats in reservoirs and rivers. I could go on about hooks. Some other time.

Dwane Clodfelder

Toad Smith discussing tactics for Big Mama with Ed Elliot, whose blue catfish of 97 pounds was a record that stood for 30 years.

ON DOWN A NEW RIVER ROAD

A well-balanced rod and reel loaded with just the right line is an object of fine function as well as beauty. The right combinations are as easy on the eye and pleasant to hold in hand as they are powerfully reassuring in battle. And the right combinations can last a lifetime.

You realize, though, that we still live in a world where cat anglers, just over 7 million strong, are mostly ignored by tackle manufacturers. I know of no rod manufactured specifically for catfish, although many rods and reels and most lines are applicable to catfishing. I know we all look forward to the day when manufacturers realize that catmen want and need rods designed for catfishing.

I insist, too, before we spend millions more on rods and reels from any company, that those rods and reels be hawked by a generation of noteworthy and respectable catmen—for every topnotch bassman like Tommy Martin, a catman like Toad Smith or some other noteworthy individual yet to be discovered.

Maybe in a generation soon coming?

Historic Perspectives

Here is a poignant prophesy about what must happen to insure a future for catfishing in North America—including a passionate plea to usher in a new day for catfish. The Catfish Guide becomes, as discussed here, the first publication in history to focus solely on catfish, following in the footsteps of the earlier In-Fisherman magazine promise to feature a catfish article in every issue—also a historic undertaking in the name of catfish. We mention once before, that like bass, trout, and salmon before them—whose champions were James Henshall and Jason Lucas, Joe Brooks, and Lee Wulff—here catfish have found their advocate.

CHAPTER 26

OCTOBER 1995

A New Era for Catfishing

An Open Letter About The Future Of Catfishing!

MY FELLOW CATFISHING FRIENDS: I'm reminded of the time our preacher, a fine Lutheran fellow, forgot to invite my Grandma Stange to a Saturday summer social at our local park. Realizing his mistake, a serious social error in a small farming community in Iowa in the 1960s, he called at the last minute to say the mistake had been inadvertent. With apologies, an invitation remained for 1 o'clock the next day.

"Too late," Grandma informed the preacher. She'd already prayed for rain.

It would be just as remiss of us not to invite you, our best friends, to a big catfish event planned for February. Coming on February 6, 1996, to newsstands near you is the *Catfish Guide,* an annual In-Fisherman publication. As I say in the introduction to the new magazine, the *Catfish Guide* marks history that I've hoped for and worked for much of my life. So far as I know, it is the first national magazine ever devoted to catfishing—a historic moment in sportfishing.

Methods for Santee-Cooper blues transfer nicely to blues in Oklahoma and Arkansas. Cat anglers just need the opportunity to exchange information.

In my mind, the *Catfish Guide* symbolically marks the beginning of a new era in sportfishing, an era in which catfish and catfish anglers finally begin to receive equal treatment and time. We see necessary changes coming on several fronts. It's about time.

ANGLER INFORMATION

Catfishermen need more information about how to catch catfish—I suppose as editor in chief of *In-Fisherman* and a hardcore catfisherman at heart, I've had the opportunity to travel and meet more catmen than most folks have. I was also in a position to observe, from a unique vantage point, the scene as the most historic period in sportfishing unfolded—a 20-year span that included unprecedented growth in general fishing information and technology, a period that spawned the tremendous popularity of bass fishing, plus a new generation of walleye fishermen, along with a renaissance in fly-fishing.

Yet catfishermen generally haven't been part of this boom. At least a good part of the problem has been a matter of press—press coverage, the powerful pen, the slick spin. Of course, bass are great sportfish. So too are trout, walleyes, and crappies. The proof, though, is in no more than people saying so; for by any measurable criteria, each fish is no more than different—although certainly a case can be made for catfish, which happen to be smarter and warier and fight harder and get bigger than all those other species. No, say it again, part of the problem is a matter of a lack of press.

Catfish, a compelling character, don't need another Ray Scott so much as they need equal time. Wherever I go, I meet catfishermen who have information to offer other catfishermen. Catmen from Tennessee know things that can help catmen from Kansas and vice versa. The techniques we use for flatheads in Minnesota, with slight modification, are applicable to flatheads in California and Mississippi. Methods for Santee-Cooper blues transfer nicely to blues in Oklahoma and Arkansas.

The problem is that catfishermen haven't had the opportunity for the sort of discourse afforded bass, walleye, and trout anglers over the past 20 years. When, for example, a new bass-angling technique is discovered, the press quickly spreads the message across North America. Catfishermen have had no such consistent way to spread information nationwide, except for continuing articles appearing in *In-Fisherman* magazine the past five years.

Those articles, while vital and certainly the groundwork for our opportunity to do the *Catfish Guide,* can't begin to rival the comprehensive coverage offered bass and walleye anglers over the years. Catfishermen need the opportunity to talk to each other, to pass along information, to ask questions and search for answers. At least a few answers to puzzling questions you have about catfishing or catfish behavior have been solved or addressed by others; you just haven't had the opportunity to hear about it.

That catfishermen want such information is apparent from the response to information in *In-Fisherman.* Corresponding with our publication of articles about catfishing, the number of In-Fishermen who fish for catfish has grown to 1 in 3 readers. You therefore join an audience of 100,000 others reading this letter about one of your favorite fish. This number, though, is but a small reflection of the larger angling world, where national surveys suggest that catfish anglers number at least 7 million, a sixth or so of the total angling force, a force second only to bass anglers, trout anglers, and panfishermen.

The *Catfish Guide* marks the beginning of a new era in the transfer of information among catfishermen.

FINE-QUALITY CATFISHING PRODUCTS

Anglers need fine-quality products targeted specifically to catfishing—Again, national surveys suggest that catfish anglers are about 7 million strong, about one-sixth of the U.S. angling force. That's a healthy market force, the last remaining plum to be picked by folks who make a living on fishing tackle and related paraphernalia.

That powers in tackle manufacturing and marketing begin to see the market potential of this group of anglers is important to nurturing this new era. The American enterprise system works. A market inspires competitive products that require advertising, which funds media coverage of fishing tackle and techniques that further fuels the market. The right advertising—that is, advertising that illustrates the status quo as well as defining the cutting edge of what's available in the marketplace—is a vital reader service.

Major manufacturers should realize that catfishermen want and need rods designed for catfishing every bit as much as their bass fishing and walleye fishing counterparts want equipment suitable to their needs. Of course, many existing rods and reels are applicable to catfishing. But we want, if you please—before we spend millions more on rods and reels from any company—that those rods and reels be hawked by a generation of noteworthy and respectable catmen. For every topnotch bass pro like Roland Martin, there's a catman like Toad Smith or some other catman of note yet to be discovered.

Turn some of that manufacturing technology toward catfish products and market it to catfishermen. In a tackle industry that has often ridden the edge of a static marketplace the past few years, the catfish market looks a lot like the bass market of the 1980s, extending well into the 20th Century.

The *Catfish Guide* marks the beginning of an era of tackle introductions tailored to catfishing.

MANAGING CATFISH AND REGULATING CATFISH ANGLERS

We need a nationwide consensus about how best to manage catfish populations and regulate the harvest of catfish—Even though catfish are North America's most widely distributed sportfish, scientific data regarding catfish population dynamics, and resulting "modern-day" management strategies for catfish, lag decades behind management of trout, bass, walleyes, and other sportfish. It's a scandal that so little has been done for this fish of the masses, while so much has been done for those fish in the eye of the media.

We need a North American catfish symposium to convene by the year 2000, where state and federal scientists and sportfishing industry personnel review current scientific advances and then leave with a multipurpose plan for ensuring a strong future for sportfishing for catfish.

Certainly regulations for harvesting catfish need to be brought into the context of these times, when overwhelming data have shown that fish populations are so vulnerable to overharvest. Yet limits and the means for harvest vary more for catfish than for any other species of sportfish.

In-Fisherman Editor and Fishery Scientist Steve Quinn has reviewed the illogical state-by-state approach to catfish harvest. For example, in Texas, catfish are "gamefish." The statewide minimum length-limit for channels and blues is 9 inches, while flatheads must be 24 inches long. These gamefish, however, may be taken by trotline, jugline, or throwline.

In Virginia, by comparison, catfish are nongame fish that may be taken in unlimited numbers by trotlines, jugs, or set poles. Snagging, grabbing, snaring, and gigging, however, are not legal. Meanwhile, in New York and California, no distinction exists between gamefish or nongame fish, but catfish may be taken all year, of any size, with no daily limit.

In Oklahoma, channel and blue cats are gamefish and can be taken only by angling, trotlines, jugs, yo-yos, and spearguns, while flatheads are nongame fish and thus susceptible to bow and arrow, gigs, grabhooks, spears, snagging, noodling, and various types of nets. Anglers can have 15 channel cats and blue cats of any size, and 10 flatheads longer than 20 inches.

In Illinois, where angler opinion surveys show catfish to be the most popular fish in several regions, regulations generally offer catfish no sanctuary, while restrictions permit harvest of only 25 mussels and 8 frogs per day.

Catfish even remain unregulated commercial fish in some states. In South Carolina, for example, a $50 commercial license allows unlimited harvest of channel, flathead, or blue catfish with gill nets, hoopnets, seines, traps, tires, trotlines, set hooks, or jugs.

I'm not calling for an end to "unconventional" fishing methods (trotlining and grabbing, for example), only that these methods be regulated right along with traditional angling methods, to prevent overharvest of those portions of populations that are vulnerable. Commercial fishing for catfish generally no longer makes economic sense in most states, given how fragile many stocks of catfish are, given too that catfish farming is more efficient, and given the large number of sport anglers vying for the same fish. Certainly, where allowed, commercial fishing needs to be intensely regulated.

Catfish Guide marks a turning point toward the more realistic management of our greatest remaining fish resource.

CATFISH ANGLERS AND THESE CHANGING TIMES

Catfish anglers need to get with the program—The average catfish angler probably believes that archaic bag-limits set by most state agencies reflect the limitless nature of catfish populations. There's no excuse for not knowing better, for not becoming involved, for not pushing to protect the future of your own sport. Catfish populations are vulnerable, not only to overharvest but to habitat problems that affect every other sportfish and wildlife population.

In-Fisherman readers who fish for catfish need to lead the way in efforts to protect rivers. Rivers and their impoundments are our primary catfisheries. We need to preserve the forested and vegetated nature of these corridors, reduce siltation, maintain adequate flows, and reduce point and nonpoint pollution. Meandering rivers and streams with trees on either side are less subject to erosion, and underbrush reduces runoff of pollutants into rivers. Trees also provide shade, and when they fall into water, they offer cover for cats to hold near.

We need to lead the way in making sure, first, that catfish are given gamefish status throughout North America.

Increasing demand for water for municipalities, irrigation, and hydropower can hurt river fisheries unless we speak up about the importance of minimum flows for fish. Low water causes low oxygen levels, producing kills during winter and summer. Water levels that rapidly rise and fall probably deter production of young catfish and the invertebrates and preyfish they feed on. Neither can we tolerate rivers so polluted with pesticides and other chemicals that harvesting a few medium-sized cats for a meal might pose a health risk.

Where water quality and habitat are adequate, catfish have a chance to thrive; indeed, they can provide good fisheries even where more fragile fish species fail. Even when habitat is maintained, however, we may still face overharvest. We need to lead the way in making sure, first, that catfish are given gamefish status throughout North America.

In most states, we also need to insist on more restrictive regulations, particularly regulations to protect our remaining big catfish. These monstrous creatures are a national treasure. No man any longer has—as a matter of conscience and (soon, hopefully), a matter of regulation—the right to harvest more than a few huge catfish in a season of fishing.

And if big fish eventually die of old age instead of harvest, where's the waste? The payment is in the 40 years of being a big fish, there to thrill men, not in the $2 a pound the flesh is worth at the market. We raise chickens and turkeys, dumb as stumps, for food. We can take smaller, more plentiful catfish for occasional meals. These fish are easily renewable. This is the logic of selective harvest, and In-Fishermen who fish for catfish need to lead the way in spreading the good word in catfish country.

The *Catfish Guide* marks the beginning of increased activism in the name of sustaining resources that support catfish populations, to thrill catfish anglers in generations to come.

Tracking Winter Walleyes! Page 104

the In-Fisherman

THE JOURNAL OF FRESHWATER FISHING

TRENDS IN BASS TACTICS Page 60

TOP TEN SMALLMOUTHS Page 68

ICE RODS FOR WALLEYE— AN EXCLUSIVE! Page 51

- Huge Blue Cats Now
- Super Stripers
- NW Ontario Muskies
- The Truth About Panfish Tackle

PLUS!

- Carp Tackle Topics • Adventures
- Science Selections • In-Fisherman TV 1996

{ Historic Perspectives

This article is the beginning of a revolution in fishing for blue catfish. Before publication, almost no one is fishing them during winter. Now-famous catfish guide Jim Moyer approaches Doug Stange in July 1993, asking to accompany him on a trip for blue cats that coming winter. The rest is history that has meant millions of catfish for millions of catfish anglers—from Virginia to Texas and California—including some of the largest blue catfish ever landed.

Don Wirth

CHAPTER 27

DECEMBER 1995

Those Winter Catfish Blues

Revolutionary Blue Cat Tactics!

WHEN YOU SPEND WINTERS in northern Minnesota with temperatures that often don't warm to zero for a month at a time, a trip to Nashville country during the middle of it all seems certain to promise reprieve. But it gets cold in Tennessee, too, so cold that we stood backs to the wind, bundled in the same snowsuits we'd worn the week before on a trek into Northwest Ontario to fish for lake trout through the ice. At least we were on open water.

Jim Moyer and I stood watching our rods set in the back of his anchored boat, while Jim Lindner stood ready with a TV camera. A hundred feet beyond the back of the boat, anchored in current by 4 ounces of lead, chunked herring impaled on Kahle or widegap 5/0 hooks lay along a 25-foot ledge.

"Water temperature?" I asked Moyer, as debris floated by. The water had risen dramatically, coinciding with our arrival from the Great White North. Happens all the time when we travel with a TV camera.

"Thirty-four degrees," he said. "A drop of three degrees from a couple days ago. That storm brought cold rain. Could be worse," he continued. "Air temp's 22°F right now. Could be snowing.

I don't think this weather will bother a bit. Can't say, though, that I'd order quite this much current. A two- or three-foot rise is perfect. But not six feet."

By this time, I was a believer, listening closely to everything Moyer said about this winter pattern for big blue cats. Not long after we'd anchored in the morning mist, a rod tip had eased steadily down. "When a big cat takes a bait like that, he's got it," Moyer said. "Not much chance to miss the fish."

It fought vigorously in the cold water, powerdiving near the boat four times against the 30-pound-test line and sturdy rod before it could be brought to net. A hefty specimen, too, a short fat blue near 25 pounds. As I wrestled the fish from the net, I noted how cold it was. "Yep," Moyer said, "just like a big old blue ice cube."

By that time, I'd seen a dozen pictures of Moyer's catches—so many cats and cats so big the photos alone would weigh a ton. A typical winter outing for Moyer (5 or 6 hours) usually produces at least 10 fish. "Sometimes, most of them are in the 20- to 30-pound class," he said. "Forties aren't rare. And occasionally 50s and 60s happen along."

Moyer had one about 80 stolen from the back of his truck one day two years ago while he slipped into a grocery store looking for a scale big enough to weigh the fish. Would have been a Tennessee record. Moyer is still as big and almost as raw-boned as he was the day he retired from more than 20 years in the Army Special Forces. I wouldn't steal an 80 from Moyer.

Surprising, of course, is that most of these huge blues are caught from heavy current in big rivers during the dead of winter and into early spring. Moyer typically starts fishing this pattern around Thanksgiving and continues until the cats head shallow to spawn in April.

December, January, February, and March—not exactly traditional months for catfish. But then what does most of the catfish world really know about what's happening in so many other parts of the cat world? I'll do an end run here to make a point. By now, most of you know we're doing a *Catfish Guide* to hit newsstands in early February. History in the making, friends. The first nationally distributed cat magazine ever.

I've had the opportunity to travel a bit in the quest for cats. Everywhere I go, I run into cat anglers who have information that would help cat anglers in other areas of the country. Tackle and rigging tips. Ideas about hooks, line, and livebait sets. Secrets about cat location by time of year. Baiting methods. Secret baits.

Problem is that cat folks haven't had the same opportunity as other anglers (say, bass and walleye anglers) to pass information around the country. New piece of bass tackle comes along and anglers coast to coast know about it in short order. Bass get good press and lots of it. Hopefully, things are about to change for cat anglers—because, as I've said, the information to change many ideas about catfishing is waiting to be discovered and told. Which brings us back to Moyer's story about big blues the winter long.

In the last year alone, Moyer boated over 200 blues above 30 pounds. And he's had similar success each of the previous four years, fishing primarily for cats in the Cumberland River below Cheatham Dam in central Tennessee, not right in the tailwater area, but in downriver sections where current runs heavily along rubble ledges that line the river channel in 20 to 40 feet of water. Moyer also has caught big blues during winter from Barkley and several other Tennessee river-run reservoirs.

And where else does this pattern work? Moyer: " Well, I'm wondering that myself," he said. "Can't say I've been anywhere it hasn't worked. But then Tennessee isn't Nebraska, and I don't know if it would work for blue cats farther north in the Mississippi and Missouri rivers. What do you think?" he asked.

Blue cats are creatures of big rivers and, these days, impoundments. They like a lot more current than either channel cats or flatheads. My guess is that wherever blue cats and river-run impoundments coincide, blue cats continue to bite

Typical Fish-Holding Sections of a Flowing Reservoirs

During winter and early spring, big blue cats run the river channel, feeding along the channel ledges. They rarely move onto adjacent shallow flats. Even the hot-water discharge area doesn't attract big blue cats, although it does draw one of the blue cat's favorite baitfish, the skipjack herring. The discharge area is a prime spot to gather fresh herring for prime cutbait.

Areas A, B, *and* ***C*** *illustrate a narrow river section about to widen and flatten for several miles before becoming another narrow section. Current increases in narrow river sections, creating prime territory for blue cats.*

Area A—*The head of a narrow river section before the river widens and flattens is a prime area for blue cats that may gradually (day by day) move up into current as they feed, but hesitate to move farther upriver into decreasing current. Using electronics, you can run upriver along the channel ledge, looking for nooks and debris that harbor fish. A particularly good area is where the ledge begins to push away from the bank to form a big shallow flat.*

Concrete barge tie-offs also gather debris. Be sure to check sections of ledge near the tie-offs. Jim Moyer often ties his boat to the back of a tied-off barge to fish the ledge below. Move away quickly if a barge captain decides to bring in another barge.

Area B—*The entire ledge is a potential holding area for blue cats. Obviously, try the ledge area near the final barge tie-off. Should be a big eddy here, too. Note also how the ledge pushes away from the bank near the beginning of the discharge area—good spot. Finally, notice how the river channel gradually deepens. The head of a deep channel area as it pushes into a shallower area may be a hot spot for big blues.*

Area C—*Note how the shallow flat bumps out below the discharge inlet—check this ledge area. Then note how the flat cuts back toward the bluff bank, creating another possible holding area. Be sure to run along the ledge near the bluff bank. Limestone outcroppings are particularly craggy and difficult to fish but often hold blue cats. Often, though, the ledges are so steep that baits must be set at the top or the base of the ledge.*

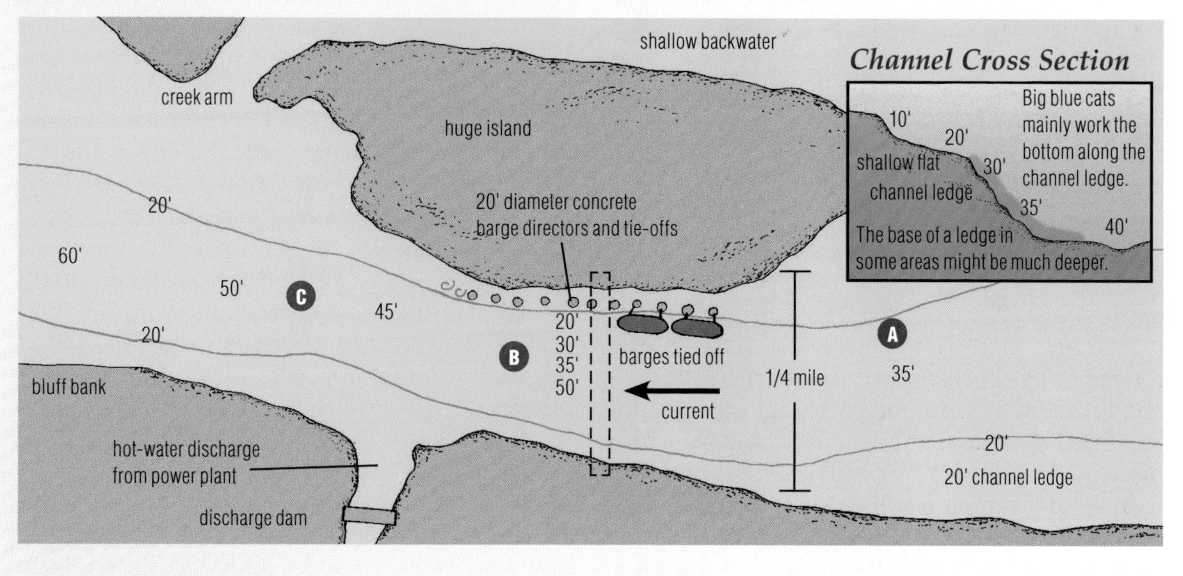

Moyer anchors over a channel ledge where the ledge begins to break back into a sharp bluff. This spot is much like the area above the bluff blank (Area C) from the previous illustration.

during winter, with the exception that somewhere along the northern boundary of blue-cat territory, the bite's going to shut down. Tennessee water, though, obviously is prime territory. So I'd be surprised if similar waters in Oklahoma, Kansas, Arkansas, southern Missouri, Kentucky, Virginia, and parts farther south don't also have monster blue cats that can be caught during winter. In fact, it may well be the best time to catch a monster from these waters—I mean a record.

Current moves food to the blues. When a dam isn't generating water, the fishing halts. Blue cats like current, and apparently, they not only don't mind cold water, they thrive in it. This may begin to unlock the puzzle of what happens to monster blues in some impoundments during summer. Perhaps the biggest fish seek colder water. Maybe that's why so many of the big blues caught until the 1960s (when dams changed blue-cat habitat and range) were caught farther north—into the Dakotas—rather than where they're caught today.

Moyer: "When I first began fishing for blues, I fished too shallow. Most of these fish are caught along ledges (channel drop-offs) at least 20 feet deep and down to 40 and even 50 feet. A channel ledge that drops quickly from about 20 into 35 feet is prime—so much the better if the ledge has old stumps and other cover. Avoid gradually sloping banks.

"Also forget fishing in big backwash (eddy) areas removed from main current. In an eddy right next to heavy current, however, work the edge right along the main current. These fish like to move along drop-offs in current running 2 mph to as fast as 7 or 8 mph. I lay baits at the top, down the side, and at the base of the ledge. I could count on two hands the number of big blues I've caught shallower than 18 feet. Yet I've taken thousands from along ledges.

"Humps near the main channel produce fish, too, so long as there's a deep ledge at the head or tail end of the hump. Check ledges around islands in main current, too."

But how far downriver? I asked.

"Again, I haven't done well in the tailwater area," Moyer said. "I don't know why. Can't even venture a guess. The closest I've caught big fish below a dam during winter is about a mile, but I wouldn't say that's an absolute, just an observation. I also haven't done well way downriver where water starts to pool ahead of the next dam. Most of the fish I catch are in the upper third of flowing reservoirs. I usually begin fishing at the lowest point in this section of reservoir. Then as the water warms in spring, I move upriver. But I think that fish can be caught even farther downriver if conditions are right. In other areas of the country, probably just depends on the actual environment the fish have a chance to use.

"Current's so important that most of the time I fish ledges in narrower sections of the river. You know, where a wider, flatter section of river suddenly narrows. Naturally, the current picks up in this section. Anywhere in a section of river like that, so long as there's a long-running ledge in the right depth, I just start fishing different portions of the ledge.

"I don't know why the cats hold where they do along these ledges, but I usually catch them in short order once I anchor. No use sitting in a spot for hours if the bite slows. I give a spot 30, maybe 40 minutes.

"Seems like blues move into an area along a ledge and use it for a while. I catch fish in the same areas year after year, but I just can't catch fish in the same spots all day every day. Spots apparently need time to gather moving cats.

"A couple other spots to check include deep-lying slag piles or rockpiles, structures caused by dredging. Blue cats like to eat mussels, too, so deep-lying mussel beds, usually at the base of a ledge, are worth fishing.

Ledge Lunch For Blues

Cut skipjack herring, the makings of a ledge lunch for big blue cats.

Egg sinkers, swivels, and Kahle-style hooks. Simple components for rigging for blue cats.

Cut or chunked baitfish threaded on a Kahle or widegap hook lies straight without spinning in current, creating a large enough offering to attract big blues. Filleted and chunked skipjack herring is Moyer's top bait. Shad, suckers, and other oily baitfish work, too.

"I use a 35-pound section of railroad track for holding in current. And I carry 100 feet of rope and sometimes need to let it all out to hold. I always have a knife handy, too, in case the anchor snags as a barge bears down on me. This is a daytime affair, mind you. I like fishing from about sunrise on, but I don't do well at night during winter."

Anchoring, I learned from Moyer, is a vital part of this system. Most anglers in his area drift for cats with bottom-bumping rigs. They move with the current, attempting to keep their baits bouncing bottom vertically below the boat. While this may be a good late spring and summer tactic in some areas, and a fine way to catch smaller, more aggressive fish, it just doesn't consistently produce bigger fish.

"These monsters sometimes are tentative," Moyer said. "They move up and mouth a bait, then wait, then touch the bait again before taking it solidly. They don't need to take all day, but they usually aren't aggressive enough to take a drifting bait. I anchor well upriver from the structure edge I'm going to fish, then let out just enough rope to reach the structure with a long cast. The play of the current against the line, sinker, and bait allows the bait to settle naturally onto the bottom. A cat can pick at the bait without feeling anything unusual."

Moyer's rigging is standard cat fare, consisting of an egg sinker weighing 1.5 to 5 ounces, depending on current. The sinker slides on 30-pound mainline above a #1 or #2 swivel. A leader testing 30 pounds runs 18 to 36 inches below the swivel. A shorter leader means fewer snags in heavier current. Moyer uses a tough line like Berkley's Big Game. And given the sandpapering a cat's mouth can cause line, he checks the leader after every cat, retying when in doubt.

A 5/0 or 6/0 Kahle-style hook is an important part of Moyer's terminal rigging. Long strips of cutbait tend to roll too much in current, twisting line. Moyer relies on cut cubes of skipjack herring. The cubed portions of fillet pack neatly onto a Kahle hook, allowing the cubes to become a big bait that gives off plenty of scent and still lies straight without spinning in current.

"Gizzard shad and other large baitfish work, too," Moyer told me, "but herring are as oily as baitfish can get. You can't buy them at most baitshops, so I catch mine the night before on a spinning outfit rigged with two 1/8-ounce white grubs tied a foot apart. Working the rig in a warmwater discharge area, I have little trouble catching enough bait to last a day or two. I've used other baits and they work, but skipjack works so well where I fish.

"I've tried livebait and all sorts of prepared baits. Cutbait continues to outperform them 100 to 1. The key to great cutbait is to keep it cool and dry. I put a metal grate in the bottom of a cooler and place the whole baitfish (scaled) on the grate. Then I put ice on top of the fish, so they're cold but not soaking in water. Fillet the fish just before you use them and cut the fillets into 1.5-inch cubes."

The rod plays an important role, too. Moyer likes a 7.5- or 8-foot E-glass baitcasting rod. E-glass is slightly slower-reacting than graphite or even S-glass, but it's tough as can be, perfect for putting an armlock on big cats. Moyer's rods are medium-fast-action models with a limber tip.

"I don't set the rods in rod holders, preferring to set them against the gunnel or against a seat in the back of my boat," he said. "The rod tip points back toward the bait at about a 30- to 45-degree angle. That way a cat can grab the bait and the rod tip gives, allowing the fish to hold the bait without much resistance. I almost always see the rod tip suddenly set down, stop, then continue down as the cat finally moves off. Pick up the rod and set just after the rod tip sets and stops, or as the cat moves off. Do it all in one swoop and a cat won't sense your presence until it's too late."

Moyer is part of history in another sense. That is, he's helping Berkley design one of the first series of rods especially for catfish. "The prototype rods I've been testing are just great," he told me recently. "We call the rods the E-Cat Series, because they're made from fine-grade E-glass. These rods are sensitive and powerful yet close to indestructible, perfect for catfishing."

Moyer often ties his boat over a portion of ledge and immediately behind an anchored barge. Note the high dirty water. Blue cats like current and Moyer has had good fishing coinciding with a 1-to 3-foot rise in water level. During our trip, the rise was closer to 6 feet, which hurt fishing for almost a week until the river dropped and stabilized.

According to Berkley, the rods will be introduced in select markets sometime during spring 1996. The E-Cat Series consists of five rods with an easy-to-understand rating system. The E-Cat #1 is a 7-foot rod on the light end of the scale, perfect for 10-pound-test line and the pursuit of smaller cats in ponds and small rivers. The E-Cat #5, a 7.5-foot rod, will handle 50-pound-test line for monster cats. For winter fishing for big blues, Moyer recommends the 8-foot E-Cat #3, or the 7.5-foot E-Cat #4.

The E-Cat #3 couples with 20- to 30-pound line and a reel like the Garcia 5600, 6500, or 7000. The E-Cat #4 handles line to about 40-pound test and couples best with a reel like the Garcia 6500 or 7000.

Moyer: "Nothing complicated about this fishing. You have to believe those blue cats are there and biting, when what you've heard has probably been the opposite. By late February in north Tennessee, I'm usually fishing for these fish in 35°F water. Five years of fishing at least five days a week for four months each year has proven this to be absolutely the best time to catch a huge blue cat. I know a lot of folks across a big section of the country are in for a big surprise."

The quality of catfish still available in a lot of river and reservoir systems is amazing—one of the greatest fish resources yet remaining in North America. As we learn more about these fish, and tell the world so more folks can enjoy this unparalleled opportunity, let's hope we also remember how old these monsters are and therefore how vulnerable.

Smaller cats are for eating. Big cats are for releasing, so fish nearing and surpassing 100 pounds remain to fill the dreams of other anglers. From Santee-Cooper, South Carolina; to White River, Arkansas; to the Red River in Manitoba, catmen should no longer tolerate stringers of huge dead catfish.

Those First Bass Of Spring! Page 50 & 66
MARCH 1996
the In-Fisherman
THE JOURNAL OF FRESHWATER FISHING
SPRING TRANSITION
CRAPPIES
LOCATIONS REVEALED
Page 120
RIGGING MONSTER CATS
PRESPAWN RIVER SMALLMOUTHS
ABOUT BIG PIKE
21ST CENTURY WIPERS
SELECT SPINNER TROUT
BAIT SECRETS FOR
WALLEYES
Page 88
Bowmount Boat
Control Breakthrough Page 44

{ Historic Perspectives

From the beginning of Stange's tenure as an editor at In-Fisherman in 1981, he maintains an open line with hardcore anglers worldwide, especially those in England and other parts of western Europe, areas that have a long history of advanced presentation techniques with live- and deadbait. This article highlights European rigging strategies that work well for North American catfish. English angler and writer Keith Lambert travels several times to North America to fish with In-Fisherman staff members and becomes a contributor to In-Fisherman and In-Fisherman's Catfish Guide. Note that it is in early 1996, at about the time this article runs, that the first Catfish Guide hits newsstands. The 102-page magazine is the first in history to feature only articles about catfish and catfishing, obviously a historic event on the fishing scene. The Catfish Guide, an annual magazine edition, still hits newstands each spring—15 years and counting since introduction.

Keith Lambert

CHAPTER 28

MARCH 1996

Suspender Rigging for Big Ol' Cats

THE PHOTOS THAT ACCOMPANY this article tell of the quest for the wels catfish by English anglers fishing in England, France, and other parts of Europe—catfish anglers, all of us, who connect with the world around us just a little better because we find passion in pursuit of catfish.

Catfishermen share a bond that traverses the many miles between continents and the many differences in species of catfish found worldwide. Letters from a missionary in Peru keep me abreast of their camp's spare-time quest to catch giant catfish of the Amazon. Several other fine contacts in South America, from Peru, Bolivia, and Brazil, also correspond about their catches. For your information, I have pictures of catfish surpassing 200 pounds, but no evidence yet verifies those 500- or even 1000-pound creatures that supposedly exist. The South American scene is one of intrigue, however, a story worth telling again one of these days. Yes, letters from Asia, too—from Thailand. And many letters from Africa, particularly Zimbabwe and South Africa.

Many of the best shore anglers in the world continue to write from England, where techniques for carp, catfish, and other species

Hardcore Angling Ideas Worldwide!

have all been refined over the past decades. Since the early 1980s, in a spirit of friendship and fellowship among seasoned fishermen, *In-Fisherman* has borrowed from their ideas about rigging. The English fishing scene, in turn, has been somewhat influenced by our approaches to fishing with lures.

Of course, many of the rigs that might be termed English rigs have had concurrent development of one sort or another here. One of my favorite rigs for flathead cats, for example, the English call the float-paternoster rig. I first saw this rig used in the early 1960s by that old reprobate, Zacker, of whom I've often written.

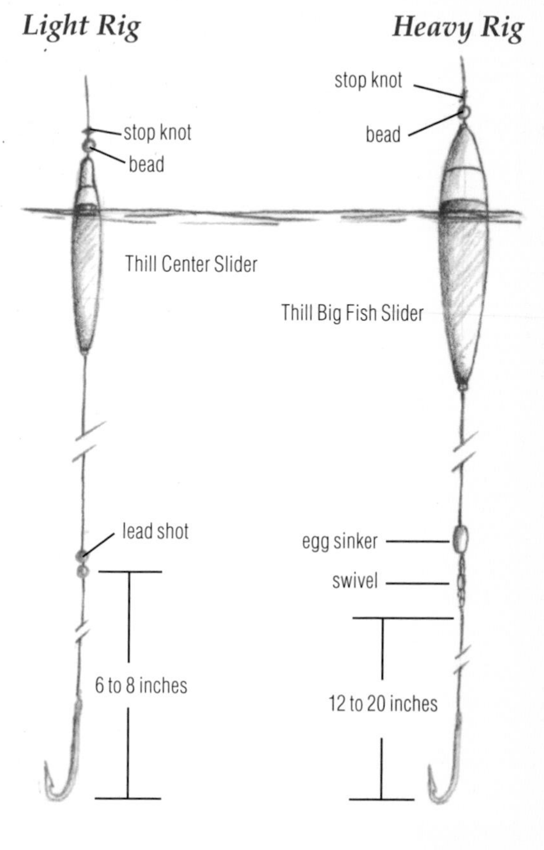

Zacker's rigging, while effective, wasn't so refined as the English version. Zacker would have been the first to admit, given his abiding interest in catching cats, that the float-paternoster rig (and variations thereof) is a better rig in many instances.

The float-paternoster rig is just one of many ways to keep a livebait up and moving, a vital element in fishing for flatheads, which much prefer livebaits most of the time. Livebait can also be the key to big channel cats in some waters. Big blues, on the other hand, usually go best for a big piece of dead something, even sometimes when they're schooled and chasing live shad. Such observations are generalities, of course.

The point remains, however, that the low-frequency vibrations produced by a struggling baitfish attract catfish by stimulating their sensitive lateral lines. Livebaits of all sizes must first be wild and super-lively, and second be presented in ways that allow them to advertise these seductive qualities. Keep a wild bait suspended just so and it feels exposed, vulnerable, and panicked, and rightly so.

Slipfloat Rigging—The simplest suspension system, of course, is just a bait tethered below a float—today, usually a depth-adjustable slipfloat. Lindy-Little Joe/Thill offers cigar-shaped float designs of sufficient size to handle livebaits ranging from 3 to over 12 inches. The classic cigar shape like the Thill Center Slider is more sensitive than the slightly more bulbous Thill Big Fish Slider, which should be reserved for bigger, wilder baits. I also prefer the classic cigar design for drifting cutbait for channel cats or blue cats, or for fishing a lighter-line livebait rig for channel cats in cold water during early spring.

Whichever float you choose to suspend your bait, the rigging goes like this: Before adding a hook and shot to your line, tie a five-turn uni-knot around your mainline, using the same or slightly heavier-test line. This serves as a sliding—that is, an adjustable—float stop. Some anglers prefer the ease of slipping on a nylon float stop or using a pretied bobber-stop knot instead of tying their own stop knots.

Slipfloat Rigging

Light Rig

stop knot
bead
Thill Center Slider
lead shot
6 to 8 inches

Heavy Rig

stop knot
bead
Thill Big Fish Slider
egg sinker
swivel
12 to 20 inches

After tying on the stop knot, slip on a 3-millimeter bead (lines to about 14 pounds), or a 4-mm or 5-mm bead (heavier line), and then the slipfloat of your choice. Then slide the stop knot, bead, and slipfloat up your line so the float suspends the bait at the chosen depth. Anchor lighter rigs with several shot about 12 inches above a hook, ranging from a #2 for smaller baits to a 3/0 for larger baits.

To anchor a big livebait for flatheads, tie in a swivel about 20 inches above your hook, which might range from a 3/0 to 7/0 or larger. The Eagle Claw 84, Mustad 92671, or a similar hook design, are functional and inexpensive. Use a file to sharpen them. Add a 1- to 2-ounce egg sinker, depending on the size of the livebait, above the swivel. The largest Thill Big Fish Slider works with a 2-ounce sinker.

Float rigs are particularly deadly in several situations. In rivers, they work well drifted through the tail end of a riffle and into the beginning of a hole, then along and around cover such as a snag. A big bait suspended and drifted through a big, slow-flowing eddy near or part of a deep hole (particularly if downed timber is present) is also a good tactic for flatheads. In ponds and reservoirs, where catfish often swim suspended, use the wind to drift a livebait through potential areas, into position from shore, or behind an anchored or drifting boat.

Float-Paternoster Rig—This rig is a top choice when the situation calls for placing a bait in the lair of big fish and waiting them out. Each of the biggest flatheads I've caught the last two years have been with this rig, placed in a big eddy just behind a huge pile of snaggy timber lining a deep river hole. With either an 8-inch bullhead or a 10-inch river redhorse sucker as bait, I toss the offering into place in the middle of the eddy, just away from any snags. Then I light a small fire and settle in for part of the night. Livebait calls in roaming fish. Every so often, prod the float to keep the baitfish dancing.

This also is a deadly rig when you're set up on a shallow point in a reservoir, in the corner of a big pond, or somewhere in the back end of a creek arm. The idea is to set baits on shallow flats near deep water—somewhere big cats roam, usually after dark.

Another wels from the River Po, this one 93.5 pounds. These fish sometimes surpass 200 pounds.

Float-paternoster rigging employs a slipfloat, so to make the rig, begin as before with the slipknot, bead, and slipfloat. The terminal leader consists simply of a 12-inch section of monofilament or Dacron with a hook on one end and a swivel on the other. Now, add a lead bottom link, a piece of monofilament with a bell sinker on one end and a swivel on the other, the swivel running free on your mainline just above the leader swivel.

The length of the bottom link determines how high the bait suspends above bottom. Run the float perfectly tight to the lead below, and an 18-inch bottom link suspends a bait 6 inches above bottom (18 inches minus the 12-inch leader). Rarely, though, should this link be tight. A little

Float-Paternoster Rig

The weight of the line varies, given conditions. For big flatheads in reservoirs where snags aren't a problem, Stange runs 30-pound mainline and a 20-pound bottom link. When channel cats are the target in a similar environment, drop to 17- or 20-pound mainline and a 14-pound bottom link. For 40- to over 50-pound cats in snaggy water, Stange usually runs at least 50-pound mainline and a 20-pound link.

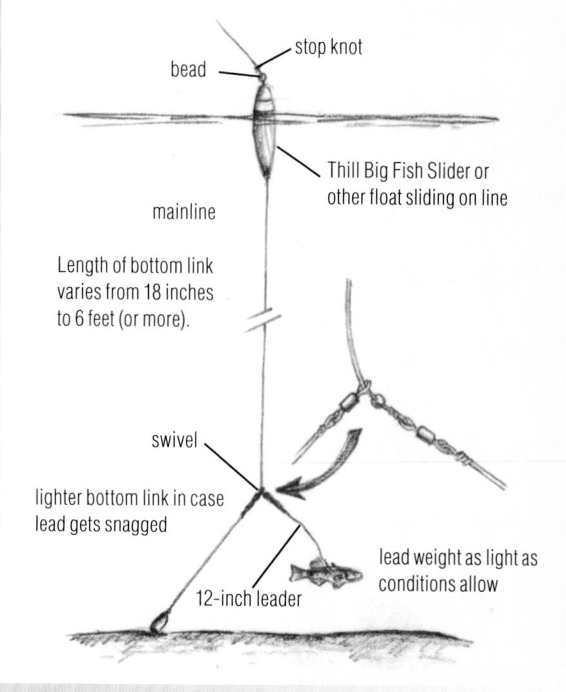

Terminal Rigging

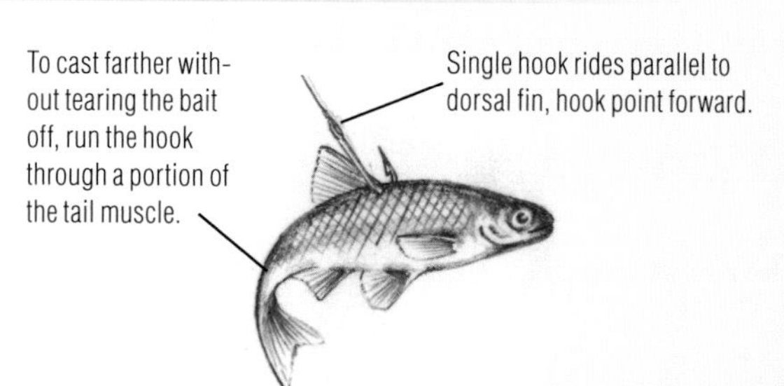

play down below allows the bait to swim in a big circle and slightly off to the side.

A tightly tethered bait tends not to swim so vigorously as a bait that believes it's going somewhere. In most situations, I run about a 24-inch bottom link. The combination of 24-inch bottom link and bait remains easy to cast with the 7½- to 10-foot casting rods I use for big fish.

The float need only suspend the bait and keep it swimming below; it doesn't have to suspend the lead (which is resting on bottom), so the float can be smaller than with slipfloat rigging. The bottom link should test slightly less than the mainline and leader. If it snags, it can be broken free without breaking off the main rigging.

Poly-Ball Leger Rigging—This is a new one for me, suggested by our English friends, Simon Clarke and Keith Lambert, membership secretary and assistant editor, respectively, of *Whiskers*, the magazine of the Catfish Conservation Group, an English organization dedicated to the cause of the mighty European catfish, the wels. Noting our *Catfish Guide,* the first catfish magazine in North America, Clarke and Lambert were kind enough to send along the latest of *Whiskers,* in which I noted explanation of the poly-ball leger rigs that are destined to work for North American cats. As you've also noted by now, the photos gracing this article are from Lambert, who is both a fine angler and photographer.

Lambert suggests that the original poly rig was developed by one of England's best catfish anglers, Bob Baldock. "Legering," by the way, is presenting a static live- or deadbait on the bottom. Our classic leger is similar to the classic English leger, and consists of a weight (egg sinker or bell sinker) running on the mainline—the mainline tied to a leader consisting of a piece of mono or Dacron, with a hook on one end and a swivel on the other. The English are as likely to fish a "fixed" lead as they are a free-running (or semi-fixed) lead, but that's a story for another day.

The idea here is simply to add a Styrofoam ball (poly ball) to the hook end of the leader in order to keep the livebait up and bobbing, as opposed to cowering on the bottom. To the end of his leader

Bob Baldock's Livebait Poly Rig

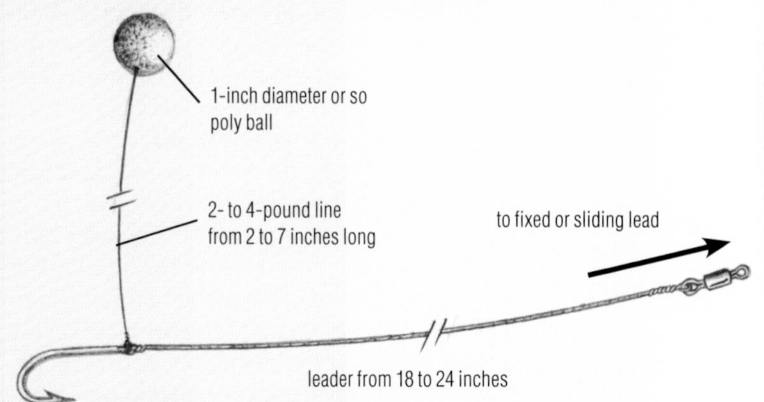

Wels eat livebait, but they are noted scavengers that eat almost anything.

Keith Lambert's Favorite Poly-Ball Livebait Rig

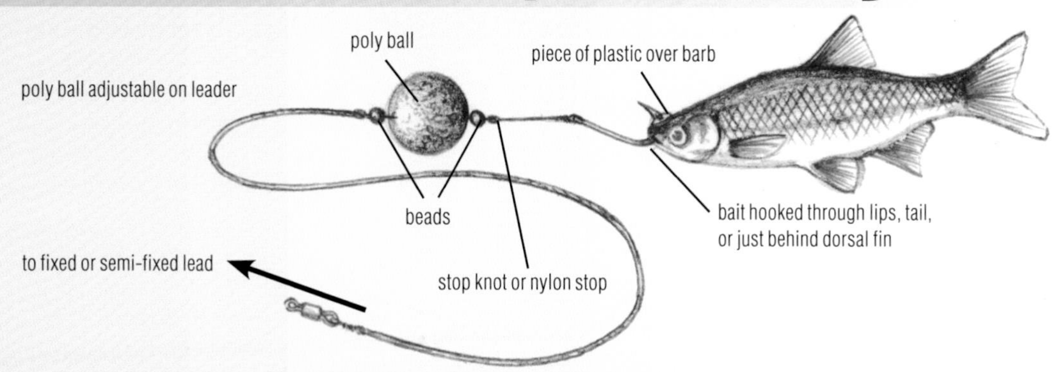

Trevor Pritchard's Alternative Livebait Rig

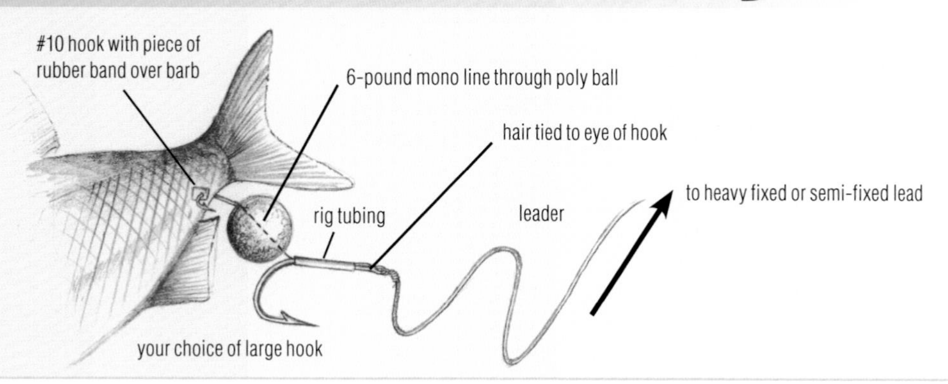

A typical comfortable bank set up in Europe.

of some 20 inches, Baldock adds a 2- to 7-inch-long piece of 2- or 4-pound line with a one-inch diameter poly ball on the end.

I gather, though, from reading Lambert's comments, that this rig has a tendency to tangle. Lambert suggests, as an alternative, a rig much like some of our suspender rigs for walleyes—only the float or poly ball is larger. Simply slip the poly ball on the leader and rig it in slip fashion so the ball can easily be moved closer or farther from the bait.

A final poly-rig modification is based on the hair rig as suggested by Trevor Pritchard. The hair rig has often been referred to in *In-Fisherman* for carp, catfish, walleyes, and pike, but is far from widely used in North America and therefore requires a brief explanation.

The hair rig was developed as a rig for wary carp. A light line (originally hair) was tied to the shank of a hook, and baits were held on the hair instead of the hook, allowing the hook to ride free just below the bait. Carp inhaled the bait along with the hook, which, riding free, much improved hookup percentage. It also ensured that carp were lip-hooked instead of throat-hooked and could be released.

In carp fishing, the baits usually are held in place on the hair (light line) with a tiny plastic cylindrical stop. Pritchard replaces the stop with

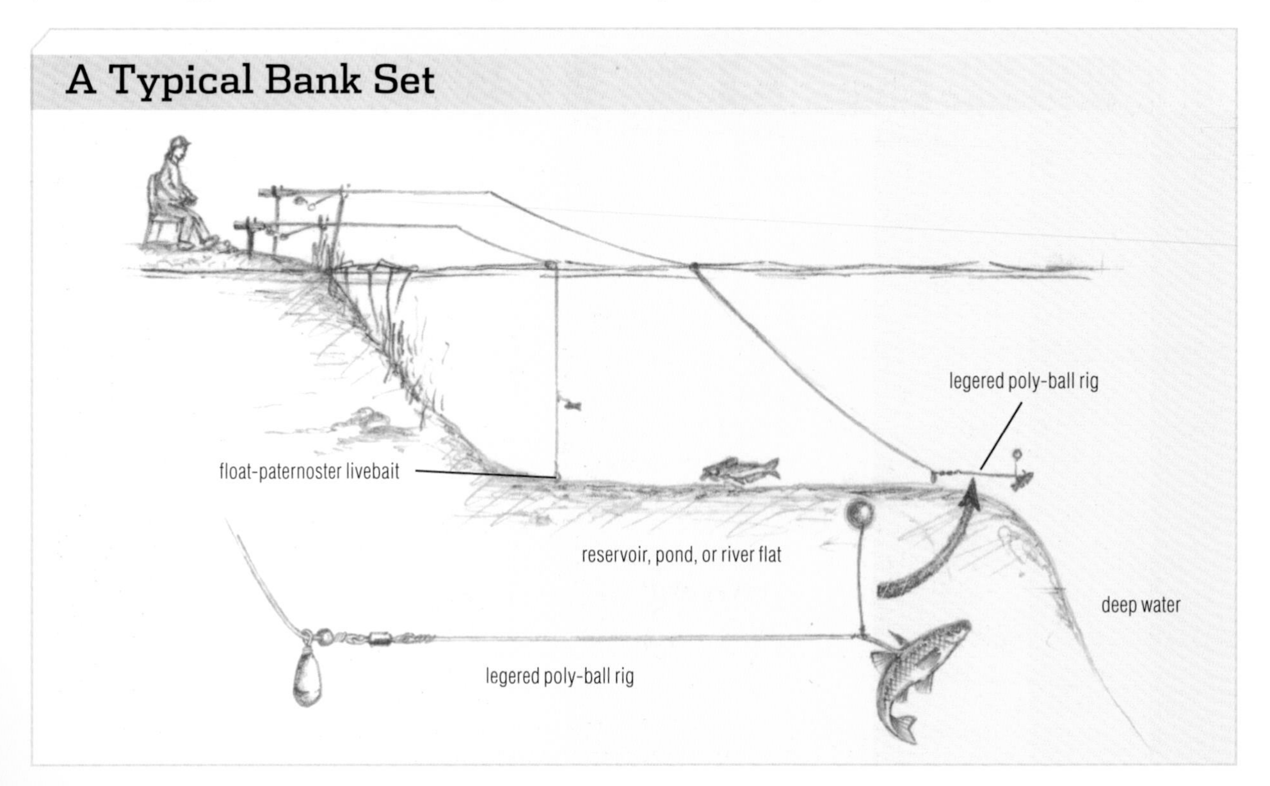

a tiny hook, which he slips through the tail of the bait to hold it to the rig. Again, the actual hook rides free just behind. The poly ball is placed between the hook and the bait, prodding the bait to move, as it must swim to keep the poly ball from tipping it.

In England, leaders often are of Dacron because it's softer and less objectionable to carp and catfish, with their sensitive mouths. Monofilament—particularly heavier mono—also more likely alerts wary fish by hindering bait movement. English fish are, however, more heavily fished and more likely to have been caught and released, and thereby are educated. Mono remains sufficient in most North American waters.

I look forward to the coming season, which I'm sure has already begun for some of you, because last season was not a good one for me. Oh, we did a grand bit of early scoring on a TV filming trip to the Red River near Selkirk, Manitoba. The fishing there can be so outlandishly easy and the fish so consistently large that it continues to amaze me, even after almost 10 years of trips there. Everyone should experience such furious fishing for huge channel cats at least once.

Should you decide to go, the hot fishing lasts from mid-May through June, then slows somewhat as fish finish spawning in July and slip downriver to hold in deeper holes. The fishing remains good all summer, though, and usually picks up again in fall when fish average several pounds larger than in spring.

The rest of my season past? Sometimes things just go way awry. We get busy at just the wrong time, so trips have to be canceled. Or, we're just about to leave and it rains 8 inches and the river goes wild. Not this year, though. I have that feeling. New rigs to try. Things just slipping into the long-ball groove.

The story goes that the famous manager of the Yankees during the Babe Ruth glory years of the 1920s, John McGraw, wandering through a restaurant where the team was eating after a game, happened past the table where a promising rookie was dining on chicken. "Son," he said, removing the plate of chicken, "better you do like Ruth over there—eat a big steak, do a big do-do (a paraphrase), and hit a big home run."

I just have that feeling. New rigs to try. Old rigs to run again. Things just slipping into that long-ball groove. Keep in touch from 'round the country and 'round the world.

The River Segre, Spain produced this impressive fish in October 1994.

{ Historic Perspectives

This is a tack-sharp, dead-on-the-money story featuring the kind of salient advice that can only be gathered from years of field experience. As long as catfish swim, anglers can find and catch them using the ideas advanced in this straightforward article. As Zacker would still say it today: "When opportunity comes knocking—don't matter how small that opportunity might seem—knock back with all the spirit you can muster."

CHAPTER 29

APRIL 1996

Cuts Means Cats

THAT OLD CATMAN ZACKER used to say his drill sergeant in World War I was the best philosopher he'd met in his almost 90 years of hard living. "Boys," the instructor used to tell his recruits when they'd strayed some, "reality will be a well-polished sergeant's boot stuck up the netherland of your anatomy if you don't pull your head out of that netherland fast." According to Zacker, this advice was so soundly drilled into him that, for the next 70 years, the sergeant's words hit instant replay each time he screwed up in some way.

Location Factors For Fat Cats In Tough Early Season Times!

Even Zacker, a well-studied commercial catman for over 40 years, considered April the nadir of the catfish year, hardly the keenest part of the season to catch cats in most parts of the country. In Canada and much of the northern U.S., ice still covers most waters like a lid on an old fruit jar. Way-up-yonder-north, catfishermen can only dream of things to come. Coming soon, of course, is just what's happening right now across most of the country, where cats are in that tenuous transition period from Coldwater into Prespawn and what becomes some of the season's best fishing.

Although we don't have all the patterns figured out on every type of water, it seems that in many southern, midsouthern, and southwestern waters, there's a way to catch numbers of big fish during the Coldwater Period, which lasts most of winter. Our December-January 1995 article, featuring Jim Moyer's methods for catching huge blue cats from riverine reservoirs in Tennessee during winter, was a breakthrough in that regard. A lot more remains to be learned, though.

Soon after the ice goes out in parts farther north, and soon after the combination of spring rains and warmer weather in March, April, and May raise water temperatures significantly in other parts of the country, cats scatter toward spawning areas. Once water temperatures settle a bit and water stabilizes, Prespawn sets in and fish numbers build in certain areas. We've covered the basics of the prespawn story before. Check our book, *Channel Catfish Fever*, if you're curious. Tune in here during May, too. The focus this month, though, is on catching cats during this tenuous transition period when "cuts" often key decent fishing.

Scattered fish, of course, always are more difficult to catch. This is a particularly difficult time to target big fish, usually the least numerous members in any population. So when they scatter, they become even more difficult to find. Smaller fish, being numerous by comparison, make up the bulk of what fishermen find during a day of fishing in April.

"Smaller," though, doesn't have to mean tiny. Depends on what a body of water has to offer; that is, the average size of the bulk of the population. Many Dakota reservoirs, for example, support huge numbers of 2- to 4-pound channel cats. That's what you catch this time of year—for the most part—in the cuts where you set up camp.

LOCATION IN PRINCIPLE

Cuts exist in various forms, but usually have in common a location removed from the main body of water. So generally, right now don't look for cats in the main reservoir, main lake, main river, or even in the main portion of a pond. Say you're on Bull Shoals, or Santee-Cooper, or Oahe Reservoir—a large body of water with a comparatively deeper main reservoir. Now, don't quit reading just because you rarely fish these kinds of waters. We'll get to your waters by and by. We need to capture here, by way of example, the general idea behind finding decent cats in any water right now.

First, detour from the main reservoir into a major creek arm, then head directly to the back of the creek arm, noting secondary cuts near the back of the arm, especially if those cuts have water running into them. Secondary cuts near the back of major creek arms usually are the warmest areas and therefore attract baitfish and gather other baits washed in by spring rains. Winterkilled shad may also stack in these areas.

If you're new at this, don't give up after checking the back ends of just one or two cuts. Some cuts draw more fish than others. Sometimes it's a one-time deal—more bait simply happened to gather there. Usually, though, some cuts draw more fish year after year—something magic about the cut. Once you've identified such cuts, you're steps ahead in years to come.

Another key spot is at the mouth of cuts, where they enter creek arms. Cats must pass through here in order to get into cuts. When the water's up into the bank brush in the main body of a creek arm, cats also roam this edge. Gets tougher to catch cats here, however, because they're scattered. It's limbline territory in most southern reservoirs.

Now, take a big step back to the point where we had detoured from the main reservoir into a creek arm. In most reservoirs with lots of cats, each creek arm will host fish. Still, as you might guess, some arms are better than others, which in turn means the cuts in those arms are the best ones to fish. The best arms almost always have water entering via a creek or river. The best cuts usually are near the entry point for such a creek or river. And the best cuts usually also have their own water-flow source. At this

Location Principle—Large Reservoirs

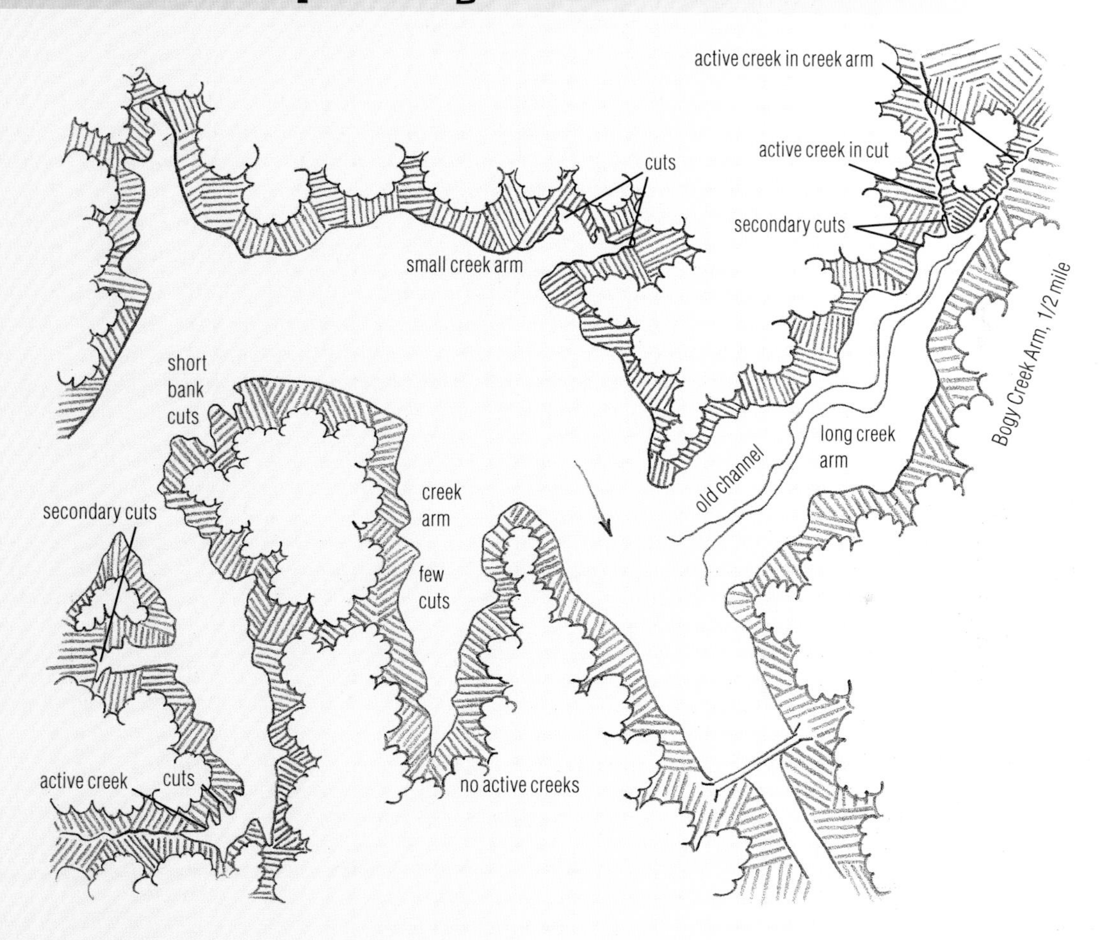

Points to consider:

- *During the transition from Coldwater to Prespawn Periods, catfish move toward warmer water in the back of creek arms. Long creek arms likely warm more quickly than short ones. Long creek arms with an active creek in the end more likely warm even faster than those without creeks.*
- *While the active creek area at the back of creek arms attracts cats, nearby cuts, especially those that also have active creeks, make the back of these arms even more attractive to cats.*
- *Sometimes feeder creeks farther from the dam warm faster than those near the dam and may therefore attract more cats.*
- *In reservoirs with plenty of catfish, each major feeder creek likely will attract cats. Some creek arms are just better than others, however. So, it's necessary to sample the fishing.*

time of year, running water always draws cats.

Finally, two generalizations that are observations, at best—not rules. In some reservoirs, the best creek arms seem to be the longest. In others, they seem to be the farthest from the dam. Again, these are observations, at best.

The rules remain these: Find the right creek arm, usually one with a creek running into the back end. Check the cuts in the back of the creek arms, particularly those that also have a source of running water. Long arms may be better than short arms because water in the upper reaches warms more quickly. Creek arms in the lower portion of the reservoirs also tend to warm faster than those in the upper reaches. Generally, move away from the main reservoir. As always, however, consider at least one major exception.

THE FOOD FACTOR

Toss one more major log into the fire that is finding cats during these tenuous times. Warmer water, particularly warmer inflowing water, usually attracts bait that attracts cats. Cuts in the areas suggested usually warm quickly and therefore attract cats. Food is primary to finding cats, but it has to be in warmer (or at least warming) water before cats feed well.

Occasionally, a major food source is somewhere other than in the cuts. In reservoirs without many creek arms and cuts, shad may spend time in the main part of the reservoir during winter instead of entering major creek arms. If a winterkill of shad occurs in the main reservoir, and the wind pushes these bloated lifeless forms into a particular portion of the main reservoir away

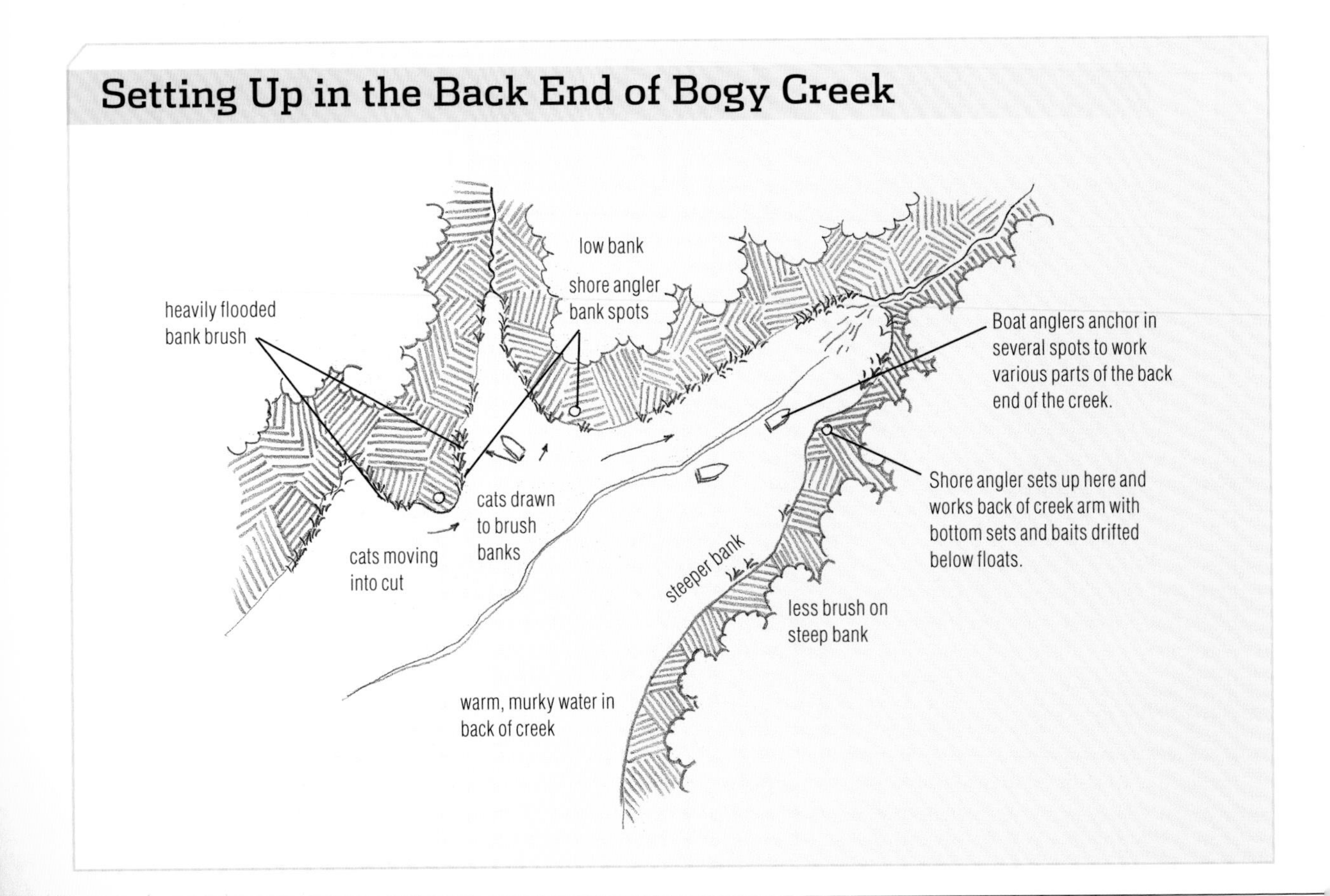

Location in Principle—Complex Lake Systems

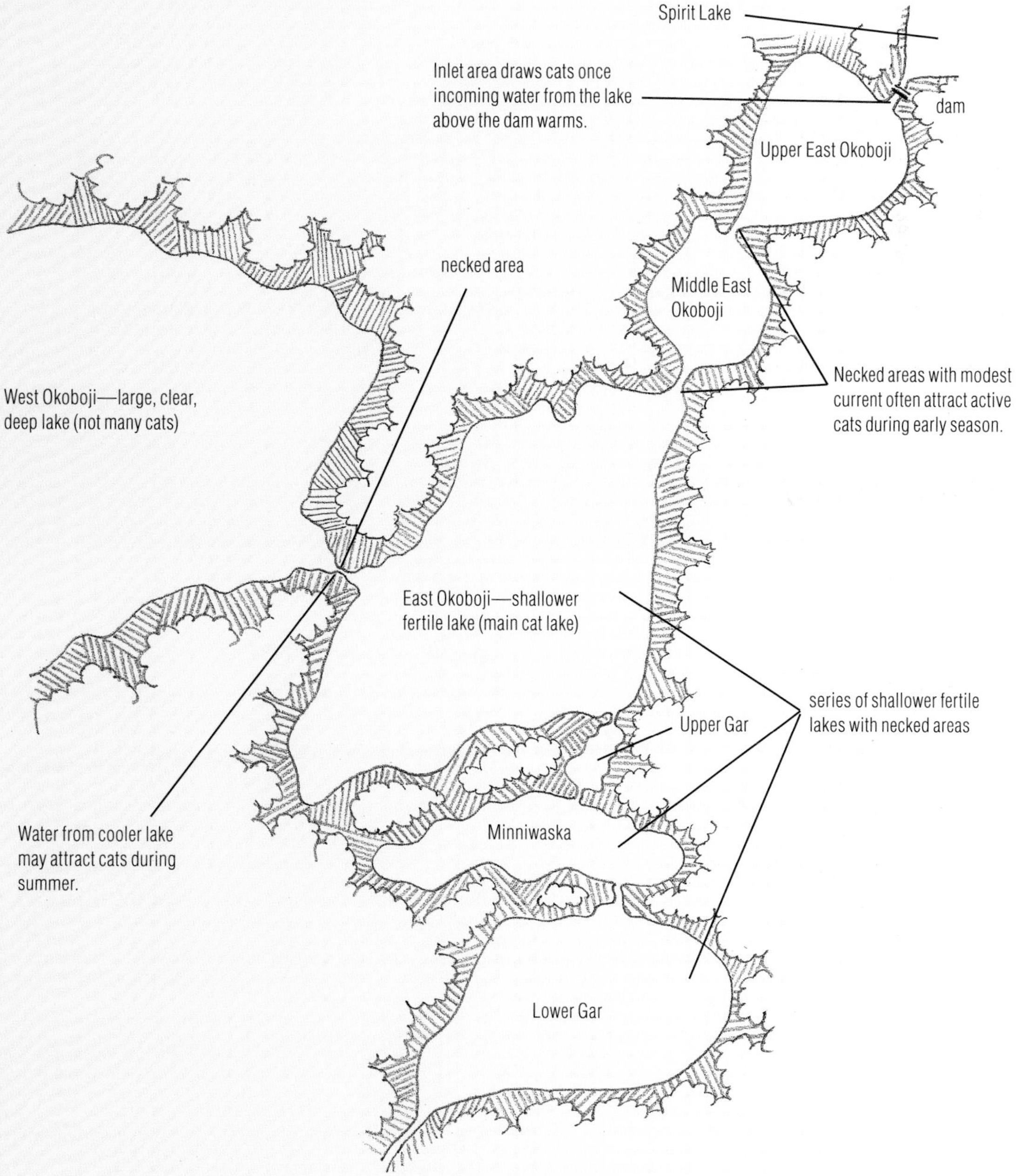

Spirit Lake

Inlet area draws cats once incoming water from the lake above the dam warms.

dam

Upper East Okoboji

necked area

Middle East Okoboji

Necked areas with modest current often attract active cats during early season.

West Okoboji—large, clear, deep lake (not many cats)

East Okoboji—shallower fertile lake (main cat lake)

series of shallower fertile lakes with necked areas

Upper Gar

Minniwaska

Water from cooler lake may attract cats during summer.

Lower Gar

Barriers like big snags and long shallow stretche gather catfish just starting to roam.

from creek arms, cats will be there, feeding as best they can, even in cold water. The warmer the water, the better the bite becomes in this area. But even in such an area, by now you know that the key to the best fishing is recognizing where some of those shad have been blown into a cut of some sort that offers warmer water.

Sometimes, too, in riverine reservoirs (often called flowing reservoirs), shad die in the reservoir portion just above the dam and are washed through the dam and down the main river channel, well away from the back ends of creek arms and creek-arm cuts in the upper portion of the reservoir. Head down the main river channel, first detouring into side channels, then into any cuts off the side channels—again, spots near the main current that carries the dead shad, but just removed enough to be slightly warmer than the main current flow.

CUTS IN NATURAL LAKES

Depends on the lake. Rules are: Get away from the main body of water and into warmer water. Running water (current) attracts fish.

I used to fish a series of connected lakes in northwestern Iowa. The largest body of water, West Okoboji, was deep and clear. As you might guess, not too many cats in West Lake, though it's connected by a necked-down passage into East Lake, which is shallow and fertile. Lots of cats in East Lake. Now we're getting somewhere. All we have to do is get away from the main body of East Lake.

No problem. East Lake is connected by a necked-down passage in the south end to Upper Gar Lake, which is connected by a necked passage to Minniwaska Lake, which is connected by a passage to Lower Gar Lake, which has a shallow outlet area leading to the Little Sioux River, one of Iowa's best channel-cat rivers. In the north, meanwhile,

Location in Principle—Simple Lakes

In simple lakes, look for incoming water from warmer sources such as marshes and feeder creeks running from farm land. Bays also warm more quickly than the main lake. Check the edge of structural elements like bulrush beds or downed timber, or set up at the mouth of the bay. Remember, too, that several days of consistent warm weather with winds moving warmer surface water into one area of a lake may draw cats to that area.

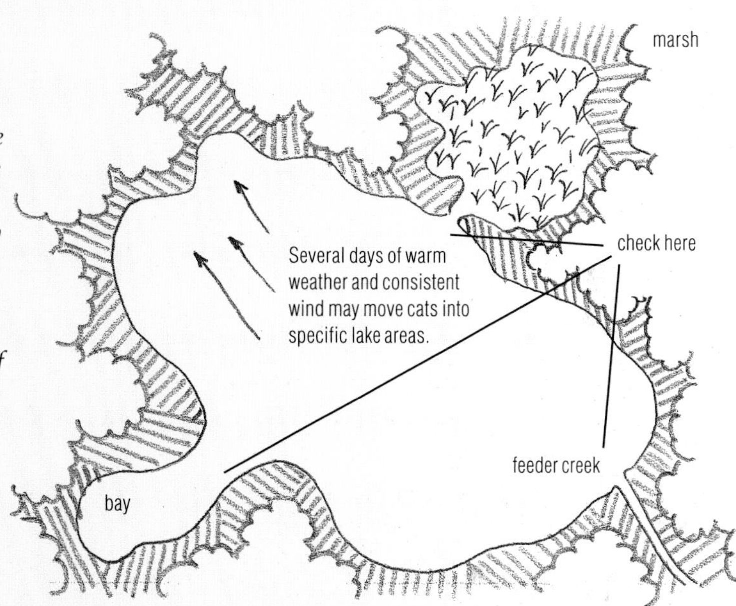

David & Cheryl Woods' One-Acre Out-Back-the-House Pond—Northeast Missouri

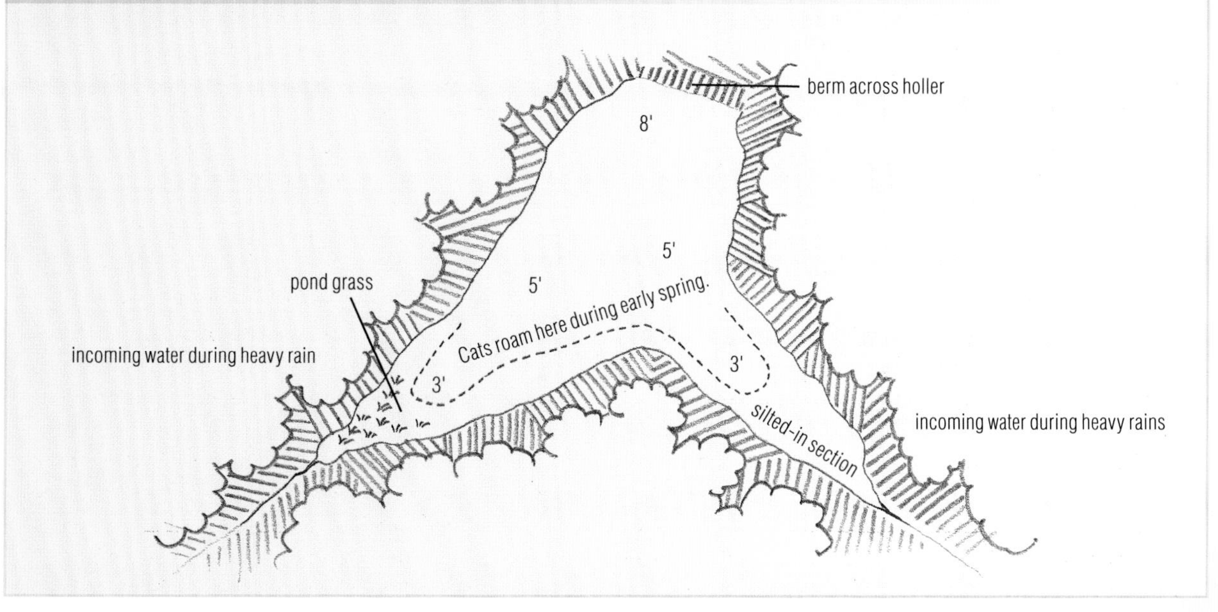

Location in Principle—Riverine Reservoirs

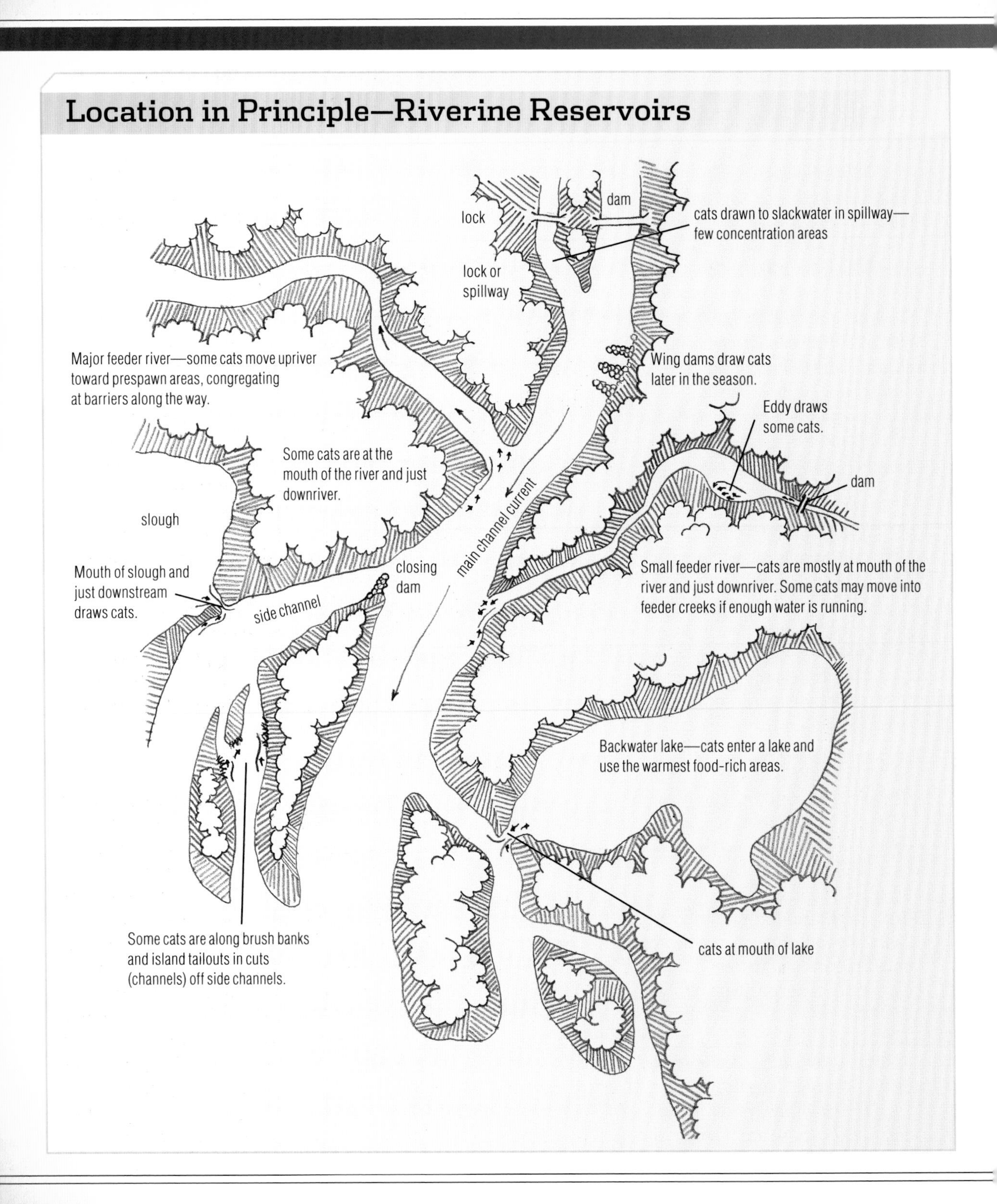

lock
dam
cats drawn to slackwater in spillway—few concentration areas
lock or spillway
Major feeder river—some cats move upriver toward prespawn areas, congregating at barriers along the way.
Wing dams draw cats later in the season.
Eddy draws some cats.
Some cats are at the mouth of the river and just downriver.
dam
slough
main channel current
Small feeder river—cats are mostly at mouth of the river and just downriver. Some cats may move into feeder creeks if enough water is running.
Mouth of slough and just downstream draws cats.
closing dam
side channel
Backwater lake—cats enter a lake and use the warmest food-rich areas.
Some cats are along brush banks and island tailouts in cuts (channels) off side channels.
cats at mouth of lake

East Lake is connected by a necked passage to Upper Middle East Lake, which is connected by a passage to what I call Upper East Lake, which has a dammed inlet stream running from Spirit Lake, a large, moderately fertile body of water.

In principle, we should first check either the mouth of the inlet area in the north, or the outlet area in the south. All the necked-passage areas should also be potential spots to catch cats, the best being those farthest removed from East Lake. While principles (rules) provide a basis for finding and catching fish, when you finally get down to it, you can't catch cats on a rule. You still have to go and see for yourself.

The mouth of the small inlet stream from Spirit into Upper East Lake is a good spot to catch cats. At ice-out, however, the water from Spirit is just too cold. Takes several weeks before this spot turns on. The necked passages immediately connected to East Lake are better early on. The fish usually are somewhere in the vicinity of the downcurrent side of the passage. Can't tell you a thing about the outlet area. I've never fished it. I'd check it, though. In lakes, current spots often draw cats most of the season.

But, you say, my lake doesn't have all those connecting lakes. It's just a big round puddle. You sure? Any inlets from connecting marshes? Any bays off the main lake? Any boat canals? Might want to set up at the point at the mouth of a bay, or check the mouth of a boat canal.

If you really are dealing with a round puddle, look for shallow bars in the west, northwest, or north portion of the lake, for these areas tend to warm more quickly than the main body of water. Don't forget the food factor, either. Several days of warm weather and a consistent breeze from the same direction may blow warm surface water into a corner of a lake, perhaps along with food for cats.

SMALL RESERVOIRS AND PONDS

Find the warmest water. Even a slight difference counts. Usually, check shallow areas just away from the main body of the small reservoir or pond. Often, these are nothing more than a corner of a pond—often a corner in the north part of the pond. In small reservoirs, always check the inlet area, which is probably shallow and somewhat silted in.

These suggestions apply even on the smallest ponds. Each April, friends and I hunt turkeys in the northeastern corner of Missouri. It's a gobbler hunt until noon—then, given good weather, we spend the afternoon hunting for morel mushrooms and fishing ponds for largemouth bass and and channel catfish. On David and Cheryl Woods' farm where we stay, for example, is a one-acre pond formed by berming a portion of a "holler," as David calls it. Truth be known, even April in northern Missouri usually doesn't mean warm enough weather to get cats going good. What fish we catch—both bass and cats—are invariably in one of two secondary holler arms far away from the deep water near the berm.

Figure the food factor, too. Lots of small reservoirs have shad kills during winter. Just after ice-out Up North, or as the water begins to warm significantly farther south, cats are where the dead shad are. Again, wind usually is a factor in moving both warmer surface water and shad into given areas. Also, pond owners often feed cats. Even though cats often aren't fed during winter, a feeding area can still attract them.

RIVERINE RESERVOIRS

While technically reservoirs, their upper reaches seem more like rivers. These include most lock-and-dam sections of the Mississippi and Ohio rivers and their immediate tributaries, plus many of the TVA reservoirs in the Southeast. As previously mentioned, in these reservoirs, dead shad often are pushed through locks or dam generators and then flow via current in the main channel past main-reservoir structural elements. Eventually, though, some of the shad also are swept into side channels, or the mouths of creek channels or feeder-creek cuts off the main channel. Most of the intense early-season activity occurs just removed from the main channel, as opposed to the far-removed activity that occurs in cuts at the back of feeder creeks in other reservoirs.

Just depends on the reservoir and what's available. The rules don't change, but the game remains a balance of what's available structurally in conjunction with the location of food and warm water. Some side channels leading to major backwater areas far removed from main current draw cats.

One of the best such areas I've fished is a half-mile-long riprapped shoreline, along a steep drop in a secondary side channel off a major side channel. (So, I suppose it's at least a mile from the main current, much as the back of a major creek arm on a classic reservoir might be a mile from the main reservoir.) The riprap is on a north shore, hit almost all day by sun, apparently helping to warm the water. Nearby are backwater ponds and sloughs that attract bluegills, crappies, bullheads, carp, and minnows. Leeches drifted below slip-floats and bobbed along the riprap produce the most channel cats. Cutbait drifted the same way produces the biggest fish.

SMALL RIVERS

This applies only indirectly to what's happening in small rivers right now. Cats remain attracted to warmer water where food lies, but few classic cuts, backwaters, sloughs, or side channels are available to move cats far away from main current. Again, cats shy from heavy current in favor of eddies just removed from main current, often congregating in barrier areas as they move slowly upriver to prespawn spots.

Barrier areas provide natural obstructions to catfish migration—shallow riffles, downed timber, the back sides of large sandbars, and any large eddies. Even in small rivers, cats are attracted to feeder creeks, sometimes running up those creeks or at least holding at the mouths of small creeks. Cats tend to run upcurrent, not downcurrent; but then the details of that story require more explanation than we have time for here.

As you might imagine, Zacker had some fine war stories, the best of which even might have been true. One favorite went something like this.

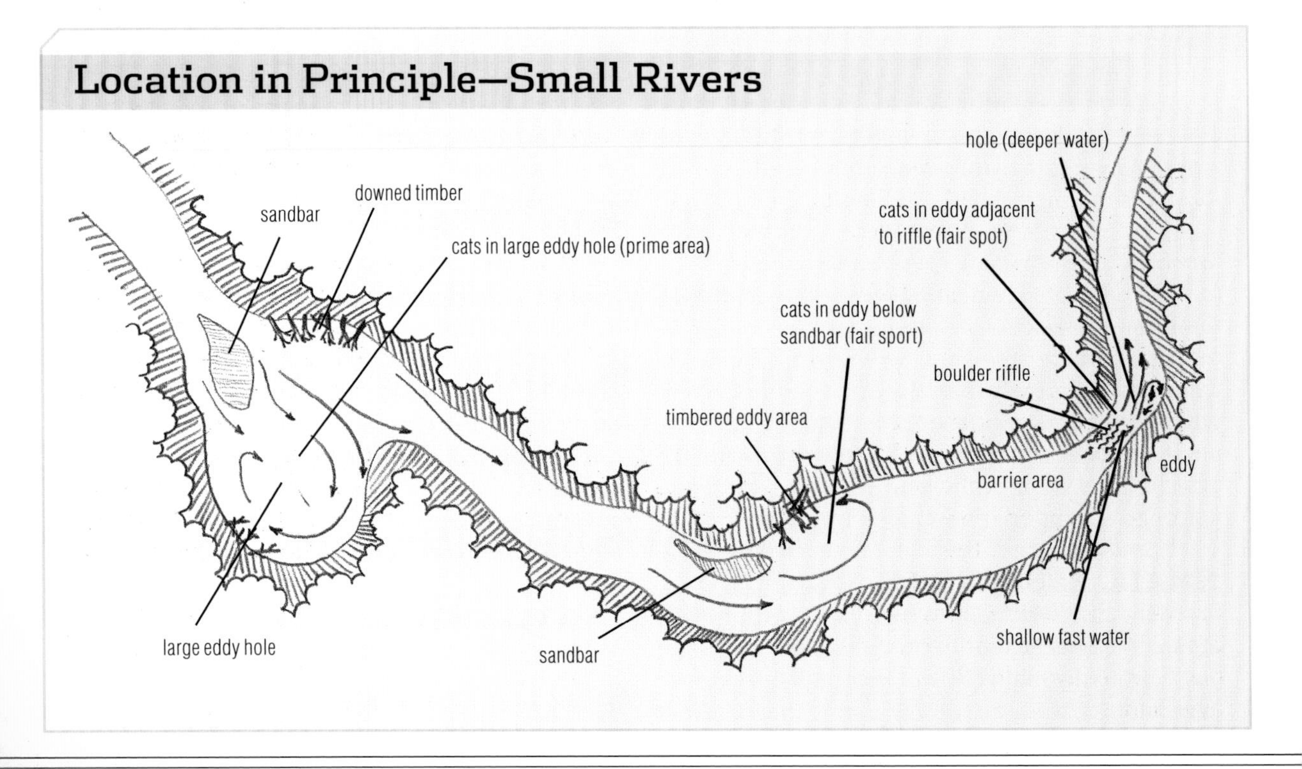

It's been a long winter, but happy days are here again We'll catch and release the big ones and keep enough small ones for a big ol' fish fry.

I can still see Zacker telling it as he sat out back of his old house on an old lawnchair, a .22 pistol resting in his lap as he guarded his garden from the starlings that liked to pull up his pea plants.

"Yep," he'd say. "Times were when we didn't for weeks eat anything that wasn't salted horsemeat or the like. Then one day, moving on down the line with part of my unit, up over a hill we came, and there standing right in the road were three chickens. As in real chickens—live ones—with real drumsticks, the kind we all used to eat with trimmings on Sundays back home. Well, the idea hit everyone at the same time. Rifles flew, packs got dropped—we chased chickens."

I'll never forget the sparkle in Zacker's old eyes as he reveled in telling about bottles of French wine being passed round while they roasted those chickens over an open fire. "To this day," he always said, "it was the best chicken I've ever had."

Then he'd end the story with an observation. "Yep," he'd say, "when opportunity comes knocking—don't matter how small that opportunity might seem—knock back with all the spirit you can muster."

That was Zacker's way of saying, live life with passion, you're only going around once, make the best of what you have even if times are tough and the going's rough. Focus on heaven and not so much on hell, for things are never so bad they can't get worse if you just sit there moping about it.

Now go catch those cats and have fun. Have yourself a big ol' fish fry. Better times and bigger cats are coming, but in the meantime, look for cuts when April sings her tenuous song.

Historic Perspectives

Just a little over a decade ago only a handful of catfish anglers across America were fishing for blue catfish during winter. This story fueled the hunt for giant fish and changed the course of catfishing forever. Today, winter fishing is standard procedure on most great blue-cat waters, including many like the James River and the Potomac, which have since developed into fisheries that may one day produce a world record. Today Stange continues to contend that the record someday soon is bound to approach 150 pounds.

Illustrations by Chuck Nelson

Jim Moyer hefts a mega blue.

CHAPTER 30

OCTOBER 1996

Countdown to Mega Blues

ANYONE READING THIS who wants to catch a blue cat of gargantuan proportions has a good chance to do so, particularly during the next five months. In at least a dozen states from California to Virginia and the Carolinas, the colder water of fall and throughout winter and early spring seems to move these monsters into areas where they're easier to catch. The resulting opportunities to tangle with fish of legendary size remain unknown to most of the fishing world. We ride here on the edge of fishing history.

World Records On The Horizon!

From California to the Carolinas, blue cats have made a comeback from the days during the '40s, '50s, and '60s, when dams changed so much of their traditional habitat. Like their ancestors, the fish today are of monstrous proportions and seemingly getting even larger. Now, too, perhaps more than at any other time in history, we are learning how to catch them.

The dimensions of some of the blue cats swimming in these waters—big lakes, rivers, and reservoirs—remain hard for folks riding the "mainstream" of the fishing world to fathom. Most anglers are used to thinking in terms of bass. Or walleyes. So it is that the largemouth and the walleye and certainly the muskie have

Virgil Agee poses matter-of-factly beside another mega blue. "Sometime soon, someone will land a blue that will make the present record seem like small change," he says.

come to be considered our freshwater monsters. Pshaww. Bass are big at 10; that's big for walleyes too; and muskies rarely reach 40. Blue cats, on the other hand?

In California, John Collins, an accomplished bass angler, is working a crawfish along the bottom in Lower Otay Reservoir. He and his partner have already boated a 10-pound bass this April morning, when . . . "I thought it might have been a big bass for a moment," Collins says. "But then it stripped 75 yards of line." Fifteen minutes later, as the fish surfaced, Collins can only exclaim, "It looks like a seal!"

Big blues really do assume grotesque proportions. Collins's fish measures only 51 inches but has a robust 35½-inch girth. Spread your arms four feet. Now make a big circle with your arms, as in, pretend you're reaching around Rosanne Barr's waistline. That's Collins's fish. "People just aren't used to seeing fish made like that," Collins says. "Really, it's almost impossible to imagine how big a fish like this is." At 82.1 pounds, the fish was the new California record, surpassing the existing record by nearly 20 pounds.

Meanwhile, suppose you were in the boat one day last year with Clarksville, Tennessee, catfish guide Jim Moyer. Moyer was the primary source to help us break the news about how mega blues can be caught during Coldwater Periods. He annually catches a dozen blues over 50 pounds and hundreds over 30 pounds. This day he is fishing a big river in Alabama. "People just aren't prepared to deal with these creatures," he is saying, shaking his head. "Add me to that list when it comes to the most monstrous of them, even after all the big fish I've handled.

"It was just one of those days that you park perfectly on a hole that has monsters—and they're hungry," he says. "The first fish we hook, well, he just spools me—250 yards of 30-pound test. Gone, like that. Spools me without so much as me turning the fish or even slowing it down. So another 30 minutes pass and I hook another one. I can tell you I don't have a net that handles a world record, for this old boy wouldn't go in no net.

"Can't tell you exactly how long this fish is. Girth? Well, hey, I'm a big guy and I don't think I could reach around it. We get a weight, though, before releasing the fish. The hog scale in the boat registers 87 pounds, but I think the fish has to be bigger. The fish has to be some 56 inches long, maybe 40 inches around. Look at the picture and you tell me. These fish are something from another world. Consider this: I've been spooled four times the past year. How big are some of these fish?"

Virgil Agee is certain some of them are kicking near the 150 mark. A seasoned catfish angler from Jefferson, Missouri, these days Agee pursues monster blues almost exclusively. "That fish two Octobers ago," he says, referring to one of the largest blues he's landed, "had me all over the Osage River." Then, as in the case with Moyer's struggle with the near-90, Agee had to wrestle the fish to string it alongside the boat. "It was a monster," he says. "But I'd seen bigger, so I decided to continue fishing instead of heading right in to weigh it."

Eight hours later the fish weighed 101 pounds 7 ounces. Shortly thereafter a fishery biologist suggested the fish might have weighed near 114 when it was caught. The Missouri record is 103, the world record 109 and 4 ounces. Virgil just shrugs. "I'm interested in records, but not overwhelmed by them," he says. "I do wish I would have weighed the fish sooner—just out of curiosity." Like Collins's California fish, this fish measures 51 inches, but is 3.5 inches more rotund, with a 40-inch girth.

Two months later Agee lands another monster blue, a fish he hasn't told many folks about. "This fish weighs—well, we'll never know for sure—but the scale says 121 on the nose," he says. "It's a world record. But, we learn after the fish is released, the certification sticker on the scale is out of date. So the fish can never be confirmed—kind of an unconfirmed world record." Agee's 101-pound fish, however, is the present Catch and Release World Record, which makes his 121 the unconfirmed Catch and Release World Record.

But the stories get even bigger, for Agee believes he'll get another shot at a fish he lost during a stretch of fall and winter fishing several years ago. "I had him boatside," he says. "I don't tell many folks the story because they can't believe such a fish exists. But I've caught 70s and 80s, and the 101 and 121. I know what these fish look like. This fish, though—well, this fish was just in another class—150 easy. I couldn't get him on board—no gaff, no way to land the fish other than kill it. I don't kill big fish. So I reached for channel lock pliers, thinking I can get a grip on the fish and run a rope through his gills. But as I reach, the fish surges—I have my drag tightened down at the end of the battle in order to control the fish. My line breaks before I can loosen the drag."

John Collins's California record, "Looked like a seal!" when it surfaced. This 82.1-pounder, a likley omen of big things to come from California, is presently no great shakes measured against fish swimming in the Carolinas, Tennessee, Kansas, Missouri, and other waters in the heart of the blue cat range.

Agee and Moyer lend a lean and persistent perspective to what we have been telling you right along for the past few years. The big blues, apparently first adversely affected by the dams of the '50s and '60s, are back in a big way—in such a big way that the fish may actually be getting as

Clarence Kerr's 103, the present Missouri record, and the world record before being replaced by a 109 from Santee-Cooper, came from that mega-blue-cat sanctuary, the middle Missouri River.

large or larger than in times past. Mega fish are there, in perhaps some 12 states, and only a few folks presently understand how to catch them. Few folks also realize the mystique that is bound to quickly envelop the continuing quest for these new-age monsters. This story should become one of the most compelling in fishing as it begins to gain publicity during the next years.

Agee: "A fish will be caught sometime soon that makes the present record look like medium change. At least, my 101 and 121 are back in the river. Those fish could weigh 150 now. And who knows what that 150 weighs?"

Collins's fish, also released back into Lower Otay, could also approach 100 pounds by now. And in many other waters across North America, fish of such mammoth proportions probably reside. Certainly, the lower Missouri River and portions of the middle and lower Mississippi, in the heart of the original blue-cat range, remain prime water for a world record.

The Missouri 103, the world record for a short time and the present Missouri record, was taken from the Missouri River below Omaha several years ago. Texas and Oklahoma waters have produced 120-pound fish on trotlines. Arkansas has monster fish, too. And I haven't even attempted (and won't here) to chronicle the catches from Santee-Cooper, South Carolina, home of the current world record and presently the best water in the country for mega blues.

Blue cats can today grow big quickly in some waters, a fact witnessed by fishery biologist Larry Bottroff, who recorded Collins's California record. Bottroff says a fin clip shows the Collins cat was part of a batch of one-pound blues planted in Lower Otay and San Vicente reservoirs in 1985. Collins's fish had grown at least 81 pounds in 11 years.

That the nature of a fish species can change as those fish age and grow is well documented, and so it appears to be with blue cats. My friend Zacker, that old commercial catman from a generation of catmen familiar with the record blue cats of the '50s and '60s, used to say simply that "little fish aren't big fish—different as night and day. Little blues," he'd say, "fish to about 8 to 25 pounds—are pesky varmints. Fun to catch and good to eat, but they're everywhere, doing everything at the same time."

His point was that some small blues might just as soon be grubbing on the bottom as nitpicking stuff off the surface. Then, too, some blues might run shad in open water, while others are snacking on snails and clams from river or reservoir flats. "But big cats are big cats wherever they swim," he'd say. And by Zacker's standards, that meant fish with a yearning for big water, deeper and cooler water, and a monster food source.

Most of Agee's fish come from some of the deepest holes in the Osage, itself a pretty good piece of water that runs into that mega-blue-cat sanctuary, the Missouri River. Much of his best fishing has been in October, November, and December. But he admits that he wants to spend more time exploring the fishing during midwinter, so long as current is present and the water doesn't freeze. It's during this period, Agee knows, that Moyer catches his big fish.

Moyer's fish, though, mostly hold along channel banks in main current in big rivers, territory from which Agee rarely catches big cats. Most of the huge cats Agee catches hold in deep holes near but not in heavy current. In each case, current remains a key factor. In rivers, monster blues rarely feed during periods of reduced water generation. Meanwhile, in reservoirs like Marion and Moltrie, which make up famous Santee-Cooper, current is an indirect factor. Most Santee-Cooper guides contend that giant blues rarely range onto shallow flats. Most of the monsters run the deep water in old channel beds, often many miles from shoreline flats.

Moyer favors depths from 20 on the shallow end into 40 or 50 feet of water. It's the bank or drop-off, in conjunction with current, that keys good fishing. Only occasionally do blues roam the shallow flat next to the drop-off, preferring instead to run the drop-off from about 20 or so down into 35 or more. Often the fish are at the base of the channel drop-off, in current that might be running 7 miles per hour. These fish are on the bottom, probably holding in depressions or behind bottom debris where the current's minimized.

As Zacker always contended, monster fish need a monster food source, not necessarily large baits or baitfish so much as lots of them. In many waters, blue cats range over mussel beds, eating the entire mussel, shell and all, digesting the soft body of the clam before eliminating the shell. Some of the fish in Santee-Cooper look like they should rattle should you shake them, they're so full of clams. Some of these fish also have anal pores the size of a 50-cent piece from having to eliminate the shells.

I believe it doubtful that monster blues run baitfish in open water; built as they are like small freight trains, they likely don't function well there. But I don't know for sure. Certainly, in reservoirs, the big boys drift suspended during certain periods. But the bigger fish seemingly feed along the bottom, keying on banquet sources of dead shad, which often are abundant during winter. Indeed, it may be the combination of mega food sources in conjunction with colder water that reduces metabolism, combining to fuel mega growth and a measure of increased longevity.

Moyer's Approach—Most of Moyer's best fishing is in the upper 1/2 to 1/3 of the river-like portions of river-run reservoirs. He rarely finds big fish in tailwater areas, because the tailwater areas available to him offer only shallow water. Thus, shad flushed through the roller dams are washed along through relatively shallow water until they tumble into deeper channel areas downriver. Big blues push upriver until they reach areas that naturally gather the most drifting shad.

Only occasionally can the best areas be identified by looking at eddies and other typical river structural elements with the naked eye. "The bank eddies are channel-cat territory," Moyer says. "It's the portion of the channel bank as it drops into the deepest part of the channel that keys where the blues hold. If, say, a huge eddy formed by a bank projection coincides with a drop-off into the channel, it might hold fish. But the eddy isn't the key."

Moyer has spent time anchored along almost every edge of channel in the 50-mile section of river that forms the upper portion of the river reservoir below Cheatam dam. "Some areas almost always hold fish," he says. "The combination of old stumps and bottom or bank depressions and other nooks and crannies helps. And often these things just can't be seen, even with electronics. You just have to fish to determine if fish are using an area. But once I catch fish in an area, it almost always continues to produce."

But not every day for days in a row. "A number of fish seem to move into an area and hold there. Pull up and anchor and toss baits out and you get a shot at those fish in short order, if they're feeding," he says. "No use staying for more than 20 minutes if you're not getting bit. And if you catch two or three fish, it might take four or five days for new fish to move in and hold in the area. Don't camp on areas. Keep moving from anchor spot to spot."

When Moyer is searching in what has proven to be a productive area, or is in a new area that he believes should be productive, he anchors for 20 minutes then moves downriver or upriver 150 to 200 yards and anchors again.

"Fresh bait's absolutely critical," he emphasizes. "I use one-inch portions of skipjack herring fillet, some of the oiliest bait there is, threaded on a 6/0 or 7/0 hook. But I constantly change my bait. I put new bait on almost every cast. That's how to call cats in from where they're holding in each anchor area. You don't always land a bait right in front of their noses, but current carries the baitfish oils downriver and the cats sense something good's in the area and move to find it.

"Most fishermen think that just because they still have bait on, it's working for them. The bait needs to be oozing. As soon as the water removes the blood and oils and turns the meat firm, I switch bait. From what I've seen, all other things being equal, this is the one thing that keys consistent catches."

Moyer anchors right on the channel edge so he can place baits up and down the drop-off. Perfect placement in a new anchor position would be a bait at the top of the drop-off and another one at the base of it—plus two more baits somewhere else on the drop-off. He holds anchor position in the swift current by dropping a 35-pound portion of railroad track on a 100-foot rope, using whatever length of rope necessary to hold nose-first in the current. We've held almost as well using a 28-pound navy-style anchor, although a navy anchor is more prone to snag.

He favors making about a 50-yard cast behind the boat to place each bait, instead of fishing it almost vertically below the boat. "Wouldn't seem to make any difference," he says, "but it does. It must have something to do with how the current plays on the length of line that allows the bait to work more effectively on a longer line."

To hold the rig down, Moyer uses a 2- or 3-ounce egg sinker above a swivel connected to about a 30-inch section of leader. From what I've seen, leader length is open to some experimentation and probably depends on the situation. It's hard to argue with Moyer's success in rivers; but particularly in a reservoir with little current, I prefer a leader no longer than a foot. The rest of his tackle consists of Berkley #3 and #4 E-Cat Series rods, which Moyer designed for them, and 30-pound-test Berkley Big Game line on Garcia 7000 reels.

"My favorite hook has always been the Mustad #37160 wide-gap design, or a similar Kahle hook from Eagle Claw—6/0 or 7/0," Moyer says. "It's a deadly hooker that lies well in current when it's threaded full of cut shad. But these days I'm a little concerned that a Kahle hook might not hold a huge fish, so I've been experimenting with the Gamakatsu #2418, an 8/0 black Octopus-style hook."

Agee's Approach— Agee prefers to fish with a lively 7- to 11-inch redspot chub, which he rigs on a 4/0 Gamakatsu #2114, the same Octopus-style hook that Moyer uses. Skipjack herring aren't available in the Osage, so Agee has experimented with cut gizzard shad. "It's great for lots of action," he says, "but the biggest fish to date have always gone for a live chub."

Agee rigs with tackle he feels fits the situation. Occasionally, he uses saltwater tackle and heavy line. Often, his tackle is scaled down compared to Moyer's rigging. His 101 was taken with 12-pound line, a 7-foot Daiwa rod, and an old Garcia 5000D reel.

"Big cats only spool you if you try to land one from an anchored position in current," Agee says. "When you hook a big boy, pull anchor and follow the fish—stay over him. Not being able to control a fish if it gets near a snag is possible, but in the areas I'm fishing, I haven't had a problem."

Agee: "One of my favorite spots is a classic big-fish hole just off main current. A shallow riffle runs just about 2 feet deep across the river, then drops sharply onto several 25- to 35-foot shelves and finally into a 50- to 60-foot hole. I motor slowly around this big hole, watching my electronics. When I see fish activity near bottom, I anchor just up from those fish.

"Nothing fancy about the terminal rigging—just a standard slipsinker rig—that is, an egg sinker, as light as I can get away with—sliding on my mainline, connected to a swivel, then a leader several feet long and a 4/0 hook. I usually run the hook through the tail of the bait just back from the dorsal fin. Sometimes I cast a bait onto one of the shelves and another into the base of the hole—just depends where the fish seem to be. And when I can't see fish on electronics, I set up the same way.

"I don't want fish to be gut-hooked, so once the rod's in a rod holder, I switch on the clicker mechanism and don't wait long to strike, once a fish has turned the clicker over a time or two. I just pick up the rod, follow the fish by dropping the rod tip as it moves off, and set. Really, once a fish takes like that, it's rare to miss it."

As we've so often said in *In-Fisherman* magazine and the *1996 Catfish Guide*, blue cats are creatures of big rivers and impoundments. They like a lot more current than either channel cats or flatheads. And as the *1997 Catfish Guide* further explores, we believe that wherever blue cats and river-run impoundments coincide, these cats can be caught during winter—just as they can be caught from reservoir systems like Santee-Cooper and an as-yet-undefined number of other southern, midsouthern, and western reservoirs.

Somewhere along a still poorly defined northern boundary of blue cat territory, the bite shuts down. Iced-up water appears to shut fishing down, at least until warmer weather gets the bite going again. South Carolina's prime. So are Tennessee and California. And we'd be surprised if numerous waters in Oklahoma, Texas, Arkansas, Kansas, southern Missouri, Kentucky, Virginia, and parts farther south don't also offer prime fishing for monster blues. They're not all going to be mega fish, but we won't be even slightly surprised if someone rolls a world record this winter.

You're not likely to have much competition. But someday soon, as the word spreads about fishing for these fish of legendary size—well, for his part, Agee likes to wear a hat that says, "Bass fishermen are just catfishermen in transition."

And then, right at deadline for this magazine, a fish likely to be confirmed as the new All-Tackle Record: Bill McKinley's 55-inch long, 41.5-inch girth 111-pound fish from Wheeler Reservoir, the Tennessee River in Alabama. We predict more and bigger fish to come.

Historic Perspectives

Things change in Farmington, Iowa, over the years, although even today it's still the weathered and forgotten river-town masterpiece of Stange's yesteryear: Catfish Corner's Bill Marsh passes on at age 71 in early 2001; Bill the Tire Man's not doing tires anymore; and the Timberline Bar's on the down-and-out. Sonny's Super Sticky, though, remains the dipbait brew against which the competition measures their product line and sales success. Stange tells a recent story of a major fishing-tackle manufacturing company that works on a dip blend to compete in the catfish market. They can make an effective product, but haven't found a way to market the product profitably—small companies like Sonny's operate on slim margins. The primary dip product this big company uses to measure the effectiveness of their new blend? Sonny's Super Sticky, of course. Although this article focuses mightily on Sonny's bait, many dipbait manufacturers to this day credit the article as the catalyst that increases sales and market share for all manufacturers in new areas of North America.

Illustration by Larry Tople

CHAPTER 31

JULY 1997

Bitchin' Blends for Channels and Blues

PERHAPS ONLY IN FARMINGTON, IOWA, a weathered and somewhat forgotten little turn-of-the-century river town on the banks of the Des Moines River, separating those most distant portions of southeast Iowa from the wilderness that is northeast Missouri, could Sonny Hootman carry on his "unholy" trade.

Folks are so downright friendly in Farmington and the atmosphere so generally way laid-back that Deputy Sheriff Barney P. Fife and Opie and Andy would hardly be noticed at all, if they parked their cane poles outside and stepped into Big Glenn Halbrook's Very General Sporting Goods Store to weigh their catch and sit a spell.

Big Glenn's place cuts the mustard a durn sight better—with stuff stocked for country folks who really go a-huntin', a-fishin', and a-trappin'—than most big-city Quick Slicks I've been in. But then no real surprise, for Big Glenn and most of the long-spell residents of Farmington have been living life pretty close to the real thing for as long as anyone can remember.

This being the heart of catfish country, no surprise either that a letter addressed only *Catfish Corner, Farmington, IA,* still is delivered forthwith and no questions asked just down the street from

"The Catfish Is
A Hideous Beast,
A Bottom-Feeder
That Doth Feast,
Upon Unholy Bait . . . "
—Old English Verse

Big Glenn's to one William Marsh, a most noted catman in these parts. Bill's been at this country livin' along the river a spell, too, and like most folks you meet in Farmington, he's a happy man who likes the cards dealt him, some good and some bad—appreciates, he does, the times he's seen and the chances he's had to have a rod and reel or a shotgun in his hands pretty much since childhood.

Then, by and by, just across the river bridge, heading west a piece before the road bends south some, where people claim to talk real Missourah—as opposed to that designer stuff that passes for not much more than South Iowan— David and Cheryl Wood run the roost on Turkey Flat, a little farm where friends and I make camp each spring, huntin' turkeys, fishin' catfish, and sneakin' up on mushrooms.

Things 'round Farmington, I'm tellin' ya, still work pretty much the way they used to—that is, pretty much the way they should. Sure enough, there's a real butcher, who from start to finish processes hogs and cattle raised no farther away than in this county; a butcher who still knows sirloin tenders from a piece of top sirloin; a butcher who appreciates the delicacy that is flank steak from a prime (not choice) bovine.

'Course, Bill The Tire Man is hanging handy, too, up at the little place he's run for more than 30 years, feet kicked up, waiting for business that in my case means changing a tire with an Osage orange spike in it. You can bet no signs at The Tire Man's prohibit entry into the garage area where he works; he really wants you standing there looking over his shoulder, talking shop. And darned if, even though I visit only once a year, the bartender up at the Timberline still doesn't always pour my drink into a glass polished on his shirtsleeve right there, and has a pickled pig's foot waiting on a napkin before I can sit down.

Farmington is a right natural setting for Sonny's, a catbait manufacturing concern of some esteem in the underground venues of the catfish world. Sonny's makes *Sonny's Super Sticky,* described by one of my hardcore catfishin' friends as "one bitchin' blend." Few who have fished it argue. Most years, Sonny and his sons mix and then sell, by word whispered among catmen, 150,000 pounds or so of this sweet brew.

Long before I met Sonny, he was already selling all the bait he could produce—and he's old enough to realize he hasn't the time in life left to want to produce more. He does a little logging, runs raccoons, travels the Midwest runnin' turtle traps for the fun of it—and he makes catbait. No more. No less. So, he could care less whether or not I am a fancy-pants writer who might say nice things about his bait. Won't make a stitch of difference whether I do or don't. Before Sonny made catbait, though, he was a catfishin' man. And long before I was an editor, I was a catfishin' man. So, Sonny and I talk the same language.

It's a fine late-April afternoon some years ago—tulips blooming in neighborhood yards—when I pull into Sonny's for the first time. As I step from my truck, on a gentle south breeze rides vestige of the beginnings of Sonny's bitchin' brew—raw cheese oozing in various volcanic stages, ripening in rows of 50-gallon drums, not far from the pole barn where the bait's finally mixed. Even at a distance, the beginnings of what is to become batches of his brutal bitchin' brew clears sinuses.

If the initial aroma carried in the open breeze is, let's say, awe-inspiring, even to an old hand at dippin', the air in the pole barn is something else. Purple haze, baby. Smoke on the water. No place for children, small dogs, and most grown men. At close quarters, the final secret ingredients render the aromatic fumes from the blend penetrating, stifling, eye-watering, edging on cut-your-wrists overwhelming. Sonny and his sons, acclimated, seem not to notice; but I need another day and two showers just to remove the residual odor from my hair.

I'd be a poor reporter if I only told you about a bait you might not be able to get in your part of the cat world. So the story here goes beyond Sonny's Super Sticky to the half-dozen or so bad brews made in the back corners of basements and

Sonny's Super Sticky

Sonny Hootman stirring up a batch of Sonny's Super Sticky, and with his son Sonny Jr., testing his fine brew bankside in southern Iowa.

Dip worm in, dip worm out, illustrating the perfect consistency of Sonny's Super Sticky.

sheds throughout the cat world. Sonny Hootman just happens to be a fine sounding-board for ideas and questions, for he has little to sell besides good fishing. And he has a world of experience in dealing with dipbaits.

Dips generally are the tool of choice among the hardcore anglers who fish with commercially prepared baits most widely called stinkbaits. That's because dips are so intense. "If there's attracting that needs doin', dips just generally do the job better than anything else," Sonny offers on the subject. "Of course, some folks think dips are harder to work with than pastebaits. (Pastes are of a dough-like consistency.) I can't see it, though. A good dip is as simple as one-two-three, and almost impossible to fish wrong."

Dips are creamy, just thin enough to require a delivery vehicle—usually a plastic worm but sometimes a piece of sponge. Also on the scene the past few years are 1- to 2-inch lengths of surgical tubing with holes.

Which delivery vehicle works best? Well now, depends, depends, depends, and who knows for sure, and even that remains open to debate. Sonny says simply that channels and sometimes blues bite just about anything that holds the essence of the dip for a time.

"I've cleaned a ton of catfish," he says. "And being a curious sort, I often open stomachs to see what they've been eating. Mice, shrews, birds—

New Dippin' Products

New products for the dippin' man. Just a squeeze between sponge and plastic dries a dipworm perfectly so it can be redipped. For those cats hooked deep, a worm hook-remover that works. And a hand lotion that does a job on dip residue. (Catfish Worm Dryer: Kewanee, IL; Catfish-Worm Hook Remover: Doc's, Parkersburg, IA; Smell Better Lotion: Tidewater Lures, Virginia Beach, VA.)

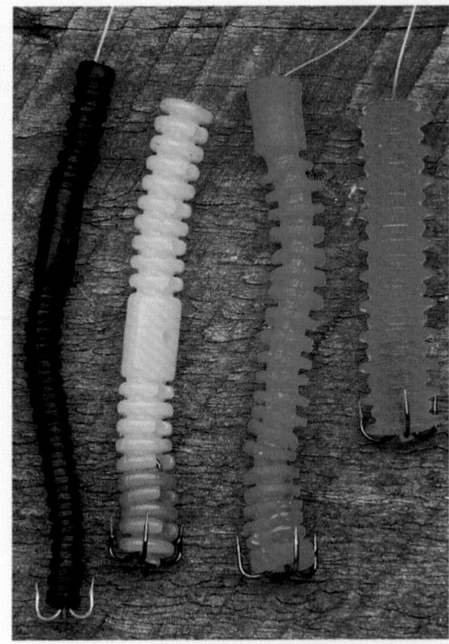

The four dipworms offered by Sonny's are representative of the worms on the market today. From left to right: The Original Catfish Devil Worm; Zipper Dipper; Super Devil Worm; and "Old Whiskers" Catfish Worm.

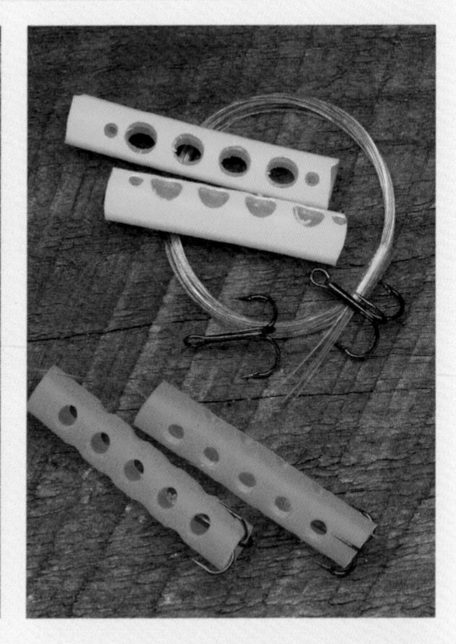

On the scene during the past five years, surgical tube worms for dipping: The Cat Tracker Tubie Worm (top); and the J & N Dip Worm.

even a bat once—and, of course, all the more typical things. Vegetable stuff, too. Like moss, or mulberries, and a little white bank tuber I call a wild parsnip, which washes from the bank when the water's up in June. So, one time I'm finding so many parsnips in fish that I decide to dig some and use them for bait. Didn't catch a thing until, in frustration, I dipped them in Super Sticky."

And on the subject of dipworms, so says Sonny: "Well, a lot of the worms on the market are there because fishermen think this or that characteristic might make one worm better than another. Mostly, though, an extra hole here or there or an extra ring on a worm, and the size of the worm and particularly the color, just don't make much difference—so long as the plastic tends to hold a good sticky bait. I don't make worms, but I sell four styles because fishermen seem to want to guess that their choice might make a difference.

"Myself? I prefer a thin 4- or 6-inch worm called the Original Catfish Devil Worm. It isn't made anymore, but before the company went out of business, I bought enough to keep selling them for a few years. Someone out there needs to make this worm. Not just copy the size and shape, but copy the plastic formula, too, for this worm really holds bait well. This thin worm holds more bait better than most thick worms, even those with really deep cuts or ring grooves, and even those with bumpy protrusions.

"But let's face it," he continues. "Dips are a top bait for fishermen who want to catch a ton of eatin'-sized catfish—for those folks who want lots of action, which is most folks, most of the time. Can't say as I've caught that many cats over 6 pounds on dips. But then, I haven't fished everywhere. Seems reasonable that situations might exist where dips produce big fish better than baits like, say, fresh cutbait. Dips, though, are mostly for folks who want to get bit and go home with a mess of eatin' cats.

"That thinner worm is just easier for a smaller cat to get into its mouth. Now, if you're dealing with bigger average cats—say, lots of 3- and 4-pound fish—then a thicker worm might be better. I haven't fished the tubing enough to comment much, although it looks like it should work. Worms, though, are just hard to beat. Sponge, I think, is fine for soupier products. But then folks should just make up their own minds. As I said, the dip's the thing."

The dipworm is pressed into the dip with a stick. Sonny likes his Super Sticky to barely drip from the worm, but he suggests that an exact consistency isn't overly important and, of course, varies with air temperature.

"Below about 65°F, I keep my bait in a warmer place—at least out of the wind. It sets up perfectly from about 70°F on up to about 80°F, at which point it begins to thin. During the heat of summer, when temperatures are above 90°F, keep it out of direct sunlight. On super-hot days, keep it in a cooler with a little ice. But then most fishing during the most intense heat of summer is during morning, evening, or after dark, when the consistency is perfect. The water's cooler than the air, too, so as soon as you dip the worm into the water, the bait sets up tight.

"In order to feel confident, most fishermen like to see a gob of dip hanging on their worm," Sonny says. "That's why 'sticky' is an important part of my formula. My bait's so sticky that most of the time is just won't come off unless a catfish eats it off. Most baits on the market are made from cheese or shad, with various other additives. Blood's popular. Sonny's offers a regular Super Sticky formula and a blood-added formula. Most of the baits are oil-based. Before making a cast with a dipbait, always dip the worm in the water to help lock the bait onto the worm or sponge.

"It helps, too, if the worm's dry. So I tell folks to carry along a towel to dry their worm each time before they redip. My bait's so sticky, though, that it usually sticks as long as the worm has been waggled a bit in the air before redipping. A wet worm requires more smooshing around in the dip to get it to hold."

Most anglers are curious about how often to dip, I say. "A sticky dip stays on for quite a while," Sonny says. "If there's still dip on the worm, you can make another cast and fish it another five minutes. Dips aren't made to sit forever, though. I wouldn't fish a bait in a spot for more than 10 minutes. That's more than enough time to call in a cat. I'd make another cast.

"I like to fish in current because the taste sensation of the bait is distributed downcurrent. 'Calling all cats!' Riffle areas in rivers are particularly productive during the head of summer. A sticky blend won't wash away quickly even in heavy current. And fishermen should know the truth—even a worm that looks like it doesn't have any dip left often catches fish. When a worm is dipped right, the aura of the bait's still there. But we're all most confident when redipping after each cast."

WHICH DIP WHEN?

Sonny has been making bait for almost 20 years. "Four or five years of correction and redirection," he admits, "and then another few years of fine-tuning." These days, quality control is most important to his bait's continuing popularity among fishermen. "I just can't afford to put any bad bait out there," he says, "not even a small batch. Fishermen just won't come back."

While Sonny is certain his Super Sticky is the finest bait on the market, he graciously grants that other folks are making bait that works, too. "Bowker's was the first to make a dip, and that was many years ago," he says. "Bowker's Original is still a fine blend—although I'd make it stickier.

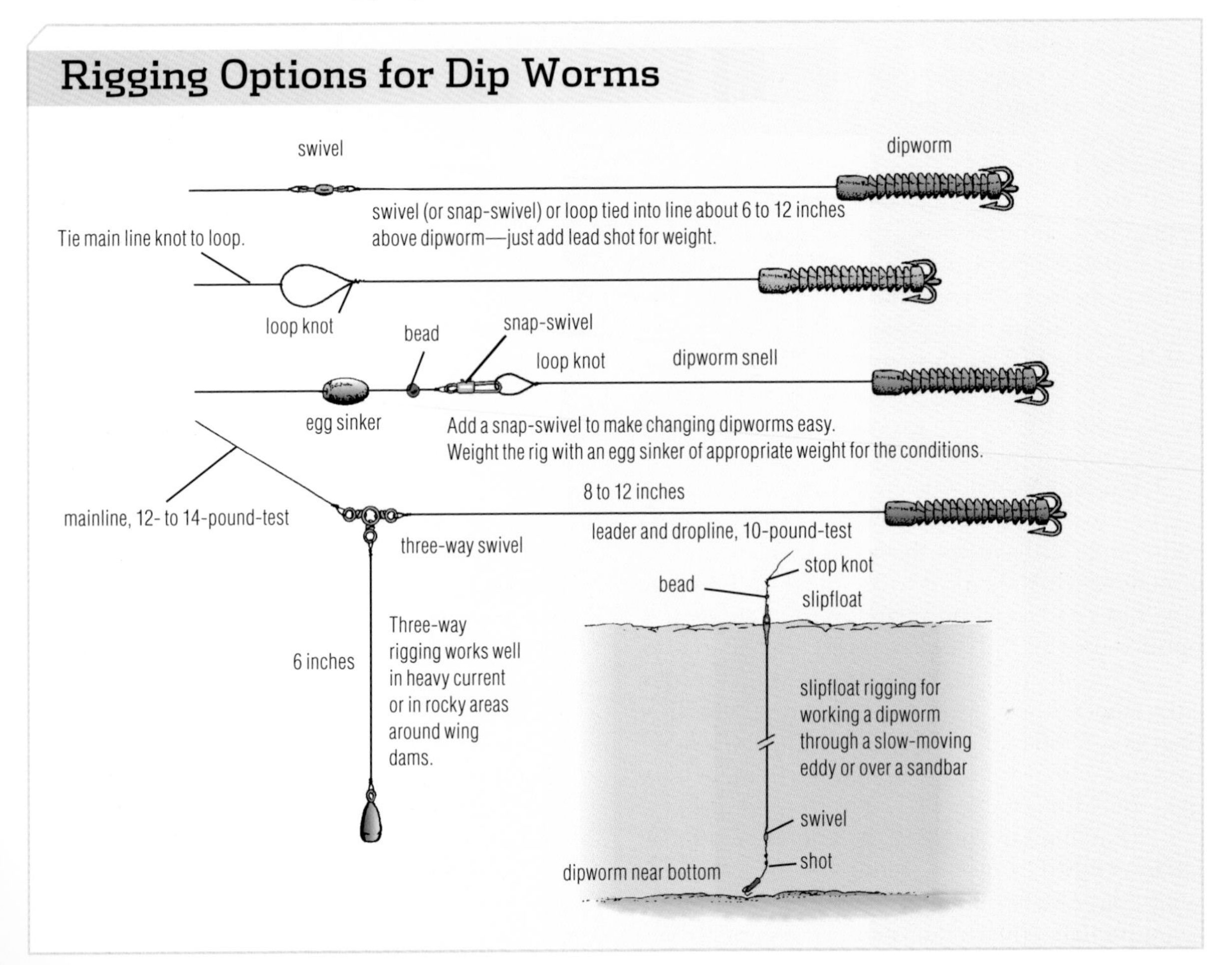

But then, maybe they'd like to make my bait less sticky.

"Doc's Original is another worthy bait. Old Doc, who's gone now, started making dips in the early 1960s, after making pastes since the 1920s. Prepared baits—particularly the dips—are pretty much of Midwest origin, spreading into Missouri, Kansas, Oklahoma, Arkansas, and Texas. Dips still aren't particularly well known in the East, Southeast, or West.

"If a company has been visible on the market a few years, they probably have a fair bait," he continues. "Fishermen should just do what I do. I always fish my Super Sticky, but I get a kick out of trying other baits. I'm always checking the competition—seeing what they're putting out there. Dips don't cost much. A good way to find which dips work best for you is to buy from a couple of top companies."

RIGGING

Whether you're after cats in lakes, rivers, or reservoirs, keep your rigging as simple as possible. The simplest rig for river fishing is to just add a lead shot or two several inches above the dipworm. Resist placing the shot too far up your line—that is, too far away from the hook—as it becomes more difficult to cast and increases the chance for snags.

The most popular rigging consists of an egg sinker sliding on the mainline above a small snap-swivel. Vary the size of the egg sinker based on current and how far you need to cast. Many anglers use a #4 or #5 bead between the sinker and the snap-swivel to protect the knot from the sliding sinker.

A dipworm snell should run about 6 inches to no more than 12 inches. Tie a small swivel, or just make a loop knot on the end of the snell. Slip the loop or the swivel onto the snap portion of the snap-swivel. Changing worms is easy if a fish swallows the bait, or if you want to try a different worm style. Have at least a dozen worms rigged and ready before you hit the water. Retrieve the worms that cats swallow when you clean the fish.

Other rigs work, depending on the situation. Three-way swivel rigging, for example, works on big rivers, particularly around rocky habitat like wing dams. Say you're running 12- or 14-pound mainline, about the standard for dipbaits. Tie the mainline to one rung of the swivel. Tie a dropline of 6 to 12 inches to another rung of the swivel. Add a bell sinker of appropriate weight to this dropline. The dip snell needs to be 3 or 4 inches longer than the dropline and, of course, is tied to the last rung of the three-way swivel. A two-way swivel, by the way, works just as well as a three-way swivel for this rigging. Tie both the mainline and the dropline to the first rung on a two-way.

Floats also work, particularly in rivers where slower-moving water runs through an eddy or pool. Keep the bait near bottom. A slipfloat helps adjust depth easily.

Cats take a dipworm by arching down on the worm from slightly above as it rests on the bottom. A big fish often grabs a bait on the first bite, while a smaller fish tests it a time or two before taking it into its mouth. Don't set too quickly when cats are pecking (testing) the bait.

This stuff is so intense that cats are curious about just what it is. When a fish has the bait, your pole tip starts to move away. Often the cat hooks itself, but set the hook anyway, and reel 'em on in. A pair of needle-nosed pliers is handy for removing small treble hooks. Doc's offers a special "Catfish Worm Hook Remover" that I intend to try this year.

Fishing with dips is just as simple as a Sunday afternoon in Farmington. Maybe Sonny says it best, at the end of his instructional pamphlet on how to use his bait: "Sure enough, the rest is up to you. I guarantee my bait will catch catfish. After a real honest effort and you aren't satisfied, your money will be refunded."

But then Sonny gets right down to core of that issue. "If such be the case, though," he says, "I do honestly believe your catfishing credibility is in question."

All Time Bass Greats! Page 116
MARCH 1998
In-Fisherman
THE JOURNAL OF FRESHWATER FISHING
TINY JIGS, MONSTER
BASS
Page 70
Crappies
Keys For
Spawntime
Page 78
NEW WAVE PLASTICS FOR
WALLEYES
Page 54
PLUS:
THE GAR WARS
JIGS FOR TROUT
THE BOOM IN RESERVOIR PIKE
FISH CALLS FOR CATFISH Page 106

Historic Perspectives

The klonk (a tool) and klonking (a method) never are the true focus of this article, but an interesting way for Stange to discuss with readers the acute sensory perceptions of catfish. This remains every bit a classic piece of entertaining instruction, as worthy of being read today as in was in that spring of 1998.

For your information, Stange and friends to this day have never successfully klonked up a flathead catfish—at least not knowingly so. They have caught flatheads while klonking, but there's never been any absolute connection between the klonking and the catching.

Other anglers come along years after this is printed and claim to be the first to discover the technique in Europe and perfect it in the States, to the tune of miraculous state-side catches. Suspiciously, they are selling klonks. We thinks the BS meter is running 100 per. Today that business is toast. Overall? Right time and place.

We remain open to the possibility that klonking might work.

Catfish worldwide share many common and exceptional characteristics, chief among them their unique sensory capabilities.

CHAPTER 32

MARCH 1998

Calling Catfish and Then Some

ANCIENT CATFISHING TACTICS rediscovered in Europe. Fish calls draw in giant wels catfish. Could similar tactics work for North American catfish? Or is this lost technique no more than indicative of a larger agenda for catfish anglers worldwide? Have we only just begun to explore the limits whereby we can attract (call) catfish by appealing to their hypersensitive sense?

The Unique Sensory Capabilities Of Catfish!

Catfish are one of the most sensitive of all freshwater fish when it comes to processing messages from their environment. Consider first their olfactory capability. Although perhaps principally a social sense used to find mates, identify school mates, and recognize home areas, the catfish's sense of smell rivals that of the salmon's, a fish which routinely travels hundreds of miles back to native streams to spawn, following only the tiniest molecular hint in water. Of more practical application to fishing is the fact that injured fish give off a distinctive molecular aura (pheromones) that catfish, using their olfactory capability, probably detect at long distance and then home in on.

Klonks. Old eastern European catfish calls.

with or at least be enhanced by the same sort of electrically sensitive sense sharks possess. Catfish can sense electrical impulses from the muscular movement of other fish. So far as we know, catfish are the only commonly sought sportfish with this ability.

With these observations as background, we are prepared for Keith Lambert, one in a handful of top English anglers who have for the past decade sought giant wels catfish throughout Europe. You might remember Lambert for his previous contribution of rigging ideas to our March 1996 article, "Suspender Rigging For Big Ol' Cats." Techniques and rigging from Europe are pertinent because fishing for wels catfish is much like fishing for North American cats.

Wels catfish are native to the large rivers of much of Europe, from the Danube and Rhine in the west, to the River Po in the south, and the Ural in the east. We may never know just how large wels catfish once grew. Scientists consider 600 pounds (12 feet long) a reasonably certain figure, a size fish that most anglers believe still might swim in some waters. Certainly, 200-pound fish are still caught today. Little wonder, then, that anglers like Lambert search for waters or portions of waters where wels may have grown old and huge, having eluded commercial and sport fishermen.

The wels shares common characteristics with all catfish. It seems to me, however, to be a fish of even wider adaptive feeding strategy than our blue cat or our flathead. For while the wels is a renowned predator of live fish and anything else that swims (including, it is said, ducks and dogs), it also frequently takes nightcrawlers, portions of dead fish, cut squid, and other pungent offerings. Our large flathead cats prey mostly on live fish, while big blue cats are known for feeding on abundant mussels and dead fish, although at times they also chase live prey.

But then, catfish also can taste at long distance, using a highly refined gustatory capability. Noteworthy is that a catfish has taste buds located over its entire body, not just on the tongue and lips. (Catfish can actually taste with their tails.) Then, too, catfish can see much better than they're usually given credit for. In clearer environments, blue cats and channel cats commonly chase shad and other baitfish in open water every bit as effectively as do stripers and other sleek predators.

Particularly important here, though, is the combination of senses at the heart of understanding how a unique European fishing tactic might relate to our fishing in North America. Catfish also possess superior auditory sensitivity, given their set of unusual bones called Weberian ossicles, which connect their inner ear to that resonator of sound, the air bladder. As a result, catfish possess a hearing range more than quadruple that of most other fish like the largemouth bass, pike, and walleye.

Hearing works in combination with the lateral line sense, which detects low-frequency water waves (below about 200 cycles per second) that can't be heard. The lateral line in catfish also is more sensitive than that of most other fish. Perhaps this is because it may somehow be connected

European Wels Common Characteristics

Keith Lambert with a wels catfish of some 90 pounds, a modest fish from many waters. This wels is a supreme predator with a mouth large enough to eat a duck, but a fish often selective enough to eat tidbits like a pack of worms, much as our flathead catfish do during certain spring periods.

The European Wels catfish (Siluris Glanis) shares many common characteristics with North American catfish, making tactics for wels applicable to our catfish, and vice versa.

LAMBERT'S STORY—KLONKING FOR CATS

Lambert: "Having traveled around Europe for the last 12 years in search of monster catfish, I have encountered many strange fishing methods. In Germany, for example, on a large lake in Bavaria, the best method for a long while was to freeline a large baitfish by first dropping it into the margins (along shore) and then allowing it to swim out into the lake.

"When the bait stopped, it was encouraged to resume swimming by gently tugging on the line pinched lightly between forefinger and thumb, all the while letting the line spill from an open spool. The baitfish could be steered by keeping the line roughly at right angles to the rod tip. By moving the rod tip, the bait could be made to cover a large area in hopes that it would find a hungry catfish. Another top method on this lake, though, was to leger (bottom-fish) floating dog biscuits. Would you believe, cats eating dogfood?

"Then in France one evening, an angler on the River Seille told me of his secret bait. He would tether a live duck in the margins at night, along with heavy line and a large treble hook. I rather like ducks, so it's not a tactic I want to employ. But I am certain that waterfowl are part of the diet of some large cats.

"Meanwhile, the mighty River Danube flows across much of Europe before splitting into the three arms which form the delta in Romania, where it spills into the Black Sea. Unfortunately, heavy commercial fishing has taken a toll on the catfish. After ten days of hard fishing, my friends and I, employing all our experience and skills, remained fishless. So when the opportunity arose to fish with one of the local experts, we took it. This man spoke no English, but a little French and the universal language of angling went a long way.

"We were taken to a wide, meandering stretch of river that lay deep between heavily forested mountains in a broad valley. Our new friend had only a crude line-winder containing a ropey-looking black line of unknown origin, but heavy break strain. He used a large rusting hook and a lead weight of around 4 ounces. A biscuit tin held his bait—black horse leeches about 6 inches long. He crammed six or seven leeches onto the hook, dropped the bait to the bottom, then raised it the distance between his nose and outstretched hand.

"We used oars to keep the boat drifting over a channel near shore, as our friend constantly adjusted the depth of his rig, making sure his bait remained about 4 feet above the riverbed. And then, to our amazement, the length of line in his hand was looped over the handle of a homemade wooden tool called a klonk. I had previously seen such a tool in photographs from old European fishing magazines, where it was described as a *butschalo.*

"The klonk is shaped like the rather thin lower leg of a hoofed animal, the backside being concave. The line in the water was held by the first two fingers of the hand gripping the klonk. Then, using the klonk like a paddle, he dipped the tool into the water and quickly and rhythmically stroked down, back, and lifted up and out, so the concave surface, which had trapped a bubble of air on the downstroke, produced an incredible *woomp*, not unlike a hippo with flatulence (I should imagine).

"If you have heard large carp 'clooping' at the surface (sucking surface film), then you have an idea of the sound. The sound from the klonk, however, is far deeper and much louder. After klonking perhaps six times, he jigged the baited line up and down gently to wave the leeches enticingly. Within this period, the boat had drifted some 50 yards with the current. He repeated the process as we continued to drift.

"At the end of the day, we had covered several miles of the Danube, caught lots of catfish, and were absolutely fascinated with our experience. Why did it work? Was the exact sound produced by the klonk important? Would other sounds work? Would the process work elsewhere?

"Our next opportunity to try klonking was several years ago while we were exploring for catfish on the River Po in northern Italy. I accompanied a film crew that included two of the world's most-noted catfish anglers, Kevin Maddocks and

Olivier Portrat. We caught many large fish, using a variety of methods. In talking with Portrat, however, a Frenchman who lives in Germany, he noted how a few modern catfish anglers were beginning to experiment with old Eastern European methods, including the butschalo. I told him of our previous experience, and we decided to resurrect the method to see if it would work on this underfished water that held many catfish.

"To cut a long story short, the method worked like magic, producing lots of large catfish, including many fish over 100 pounds. One of

Klonking In Action

Another application for klonking, this time with the angler calling catfish as he drifts downriver along bankside cover.

Klonking on the River Po, Italy. Note how baits are being presented by several methods, while one man calls cats. Meanwhile, the boat drifts downriver as the anglers consult sonar to stay over the river channel.

the advantages of klonking is that it works while drifting with current, allowing for covering large expanses of water. Why catfish respond to this amazing sound passing over their heads I'm not sure. Are they antagonized into attacking? Does the noise resemble catfish feeding at the surface? So many questions remain. We do know, though, that as one might expect, cats wise up to the method if it's used often. Good runs (fishing spots) must be rested for a period before klonking again draws fish."

KLONKING IN AMERICA

Klonking hasn't been tried in North America in exactly the way described by Lambert and as generally practiced in old eastern Europe. Of course, it will be tested this season, by us and perhaps by some of you. The old East Euro method, though, may not be so important as the general idea (or process) behind the method, as it applies to catfish senses as we know them, whether the catfish be North American or European—or Asian, African, or South American, for that matter.

Catfish fall on the hypersensitive side of the scale in every sensory category except vision, and we're not too sure about that one. Whether the catfish in question be European, North American, Asian, or South American, they can smell better and taste better (by logarithmic proportions) than most other freshwater fish sought round the world. And so what strange things (in other words, unusual by most other angling standards) do anglers do to attract (that is, call) and catch these fish?

I told you years ago how an old friend taught me as a lad to gather cowpies that had begun to dry just so, then to sack them and weight the sack with rocks. The sack with the bowel-fermented moo pies was then placed at the head of a major river hole during the Prespawn Period (May and June)—prime time when catfish migrate upstream toward spawning grounds. I was never offered an explanation other than this would stop migrating catfish in the hole, ensuring great fishing during Prespawn.

I later surmised that the tactic should work anytime during summer (after Prespawn), when rain raised water levels enough so catfish again moved from river hole to river hole, redistributing themselves around portions of a river. But I never found enough time to test this tactic to my complete satisfaction. And I haven't heard from many others who have tried such tactics. I suppose even the strangest among us hesitate to sack cow chips in broad daylight.

Similar tactics reign supreme in portions of the catfish world, however. Consider our coverage by contributor Ned Kehde of the bean-dipping scene in Kansas and Texas. Five-gallon pails of soybeans, milo, or wheat are soaked and allowed to ferment for, say, a week. The result isn't quite bootleg whiskey, but is potent enough to be used as chum to attract and hold channel catfish in reservoir areas where they would otherwise roam too far and wide to be caught in numbers.

Catfish, we must consider, are just being discovered (or rediscovered, as the case may be) in Europe and in North America. Only during the last decade or so have modern anglers begun to appreciate what a challenge and what an opportunity these unique fish offer. So, too, are even the most astute anglers just beginning to understand how the unique senses of catfish can be toyed with in the extreme, in order to catch them. Attracting catfish via their hypersensitive sense of smell and taste are one way to call these fish.

Klonking, as we understand it now, probably is just another way to call catfish, in this case via their hypersensitive senses of hearing and feeling. It's a way of talking to our catfish friends, asking them—pleading with them—to come have a look-see at what we're offering. This area, even more than our experiments with scent and taste, remains little tested, however.

Or is it? Actually, we've already discovered ways to call fish with vibration, although we often don't realize what we're doing or when we're doing it. We tether lively bait just so on various rigs, for example, so they wiggle and waggle an attractive low-frequency tune that calls catfish through their lateral lines. We know this works, but we rarely express what we're doing in terms of "calling cats."

Really, we've only begun to scratch the surface in this regard. I agree that common logic holds that outboard-motor noise repels fish, for example, but my actual experience after decades of fishing is that the opposite often is just as likely the case. We simply need to be open to seeing a cause-and-effect others reject outright.

Perch, in particular, are attracted to motor vibration, especially in dingy, shallow lakes. Anglers often increase their catch by leaving their motor idling as they fish. Perch also often are attracted to the drilling vibration of a gas auger on ice. On one occasion, in order to continue to catch perch when no one else around was catching them on Devils Lake, North Dakota, one angler (Toad Smith) drilled hole after hole while the other angler (me) continued to fish.

I suspect, therefore, given how much more sensitive catfish are to vibration, that they can be attracted by all sorts of similar low-vibration calls that appeal to the catfish's lateral line. We just don't leave ourselves open to the possibility—haven't even really begun to experiment with the idea.

Coincidental evidence? Well, of course, although I really wouldn't call it coincidental. Many anglers, for example, know how well catfish respond to vibrating baits. Walleye-style spinner rigs have long been a hot option for catfish in natural lakes and reservoirs. My first experiences date back to the late 1960s, when anglers began trolling early versions of tandem-hooked spinner rigs coupled with crawlers for walleyes in Iowa lakes and in Missouri River, South Dakota, reservoirs. All those early baits were equipped with small spinners (#1 or #2). They produced as many catfish as walleyes—and still do today.

Of course, the spinner thing just generally hasn't caught on across the country. Professional walleye anglers often seem surprised when, during tournament competition on waters where catfish reside with walleyes, their catches include huge numbers of catfish. Hey, it works everywhere, but like many topics in catfishing, it hasn't been widely written about.

We've learned along the way, incidentally, that bigger calls (spinners) often call cats best. No surprise then that catfish also love those other vibrating fish calls—crankbaits. During summer, they crunch them with relish on small waters and large, in running water and reservoirs. Catfish often love rattling baits, too.

But what about klonking, you still may be wondering? Will it work here? Yes, I say, but again, the idea behind the specific process is more important than trying to duplicate the exact practice as defined in Europe. The right vibration and sound call catfish. That's the idea. The sound and vibration produced by klonking are at least one sort of call that works for wels catfish.

Other calls of this sort will be discovered in Europe. I envision European anglers standing along shore calling catfish with the noise produced by, say, a boat paddle *woomped* gently and rhythmically on the water. I can see American anglers doing the same thing to draw flathead catfish from a big eddy near a major river hole.

But maybe a paddle woomping the water won't work best. Maybe it will be the dull rhythmic thump from a big stick pounded on the bank near where cats reside and where our baits are placed. Paddle-woomping is, by the way, already a tactic used by some fishery workers to call muskies to net during spring spawning runs. But then, merely walking heavily along a bank also calls catfish in ponds—the vibration indicating feeding time.

Just begin to open your minds to the possibilities. Rattling floats? An obvious one. Spinners used in conjunction with dipbait and dipworms? Absolutely—not so obvious, perhaps, but already happening.

We have just begun to explore the limits whereby we can attract catfish by appealing to their hypersensitive senses.

The Latest Muskie Mystery! Page 36
APRIL 1998
In-Fisherman
THE JOURNAL OF FRESHWATER FISHING
SCOUTING SPRING
BASS
Page 60
Critical Concepts for
Walleyes
Page 48
PLUS!
MASTER ANGLER AWARDS
TRACKING TIGER MUSKIES
ALL ABOUT SPAWNTIME BLUEGILLS
AMBUSHING TRANSITION SMALLMOUTHS
A Lure For Catfish Page 98

Historic Perspectives

Stange is on a mission on behalf of catfishing and catfishermen, hoping to convince anglers that fishing with artificial lures is more than passing fancy—is indeed a sturdy option, at times better than fishing with live, dead, or prepared baits. He also is needling lure manufactures to take note: Catfish anglers 7 million strong, according to a national survey, represent a large, untapped market. Only bass, trout, and panfish anglers surpass catfishermen in numbers. Walleye anglers number about 3 million. No other groups come close—and all the noted market groups are already tapped.

Change comes slowly at times in catfishing. Stange notes that today most catfish anglers are still just beginning to ponder the possibilities—and major manufacturers, true to past performance, largely ignore catfishermen.

CHAPTER 33

APRIL 1998

A Lure For Catfish

THE LURE CONNECTION to catfishing isn't something new; it's like so many other topics in catfishing, where most stories over the years have gone largely unreported nationwide. So how could every average Cat Joe know?

Artificials Are A Natural For Catfish!

Lures aren't necessarily better than livebait, deadbait, or prepared baits. Sometimes, though. And therein lies the beginning of a story that continues to develop. Lures just make sense for catfish. When it comes to processing messages from their environment, catfish are one of the most sensitive of all freshwater fish. Their sense of smell rivals that of salmon, which routinely travel hundreds of miles back to native streams to spawn, following only the tiniest molecular hint in water.

Of more practical application to our fishing is that injured fish—and other baits like crawlers, grasshoppers, and crawfish—give off a distinctive molecular aura that catfish, using their sense of smell, detect and then home in on. Catfish also can taste at long distance, using their highly refined gustatory capability. Catfish, after all, have taste buds located over their entire bodies, not just on the tongue, lips, and barbels.

Leadhead Jigs, Cranks and Spin Options

Leadhead jigs can be fished as a classic lure for catfish, as when a bucktail jig (tipped with or without bait) is cast into a tailwater area teeming with catfish. Or they can be used as a tool (a sinker) to anchor livebait or deadbait in position so a catfish can eat it.

One of the most prominent jig options was written about by In-Fisherman contributor Ned Kehde, who described how some Kansas anglers flip jig-and-crawler combos for flatheads spawning in holes in riprap habitat along causeways and at the face of dams. This tactic is a potent option anywhere cats hole up during spawntime, not just in reservoirs, but in rivers once cats move into holes in either snags or cutbanks.

A jig also can be coupled with a slip of cutbait or a livebait. Doug Stange sometimes uses a 2-, 3-, or 4-ounce saltwater jighead to anchor a big baitfish (hooked in the tail) right below the boat when he's anchored near a snag that holds flatheads. This rig also provides good control when you're flipping and dipping a big bait right into a snag for flatheads, a tactic that sometimes even works during the day when flatheads are really cranked during Prespawn, once water temperatures have shot up into the 70°F range for the first time in the year.

(A) *Classic bucktail jig tipped with a slip of cutbait, an option for cats feeding on shad, minnows, or other baitfish.*

(B) *A 3-inch strip of cut baitfish fillet—one of the best all-around options for channel and blue cats in almost any situation, whether the fish are on bottom or suspended.*

(C) *A livebait anchored by its tail, so it struggles away from the weight of the jig.*

Leadhead Jig Options

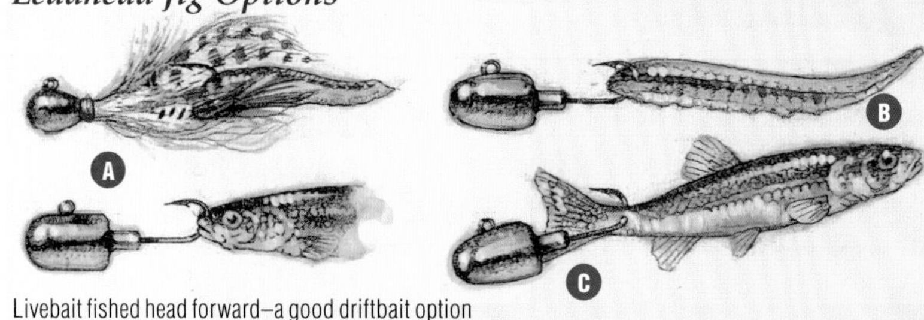

Your Own Spin-Drift Rig for Big Blues

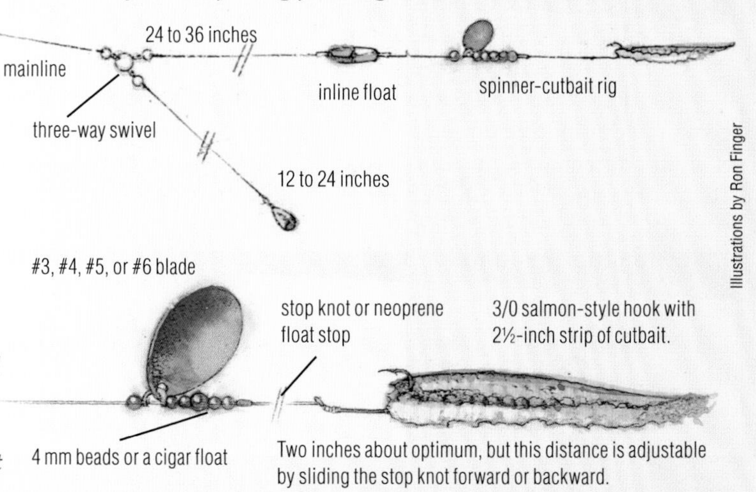

Illustrations by Ron Finger

One Hot Combo For Cats?

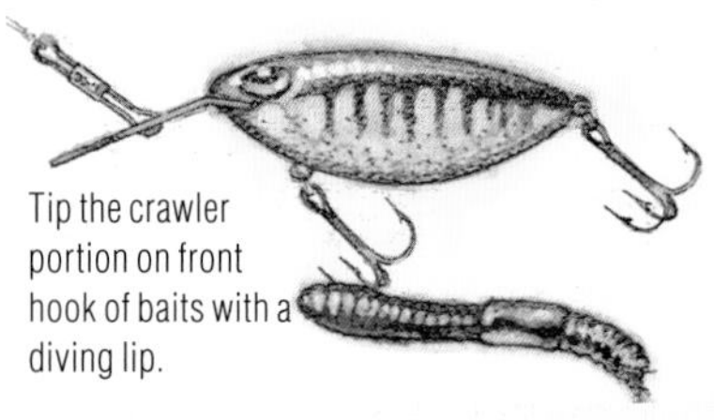

Tip the crawler portion on front hook of baits with a diving lip.

A combination of crankbait tipped with a portion of crawler, a common choice for walleyes during the 1950s and 1960s, has enjoyed a recent rebirth of popularity in some areas.

Then, too, catfish possess a range of hearing more than quadruple that of fish like the basses, pike, and walleye—in large part, because of an unusual set of tiny bones called Weberian ossicles, which connect the inner ear to that resonator of sound, the air bladder. Hearing, though—and this is important to the theme of this article—works in combination with the lateral line sense, which detects low-frequency water waves (below about 200 cycles per second) that can't be heard.

The lateral line in catfish also is more sensitive than that of most other fish, perhaps in large part because it's enhanced by the electrically sensitive sense sharks possess. Catfish can sense electrical impulses from the muscular movement of other fish. So far as we know, catfish are the only freshwater sportfish with this ability.

Vision, too, plays keenly in this topic. Cats often get a bad rap in the vision department, even though every bit of practical evidence suggests they can see well. Cats, once again, are just more versatile than those other predators. They feed effectively in dingy water where other fish might starve. But when waters clear, they also use vision to run baitfish, to corner crayfish, to pick at surface insects, and much more. I suggest, too, that they have color vision, even though some science texts suggest otherwise.

Whether or not catfish possess color vision, though, is incidental to our course. The idea is that catfish can see well and use vision in conjunction with their other super senses to thrive in most waters. That's one reason they're so widespread, so adaptable, and therefore so successful in North America and as a group around the world. It's also the reason that catfish sometimes respond to lures as well as and sometimes better than many other popular predatory species.

Better than, say, walleyes? Sometimes. Certainly as well as walleyes in many instances. And again, that isn't hard to figure, for when the two fish square off in a sense-for-sense showdown, the

The Classic Spinner Rig for Cats

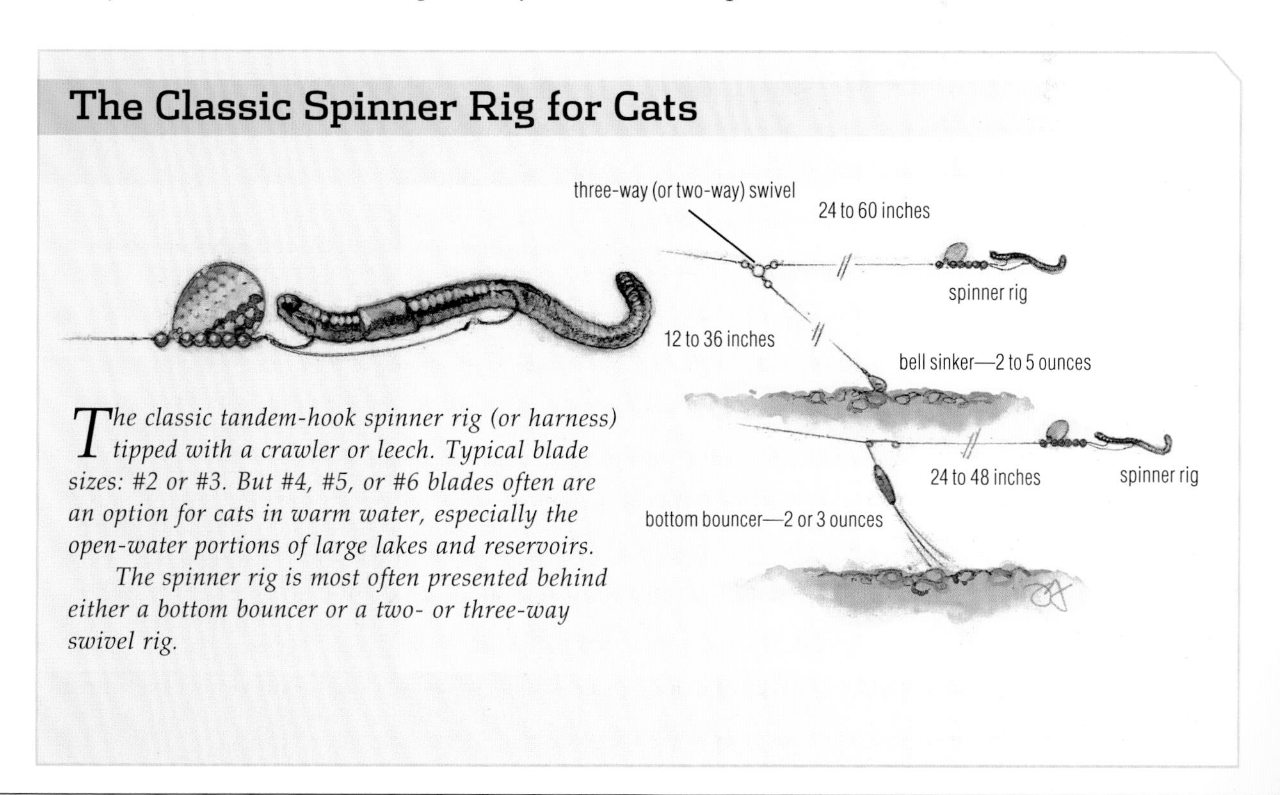

The classic tandem-hook spinner rig (or harness) tipped with a crawler or leech. Typical blade sizes: #2 or #3. But #4, #5, or #6 blades often are an option for cats in warm water, especially the open-water portions of large lakes and reservoirs.

The spinner rig is most often presented behind either a bottom bouncer or a two- or three-way swivel rig.

Spinner-livebait combos have been triggering catfish in many waters since the late 1960s. Yet today such rigging is mostly underused in most areas.

catfish wins in every category except vision—and, truth be told, we're not really sure about that one. Let's just say that it's uncanny how relatively similar the two species are in their response to lure presentations. They both relish combo lure and livebait presentations—like spinner-livebait and jig-and-bait combos. And they both are extremely sensitive to vibration patterns and noise produced by crankbaits.

Admittedly, though, these super senses of the catfish also make them much different from walleyes and other predators. Anglers interested in optimum catches always have to factor in the chance that livebaits, deadbaits, and prepared baits might, in the situation at hand, be a better option than artificial lures for catching cats.

That's not quite so much the case with most other fish, although, of course, livebait can be a vital option for walleyes and most other predators. And pike, to pick only one example, sometimes relish deadbait. My objective isn't to convince you to fish with artificial lures so much as to awaken you to the option.

THE COMBO CONNECTION

One of the finest lures for catfish is a combo lure + livebait that, again, just makes sense and has long been catching catfish in certain areas of the country. Catfish are extremely vibration-sensitive. The essence of spinner rigging is to attract fish via vibration, along with visual cues (flash). Add a crawler or a leech, though, and powerful scent and taste are added to an already potent visual and vibratory package.

Especially during late spring, summer, and early fall, the same style of spinner rigging popular for walleyes is one of the better baits available for channel catfish in many waters. I refer to crawler-harness-style rigging with two or three hooks in tandem following the spinner. This rigging developed as an adjunct to the popular 1960s Red Devil spinner style composed of a spinner and a single hook.

I first used a coarse version of the tandem rigging after finding them in Red's Tackle Shop at Big Bend Dam, South Dakota, during the mid-1960s. Then, during the early 1970s or so, when this rig was beginning to catch on I fished with a dandy version of it, the Bena Rig, made by Greg Bena of Sutherland, Iowa. The Bena Rig was, even at that early date, tied fine enough to compare with the best commercial spinner rigs on the market today.

I offer dates relative to this issue because already back then, anglers fishing on Lake Sharpe and Lake Francis Case in South Dakota were routinely bagging combo stringers of walleyes and channel catfish as they drifted spinner rigs and crawlers behind early-day bottom bouncers. See? This is no recent deal. Too, one of the finest stringers of big channel cats and big walleyes I've ever witnessed was caught in the mid-1970s by

Trolling Crankbaits for Channel Cats in Smaller Rivers

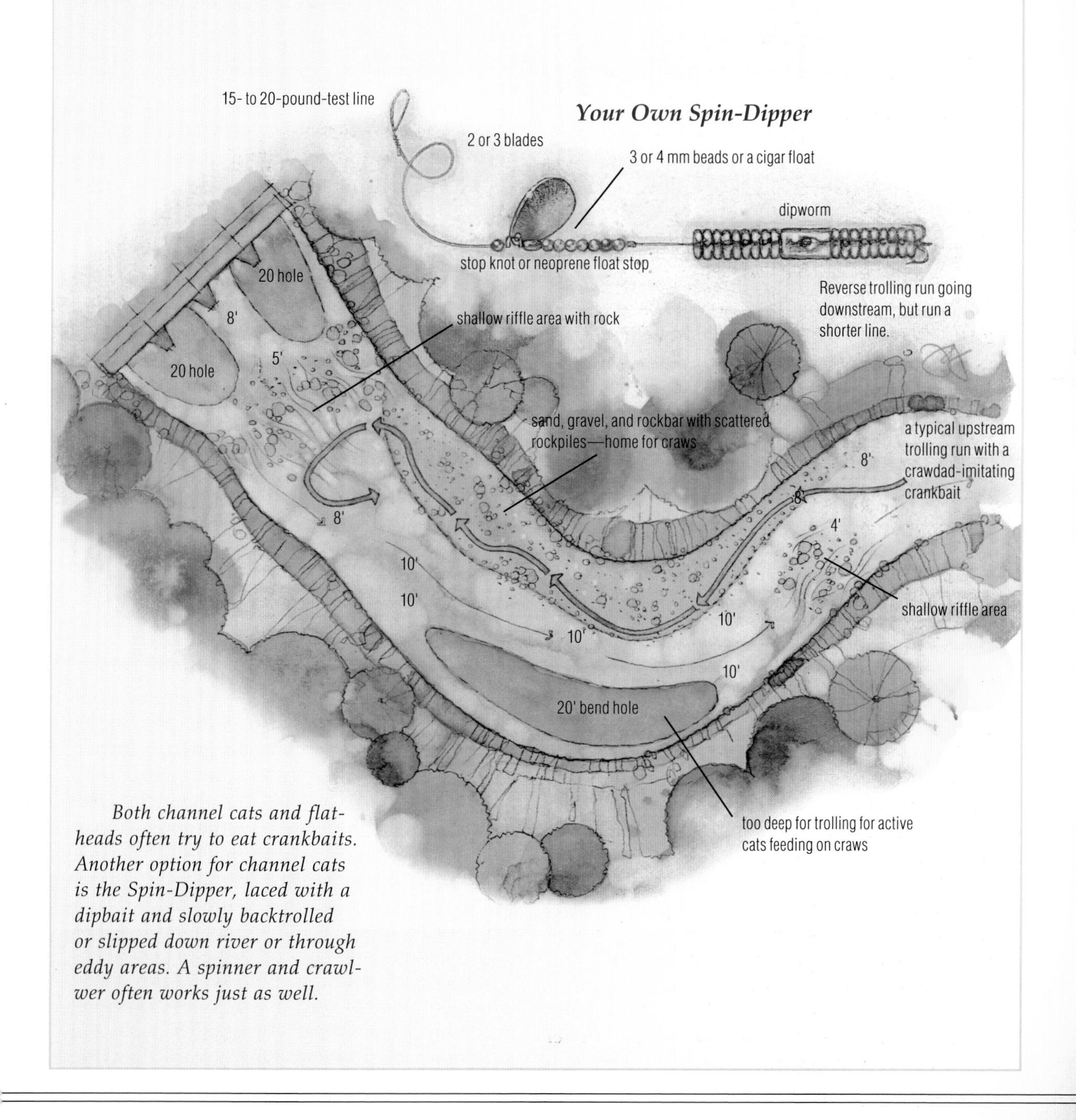

Both channel cats and flatheads often try to eat crankbaits. Another option for channel cats is the Spin-Dipper, laced with a dipbait and slowly backtrolled or slipped down river or through eddy areas. A spinner and crawlwer often works just as well.

longtime In-Fisherman, Iowa's Fishing Professor, Jim McDonald, using the Bena Rig and crawlers on Storm Lake, one of Iowa's shallow, fertile, natural lakes.

This rigging and an almost endless variety of modified rigs produces catfish (or could produce catfish) for those who apply it in the right situations. It's a superb rig, for example, for walleyes and channel cats in portions of the Great Lakes during much of summer and early fall. Use a larger blade (#5 or larger) in this instance, though. More thump to call fish roaming vast portions of open water.

Meanwhile, on large rivers like pools of the Mississippi and Ohio rivers, the rigging works for walleyes and cats holding on or near wing dams. During summer, though, walleyes often prefer a crawler presented without a spinner, whereas catfish seem to prefer the spinner combo. When things get difficult along wing dams and closing dams, by the way, don't forget to try leeches. Catfish love leeches. And often they can find your leech presentation easier when it's trailing behind a spinner.

During summer, I've also caught channel cats with a spinner-crawler combo, using a controlled boat drift while bottom bouncing the spinner rig and bait combo along the deep channel lip in pools #3 and #4 on the Mississippi River. And it's been a productive rig fished on a static line behind a boat anchored just off riprap banks buffeted by heavy current on the Missouri River near Sioux City, Iowa. Use crawlers in conjunction with the spinner rig to catch channel cats. Fish a dead chub or a strip of cutbait, and flatheads also happen along. And, again, when things get tough, don't forget to try leeches. Hold the rod so the rod tip is at a right angle to the main current, occasionally lifting the rod tip in order to keep the spinner spinning and attracting cats.

Some semblance of this spinner rigging should work almost anywhere cats swim—trolled, cast, or drifted in natural lakes, reservoirs, and large rivers across North America. As an addition to the drift rigs used by Santee-Cooper, North Carolina, catfish guides, for example. Instead of a crawler, I'd use a strip of cutbait behind a big spinner to call big blue cats and an occasional fat flathead. Again, spinners call cats and the addition of bait intensifies and focuses catfish reaction.

Other combo connections? A spinner in conjunction with dipbait, you say? A guide from Wisconsin (I lost his card and therefore his name) has confided that he adds a spinner ahead of a dipbait worm during summer. He anchors in current above a snag or a hole. Then he dips the dipworm portion of the spinner-dipworm combo into his favorite dipbait and flips the rig out so it holds in place just in front of the snag or at the head of a hole—calling all cats with vibration, scent, and taste.

Really, the opportunities with spinner combos are limited only by your imagination.

CLASSIC ARTIFICIALS—CRANKS FOR CATS

No surprise, given how sound- and vibration-sensitive catfish are, that they crunch their share of crankbaits all across the country—crankbaits of various styles in lakes, rivers, and reservoirs, mainly during summer and into fall, but also throughout late spring on some waters.

In Wisconsin, guide John Kolbeck (Stevens Point) keys on a crankbait pattern for channel cats on the Wisconsin River. He flatlines Rebel Crawdads and Storm Wiggle Warts as he trolls along and over appropriate rock lips and humps where channels are searching for crayfish. Lipped baits with an intense wiggle carom off rocks and get hung less often than baits with shorter lips. Not surprisingly, he likes crab-colored lures, brown and orange being his favorite combo.

The best areas are those with mild current and plenty of rocks. By consulting his sonar, Kolbeck keeps lures running shallower than about 8 feet. Let only enough line out, he advises (usually 50 to 75 feet of 10-pound test), to keep lures barely ticking bottom. No need to worry about keeping lures away from the boat. Cats aren't boat-shy. An occasional snap of the rod tip in crack-the-whip

Bumping Bottom For Giant Cats

The Mann's Stretch 20+, Virgil Tagtmeyer's preferred crankbait for bumping bottom for giant cats in the headwaters of Lake of the Ozarks and Truman Reservoir.

Keown's Minnowbait Rig

Where for Tailwater Cats

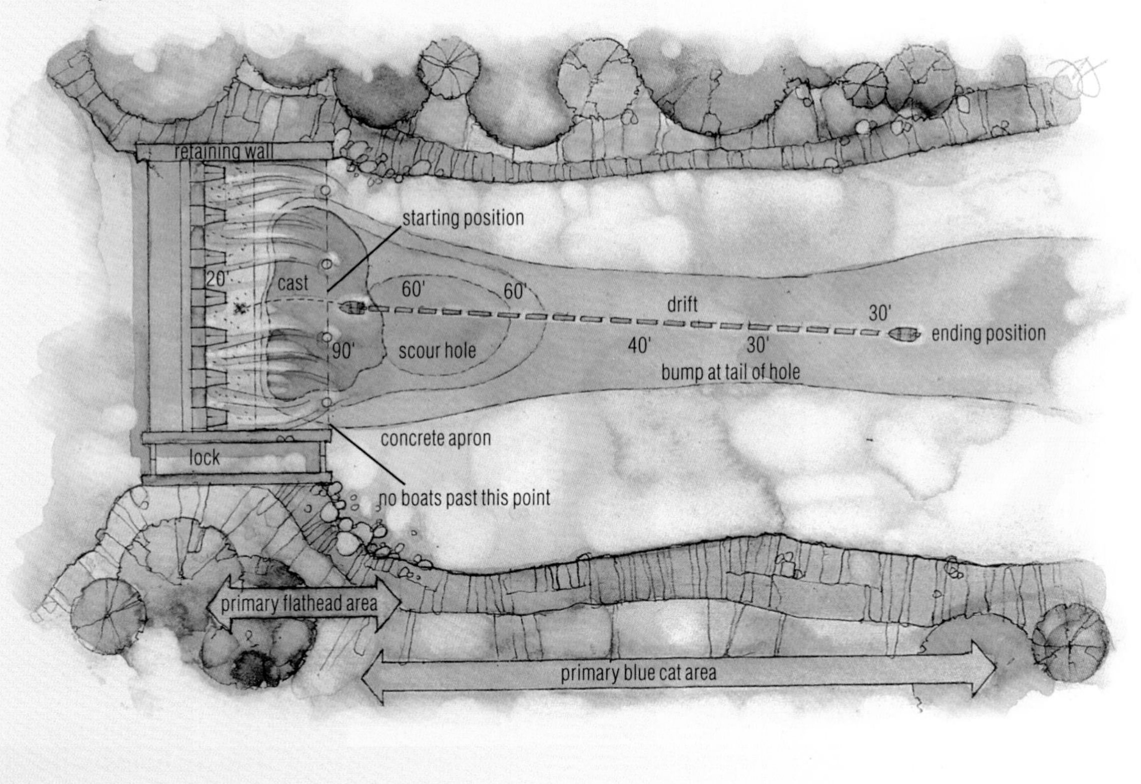

Flatheads and channel cats are particularly attracted to heavy-thumping lures.

fashion often helps to trigger them.

Meanwhile, in Missouri, Virgil Tagtmeyer since the early 1980s has been using cranks to catch cats from the waters of the Osage River. At first, he used Natural Ikes and Bombers weighted to get down into river holes lying 20 to 30 feet deep. Today, he relies on the Manns 20+ to troll deep in the waters below Truman Dam, at the headwaters of Lake of the Ozarks. One day during May last year, Tagtmeyer boated a 77-pound blue cat that had engulfed a Mann's 20+. Then, as the day progressed, a friend added three 40-pound-class flatheads to their bag. Several more cats rounded the take at 209 pounds.

Tagtmeyer suspects that the catfish he targets leave deep holes at night and spread over shallow flats as they search for food. During the day, the fish concentrate in holes, particularly holes at bends in the old Osage River channel. The drop-off can be from 4 into 30 feet of water. On sunny days, though, the cats usually lie from 20 to 26 feet deep. Of course, if Tagtmeyer marks a big fish on sonar, he moves his lure to that depth. And if baitfish schools are running at a given depth, he trolls lures at that depth.

During 1993 and 1995, the current in the Osage was too brisk to work lures into good spots, so Tagtmeyer fished the big water of Truman Lake, where he trolled over expansive mudflats mostly devoid of timber. During both 1993 and 1995, he caught flatheads and blue cats weighing up to 30 pounds.

Tagtmeyer prefers to troll with a superline, 28-pound-test Spiderwire Fusion, but he always employs a wire leader to protect this thin line near the lure. It takes about 90 feet of line to take the Manns Stretch 20+ into 20 feet of water, where one day not long ago he hooked a fish he couldn't move off the bottom. Once anglers begin to troll lures in similar situations across the country, Tagtmeyer believes catches of monster catfish on lures will become common.

And then in Kentucky, guide Jerry Keown catches dozens of flatheads and blue cats in the 40-pound class, along with lots of stripers, during summer, as he drifts minnowbaits below the Cannelton Dam on the Ohio River. Keown prefers floating baits like the Smithwick Rattlin' Rogue because they exhibit an erratic action in current. He uses a Carolina rig to keep this bait on or near the bottom—a two-ounce egg sinker above a #5 barrel swivel and 18-inch leader with a snap and the minnowbait.

Regulations prohibit boats from entering the 100-foot zone below the dam, so Keown uses a flippin' stick and 20-pound line to fire long casts at the face of the dam. Letting the lure drop to the bottom, he then slips his outboard into neutral and lets the current carry the boat downstream. As the boat drifts, he snaps baits forward a few feet, then lets them work on their own in the current before he snaps again. After drifting 200 or 300 yards down the river channel, he motors back to the dam.

Most of the flatheads are caught in the first 100 yards of the tailrace—from the face of the dam to the tail of the scour hole, where relatively slack water builds along the bottom before boiling downstream. When the first dam gate is open and the current's ripping along the retaining wall, though, some of the biggest flatheads also hold tight to the wall in water almost too fast to fish. Meanwhile, most of the blue cats hold in faster water along the channel ledge downstream from the first hump below the scour hole.

According to Keown, you can throw out the book on location when striped bass are rampaging on the surface—a half-acre mass of 7- to 15-pound stripers smashing into massive schools of gizzard shad. The bait's flying, the stripers are slashing, and the cats—both blues and flatheads—are gorging on the dead and dying baitfish that drift down. The only drawback is trying to decide whether to cast unweighted baits for stripers or weighted baits for cats.

And so the defense rests for now. We offer, as evidence, dozens of contacts with hardcore catfish anglers who, over the years, have discovered patterns that rely on artificial lures. Evidence from anglers North, South, East, and West. Anglers using combo systems that couple bait with lures. Anglers using jigging spoons, rattlebaits, traditional crankbaits, streamer flies, leadhead jigs—even surface baits. Anglers catching catfish, not just by accident, but by design. Because, given the super-tuned senses of catfish, lures just make sense at certain times, during certain seasons. As is so often the case with catfish today, we just have to be willing to open our minds to the possibilities.

Swimbaits and Crankbaits

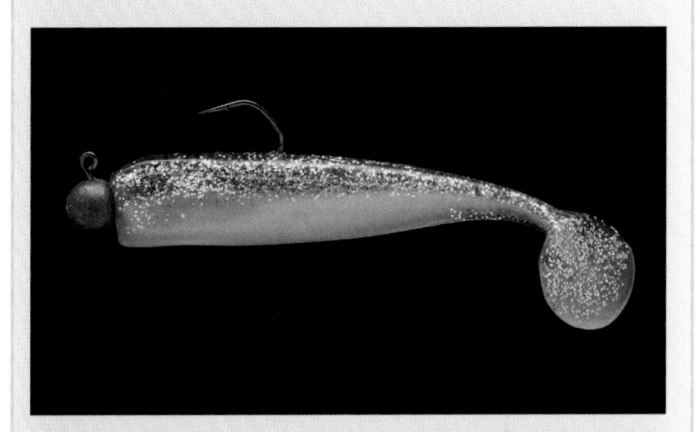

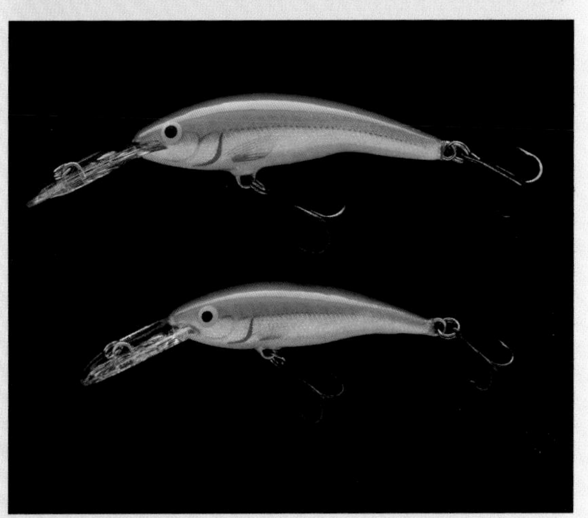

Along with many crankbait styles, swimbaits have also proven productive for catfish, particularly flatheads.

{ Historic Perspectives

This is a follow-up perspective on the dipbait scene several years after an earlier article (Chapter 31: "Bitchin' Blends") gets a real buzz going in catfishing circles. Here again, though, we take a step back to the future, for most of what Stange suggests as the potential for sales of dipbaits, and subsequent increased catches of catfish by catfishermen because of it, hasn't happened, but still could and should, as a matter of reasonable course. Dips, after all, remain one of the handiest and most economical bait choices available—and the produce big catching in the right situations.

CHAPTER 34

FEBRUARY 1999

D-Day for Dipbaits Nationwide

THE POINT REMAINS that channel catfish in Pennsylvania aren't different from channel catfish in Iowa and Nebraska. Yet in the past 20 years, hundreds of thousands of pounds of dipbaits have been used each year to catch ton after ton of channel cats in the Midwest, while the market for dips has remained piddling in Pennsylvania and other parts of the East and Southeast. Dips aren't popular in the West, either. And they've been only modestly popular in some sections of the deep South.

Dipbaits And Related Paraphernalia—Ready To Go Ballistic!

So a virtual dipbait vacuum still exists out there. Given just a little coverage, though, and suddenly the dipping world looks a lot like it's ready to go ba-ba-boom.

Our coverage of this topic in *In-Fisherman* several years ago was the first national coverage of the dipbait scene ever, so far as I can find. Sonny Hootman, whom we talked about in that In-Fisherman article, sells Sonny's Super Sticky, a dip that for some years has been all the rage among a hardcore contingent of anglers in the heart of the Midwest. Sonny manufactures and sells his popular bait from his home (well, not literally) in Farmington, Iowa.

"Amazing," he told me last fall. "Thought I'd seen it all. For the most part, we could just supply the growth in the market we already served. And now, all these folks are calling from other parts of the country. My boys and I were brewing 100,000 pounds of bait a year just a couple years ago. We've had to almost double our production, and we just can't keep up. We have no down-time to go fishing. I'm not sure I like this."

Meanwhile, Mark Mihalakis, manufacturer of the Cat Tracker line of dipbaits, has been working to open new markets for Cat Tracker baits in the Carolinas, Tennessee, and other parts of the Southeast. "Almost everyone who discovers the bait is catching fish on it. Lots of fish," he offers. "And not just channel catfish. Blue cats, too—some big ones—are falling for baits on Santee-Cooper (South Carolina) and other waters. It's no surprise to folks who fish the baits in the Midwest. But it's like a revelation to anglers in the East.

"Here, after all, is this really deadly-smelling stuff these far-flung anglers have been hearing about via the grapevine all these years—and finally someone on a national level says this stuff has the potential to work everywhere catfish swim. So, for the first time, lots of new anglers are trying it. And, of course, it works. Right off, these new folks are wondering how long they can keep their discovery a secret on the waters they fish."

Well, not that long, we think, in the grand scheme of things. But still, it will take years before the baits become as popular as they are in the Midwest. And there's even room for major growth in the Midwest. So, really, we have no way to accurately judge just how big the market might be once it gets rolling nationwide.

Fun to try, though. Almost 8 million catfish anglers out there. It's a rare angler who wouldn't find some use for the bait where he fishes, sometime during the year. One guide on a Kansas

A Few Dipworms

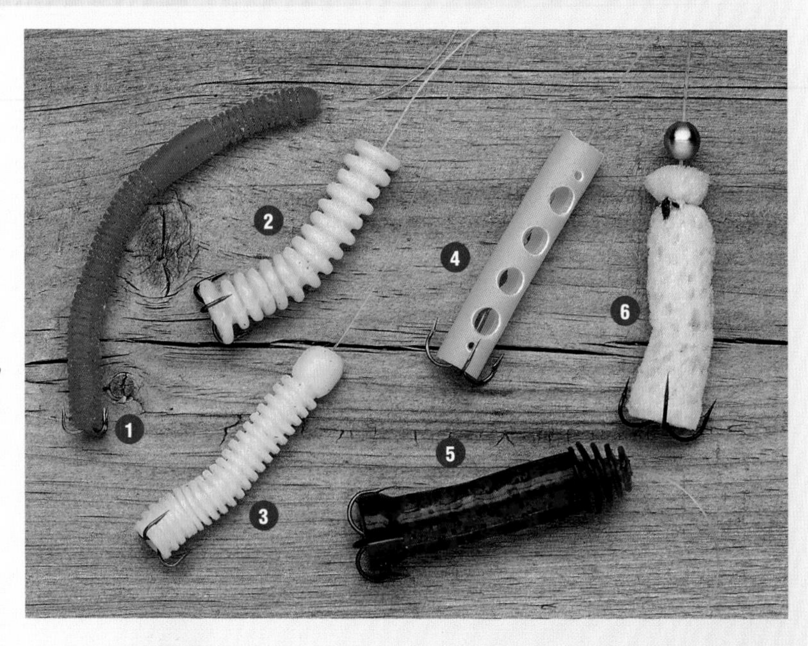

(1) *The Original Catfish Devil Worm, the longest, thinnest worm, is available from Sonny Hootman—only while they last.* ***(2)*** *The traditional Catfish Charlie worm.* ***(3)*** *The classic Uncle Josh Catfish Worm.* ***(4 & 5)*** *The Cat Tracker Tubie Worm (surgical tube) and the new Tubie 2000, a cross between a surgical worm and a classic plastic.* ***(6)*** *The W-D-3 Dipworm is a "spongy" worm that floats.*

reservoir went through 600 pounds of dip in his business last season.

But say a pound of dip per angler per year is the maximum average potential per year. Say, too, that Sonny's average production of around 100,000 pounds of bait a year (other manufacturers aren't willing to share such information—my guess is that Sonny's the biggest dip baron on the planet right now) is about right among dip manufacturers. Might be 10 manufacturers out there right now. That's a million pounds—way maximum—being produced right now in a potential market almost 10 times that.

It's impossible to spend time in catfish country and not be able to feel (or smell) these winds of change. Consider, too, the paraphernalia used to fish dipbait. More room for growth. Plastic dipworms are almost as hot as bass plastics. The standard worm has been about a 4-inch piece of plastic about 3/8 inch in diameter with horizontal grooves running the length of the worm. A snell portion of about 20-pound monofilament is run through the center of the worm and a #6 or #8 treble hook is tied on terminally and then pulled tight against the base of the worm.

Folks are catching so many fish on the worms, that most good anglers are at least bending down barbs on the trebles to make them easier to remove. The best bet, though, when a hot bite's on, is to switch to a single hook, like a #1 or #2 Octopus-style. Again, bend down the barb, for catfish fight hard enough to ensure a tight line throughout the battle. I've used barbless single hooks on 50-fish days and never lost a fish.

A tip in this regard, too, is to switch to lighter line, particularly on smaller waters. We buy worms in bulk and then tie our own snells, usually with 14- or a maximum of 17-pound line. Lighter line makes the baits easier for cats to eat. Actually, 12-pound test's about right during early spring, when the fish are tentative. Just have to be willing to retie the terminal portion of the line more often than with heavier line.

Plenty of room for innovation among the worms that are offered, too, although how much of a factor worm design is in actually triggering catfish will continue to be debated. Everyone agrees that the worms must be able to hold bait. But anglers certainly don't agree on just how much bait's necessary.

Hootman: "One reason our bait's so popular is because it's so sticky. Fishermen want to see plenty of dip hanging on. But dipping every five minutes isn't always necessary to catch cats. The essence of a good bait remains on the worm for a time, even when the dip seems to have washed away. Especially in heavy current, catching cats on worms with almost no visible dip is common.

"Again, though," Hootman continues, "most folks just feel more confident with an obvious wad of dip on the worm. When in doubt, I dip. And I'm not just trying to sell bait. I want folks to catch fish."

To date, almost any worm introduced has enjoyed immediate sales success. Mark Mihalakis: "The Egg Worm we introduced two years ago sold like hotcakes at a Boy Scout breakfast. We added a bulbous end at the top of a standard worm, so the head of the worm breaks current just enough that more bait sticks to the business end of the worm. We also introduced a surgical tube worm, the Tubie Worm, that sells well. The plastic's just a little softer and the hole's a little bigger than on most tube worms on the market. Sales of tube worms are way up, by the way. Just two years ago, almost no one was buying tube worms.

"New for this year is the Tubie 2000," he goes on, "a cross between a standard dipworm and surgical tubing. It has a little ribbing at the top end, which is slightly bulbous, as on the Egg Worm. The rest of the bait is a tube, made from soft plastic, not surgical tubing."

Hootman, who doesn't manufacture worms but does offer four different styles to his customers, thinks someone should be making a longer, thinner worm. One of his favorites is the old Catfish Devil Worm, a thin 5-inch worm. Because it's so long, even though it's thin it actually ends up holding more bait than most other worms.

I've used the worm for two seasons now. As

Selected Commercial Baits, by Steve Hoffman

(A) Berkley—Chemist John Prochnow says Berkley's Catfish Paste and Power Liver lures are a clean and effective alternative to attractor baits. "In all of our field tests," Prochnow says, "we caught as many or more channel cats with our paste as with natural chicken livers." Berkley also offers a PowerBait dipworm and plans to introduce a dipbait in 1999.

(B) Bob's Cheese Punch Bait—Punch Bait lies between doughs and dips on the firmness scale. Instead of molding the bait on the hook or applying it to a worm or sponge, use a stick to "punch" a small treble hook into the bait, then pull it out.

(C) Bowker's—Joe Bowker developed the first of all commercial dipbaits in the early 1960s. Roger Bele follows that same recipe today. Bowker's recently introduced a shrimp formula that Bele says is less odor-offensive than the original and more effective in cool water. Bowker's offers sponge strips that can be cut to size—also a 10-minute video demonstrating the use of dipbaits

(D) Cat Tracker—Mark Mihalakis says the five flavors of Cat Tracker dipbaits are produced from different cheeses. "Some cheeses have a firm texture when ripe," he says, "while others are rich and creamy." Mark's Magic Additives are powdered products that can be added to dips to produce a firmer texture or a different scent and taste. Cat Tracker also offers several dipworm styles.

(E) Catfish Charlie—Cheese, blood, and shad-flavored dip- and pastebaits. Eileen Holub says the bait's consistency can be modified for year-round use. The shad formula contains 40 percent ground shad and is popular with anglers who traditionally have used sour shad in spring. Catfish Charlie also offers a dipworm.

(F) Doc's Catfish Bait—Doc Schaulk began the prepared bait business in 1927 when he

A

B

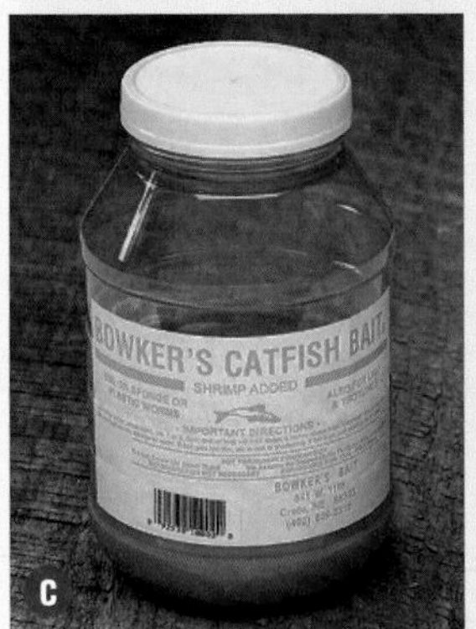

C

D

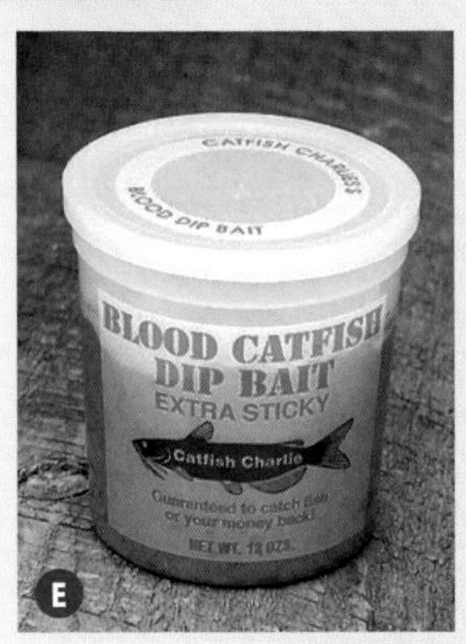

E

manufactured his original paste. Doc's Catfish Getter Dip Bait was introduced in the early 1960s. Today, owner Bob Hosch offers a liver-flavored bait in the original consistency, and cheese and blood flavors in three consistencies—also sponge hooks, dipworms, and a dipworm hook-remover.

(G) Lucky-7—*John Down says his Dunkers cheese-based dipbait is sticky enough to adhere to worms and sponges in cool or warm weather. He also makes the Dunker Dip Worm.*

(H) Magic Bait—*According to Scott Hampton, Magic's Hog Wild dipbait is a hot-weather superstar but scratches cats in cold water, too. Magic Bait offers sponge hook rigs with #4, #6, or #8 treble hooks.*

(I) Rusty's—*Rusty Ryan is stirring up the same dipbait he's been producing for more than 20 years. The bait works on sponge or dipworms, but Rusty says it's even more effective with his worm and sponge combo, which lifts the hook off the bottom.*

(J) Sonny's—*Sonny's Super Sticky dipbait is available in regular or blood-added formulas. Four styles of dipworm are available.*

(K) Uncle Josh/Little Stinker—*Little Stinker tube baits are molasses-based. Mr. Catfish products are cheese-based with blood formulas available. The tube formula is thicker—it can be squeezed like toothpaste into a hollow soft-plastic lure. Sponge hooks and dipworms are available.*

(L) W-D-3—*Wayne Schefsky says his dipbait floats. "When the floating bait is used with our floating worm," Schefsky says, "it suspends above weeds, snags, and silt." Temperature has little effect on the bait's consistency.*

Talking Trash

By now most of you have met In-Fisherman Editor Steve Hoffman, who also is the editor of our catfish publications. He's a crafty young feller and a good sport. Sharp as a new polished tack and a pretty fair angler. Better than fair, in his mind. Getting better, I'll grant him.

We're out last summer with Mark Mihalakis of the Cat Tracker company, wading wet for catfish in a small stream not far from our office. Me? I'm working, of course. Shooting pictures to capture this historic event.

Of course, the fishing's pretty good—easy, actually. And right away, don't you know it, as all these young fellers are wont to do these days, Hoffman's talkin' trash. "Boys, boys, boys, wouldja look at this, yettanother catfish. And a big un," he's saying, with a Howard Cosell swagger in his voice. "Maybe the biggest ol' catfish to ever come from this or any stream of any size, anywhere in this country. Just call me Catfish Kid. Just call me Mr. Catfish. One of the most astute catfish anglers of this or any age. Tell you what, if Bill Dance calls, tell him to cool his jets; my agent will be in touch."

After a half hour of all that lip, and me sweatin' and shootin' photos, well, that kind of uppity is uppity enough. So I say, "Hold it there, Spiffy. Take the camera and shoot me."

"But you don't have a rod," he says.

"Not a problem where I learned to fish," I say.

So I pick a tree branch. Cut myself 8 feet of line. Add a hook. Catch a grasshopper. And in three minutes I'm swinging a catfish bankside.

"Cost per catfish catch-ratio, 4 cents," I say. "Let me know when you can break 50 cents."

Said he'd get back to me.

The big stick in action.

Hoffman catching cats and talking trash.

Hootman suggests, it works well throughout the season, but really seems to produce well during spring, when the water's still cold, or at least cool. Hootman: "I still have a stock of these worms to sell. But another year or so and the world will be without a longer, thinner worm."

Fishing these baits really is just easy. *In-Fisherman* and *Catfish In-Sider* Editor Steve Hoffman and I spent an afternoon fishing with Mark Mihalakis on a local creek late last summer. We slowly motored upriver for several miles and then fished our way back down, wading wet in shallow sections. In deeper areas, we stopped for 10 minutes or so at each riverbend or river hole with woodcover. Using two anchors, we anchored the boat parallel to current about 50 feet upcurrent from the snag—so each of us could fish a portion of the snag.

Hoffman began using a single hook with a lead shot to anchor his bait choice, a portion of cut sucker. Meanwhile, Mihalakis tied on a prototype of his new Tubie 2000, and I tied on his surgical tubeworm, the Tubie Worm. We each added a lead shot 8 inches above our bait and began dipping.

We all caught channel cats right along, but we soon found that fishing the dipbait (Cat Tracker Sewer Bait) was just easier and more cost-effective in this situation. When cats are biting well, a 15-ounce tub of bait could produce a couple hundred dips and 100 cats for pennies a catfish. Unless you seine your own chubs—which takes time—livebait and cutbait's substantially more expensive.

That's not to say, of course, that cutbait isn't the versatile option that we've long contended. In many situations, it's a better choice than dipbait. Good as dipbait is, it's not magic and doesn't always produce as well as a natural bait. Too, so far as we know, cutbait still generally remains a better bet for bigger catfish. Perhaps not in all situations but in most. But some big cats are being caught on dips. Give us more time to experiment, and we'll soon know a lot more about just when to use which bait for which catfish species in certain situations.

The dipping story should get hotter as the topic continues to catch on in other magazines and across the country.

The dipping story should get hotter as the topic continues to catch on in other magazines and across the country. You might as well be ahead of the crowd, experimenting with the baits available out there, until you find the one that's just right for where you fish.

Of course, there's more to all this growth than just talking about the baits within articles. Products can be sold by word passed from catfish angler to angler only so long before, as we suggest, some sense of secrecy tends to erase part of the trail. A few dip manufacturers already may have as much business as they want. The rest need to advertise, which is the traditional means to preach the good word to a market group.

Hootman, on the other hand, is an exception, at least for now. "I wouldn't dare run another ad," he says. "Can't keep up with the demand now."

Hootman, the dipbait baron (Baron von Sonny) would look good wearing a little French beret as he wanders his vineyards—row after row of 50-gallon drums filled with festering cheese. That fine Super Sticky vintage from 1998 was a very good year. Demand for the 1999 crop is bound to far exceed production.

CONTROVERSY: Fishing For Spawning Bass!
In-Fisherman
THING FOR
SMALLMOUTHS
RECORD
WALLEYES
PLUS!
• SPOON SPECTRUM PIKE
• KEY CRANKS FOR PRESPAWN BASS
• QUEST FOR MONSTER FLATHEADS
• TARGETING PRESPAWN BLUEGILLS
Tackle For Shallow Crappies!

{ Historic Perspectives

"I pick up the phone and these characters are there," Stange says. "In some cases, I talk with them only once. Occasionally, though, the conversations continue over the course of years. This is about one of the most curious characters I meet over the phone." Some have called this one of the best short stories written about the impassioned pursuit of large fish, a modest catfishing version of The Old Man and the Sea. Stange also is at his best writing in favor of the conservation of big catfish in the last part of this: "I am disturbed that most fishermen who presently fish for this fish still by tradition treat it as an unlimited commodity, instead of a limited national treasure," he says. And much more—much more.

Illustrations by Ron Finger

CHAPTER 35

MARCH 1999

Let Each Man Find His Own Way to Flatheads

NO MAN OF HONOR WOULD FAIL to keep a secret when the secret is held at the behest of another catfisherman—and it regards flathead catfish of supreme consequence. But the reason not to tell the story—never mind that some details regarding names and places remain secret—passed with the man several years ago. I did not know for certain of his death until recently when a relative of his called to ask why my name and number had been one of only a few names in his meticulous diary of his last years. Most of the notations in the diary related to his fishing.

Monster Catfish Beyond Imagination!

I was at once surprised and, at first, admittedly suspicious that the man would share his secrets. I just picked up the phone that day in December 1991. He was someone who, it became apparent, caught huge flathead catfish. Until about two years ago, we talked a time or two each year, until that last year, when we spoke quite often. We never met and never will. He was satisfied, he said, after reading my stories about catfishing, that I was the one to talk to. He also, at that time, had been saddened by Toad Smith's death that fall. Through my stories he had known Smith as a kindred spirit—another plain-speaking catman who lived the good fishing life in his own way.

No need for fame or fortune when life is so short, my new friend would say, echoing Toad's sentiments. I suspected he sensed his own mortality in Toad's passing, for he was, I gathered, older and was not in good health. He wanted to talk with someone, but reckoned he would tell no one who might short-circuit his quest for flathead catfish of otherworldly proportions. I soon became convinced that my new friend was telling the truth, although I still can't verify a thing. I have asked for but so far have been denied access to his diary.

My long-distance friend was the kind of man many of you would call a fanatic. Once many years ago, a man who you might suppose was like him was said to live in a cave in the wilderness near a western reservoir where huge brown trout swam. He was said to stay for weeks at a time in the cave during fall, sleeping during the day then fishing all night. He bathed by breaking thin ice on the edge of the reservoir near his cave. Likely he ate locusts and wild honey like John the Baptist, for all we know. But we know that he caught huge brown trout on a lure of his own design. We know all this about this fanatic because he told everyone who would listen that he was a fanatic who would catch the world-record brown trout on a lure of his own design.

I have learned to be suspicious of fanatics like that—too much agenda.

My friend, by comparison, was without agenda, save one that had little, by his choosing, to do with anyone besides himself and the fish he sought. He was crazy in that sense—so crazy, in fact, and getting crazier those last years, I suspected that even if he were to realize his dream, his agenda of catching a world-record flathead, he would not share the event and the fish with the world. His intent in the beginning was not to tell the world until he could show the world the fish. State records meant nothing. He talked in passing of several 80s, a mid-80 or two, and one that nudged past 90. By my calculations, that meant he'd set records in each of the three states where he fished and probably had broken his own record in one of them.

But it was two fish he had hooked that shaded our every conversation and swam forever with him. When he awoke in the middle of the night, the fish were there. First thing in the morning, during any pause in a never-too-busy day, and last thing at night, the fish were there. One fish, he told me, he always pictured as it first wallowed on the surface as he had brought it up from a river snag, his headlamp illuminating the fish's huge maw and then the length and breadth of its body. That fish was up and gone in seconds. Hadn't even realized it was hooked as it eased to the surface in order to disgorge the carp that was sticking in its craw. The two-pound carp, crushed and a speck in the fish's gaping mouth, just popped free, along with it the 12/0 hook.

My long-distance friend was the kind of man many of you would call a fanatic.

The incident with the other fish—which actually was the first of the two huge fish he encountered—was a more calculated affair. Both man and fish realized their predicament by the end of the 20-minute tangle, which transpired below a roller dam near the downtown area of a fairly large city. This is an area off-limits to fishing by virtue of no boats allowed and no place to stand and fish within 150 yards of the roller dam. Only occasional fishermen gathered on the remains of a pier that once docked boats. The key to catching fish was reaching the area below the dam.

I note, because it may help to understand our friend, that he apparently had a degree in engineering and had been a corporate executive of consequence before being squeezed out in one of the hostile takeovers of the 1980s. He was as ingenious as he was focused. And his focus now was flathead catfish. In the bed of his pickup, he carried a large livewell disguised as a tool rack. He had modified a digital grain scale to weigh fish in a sling made from mesh decoy sacks lined with rubber netting. The problem was moving a big fish to the truck to weigh it, for as I've said, he was no longer a young man. So he designed a portable electric winch powered by a small gel battery, the entire package weighing less than 20 pounds. With two bolt attachments, he could fasten the winch anywhere. With the fish riding in a heavy canvas sack, he'd winch it up the bank to his truck. Then, reattaching the winch to a portable arm on the side of the pickup box, he'd lift the fish into the tank. He could winch anything anywhere if he had a mind to.

Because he couldn't handle nets large enough to land big fish, either from a boat or from the bank, he modified an eight-foot kayak by adding, as he described it, a fish ramp on one end. With his boat anchored along a river snag or at the head of a deep hole, the partially water-filled kayak would float in the water alongside the boat. Then, as best as I can surmise, a hooked fish was led to the ramp at the end of the kayak. It would swim forward into the kayak, lodging its head under the front deck as the kayak popped back up. The kayak could easily be winched into the boat or up a bank.

Our friend also was as calculating as he was focused. There was little else in his life those last years except the pursuit of catfish. It did not surprise me that one of his strategies for the tailwater was devised only after 20 nights in a row of fishing the area during early summer. He noted a trend in the water discharge schedule that lasted only that summer, a summer of particularly high water.

For reasons he could get no one to explain, about 4 a.m. each morning, one of the rollers nearest the wall on one side of the dam would shut down for about an hour until sunrise. Within minutes, a huge eddy swept in a circle back toward the dam along one breakwall. This offered a 40-minute window of opportunity. A carp hooked in the top of the tail with a 12/0 hook might—just might, with the right prodding—be persuaded to swim the 150 yards along with the current sweeping the wall into the area below the dam. Although this tactic produced fish of some consequence—several 60s—it produced no monsters, probably because the window was so limited and did not open in subsequent years.

The tactic that eventually produced the monster also was a matter of common sense and compromise. With limited options to reach the tailout with livebait, he read surf-fishing manuals to identify the tackle needed to cast deadbaits into the tailout. Soon he was outfitted with a 14-foot spinning rod and a large-capacity spinning reel. With the right coordination, he could deliver 10 ounces of weight from the pier to the rear of the tailout area. This tactic, however, also had its window of opportunity, one based on recognizing a tendency of the flathead catfish. In many waters around the country, flatheads feed predictably on deadbait only during a period nearing the middle of Prespawn, a time when they often feed so aggressively that they take almost any food, including deadbait. In a typical year this occurred around the first of May on the river he was fishing.

I don't remember which make and model 5/0 hook he used, but the rest of his terminal tackle was of breakaway design, a rigging we have suggested is applicable in tailwater situations. He preferred a two-way as opposed to a three-way swivel, because in current a two-way doesn't twist the three lines at the swivel connection the way a three-way does. His mainline was a stiff 30-pound mono, one of the German lines, probably Ande, but perhaps Maxima. (In those days, he had no experience with superlines.) The sinker dropper was 24 inches long, rated at 14 pounds, and was of softer and thinner monofilament like Berkley XL. The hook snell was 12 inches of stiff 40-pound line, again, one of the German lines. The snell line was tied to the rung of the two-way swivel connected to the mainline. He fished barbless with the hook hand-honed to catch flesh and easily sink in.

Flathead catfish, I contend, are the pre-eminent big-game fish of freshwater and should not be treated like smaller gamefish.

When huge flatheads feed, they can be tenacious. While there is, for example, nothing particularly natural about a carp tethered on a limbline, poleline, or trotline testing 500 pounds and anchored to something that won't move, such rigging isn't much of a deterrent to flatheads that want to eat. Even with no give after the fish takes, the fish just won't be denied until something gives—either the line (seldom), the anchor point (occasionally), the hook (quite often), or the fish.

During about a two-week period, our friend was somewhat assured of triggering flatheads so long as he could get the cutbait into the tailwater area. The rig then sank to the bottom where the drop sinker snagged and held the bait in place until a catfish took it. A big flathead that took the bait would set the hook as it struggled against the lighter sinker dropline before breaking the dropline. The fish was then free to be fought in. It wasn't all that easy, of course. When no fish bit, the sinker had to be sacrificed each time the rig was reeled in. This process took time. Sometimes the baited hook snagged and the entire rigging was lost. Another problem was not being able to keep smaller fish from taking the bait. When big fish are on the prowl, though, small cats usually don't move. Still, it's possible that the monster that took his bait in the tailwater late one night had eaten a smaller channel cat that had taken the deadbait and struggled there until the monster flathead found it. In such a case, the big catfish probably wouldn't be hooked but just played for a while before disgorging the channel catfish.

The lesson our friend learned that night was one almost every catman who has ever dealt with monster flatheads learns in one of those first encounters. Big flatheads in close quarters are like no other fish in freshwater. They aren't quick. Struggling against appropriate tackle, they don't fight that long. But they are a bull of a fish. And it seems that almost no angler can imagine the tackle necessary to subdue a large flathead until the angler has been completely beaten, has had his first choice of what he assumed to be tough tackle completely dismantled in a close-quarter encounter.

After breaking the line on the breakaway rig, the huge cat casually swam the 100 yards from the tailwater toward the pier. "I knew the fish was huge," he told me. "I already had taken 60-pound fish from this spot on slightly heavier tackle and live carp. As the fish neared I tried to lift it and just couldn't. The fish stopped right there below me. I'd lift and nothing would happen. Then I'd lift again and again. Finally, it just started swimming downriver, steadily taking line until it hit the edge of a big eddy, where it began to swim back toward me. As soon as it did, it started coming up.

"The problem was the tangle of wood washed in along the riprap," he continued. "With the fish moving toward me, my line hooked a heavy branch. I guess I panicked. I pulled, the branch bowed, the fish kept coming up, the branch broke, and the fish went berserk, swimming right up the 30-degree angle of the riprapped bank below me, going crazy there on those rocks right below me, the scene set by a street light on the pier. I have never seen a flathead so large, nor a fish so wild."

Back into the water, the fish tossed itself. Our friend lifted again, but the line had looped around the tip of his rod. The fish ripped the rod tip down, the tip snapped, and the sudden shot of tension, released as it was all at once as the tip popped, was too much for everything else to catch up. "Everything just froze," he said. "The reel just froze, and the line cracked like a shot." Then, sitting there—for he had stumbled—he watched the fish thrash back to the surface, wallow through a half turn back toward shore, and then proceed to swim half a body length back up the riprapped bank before launching itself back into the water and disappearing. "Try to forget something like that," he said, "especially when this fish was, well . . . "

How large these two fish were he was hesitant to say, for he had begun, over the years, not to trust his own judgment in matters where no experience was concerned. He told me earlier on, when his biggest fish ranged up to 50 pounds, how ill-prepared he was to estimate how large substantially larger fish really were. Wallowing in the water, his first 60 looked like another 50, he told me. But with the fish lying belly on the bank, its girth was apparent. The fish was an inch longer than the 50, but three inches wider. The ability to accurately estimate such proportions and resulting weight of huge fish comes only from experience—having the fish on the bank, checking the exact weight, and noting inch-by-inch dimensions.

Through conversations over the course of several years, he would always skirt the issue of the estimated size of these fish. I knew he had figures in mind and through those conversations we finally arrived at—and he finally tenuously agreed with—conclusions based on circuitous calculation. One reason he wouldn't suggest size was because he was at first hesitant to believe the fish could be as large as he wanted to say. His initial target weight for huge fish, after all, had been

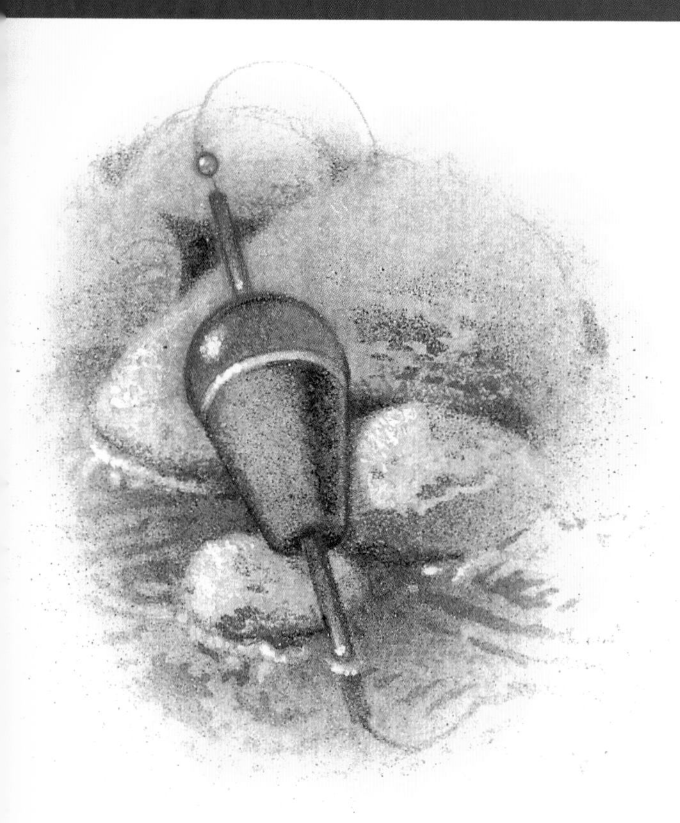

100 pounds. These two fish had been much larger.

I reminded him that fish of the size he might be suggesting were reported to swim in some waters in the 1800s. But weren't those blue cats? he would ask. Yes, so we are told, I would say. But I offered that many of the old accounts were in question on some counts, including fish weight and species. So at least some of the 200-pound-class fish suggested by some old reports could have been flatheads. By that logic, we both agreed, some of the fish also could have been larger than those old reports suggested—no particular reason the reported fish should be the largest fish of their day. And why couldn't fish like that be swimming in some—perhaps quite a few—waters today?

It was a monumental thing for him to finally feel comfortable saying out loud and with conviction what he had been thinking for a long time. The flathead that danced below him on the rocks that night in May was as large as he was and a little more—between 140 and perhaps 160 pounds, with his best estimate resting at about 150. The other fish was 120 to 130, maybe more, but probably not much less. With that one, he was certain he could judge length and width in relation to the snag and the boat. He granted, though, that width can be deceiving without being able to see belly and chest depth.

"Amazing," I said.

"Yes, but I could still be wrong," he backtracked.

"But you're probably right; go ahead and say it," I said.

"Yes, I think those numbers feel good," he said.

This is a good story now, for catfish anglers are for the first time in over a century beginning to get back in touch with this monster of a fish, this predator supreme. Even fishery scientists in most states admitted at Catfish 2000, the first scientific catfish symposium in the history of catfishing, that they just don't know much about flathead catfish populations. We recently tried to complete a state-by-state survey to find out where the best waters were to catch state-record or world-record flatheads. Most states couldn't provide much information because little surveying has been done.

By anyone's calculation, though, within the last two decades, state records have been set in 28 of the 34 states where flatheads swim. Those states range from Wyoming, where flathead numbers are negligible, to Kansas, where huge flatheads are so numerous they could be considered a commodity equal to the annual corn crop if the opportunity to catch them were marketed. And, a new world record was set there last year at 123 pounds.

But then, in so many states, particularly across the South, the flathead isn't even by statute considered a sportfish. I think money still changes hands in some political circles to keep catfish, including flathead catfish, in their place, which is at the beck and call of commercial concerns. I am disturbed that most fishermen who presently fish for this fish still by tradition treat it as an unlimited commodity, instead of a limited national treasure.

Here we have one of the largest and most

superlative sportfish in North America. No other fish in freshwater approaches it as a predator supreme. Certainly not the largemouth or smallmouth bass, not the king salmon or any other coldwater fish, not the muskie or pike. None of those fish even comes close. Yet in states like Iowa, to pick just one, a hunter is limited each season to perhaps a deer or two, while anglers can keep an unlimited number of large flathead catfish. I suggest there are many more deer in most states than there are big flathead catfish, that deer are a much more abundant commodity than these fish. Yet we protect one with the full resources of game and fish departments and mostly ignore the other.

Saltwater anglers, meanwhile, term some fish gamefish and other fish, like bluefin tuna and marlin, big-game fish. Flathead catfish, I contend, are the pre-eminent big-game fish of freshwater and should not be treated like smaller gamefish—and certainly not as commercial fodder. Present harvest numbers still work in some areas because so few anglers fish for this incredible fish. That's changing. Bass and other sportfish are one thing, flathead catfish quite another. Much as I love all those other fish, none of them quite approaches the flathead. It really is the king of freshwater sportfish. It really is the pre-eminent freshwater sportfish of today and the future. It's one of only a few freshwater big-game fish, the others being the blue cat, alligator gar, and several of the sturgeons. Eventually, this is going to catch on. Eventually, we will appreciate our big-game fish, especially this flathead.

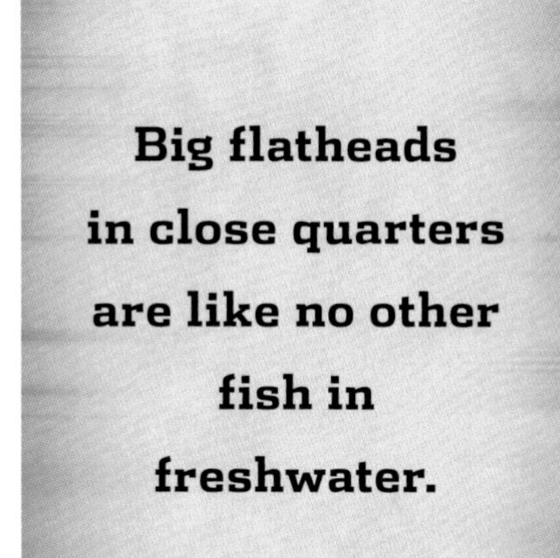
Big flatheads in close quarters are like no other fish in freshwater.

Our friend realized this. An increasing number of those of you who are reading this do too. Kansas anglers Red Rheums and Gary Van Pielt are the first two limbline and trotline anglers I know of who catch big flathead catfish on such tackle for the great sport it provides. They keep smaller fish for the table, but they release those patently unusual fish, the big ones. A few rod-and-reel anglers are beginning to release these fish, too, in order to help sustain this incredible fishery that is bound to catch on among more and more anglers. Hopefully, fishery managers in many more states soon will understand this unique fishery and enact measures to better regulate it.

Near the end, he suggested that I might one day, when it no longer mattered, tell some of his story, perhaps to make a point about flathead catfish. He got a kick out of the idea that enough clues might be woven into such a story to provide hints at where he fished. But he was steadfast in not wanting to tell too much. "These fish deserve better than shortcuts," he said. "Let each man find his own way. It should be enough to know the fish are there." So you know quite a bit about our friend. You may even have crossed paths with him and fished over the same fish. And you believe or don't believe that the fish are there.

Then, during our last conversation, I said again without really thinking about it: You're not going to tell anyone when it happens, are you? And he just remained silent. Suddenly, it hit me, the feeling—the realization—just overwhelmed me. It had already happened. He wasn't about to share everything with me. I said, you mean you couldn't even say something? How big have they been? I asked.

"At least a few fish are as large as you can imagine," he said—I could almost hear him smiling. "You know that. Someday the world will too."

Historic Perspectives

"Put a hot round a skimmy below their principles. Powderburns on the crotch of yer pants will gettcherself a case of getmovin's, by golly." Indeed, indeed. Zacker, that old-school catman and flatland philosopher, has that dead to rights based on personal observation and participation, as Stange explains in this article, adding a bit of flavor to what is a thorough characterization of the hottest fishing period in catfishing—the Prespawn Calendar Period, in all its subtle moods and meanderings. Any catfish angler looking to time the best fishing of the season need read no farther. Just a step beyond any of the good times is a sturdy lesson to learn about how to catch catfish.

Stange notes with curiosity that Larry Tople's rendition of Zacker in the lead illustration is perhaps the only time he doesn't get it quite right, for Zacker never carries an extra pound in his life—is always as skinny as a church mouse and as wiry as a puma. Zacker does shoot cracksure from the right, so the billy club measuring its justice from the left is accurate. And, don'tcha be thinkin' "a skimmy" is a word pair worth reviving—as in, "just a skimmy between yer cheek and gum?" Or, "The cast went just a skimmy left of dead center?"

Illustrations by Larry Tople

CHAPTER 36

APRIL 1999

Moon of the Rutting Catfish

Timing The Prespawn Bite Right!

THAT OLD COMMERCIAL CATMAN ZACKER, whose ashes are scattered on a bluff overlooking the Missouri River in South Dakota, used to tell me he could count on making "whiskey money" from his catfishing at least three seasons each year. Whiskey money wasn't drinking money. Matter of fact, old Zacker rarely touched the stuff. The saying came from his early years when he ran with bootleggers smuggling whiskey from Canada into Montana and then through the Dakotas. There, on his own turf, Zacker and the boys passed the cargo to others who moved the goods south toward Kansas City, or east toward Rock Island-Moline.

"Whiskey money" was his payment for services rendered, which was enough to let him live well for months at a time. Zacker traded his highfalutin' life as a bootlegger for a safer existence as a fisherman after he was bushwhacked by rival whiskey runners. What really made him mad about that deal were the bullet holes in his new oilskin coat. He spent the next 50 years living the good life on the wild river, before all the dams, learning to live with the monstrous changes inflicted by those major obstructions.

Calendar Period Regional Timetable

The timing of the channel catfish Spawn Period illustrates the general region-by-region progression of the Calendar Periods. Region (latitude), water temperature, weather trends, length of daylight, and competition for habitat are just a few of the factors influencing the exact timing of the spawn. Not all cats, even of the same species, spawn at the same time, even in the same body of water. While the bulk of adult fish on a given river may spawn during a few days of ideal conditions, some still spawn early and some late. Some cats may not even spawn every year. Regionally, the onset of spawning may begin in mid-April in the extreme South and Southwest and as late as early August in southern Canada.

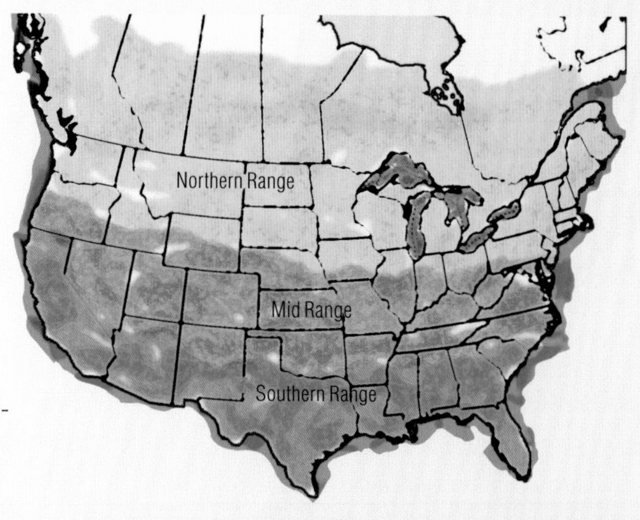

"Best time of the year for nets (usually hoop nets) in the southern Dakotas and Nebraskee was from late April or early May through June," he'd say. "'Course it all depended on the weather. But about late June or early July, cats would start to spawn and lay low for weeks, sometimes a month. Usually by mid-August we was back on fish, maybe for two or three weeks or so before things started to slow again. After that, it was our turn to lay low until gig time, when ice first come on over deep hidey holes where cats gathered to spend winter."

Soon enough, the ice was too thick and the fish too hard to get at until spring. Zacker trapped furbearers or shot market geese during fall, to tide him over until gig season. And he'd tend bar at the Yahoo Tavern down the road, if he had to, during winter, to get by till spring. Friday and Saturday night in a little river town in South Dakotee could be a real hoot and a holler back then. Town Marshall didn't pay no never mind to fisticuffs until someone started shooting.

Zacker was known as a hard case, good with a billy club and a pistol, so he always had work behind a bar when he needed it. Wielding one instrument of destruction in each hand, "Ya holds troublemakers at bay with the pistol while ya beat 'em (toward the door) with the billy club," he'd cackle and laugh, and dance half a jig, remembering the good old

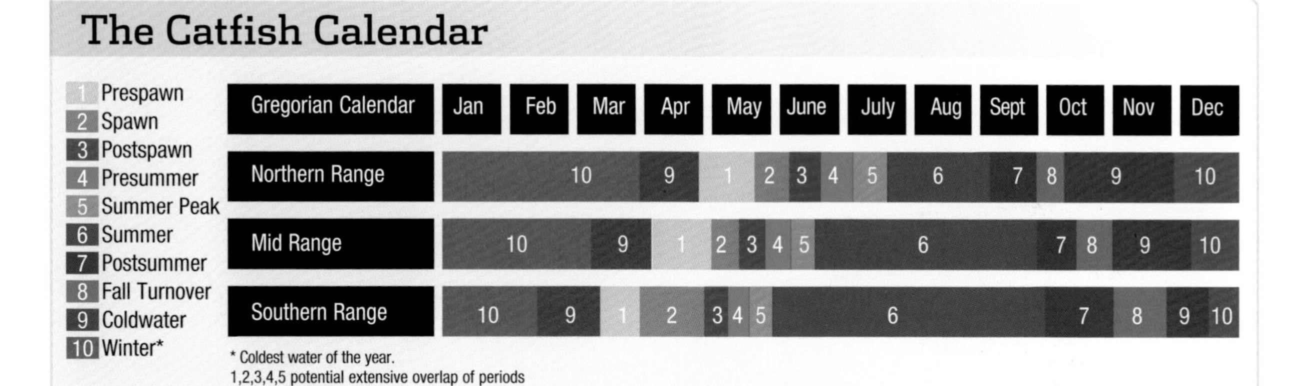

The 10 Calendar Periods of fish response vary in length from year to year. Unusually warm or cool weather affects the length of the periods. They can vary as much as 4 weeks from one year to the next. The periods aren't based on the Gregorian calendar, so they don't occur on specific dates each year. Instead, the Calendar Periods are based on nature's clock.

In addition, they vary by regions of the country. The rivers of the South experience an extended Summer Period and a brief Winter Period. In contrast, rivers along the U.S.-Canadian border have extended Coldwater and Winter Periods. Channel cats in Florida or Texas could be in the Spawning Period while those in northern Minnesota are still in the Winter Period.

Unusual about the catfish calendar is the long period during which individual cats in a population may be in one of 6 different periods. In most situations, this doesn't affect fish location and fishing patterns.

Finally, we have much to learn about catfish. This calendar is based mainly on channel catfish, although these divisions probably also come close to being representative for flatheads. We are in the process of working with fishery scientists for a better understanding of the calendar progression for blue cats.

Typical Spanwing Months by General Latitude

Area	*Months*
Florida	*April-early June*
Alabama-Georgia	*May-June*
Texas-Oklahoma	*May-June*
Kentucky-Tennessee	*June-early July*
Missouri-Illinois-Iowa-Ohio	*June-mid July*
Minnesota-Wisconsin-Michigan	*June-early August*
Manitoba	*July-early August*
Arizona-California-South Texas-Mexico	*April-early May*

In-Fisherman Editor Steve Hoffman poses with a channel cat from the Red River, Manitoba. In preceeding pages, In-Fisherman Editor In Chief Doug Stange holds a flathead from the Minnesota River. And guide Jim Moyer holds a blue cat from the Cumberland River, Tennessee. We know much about how channel cats and flatheads progress through the prespawn and spawn process, but not so much about blue cats. Flatheads, meanwhile, are a little-understood quantity during late winter and early spring, while blue cats are more predictable then. In the right conditions, we now know that channel cats often bite all year. So much still to learn about catfish.

days. "An' if they still wasn't backin' out the bar fast enough, ya put a hot round a skimmy below their principles. Powder burns on the crotch of yer pants will gettcherself a case of getmovin's, by golly."

Moon of the Rutting Catfish is what Zacker called the full moon of late June or early July, which signaled the end of the best time of year for netting catfish—more catfish movement up until then than at almost any other time of year. Soon after that moon, according to Zacker, cats just stopped. First the nets would go dry of channel cats and blues. Then flatheads would disappear. Zacker usually hung up his nets during July, before setting again in August and into September—long as his time on the river paid the bills.

Zacker's Moon of the Rutting Catfish might occur as early as April, for those of you who get a chance to fish for blue cats in the Deep South. The moon of May is more likely the rutting moon on most of the waters in the South and Midsouth. Meanwhile, channel cats may spawn as late as July in parts of the North Country USA and Canada.

MAJOR MARKER IN THE YEAR

Zacker's rutting moon isn't exacting science. Granted, of course, science is still running a little behind the times in research of catfish. Science, as a matter of fact, doesn't make much of a definitive statement about the moon's influence on spawning. I don't claim to know. I'm always the skeptic, even when it's Zacker doing the pronouncing. So even after at least 20 years of observation, I wouldn't want to say that Zacker was right—that catfish spawning activity peaks around a yearly "rutting moon."

Seems to me that in a year when a full moon occurs during the last weeks of April, May, and June, spawning might just peak in various parts of the country about then. But surely, time of year, water temperature, and other water conditions have as much or more of a bearing on spawning as does the full moon. Seems logical, however, when all the right conditions coincide, including perhaps a full moon, the onset of spawning is a foregone conclusion.

But that's really not the point. The key to

fishing during Prespawn and into the Spawn Period isn't an exact definition of when catfish spawn. You need a clue, though. The spawning event, you see, is the major marker dividing the season. It's the defining moment in the catfishing year. So you need a clue—the closer the better—in order to make judgments about how the season's proceeding, and how and where you should be fishing based on how the season's proceeding.

The spawning marker is, for example, a major factor in planning fishing trips. Timing can be everything during most periods, but particularly this one. Say, for example, that you've planned a pilgrimage to see the channel catfishing on the Red River below the Lockport dam near Selkirk, Manitoba. I say pilgrimage because this place is a Mecca of sorts for catfishermen. Anglers really do have to see this unique fishery, the incredible numbers of big channel cats, to believe it. Eventually, most serious cat folks will go at least once, even if they live near the shores of other fantastic catfisheries like Lake Texoma or Santee-Cooper.

This treasure of a fishery, however, plays by the same rules as any fishery in North America. Weather and water levels affect the fishing, but those variables always are set against the backdrop of when spawning typically commences. When conditions are right, the best fishing occurs during Prespawn, beginning in early to mid-May and peaking during mid-June. During what I call the "prespawn peak," most of the fish hold in the tailwater below the dam, or in holes or along shoreline breaks within a couple miles below the dam. As spawning approaches in late June, more and more cats drift back downriver to spawn, usually in a huge marsh off the main river.

Of course, all the fish don't spawn at once, so fishing can still be good during, say, the second week of July. But if I had to plan a trip and I had a choice, I'd be there the second week of June instead of during the second week of July. Usually by late July and into early August, the fish settle into a summer pattern—fish holding in scour holes up and down the river. Move from hole to hole and the fishing can be almost as good as during the June peak.

But it's difficult to beat the fishing during the prespawn peak. Some would protest and say the bite can be just as good and the fish average larger during late September. Agreed. The September bite, though, doesn't occur with the consistency of the bite during the prespawn peak. Certainly, no distinguishable marker exists in September to mark just when that bite might begin or peak. That, by comparison, is the magic of the spawning marker and the prespawn peak that precedes it.

ONLY THE TIMING CHANGES

This same set of circumstances plays in every fishery in North America, with only the timing changing. It isn't enough to know that you're going to a great fishery; you need to be there at the right time. So if you're traveling to a distant spot, you need a reliable contact in the area—weather and water conditions might push the peak forward or back in an exceptional year. Too, extremely high water often makes fishing difficult, although almost never impossible.

Weather plays an even more important role when a trip must be planned at the beginning or end of the Prespawn Period. Several years ago, for example, we planned a trip to Santee-Cooper during early April, choosing that time in hopes of catching the tail end of the cold-water fishing for big blue cats, and the beginning of prespawn for flatheads. We managed to catch some good fish of each species. But we didn't see the kind of peak fishing we would have had for blue cats if we'd planned the trip for early March. Peak prespawn fishing for the flatheads required being there about the beginning of May. Again, such planning requires an understanding of when the different catfish species spawn in a body of water. Spawning is the major marker in the fishing year.

DIVIDING THE PRESPAWN SEASON

Some of the year's best fishing for most fish species occurs during Prespawn. Catfish anglers are particularly lucky because catfish go through one of the longest Prespawns of all freshwater species.

Prespawn for pike, for example, often lasts only weeks, from ice-out until water temperature nudges past the low to mid-40°F range. Sometimes pike finish spawning in marsh areas before the ice is off the main body of water. Prespawn for walleyes often lasts a little longer, from ice-out until temperatures nudge toward the mid-40°F range. Prespawn for largemouth bass, meanwhile, is a more extended affair, lasting for a month or even two months in many parts of North America.

Fish tend to be aggressive and searching during the middle stage of Prespawn. Anglers who understand the basic nature of the species they seek find it easier to locate fish. Once they find fish, they usually find them feeding aggressively. Again, Prespawn lasts for two or three months for catfish, offering anglers an extended period to fish for potentially aggressive fish. As a result, this is one of the finest fishing periods for any species in freshwater.

The entire Prespawn Period, though, doesn't offer the same potential for fine fishing. While prespawn for pike is too short to subdivide, prespawn for catfish needs subdivision. Only then can we begin to categorize some of the tendencies of catfish during the different Prespawn Periods. Only then can we begin to make judgements about how weather and water levels are affecting the natural prespawn progression—and naturally, how weather and water conditions might be affecting catfish and catfishing. Only then can we begin to predict, as one season becomes two seasons, becomes many seasons, where each of the catfish species is likely to be when, and how and on what they are likely biting, based, again, on how the prespawn season is progressing.

Experience counts, but it's more than mere time on the water. We need to place our experiences within the framework of a set of distinguishable markers—divisions in the season. We can tell you things to look for to begin to understand the waters and the cats where you fish. In particular, you need to recognize what I've already referred to as the "prespawn peak," a one- or two- to three-week period of exceptional fishing that no catfish angler should miss.

EARLY PRESPAWN

The spring season begins as ice leaves or early spring weather arrives. Early spring usually means continued cold and turbid water. Channel cats and flatheads remain mostly inactive, holding in deeper water. Blue cats in many southern waters, however, probably have been feeding consistently during much of the winter. Eventually, rising water temperatures stimulate channel cats and flatheads. They stimulate blue cats, too, but cause them to move

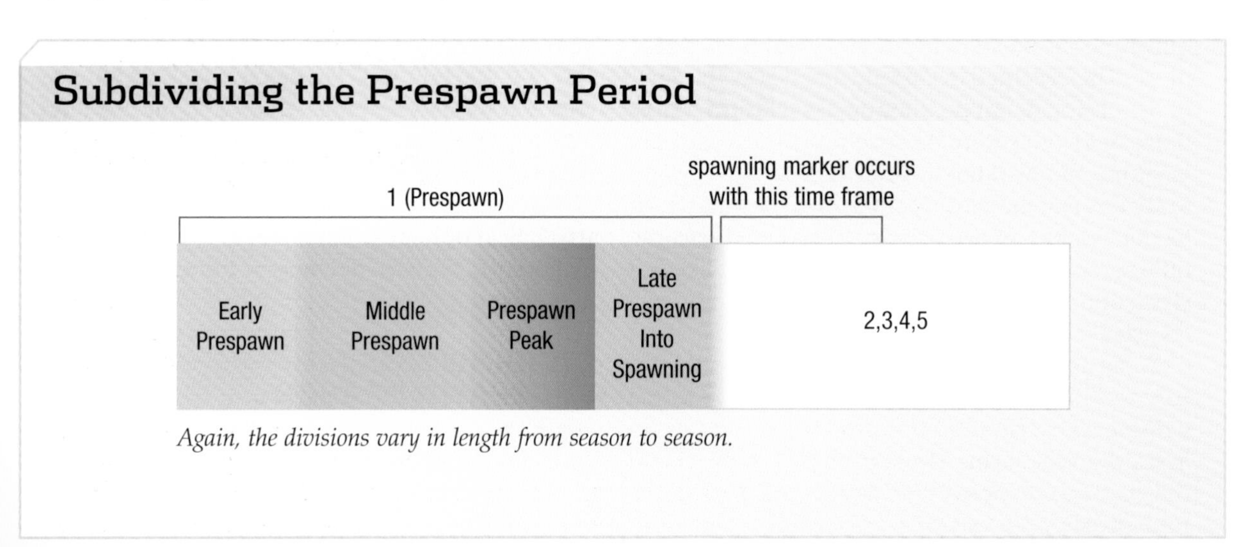

Again, the divisions vary in length from season to season.

out of winter patterns, making finding them more difficult for a while. This is the early portion of the Prespawn Period.

In southern regions, where water temperatures have been in the 40°F and 50°F range during winter, channel cats and flatheads might start feeding when water temperatures reach the low 60°F range. In northern regions, 50°F temperatures put channel cats on the prowl. The truth is, no one seems to know exactly when flatheads start feeding. My guess is that in most waters across the South, they feed periodically during winter.

But we just have a lot to learn yet about what happens during different seasons on different bodies of water relative to the different species of catfish. In the North, the first flatheads I've caught have been in small reservoirs, with water temperatures in the upper 50s. In rivers, there's no consistency to the fishing until temperatures rise into the 60s, although you might scratch a fish before then.

Understanding the Calendar Periods is one basis for learning the patterns of catfish and developing the skill to find them. The calendar serves as a reference. Understanding that fish progress through distinct periods of activity that vary only in their length from year to year, based on changes in weather, allows anglers to note similarities and differences in fish behavior from one activity period to the next.

One overriding factor in discussions among anglers, therefore, is the Calendar Period under which the discussion takes place. It does little good for catfish anglers to discuss the productivity of a certain baitfish, for example, without first noting the Calendar Period in question. Just because bullheads are productive for flatheads during one Calendar Period doesn't mean they will be good during another.

MIDDLE PRESPAWN AND THE PRESPAWN PEAK

Zacker, of course, didn't need to monitor water temperatures to know when spring was busting out of its britches. It was in the air, as folks say. No more weekly whipsawing from nasty to pretty nice. Suddenly the weather's just nice, often for days in a row. Spring showers are cool instead of icy. Dandelions glow in the sunlight—green grass growing; nightcrawlers out in force; trees budding; frogs in evening chorus; turtles sunning on shorelines. The world's alive. And catfish are moving. This is the middle portion of the Prespawn Period.

In rivers, the movement is upriver, often into feeder streams, or even into smaller feeder streams off larger ones. As the water warms, metabolic rates climb. Initial movements are motivated as much by the need for food as by any sense of spawning fever. Along the travel path, barriers stop cats and gather forage. Temporary barriers include logjams, prominent wing dams, and large sand bars with tailout holes. Dams—permanent barriers—almost always gather large groups of fish. Exceptions seem to be those dams with exceptionally shallow tailwater areas. Fish hold at barriers, feed, and then seem to move on. Prominent barriers, though, continue to gather traveling fish, probably initially as they move upriver and then when they drift back down.

Reservoir catfish move, too. Indeed, in flowing reservoirs like Santee-Cooper, blue cats often move miles from lower lake Moultrie, through the long diversion canal into upper lake Marion. Once in Marion, they mingle with resident fish and often feed on mussels on windswept points and shorelines. Flatheads, meanwhile, often begin to move along deep creekbeds, stationing in prime spots.

In other reservoirs, flatheads follow creekbeds from the main reservoir into shallow creek arms. And in still other reservoirs, they patrol along riprap at the face of dams or along causeways. The best causeways early on are those along north shorelines, because they get the most sun. Later, I'm not sure that anyone has determined why certain causeways are better spawning spots than others. My guess is that the best early spots tend to be shallower than spawning spots, which should be near deeper water. But like so much of what I'm alluding to here, the specifics are a story for another day.

The earliest prespawn movement in reservoirs is by channel cats, which often gather to feed on winter-killed shad in windward bays shortly after ice-out and continuing for several weeks. Eventually, during middle prespawn, many of the channel cats move out of bays to feed on windward points that poke into the main reservoir. Or they gather along almost any reservoir barrier that offers current flow. In flowing reservoirs like the lock and dam systems of the Mississippi and Ohio rivers, for example, some of the best spots are near the mouth of side-channel areas. These are secondary current areas as opposed to areas that get heavy current. Most of the channel cats in Santee-Cooper, on the other hand, seem to reside in the several-mile-long diversion channel, which often has heavy current flow.

The prespawn peak begins several weeks into the middle Prespawn Period. Catfish continue to move into prime feeding areas where fish already have gathered and are feeding aggressively and, often, more and more competitively. Fish that move on continue to be replaced by other fish. Depending on weather and water conditions, and on the number of fish available in a body of water, the peak usually lasts at least two weeks. But these two or three weeks of exceptional fishing also are surrounded by potentially good fishing on the front side, and at least fair fishing on the back side.

Early is Late

In late fall, channel catfish often act a lot like they do in early spring, only they're heading in different directions. Immediately after ice-out last spring (water temperature 45°F), for example, channel cats were still holding along drop-offs into the basin of a lake we fish year-round in Minnesota. Occasionally that day, fish would move up onto a shallow flat near where a shallow feeder river enters the lake. A week later (water temperature 55°F), fish were already moving upriver. Many other fish had moved onto shallow flats or were holding around modest current areas near necked areas traversed by bridges.

Late last fall we broke ice to fish the same areas. The fish had vacated the river and main-lake flats and were holding in 30 to 40 feet of water at the base of the drop-off into the main-lake basin. This also is where we find the fish after ice-up.

LATE PRESPAWN INTO SPAWNING

Eventually, as the season progresses and water temperatures continue to climb into the mid- to upper 70°F range, the urge to feed is tempered by the need to spawn. Cats begin to drop away from prime feeding areas toward spots where spawning commences. Fishing success tapers off at first, then often really slows. Sometimes, though, when feeding areas and spawning areas coincide, anglers see no rapid decrease in fishing success. I suspect, too, that all adult catfish don't spawn each year, and that's the reason fishing often continues to be pretty good on waters with many cats.

Probably the most obvious spot where fishing tails off is in a tailwater area. Fishing often is spectacular during the prespawn peak, begins to slow, then goes dead from one weekend to the next. Most of the adult cats just drop downriver, and suddenly the tailwater is mostly the home of smaller cats. Catfish continue to feed during the Spawn Period, however. Anglers just need to be near spawning cats. Another story.

Remember, too, that each catfish species progresses through these phases of prespawn at different rates. As spawning approaches, fishing for channel cats declines before fishing for flatheads does. Tailwater fishing for flatheads can still be good even though fishing for channel cats is in a funk. When it comes to blue cats, my impression is that our understanding of the world according to this fish is running behind our understanding of channel cats and flatheads. I won't presume to tell you exactly how blue cats approach the Spawn Period relative to the other species—what temperatures are key.

Always, too, you must note a reckonable interaction between the different catfish species. Channel cats are on the prowl before flatheads, so some areas host fine fishing for channel cats until flatheads arrive. But flatheads almost always dominate channel cats. When flatheads move in, channel cats usually move out.

Or, channel cats time their activity to occur when flatheads aren't active. In rivers with good populations of flatheads and channel cats, it's easy to tell when activity for flatheads is peaking, because flatheads dominate snags that held channel cats earlier and will hold them again later. When flathead activity is peaking, they also are likely to bite 24 hours a day, although the biggest fish still seem to be nocturnal. During this period, channel cats tend to move out of snags onto river flats. During summer, flatheads almost always feed at night, while channel cats (except for the largest fish) do most of their feeding during the day.

In a place like Santee-Cooper, both blue cats and flatheads dominate channel cats, perhaps the reason channel cats aren't numerous in the far reaches of the huge reservoirs, but tend to be confined to the area in and around the diversion canal. Once channel cats were the dominant fish at Santee-Cooper, however, and in recent years their numbers seem to be rising. Not many big channel cats there right now, though. Again, different species of catfish interact with each other, influencing total behavior. This too must be factored into the game that is catfishing—and must be played against the backdrop that is fishing during the Prespawn Period.

Zacker would object at this point. Too much calculating. Too much thinking. "A man just gets to havin' a sense about these things," he'd say, his way of saying that eventually we learn from experience. But he spent so many years on the water. Most of us don't get out as often as we'd like. We have to be a little more calculating in order to make sense of what's happening when we do get on the water. This is where catfish anglers begin to make sense of fishing during the finest fishing period of the year, the Merry Moon of the Rutting Cat.

Master Angler HUGE Fish! Page 136
APRIL 1999
In-Fisherman
THE JOURNAL OF FRESHWATER FISHING
DARTING FOR PANFISH Page 100
OUR TOP TINKERING TIPS FOR BASS Page 54
PLUS!
• MOON OF THE RUTTING CATFISH
• MUSKIE RELEASE TACTICS TODAY
• GREAT LAKES OUTLOOK FOR SALMON
• RESERVOIR WHITE BASS
THOSE POSTSPAWN WALLEYE BLUES
Bass Attitude by Latitude

{ Historic Perspectives

This essay from the In-Side Angles column in the front of In-Fisherman magazine is one of over 150 that Stange writes in his time as either Executive Editor or Editor In Chief. The lead column should, he says, set the scene for the issue, not by reviewing the articles that are in the magazine—readers can do that for themselves—but by setting a broader context for the columns and features, or by offering information that readers can't get by reading those items. It's just his take on a familiar aspect of doing a magazine. This essay, meanwhile, is an example of the kind of writing he frequently offers there, to show how these items so often connect naturally to catfish and catfishing. Indeed, reading a fair share of these essays, one might easily conclude that many, if not most, are a direct result of his love of catfishing and the kinds of things that happen as a matter of course in being a catfisherman.

Illustration by Lee Stroncek

CHAPTER 37

APRIL 1999

Taking Time

I WILL NEVER FORGET A FRIEND telling me about the time he forgot a fish. The fishing was so good and he was in such a hurry to catch another and another, he realized that, although he had caught a good fish some hours back, he just couldn't remember much about catching it. It was like not having caught the fish at all, not being able to remember much about it. He'd been in such a hurry to get somewhere that he'd gotten there without getting anywhere at all.

I worry that campfires (or cooking fires) are among the most frequent fatalities in the rush that fishing can be today. My last seminar audience of the 1999 season was a group of several hundred who gathered to talk about walleyes. A show of hands revealed that less than a tenth of the crowd during the last season had taken time to do a shorelunch, or just to camp and gather around an evening fire over which some of the fish of the day were cooking.

There's something special about campfires and their connection to people who spend time outdoors. Our ancient ancestors ended

There's Something Special About Campfires—Cooking Fires!

Double dipped and deep fried. Dust the fish in flour, dip in an egg wash, then roll them in Panko bread crumbs or corn meal. Classic shore lunch.

each day with a cooking fire, a campfire. Today, though, many fishermen never experience a fire site (even a gas stove cook site) except as a matter of incidental course by way of shorelunch prepared by a guide. Often it's the best fish they've ever eaten and one of the most memorable parts of their trip.

Perhaps this is especially true for children. Taking kids fishing is one thing—a big thing. Further introducing them to the ancestral experience that was a natural part of hunting and fishing for many previous generations is quite another. Serious intent to catch, dispatch, and cook at least a part of the catch was the original essence of being outdoors, fishing and hunting. One of the integral reasons that most of your grandparents fished wasn't just for sport, but to harvest fish for the table.

Fishing still works best when that connection remains, although, of course, today we have no need to harvest more than a meal of fish on most outings. We just have to take time, even if it's an hour away from fishing at noon, or an hour less fishing in the evening. We just have to take time even if the fire is no more than a camp stove on a picnic table at a common state campsite.

Taking this kind of time suggests only that fishing is more than the actual event, and the actual event is more than a rush to attain some certain number of fish—although I have to admit, some is always better than none.

Baked Fish for a Rainy Day

This simple and versatile recipe from Chef Lucia Watson is easy to prepare over hot coals. On a rainy day, build your campfire under a tarp to warm up while lunch cooks. If you need to come in and dry off, bake the fish in the oven. I prefer to leave the fish whole, as the bones add flavor and help the fish to retain moisture, but this works well with fillets, as we've shown here. If you know your wild mushrooms, be sure to try our variation. Delicious!

For a whole fish, scale, gut, and rinse the fish. Place a generous helping of herbed butter in the cavity, sprinkle with salt and pepper, and layer the lemon slices in the fish. Close up the fish and wrap in aluminum foil. Buried in coals, or in a 350°F oven, the fish takes about 10 to 15 minutes to cook.

For fillets, lay each on a piece of aluminum foil. Smear a generous helping of the butter over the fish, sprinkle with salt, pepper, and the breadcrumbs. Place a few lemon slices on top. If cooking in the coals, cover the fish completely in foil and nestle in the coals and cook for about 10 minutes. If using an oven, wrap the foil up around the edge of the fillet but leave the top open slightly; cook the same amount of time—about 10 minutes.

For an added treat, wrap a serving or two of small to medium new potatoes in foil with about 2 tablespoons of olive oil , salt, pepper, garlic, and a sprinkle of herbs. Buried in hot coals, they take about 30 minutes. At home they cook in about 30 minutes at 375°F.

To serve two. . .

one 2 lb. catfish (or two fillets)
2 tbsp. herb butter
one lemon cut into rounds
salt and pepper
1/4 c. breadcrumbs (if using fillets)
new potatoes
olive oil
1 tbsp. mashed garlic or
garlic powder to taste
salt and pepper
fresh or dry herbs

Historic Perspectives

In-Fisherman is sold to a large magazine-holding company, Primedia, based in New York City. In-Fisherman suddenly is one of 250 other magazines, from Seventeen to ImportTuner and Chicago. Shortly thereafter Stange attends a meeting of Primedia publishers and top editors that takes place on Madison Avenue. Here stands a small-town Iowa boy, looking up at the New York skyline. You might excuse him for thinking, "Holy hanna!" Getting on an elevator to go to a morning meeting, everyone with name tags on, riding with him are the publishers of New York Magazine and Chicago. "Whoa," he thinks. But surprise: One of the publishers notices his name tag. "You're at In-Fisherman," they note. "You're actually doing books, videos, radio and TV, internet, besides publishing magazines? How do you pull all that off?

It seems that In-Fisherman is the poster child for where Primedia executives want the rest of the magazine crowd to go. Later, Stange rises to accept an "Integration Award," as the most admired multimedia company in freshwater fishing, this in front of several hundred of the top magazine people in North America. Heady stuff for a catfishin' boy!

CHAPTER 38

MAY 1999

A Mess of Catfish On My Mind

MAYBE THE WORST THING you can do is make this complicated. Really, most of the time, catfishing just isn't. Or doesn't have to be. Go after whatever's available—channel cats, blue cats, or a flathead (one should be enough). My choice would be to fish a river, but then again, maybe not.

One of the best spots I have near me is a reservoir disguised as a lake. You have to search to find the dam, and when you find it, it's one of the few in catfish country that never attracts any catfish. It's positively un-American. Not much of a tailwater there. Not much of anything there except the dam. So the place to look for channel cats (and I imagine blue cats if any happened to be in this body of water) is around bridges, which is a pretty common pattern on lakes and reservoirs.

I Never Fish So Well As When I'm Hungry—A Mess Of Eaters On My Mind!

LAKE AND RESERVOIR BRIDGES

We've spent the better part of 10 years telling you to stay away from river bridges because that's where everyone fishes. Once the catfish holding by a river bridge are fished out, it takes a spell of high water before more of them gather below that old bridge.

Bridges on lakes and reservoirs are another story. Bridges there usually are built across necked areas that mean current, which draws catfish, especially early in the year. Often as not, these spots produce some fish three seasons long.

The problem with bridges can be boats going under and cars and trucks traveling over. Dust. Gravel. Little spill-splash from cattle and hog trucks. I can testify too that no-stretch superlines really don't, after a boat ran over my Spiderwire Catfish last spring, the prop winding the line up so fast that my rod looked like an arrow launched from a cannon as it took off from its perch in a forked stick. Bridge graffiti, too. Such literacy. Such sense of verse. Such a range of topics. Even politics: "Clinton to Congress: Yank my doodle it's a dandy."

One of the most productive bridge spots connects shallow with deeper areas. Could be a marsh area on one side of the bridge connected to the main lake. The cats usually hold in the main reservoir during winter, but are drawn to the current from the warm run-off coming from the marsh in spring and on into summer. Most of the cats hold on the downcurrent side of these spots. Usually the current flows from the marsh into the main lake, so most of the cats hold on the main-lake side of the bridge.

The best bridge spots usually connect major parts of lakes or reservoirs. The best bridges almost always are those connecting the deepest lake or reservoir section to another smaller or shallower section. Most of the cats hold in the deep lake during winter, so the bridge is a major traffic area as cats move into shallower lakes during spring and early summer. Again, though, even modest current continues to draw some cats most of the year.

PONDS

You should be so lucky as to have access to a 1- or 2- or 10-acre pond full of channel cats. Should you have such a pond, particularly a small one, you probably shouldn't, as one of my friends did, stock the pond with a fat old flathead from a nearby reservoir. He thought he could catch the flathead again whenever he wanted. But he couldn't, and pretty soon he had a pond with a fat and apparently quite contented flathead and few channel cats. In fact, almost none. And those that were left were so scared that they just crawled up on the bank one day and surrendered.

The best spots in most ponds are anywhere almost anything sticks out or sticks in. Stick-out spots are anywhere a point pokes into a pond. An obvious example is David and Cheryl Wood's pond on their farm in Missouri where I goes a-turkey huntin'. David and Cheryl built their pond shaped like a big elbow. So when David gets a hankerin' for a catfish dinner, he drives his mobile deer-blind (his pickup truck) down to the elbow where he has a little spot mowed for his lawnchair. It's positively American, or at least Missouri American. Cats looking for food naturally filter around stick-out spots like David's elbow point.

And soon enough, Cheryl walks down to the pond, wakes David up, and catches him a catfish for dinner. Stick-in spots, on the other hand, are the corners of a pond and the inlet area. Some inlet areas even have a little running water, which naturally draws cats. Inlet areas also warm quickly during early spring and are the first to draw catfish. Corners of ponds, meanwhile, tend to congregate cats that naturally bunch up there as they search along the shoreline.

One fairly unusual tactic to attract cats to where you're fishing is to run in place on the bank. No, I'm not kidding—although I don't recommend this until the fishing slows at any spot where you set up. Now I'm not going to explain this, because I hear you snickering out there. You think I'm plum crazy.

Well, I am not. 'Course, if anyone sees you trying this they'll think you're loco, too, so you can join the club. But just you go ahead and write me a letter with a big apology if this isn't the gospel, as it works, sometimes. Go ahead, now. I'm saying when things finally get tough and you're so catfish hungry you stoop to trying it and it works, you'll be embarrassed and feel guilty for calling your old buddy a crazy yahoo.

RIVER BARRIERS

This is the best time of year to be floating or walking a nice stretch of small to medium-sized river. In most parts of the country, the cats haven't spawned yet, and they're cranked—movin' right along upstream, they are, for the most part, stopping along the way to feed when they hit river barriers. The best barriers are major river snags (tree tangles) in conjunction with a big river hole just downstream from a long, flat, shallow section of river. Smaller tangles also draw some fish.

This is prime time for walking or drifting far and fishing fast. Say you're boating. Usually the plan is to motor upriver, noting potential spots as you pass, then fish as you motor back down. At each spot, anchor so the boat stops 50 feet or so in front of (upcurrent from) a snag. From this position, pitch baits just in front of and alongside the snag. The most active cats patrol the front and current-wash side of the snag. Usually doesn't take more than a couple minutes to get bit. Then it might take another 5 to 10 to call a few more fish out of the core of the snag. Don't stay much longer, even if the spot looks too good to be true.

Any spot you find that looks that good, by the way, is probably prime for flatheads after dark. You should also be catching some flatheads during the day on prime rivers with lots of flatheads, providing that you're fishing with cutbait part of the time. Most of the flatheads that bite during the day, though, are running with channel cats. Usually they're smaller flatheads—up to around 15 pounds, in my experience.

Fine fishing and dinner to boot.

The big boys dominate the best river spots at night. The best river holes almost always are associated with major timber snags. The exception occurs upstream near dams, where snags don't likely form, so flatheads just drop into the core of deeper holes. The last two years, we have taken some larger flatheads from these types of holes during the two hours before dark. I would have bet those fish wouldn't bite before dark. Goes to show how little any of us knows about everything that has to do with anything about catfish. I'm willing to learn whatever those cats are willing to tell me. I just wish I could get into listening distance more often than I do.

The point is to keep moving. We usually try to fish four or five spots in an hour. Takes time to up anchor and move and re-anchor. Second time out, we know better than to stop at the marginal spots we fished the first go-around. Good spots, it's somewhat redundant to say, produce nicer fish. Marginal spots often are full of peckerwoods that don't dare run with the big fish. Sometimes, though, when we're looking to deep-fat fry a bunch of cats whole, those pounders are just right. I fillet most of the catfish I creel if they weigh more than 2 pounds. Smaller fish cook up just as well skinned and pan-dressed. A couple of those channel cats deep-fried, two ears of buttered corn, a scoop of red beans and rice, and a hushpuppy or two is about as good as it gets for a catman believer.

TAILWATERS

Tailwater areas get better and better as spring progresses into early summer. By the time water temperature cracks into the 70°F range, cats are going crazy—and much of the party is taking place in tailwaters. Depending on the tailwater, you might find channel cats, blues, flatheads, all three, or some combination thereof.

If there's a problem with tailwaters, it's that it's sometimes difficult reaching the fish that hold in the fast-water areas right below the dam. Much of the feeding takes place there as cats push into current breaks formed by obstructions on the bottom, or by the way the water gathers as it's released from the dam.

Even just downriver from the dam, though, to be successful you must read current, watching in particular how different currents meet to form an edge and an eddy. Most of the cats hold along these current edges or roam through eddy areas. Some also move right up on shallow shoreline flats, sometimes swept by large eddy areas, but usually the current isn't super-swift here. These are prime flats for presenting bait below a float (a lighted float at night).

If you've never fished a tailwater area and the process sounds puzzling, don't be put off, just go and have at it. Usually this time of year, so many fish are there that you're bound to catch something. And while you're at it, you're getting a feeling for where other folks are fishing and perhaps beginning to see why they're more or less successful than you are. Most cat folks are willing to help. They're not going to give up their fishing spots, but they might explain what they're doing if they're catching fish. At least the channel-cat boys will. The flathead crowd tends to be more tight-lipped.

THE OLD ONE, TWO, MAYBE THREE

I wouldn't go anywhere this time of year without fresh cutbait and at least one top dipbait. That's the basic one-two punch for blue cats and channel cats, and as I said earlier, flatheads sometimes take fresh cutbait. If you're serious about flatheads, especially the big boys after dark, add big livebaits to your bait stock.

Fresh cutbait can be freshly killed shiner or sucker minnows, or shad about 4 to 5 inches long. My preference is for larger chubs, shad, or suckers, with the sides filleted off and then cut into 1-inch strips. In a pinch, four or five smaller minnows impaled on a hook also works, sometimes. Keep the bait on ice until just before you use it.Hook a 4-inch minnow through the tail, after trimming off the tail so it doesn't catch current and make the bait roll and tangle. Crush the head of the bait or cut the head off to get juices flowing. Don't try to hide your hook. Cats rarely care about hooks. Leave the hook point exposed so it's easy to set the hook.

Big snags usually hold lots of catfish, including flatheads, when they're present in the river. Cutbanks with little cover usually produce small fish, which is fine if you're looking to deep-fry a bunch.

Fresh cutbait!

Livebait!

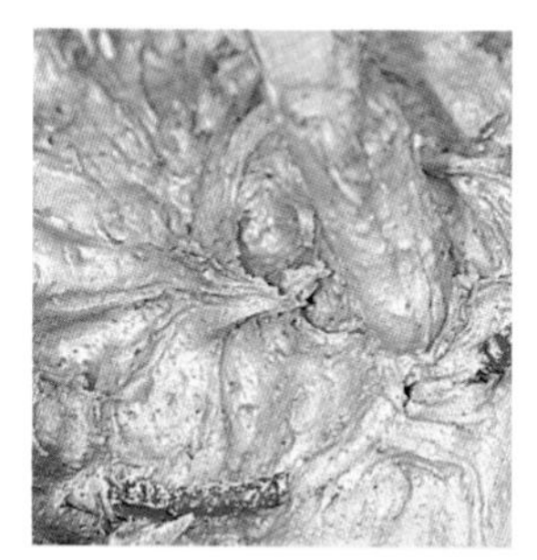

Dip!

I enjoy gathering bait. Never know what you're going to dredge up in a seine—boots, turtles, tires, cans, and the occasional ticked-off muskrat. If we have time, we find a small creek where it runs into a larger river, lake, or reservoir. In small rivers, if the water level's down, we seine the edges of holes right in the river. Might even end up with the makings for turtle soup or chowder. Release all muskrats, boots, and tires. (They're out of season.) When time's short, buy the biggest bait you can find at a baitshop. Baitshop bait isn't an option every place in the country, though, especially many places in the East and West.

Another option is to catch chubs by hook and line, using tiny portions of crawler or liver on a #8 hook. Good spots include under bridges, over creeks, or in holes in small rivers. Get the chubs biting by chopping a couple crawlers (or liver) into bits and tossing a palmful of bits into the hole. Chubs are voracious once they start feeding. Use a float to suspend bait for chubs. Fish on the bottom for suckers. This is a good way to get big baits for flatheads, too. Other top baits for flatheads include bullheads, bluegills, green sunfish, and small carp.

If a body of water has channel cats and flatheads, or channel cats, blues, and flatheads, I start fishing with a piece of cutbait. It's the only consistent way I've found so far to tempt flatheads, along with channels and blues. The dominant fish in the area usually bite first, and usually that's the flatheads or larger channels or blues. Start with dipbait and, my thinking is, you'll likely spook the flatheads and not be able to catch them even if you switch to cutbait after fishing with a dip.

If it's just channels and blues you're dealing with, start with either bait; then when fishing slows on one option, present the other. Often you'll scratch an extra fish or two from a spot by switching baits after the initial flurry subsides.

I've been experimenting, too, with first presenting a dipbait from one company and then, after the initial flurry, switching to a dipbait from another. I also tried beginning with a dip from one company and switching to a different blend from the same company. The first dip gets bit good. Then things go downhill.

Some of the dips I've used with good results include those from Bowker's, Catfish Charlie, Cat Tracker, Sonny's, and Uncle Josh. I fish dips either on dipworms or surgical tube worms. Those companies also sell dipworms.

The old one-, two-, and (maybe) three-punch presentation works in other places—indeed, most places. Works in front of or behind wing dams and closing dams on large rivers. Works on flats in large rivers and reservoirs. Works in conjunction with drift techniques along channel edges in large rivers. Works on pay ponds in Ohio, Kentucky, and other states. Works along riprap in heavy current on the channelized Missouri River from Sioux City down to St. Louis. And more, more, more. We just can't get to everyone's specific situations right here, right now. I will, however, leave you with a story about flatheads.

LESSON LEARNED

The lesson finally set in about July 1988. We motored upriver and downriver, fishing for channel cats during the day, all the while noting major river snags that might hold big flatheads, so we could set up and fish at night. Camp included a tent to fend off mosquitoes when we wanted to sleep, a campfire that eventually burned low, and a sandbar with enough driftwood for the campfire. Some spots are great camping spots, others are the pits. This one was a small sandbar across from a deep riverbend with a lot of rock and not much timber. I've learned that riverbends and rock are fine up closer to a dam, but timber is the key to flatheads in small and medium rivers farther downstream. That, though, isn't the lesson I intend to leave you with.

Fishing isn't good that night—no runs in hours. Having been up some 20 hours, by about 2 a.m. I can't stay awake any longer. This night I'm fishing with my son who's 8 at the time. He had long ago snuggled into his sleeping bag. Leaving two lines set, I climb into the tent. No sooner am I in my bag than zzzzzzzzt, zzzzzzzzzzzzzzzzzzzzzzztt. A fish is running line off against the clicker. So I get up, unzip the tent, hustle to the rod, check it, attempt to set on a fish, and miss. Dirt.

Rebaiting with a big sucker, I toss the line out and climb back into the tent and my sleeping bag. Not two minutes pass. Zzzzz-zzzzzzzzz. Zzzzzzzzztt-ttzzzzzzzzttttt. Geez. I climb out and repeat the procedure. Three more times. The fish are just crushing the head of the bait and toying with it. Finally, 3 a.m., exhausted, I reel in both lines. I'm so tired I decide to leave each rod in a rod holder set bankside, with the lively baits dangling in inches of water just beyond the end of each rod tip. Ah, peaceful sleep.

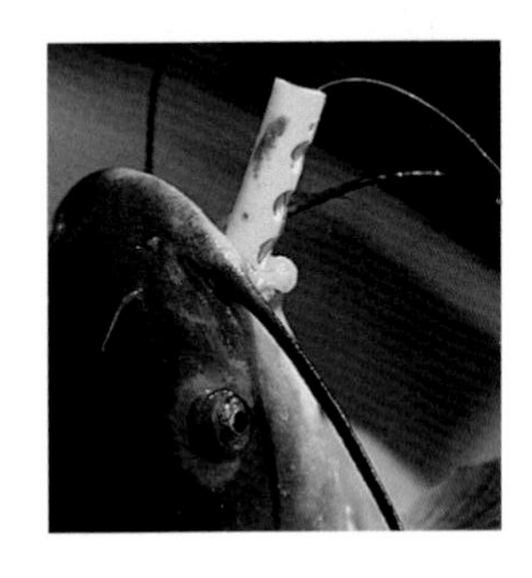

Dip-Rigging

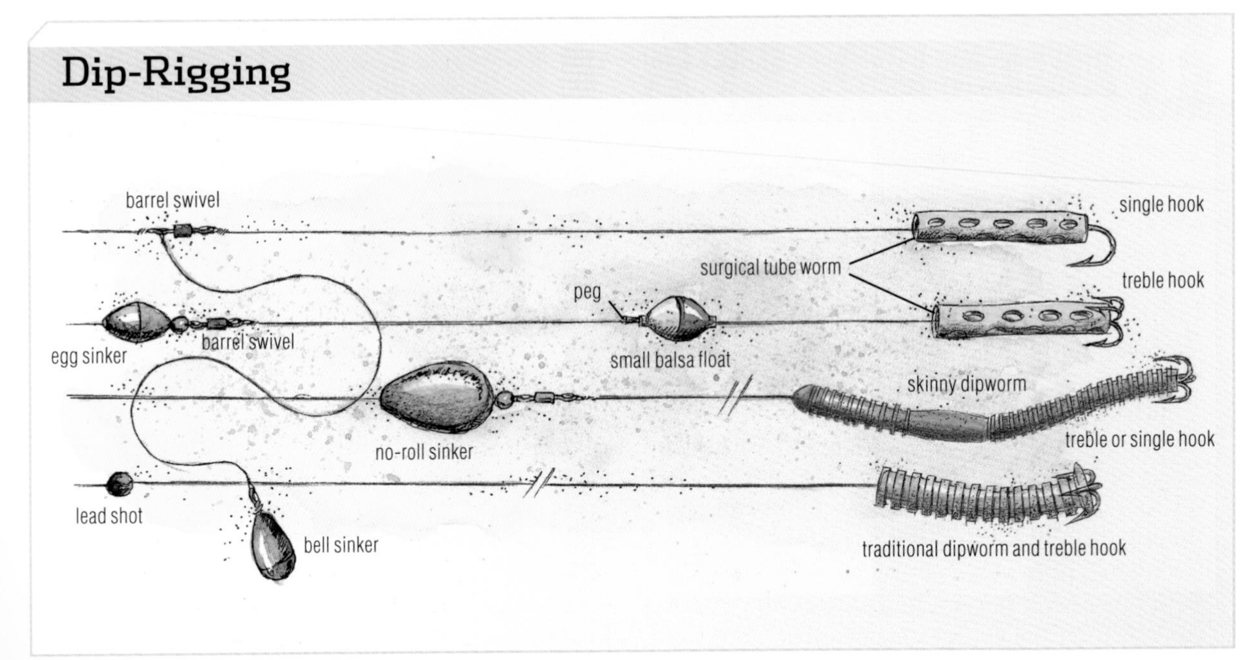

At 6 a.m., I'm in need of coffee. Stirring the fire coals I notice that both lines are out. What? Didn't I reel them in? I double-check my recollection of the final events of the night. But both lines are out and at least one is pulsing. Fish on, for heaven sakes. Tightening up I can feel the fish, but soon realize it's lodged in the snag across the river. No way to get the fish out, so I break the line. The other line has just been run out—almost 80 yards of line off the reel. The big sucker that was on the line is gone.

I check the sand around the rods. Raccoons? No. Turtles? Probably not. Turtles usually eat right there. Would flatheads wallow in that shallow? My old buddy Zacker used to tell me that when frogs ran into the Missouri River backwaters predam era in the Dakotas, he often saw flatheads so shallow after dark that their eyes were out of the water.

The moral is that while I usually don't recommend setting lines that shallow, flatheads can feel struggling baitfish in shallow water and will move in bankside to get them. A few times after that, I've caught flatheads by setting struggling baits with no more than 4 feet of line dangling beyond the rod tip, the bait in perfect position near the surface of the water near the edge of a deeper hole, the rod set firmly in a rod holder, the reel clicker on. That this works in the right spots shouldn't be a surprise because this is how bank pole anglers set their baits, whether by limbline, poleline, or logline. Flatheads are an amazing predator. Catfish are amazing fish.

A fair number of you write from time to time, requesting the jambalaya recipe Toad Smith and I used to do bankside at midnight on the first campout trip of the year.

Whack one catfish of about 5 pounds and cut the fillets into one-inch strips (or cubes). In an 8- or 10-inch cast-iron skillet, add a tablespoon of butter, a medium onion chopped, a clove of garlic chopped, and a big splash of white wine (chicken broth works too). Cook the onion over medium heat, stirring for about 3 minutes. Add chopped tomatoes and reduce them to pulp by cooking about 5 minutes.

Add two or three 12-ounce jars of medium or hot salsa and a little more wine, plus cayenne, black pepper, and salt, to taste. Cook on medium-high to reduce the liquid by half, about 5 minutes. Reduce the heat to a slow simmer. Add the strips of catfish, cover, and simmer 8 more minutes. Stir once gently. Garnish with chopped scallions. Serve over rice or a big bowl of grits.

Historic Perspectives

This article about fishing for flatheads during fall is written in what is now recognized by some as classic Stange style, a bit of reflection coupled with story telling, hardcore field experience, and notes about science.

It's just decent writing, really—relax, have fun, and learn something at the same time.

Meanwhile, changes continue at In-Fisherman. Stange assumes command of the editorial direction of all aspects of the company, working closely with Publisher Stu Legaard.

By this time, Editor Steve Hoffman takes over most of the day-to-day business of staying in contact with the catfishing world. Hoffman joins In-Fisherman as a staff writer in 1996, becomes an editor in 1997, managing editor in 2001, publisher in 2004, and group publisher for all Intermedia fishing titles in 2008. Not bad for another catfishing boy from Iowa. From 1998, Hoffman serves first as the primary editor for Catfish Guide and Catfish In-Sider and then covers most of the catfishing writing for In-Fisherman until 2004, when Dr. Robert Neumann takes over.

CHAPTER 39

OCTOBER 1999

Just Waiting on a Friend

Those Last Flatheads Of Fall—And The First Flatheads Of Winter!

FRESH FROM A MORNING HUNT, I have a brace of mallards or wood ducks and perhaps a squirrel or two ready to be picked or skinned clean as the catfish line does its work. I am a fair shot and fisherman and I surely enjoy cooking and eating wild game and fish, well beyond the reasoned expectations of the quite proper crowd I occasionally rub elbows with these days.

I have a primal streak that runs feral true. God help me, I surely love what little is left of wilderness. And, more often than not these days, the easiest place to find even a little of it, not far removed from the city, is somewhere along a stretch of catfish river. I tell you again that I have often fished within miles of millions and have never seen another fisherman on some of these rivers that account for much of the remaining wilderness in North America.

Eventually this day, I'll build a fire bankside, brew fresh coffee, and sit there in the afternoon sun, back against a fat old log. Surely, mountain man Jim Bridger did the same as he worked his way over Union Pass, Wyoming, on his way down into Jackson Hole. Can't snooze long, because sooner, not later, when the spot's right, it will happen—often quite often and quite often big. Bridger's evening meal may have been tenderloin of elk.

Mine this day, if I do things right, will be a portion of flathead catfish fillet along with fowl and hare.

Some of my most pleasant and memorable days of catfishing have been on sunny October and early November afternoons when gusty southwest breezes whisked leaves across the water as I watched lines set in key spots along a deep river hole. The largest flathead of my life came calling about 6 one evening on just such a day in early October. The fish and I both sat bankside, huffing and puffing, me almost wetter than the fish, after wading up to my knees in the chilly water to grab her and drag her to shore, all the while being thoroughly thrashed by that wild old fish.

I sat, my wet butt on the sandbar, rubbing the rasped-raw knuckles of my left hand. The light was soft and setting fast as I removed the hook, took a last look, and slid the fish on her flat belly back into shallow water. She let me know what she thought of our brief affair by thrashing me once more with her tail as she headed back into the hole.

Forty-five pounds, I estimated. Just after dark I managed a smaller fish, my final flathead of the 1991 season, which joined the squirrels and ducks in my celebration of Selective Harvest. The flathead is one of the finest eating fish in freshwater. It's also our premier predator, our preeminent freshwater big-game fish, growing as it does to well over 100 pounds. No other freshwater fish quite approaches the unique character of this one.

THE TRANSITION SEASON

You who love catfish of course recognize that we have learned so much very quickly during the last years, about fishing for catfish during the transition period from fall into winter. Next time we talk even more about catching catfish right throughout the core of winter into spring. Only in the Far North do catfish sometimes become supremely difficult to catch once the water turns frigid. Even in the North, however, certain pits, ponds, reservoirs, and rivers produce at least some catfish for anglers who know what they're doing.

But while we know quite a lot about catching channel and blue catfish throughout fall and winter, the tune we sing about flatheads isn't quite so harmonious. In the North, on the rivers large and small where I do most of my fishing, early fall—September—is prime time for flatheads. Most years, the fishing usually peaks, however, in early October, or in mid- or even late October, if we have with a prolonged period of Indian summer.

The Indians certainly had it right. Apparently at least part of the background for our use of the term, Indian summer, came from the belief of some Indians that a spell of mild fall weather was a great gift to an honorable people as they prepared for winter. Hardcore work ceased for favored activities. The Chippewa hunted waterfowl and deer. The Lakota hunted buffalo, and perhaps elk and antelope. While the weather lasted there was great celebration. Should catfish anglers do less than claim vacation when such weather sets on in October and November?

Generally, fishing for flatheads shuts down by mid-November on most waters in the North. In much of the South, it sours by mid-December. But we have much to learn. Catching flatheads isn't impossible then, just generally more difficult than catching channel or blue cats. Anglers fishing cutbait for those other cats occasionally tempt a flathead. At least some of these "mistakes" I've witnessed have been impressive fish—unusually well conditioned and girthy, looking like cornfed hogs. Perhaps a flathead has to be really fat to function in cold water?

Occasionally, too, anglers stumble on the large winter congregations that often gather in riverholes and in reservoir channel beds, tempting some of those fish with a jig or some other bait. At least some of these fish bite, although much of the photo evidence that has appeared over the years probably is of fish that have been snagged, sometimes inadvertently, other times with intent. So until recently, evaluating the true potential of this winter "bite" has been difficult, because the quality of the input hasn't always been honest.

Perhaps more than anything, at this point we're just victims of ignorance about this fish

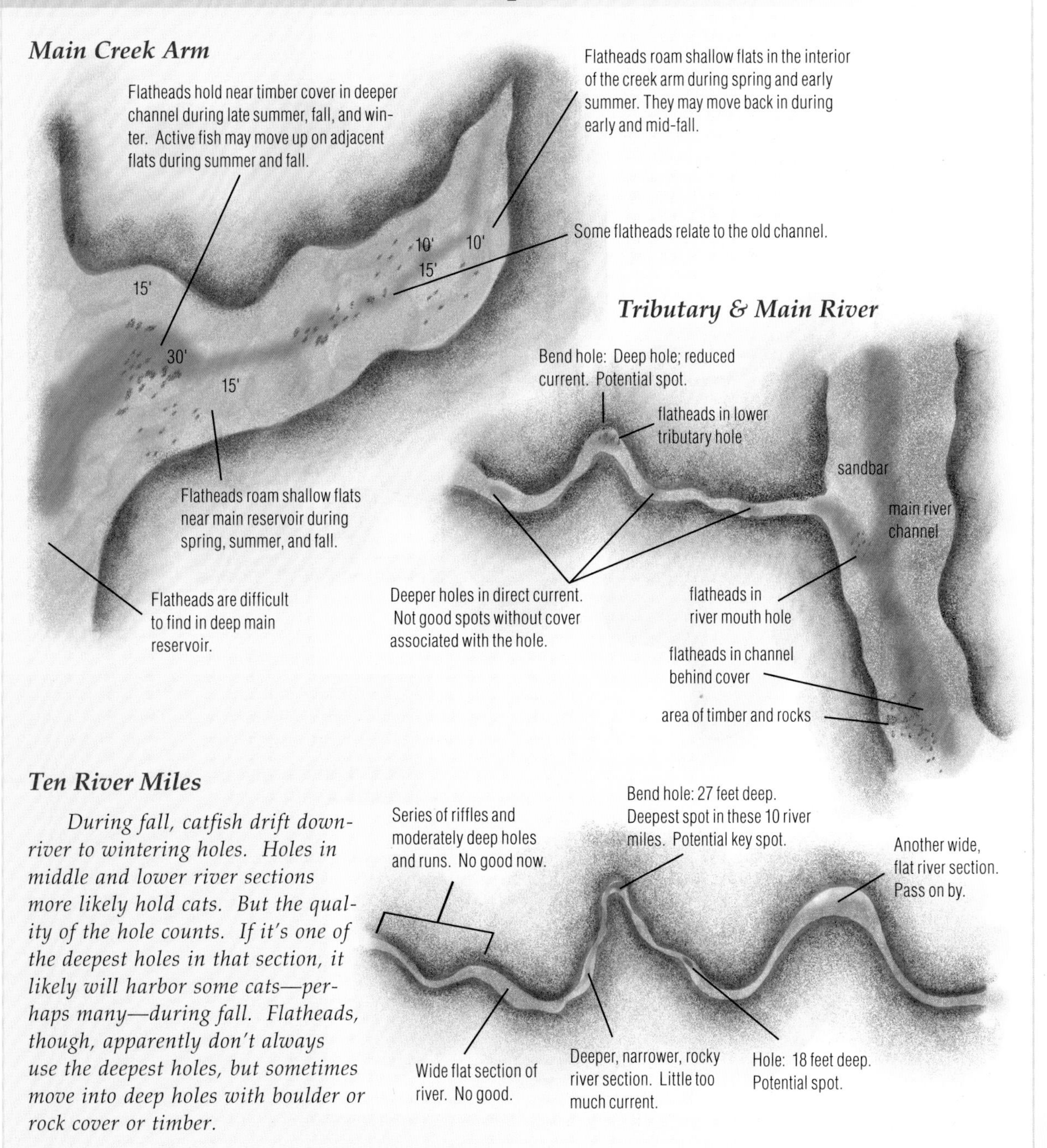

Where The Flatheads Hold Up
Main Creek Arm
Flatheads hold near timber cover in deeper channel during late summer, fall, and winter. Active fish may move up on adjacent flats during summer and fall.
Flatheads roam shallow flats in the interior of the creek arm during spring and early summer. They may move back in during early and mid-fall.
Some flatheads relate to the old channel.
10'
10'
15'
15'
30'
15'
Flatheads roam shallow flats near main reservoir during spring, summer, and fall.
Flatheads are difficult to find in deep main reservoir.
Tributary & Main River
Bend hole: Deep hole; reduced current. Potential spot.
flatheads in lower tributary hole
sandbar
main river channel
Deeper holes in direct current. Not good spots without cover associated with the hole.
flatheads in river mouth hole
flatheads in channel behind cover
area of timber and rocks
Ten River Miles
Bend hole: 27 feet deep. Deepest spot in these 10 river miles. Potential key spot.
Series of riffles and moderately deep holes and runs. No good now.
Another wide, flat river section. Pass on by.
Wide flat section of river. No good.
Deeper, narrower, rocky river section. Little too much current.
Hole: 18 feet deep. Potential spot.

During fall, catfish drift downriver to wintering holes. Holes in middle and lower river sections more likely hold cats. But the quality of the hole counts. If it's one of the deepest holes in that section, it likely will harbor some cats—perhaps many—during fall. Flatheads, though, apparently don't always use the deepest holes, but sometimes move into deep holes with boulder or rock cover or timber.

Photo by Doug Stamm

were lethargic and grouped. The boys could spear a fish without spooking those lying nearby.

These consolidated fish need protection from harvest during winter. Certainly, they need protection from overharvest. The problem remains that we have little definition of what constitutes overharvest in most areas. Even in conservative states such as Minnesota, the limit on most waters is 5 catfish of any species, never mind that those 5 fish could be 40-pound flatheads with a combined age of well over 100 years.

Never mind, too, that these fish might be taken from a winter concentration that numbers in the hundreds—fish that, once spring arrives, spread throughout the river and its tributaries to provide recreation for the masses. But I'm reaching here. The only thing I know for certain is that we need to learn more in order to protect this incredible big-game fish.

Some of the most definitive research on river patterns remains the work by fishery researchers Kevin Stauffer and Brad Koenen of the Minnesota Department of Natural Resources. In a project that began in 1993, they sampled via electroshocking the resident catfish populations in the upper portion of one of the state's best cat rivers, the Minnesota. "We'd sample a pretty goodlooking hole without bringing up a catfish," Stauffer told me as I prepared an article for the next year. "Then we'd sample another hole and bring up hundreds of fish. Depth was the primary variable. Almost

during the transition into and throughout winter, somewhat in the way most anglers once believed all catfish in every body of water became dormant during late fall. We're hoping to spur investigation. Or we're hoping to hear from folks who already know but haven't had the opportunity to share what they've discovered. Soon enough, we'll know much more about flatheads in frigid water.

CONSOLIDATED CATS

We already know something about how they behave in some waters during most of fall. Flatheads soon begin moving to spots where they spend winter. In rivers, some of the best holes, those with plenty of depth and enough current, hold large numbers of flatheads. Consolidated cats. And so long as the hole isn't filled in by changing river dynamics, they continue to gather in the same holes year after year. So it was that old commercial river boys like Zacker would gig these fish at first-ice each year. It was some of the most profitable fishing of the year because the fish

97 percent of the cats we sampled came from holes deeper than about 22 feet."

Most of those fish, however, were channel cats. Indeed, their tally that year was 2,670 channel cats and only 15 flatheads. Why so few flatheads? I asked. I told them I could catch flatheads from the Minnesota River in October, but almost never in November. Occasionally, though, I could still catch channel cats in November. They theorized, "Perhaps flatheads winter in shallower holes with timber. Or perhaps the fish just don't respond to the type of electric current we were using."

But I fish those kinds of spots, I said. I just don't catch flatheads once the water starts to get really cold. "Then perhaps the fish have migrated farther downriver. Perhaps, too, the flathead's metabolism slows faster than that of the channel cat."

The migration hypothesis also has been suggested by old-school commercial catfishermen like Tommy Burns of Lawrence, Kansas, who spent a lifetime on the Kansas River. He suggests that so long as the river is running high, as the water cools during October, flatheads move en masse downriver toward the Missouri. He thinks that during such high-water years, most of the fish spend winter in the Missouri then migrate all together back upriver in spring. He talks of often seeing groups of flatheads hundreds of yards long, moving along the surface upriver during spring.

In low-water years, however, the fish don't migrate back to the Missouri, Burns says, but drop into deeper holes in the vicinity of where they spend summer. Given that big flatheads often are found in major holes throughout summer, we surmise that most of these fish don't move much at all over the year, if Burns is correct about what the fish do during low-water years.

My own fishing experience during successive low-water years suggests that he might be right. Often the flatheads in these holes quickly eat most of the forage, which makes them easy to catch. This was Burns' point about fishing during fall in low-water years on the Kansas. A low-water fall that slid into first-ice season produced some of the year's best fishing, if the angler knew where wintering holes were located. It was Zacker's point, too, about fishing the holes at the mouths of streams and rivers that entered the Missouri in South Dakota and Nebraska.

Even in low-water years, many of the flatheads in, say, the lower third of a tributary river still have enough water to drop down to the mouth of the tributary. Once they hit the big river, they apparently prefer to slide downriver—rarely moving upriver from the tributary. So again, the effect is to group fish into primary holes.

The key to fishing during fall is the same as during summer, only more so—find the right hole, but there won't be many. Identify the location of potential holes by surveying a large section of river during summer. Once that's accomplished you have a good shot at finding and catching fish during fall, so long as the water isn't high, dirty, or extremely cold.

In at least some reservoirs during fall, flatheads begin to move back into creek arms as the water gets colder. They don't like to move long distances in reservoirs unless they have to find food. Seems to me that the lives of lots of fish center on major creek arms. They move in during spring and stay much of the summer, perhaps moving out as do crappies, bluegills, bullheads, suckers, and other bait, when the water becomes too warm later during summer. Once they drop out of the creek arm into the main reservoir, they don't go far. Then, during fall, they move right back in, leaving as the water turns frigid by late fall and early winter.

FISHING

Livebait or fresh cutbait continues to be the key to catching these fish. I've never had success with prepared catfish baits for flatheads. Crawlers work well during some spring seasons, but I haven't done well with them during fall. Frogs can be good sometimes, but they're not magic. Cutbait—1-inch strips of freshly filleted sucker or some other oily baitfish—works just as well, particularly if you're after channel cats, too. But if you're really targeting flatheads, livebait's the way to go. Livebait also seems to work well for channel

Photo by Doug Stamm

during this season.

I hook my livebaits just under the skin about halfway between the dorsal fin and tail. I match hook size to bait size, so at least a 7/0 hook (better a 10/0) is necessary for the largest baits. A 5/0 works for smaller baits. I still use hooks I've been using for over 20 years, the Mustad 92671 and Eagle Claw 84. Other companies make similar hooks. Touch up the points with a file and bend down the barbs slightly to make running the hook through the baitfish easier.

cats when the water really starts to cool down.

Creek chubs are good during fall. In spring, on the other hand, chubs haven't worked well for me. Particularly just before spawning, when the males have horny protuberances on their heads, chubs are really fragile and die easily. They also aren't active baits then. By fall, though, chubs become hardy as can be—wild. Big ones measure 8 to 10 inches. The bigger the bait the better, when the water's still in the 60°F range. Six- to eight-inch baits are fine as the water cools into the 50s and upper 40s.

Bullheads also are a top bait, perhaps the best on many waters, but they're hard to get during fall. Seven- to ten-inchers are fine early on. Later, 6-inch baits are better. Wild suckers are good, too. So are narrow-bodied panfish like green sunfish. And in waters where shad are forage, I suppose they remain an option during fall, though I haven't had much experience fishing with live shad

Typical terminal rigging consists of a bell sinker running freely on the mainline, stopped by a swivel about 10 inches above the bait. I use at least 50-pound mono for flatheads, even during late fall—or 30-pound line in a reservoir without a lot of snags. Snags and flatheads are a pretty common couple, though.

The 10 inches of leader will be of 80-pound superline—Spiderwire Spectra 2000, Berkley FireLine, PowerPro, or Cortland Spectron. Superline is more supple than mono and therefore makes a better leader. Superlines also make a fine mainline, but it's expensive by comparison to mono and not necessary for this particular seasonal affair with flatheads.

In 1994, I wrote: "Active cats often move to the head of a deep hole to feed, but during late fall they usually don't swim up into heavy current or move shallow enough to enter a riffle. Set at least one bait at the head of the hole in deeper water just away from current. Set another in the middle of the deepest part of the hole. Set others in slack, deep water alongside the hole."

Still good advice. Most of the big boys I've caught in rivers, however, have been in that part of a hole where sand meets rock. One of the best holes I fish has a sandbank on its inside bend, with broken granite on the outside. Most of the inactive fish are holding in the granite crags, but when they feed, they swim right along the sandbank's drop-off. If you're on a good hole, just wait them out.

MORE FISHING

Can't claim to know exactly what the best part of the day or night is for flatheads, where you might be fishing. Most of my fish are taken from around 3 p.m. to 8 p.m. Wherever you fish, I'd be surprised if the hour before and after sunset wasn't a key period, particularly as the water continues to cool toward late-fall lows.

Lots of reservoir anglers tell me that they do well the first part of the night, during the last part of fall. The first part usually is no more than an extension of summer—with some of the best periods running throughout the night and into midmorning, as opposed to afternoon into evening. I haven't done well in the morning during middle and late fall. And I haven't done a lot of fishing late into the night during this period.

The fall transition also suggests a change of fishing tactics relative to changing location. In comparison to summer quests—when sitting too long on any spot is unwise except at a big-fish hole after dark—fishing during fall often is a waiting game at a good deep hole, at least in smaller rivers for flatheads and channel cats. In bigger waters, blue cats still may demand frequent changes in angler location, in order to find fish that often move from one day to the next.

Cold, of course, is all about perspective. During that February of 1991, I left Minneapolis at 10°F below zero, arriving in Miami en route to a photo shoot in the Florida Keys on a 70°F morning. Over a double shot of espresso, one of the baggage men on break told me that come January, when the water temperature in all those Miami canals drops into the 70°F range, channel cats just sort of seem to go on strike.

Somehow I doubt that, for we'll soon tell you how to catch channel cats at first-ice and beyond. And we'll share what we know about catching monster flatheads during the dead of winter. First, though, I'm planning to celebrate another fall. Hope that log's still laying on that sandbar across from my favorite granite hole. I plan one day soon to park there in the afternoon sun, set a line, and brew fresh coffee over a little driftwood fire. Hope to be plucking a duck or two while I sit. Might have my Winchester 9422 sitting up against the log in case a fat squirrel gets to dancing around in one of those oak trees across the river there. All the while, I'm just waiting on a friend.

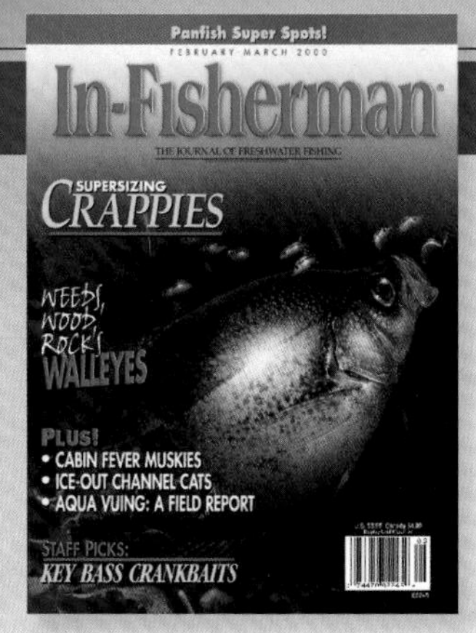

Panfish Super Spots!
FEBRUARY-MARCH 2000
In-Fisherman
THE JOURNAL OF FRESHWATER FISHING
SUPERSIZING
CRAPPIES
WEEDS, WOOD, ROCKS
WALLEYES
PLUS!
• CABIN FEVER MUSKIES
• ICE-OUT CHANNEL CATS
• AQUA VUING: A FIELD REPORT
STAFF PICKS:
KEY BASS CRANKBAITS

Historic Perspectives

Just curious, that's all. And in a mood for a meal of fresh channel catfish after several months of being stuck in the office, not getting to visit any southern waters all winter. Just curious how soon after ice-out channel cats might start biting in a known hot spot? Just curious what some of the better baits might be—and would they change as spring progressed?

Just curious, that's all.

So Stange keeps a close watch on the ice conditions at a reservoir with lots of channel cats, begins fishing on the day of ice-out, and continues fishing until he proves something about fishing for ice-out channel cats. And by golly if he doesn't surprise even himself.

Illustrations by Jan Finger

CHAPTER 40

FEBRUARY 2000

Five Days at Ice-Out

THE HOT SPOT I'LL BE FISHING when I can for the next couple weeks is a bridge area connecting two portions of this reservoir in Central Minnesota. Large numbers of catfish winter in the deeper reservoir section west of the bridge, then move through this bridge pass on their way into the shallower portion east of it. Many cats also move up a small river that flows into a section of the deep portion, but you need a boat to fish the better ambush spots. I'll be keeping things simple, fishing from shore. Perhaps next year, we'll track the progressive movements of channel cats up the small river starting at ice-out.

Channel Cats—A Case Study!

On lakes and reservoirs, by the way, bridges can be prime spots for contacting channel catfish, particularly from spring into early summer. Bridge spots with current during summer often produce fish all summer long. Some of these areas also get going again during fall, as catfish migrate back to deeper wintering areas.

Fishing in these areas almost always is best on the downcurrent side of the bridge, unless the upcurrent side offers much better habitat, such as a deep hole or cover like logs or brush. Sometimes cats also like to hold around nearby docks that attract minnows.

March 30, 1999—Water temperature 39°F. Air temperature 50°F. Light westerly wind, partly cloudy.

It's a little cool out, but after a long Minnesota winter, wetting a line is a pleasant experience. This is a Tuesday, and I've bumped away from my desk at noon to get in a couple hours of fishing during the warmest part of the day. As I walk down to the edge of the water below the bridge, I see light current moving under it from the west (deeper side) to the east (shallow side).

The channel under the bridge usually runs 5 to 6 feet deep, but the water is up a foot or so. The channel cut widens as it moves out from under it, shallowing slightly to 6 feet. The channel stays deeper toward the south bank. Indeed, to the north, a 3- to 4-foot-deep bar extends from the shoreline into the channel. Beyond the bar, where I'm fishing, the water pretty much runs 5 to 6 feet deep.

My baits this day by necessity are nightcrawlers, for I've been unable to find chubs or suckers in any of the area baitshops to use as cutbait. In Minnesota, most folks won't be needing bigger bait until they begin fishing for pike and walleyes in May when the season opens. Fishing for channel cats generally doesn't register here. The fellow in the baitshop finds me a bit strange when I admit I'm going to fish for channel cats. Most folks just don't understand cats here. It particularly doesn't register that someone might fish for them when the water's so cold.

So crappie minnows are all that's available at this baitshop. Now, I've often caught channel cats by using four or five small minnows on a #4 hook, but this shop has only microscopic minnows for sale. It would take 700 of them to make a decent presentation. Hopefully, I'll be able to pick up cutbait for my next fishing session. I also have along with me two popular dipbait blends, Sonny's Super Sticky and Cattracker's Sewer Bait.

Looking at my watch, I'll be making my first cast at just about 2 o'clock. I'm using a fat crawler run through several times on a #1 hook anchored with a 1-ounce bell sinker, held about 6 inches above the crawler with a single BB lead shot. Twenty-pound Spiderwire Fusion or Berkley Fireline (I don't remember which) is on this long spinning rod-and-reel combo I otherwise use to longline for walleyes. Not much cover here, and I'm not expecting anything I can't handle. Big fish here rarely top 10 pounds and aren't likely to put up a mighty tussle in this cold water.

I place my first cast on the edge of the eddy and the deeper water along the bar running slightly northeast from the bridge. While the current here isn't heavy enough to discourage cats, at least some fish still almost always relate to current edges. Tightening up my line, I place the rod in a forked stick left over from the previous fishing season. Looking out into the lake beyond, I can see the ice is only half out. Another day or so should do it. This really is an ice-out challenge.

I don't even have time to sit down on my cooler. In no more than a minute, first bite. Easy now. Drop the rod tip slightly toward the fish but still keep the line relatively tight. *Wumpa, wumpa,* I can feel the fish has the bait in his mouth shut tight. The *wumpa, wumpa* is the fish moving his head left-right as he begins to move slightly. I ease the rod tip along with him for a foot or so, then set. Yes. Fish on. Near shore the fish, which is a solid 2 pounds or so, puts up a determined fight, running left, then right, then diving for the riprap at my feet. He looks so fine on my stringer. Catfish for dinner tonight. Yahoo.

Before I have time to decide on a recipe, I have another fish on. From the same spot. On a crawler. This one bites differently—*punk, punk, punk* (the fish's pinning the bait against the bottom trying to pick it up). Then thunk, finally gets it into his mouth and moves off about a foot. Won't move farther, but I can still feel the fish, so I set and connect. This one's about 1½ pounds. Nice fat fish. The fins on both fish are covered with leeches. They apparently spent a fair part of the winter resting on the bottom somewhere.

In the next 15 minutes, I catch two more cats and miss one. Need one more fish for my limit, and it takes another 20 minutes to catch it. By this time, since I'm not getting bit right away after casting out, I'm trying different spots, hoping cats are also positioned elsewhere in the current area. After trying four other spots, I cast back to the eddy edge to catch the fifth fish, my big fish for the day at perhaps 4 pounds.

Time to try the dipbaits. In the 50°F air temperature, neither dipbait stays on a plastic dipworm well. Should have taken care to keep the bait warmer. Should have added a little vegetable oil to the dips to loosen them up. Too late now. I have enough bait on the worm, though, to fish it. The essence, that is the taste and smell, is what counts.

No bites. I note, though, that the bite was already dying before I began to fish the dips. Did I clean out the cats holding in the area? Did I hook the five fish and spook the others? I can't get a bite. Switching back to crawlers, I still can't get a bite. So far, I've been fishing for just over an hour. I move to the upcurrent side of the bridge. Nothing. Back to my original position. A bite. The fish is a small carp. Then a perch. Then a small walleye. No more cats. I take all five catfish home for the larder.

April 3: Stiff east by northeast wind blowing into my spot and against the current flow. Water temperature 40°F. Air temperature 34°F. Heavily overcast skies. All the ice is out.

The water appears to have cleared since my visit four days ago, but the wind has almost stopped the current flow. Couldn't get cutbait, so I'm relying on crawlers. Sure would be nice to at least try the cutbait.

I make a cast to the hot spot but can't get a bite.

I try casting to different spots, letting the bait work in each one for about five minutes. Thirty minutes pass. It's too cold to sit in this wind any longer, so I try the opposite side of the bridge. At least I'll be out of the wind. No bites. Back to the other side of the bridge for 20 minutes. No bites. This is the first time I've fished this spot over the course of two years and perhaps 10 visits without catching a catfish. But then, I didn't try the dipbaits.

April 7: Mild (55°F) but windy (15 to 20 mph) from the west. Water temperature 44°F.

The wind is moving current steadily from west to east under the bridge. The water's clear, though, and I immediately catch a 2-pound catfish by casting a nightcrawler to the eddy edge, which was the hot spot on day one. Staff Writer Jeff Simpson is fishing with me today. Takes 10 minutes for him to get our next bite. He swings and misses, then shortly afterward, so do I. The fish are tentative, bumping the bait against the bottom, probably to taste it, then barely picking it up. But then they won't move off so it's hard to get an angle on them to ensure a hookset.

We catch five fish over the course of the first hour, missing a total of three fish. I fish dipbait for 15 minutes but don't get bit. Then, for reasons unknown, redhorse suckers move in, and we absolutely can't catch another cat. We try many different casts to different locations, but all except two of the fish and one miss have come from the general area of the eddy edge that's been so productive. Again, no cats on the upcurrent side of the bridge.

Seems cats are present when we arrive, then we either quickly catch the ones that are present or catch a good share of them and spook the rest. Simpson scores big-fish honors this day, with one about 4 pounds. The rest run 1 ½ to 2 ¼ pounds. Take two fish home to eat.

April 11: Wind at about 15 mph from the north-northeast. Air temperature 34°F. Water temperature 42°F. Overcast.

This is Sunday and, as difficult as the weather is today, it had been worse on Saturday, when the wind was even stronger from straight east. Given my experience with the poor fishing when the wind was blowing into my spot on April 3, I had decided not to fish Saturday, in hopes that on Sunday the weather would moderate. That might have been a mistake (and I had wanted badly to fish two days in a row to see how it affected the fishing), for I proceed, beginning at about noon, to catch five fish in 40 minutes, before—as now has become typical on each trip—the fishing slows. In the next 20 minutes I miss another one, then catch a final fish.

This is the first day I've had cutbait along, but because I've been fishing each previous day with nightcrawlers, I decide not to use the cutbait until I can no longer catch fish on crawlers. The last fish is on cutbait. But it takes almost 20 minutes to catch it.

My guess is that the fish that are present would bite cutbait as well as crawlers if it were the first thing I presented to them. But I'll never know for sure. Certainly, my hot spot is worth a bunch of quick fish before the fishing slows. Again, it's impossible to determine whether the slowdown is due to removing most of the fish or spooking the remaining ones. That's why I wanted to come here two days in a row. Would the fish build back up in the spot that quickly?

It's curious how fish can be so hot, even in difficult weather conditions, that they go immediately and then shut down completely. I haven't tried dipbaits today because of the air temperature. Haven't caught a catfish yet on one of the dips. Yet dips have proven to be a hot option in this spot during summer. The earliest I've caught fish on dips here is early May, with water temperature hovering around 55°F, air temperature in the 60°F range.

Perhaps current made the difference on this otherwise difficult day weatherwise. Even with a cold wind blowing in, the increasing water level over the last weeks has made the current run steady and fairly strong. The weather report is for calm, mild conditions with temperatures increasing to 65°F by Wednesday, April 14, which will be the final day of my experiment.

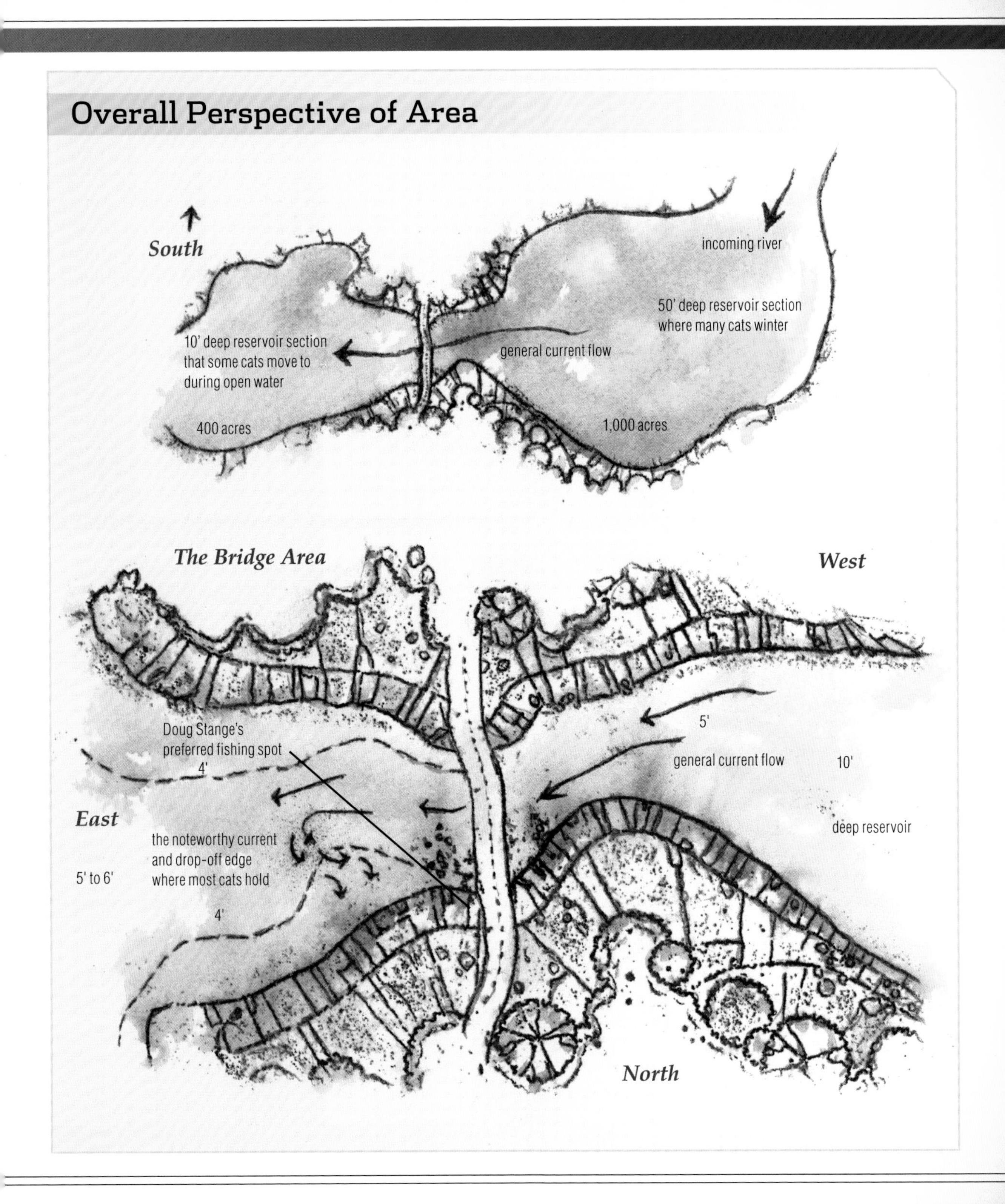
Overall Perspective of Area
South
incoming river
50' deep reservoir section
where many cats winter
10' deep reservoir section
that some cats move to
during open water
general current flow
400 acres
1,000 acres
The Bridge Area
West
5'
Doug Stange's
preferred fishing spot
4'
general current flow
10'
East
deep reservoir
the noteworthy current
and drop-off edge
where most cats hold
5' to 6'
4'
North

April 14: Clear, calm, air temperature 60°F. Water temperature 46°F.

I'm here late this day, making my opening cast at 3 o'clock. What a beautiful day. After taking the water temperature and noting the increase, I'm ready for my first cast, which will be with a piece of freshly cut sucker. My plan is to alternate casts between cut sucker and nightcrawler. As usual, I catch a fish within minutes of my first cast to the current edge area. Typical 2-pound cat. I mention at this point that, having cleaned these fish over the course of the last weeks, the only food in their stomachs was portions of the crawlers I've been using to catch them. Still, these fish are fat as can be, and obviously they're ready to feed. Five of the fish I've cleaned have been males, two females.

The second cast, this time with a crawler, produces another fish, within about five minutes of splashdown. This day I total six more fish (eight in all, with two misses) before the catching dies. This takes place within an hour of my arrival at 3 o'clock. I fish until 5 o'clock without another hit from a catfish, although I catch two carp and several suckers, plus a bluegill and a perch, all on crawlers. Ten to fifteen minutes of fishing with dips doesn't produce a fish.

OBSERVATIONS

While dipbaits haven't been a productive factor in this experiment, I've caught enough catfish on them shortly after ice-out to suggest that you keep them on hand. The main ingredient in fishing them successfully at this time of year might depend on what the cats are eating. Sour baits work well in rivers and reservoirs with winter-killed shad, and cats move in after ice-out to feed on them. But dipbaits also often work well in these areas at this time.

Air temperature seems to be a factor, too. Below about 55°F, unless you take particular care to keep dipbaits warm, they just don't stick well. Toad Smith used to suggest a little plastic squeeze bag of the stuff held under each armpit. I'd keep the vats near the heater in the truck, then alternate between two vats, keeping one wrapped in newspaper or a towel in a cooler, while the other one's near the heater.

Nightcrawlers remain a readily available and potent bait for cats in early season—not just for channels, but for blues and flatheads, too. I'm guessing that crawlers are particularly overlooked during early season for those last two species. Bullheads could be a problem on some waters, but then, I don't mind a mess of bullhead fillets just after ice-out.

So, I wouldn't recommend being on the water anywhere during early season without fresh cutbait, so long as it's available. It remains, in my mind, overall the most consistently productive natural bait over the course of the season for channel cats and blues. Sometimes early on, sour baits outfish it. The best sour baits are dead shad gathered along the shore of a river or reservoir where you're fishing. Keep them in plastic bags. Doesn't hurt if they get a little bit warm, but if they're already soured, don't leave them in the sun any longer because they just deteriorate. If they aren't sour enough, leave them in the sun for an afternoon or two.

My favorite sour bait remains winter-killed carp or buffalo. We're talking real sour stuff here. One 5- to 10-pound fish goes a long way filleted and cut into strips. Slip your hook once through the tough outer skin once the scalers are gone. Often these baits last for a half dozen fish. I've caught a fair number of channel cats just on the skin alone—no meat left on the bait.

I'll experiment more next year and in years to come. Remember, we're always interested in what you're doing, too. Drop us a note. I keep saying that we don't know everything, that catfishing is an ongoing project—a work in progress. But if we can catch cats at ice-out in Minnesota, you have a good shot at fish where you live, too.

Nightcrawlers are a consistently productive bait right at ice out and for several weeks after, often even better than sours or fresh cutbait.

25th Anniversary
In-Fisherman
THE JOURNAL OF FRESHWATER FISHING
SPECIAL ISSUE
America's angling legends talk fishing 2000.
Al Lindner, Ray Scott & Johnny Morris: Millennium Men

Historic Perspectives

Oh, boy, the mail that this one generates in March 2000, a Special 25th Anniversary issue, one of the most read In-Fisherman magazines of all time. On the cover are Bass Angler Sportsman Society Founder Ray Scott, In-Fisherman Founder Al Lindner, and Bass Pro Shops Founder Johnny Morris—Millennium Men, the cover copy states. The purpose of the issue is to allow America's Angling Legends to offer perspectives on their particular areas of angling expertise.

So Scott talks about the future of bass fishing and Morris talks about trends in marketing and merchandising. Doug Hannon, Billy Westmoreland, Harold Ensley, Denny Schupp, Roland Martin, Spence Petros, Dick Pearson—and many more, from Bill Dance to Homer Circle, Jim and Dick Cabela, and Earl Benz—all take up the torch to offer their vision of how things might unfold in the new millennium.

So it is fitting for Doug Stange, the first man of catfishing, to take up the cause for catfish. This is a rant by name today. But catfish anglers love it and letters pour in by the hundreds.

CHAPTER 41

MARCH 2000

Well, Maybe Catfishing Could Change Just a Little

JUST THIS ONCE I'd like to write something addressed only to catfishermen and not have to worry about what the rest of the world might think if they happen along. I'll make it short, too.

Look folks. Truth is, we have one of the best things going in the fishing world right now, so be cool. That is, why get so upset—indignant even—that so much of the rest of the world doesn't quite get it? It's like this. Guy moves to the suburbs to get away from the traffic, the congestion, the concrete, the rat race of the city. Starts telling everyone else how great the suburbs are. Can't shut up about it. Pretty soon, everybody's moved to the suburbs and the suburbs are the city—same traffic, same congestion, way plenty concrete, and lots of rats (disguised as neighbors).

No, one of the best things about catfishing right now is that it's not quite so much like the rest of the fishing world.

On plenty of rivers, I still can put a boat in and float for hours without seeing another angler. I've never seen boat-ramp rage on catfish water. On walleye water, it's a different story.

Hey, While You're At It—Bite Me!

It's pretty nice, too, that in about five minutes I can name 50 spots where I have a realistic shot at catching a 30-pound blue cat—in one outing. 'Course, I can name about 15 spots where I have a good shot at catching an 80-pound blue or flathead—in one season. Maybe 100 spots where a feller could get a 60. Maybe half a dozen where enough 100s swim that I might connect in less than a decade. That's some pretty primo fishing, man.

On most catfish waters, I also don't have to worry about getting run over by a bass or walleye boat going 7,000 mph. And by golly if it isn't just pretty nice, when I'm cleaning catfish back at the dock, that I don't have to worry about some self-righteous sort telling me I'm a sinner for keeping some pansized fish. If that's sinning, you'll have to get in line.

And you want to change all that by convincing all those bass and walleye boys, nice fellers though they are, to join us?

Well, all right, maybe catfishing could change just a little.

Would be nice to sit down on Saturday morning and watch at least one good catfishing show. Might even be exciting—which would be a fairly new concept for many TV fishing shows these days, where the apparent *modus operandum* seems to be catching endless bass after bass while circling a private pond. Hell's bells, none of us short-legged old cat boys could ever even get permission to fish there anyway. The owners in that big fancy house on the hill would sure enough sic the Doberman on us before we ever made it past the gate.

Might be nice, too, if we had some guarantee that the fine fishing we're having is going to continue.

I mean for every 700 biologists doing studies on bass, trout, and walleyes, we're lucky if we have 2 working on catfish. And sometimes it seems those guys are shipped off to the equivalent of Siberia in their respective states. "There's a phone-call from where? From who?" the guy at the State Capital office desk asks. "Thought that little flea-bitten spot was in the next state? Thought old crazy Harley was dead? Oh, that's right, we've got him working on catfish."

Of course, I jest. But not so much.

Leveling the playing field sciencewise would require taking the number of anglers who say they fish for a certain species and divide it by the number of biologists dedicated (in some small degree) to that fish, to arrive at a fish/biologist ratio. Last National Hunting and Fishing Survey suggested that 13 million anglers fish for bass, 9 million for trout, 7 million for catfish, and 3 million for walleyes. You get the picture.

But maybe not the whole point.

Given the obvious bias in the fish/biologist ratio over the last 30 years, surely affirmative action's in order for at least the next 10. I say, dedicate 8 of every 10 biologists out there to studying catfish in order to start catching up. Truth is, we have enough bass data backed up and stacked up and still being analyzed to last for another 5 years anyway.

While we're at it, let's make it a felony to whack more than one giant catfish a year, countrywide.

A rule like that might help us catch up regulationwise, too, because if we had the appropriate number of biologists dedicated to catfish during the last 30 years, it might already be at least a misdemeanor to kill as many monster catfish as are killed in some places today.

Or let's just make it a rule that the angler has to be at least double the age of the fish in order to kill it.

The average age of a 50-pound flathead is probably around 30 years from many waters, so a fisherman would have to be at least 60 in order to kill a 30. Or you get whacked with a felony charge. Same as you robbed a bank with a gun. Cause that's just what some folks are doing, robbing the almighty bank of our catfishing future, hanging five or ten 40- to 60-pound flatheads on a board to take a picture and then do a giant fish-fry.

Some of these folks are armed and dangerous.

And you can't tell me otherwise until we get enough scientists working on catfish to have the data to say it isn't so. Could be I'm wrong. Could be we can kill some big fish from some waters each year. But when you're cutting boards with a buzz saw, you err on the conservative side where your fingers are concerned.

Evidence being what it is with other fish, it will be uncommon science, indeed, if data finally suggests we can kill so many big fish without jeopardizing our fishing. I find myself wondering if even one fishery chief in any state can look any catman in the eye and say that our present course relative to the harvest of big catfish makes good sense, much less good science.

More like nonsense in the absence of not enough science.

Do an executive order. Oh, I know, you probably can't do those. But do one anyway. Do something. Just declare a moratorium on killing lots of big cats until we have our science ducks in order.

But then I get these letters from time to time—*Dear Mr. Fancy-Pants-Writer-Man:* You ever really caught a catfish in your whole stinking life? If you're so smart and such a hottytoddy sportsman, such as you seem to claim, how come you and your fancy-pants magazine feature trotline fishing, and limbline fishing, and jug fishing—even grabbing catfish? If you were a true catman, you wouldn't encourage the demise of catfishing by these archaic means of raping our waters. *Signed:* A True Catman.

Well now, hold on there. The way I see it, one of the unique things about catfishing is the various traditional means by which we can practice it. These traditional methods add flavor and diversity to the sport. We have great freedom in being able to choose from among so many different ways to fish. It's just as challenging to set an effective limbline as to make an effective set with rod and reel.

But yes, of course, trotlining and limblining can be much more efficient than rod-and-reel fishing. We want to keep some of the freedom but regulate the harvest. Let Mr. Limbliner practice his art, but regulate him so the overall harvest equation is fair and fits within parameters that protect catfish populations, giving due weight to the fact that rod-and-reel anglers vastly outnumber limbliners. When we can, let's allow folks to fish but harvest selectively.

Give me a break with this "true catman" stuff. Somebody's always trying to paint someone else into a little corner. What is this, Leningrad, 1950? I understand your concern, but for being so narrowminded, why don't you just bite me. Yeah, right there.

But then politics also continues to play an unfortunate role in our collective catfishing.

Somebody's getting paid something under the table somewhere when you still have commercial boys fishing Holy Hanna out of a tourist Mecca like Santee-Cooper, which should be the most unbelievable rod-and-reel catfishery in North America. Oh, Santee's good, all right. One of the best. And I acknowledge that some data suggests that commercial fishing might be good for Santee Cooper.

Just do something like this:

Cut the commercial take by half over the next two years, and then by half again over the next five. But guides and the rest of the rod-and-reel crowd have to give a little, too. Also intensely regulate the rod-and-reel take of large catfish. Inside of five years, South Carolina could take a tiny part of the extra bajillion dollars they'd make from increased tourism traffic to Santee-Cooper and buy out most of the commercial boys, who by their own account aren't making much of a living anyway. If you think catfishing is good at Santee-Cooper now, you haven't seen anything.

In case you're thinking I don't much like commercial catfishermen, wrong.

A few of my better friends have been commercial catfishermen. The ones I've known aren't just good folks, they're some of the best to be with for a day or two on the water. Full-time commercial fishing is extremely hard work and takes an uncommon understanding of what makes a fishery tick. It takes extensive time on the water. No one spends that much time on the water for more than a few years without an abiding love for what they're doing.

Commercial fishing has its own grand tradition that's closely tied to our sport. We intend to cover it from time to time, just like we cover every other aspect of the catfish scene. We probably need to continue it on some waters, but commercial fishing generally doesn't make economic sense anymore, given the large number of sport anglers vying for the same fish and the price the commercial boys are getting for those fish, in the face of competition from catfish farmers.

Commercial fishing probably makes sense as a way to help regulate fisheries in response to scientific data that suggests the need for the removal of portions of fish populations that anglers aren't catching. Certainly, though, the fishing needs to be intensely regulated, so we really know what's being caught. Perhaps we'll end up with a limited number of "government" commercial fishermen, just as we have government professionals who trap problem wolves and cougars.

There's more, of course, much more for another day. But before I go:

• To all you narrow-minded, short-sighted, can't-see-the-present-or-the-future tackle distributors out there who won't stock catfish rods, even when a primo company like St. Croix steps forward and makes a superior product like the Classic Cat series. Why don't you BITE ME!

• To you folks at the Catfish Institute, the organization in charge of promoting farm-raised

Steve Hoffman: Catfish Tackle Trends

Not so many years ago, the only products designed and marketed specifically for catfishing were prepared baits like dips and pastes. Despite the popularity of catfish across the country, the tackle industry viewed catfish anglers as an unsophisticated group who were unable or unwilling to spend money on boats, tackle, and accessories. Lacking species-specific products, catfish anglers made do with rods, reels, and terminal tackle designed for heavy freshwater or light saltwater fishing.

Increased media attention during the past decade, though, has given catfish anglers a voice that the tackle industry can't ignore. Several rod series have been introduced in the last few years that were designed with input from In-Fisherman and veteran cat guides. The rods are strong and durable enough for heavy use and big fish, and most importantly, they possess the kind of actions appropriate for most catfishing situations. Even companies with general-purpose rods have begun to advertise appropriate models in publications like Catfish In-Sider.

No manufacturer currently offers a reel designed for catfishing, but many offer models with the large line capacities, bait-clicker mechanisms, and powerful gear ratios that big-cat specialists need. And again, they're marketing those products to catfish anglers. Same's true for line and terminal tackle, though some companies have repackaged existing products like line and hooks with a catfish-specific label to appeal to catfishermen.

Part of the problem faced by these pioneering companies is that distributors and retailers are unwilling to change, after decades of stocking inexpensive tackle because it was the only available option. Catfish anglers looking for fine tackle, whether it's premium hooks or a high-end rod, shouldn't settle for less. Encourage local retailers to stock the equipment you want, or shop around until you find it.

catfish—you folks who don't want anything to do with catfishermen because you're scared it will hurt your image. Hey, bite me. In fact, why don't you bite me twice, once on each side! And then bite me again. BITE ME!

• And to you folks in states trying to eradicate flathead catfish, especially those willing to let people use electricity to do it, get real. The flatheads might be an unfortunate introduction, but they're present now, and they're not going anywhere. So learn to live with it. And while you're at it, bite me!

• To all you folks who want to straighten every creek, cut down every tree, tile every marsh, plow right up to the edge of every river, all to lose money producing more corn at $2 a bushel. Hey. Bite the big one!

• To all you politicians who spend our money on everything else and won't help farmers even a little so they don't have to farm every marginal acre, bite me!

• To all you TV fishing stars who don't know how to hold a catfish. Bite me!

• And the biggest bite me of all goes to me, for being such a whiner. It was fun for a change, though, and I'm not taking back one word. And if you don't like it . . .

That Was Our Dad: Toad Smith

John Smith:

Doesn't surprise us anymore, even almost a decade after my father's death, that people still say nice things about what an impact he had on their fishing. My father was also a real character.

One of his favorite tricks when my brother Elliot and I were younger was taking us fishing all day and into the night. Then we'd clean fish for another hour. We'd stay at it as long as he'd let us. By 10, we were so shot we could hardly see. So he'd tuck us in and then ask, "You guys up for fishing in the morning?" Well, of course.

So he'd set our alarm for 6 a.m., only he'd turn the clock ahead six or seven hours. We'd be dead asleep for an hour and the alarm would go off. Oh, boy. We could hardly open our eyes, but, not wanting to be late and left behind, up we'd get, pull on our clothes, and hurry into the kitchen to grab a bowl of cereal. Then out we'd go to the car to wait. And wait and wait—while he was lying in bed chuckling. That was our dad.

After he had his first heart attack, doctors said he'd never hunt or fish again. Dad would have none of that. That's when the great friendship developed between him and Doug Stange, Editor In Chief of In-Fisherman. They both loved to hunt and fish. Dad used to say Stange was the only one who would take him fishing right after his heart attack, because everyone else was worried they'd end up in the morning in a motel room with a dead guy.

Stange, of course, was the one who really made Dad famous, by writing about the wild times they had catfishing. And it was Stange who convinced Dad that he could be a writer and lecturer about hunting and fishing. Those, I think, were probably the best years of Dad's life. I know lots of people think that the tales of those times as they appeared in In-Fisherman were some of the best writing ever about catfishing and the catfishing life.

Monster Fish of 1999!
April-May 2000
In-Fisherman
THE JOURNAL OF FRESHWATER FISHING
BLUEGILLS:
THE SPAWNING FLING THING
PLASTICS, SPINNERBAITS, OR JERKBAITS FOR
BASS
PLUS!
• SUPER SIZE-LIMIT MUSKIE
• BENT WATER CATFISH
• NO KILL SMALLMOUTHS
WALLEYES
"Afloat" For Early Season

Historic Perspectives

Early season catfishing, as simple as it gets on small streams, but with right-on-the-target tactics for catching enough channel cats from high, dirty water to do a fish-fry in turkey camp—that's the essence of the writing here.

The opening paragraph is as true as can be, but with the passing of Catfish Corner Bill Marsh in 2001, and with these changing times, we'll not see those days again. Marsh is in his prime a topnotch angler, hunter, and all-around gentleman who is at his best putting on a fish-fry for a crowd. That's Bill on the opposite page, Catfish In-Sider hat on, in his basement hideaway, talking with Stange after they spent the afternoon fishing.

CHAPTER 42

APRIL 2000

Simple Does It for Channel Cats in Bent Water

I HAVE TOLD YOU BEFORE that a letter addressed simply Catfish Corner, Farmington, Iowa, 52626 will be delivered straightaway, no questions asked, and with an appropriate measure of respect to one William Marsh, who lives on the right bank of the Des Moines River, just across from the farthest corner of northeast Missouri and just a skip or two from downtown Farmington, such as it is.

Scratching A Mess Of Catfish In Tough Times!

Farmington isn't just Small Town, U.S.A., it's Small River Town, U.S.A., so far off the main trail that you'd have to travel 90 miles to get a double cappuccino. In these parts, a knack for hunting, fishing, mushrooming, being a good neighbor, and running a proper fish-fry still count for quite a bit. And when you have the knack for all of the above as Bill Marsh has had for a spell approaching a good half century, well, folks just naturally sort of take it all for granted.

After all these years, Bill would be the first to tell you that a little moderation tempers life just right, even where catfish are concerned. In that regard, Bill and his son Tom haven't found too many ways to make catfishing complicated, though you'd be hard-pressed to slip a new trick by them without its getting their due consideration, usually long before the rest of the crowd. They were several years ahead of the rest of us on the circle hook thing as it pertains to the limblines they like to set for the big flatheads that migrate upriver during June. But that's another story. Let's take this one month at a time.

By the time I wander into Farmington about the middle of April each year, the turkeys are gobbling real good and just itchin' to get a load of buckshot in the britches. That's morning detail. After lunch, the target's catfish.

The problem around Farmington this time of year often is the problem just about everywhere this time of year—rivers all uppity and bent so out of shape that most folks can't seem to figure a way to catch enough channel cats for a decent fish-fry. A decent fish-fry is important any time of year, but especially in turkey camp. It's a tradition for heaven's sakes.

With rivers bent big-time, Wild Bill says that first off a feller has to be realistic about what he can expect to catch. "Oh, sometimes when conditions get just right after a pretty good spell of high water, and the water starts to settle and clear just a bit—along with a steady rise in water temperature, well," he says, "those cats might just get goin' real good. Early on, though, when the water first rises and looks darker than chocolate milk—especially when it's still cold—it might take three afternoons of fishing to get 10 pounds of fillets.

"Sometimes we set a short trotline—maybe a 10-hook line," he says, "but usually we just walk a bank along a flooded creek or flooded backwater connected to the main river, fishing along the bank as we go. A lot of these creeks or cuts are so small that this is the only time catfish move into them. Some backwater spots are the same. Cats are hungry after a long winter. They run out of the main river where the current's difficult, into these creeks and backwater spots to feed."

The best creeks are more than a mere dent in the shoreline with a little water running in, although even spots like that may draw a few catfish as they slip away from the main current and search for food. But neither are the key creeks active feeder creeks that cats move into to run upriver and eventually spawn. That's another proposition, an important one, that we touch on in a sidebar.

Most of the key creeks are dry or little more than a trickle of water, most of the year. Some of them are ditchlike, the remains of the ends of small creeks. Others look like creeks for oh, say, a quarter mile as they wind through river bottom land, then just stop where a marsh or series of low spots were filled in and tilled to drain run-off from what's now farm fields.

The river bottom connection is important, because that's usually the extent of the good fishing. Meanwhile, the main river's high—maybe very high—but not breaking bank level and flooding adjacent river bottoms. When that happens, catfish spread into acres of river bottom and adjacent farm fields and become difficult to find and catch.

Marsh: "Most of these spots have mud banks. Cats move in to eat the worms that wash out of the banks, or wash into the creek from surrounding fields. This is just about the first big nightcrawler and angleworm run of the year, too, the first time it's warm enough so that a warm rain brings lots of worms to the surface to breed and feed.

"Cats that have just moved into a creek often are skinny. Then again, we catch some little fish that look like those ocean puffer fish you see on the Discovery Channel—so full of crawlers they're almost going to burst. But they keep right on eating.

"As you might expect, it's tough to beat crawlers as bait, although sometimes we use cutbait (one-inch pieces of chubs or suckers) and do just about as well. Dipbait like Sonny's Super Sticky, manufactured by Sonny Hootman and his boys right here in Farmington, works fine but produces better as the water warms. If you can't get other baits, you can sure catch some fish on dips.

"The key as always is to fish where the fish are, and usually that's right along the bank. I mean,

Feeder Creek Pattern

Dipbait manufacturer Sonny Hootman, also a resident of Farmington, Iowa, concentrates on small feeder creeks during the portion of early season when larger rivers often are bent out of shape. Hootman: "Higher water can be an advantage because it gets channel cats moving way upriver, out of major feeder rivers into secondary rivers and into tiny feeder creeks. Feeder creeks tend to clear a lot faster than larger portions of river.

"One portion of a creek we fish is at least 20 miles removed from a secondary river, which is another 15 miles removed from a major river, which is another 50 miles removed from the Mississippi. Fishing a tiny creek isn't much different from fishing a larger river. Concentrate on holes below shallow riffles and pay particular attention to any cover like fallen trees that reach just into the hole. We walk upriver, fishing each hole and piece of cover as we go.

"Some holes can really get a lot of catfish stacked in them. The best usually produce year after year unless a flood changes its nature. Some years, though, the cats tend to be farther upriver or downriver. As usual, unless you're catching lots of fish, it pays to move around and check other areas.

"Lots of these tiny creeks have fish in them all year, but by summer, it takes a pretty good spell of high water to get cats replenished in sections of creek that are heavily fished. Most of these creeks rarely get much pressure, but access can be a problem. They're too small to float, so you need permission from landowners."

Sonny Hootman casting into a hole below a riffle on a portion of feeder creek many miles removed (upstream) from a main river.

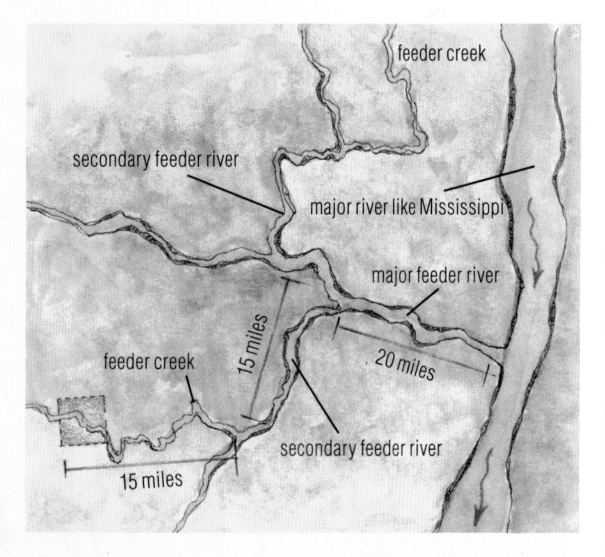

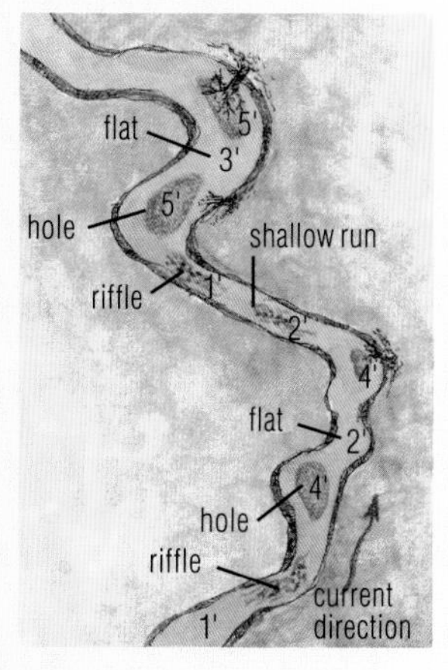

sometimes right under your feet. We catch fish in a foot of water, other times in 3 or 4 feet of water, but usually right along the bank—not out where most folks want to cast to in the center of the creek channel."

This pattern isn't so different from the cutbank patterns that sometimes develop during summer when it rains hard. Cutbanks are mud and clay banks that get cut into as current washes out an inside bend. Rain brings crawlers to the surface and to the edge of the bank, where they either get washed in or are in dirt that peels off the bank. The problem with fishing crawlers during summer in a lot of main river spots is that you're bothered by other fish—bullheads, chubs, suckers. A lot of times, cutbait or dips work best during summer, even though the main target of the cats might be crawlers.

Brush and other obstructions can also concentrate catfish as they move along a bank. Marsh: "Pay particular attention to brush and downed trees. Check right where these intersect the bank

Wind Current Patterns in Reservoirs

One of the better early season patterns in reservoirs develops as a combination of wind and baitfish, like shad, which often die during winter. Channel cats stay deep until after ice-out, so as shad die, their numbers tend to build in shallow water, particularly in shallow feeder creeks.

Immediately after ice-out, catfish move into shallow creek arms or other backwater areas that warm more quickly than the main reservoir. Most of these areas have some dead baitfish. Soon, however, catfish clean out these areas.

As water in the main reservoir continues to warm, cats move closer to and then into the main reservoir. Warming winds—usually southerly, but also sustained northerly winds so long as they aren't strong, cold blows—set shallow-water current in motion in windward reservoir areas. The wind current concentrates dead baitfish from the main reservoir onto shallow flats. The longer a modest wind moves water in one direction, the better the fishing can be on windward reservoir flats.

Although catfish can be found on main reservoir points and in shoreline pockets, often in water 1, 2, or 3 feet deep, key areas still tend to be the shallow flats at the mouth of shallow creek arms and other backwater areas. Sour shad are the classic bait, but dipbaits and nightcrawlers also produce lots of fish.

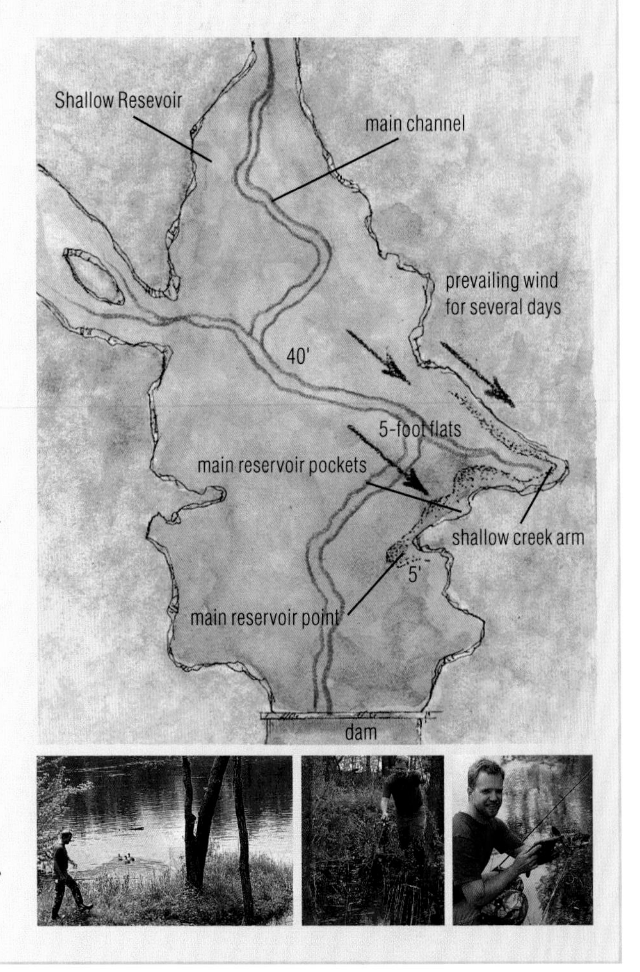

instead of keying on where the brush sticks farther out into the creek. Usually, though, key bank areas are a bit deeper than surrounding areas.

"No fancy rigging necessary to fish this situation effectively," Marsh says. "Sometimes, like I say, we just walk the bank and flip a crawler right up along the bank in front of us as we move along. Might make, oh, a 10- to 15-foot flip, using the weight of the crawler on a #1 Aberdeen hook to sink slowly along the edge of the bank. I think the most effective way to fish is probably with a small float. Makes it easy to see where your bait is and where it's heading when you move it.

"Cast up the bank 20 feet and let it sit for a minute. Doesn't take long if cats are in the vicinity. Then reel the float toward you 5 feet and let it sit for another minute or so. Move it one more time before walking a little farther and making another cast. Of course, if you're catching fish, stay right where you're at. Cats can sense a bait's in the area, either by using their taste and smell sensors or by feeling the movement of the crawler. We just slip the hook through a crawler about three times so the bait has some wiggle room. I think this helps attract fish.

"No fancy floats necessary, either, although I certainly don't have anything against a pretty float. We use a few of those fancy Thill floats, particularly Center Sliders. But cheap plastic floats—that is, floats that set at a fixed spot on your line—work fine, too. So do those classic round red-and-white plastic bobbers that have been around for ages."

Marsh likes to begin with the bait riding about a foot down. "I think cats are moving up and down the bank as they swim along the bank," he says. "They're just as likely to find a bait suspended up a bit higher as to find one set deeper. And it's a lot easier to cast and fish a fixed float when it isn't set so deep.

"Fish goes 'thump,' takes the bait, and the float jumps and then starts to move. Ease the rod tip along with the fish, and set with an easy sweep once the cat has moved a foot or so—when you have an angle that assures a hookset in the corner of the mouth."

Simple as that. Bill drops his fish, which usually run a pound or two and perhaps up to about 5 pounds, into a 5-gallon bucket as he works his way along. I've used a wire fish basket in the same situation. Just pick up the basket each time you progress along the bank. It's lighter to carry than a bucket. Takes too much time to get fish on and off traditional stringers.

Ever catch any big cats in this situation? I ask Bill. "Not so often," he says. "Bigger channel cats usually are taken on trotlines. Must take bigger fish longer to decide to hit. Or perhaps they're feeding at twilight or after dark. This time of year, we're usually home by that time."

Once the water starts to drop, cats vacate these marginal creek areas. According to Marsh, the mouth of these creeks, where they enter the main river, usually are good for a mess of fish at this time. By now it's also time to start checking obvious eddy areas formed by obstructions along the bank in the main river. Time, too, to start checking eddy or backwash areas in tailwater areas below dams.

But then, once this river pattern starts to crumble, all kinds of catfish patterns in lakes, rivers, reservoirs, pits, and ponds are in full spring swing. This is all about scratching a mess of cats from bent water during that marginal time before the heart of the season begins.

Lizard Lovin' Largemouths! Page 48
June-July 2000
In-Fisherman
THE JOURNAL OF FRESHWATER FISHING
SUPER GRUBS FOR BASS Page 74
SLICK RIGGING WALLEYES Page 67
PLUS!
- Top Tactics For Salmon
- Bad Bucktails For Muskies
- Last Letters Of A Catfish Man
- On Top For Carp

KEYING ON CRAPPIE SENSES!

Historic Perspectives

The writing style you find here is modeled after Michael Shaara's writing in his novel, The Killer Angels, about the Battle of Gettysburg in the Civil War. It becomes one of Stange's favorite ways to tell a story. You find it also used to write Chapter 35, "Let Each Man Find His Own Way to Flatheads."

From publication of the first Zacker story in 1985, readers over the years continue to ask if Zacker is a real character or made up by Stange to prove various points. Why always no more than hints of where he lives—no more than the use of the singular name? And why never any photos, but only cartoon-like caricatures? Stange insists that if you read through all the stories in this book and pick up on all the various hints about his life, then study this final epitaph, you can find your way to Zacker's grave if you so desire.

Whether or not you ever do, Zacker remains as real as a good story can be—forever part of the literature and the history of catfishing.

Illustrations by Ron Finger

CHAPTER 43

JUNE 2000

Zacker's Last Letter

HE LOOKED OUT TOWARD the Missouri River, big reservoir now, lying well down below the rolling prairie bluffs where he sat on the porch of his house built for him by the government boys in the 1950s, when the reservoir flooded the river village where he and a few others lived. He could still see in his mind the outline of the old river, the big timbered bends, ancient cottonwoods, massive sandbars, maze-like backwaters. He remembered the old boys who would always see his boat laboring upriver, would always have time to walk down to greet him at his dock, wondering how the fishing had been. He straightened himself in his chair, drew the table closer, thought, I have lived longer than most, have seen some fine times, but this is all passing too quickly, I must write this letter, one small remembrance.

He had several days ago returned from a fishing trip with the boys, as he called them, Otis "Toad" Smith and Doug Stange, younger fellas who loved catfishing and who had befriended him, a solitary old man, who also loved catfish and the places where catfish live. The boys were hardcore catmen, and then some, and not the slightest bit judgmental, as were many of the other anglers of this new generation, who seemed to hold his old profession as a commercial catfisherman in high disregard.

Life And Times In Catfish Country!

For more than 60 years, he had lived a wild life on a wild river, doing what he had to do—loved to do—making a living hunting, trapping, and fishing. Most springs brought savage flooding that chiseled new form into the riverscape. The intricate backwaters on huge river flats were like a puzzle to most men. Yet a river channel, a main highway, always ran through it. In those days, his big river was still the biggest small river in the world, with obvious river characteristics like riffles, holes, and runs. Catfish were everywhere, depending on the season, depending on water level, just . . . depending. His ability to read those "depending" conditions kept him in business.

He looked at the paper on the small table, held the pencil tightly, almost began to write, thought, My life was more than a matter of choice; it was a matter of course. Those were years when people in cities, towns, the surrounding countryside—farmers and ranchers—needed his harvest of furs to keep warm and look fashionable. Those were years when people relied on his fish to spice their so-common farm larders of pork, beef, and mutton.

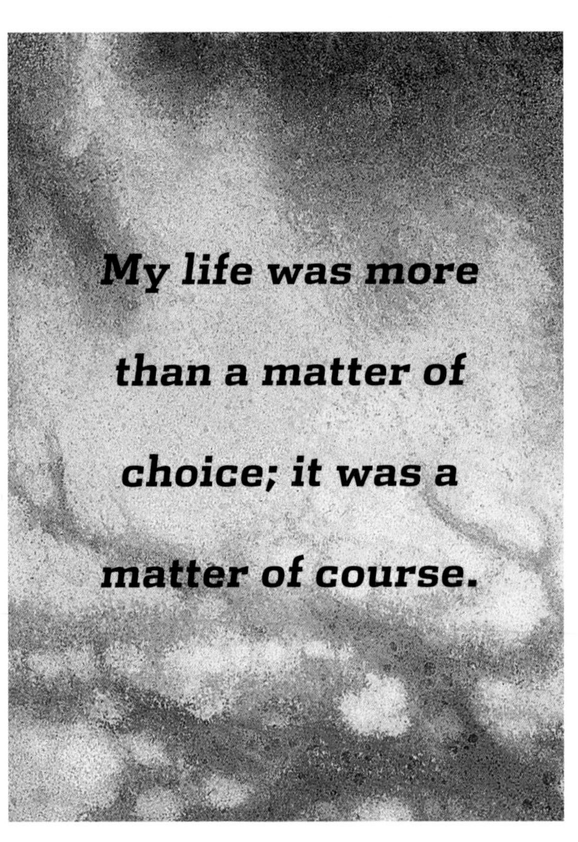
My life was more
than a matter of
choice; it was a
matter of course.

Indeed, he remembered it all, smiled, thought, The Friday night fish-fry, that was something, a religious event in most small prairie towns where the preponderance of immigrants were Catholic. Small carp, buffalo, and catfish came to his nets and were gutted, skinned, and kept on ice from his icehouse on the bluff above his makeshift dock. He spent January putting up enough ice to last the year. No shortage of hay in this country to insulate ice. Occasionally, he'd sell ice to passing fishermen, for pennies or a nickel, depending on the size of the blocks. Or he'd trade ice for tobacco—sometimes, too, to locals for fresh vegetables, milk, butter.

He shifted his chair to face the setting sun, realized he had not eaten since morning, felt a touch of hunger, thought again, Those fish fries. The surrounding towns were no more than a few houses, maybe a store, a church, a bar, and a ball field scratched out of the prairie. People spent their meager free time at church or in the bar and, on a summer Sunday after church, watching the local gaggle of farm boys play the ball team from one little town or another up the dirt road.

Likely as not, the local priest was the umpire, pardoning sins in the confessional before morning mass, knowing he'd be back in business soon enough, after listening to the powerful language on the field that afternoon. "Jimmy, me boy," Father McGucken would observe in a thick Irish brogue after Jimmy Cutler struck out, "I believe it fair to say the opposing pitcher has not been sired by a dog."

And, oh, the fistfights, fueled by bets on the game. Eventually, everyone gathered at the bar, and passions passed as the barley did its work. His ice cooled the beer, too.

But it was the Friday Nite Fry that brought the people together. Oh my, how many fish had he cleaned over the years? He stretched his fingers, looked at them, bent now from age, arthritis, saw the scars, remembered the worst of the wounds, thought, So many stories in an old man, the reason to write the letter. He would like someone to relive a few of the best of them.

That was one reason he enjoyed his time with the boys. They loved the stories. Could see in their minds the great fish, the great catches, the hard work, the hard times, the battles over territorial fishing rights, the feuds that occasionally turned deadly, the life-and-death struggles with the river, the floods, the droughts, the great flights of ducks and geese in fall, the unlimited freedom of his life.

Hard times but good times. And always the freedom of the river.

He would explain—with the boys listening politely, for they'd heard much of it before—how small carp and buffalo were scored to the bone with quarter-inch diagonal cuts, then scored again in a second series of quarter-inch cuts diagonal to the first; rolled in flour and cornmeal once, then again, before being deep-fried crisp in hot lard. The smaller catfish also were dredged twice, then deep-fried. They were the best fish he had ever eaten, served with pickled beets, sweet pickles, and boiled potatoes in fall and early winter, served with huge slices of beefsteak tomatoes, sweet-vinegared cabbage slaw, boiled onions, and sweetcorn in summer.

Not only had the boys understood his love of harvest, the common sense of it all, but they could have been him had they been born into previous generations. Hard times, but good times. And always the freedom of the river.

He thought then of the end of it all, his own gravestone ready to be planted in the little Boothill out back, saw in his mind the face of the marker: Here Lies . . . Zacker. Worked The Old River. 1900 - ____. Someone would have to finish. Probably one of the boys. He thought again of his most recent trip with the boys, wondered, Was it my last? If so, it was a good one, no rain, few mosquitoes, decent fishing, pleasant nights alongside campfires, which he dearly loved. For 50 years he'd slept on the ground on one riverbank or another as he waited for the nets to do their job. Then, well before the sun rose, he'd shake the dew from his knapsack, build a small fire, boil up coffee and fry bacon, softening his hard biscuits with grease from the pan.

He looked again at the paper, set the pencil aside, flexed his fingers, considered rolling a cigarette instead of fixing something to eat, wondered, How do writers put to paper that stuff they write? Must be painful work at times.

Searching the horizon, he saw a boat far upriver. Walleye fishermen heading home. Walleyes thrived in the reservoir now. Catfish had dominated the wild river. The carp came later, in the 1920s, as he remembered it. The buffalo fish had always been there, still were. The cats were there, too, just more difficult to get at during summer. Nets were useless once the river became a reservoir, except in spring when the fish pushed into backwater areas. Few men fished these waters for catfish anymore. He'd showed the boys, who made good catches on nightcrawlers one spring. Seeing the boys into lots of catfish, he longed for his nets. But his nets were gone.

He smiled, thought, Darn those boys, they do run with better fare and sure do treat a growly old man just pretty dandy. Smith had rigged for him a padded lawn chair he could perch securely on the front deck of Smith's boat. He would sit looking forward, as the boys motored slowly upriver, checking catfish habitat as they went.

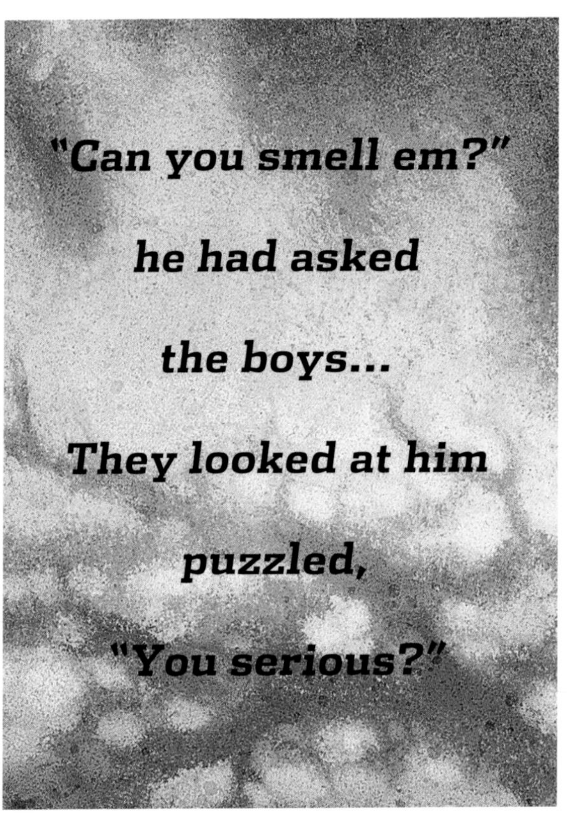
"Can you smell em?"
he had asked
the boys...
They looked at him
puzzled,
"You serious?"

He offered advice freely as they traveled, was never bashful with the boys. "Now lookee there," he'd say, and the boys would stop the boat, shut down the engine, listen. "All those turtle tracks in the sand. Now you boys maybe do, maybe don't know it, but when the river rises once turtles have egged, there's bound to be fishing for channel cats over those sandbeds, mark my word. And when those turtles hatch about August, scratch their way out of the nest and scurry down to the water, there's bound to be catfish waiting, mark my word."

He taught the boys to watch the surrounding terrain. Woods might line the riverbanks for several miles, interspersed with a small patch of farm field here and there. "Watch for an extensive grassy plain," he'd told them. "By midsummer, grasshoppers are a big draw for channel cats. Fish the river sections just down from grassy plains. Cats migrate for miles to hold in riffles and eddies just down from spots like that."

Of course, the boys knew their stuff, certainly could find catfish as well as anyone on any river. He removed his old hat, rubbed his head, watched the last of the sun set, thought, Yes, the boys had the idea: Look first, fish later. Some days, especially on new water, best look for hours and hours without ever fishing. Check the depth of holes, get a gauge on how much blowdown timber was tucked near or, better yet, in a portion of a goodlooking hole. The boys would stop the boat and cast a line with only a sinker, counting down the sinker to judge depth, then dragging it back to judge the width and breath of a hole, how much timber was present below the water, and so on. Three or four casts and they were on their way again, to search more water.

Timber on a river flat was a waste of time unless the target was eater channel cats. The bigger the hole, the deeper the hole, the more tangled the timber, and the deeper the timber was pushed into the hole, the better. The rule for flatheads, though, was always timber first, depth of hole later. That is, give a man a shallower hole with a snarl of timber, and he's bound to find more flatheads than a man fishing a deeper hole with only a little timber. Of course, rules could always be broken.

He rose from his chair, straightened up as best he could, lit that cigarette, would settle for coffee, shuffled inside, remembered, Older timber was important, too. Channel cats would hold in newly downed timber, but rarely flatheads. That too was an old rule. The nooks and crannies, the hollers and holes in old timber gave smaller fish a place to hide. Flatheads were there to feed on the smaller fish—larger fish, too—for big snags, especially those big enough to stick well out into current were sure to stir the surface of the water, creating foam and trapping flotsam that carp loved to suck. And flatheads loved carp. Loved drum, too. And bullheads, although it was a rare river where bullheads survived for long in the presence of a fair population of flatheads.

As the government
boys continued
to tame his river,
he moved to the
wild stretches that
remained.

He poured the coffee, shuffled back to the porch, saw the picture on the wall near the door, thought, That trip, those fish, that was his first time years ago with the boys. The three of them had rounded a big bend on a new section of river and suddenly stood transfixed at the sight, the massive logjam lining the length of the bend, the perfect gravel bar where they'd camped that night on the curve opposite the bend, still saw it all as clearly as if he were there now, thought again, This one wasn't just a big, deep, bend hole, filled with timber. The secret was, it was the only massive timbered hole of its kind in a huge section of river. For three miles downriver and at least three more upriver, nothing could compare with this hole.

Quality habitat in a confined river section, the boys called it. Then he'd asked them, "Can you smell 'em?"—had asked the boys, who at first didn't think he meant what he was asking. He'd insisted again, repeated the question, and they'd looked at him puzzled, had asked, "You serious? Don't smell anything but river, maybe dead fish." That was the first they'd heard of it, but they both knew the smell from long experience fishing, just didn't make the connection. Most seasoned anglers know that smell but don't quite make the connection. But it's there as certain as the sunrise. Just have to recognize it for what it is, what it means, the presence of fish, not just predators, but prey, the smell oozing from the water, carried by the natural flow downriver.

Just like the great predators themselves, he knew from experience that flatheads would migrate for miles, passing marginal hole after marginal hole in mile after mile of river, then know apparently from taste and smell that this was summer home, or winter home, or that they should just stay for a while because there was prey aplenty. He'd once caught the same gnarled old male flathead catfish four years running from the same river hole, same time of year. Sure enough, there, suddenly after 10 sets in the hole, the calendar would turn up June, and that fish would be there, skinny as can be; and he'd let the fish go, maybe catch it one more time, then not see it again until next year.

Dinner on the fire—literally. Get a big bed of oak coals glowing and lay the steak right on top of the coals.

Zacker's Life & Times

Addendum—After listening to Zacker tell his stories, we encouraged him to do a journal about some of the best of his life. Each time we'd ask how it was coming, he'd say, "Sure enough, you boys can collect the royalties; I'm working right along on my last letters." Not to be. So far as I know, Zacker never did put pen to paper, never did record the great stories of his life. So, over the years, I have taken to telling some of them. The most recent previous tale was all about Camp Catfish, in the May-June 1994 issue of In-Fisherman *(Chapter 21, herein), written not long after Zacker passed on at just past 90 years of age.*

It's impossible to forget those days. As I said in that tale in 1994, "Some time late into the night, so long as the cats weren't biting, we'd all drift off as the fire burned low and the early morning light sneaked over us, along with a morning chill and a bit of fog. Usually, a big fish would have run all the line off one of our reels. Toad would reset the lines and then as the sun cracked the horizon, I'd poke the fire and set coffee brewing.

"Sitting there with first coffee was the quietest part of the day. No one said much until the caffeine got coursing just right. What would this day bring? And another night? Big fish? We always hoped for such a fish or two. Lots of fish? That was always nice. Whatever the new day brought, our times together were always the best that life could offer at a price we could all afford."

He'd been there, too, downriver a hundred miles, in those years from about 1950 through 1960, living in a small house just off the Missouri river near Yankton, South Dakota. As the government boys, the dam builders, continued to tame his river, he moved to the wild stretches that remained. Blue cats had never been a fish he could depend on, although a fair population ran far up the wild river from time to time.

He'd told the boys stories about the fishing that developed in the 20-mile section of river below the Gavins Point Dam, just upriver from Yankton. The river had always been full of sandbar holes, but those that appeared downriver from the new dam were particularly deep, often with stairstep ledges. "Those big blue cats," he'd told the boys, "like the deepest water they can find, especially when the water's cold. Fish along the deepest edge near the core of the hole, or you won't catch anything but channel cats and drum."

He paused, trying to decide exactly what he'd told the boys about blue cats, decided, Must have told them the four deepest holes in all that river held the biggest fish. The monsters held in those holes from early winter through late spring, then seemed to disappear in May or June, just about the time most anglers got serious about fishing. Still, boys like Ed Elliot and a few of his friends, good fishermen those boys, had caught their share of big ones. Elliot held the world record for a good spell, from 1959 on. Ninety-seven pounds, as he recollected. Saw quite a few fish in the 70- to 90-pound range. Most of them never brought in. Heard tell of a 115 snagged at the mouth of the James River below Yankton.

The sun now set, he still sat on the porch, still stared at the paper on the desk, thought, Mostly, it was the campfires he missed, his lawnchair sitting just close enough so he could poke the fire as Smith added a log now and again and Stange stood listening attentively for a clicker to go on one of the reels. Some nights about midnight, they'd eat cold fried chicken, drink sodas. Other nights they'd do dinner on the fire, maybe fresh catfish, sometimes steaks. No pan necessary for steaks, just get a big bed of oak coals glowing and lay the steaks right on top of the coals, the coals so hot the meat wouldn't stick as the steaks seared. A quick turn and the steaks were finished.

Predictable as a sunset, he'd always gnaw off a big piece of steak, then mumble to Smith, "What the hell are you looking at?" Just as predictably, Smith would say, "Never saw anyone with two teeth eat a steak before. Maybe the funniest thing I've ever seen. Maybe better feed you hamburger next time." "Had a face like yours," he'd get right back after Smith, juice running through his whiskers, "I'd shave my butt and walk backwards. Used to have a bunch like you up the holler where I lived. Came from a long line of brothers and sisters." All that kind of "witty reparte," as Stange called it.

A warm south breeze pushed over the distant reservoir, up onto the prairie plateau where he sat now in the moonlight on his porch. This remained barren country, too dry for most modern agriculture. Sod farmers long ago had been replaced by ranchers who these days lived in the city 40 miles up the road. He counted the few familiar lights in the distance, thought, It was the wilderness passing that bothered him most. More and more people needing more and more room, each generation less connected to the land and water, not knowing how the world had been, each generation willing to sacrifice a little more of the wilderness that remained.

He reckoned that before long, the little wilderness that remained would be worth millions, thought, Then it will be controlled by very rich men. And we will have come back full circle to where we started from, no better off than our ancestors in the old countries, who answered with their lives to a king if they were caught hunting or fishing on his land. He didn't know the answer. Just knew that in all those years, it wasn't only the fish he had been after. He'd sought the best that life had to offer in wild country, had found what he was looking for, had paid the price such a life demanded, had gladly paid with his life.

SLOW ROLLING SECRETS FOR
BASS
TRANSITION TO NIGHT BITE
WALLEYES
A MUSKIE EXPERT PICKS
TOP BAITS
TOP TIME

Historic Perspectives

Here's another story set with Toad, Zacker, and Stange fishing bankside after dark and it's a good one, indeed, one of the most memorable of the bunch— "a real pickler," Zacker would call it. It's probably the last one ever to be written in this context.

On another front, by this time in 2000, Stange is back into doing TV, having been out of the television mix for 4 years, this after directing the TV department for many years during the late 1980s and early 1990s. Few realize that the first modern-style outdoor video of all time—not just the first fishing video—is created by In-Fisherman in 1986: Ice Fishing Secrets. Stange does the writing for this video and appears onscreen.

Meanwhile, the first catfishing video—Channel Catfish Fever—is chiseled from work done by Stange and Toad Smith, on video footage shot from 1985 through 1989. Channel Catfish Fever hits the market in 1991 and is the largest-selling catfish video to date. It's still on the market, offering classic instruction in the art of fishing for stream catfish. Its instructional counterpart, the largest-selling catfish book in history, Channel Catfish Fever, is on the market at about the same time.

Illustrations by Larry Tople

CHAPTER 44

AUGUST 2000

Bojangles, Campfires, and the Nite Bite for Big Channel Cats

A SMALL FIRE IS THE CENTER OF the universe as darkness falls and anglers like you and me sit silently, patiently, on a sandbar opposite a big riverbend hole, listening for a reel clicker to call evidence of a whiskered intruder. Some nights the action begins at dark and continues for hours. Occasionally it peaks late at night, while at other times the action never begins and the night is tempered by no more than a fish here and there. A final short round of action is typical, if not guaranteed, during those hours before sunrise, the increasing light apparently signaling a last chance to feed before another day dawns bright and hot.

Another Cozy Campfire With Friends!

Lots of you have asked, so I thought I'd take time to answer: Fishing at night has for me never been a consistent connection to larger channel cats, even during the hottest part of summer. Occasionally, yes. Most times, no. So after more than 30 years of spending hundreds of nights on the prowl, I believe that no overwhelming big-fish pattern prevails. A minor pattern here. A minor pattern there. Just depends. Fishing at night is, however, good enough to be worthy of note. And even if it weren't, I'd still do it just for the excitement and the chance to share a campfire with friends.

Now I know a few of you like a little story with your catfishin', particularly if it includes my old buddies Zacker and Toad. Well, one night we'd had ourselves a big ol' midnight feast of cold Kentucky Fried, and the bone piles built up pretty good here and there around our campsite on a sandbar. Feeling fat and sassy, we all settled in for a snooze before morning light broke.

Roundabout first light I heard rustling in camp, peeked out of my sleeping bag, and there was a big ol' raccoon, butt toward me, tail waving high in the air, not 10 feet away, digging in one of the bone piles. A big, dominant male he was, with a set of bojangles like an old Hereford bull; so it wasn't any surprise that when I tried to shush him out of camp, he would have none of it—would just turn, bare his teeth and hiss. He was diggin' those chicken bones, doing the breakfast shuffle, counting his blessings, such as they were.

Soon enough everyone was awake and watching this old boy chewing bones. Funny thing was he'd get grease on his paws—even his feet—and sand would stick to them when he walked. Annoyed, he'd stop and then stick way out and up, toes pointing straight as arrows, first one back leg, then the other, and would try to kick off the sand by doing a pathetic three-legged dance—all the while his tail, big butt, and those old bojangles shaking left-right, up-down. Well, we all got to laughing so hard Zacker finally had to get up and water the bushes, or else.

We fished the next day and didn't think much about our buddy Bojangles until we set camp on the same sandbar that night. Now, Zacker always carried a pint XXX bottle with him for his arthritis. So just after midnight, Zacker sets this trap—three big yummy-looking chocolate brownies, frosting and all, laced with two sturdy shots of his Russian XXX, mixed neatly in a coffee can set 30 feet away on the sandbar.

Well, it didn't take two hours for that old beggar Bojangles to hit camp. We all awoke to a ruckus and a mournful whoOOO-chip-chip-chip, whoOOOoo-chip-chip, which I guess is coon talk for "How dry I am," or maybe, "The last word in lonesome is me." As we peered from our bags, Zacker shined a flashlight toward the ruckus. Bojangles was sitting flat on his butt, tail sticking out at an odd angle between his legs, fur all messed up with chocolate frosting along one side of his face, the can held tight between his paws and legs. His eyes shining in the light, his head would nod a little left and then nod back a little right. *WhooOOOooo-chip-chip-chip.* Have you ever seen a raccoon grin?

Finally, ol' Bojangles stumbled down to the water, intent on swimming the river. He started, then hit the first part of the current, which turned him, and he swam in a circle, hitting the shoreline just about where he started. He stood there for a moment, a little wobbly, considering this odd turn of events: *"But I just left here a moment ago."* After two more tries, exhausted by his circuitous activities, he just flopped himself down on the sandbar and went to sleep. Ever heard a raccoon snore?

Raccoon critters aside, I was about to make observations about the night bite for big channel cats. Typical were our early experiments on the Red River below the Lockport Dam just north of Winnipeg, Manitoba, now the most famous channel catfishery in the world. Toad Smith and I first saw this portion of the river on a June day in the 1980s. We'd heard tales of the fishery and went to check it out. Caught some 40 channel cats that day that surpasses 18 pounds. Unbelievable. Still is.

That was sort of the beginning of the new age of catfishing on the Red in Manitoba. A few articles alerted anglers to the fishery, and the rest is history, including Manitoba's proactive plan to protect the unique fishery, beginning about 1990, with restrictive harvest regulations.

By about 1987, having caught hundreds of 15- to 24-pound channel cats from this fishery during many day-trips, Toad, Manitoba friend Ted Jowett, and I began to wonder if we weren't missing the big fish. We resolved to spend a few August nights fishing, to check out a nocturnal bite for big cats.

We fished eddy areas below the dam, as well as the head of prominent holes up and downriver.

One night we caught 28 fish. Toad always counted. Couple small fish and 24 fish from 14 to 23 pounds. Never saw another angler after midnight. Never scratched a fish larger than we would have caught during the day. Seemed the fish never stopped feeding, no matter the time of day, until most of those holding in an area had been caught. That is, if you fished an eddy area below the dam one night, the catch would be drastically reduced the next night. Same thing for fishing the head of a major hole two nights in a row.

The fish in this portion of the Red have gotten larger over the years, but it has everything to do with harvest protection and little to do with time of day. But then, I haven't conducted the same sort of experiment in recent times. I'd expect today, though, to catch a fair number of 15- to 26-pound fish, as well as a few pushing beyond 30, especially during September—the same sort of fish you'd catch during the day.

We did learn interesting things about fishing at night: The Red has a good flow (at least a consistent one) most of the year, even when the water's down during summer. Once you move downriver from the tailwaters, the river probably averages 150 yards from bank to bank. Some of those shorelines have a distinct lip connected to shallow flats that connect to midriver holes. So, say a shoreline has a lip that drops immediately into a foot or two of water, connected to a flat that runs 3 to 8 to 11 feet deep, which then drops into a hole maybe 15 to 20 feet deep.

If Toad Smith has a legacy in catfishing, something he introduced to the sport beyond his huge personality, it's float-fishing. Toad was using floats when I first heard of him in the early 1970s. Today, drifting cutbaits below a float is popular on the Red and in a few other areas of the country, but it was entirely unheard of back then.

We anchored at the head (upstream end) of major shallow flats and used the current to drift baits over those flats. No need for a lighted float. Just keep your reel in freespool and monitor the drifting float with your fingers as it moves downriver. You can easily feel a fish take the bait. We could easily drift baits for more than 100 yards downriver before reeling in and beginning again. Set the bait below the float so it just bumps bottom most of the time. If the depth changes and the bait drags or floats a foot or so above bottom, cats still take it. The float not only keeps the bait moving but also keeps it from snagging.

Those flats held a lot of fish at night, and they still do. The surprise was in how many fish pushed right up against lipped shorelines. It seemed like the action peaked in the hours before sunrise, as before, although we also caught fish along those edges during the day. Twenty-pound fish in just a foot or two of water. In 1987, we shot TV shows on consecutive early mornings by fishing from shore on spots like this. I shot one show with Toad, the other with Englishman Duncan Kay. The portion of the filming where Toad and I stood in hip boots drifting baits downriver along those lipped shorelines was never shown; the other action eventually made it into some of our early videos.

That style of fishing isn't unlike the fishing that transpires this time of year on major river systems like the Mississippi, where falling water levels make it possible to anchor or wade and drift floats over the shallow portions of sand- and gravel bars on or near wing dams. Again, cats push up onto these flats to feed at night. It isn't unusual to catch 50 fish a night, but it's rare to get a fish surpassing 10 pounds. The best wing dams seem to be on inside riverbends, although that isn't a hard rule. The most popular baits are grasshoppers, nightcrawlers, and dipbaits. Most of this is close-range fishing, and anglers seem to prefer lighted floats; but the times I've fished this pattern, I didn't find them necessary.

If there's a class of water where an angler has a fair shot at bigger channel cats at night, it's on bodies of water that have a good population of flathead cats in conjunction with channel cats, just the situation we were fishing that night old Bojangles The Bandit wandered into camp. Because of their aggressive predatory nature, flatheads rule these waters, moving all but the biggest channel cats out of primary feeding areas. So, when flatheads feed during the day during prespawn in May and early June, they hold near large snags and move channel cats into snags on river flats.

Once summer arrives, flatheads feed mainly after dark, prowling areas with large snags in conjunction with deeper river holes. Most average-sized channel cats do most of their feeding during the morning, after flatheads stop feeding and hole up for the day. Only the largest channel cats aren't intimidated by flatheads. So, only the largest channels prowl right along with the flatheads after dark.

Not that you're likely to connect with many big channel cats on these waters after dark. Just doesn't seem to be that many large channel cats on any body of water except the Red, though we still have much to learn in this regard. I'm hoping to provoke thinking about this subject and to encourage feedback about what you've seen. I keep telling you we don't know everything there is to know about catfishing. Channel cats inhabit waters in 44 states, and I've fished only in about 30 of them.

After dark on these waters, I target them by fishing with deadbait, which flatheads tend to ignore in favor of livebait, the livelier the better. Actually, big channel cats will take either livebait or deadbait, but in my estimation, they tend to prefer fresh cutbait. A typical good set would be with a freshly killed shad or, on the rivers I usually fish, a freshly killed sucker about 8 inches long. I cut off the head and snip off the tail (so the bait casts well and lays well in current) and make a series of cuts to the backbone on one side of the bait.

Using a hook like a 3/0 Mustad 92671 or Eagle Claw 84, my favorite hooks, I slip the hook through the tail of the bait, leaving the point exposed. I usually use a simple set rig consisting of a bell sinker (sliding on my mainline) pushed right up to the bait. No need for a leader between hook and sinker. Then I set the reel on freespool with the clicker on and put the rod in a rod holder. I've been using Tite Lok bank sticks for about 5 years. They're expensive (around $35 retail) but so sturdy they're bound to outlast me. Of course, a guy can get by with a forked stick.

The main mistake anglers make at night is to let cutbait sit too long without tending it. You know how it goes. You set several lines as the sun goes down. Nothing happens for a half hour—so you let the lines sit. After all, they haven't been hit. The key is to fish cutbaits aggressively. Let a bait sit for 20 minutes, then reel it in and freshen it up.

Cutbaits work because they exude juices (blood and oil) that attract cats. Freshen the bait (reactivate it) by making a series of cuts on the other side of the bait, then cast to a different spot. Twenty minutes later, reel in the bait and step on it to squash it a bit, reactivating it again. Then make another cast. It's unusual to go an hour at the beginning of the night without getting bit. By then it's time to flip that old bait into the woods for the coons and put on a fresh piece.

As I've said, when you're set up on a good hole that hasn't been heavily fished, it would be unusual not to get action during the first hour after dark. That's usually a hot time for flatheads, too, so I usually also have a livebait such as a lively bullhead set out for flatheads. If nothing's happening during the first hour or into the second, chances are it's going to be a long night. Sometimes I just take a three-hour snooze by the fire through the middle of the night, in order to be ready for the peak period that usually begins about the time light begins to crack the eastern horizon.

By this time, your baits having been set for several hours, it's time to freshen them, then stir the fire and make coffee. I've often gone an entire night without any serious fish, only to get into a few nice ones just before dawn. If they don't bite then, chances are you're on a real bummer of a hole, at least until the water rises again and cats have a chance to move back in. This pattern continues into early October in the North Country, and well into early November in parts farther south.

I've also fished many lakes and reservoirs after dark, my favorite spots being necked-down areas with a bit of current. The when-fish-bite patterns on these waters are similar to those I've already mentioned. Again, at night I've caught lots of nice fish, but only occasionally, and unpredictably, larger fish. Across the South, of course, fish bite during the day as well as at night, but the oppressive heat keeps anglers off the water most of the day.

One trick I've used on lakes is a cocktail bait, which consists of a piece of nightcrawler in conjunction with fresh cutbait. At first I thought the double bait would double my chances to interest cats that wander by. After a while, I realized that small fish—perch, minnows, bullheads, small cats—were constantly after the nightcrawler. This activity apparently attracts larger cats, which move in and take the cutbait. Other anglers fish a different version of this same rig by just dipping their cutbait in a good dipbait. All sorts of fish are attracted to rotten cheese. And when bigger fish move in, whether attracted by the activity or the cheesy aroma, they have a sturdy piece of cutbait to eat.

So, fishing after dark, in my estimation, only modestly increases the odds of catching larger channel cats, and then only in a few predictable situations. Still, those situations are an important part of the game, particularly if you have access to rivers and perhaps reservoirs where flatheads dominate. Don't expect to catch many channel cats in those waters, but the ones you catch likely will be good ones.

What qualifies as a big channel cat varies by region. With the exception of the Red River, a 10-pound channel is a good fish, indeed. Of the 7 million catfishermen out there, most of whom are fishing for channel cats, I'd bet no more than a percentage point of them have caught a 10—much less a 20. Imagine then the difficulty in breaking the 58-pound world record. We're working on verifying the handful of 50-pound fish on the record books. Chances for new world-record flatheads and blue cats seem good, but the present channel cat world record may stand for a long time.

Reasons for fishing at night go well beyond the slightly improved chances it provides for taking larger channel catfish. Our ancient ancestors ended each day sitting around a campfire. You can almost feel the vibrations across the ages as you consider the stars, the night sounds, the catfish, and have a chance to cross paths with critters such as old Bojangles, and characters the likes of Zacker and Toad Smith.

Bojangles, I have to tell you, was the next morning looking very much the worse for wear. The old boy was still snoozing sprawled on his side, tail pointed south and legs headed east, as I began to poke the fire. "Maybe he's dead?" Toad wondered, as he looked out from his bag. Then a leg twitched, his head raised, and the old boy righted himself. "Just hung over," Zacker said. Such a sad looking raccoon. Face still matted with chocolate and sand, he began a long, slow, shaky walk down the sandbar, tail no longer raised jauntily but dragging in the sand.

"Probably never eat another piece of chocolate cake," Toad said.

"Been there, done that, lesson learned," Zacker said.

Only on a sandbar in the wilderness with these guys, I said to myself. Oh my, it was always hard to tell what another day would bring.

MONSTER FISH OF 2000!
April-May 2001
In-Fisherman
THE JOURNAL OF FRESHWATER FISHING
"FORAGING" FOR WALLEYES
COLOR PATTERNING BASS
PLUS!
• Drop-Shotting Bass
• Minnowbait Muskies & Pike
• Cover Principle Crappies
• Conquering Catfish
• Fishing Ultralight Today!
The "SECRET" Return of Great Lakes WALLEYES!

{ Historic Perspectives

Kansas City, Omaha, Chicago, Pittsburg, Cleveland, and smaller cities—Stange travels widely during the late 1980s and 1990s talking to sport show audiences about catfish. Modeled after a popular seminar topic he sometimes uses, this article addresses the most fundamental problems every catfish angler faces with a straightforward confidence born of years in the field experimenting with solutions. Stories from the field seal the deal.

Stange also is one of the speakers at the First International Catfish Symposium, which In-Fisherman helps to organize, held in Moline, Iowa, in 2000. The 2nd International Catfish Symposium is in St. Louis, Missouri, in June 2010. In-Fisherman again helps to organize the event.

Illustrations by Peter Kohlsaat

CHAPTER 45

APRIL 2001

The Best Told Mistakes of Every Catman

MARION BRINK, THE SAVVY PRINCIPAL in the school where I first taught science so many years ago, shared with me one of his strategies for dealing with parents who called to complain about how little Johnny said he was being mistreated at school. "Listen," he'd tell parents, "If you promise not to believe everything Johnny says about what goes on at school, I promise not to believe everything he says about what goes on at home." This usually was at least sobering enough to get the conversation between parents and principal started with some measure of mutual respect.

The conversation here is more straightforward and, I assure you, I respect you, even though I know a good many of you out there. Not likely to be much debate about typical problems facing many of the catfish anglers I meet at sport shows and when

Catfish Make Mongo Smile!

I'm fishing. Many longtime readers have already recognized these problems and have conquered many or most of them. Catfishing isn't difficult. It can be learned. If I can be fairly successful, so can you. And, heaven knows, I have a lot of friends who, well, if they can learn to be fairly successful, it's absolutely certain that you can too.

Indeed, I like a challenge, so we might pretend just for this article that we're teaching Mongo how to catch catfish. If you don't know Mongo, go to your favorite video store and rent *Blazing Saddles*. Don't just rent it, watch it. You probably need a good laugh, anyway. Let's just say that Mongo is a rather large and somewhat slow-witted individual, played by an ex-professional football player who eats a lot of beans (it's a western) and subsequently farts like a racehorse on steroids. I say, nothing like a little flatulence in a story line to get a movie on the right track. To heck with the critics, that kind of stuff's thumbs up by me. Anyway, I was about to say that Mongo's a likable sort. And he's teachable. Good Mongo. But, Mongo, put the horse down. (OK, forget the Mongo idea.)

DON'T HIDE HOOK

It isn't that catfish aren't intelligent. Indeed, science suggests that they're among the most intelligent fish among those we usually write about, way smarter, in many ways, than pike and walleyes, notably smarter than bass and trout, and just about on an even plane with carp. But catfish with no experience with hooks, which is most of them, bajillions of them—they haven't a clue what a hook is. Admittedly, though, catfish that are caught and released probably learn to associate hooks with danger, but even that takes an unknown.

So no sense to hide a hook in order to fool a catfish, even though it seems logical to a lot of catfish anglers. The entire process isn't just a waste of time, it's one of the main reasons anglers don't get a good hookset. Everything I say here has exceptions, of course, but in most cases, leave the hook point exposed, so that when you set, it immediately and easily moves forward into catfish hide.

"But," a skeptical angler asks, "won't the fish feel the hook when it picks up the bait?" Yes, maybe, but so what? It still won't know what a hook is and isn't going to care, given everything else it's perfectly comfortable grabbing and swallowing. Cats pick up crayfish that bite and scratch. They eat spiny bullheads like so much popcorn. And when they suck food off the bottom, they often inhale a good bit of debris—sticks and pebbles—right along with the good stuff, sometimes rejecting the junk, but other times swallowing it all without flinching. Getting rid of that stuff might be a different story, but then I don't know, I've never asked a catfish.

So, when fishing a nightcrawler, one of the best baits in a lot of waters in April, leave the point exposed. Yes, no matter what Grandpa said. Just run the hook through the crawler four or five times to get the juices oozing and calling in catfish, but don't run the point back into the crawler.

When fishing a piece of cutbait, like a one-inch strip of filleted shad or sucker, run the point through the skin in a corner of the bait one time, again, leaving it exposed. In running the hook through, be sure no scales are impaled on the hook point, which makes setting it past the barb difficult. And so on and on with all the baits you might fish, from grasshoppers to chicken liver. The exception would be pastebaits and dipbaits, which are so soft that the barb pushes through immediately on the set.

On this same angle, many anglers also tend to use smaller hooks than they should, thinking fish won't see, or that it's easier to hide a smaller one. In general, use the largest hook you can get away with, given the type of bait you're using. Larger hooks offer more gap, which generally means a better set. When fishing with one big crawler, go with at least a #4 hook, better a #2. Fishing two or three crawlers calls for at least a #1 or 1/0. A big grasshopper takes a #6 or a #4. For chicken liver, which to tell the truth, I rarely fish with for reasons discussed in the next section, use a #1 or 1/0. For chicken liver, leave a 10-inch tag end on your line after tying on a single hook, and use the tag end to wrap the liver on the hook. Finish off the wrap with a half hitch to hold everything in place.

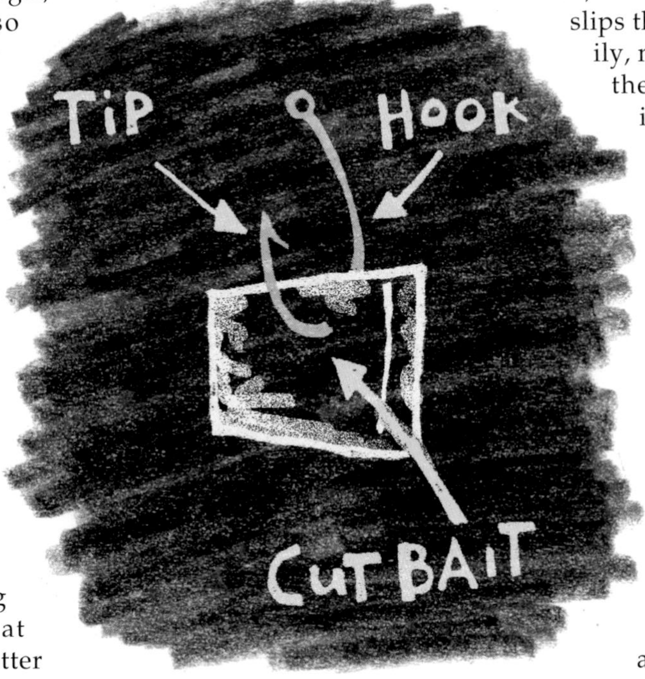

It's particularly important to use larger hooks with livebait. The smaller the hook, the smaller the gap and the more likely it will set back into the bait, making it impossible to get a hookset. Even when larger hooks set back into the bait, they still often have enough gap to break free and find flesh. For 8-inch suckers and 6- to 8-inch bullheads, I use at least a 7/0 hook; for bigger baits, I go with a 10/0. Mustad's 92671 is one of the few hook styles in sizes up to 10/0. Most others are available in sizes up to only about 7/0.

Hooks don't need to be particularly sharp in order to set into the soft mouth of catfish, but a modestly sharp hook slips through a bait more easily, making less of a mess of the bait and causing less injury to live minnows. But don't get carried away, especially if you're after flatheads with big livebaits. Needle-sharp hooks snag into wood debris too easily. They also sometimes puncture a baitfish again and again as it swims impaled on it. Sometimes, too, a needle-sharp hook sticks right back into a baitfish when you reel in to recast. Keeping a good, big baitfish as lively and healthy as possible is important. And many times, they aren't that easy to come by.

ABOUT SECRET BAITS

There aren't any—secret baits. Not chicken liver, beef blood, chicken blood, frogs, grasshoppers, baby turtles, rotten cheese, semi-rotten cheese, shad guts, shad gizzards, yak meat, or medicated monkey meat. There are many fine baits, some that work better than others, given time of year and body of water. A few baits, experience has shown, tend to be top choices during most seasons on almost any body of water.

Fresh cut-up baitfish—cutbait—is one such all-season choice, a consistent winner for blue and channel cats and, in some instances, for flatheads.

The last time Toad Smith and I fished below the famous Lockport Dam on the Red River just north of Winnipeg, Manitoba, we had a typical experience relative to other catfishermen fishing the same water with a supposed secret bait. This was early June, the water in perfect shape, the cats feeding heavily in prespawn mode. We had a great first day of fishing, landing at least 40 fish from about 18 to just over 25 pounds.

We came off the water a bit early, and Toad, naturally, struck up a conversation with a couple of cat boys who said they were seasoned catsters. Been fishing cats in Kentucky, Tennessee, Indiana, and them there parts for over 30 years, they said. Knew just about everything there was to know about catching cats. And had come on up to Canada to see what all the fuss was about. Well, they said they were rightly impressed with the fishery and the fish, which they had pretty much just about conquered on this particular day, thanks in part to their secret bait.

Well, now, Toad just had to know, What would that be? "Rotten chicken livers," they said. Had to be aged to the point of deterioration in the midday sun. Kind of difficult to fish, ain't they? Toad asked. They said they spent the time it took to tie the livers up, held together in nylon stocking. Tedious, they said, but worth it.

How worth it? Toad wanted to know. Ten fish, they sort of whispered, not wanting any of the other anglers at the ramp to hear. All more 'n 20 pounds. Then, "Here, we have a few extra baits we'll share with you." That's when Toad, being the honest, helpful sort he was, always wanting others to catch as many catfish as they could, said well, thanks but he'd caught 25 fish to 25 pounds all by himself and took an hour nap in the boat to boot at noon, and all on simple old cut-up suckers that didn't stink too bad and were easy as can be to fish. The catsters were, in no particular order, indignant, offended, PO'd, and beyond believing that anyone could have possibly outfished them or their secret bait.

We're lucky that catfish are abundant across most of the country. So, some cats aren't all that difficult to catch in most places. That can be a problem, because anglers get to catching a few fish and then assume they've chosen the only bait that works, when another bait might produce five times as many fish in the same situation. I keep talking about fresh cutbait, which we usually fish in one-inch strips, after filleting the sides of a baitfish that's been kept cold in a cooler. I keep talking about it, because we've generally done so well with it almost everywhere we've fished it, often enough in direct competition with the other "hot" baits that are supposedly producing cats galore. I wouldn't go anywhere on a major trip for channel or blue cats without fresh cutbait in the cooler.

But, granted, cutbait's not magic either and at times, other things produce more fish. Even chicken livers are OK because they're bloody, and bloody baits, like pure coagulated blood, are attractive to catfish. Chicken livers are also easy to get. But if you can get fresh livers, I say roll them in seasoned flour and sauté them in butter and serve them alongside a mess of hushpuppies drizzled with honey. Now that's good. And more productive than fishing with them, at least by my measure, for in 30 years of occasionally fishing them alongside other baits, I've rarely seen them be the best thing a feller could be fishing. Same with shrimp. Work fine, often as not, but rarely the best choice. Same with wieners dipped in one concoction or another. But the point is, a few cats can be caught on just about anything. Dip a sponge in gasoline and see if you can't catch a catfish or two when the bite's on. A friend caught a cat with a cigar butt in its stomach. But then it was a CAO Churchill, a pretty classy cigar.

We know a lot more today about dipbaits, too, which aren't to be confused with pastebaits. Pastebaits are thick enough that you have to work the paste into a ball with your fingers. Then it's fished on a treble hook. Paste is handy to keep around, but it hasn't proven to be as consistently effective as dipbait, which has a looser consistency and needs to be fished on a "carrier," such as a plastic dipworm or piece of sponge.

All the good dipbaits I know have rotting cheese as a basic ingredient. But there's a real art to this business; this isn't just mixing up a bunch of slop. Each company has its own secret procedures and pet ingredients that make, say, Sonny Hootman's Sonny's Super Sticky just a little bit different from Cat Tracker's Sewer Bait.

These baits can be the hottest thing going, especially for channel cats. Blues bite them, too, although it would be hard for me to say at this point that something else might not produce better in those same situations. Just don't know for sure. We also know cats eat these baits in cold water, not just during summer, some of the secret during cold weather being to get the baits into a consistency that stays on a dipworm well.

My original opinion about dips generally not being a top bait for big cats still stands, although certainly they do account for bigger fish in some waters. An angler always has to weigh how many more larger fish he would catch—if big fish alone are his intent—if he would fish something else instead of the dip.

"Doug, you're right," says Sonny Hootman, who manufacturers his famous bait in Farmington, Iowa. "My bait produces lots of fast action for eater cats, but fish generally top out at, oh, say, 6 to 8 pounds. Occasionally, someone will latch onto a good one. Been some monsters caught, too. So it's a good choice for fast action—and an outside shot at a bigger fish. I'm the first to say I'd probably fish something else if I was after only big cats. But then the reason my boys and I can't make bait fast enough is that most people want action."

Maybe the biggest mistake of all relative to dipbaits is not using them. Half the country still hasn't discovered dipping. Hardcore dippers mostly reside in the core of the country, from Kansas to Indiana. Most of the catfishermen in the East, Southeast, Deep South, Southwest, West, and Canada have never yet "cut the cheese."

DON'T LET CATFISH RUN

It follows somewhat logically that if catfishermen assume that a cat knows what a hook is and will drop a bait if it feels one, they also will worry that a catfish might "feel" them on the end of the line once a fish picks up a bait. So everytime a fish gives a tug or pull or makes a run, they flip the reel into freespool and feed line, a mistake most of the time.

Feeding line usually just causes problems, especially in current. Try feeding line to current without having a bite. Feels just like a fish taking line. Feed 10 feet of line to a catfish, and usually about 6 to 7 feet of that is excess line bowed in current. Try to set, and all you get is slack line. So, quickly reel the line tight and set again. Maybe on the second set, if the fish is still there, it gets hooked.

Cats usually not only don't know or care that you're on the other end of the line, but they also actually seem to respond favorably to having you there. That is, if you keep the line modestly tight so the fish has something consistent to pull against, the fish, too, usually continues to pull consistently. That's another subject, but this is one reason setlines work well for catfish. And along yet another angle, it's the reason circle hooks also work well.

But you do want the fish to move away from you slightly before setting. It should at least turn so the hook slides across its mouth. So most of the time, all an angler needs to do is ease the rod tip along with the catfish as it moves away, all the while maintaining steady pressure on the fish. Once the rod tip has eased along down a foot or two, set the hook. When you're used to doing this, keeping your rod tip at a right angle to the fish when you're monitoring bites becomes natural, so you have room to move the tip with the fish.

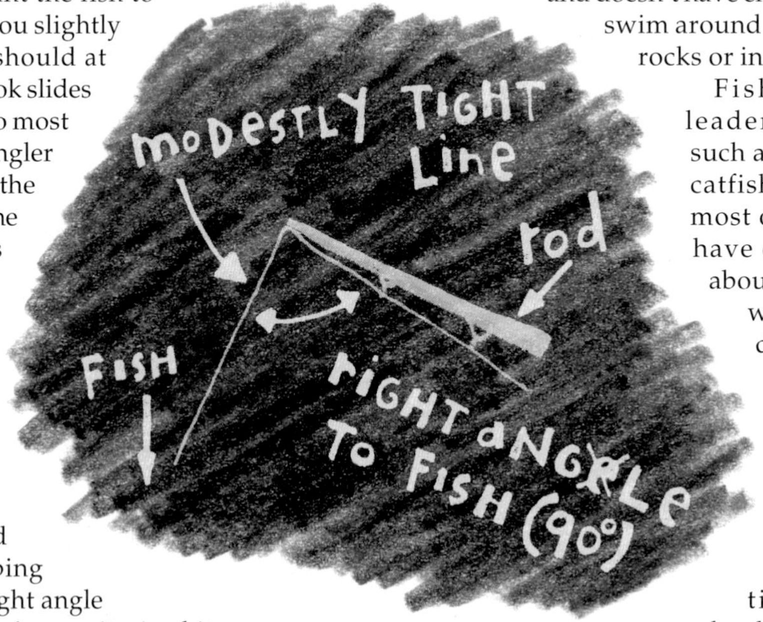

Sometimes it's necessary to give line in order to get a fish to take. Occasionally, flathead cats seem to be so picky that if they feel any pressure they crush the bait and just drop it. Sometimes, in that situation, pulling the bait away from a fish actually seems to make them mad enough to pick up the bait more firmly. With fish and fishing, you never know everything. Many situations call for a modification of this basic rule; but the rule still remains—don't feed line.

SHORTER LEADERS, NOT LONGER

A leader of a certain length is rarely a critical factor in catching more catfish. Use the least amount of leader you can, which, surprising to most fishermen when I tell them, often is no leader at all. Particularly for channel cats, just let the sinker slide all the way down to the hook. This is a precise way to fish. The advantage is that the baited leader doesn't wave around in current and get snagged. Or when fishing a livebait, particularly for flatheads, it stays close to the sinker and doesn't have enough leader to swim around and get under rocks or into timber.

Fishing with a leader, though, is such a "thing," with catfish anglers that most of them never have even thought about doing otherwise. They just do it. Part of the thinking here is kin to worrying about a catfish sensing that the sinker's in combination with the hook. But a catfish doesn't know or care what a hook is. A sinker is just another rock, as far as a cat's concerned.

I usually fish with about a 6-inch leader for flathead cats, unless I'm fishing in heavy cover. It's bait movement that attracts flatheads. Say I want my bullhead to move as much as it can, but not so much that it gets snagged. In this instance, I'll probably have a 3- to 5-ounce (maybe even an 8-ounce) bell sinker sliding on my mainline, and a barrel swivel tied in 6 inches above the hook to stop sinker from sliding.

Blue cat ace Jim Moyer of Clarksville, Tennessee, a longtime contributor to our knowledge bank at In-Fisherman, has convinced me that a leader of about 2 feet or so when anchored in current during cold-water periods helps attract blue cats. He anchors above a hole or a structural element, then casts the bait downcurrent 100 feet or so. Apparently, the extra leader allows the bait to move a bit in current, attracting more blue cats. Moyer, of course, pays occasionally for his extra leader with extra snags, but he pours his own sinkers by the ton.

MORE MISTAKES

Some of the mistakes I've mentioned here rank as modest meanderings compared to the more overwhelming mistakes we've covered in other articles. In rivers, for example, there's a time to move and fish a variety of spots, seeking active fish, instead of just parking by the first bridge you come to; nothing I've noted here compares to being in the wrong place at the wrong time. None of these mistakes mean anything if you're not first on catfish.

Granted, once you're familiar with a 10- to 20-mile section of river, there's a time to sit around a campfire at night and wait them out, especially if your quarry is big flatheads. But you can't sit just anywhere. You need to have surveyed a section of river by actually fishing it to make a good judgment about the quality of spots you intend to spend the night fishing. This is a story I covered in the March 2001 issue of *In-Fisherman*. It's also a story we cover in our book, *Channel Catfish Fever*.

The right tackle's important, too. Doesn't have to be all that expensive. A modest investment in good rods and top-end reels that will last for decades (unless Mongo sits on them) makes fishing more fun and more effective. It's common for catfishermen to be way undertackled when they begin. Eight- and ten-pound line and whoopee noodle rods are for small cats in ponds and creeks, but they won't land much for you in most other environments. Certainly, yourarely land a bigger fish with such tackle.

There's a time to experiment with a variety of baits. You learn as you go about appropriate fishing lines and various other tackle items. There's a time to fish all night instead of pressing the issue during the day. Just as there are times to fish during high-percentage periods at dawn or dusk, instead of trying to do a 24-hour thing.

All the problems, all the potential solutions, all the extra catfish, and in the meantime, all the fun, are the reasons I fish for cats and subsequently write about them in hopes of helping others catch more fish. There's enough to write about, enough fish to catch, enough stories to tell, to last a lifetime.

Like the little boy who showed up late for Sunday School one day. His teacher asked him why he was late. He sort of shuffled his feet around for a moment, then said, "Well, I started out to go fishing instead, but my dad wouldn't let me."

His teacher smiled. "Now that's a fine father," she said. "He was absolutely right not letting you go fishing on Sunday. Did he explain to you why?"

The little boy nodded. "Oh, yes. He said there wouldn't be enough bait for both of us."

Historic Perspectives

Over the years, Stange fishes many of the best catfish waters in North America, from Santee-Cooper to Texoma, from the Red River of the North to the Red River of the South. Yet, true to his roots, his favorite waters remain the kind of secluded small streams that can be waded wet during late summer. That's where and how this story unfolds—another tale of good times in simple places close to home.

On the larger scene, doing TV and radio, delivering seminars and in writing other In-Fisherman magazine articles not included in this book, Stange often returns by one method or another to the theme offered in his first catfish article for readers of Fishing Facts magazine over 25 years before. He puts it like this:

In one All In The Family episode, Archie Bunker stands, cigar in hand, next to his favorite living room chair, lecturing his wife, Edith, on his difficulty in getter her to understand the obvious logic of his ways. "The problem," he tells Edith, "is that I explain in English and you listen in Dingbat."

So, too, does the easy logic of the ways of catfish in rivers often pass by the casual river angler. They find a bridge, park their vehicle, and walk down and plant a lawn chair. You have to move—to walk—to begin to judge the comparative merits of the river structural elements. By now you already know that, but not long ago this logic is just an idea in one man's mind.

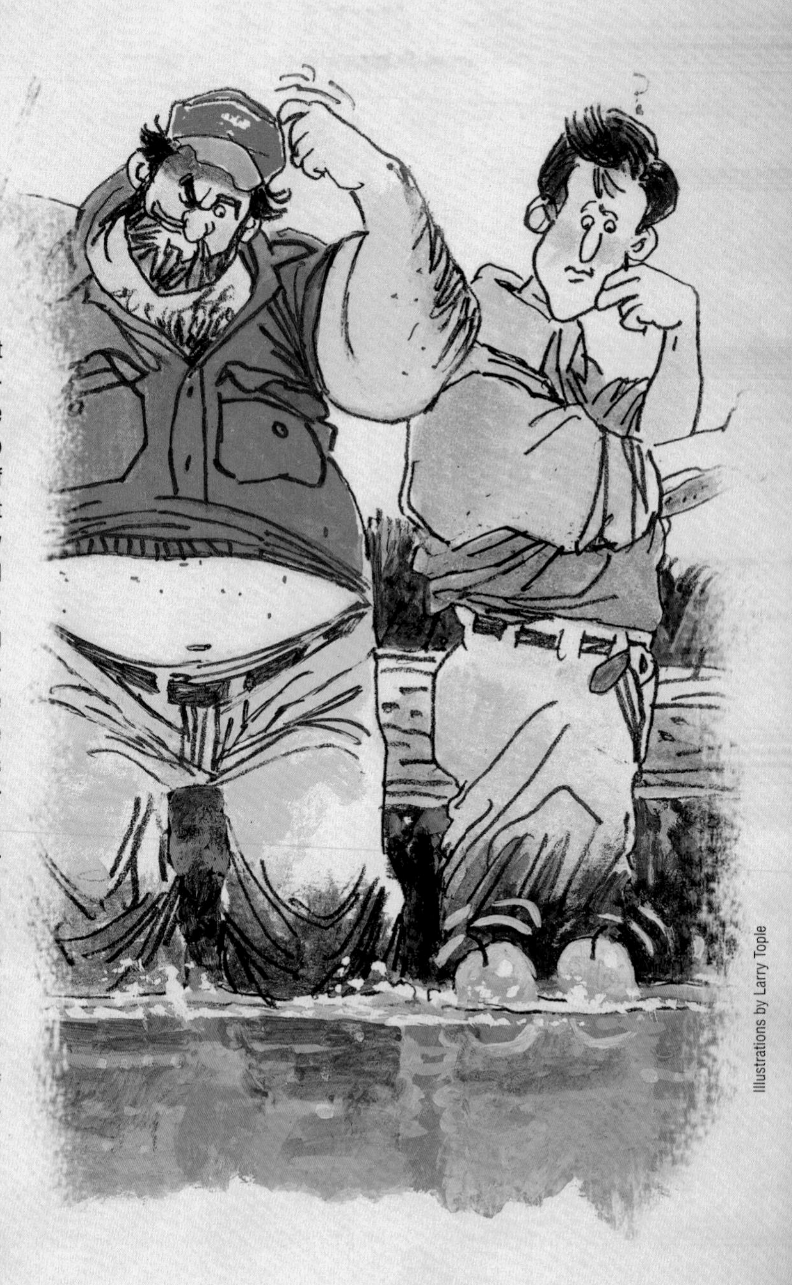

Illustrations by Larry Tople

CHAPTER 46

AUGUST 2001

Knee Deep in Channel Cats

This Baptism Brings Anglers Back To Life!

AT MY AGE I'M BECOMING FORGETFUL, which seems distressing until one begins to think of all the things better off forgotten. That's the way it is a lot of the time. What appears to be a problem often isn't much at all when you finally gnaw right down to the applecore. Which reminds me of a day on the water—I still rarely forget much about fishing.

Toad Smith and I were wading wet, playing cool cookies, I guess you could say, standing knee deep in the thick of the action, midstream, dressed in our best cat duds—old jeans, worn tennies, old socks, and so on. I remember Toad's shirt that day, a faded red knit polo thing that didn't quite cover the entirety of his tummy, much less the top of his "asky when he'd bendoversky," which of course he did to land catfish. That's when I'd turn my head away from the shine and yodel out, *"Moooooon Over Minnesota!"* a small tribute to the river we were fishing. We were, per usual, having a good time of it, what more can I say.

I also remember Toad's attire, because—and I have told this story before—we had stopped in town at a diner to get a cheeseburger and fries before fishing and had discovered right off that we could just go from vehicle to vehicle in the parking lot and pick plenty of grasshoppers off the grills of pickup trucks and the occasional Caddy; it's still mostly Ford, Chevy, and Dodge pickup trucks parked at diners in most farming communities, with some of the old retired boys driving Caddies—truth is, to this day, I have never fished a hopper off a Mercedes Benz.

That's when the biker lady stepped from the diner, toothpick in mouth, flexing arms like power pistons from out of a Grateful Dead T-shirt with the sleeves cut off at the shoulders, a snake-and-skull tattoo on one bicep, her blond hair in the kind of tight bun reminiscent of one of the *führer's* women in a Nazi war documentary. She took one look at Toad, dressed as he was, looking, I suppose, for all the world like a homeless person, there picking grasshoppers one by one off the grill of her truck, which carried her Harley in the pickup bed. Pathetic, she must have thought, and she slipped a wad of bills from a pants pocket and offered him $5 to get a hot meal and maybe a shower—along with a wink and a "then why don't you come see me sometime."

A tight little pained smile creased Toad's face. Little beads of sweat broke out all along his brow. It was the only time I ever saw him at a loss for words, the only time I ever saw him shrink from a situation. "Opportunity knocked and you failed to answer," I said.

"For a moment, I saw my life passing before my eyes," he said.

But I digress, for I was about to make a connection, if you would return momentarily to the first paragraph, exactly to the part about gnawing to the applecore, about to make a connection about apples. For it was that late afternoon that we stood, as I've said, knee deep along the edge of a sandbar, when, what from upstream should appear but two green apples floating downriver. I don't remember either of us saying anything, just looking at each other, strange, as in how did those green apples happen to be floating buddy buddy downriver—and from whence could they have come?

Toad grabbed one, as did I. Perfect late-summer green apples. "Yum!" I said, cracking off a bite. "Special delivery from above," Toad said. "At least from upstream," I said. "That's what I said," he replied. "Probably laced with arsenic," I said, "then dropped in the water to clean from the gene pool anyone sensible enough to wade wet for catfish." "Probably someone against folks having too much fun," he said.

Too much fun is just about the only way to describe wading wet for cats in August and September, months that might seem like the bottom of the barrel for catching fish. Hotter than Hades. Rivers threaten to go dry. But the hot weather just kicks cats into overdrive, and the low water just makes cats easier to find and rivers easier to wade. For those willing to hang loose and wade right in, this baptism brings many an angler back to life. Most of us, after all, are pretty much just a wet step removed from being carefree kids again, brimming with enthusiasm, full of anticipation and curiosity.

Make no mistake, this too is a fine way to corner catfish. Pick just about any section of river with plenty of decent holes. As you know, rivers run in a continuous series of riffle, hole, run configurations. Some series of riffles, holes, and runs are better than others. Some sections of river also have more good series of riffles, holes, and runs than others. By late summer, many cats have moved to the best holes, often deeper holes associated with wood cover.

Lots of small streams, though, don't offer much cover other than deeper water along cutbacks or in the core of holes. Sometimes that water's only two or three feet deep. Try to find river sections that average slightly deeper than surrounding portions of river. It's not unusual to have many of the cats from, say, a three-mile section of river, holding in a half-mile section where the holes are just six inches or a foot deeper, on the average.

One of Toad's favorite small streams in Iowa was like that. It's a tiny stream a hundred miles and five tributary intersections removed from the Missouri River. By August, the stream wasn't more than 20 feet wide and two feet deep in most places. Most fish ran about a pound. But a good afternoon of wading might produce a dozen to three dozen fish. That's good sport and good eating, too.

Bigger rivers are better overall, of course. They just have more fish of a bigger average size, along with a shot at one that might surpass 10 pounds. Lots of anglers wade wet, for example, on sandbars formed by wing dams in the upper and middle Mississippi River. Cats move up on the sand to feed on all sorts of critters, including crustaceans and insect larvae and the minnows that eat the larvae. Perhaps the best presentation is to drift a bait below a slipfloat set just deep enough to keep the bait tumbling along over the sand. The best catches are almost always at or after dark, or up until about 9 or 10 in the morning.

This is one time of year and one situation where fresh cutbait doesn't stay fresh for long stashed in a plastic bag in your back pocket.

The Minnesota River, where I've learned so much about catfish over the years, runs for some 300 miles across Minnesota. It has served as such a fine proving ground for catfishing techniques because it's a classic river, so much like portions of hundreds of other rivers across the country. Long shallow stretches are interspersed with sections having more gradient, where the water runs faster over riffles, into holes, and on through long runs. Lots more gravel and rock there. Lots more wood cover. These are the stretches to target. Might be 10 or even 20 feet of water in some of the deepest downriver holes, but most holes run 4 to 8 feet deep.

We usually walk upriver, then hustle back downriver once we've finished fishing the best spots, only stopping to refish a few of the top spots on our way back to the truck. Occasionally, especially if we get to the river during early afternoon and don't expect the best fishing to occur until late afternoon on toward dark, we'll walk downriver first, noting the best potential fishing areas as we go. It's typical to catch small fish and an occasional decent fish all day long. The best fishing, though, usually is up until about 9 or 10 in the morning and after 5 or 6 o'clock in the afternoon.

I love to drift a bait below a slipfloat this time of year, with the low flow just moving the float and bait along slowly through potential spots. Any float will do, but those simple walleye-style slipfloats with a stem are more visible at a distance. On streams, I use a bass flippin' stick and 12- or 14-pound line on a casting reel. On larger rivers, I use a Euro-style rod like the 11-foot Aurora, with a casting reel filled with 14-, 15-, or 17-pound line. The longer the rod, the higher the rod tip can be held above the water, which helps to keep line off the water for a truer drift for the float and bait.

This is one time of year and one situation where fresh cutbait doesn't stay fresh for long stashed in a plastic bag in your back pocket. Cutbait works, though. Hoppers can be good, too, and so can dipbaits. Hoppers keep well in a plastic bag or a small jar. Just duct tape a shower curtain ring to a jar and hang it on your belt. With a plastic bag, just run a corner of the top of the Ziploc-type bag through on the shower ring and, again, hang it on your belt.

A regular stringer works to keep a few fish. Toad used a wire fish basket tied with a stringer to his belt when he was standing in the water. Usually, he'd just carry the basket by hand and lay it in the water near shore as he fished. The basket was perfect for smaller cats; we didn't keep big cats anyway, unless we happened to catch a flathead of four or five pounds. Good eating. Just about the perfect size for a meal for two.

I mention the basket, because it also was a handy way to carry dipbait, usually in a glass jar. Dips, of course, get pretty runny in hot weather, and the cooler water keeps them in a little better consistency. Thicken runny dips just a bit with a binder such as flour.

Dealing with dips midstream isn't easy, because you must unscrew the lid on the jar, then drop the

plastic worm in and dip it with a stick. Dip worms also hold dip best if they're dried off a bit just before dipping. Most anglers hang a towel on their belt or tuck it in a back pocket.

The point is, you just don't have enough hands to accomplish everything easily in midstream. So most anglers doing the heavy dipping routine wade wet, but usually stand along the edge of the water to make presentations. They set the dipbait on the bank. Or if they're carrying a cat bag over their shoulder, they set the cat bag containing the dipbait on the bank. Dips, which are mostly made from rotten cheese, are a potent bait during late summer.

This is prime time to hold a bait right in a riffle area, often in less than a foot of water. Active cats move right into the shallow riffles to feed. If you're drifting a float, just let the float and bait tumble right through the riffle. A cat will grab the bait as it bounces through the riffle or grab it just as it enters the beginning of the hole below the riffle.

Well, one hot August afternoon, a couple local hot shots and their girlfriends in a hot-rod '57 Chevy headed up that gravel road north of town.

To hold a bait in the riffle, use a simple slipsinker rig with a heavier than normal (for low water) sinker, say a bell sinker of at least an ounce and probably more like two ounces. Cast the bait right into the fast water and let it settle. Get it to hold right in the fast water. The taste molecules from the bait are carried down into the hole to the cats, which shoot right up into the fast water to grab the bait. Hold your rod tip high, so that when a fish grabs hold you can drop the tip toward the fish a foot or two before setting. Don't feed line to the fish. Just drop and set. Don't have your reel in freespool. Hold on tight. These fish often are really smokin' along when they grab the bait.

Now you know I could go on talking about different situations and telling all kinds of stories. Seems to me this isn't one of those situations where most of you need all that much instruction. The point is to go. Imagine all the younger cat anglers out there who have never tried wading wet. Think of all the fun they'll have, all the things they'll discover. And all you old boys who have done this before back in your more "instructive" years, well, think you can drag those old bones out of an easy chair for one more round? Might be the most fun you have all summer.

OK, one story. The closest catfish to me in my junior high school days were eight miles or so north of the small farming community where I lived. A narrow gravel road led over a small bridge across a small river, the Little Rock, to be exact. That's where I caught my first catfish, wading wet.

Well, one hot August afternoon, a couple local hot shots and their girlfriends in a hot-rod '57 Chevy headed up that gravel road north of town. I know because, going about 200, they almost flattened my friend and me as we peddled our bikes up the road toward the bridge, fishing poles in hand.

Now, the road narrowed a few miles from the bridge, where the hot-rodders had to slow down as they pulled up behind a tractor. Eventually, a wide spot allowed the farmer to graciously pull to the side to let the speed wagon pass, which they did, laying on the horn and spraying gravel. Arms with middle fingers extended also went out the car windows as the car spun around the tractor. Up yours you hornytoad-headed old farmer!

The rest is history, as they say. The hot-rodders pulled up to the bridge and piled out, intent, apparently, on a little wet wading of their own, likely without swimming trunks. Well, the farmer continued on down the road, eventually reaching the bridge where the '57 Chevy was parked, windows rolled down to keep the car cool. As the farmer passed, he just pulled the lever on the wagon he was hauling, a manure spreader. We got to the bridge just in time to witness that "thems that deserves it sometimes gets theirs in the end."

Historic Perspectives

With the retirement of Publisher Stu Legaard, Mike Carney takes over. Working closely with Carney, Editor In Chief Stange, and the rest of the staff, forge ahead on all fronts in order to maintain the presence of In-Fisherman in the fishing world. Part of the agreement in selling In-Fisherman in 1998 is for Al Lindner to appear on In-Fisherman Television through the 2002 viewing season. With no one available to take over the on-camera work, Stange does so, thus immediately increasing the on-screen presence of catfish.

Looking back on the In-Fisherman TV scene, we note that Stange appears in the first catfish segment ever shot for In-Fisherman in 1985. He and Toad Smith appear together in 6 segments from 1988 through 1990. Over the years Stange appears in more than 30 segments featuring catfish and in more than 10 videos, some of which are still on the market. By this time, Steve Hoffman is the other In-Fisherman personality doing on-camera work with catfish. Today, Stange, Rob Neumann, and Hoffman continue to do catfish segments.

Asked what his favorite catfish segment of all time is, Stange says, “Night Flatheads, vintage 1989, with Toad Smith and me eating Kentucky Fried by campfire light on a warm July night and catching the heck out of some pretty good ones. That one still tugs at the heart enough to bring a tear to the eye.”

Illustrations by Larry Tople

CHAPTER 47

DECEMBER 2001

Dances Along the Great Divide

IT HAPPENS TO ALL OF US ALONG THE WAY, this walk we love, this good life that is catfishing. It's Biblical, actually. Proverbial Biblical. No sooner do we get to thinking we have these crazy catfish figured and something just awful happens to humble us, the foolhardy, with the fish (or the weather) beating the bejeebbers out of us, leaving us standing doing that bbabalubabeebeebeebee thing, with our finger up and down between our lips. Pass me a little beeny with a propeller on top. Pretty, it isn't. Pathetic, it often is.

The Best Of Very Bad Times!

I'll not forget Toad Smith standing in the firelight that night so many summers back, the two of us younger sprouts then. Ace catmen? But of course. Many a big channel cat under our belts, by that time. Pro's pros, we were. Catfishing prodigies. I had even been writing a bit about catfish and catfishing by that time, so we obviously knew what we were doing, had to know what catfishing was all about.

Seemed logical and easy, this business about finally getting serious about flatheads. No problem. We beat most big channel cats by spooling up with 17-pound line, sometimes going to 20-pound at the heaviest, to pull fish from cover. Toad could pull channel cats from cover. In his prime he lifted a little, could benchpress 350, could squat nearly a half ton. Catfish, smatfish. Bring 'em on and we'll kick their . . . aaaactually, the fire scene took place along a sandbar on a fair-sized river in Minnesota. Flatheads there run to about 50 pounds. The average good fish on a good night was, and still is, a 30.

What to spool up with? Toad had a batch of 40-pound mono. Well, after fishing with 10, 17, and even 20, for our entire lives, 40 looked like rope. I looked at Toad. He looked at me real serious, wrinkling those bushy eyebrows. "Nothing in this river could break that! Hell's bells, a mako shark couldn't chew through this stuff!"

So there Toad stood in the flickering firelight, up to his knees in the water, looking off into the blackness beyond the edge of the light, rod in one hand, foot of broken line dangling from the rod tip. We'd set up on a sandbar opposite a huge timber snag, some 10 feet of water running along the face of the snag. Prime territory. Big suckers for bait. Big suckers. Placed as accurately as we could lob them to the face of the snag, the baits held in place in current along the face of the snag with 5 ounces of lead, the reels placed in freespool, clickers on, rods in bank sticks, just waiting.

That first bite was a classic: "Zzzzit! Zzzzzt!" Old big boy crunched the bait and refused to spit it. Then, "zzzzzzzzzzzzzzzttt," began slowly and steadily to move off. Toad's rod. Agile he was for a big fella, like a pheasant dog on point, what with five cheap colas and 10 Oreo cookies—sugar high—under his belt by that time of night, sand flying, heels clicking, as he raced into action, grabbing the rod, quickly and carefully placing the reel in gear, waiting ever so momentarily . . . and then—I can see this all happening as if replayed in slow motion—the hookset, mighty hookset, with Toad taking three steps back to recover from his own momentous upward sweep.

And then the rod stopped, Toad stopped, everything stopped, and the world for a moment stood still. Something had to give. Suddenly, Toad was like a huge tree bending in a strong wind, bending down, then pulling back, then back down, until—one step, two steps forward, the rod now pulled down and pointing directly at the snag, Toad stumbling farther forward, slipping, helplessly, into the water, rod and reel now extended at arms length, Toad about to lose the rod. The line snapped like a .22 caliber pistolshot in the night.

Toad's immediate observation was, as you might imagine, less than poetic. He further explained, quite graphically and with animated (frantic, actually) arm movements, once he returned fireside, that when he was a mere child working for fishing money, he had been shoveling manure in a farm feedlot and found himself on an approximate straight line between three bulls and a farmer rattling feed buckets, the result being approximately what he had just experienced—a real basic butt-kicking rodeo stampede in progress.

Butt kicked by catfish.

Actually, this all began with a letter from Lee Marek, Dixon, Missouri, who recalled my telling the Toad story once before, a story in which I had simplified and pacified Toad's comments following his flathead ordeal into a succinct "Kicked my butt," in referring to the results of that first encounter. The "Kicked my butt" reference is what inspired Marek to tell me about his got butt-kicked bout.

Seems he and his buddy Elva Sinden were fishing the Osage River two miles upstream from its mouth. To set the scene, picture, in Marek's words, "Two good-looking old fat men in bib overalls sitting comfortably in a big jonboat anchored up perfectly on a good deep hole." Marek, as he tells it, sports a thin gray beard and wears granny glasses. Even then he can still barely see beyond the end of his nose. Mr. Magoo comes to mind. He also wears a favorite fishing hat, a distinctive narrow-brimmed camo jungle hat (probably left over from 'Nam).

So there they were, this pair, anchored at the head of a 32-foot hole, current running heavy, the boat about 30 yards from shore. This is where Marek turns outdoor writer in his description of events: "I had cast out my 'Brute Forcin' rig, consisting of a super-strong 8-foot Eagle Claw Star Fire Trolling Rod, with a Penn 320 GTI reel loaded with 40-pound Berkley Big Game. A 3-ounce egg sinker held down a sliprig with a 5/0 Eagle Claw Kahle hook. I favor these hooks. The bait was a 5-inch piece of golden eye fillet, which I had scaled and cut into a baitfish shape. I think this bait offers the shape, flash, and odor of a fresh baitfish."

Marek continued: "The current was too strong for the clicker to hold on free spool, so I left the reel engaged, ready for action. I had the drag set heavy—so it would barely slip—and had cast about 70 feet downstream. The rod was in a rod holder set so the rod tip was just off to the side of the boat."

The boys had barely settled in for a cup of coffee, the way Marek tells it, when suddenly the rod tip bent down and back and set to bouncing. Line began to peel off steadily downriver against the heavy drag. Struggling, Marek managed to wrestle the rod out of the holder. No need to set the hook. Elva reeled in the other lines.

"Fetch up the anchor," Marek cried. "I can't stop this fish."

With the anchor up, the fish pulled the boys downstream at a clip slightly faster than the current, all the while still steadily taking line. "Tighten the drag," Elva said. "Don't let him get too far away and snag up."

Savvy advice, Marek thought. Reaching around with his left hand, he cranked down on the star drag, until it was just about all he could do to hold on. Sweat rolled down his forehead, and his hat had flipped back in the fashion of a rodeo rider, Yeehaa! They continued headlong downriver, passing a woman on a dock, who stood for a moment, mouth agape, astonished, then ran for the house, the sight of two old fat men, one of them grunting like a bison in heat while hauling on a huge fish, apparently more than she had bargained for on a quiet Missouri evening.

Finally, progress? As Marek stood with the rod doubled over, the fish turned and headed toward shore. They were at least 250 yards downriver at this point. Suddenly, another change of direction, the fish pulling hard upriver for the first time. As the fish burrowed deep, with the drag so tight it would slip only grudgingly, the fish surged again, dragging Marek around the back of the boat.

"I was losing my grip and my hand was cramping," he said. "I had to do something, so I slipped my left hand under the reel, spreading my fingers to get a better hold. Relief. That's when my middle finger slipped up onto the spool and, as the fish made another lunge, the level wind caught the end of my middle finger and squashed it against the sideplate."

So instantaneous and overwhelming was the pain that Marek couldn't talk, couldn't utter even a word, could only swing his head back and forth in pain, face red, eyes bulging, teeth clenched, a low guttural moan barely escaping from somewhere deep inside. The tip of his finger pinned flat against the sideplate blew up like a small balloon and turn black. Blood started oozing then spurting like an oil gusher from around the fingernail.

He staggered sideways, mouth still agape, eyes tearing, unable to utter a word, trying to show Elva the predicament. "That's when it got worse," Marek says. "To my horror, Elva, panicked by the sight of the bulging black finger, grabbed a towel and grabbed the line. He was going to try to break the line by hand. By hand, the numskull. Fifty-pound line. Elva, let me tell you, couldn't break 10-pound test if he tied it between a telephone pole and a speeding truck. Ahhh, ahhh! I still couldn't gather the strength or the composure to do anymore than weave my head back and forth in agony, frothing at the mouth, in near delirium from the pain. Every time Elva yanked on the line, more blood spurted from around my fingernail. I had the fish, the fish had me, and now Elva was spastically yanking on both of us.

"Just when matters couldn't get worse, Elva let go and unsheathed his knife. All I could mumble and moan was 'Augh! Augh!' as he came for me. "Shall I cut it?" he shouted at me as he stood there huffing and puffing in excitement, his face about two inches from mine. "Shall I cut it?"

"My finger off?" I yelped.

"The line, you moron! The line!"

"I squinted at my finger, tears streaming. I felt again the strength of the great fish. How big could it be? Over a hundred? Certainly the biggest fish I'd ever hooked and probably ever would. I waited a moment longer, the fish didn't budge, blood oozed, it hurt so bad my hair hurt. "Cut it!" I moaned. "Oh, please, cut it.' "

Marek and Elva live with the dream of the monster that was. Elva observed, correctly, that this fish had been in control of the situation from beginning to end, about 12 minutes. "It was shortly thereafter," Marek said, looking back on this miserable affair, "that I remembered Toad's immortal words, 'Kicked my butt.'"

BUTT KICKED BY CATFISH

Prevailing conditions also conspire to kick butt. Our old friend Zacker, an outdoorsman in the largest sense of the term, lived through the famous Armistice Day Storm of 1940, as it spread through the Dakotas that day in November. The Dakota storm apparently moved more slowly than the subsequent killer storm that overtook Minnesota and other parts of the Midwest. Still, Zacker, hunting geese on a sandbar in the lower Missouri near Yankton, South Dakota, barely had time to gather in decoys as he realized this was no typical storm a brewin'. Leaving the decoys on the bar, he rowed for the main shoreline, making shore just before the squall line swept across the river, savaging everything in its path. He and a friend spent the night huddled below their overturned boat, walking to safety the next afternoon. He said the thing that saved them was that the ground was so warm from the unusually warm fall weather that preceded the storm, which dumped 20 inches of snow and dropped the air temperature by 80 degrees.

That wasn't a direct catfish connect to dreaded conditions, though. Still, Zacker, the consummate commercial catman for almost 40 years during the 30s, 40s, 50s, and 60s, had his share of fishing dramas, many of them weather related. In one instance, both the weather and the fish conspired to have him "Dance the Great Divide," as he used to call a close call with death.

I make no claim to knowing the exact details of this adventure, it having been mentioned only a time or two in passing as we shared a campfire with Zacker late in his life. I gather, though, that Zacker used to pilot an old wooden 20-foot flatbottom boat, powered by a one-lung something-or-other. He towed a sleek 14-foot wooden rowboat, a classic for those times, behind the bigger boat. He used the big boat to haul his catch to dock, while he worked his lines with the maneuverable rowboat, once he was in the general fishing area. Zacker, although a small man, was a powerful sort, weathered and hardened by years of rowing and other outdoor work. Often as not he worked alone, braving the elements with wit and wile.

One of his favorite sets for big catfish, which he apparently often sold to be placed on spits and roasted in the manner of a hog or small calf, was a deep set along a portion of the old river channel, by then some 30 feet deep and at least a quarter mile from shore after the old river became a reservoir. Picture, too, the cold-weather clothing of the time, for this tale transpires during the last vestiges of fall. Pelt coats weighing 40 pounds or more had given way to heavily tanned, oiled, and waxed leathers, usually blackened by the oiling and waxing. A typical coat was about 3/8 inch thick overall with heavier patching along the seams, collar, and coat margins. One of these waxed leathers often weighed 20 pounds, and the wearer depended on it, quite effectively it seems, to shield himself from the elements, while wearing heavy wool clothing underneath for insulation. So Zacker was dressed that day in late October as he check his deep trotline sets for one last time before settling in to trap and hunt for the remainder of the year.

Zacker was a stubborn, hard, determined man, as a matter of course. When he fished, he fished all day, every day, until he had the fish he needed, the conditions rarely of consequence. He didn't question the day, just went, unless it was literally impossible. If conditions worsened along the way, he settled in, just worked longer and harder until he finished. Or he made crude camp, until he could complete the task at hand and return home. Ten miles downriver might mean a sunset return on a good day, a return days later in difficult times.

This day was difficult from the start. The flatbottom labored downriver through four-foot seas, the wind blowing sleet at a cross-current from the north, this portion of reservoir running downstream in a general southeasterly direction. Zacker set course, sticking to the sheltered north shore, traveling from point to point, moving through backwater areas when he could. He beached and tied the big boat a half mile upriver from his sets, so he could row with the heavy seas to reach his sets.

His options after running each set depended on his catch. The plan apparently was to gather the catch, then, if the catch was good, with the boat running heavy, to row to the nearest sheltered shoreline, stash the catch, along with the setline (for again, this was the last run of the year), then row back to gather the next set. After running all the sets, he would row back upriver to the big boat, then run downriver to retrieve the entire catch.

What I know is that the heaviest weight on a line was set upcurrent, each line running about 50 yards downcurrent and holding only about 5 hooks. The sets were marked at the downcurrent end with a marker line connected on the surface to a quart whiskey bottle. The upcurrent marker was smaller, a pint bottle.

These were sets for big fish, not numbers. The hooks were large, even for the time, running bigger than the 12/0 O'Shaugnesseys of our day, this at a time when big hooks were equated with big fish, in no small measure because the baits often were large, carp and smaller catfish, usually dead and weighing around a pound. The catch might be flathead catfish and, I gather, big blues, even though blue cats today do not roam this reservoir. I gather, too, that big fish were not always weighed and sold by the pound, but were simply sold as "big fish" when the dressed carcass surpassed about 25 pounds. A much bigger fish might fetch more money, but not much. Big was big enough.

Zacker began by lifting the quart whiskey line and the lighter downcurrent weight, usually a rock of ten pounds or so, and cutting the rock free. Any hooked fish, while probably not played out, were by this time resigned to being tethered to hook and line and generally were resting on the bottom, facing current. Once the downcurrent line was free, Zacker would, on calm days, fight in the fish nearest the end of the downcurrent end of the line, then pull the boat upcurrent farther along toward the heavy weight. In heavy weather, the process was reversed, with Zacker cutting the downcurrent weight, then rowing upcurrent to begin the process of fish removal by drifting downcurrent. He would struggle to lift a portion of the upcurrent line along with, hopefully, the first fish, the weight being too heavy to lift along with a fish. Gathering in the first fish, he held tight to the line still connected to the heavy weight, measuring his movement downcurrent by slowly releasing his grip on the 500-pound line.

Only with the fish in the boat did Zacker row back upcurrent to attempt to lift the heavy upcurrent weight. Usually the weight was just cut and left, with a new end added to the line before the next set. I do not know the weight of the upcurrent rock, but guess they surely surpassed 25 pounds and may have been as much as 30 or 40.

On this day, Zacker struggled past several hooks without gathering a fish, slipping downcurrent almost out of control as the wind howled and threatened to tear him away from the main line still held fast below by the heavy weight. It was then, as the wind gusted, that Zacker lost control of the line, slipping to the boat floor, the line sawing over the gunnel, as the boat, caught by wind and current, surged over a huge swell. Without thinking, he struggled to get up, the line peeling across his back as a hook snapped like a bow-shot arrow over the gunnel, catching him in the lower part of his back, the huge hook sinking through 3/8 inches of leather coat, at least an inch of straining human flesh, and back through another 3/8 inches of coat.

Epic moment. Lightning flashed across the dark day as wind drove sleet horizontally across huge swells. Zacker raised himself for a moment midboat, assuming a wrestler's hunched stance, reaching for the heavens, arms and fingers curled, head thrown back in agony. "I didn't have time to scream," he said. With his back to the agony of hook and line, a swell pulled the line taut again and smashed him against the opposing gunnel. "The next swell would rip me from the boat and I would be gone," he remembered. "But the impact of the hook and line had ripped my coat open and my knife, sheathed on my belt, was already unlatched. I grabbed the knife with my right hand as I reached with my left to find the line, straining against the line taut to the hook in my back. I remember one long loud scream of agony as I swung the knife.

"I was free. Cutting the other end of the line, I slumped into the boat." The hook wouldn't be removed without a lot of whiskey more than a day later. "Ruined a good coat," he observed there at that campfire so much later in life, as he looked back on one of his many Dances Along the Great Divide.

And what might your story be?

» THE CUTTING EDGE WORLD RECORD CATFISH!
DECEMBER 2004
In-Fisherman
THE JOURNAL OF FRESHWATER FISHING
HOTTEST NEW
BASS
LURES
» WORLD CLASS PICKS
FOR RESERVOIR CRAPPIES
WALLEYES ON BIG WATERS
BIG BASS–NEW HOT SPOTS
READING WINTER PIKE
PLUS! SCIENCE SECRETS ADVENTURES NEW STUFF CHOWDER
THE SPIRIT OF IN-FISHERMAN » PAGE 6

Historic Perspectives

It is the winter of 2003 when Cody Mullinnex pulls the world-record blue cat he names Splash from Texoma Reservoir, takes great care to keep it alive, and donates the fish to the state of Texas for display. Splash becomes the most famous catfish of all time, perhaps the most famous world-record fish of all time. The fish appears with Mullinnex and Stange on In-Fisherman Television in 2004. Splash dies in 2007, from an infection from an old hook wound.

True to Stange's prediction, another world-record fish is pulled from the lower Mississippi River several years later, a fish weighing 125 pounds. We await fruition of Stange's prediction of a fish approaching 150 pounds. He believes at least a dozen waters exist where such fish might swim.

Catfishing remains a vibrant sport due to obvious factors. Channel catfish swim in 44 states and 5 provinces, so they are widely available. In many areas they're abundant, offering fishing that allows harvest as well as fishing for trophy fish. Flathead and blue-cat waters also offer the opportunity for harvest, but these fish grow to be the third or fourth largest freshwater sportfish in North America. Only white sturgeon, alligator gar, and lake sturgeon get bigger. Catfish are colossal in size and character, a point made often by the author over the years.

CHAPTER 48

DECEMBER 2004

150 or Bust!

THE UNDISPUTED WORLD-RECORD BLUE catfish of 121.5 pounds caught by Cody Mullinnex of Howe, Texas, late last winter is one of the most magnificent creatures I've seen. "Splash," as the fish is called, measured 58 inches by 39 inches, longer and a little leaner than most other huge blue cats that have in recent years approached or held the record. Some past world-record-class blue cats have had the proportions of a 50-gallon drum. Splash looks more like a world-class athlete of gifted proportions—an in-his-prime, sweet-on-his-feet Mohammed Ali, as compared to the hulking George Foreman in his later heavyweight years.

Rolling A World Record Blue!

Swimming slowly, effortlessly, in almost suspended animation in the 24,000-gallon tank at the Texas Freshwater Fisheries Center in Athens, Texas, Splash looks to be a healthy younger fish with a ways to grow, yet. If records from the 1800s are to be believed and a 15-year trend in big-blue catches from around the country are apt indication, then my prediction of a fish weighing in at 150 pounds may become true before long, the Shrek of blue catfish.

On that fateful day, the 14-foot Shakespeare surf rod buckled from the tip down to the butt in the rod holder, which had been placed in the sandy bank of the south Lake Texoma shoreline. Mullinnex lifted against the heavy fish as it surfaced, rolled, and flipped its great body out there 100 yards from shore. "Just a half hour before, I'd landed a 56-pound blue," he said. "This fish was way—I mean, waay—bigger."

The battle lasted about 20 minutes, man and 20-pound-test line against mammoth fish. Mullinnex didn't get a good look at the fish again until it was right along shore. "I saw it close up and thought, 'This fish is a hundred pounds,'" he said. He went right in after it to push it over, then onto, a shallow shoreline shelf.

"All I knew was that it was huge. I just kept thinking a hundred pounds," he said. "That's when I used my cellphone to call Jason (longtime fishing partner, Jason Holbrook). "'I need help,' I told him. 'And bring the 100-pound scale.'"

Holbrook and Mullinnex grew up fishing, spending a lot of time together along the shores of Lake Texoma about a half hour from their home. "For the last 20 years or so, we have been fishing specifically for big cats," Holbrook told me. "People are catching a lot of 50- and 60-pound blues these days—quite a few into the 80s, actually." Holbrook held the Texas state record for several years with an 80-pound-class blue.

So Mullinnex and Holbrook are no strangers to big catfish. This was no purely lucky catch—man fishing with Snoopy pole and wiener off a marina dock. This was world-record by design—at least as much design as is possible in such instances.

Holbrook and I have corresponded over the years, he sending me a letter in 1996 asking about the best hooks for shorefishing. Curiously, I'd called him the week before Mullinnex caught the fish, just to see if he was fishing and how things were going.

As Holbrook and his brother helped Mullinnex, the fish bottomed-out the 100-pound scale. "We'd actually talked 'what ifs' before many times," Mullinnex said. "I mean, this is what we were fishing for. Something like this is always a surprise—yet it wasn't a total surprise. We knew that fish like this were out there. We knew our fishing system worked. So here we were, and here the fish was. It happened. And now what?

"Well, we release 95 percent of the fish we catch—certainly everything above 20 pounds. It makes no sense to kill such incredible fish. Big fish are priceless, swimming out there alive, inspiring further hope that someone else might come in contact with them. The only way we can grow these monsters is to release all the bigger fish so they can continue to grow. Our immediate concern was to keep this huge fish in good shape, weigh it, and then release it. We used Jason's big stainless-steel beach cart filled with water to transport the fish."

So Mullinnex became not just world-record holder, but the first angler of such status with the conscience and concern to keep a high-profile record fish alive. It was at a local tackle shop where the fish was finally weighed that a conservation officer suggested the fish be donated to the Texas Freshwater Fisheries Center, to be on display and inspire those who visit.

Mullinnex agrees that his record probably will eventually fall. If it does, both he and Holbrook won't bet against the fish coming from Texoma, although there are plenty of other great blue-cat fisheries around the country. It's likely fish of this quality swim in at least a dozen areas of the country, almost certainly in portions of the middle and lower Mississippi, the lower Missouri, the lower Ohio, and sections of rivers and associated reservoirs that connect with these rivers. The Tennessee River is a top bet. The Osage. The Cumberland. Along with traditional monster-fish-producing reservoirs like Santee-Cooper. Many other Texas reservoirs and some in Oklahoma, too, as well as others in the Southeast. And up-and-coming reservoirs where the fish haven't been that long but have already proven to grow huge quickly—places like southern California.

But I begin to digress in a direction I love to head. You can return another day to hear me tell stories of the ongoing search for world-record-class catfish. The story here is the straightforward system that Holbrook and Mullinnex use to catch a ton of blue cats from shore each winter.

ABOUT TEXOMA AND RESERVOIR BLUE CAT LOCATION

First, a bit about Lake Texoma, which straddles the Oklahoma-Texas border a little more than an hour north of Dallas. Gizzard shad and threadfin shad key catfish location in this huge reservoir. The story here is somewhat the same for other reservoirs in the country.

During much of the year, bigger blue cats hold in the deep water associated with the main-reservoir channel, or along deep cuts at or near the mouths of creek arms. During winter, though, beginning in November—certainly by mid December—as waters cool through the 60°F range and into the 50°F and even the 40°F range, shad move into the headwaters of the Red River and into the shallower portions of creek arms. Of course, some blue cats stay deep most of the year, including during winter. Still, lots of fish also follow some shad shallow.

Splash was caught in the Big Mineral Arm of the reservoir, which pokes south from the main east-west run of the Red River and the main portion of Texoma into north Texas. Holbrook: "The Big Mineral Arm's about 8 miles long and we mostly fish the lowest end—that portion in the Hageman Wildlife Refuge. Most of this area's no more than about 10 feet deep. Most of the fish follow a gradual drop-off line somewhere off the shoreline, especially windward shorelines where the shad stack up. You don't always have to fish facing into the wind, though. Just generally consider which way the wind's been blowing for several days before you fish. A wind switch doesn't hurt, so long as its general direction has been into a shoreline for several days. Even this isn't an absolute predictor of where the fish might be. They can be wherever they want. They just roam trying to stay with the shad. The main thing is to get out there and fish."

Mullinnex: "It's no secret where I caught the fish. I originally highlighted the general spot on a map for anyone to see. It's where we fished to shoot a segment for the In-Fisherman television show for 2005. There's no reason to keep such a secret, because the spot's not a secret. It's a good place to fish, but there are 20 other places just as good, just about like it, around the lower end of this creek arm—which, as Jason said, for the most part gets no deeper than about 10 to 15 feet. Splash bit about 100 yards from shore, but the water out there was only about 5 or 6 feet deep.

"A foot or two difference in depth can make a difference, sometimes. The bottom's mostly sand, with washout edges here and there that offer a little bit deeper water. Sometimes these gradual drop-off edges help to gather some fish. Lots of places that we fish, you can wade out 30 yards or so to make an even longer cast, checking for a drop-off. Cast out and count the weight down. You can pretty well guess how deep it is. Still, tremendously long casts aren't always a key. Sometimes we catch fish 50 yards out. It still pays, though, to be able to make long casts. That's one reason for the surf tackle."

Holbrook: "In the end, after you get the basic presentation system worked out, catching big fish is a matter of percentages—picking the right spot, to be sure, but also how often you fish, how many rods and lines you put out, having fresh bait, and so on. The day we fished with you, for example, we set up on the same location where Cody caught the record. Yet, that day, as you remember, friends fishing 200 yards south of us were into way more fish than we were. The biggest fish they caught was only about 20 pounds. They must have caught 60 fish that day. It was nonstop action for them, while we caught probably two dozen fish in about 5 hours—and our big fish was about 20 pounds, too.

"Once we pick a spot and use our beach carts to haul all our equipment down and get set up, well, we've made a pretty big commitment to a spot. It isn't that easy to pick up and move a bunch of times. We usually have a set of at least 15 rods—sometimes more—spread up and down 100 to 200 yards of beach. Sometimes the fish seem to be in one spot along the beach more than in others. Sometimes the fish are just spread everywhere. You just have to get out there and get plenty of baits out, so the fish have a chance to tell you where they're at."

The guys gather fresh shad by throwing cast-nets in the back ends of creek arms the night before they fish. "Fresh bait's certainly important," Mullinnex said. "First, it's firm, so it doesn't throw off on a long cast. Secondly, it just fishes better—attracts more fish. Keep it bagged and on ice. We often go through at least 100 baits on an outing."

World Record Terminal Rigging

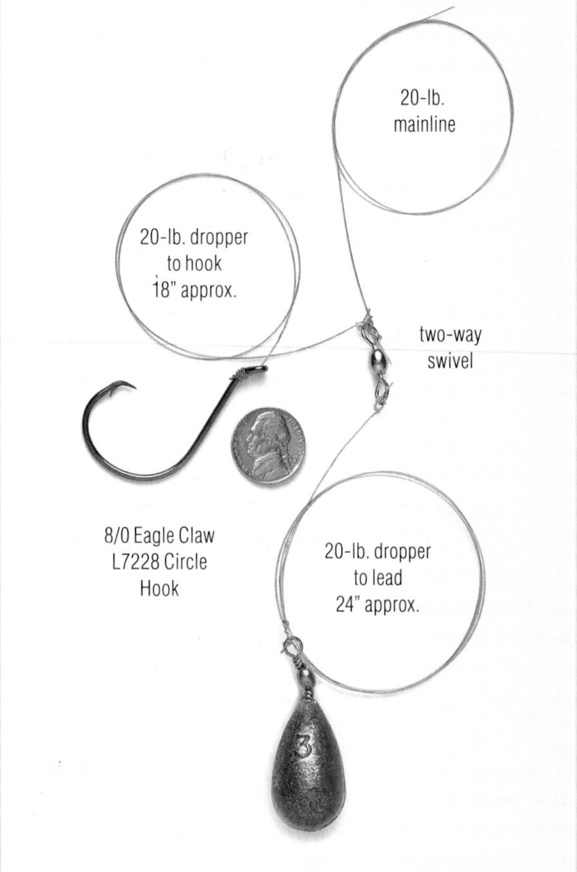

20-lb. mainline

20-lb. dropper to hook 18" approx.

two-way swivel

8/0 Eagle Claw L7228 Circle Hook

20-lb. dropper to lead 24" approx.

Holbrook: "The other places that produce fish on Texoma during winter are deeper, shorter creek arms closer to or directly connected to the main reservoir. Points at the mouths of or inside these creek arms often produce fish. Again, the fish are searching for shad.

"We fish almost entirely during the day in the shallow portions of Texoma, where the water's usually dirtied by wind. Some anglers fish at night in the deeper creek arms, where the water's much clearer. The Big Mineral Arm isn't the only shallow area. Wherever you can get at shallow shoreline in the upper end of the reservoir, you may get into fish. Lots of that area, though, is only accessible by airboat."

TACKLE

Since scoring the noteworthy catch, Mullinnex and Holbrook have refined their tackle just a little, with the help of the people from Berkley, Shakespeare, and Eagle Claw. Some of their old 14-foot fiberglass Shakespeare Alpha Big Water spinning rods (ABWS 514-2M) have been replaced with 12-foot Ugly Stik Custom Graphite Surf Rods (USCSSP 1112-2M).

"No question the graphite construction of the Custom Ugly Stiks helps to whip 8 ounces of lead out farther than you can cast with the longer fiberglass poles," Mullinnex observes. "The rods are a lot lighter, too. We still fish with some 14-foot fiberglass poles, though. We proved you can fish effectively with the fiberglass poles. If you want to kick it up a notch, try the Customs. They're a great-looking rod, too."

The reel of choice is the Shakespeare Prius Bigwater Spinning Reel, the P480, which is the largest available and can hold 200 yards of 30-pound monofilament, or about 300 yards of 20-pound. Holbrook: "Snags aren't much of a problem in most of the areas we fish. We also often need to make long casts, so we want to fish with the lightest line possible. Twenty-pound Berkley Big Game is perfect. Go any lighter and you snap sinkers off on a cast. Go heavier and it cuts casting distance. The 20-pound's heavy enough to land huge fish. Cody proved that."

The terminal rigging they use is a dropline of about 24 inches, tied to the end of a two-way swivel which is tied into the mainline. The weight is added to the end of the dropline. Meanwhile, a hook dropper about 18 inches long is tied off the top rung of the two-way swivel. They use 8/0 Eagle Claw L7228 circle hooks.

After making the cast, the drag on the reel's set so it gives gradually by pulling line just above the reel. The rod butt is placed in the rod holder, with the rod tip up at about a 45-degree angle to the water. They keep a tight line to the bait. When a fish eats the bait, the tight line makes the hook point catch flesh. As the fish moves farther, the combination of the stretch of the line and the bending rod in the holder keeps the hook point digging in and finally setting.

Mullinnex: "There's no way for fish to reject the hook, unless for some reason the hook point happens to get covered by a portion of the bait. It's fine to let an aggressive fish load the rod before picking the rod out of the holder and reeling. No need to set the hook. When fish aren't aggressive, but you can tell one has taken the bait and is just lying there, just ease the rod out of the holder, point the tip out at 45 degrees and start reeling. No setting. Just get the rod to load. Remember that the drag has to be set firmly enough to keep the line taut, yet just loose enough so it will give, if a big fish eats and surges off before you can get the pole out of a holder.

"We usually monitor all the rods from a central position on the beach. If we get the rods really spread out, an angler monitors a particular stretch of shoreline. With the surf rods, you can see the rod tips from quite a way to tell if fish are there. We constantly walk up and down the line of rods, occasionally moving the baits in a little bit. Sometimes a bait gets into a spot that makes it hard for a fish to reach, so it's important to reposition the baits occasionally by moving them just a bit.

"We also sweeten our baits at least every half hour. Just reel the baits in and give them a pinch to get the body juices flowing. Don't hesitate to switch baits. Fresh bait triggers more fish.

"Most days we're set up by sunrise. Some days there's competition for spots, but not too bad, so far. Really, almost every foot of shoreline in the Hageman Refuge can produce fish. If the bite's not happening, we might move to a different spot for the afternoon or evening bite."

"So, did fame and fortune come calling along with the record?" I asked Mullinnex.

"Well, not exactly," he admitted. "The award ceremony by the state (Texas) was fun. You know that— you were there at the Fisheries Center in Athens. The fish got featured in a lot of papers, especially around Texas and Oklahoma. *Sports Illustrated* ran a short item on the record. You put us—Holbrook, his brother, and Mullinnex—on the cover of last year's *Catfish Guide.* That was exciting. Got lots of great comments about that. The aforementioned tackle companies helped us out. We shot a short television segment with you on how we fish. That was great. Now this story. But I really didn't make any money on the fish.

"The best part to this day is knowing the fish is on display in Athens. Hearing about all the people that drive to Athens just to see Splash. Hearing all the wonderful comments about how incredible the fish is, swimming in the tank and showing off for everyone. Knowing that the fish inspires at least some people to think about not killing big fish. It's been a great year—just a great year, and we're happy to be able to help others catch more catfish, if we can."

I was at that point reminded of the P. S. on Holbrook's 1996 letter to me, in which he'd told me about his fishing. It said: *"I am going to beat that 111-pound world record this coming winter. So be ready to hear from me again."*

Obviously, it took more than a winter, and it didn't happen to Holbrook, but to his best fishing friend. Holbrook couldn't have been happier. I wouldn't bet against it happening to one of the guys again. Holbrook's turn, this time. After that, since Holbrook and Mullinnex are both just 28, maybe time for Mullinnex again.

I can see it now on T-shirts across blue-cat country: "150 Or Bust!"

Historic Perspectives

This article written for the 30th Anniversary issue of In-Fisherman in 2005, addresses the overall topic of this book, eventually becoming its model, as the author offers a long look back at his involvement in the catfishing world.

We interpose here—for it works as well here as anywhere—the story of the first time Stange and Toad Smith see the now-famous Red River channel cat fishery at Selkirk, Manitoba, just north of Winnipeg. It's early June 1985, so about the time Chapter 1 of this book is unfolding. The boys have fished their way up the Red River from Breckenridge, Minnesota, to Grand Forks and Drayton, and are fishing in the Emerson area. They talk with a couple anglers who relate this story: "We drive down the hill on the west bank of the river just below the dam, past Lilly Ann's to the boat landing, where two large tents are set up. Nobody's fishing below the dam. Nobody.

We enter one of the tents and find women canning something. It's catfish. In the other tent, men are cleaning giant channel catfish. They tell us there's no limit, that the fish are biting just like they usually do—more 20-pound fish than you can handle. On the dock is a 20-foot-long stringer made out of 1/4-inch chain link with big fish waiting to be processed. The canned fish are eventually loaded into a trailer and it goes back home to Iowa."Smith and Stange go to see for themselves. The tents are gone, but true to the story no one else is fishing. They head out to test the water for themselves. That first morning they total more than 40 fish surpassing about 18 pounds, with the biggest fish going about 25. Unbelievable.

It is the beginning of publicizing this fishery. Talking with Manitoba fishery officials, Stange calls the fishery not just world class but an international treasure, the rarest of rare finds as fisheries go. With the increased fishing pressure that accompanies writing about the fishery, Manitoba implements harvest regulation that prohibits taking any big fish. It's one of the wisest proactive moves ever made to protect a unique fishery. The fishing is as good today as when the boys first got there in '85.

CHAPTER 49

JUNE 2005

30 Years on the Road to the New Age of Catfishing

I HAVE BEEN WRITING about catfishing for over three decades. My first published article appeared in *Fishing Facts* magazine about 1975, several years before I began to write for *In-Fisherman.*

Others have written about catfish over the years. But when I was growing up in the 1950s and early 1960s, virtually no information was available about catfishing. Meanwhile, Joe Brooks was writing beautifully and instructively about trout in *Outdoor Life.* Jason Lucas was helping to make bass the most popular sportfish in North America, with his passionate columns in *Sports Afield.* Eventually, Homer Circle, another master of the craft, would take over for Lucas at *Sports Afield.* And all through that era, Buck Perry was changing the way some anglers approached the overall fishing process with his book, *Spoon Plugging* and his writings for *Fishing Facts.*

Perry really was the only one from that era who had a formula for teaching how to fish successfully—at least until *In-Fisherman* came along. As the years proceeded, we found that Perry was generally right about everything, but many of the ideas needed tinkering. Perry also didn't specifically address the world of catfish.

Others Have Written About Catfish . . . But!

Being a student of Perry's, I attempted in the early 1970s to adapt his terminology and thinking to the process of finding channel catfish in rivers. So the deepest water (the holes) was the home of the catfish (their sanctuary), and I looked for migration routes from their home to the feeding grounds nearby. In broad theory it sort of worked, so long as the hole an angler chose to fish was a good one.

In the 1960s, though, before I discovered Perry and modified his thinking and finally arrived at my own workable way to approach river fishing, I fished like so many of the people still out there struggling today. I'd find a hole or park by a bridge and set up and sit there, dreaming of all the big catfish that just had to be waiting for my bait. Sometimes I'd even move a time or two during an afternoon and luck into some fish. I also went through the "bait thing" just as certainly as everyone else did. There had to be a magic bait, didn't there? Shrimp, perhaps? Chicken livers? Bowkers was my first experience with dipbait. Along the way, I began to see that some areas produced fish while most did not, and that bait, while important, was surely secondary to being on fish.

A moment that is as clear to me now as when it happened that day in June so long ago—I must have been about 13 years old—was when I biked to the Little Rock River, about 9 miles north of my home in Northwest Iowa. That June the water in this little river was low and remarkably clear. There was a tree leaning over and into my favorite fishing spot. I crawled out onto the tree for a look and was surprised that my perfect hole was actually almost entirely shallow and not much of a hole at all. Furthermore, there were no catfish. Not one. I had spent many days fishing this area over the years,

A classic Larry Tople illustration capturing Toad Smith, the Mighty Toadmonster, in action, racing toward a "clicking" reel as we waited for flatheads around a midnight fire sometime during the late 1980s.

believing it surely to be the home of giant catfish.

As I walked downriver that day, I could occasionally see fish holding in the relatively deeper water along cutbanks, usually below faster-running water—shallow areas called riffles. It would be years, though—the 1970s—before I accepted that rivers run in a continuous series: riffle-hole-run; riffle-hole-run; with only a few of the holes being prime habitat for catfish. The best holes usually were deeper—often the deepest holes in a section of river—and usually had other associated habitat such as timber snags and, perhaps, boulders or other cover.

That summarizes the thrust of my first writing about catfish, that the smart catfish angler should walk (or float) quickly and cover a lot of water, surveying large stretches of river, looking for the best catfish habitat which, once found, almost always produces the best catfishing. No need to spend time fishing most river areas, because most areas hold few catfish. Catfish, especially larger ones, congregate only in the best habitat areas. With experience, many marginal areas can be sorted out visually, without even fishing. Again, walk far and fish fast. Catch the active catfish and move on, unless your target is giant catfish, in which case the strategy might be to return during prime time, such as at night, and wait them out. By that time, anglers should know that the place they park is prime territory for big fish.

I began to work with In-Fisherman in 1977, writing the Bits and Pieces column. Catfish weren't my only interest. I fished extensively for walleyes, smallmouths, muskies, panfish—really anything available, including carp. I joined In-Fisherman fulltime in 1981, and made my case for including catfish in *In-Fisherman* magazine. The first article appeared in 1984, the June issue, Book #55. It was a 12-pager outlining fundamentals for catching channel catfish—location in rivers, reservoirs, pits and ponds, along with standard presentations for catching catfish from those environments.

Many more articles followed, until we eventually promised (as we do to this day) to feature at least one article on catfish in each issue of In-Fisherman. So far as I know, it was the first time in angling history that a writer had a free hand to write extensively about a group of fish that had received only occasional attention over the years. I wrote primarily about channel catfish and flatheads, touching on blue cats only a little because in those early years, I didn't have much opportunity to fish for them.

This remains Stange's favorite Tople rendition of "The three skunks" sitting around a fire.

Along the way, two characters helped sell catfishing, not just to longtime catfish fans, but also to a larger audience that had never considered catfishing before. Zacker was a crotchety old commercial fisherman and river scoundrel with a curious and colored past. Otis Smith and I discovered him (or he us) in our wanderings in search of catfish in the 1980s. Zacker had long been a solitary man, but he was nearing the end of his life, and Otis and I just sort of naturally connected with him. He really never told anyone but Otis and me about his remarkable life in the outdoors, in what was still, in his day, wild country. Soon enough we were "his boys." That's the three of us pictured by Larry Tople in

Larry Tople has been In-Fisherman's cover artist for 30 years, a remarkable stint and surely an important part of the success of the magazine. Larry loves doing caricatures that captured the mad escapades of Toad, Stange, and Zacker.

the lead illustration for this article.

One of my first stories about catching big flatheads intertwined Zacker's plainspoken advice about big fish with a storyline that included some of his retrospectives on life on the big river, before the dams. We received more feedback on that article—Zacker Bring A Bigger Cat—than any article we published that year.

My other catfish conspirator was Otis Smith, better know as Toad, a longtime acquaintance from my days as a schoolteacher in Iowa. We didn't become good friends until after he suffered a life-altering heart attack in the 1984. He was simply the most memorable character I've ever known, a kid in the body of a large man who was always on the edge of his next practical joke, an easy man with a handshake and a gap-toothed smile, never at a loss for a story, easy to get to know—and knowledgeable about catfish to the point that, once I began to bring the Mighty Toadmonster into my writings, he became larger than life to most catfish anglers—indeed, to the point that even today more than 10 years after his death, about once a month someone calls or writes wanting to talk with him.

I used Toad as a sounding board for ideas and he easily played the part of expert, which he was on all things practical. A lot of what I thought and wanted to say on a more progressive note always

sounded better coming from him, and so that's the way I often chose to say it. Funny how well people listen when it's just the right messenger carrying the message. Funny too how successful you can be in changing ideas or making points when it doesn't really matter who's getting credit for the progress.

Of course, stories remain to be told about my adventures with Toad and Zacker. Perhaps someday when I get a little time they can become the final chapters to a book I'd like to write. I'm going to take a moment to show you how I might assemble a typical story. First, we need an introduction, which might go something like this.

The moon quickly became a full golden orb that evening on the river in August 1989, a contrast *to the morning sunrise, which had been an almost vicious blood red. A vicious sunrise, Zacker announced, meant rain in every other month except August, always "bonedry as hell" in his native South Dakota. Zacker, approaching 90 at that point, was rarely wrong about the weather or anything else outdoors, and he didn't need a weatherman, reading sign like a native 19th century scout from experience born of more than 50 years outdoors on the Missouri River doing commercial deeds of one sort or another, almost always legal, because, as he'd tell it, "almost everything was legal on the river in them days."*

Zacker was no shrinking violet. He spent time as a bootlegger in his younger years, a lower-ranking member of the western outlaws of the day, moving the goods from Canada into Montana, through one of the Dakotas and Minnesota, on to a pickup point in Wisconsin; or sometimes down through eastern Wyoming and into Nebraska, then on to Omaha by the northern route through Valentine and O'Neill, the whiskey, depending on the route, eventually headed for Chicago or Kansas City.

His life changed in a moment when he was bushwhacked and a load highjacked in a double-cross. He was left for dead in a roadside ditch in eastern South Dakota. Not daring to see a doctor, he tumbled himself into a railroad car and made it to Sioux City, then on to a farm place along the Missouri River near Yankton, all the while holding in his bowels with his hands, the hole eventually stitched with catgut by a friend who did the same for horses marred by barbed wire. It was the beginning of Zacker's somewhat tamer life on the Missouri River, trapping, hunting, fishing, and bartending during the dead of winter.

So, now that the reader knows a bit about Zacker, it would be Toad's turn, the idea being to set the scene, set a mood, and also to seal the character of these two overwhelmingly unique men, whom readers would have the fortune to spend a night with on the river. These sorts of stories, I've been told, left readers with a sense that whatever transpired, a deep friendship ran through it all—and so it did. Advice about fishing tactics, conservation, or life outdoors in general, offered in such a setting, coming from characters that loomed a little larger than normal life, was compelling and unforgettable.

It seems a mistake, sitting here now, that I haven't written in recent years in a similar vein about catfishing. Zacker and Toad, though, have

Finding Catfish in Rivers (circa 1984)

Snags or deep holes are catfish homes or holding areas in smaller rivers. The catfish in these areas usually aren't actively feeding, so it makes sense to fish other areas first. Still, make sure you're at least fishing in the vicinity of a good catfish holding area.

Once you've found this, generally walk upstream to a steeper-gradient riffle area ***(AREA A).*** *Drift a bait through the area and into the pool* ***(AREA B)*** *immediately below. Continue fishing by checking backwash areas associated with the riffle* ***(AREA C).*** *Make sure to fish other backwash areas* ***(AREA D)*** *and the tail end of the pool* ***(AREA E).*** *The last places to check are the deepest part of holes or the water in front of, or behind, snags.*

Repeat this procedure in a riffle area immediately below a catfish holding area. The same basic procedure applies to fishing large rivers, where only the scale changes.

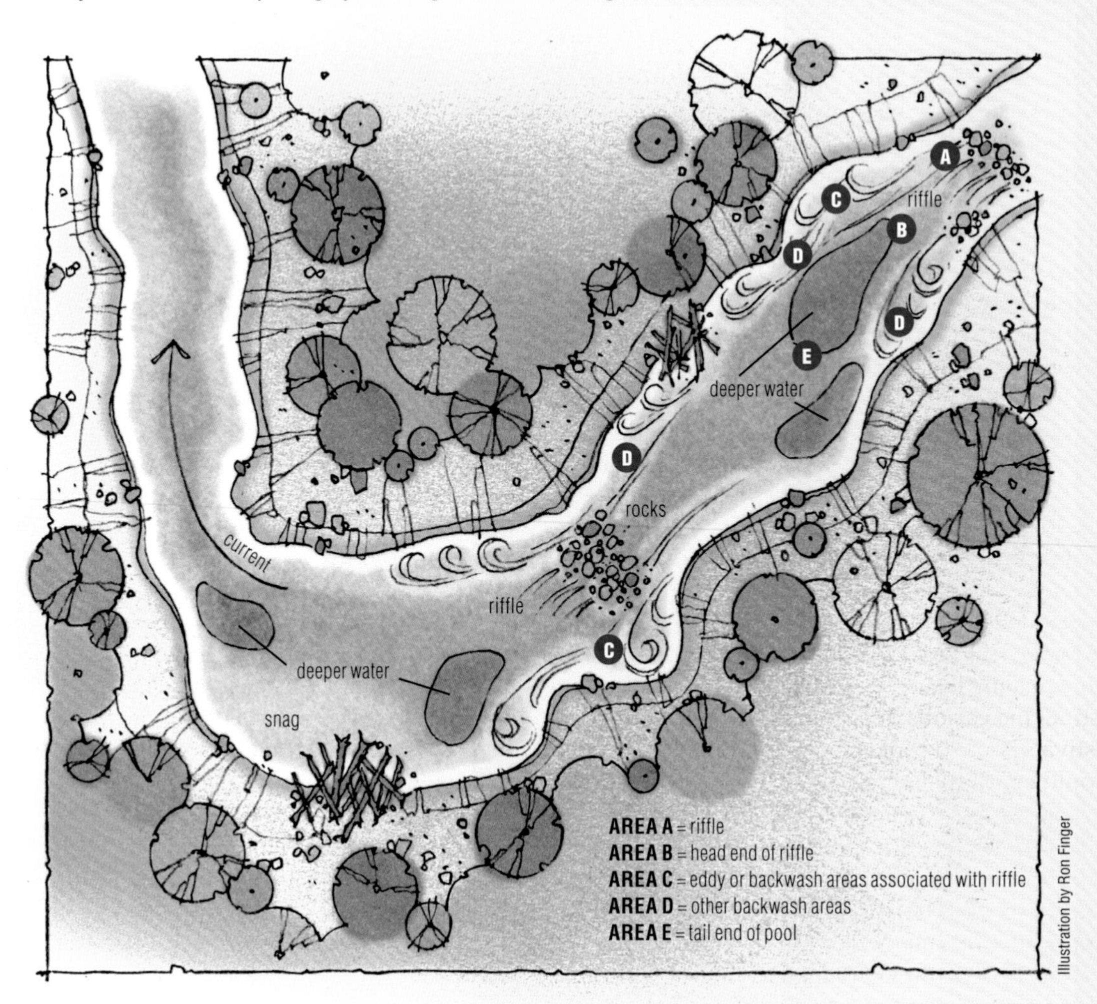

been dead for over a decade. In the meantime, my world has also changed and I no longer have that much time to write. Along the way, Staff Fishery Scientist and Editor Steve Quinn also began to offer advice about catfish. Eventually, our present In-Fisherman Publisher Steve Hoffman was hired as an editor, to take over many of my duties related to writing about catfish and catfishing.

Catfishing has changed, but still not so much as most of the rest of the fishing world. Can you imagine an ESPN Catfish Saturday? I surely can, even though I know it's not bound to happen soon. Would that I could have the opportunity to produce and direct such programming. Can you imagine what could be done with the larger scope of the catfish world, the sweeping history of it all, the hunt for truly giant fish, all the various down-home settings, the catfish festivals, catfish cookery, the unique characters? It would be fascinating.

Part of the problem in catfishing, even though they remain one of the most popular groups of fish in North America, is the lack of industry advertising and overall industry interest targeted at catfish anglers. Catfish are of merely passing consequence and fall under the very large shadow of the main market, which targets bass. The fact that walleye tournaments and walleye fishing have been quite successfully marketed within the fishing world, though, serves as notice on what could be done with catfishing. The base of walleye anglers is just over 3 million, while at least 7 million catfish anglers are in the marketplace. Would that I had another lifetime to help make this all happen.

Would too that we could have continued with a subscription-based magazine about catfishing, our original *Catfish In-Sider,* which debuted in 1994 at 4 issues a year. Most publishing formulas depend on a combination of advertising and subscription revenue to make a go of it. With minimal advertising in the mix right now, the best we can hope to do is continue with an annual *Catfish Guide* in April each year.

Certainly, catfish and catfishing have become much more mainstream in the last 15 years. Quite a few articles now appear in national and regional magazines. Some books are on the market, the best I think still being our original *Catfish Fever,* and our first two books in what is to be a four-book In-Fisherman Critical Concept series, discussing fundamentals (Book 1), location (Book 2), and various presentation methods (Books 3 and 4) for catfish. A quick look on the web also turned up at least a dozen sites focusing specifically on catfish.

Catfish have also made progress on other fronts, especially in regard to regulation and management. The biggest thing still missing in some southern states is statute recognition of catfish as sportfish or gamefish, which would require those states to manage the fish more conservatively, as is generally the case in other states—establishing limits based on science and, hopefully, also to give more protection to larger fish. I could go on at length about this, as

Advice On Rigs and Riggings (more from 1984)

Catfish rigs can be simple or involved, depending on the bait used and where the rigs are fished. Three simple drift rigs are:

(1) *Hook and split-shot rig: Add split shot 8 to 12 inches above a bait. Hook size should match the bait being fished.*

(2) *Hook and egg-sinker rig: Slip an egg sinker onto your line and pinch a split shot on to hold the egg sinker in place. A swivel can be used in place of split shot.*

(3) *Slipbobber rig: Tie a bobber stop knot onto your line, and slide it up to the depth level you want to fish. Add a small plastic bead and the slipbobber onto your line. Pinch on split shot for weight.*

(4) *A simple "set" rig: Starting with a three-way swivel, tie your line to one rung and dropper lines of about 8 and 24 inches to the other rungs. Add a bell sinker to the short drop line, and a hook and your bait to the longer line.*

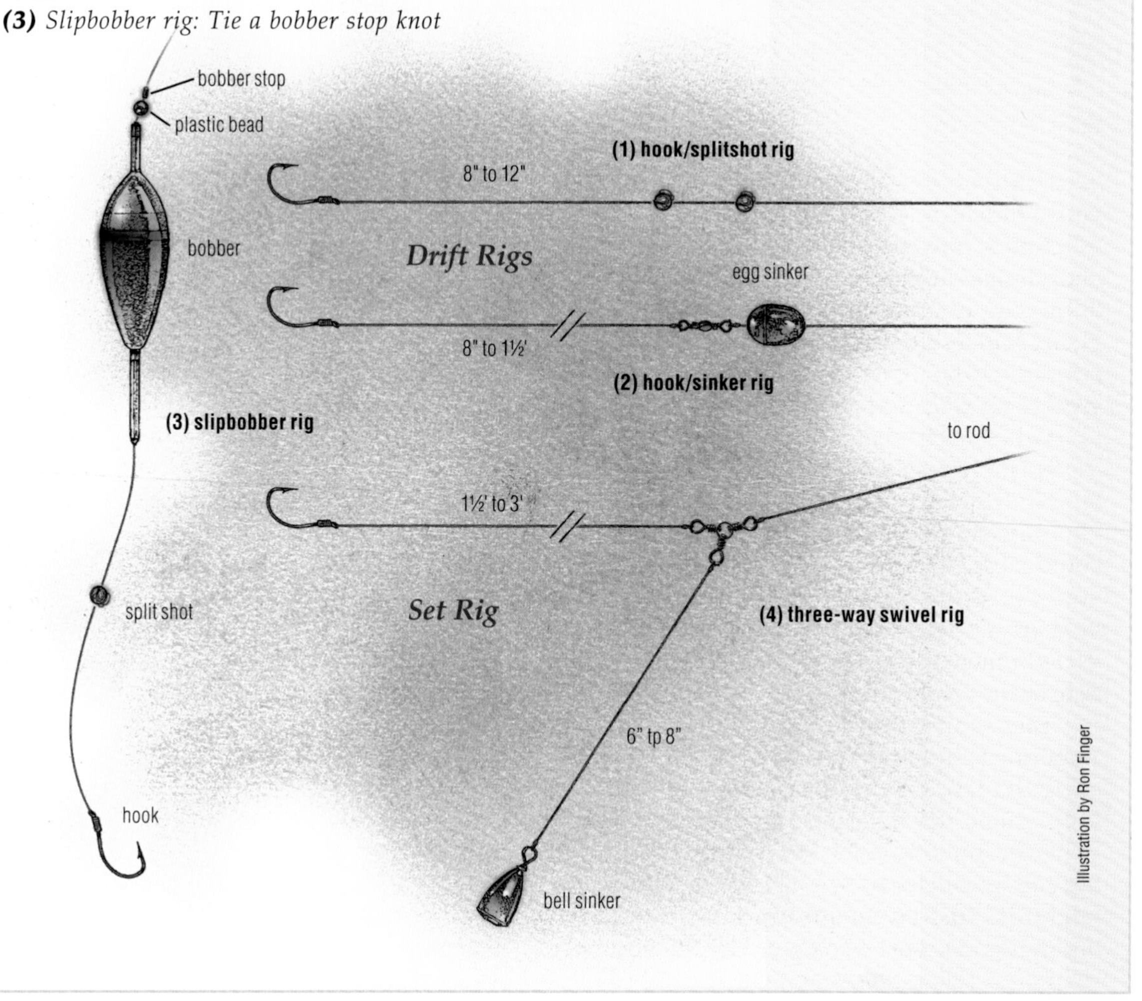

I have over the years and hope to do again as we move forward.

Catfish are popular because they're one of the most remarkable groups of fish in North America. Channel catfish are one of the most widely distributed of all freshwater fish. And they're abundant in a huge number of those environments, yet always challenging to catch because they are unique in their sensory abilities—finely tuned packages of hearing, smelling, tasting, feeling, and vision, superior to most other fish on all sensory counts.

Catfish also grow big and fight hard; indeed, the biggest flathead catfish and blue catfish are among the largest sportfish in North America. Even channel catfish commonly grow to 20 pounds in many environments, a weight approaching the record size of bass and walleyes.

Suggesting that catfish are, in many ways, superior to most other fish isn't being especially proactive in favor of catfish and doesn't denigrate those other fish; it's simply reporting the facts.

For what it's worth, in my mind, all along the way these 30 years I had an opportunity to fight authority (the status quo) and, while authority hasn't always won, it has been darn slow to move most of the time.

Suggesting that catfish are in many ways superior to other fish is just reporting the facts.

Stock-Still For Bass! Page 24
AUGUST | SEPTEMBER 2007
In-Fisherman
CATFISH
On A Summer Breeze
Slash The Ripper PIKE
PLUS!
GIANT CRAPPIES—LESSONS LEARNED
BAIT-SET TROLLING SECRETS
LEADCORE WRINKLES FOR WALLEYES
Turbo-Trolling Walleyes!

Historic Perspectives

It's fitting that this book ends with the author on a small stream. It's also fitting that Toad Smith is part of the story, for theirs is a friendship for the ages. What better way to head into the sunset in catfish country than fishing with a friend? So here's the author writing again about one of his favorite topics, yet it's still clever and full of life. As we end, what might be the most memorable line in this book? Or, what might be a fitting synopsis for all the writing offered here in favor of catfish and catfish anglers? Possibly some variation on the last sentence in the story, Camp Catfish? Zacker, Toad, and Stange have spent another night around a fire on a sandbar, waiting for catfish—and the story ends like this: "Sitting there with first coffee was the quietest part of the day. No one said much until the caffeine got coursing just right. What would this day bring? And another night? Big fish? We always hoped for such a fish or two. Lots of fish? That was always nice. Whatever the new day brought, Camp Catfish was always the best that life could offer at a price we could all afford." That's the heart and soul of this book. That's the fishing we all know and love. Catfishing is the best that life can offer at a price we can all afford.

Illustrations by Larry Tople

CHAPTER 50

AUGUST 2007

Channel Cats On A Summer Breeze

THE STREAM SECTIONS I REMEMBER vividly, having walked them and fished them for more than 40 years, stretch beyond reality into imagination. Sometimes, thinking about where catfish hold so predictably in these waters, I dream of trips to rivers in parts of the country I haven't yet visited.

One recurring curiosity is about fishing the Little Missouri River in western North Dakota. It is because I have long been interested in the history of the Plains Indians; so I wonder about them fishing the river as they camped in those years when they roamed the area.

There's no record of any such fishing, but I get there by leap of fact and faith: We are told about General Crook and General Custer as they pursued the Lakota and other allied Indian factions in the period before and, in Crook's case, after Custer's annihilation at the Little Horn River in late June 1876.

By the time of Custer's death, Crook and his command in pursuit of the Indians from the south, up into Montana, had already been kicked in the pants and pushed back into camp in

Late Summer In Catfish Country — As Good As It Gets!

SHAKE A LITTLE TAIL FEATHER, BABY.

Wyoming on Goose Creek, at the base of the Big Horn Mountains. The record indicates the men fished Goose Creek by various means, including hook and line—but more often in the way the Indians usually fished, by herding the fish with their horses, running them upstream or downstream into shallow areas where "fishermen" waited. Thousands of fish were caught during the weeks Crook was in camp.

Those fish probably were cutthroat trout. The Little Horn (or Little Bighorn), which runs into the Big Horn, which runs into the lower Yellowstone, has channel catfish as well as trout. Custer's men didn't get time to fish, but surely some of the Indians did from time to time—and so it's no stretch to imagine them occasionally fishing the Little Missouri, which also was a fundamental part of their terrain.

I have read that the Little Missouri by late summer often is so shallow that it's difficult to float by canoe. But that's true of many small streams in North America in a typical August, until the September and October rains gather. I know something of the Little Missouri from photos of it set in the surrounding terrain, so it's easy to imagine the stream—the riffles, the holes, the runs—and where the fish would hold.

I could catch a mess of channel cats for an evening meal and overnight encampment on a bank of the Little Missouri. I'm confident because I've not been anywhere else in North America where small-stream fishing isn't the same type of small-stream fishing that I grew up with in Iowa in the 1960s.

The stream I fish most often now in Minnesota is so secluded in certain sections that it wouldn't surprise me if a Pterodactyl flew overhead. This comes to mind because I am watching TV the other night, flipping from channel to channel, and suddenly on a sci-fi channel two time travelers are walking somewhere in open country and a Pterodactyl swoops from above and clips off the top half of one guy, leaving only two legs topped by a part of lower torso spurting blood in great burbling leaps toward the sky. Cool.

The catfish in my Minnesota stream hold in the same places the catfish did when I last fished a small section of the upper Des Moines River in Iowa before my old buddy Toad Smith died. Those fish, meanwhile, held in the same places the fish did in my boyhood streams, Otter Creek, the Little Rock River, the Big Rock River, and the Big Sioux. Well, maybe leave the Big Sioux out. The fishing's almost the same, but you get to tinkering around in little-bit-bigger rivers like the Big Sioux and the fish get spread out a bit more and become more difficult to pin down—the story begins to change.

Well, not that much, come to think of it, especially in the uppermost sections of the river near Sioux Falls. That's a salient point, here. We have creeks and small streams and the smaller upper sections of bigger rivers that all function alike, whether you're in New York, Michigan, Alabama, North Dakota, or Florida. Except in Alabama you might have to watch out for snakes—maybe 'gators too in Florida. Might actually be a rattler or two along the Little Missouri. Have to check on that before I go.

That day now more than 17 years ago, Toad is using 10-pound line on a spinning reel on a 6-foot rod to flip a grasshopper and a classic red-and-white round bobber into likely spots. The hook's an Aberdeen, probably a #4 for big hoppers or a #6 for smaller ones, held down by a lead shot about 6 inches above the bait, which is riding about 1.5 feet below the bobber. Meanwhile, I'm using an ancient 9-foot fiberglass flyrod with an old flyreel. I have a short section of monofilament leader tied with a nail knot to the flyline—and the same terminal setup as Toad's (minus the float).

These are simple yet effective rigging options wherever you fish. You ever see a happy duck walking through the barnyard? A waddle here and there and always a little butt wiggle—a little tail-feather shake—along the way. That's Toad and me walking along that stream that day. It's easy to catch fish in this setting and it feels good. Catch fish, talk smart, have fun—shake a little tail feather, baby.

I'm following Toad as we walk upstream. Our system that day is for him to fish through areas first, making a pitch and a short drift or two with his rig. Then I follow, fishing more thoroughly by dabbling the bait vertically into and through the highest percentage spots.

Given that we're both wading wet in jeans and tennis shoes, I wade right into the stream to reach the critical spots. At that point I hold a bait in a spot until I'm satisfied no one's home—or at least no one's going to bite. Or I make the same

WHITE HAIR FISH
LIKE LAKOTA!
...BUT LEGS
LIKE GHOST.

5-foot drift 5 times in a row in less than a minute, before moving on.

In a mile river section it isn't unusual to find a dozen decent spots with a little bit deeper water and catch a couple dozen fish. It certainly isn't unusual on my Minnesota stream to have a 20-fish afternoon, fishing at a leisurely pace. I fish a little slower these days. Twenty fish doesn't seem that many fewer than twenty-five, like it used to in the old days.

One of the biggest channel cats I've seen caught from a tiny stream was brought to bank by Chef Lucia Watson last year as we filmed an In-Fisherman TV segment about selective harvest. That fish probably weighed 6. Most fish weigh a pound or two. As was the case with Lucia's, most big fish are in portions of streams with close access to lakes or larger rivers. This fish was about two miles upstream from where this little river dumps into a small reservoir.

Another way to walk a stream with a friend is to take turns fishing each spot as you go. Or, if you're in a hurry, you can hopscotch each other, fishing every other hole or good-looking spot along the way. But it's fun to watch someone else fish a spot, anticipating what's going to happen and, perhaps, giving commentary on what they're doing right and wrong. Toad could talk trash with the best of them. I'd listen for a while, catch a catfish, then turn and look at him with all the feigned disdain I could muster: "Bite me!"

Told a story once about fishing with In-Fisherman Publisher Steve Hoffman when he first came to work at In-Fisherman. He was hired originally to be the new editor of *Catfish In-Sider* magazine. We're fishing with Mark Mihalakis of the Cat Tracker bait company, wading wet for catfish in a small stream in August. Me? Well, I'm working, shooting pictures to capture this historic event.

Of course, the fishing's pretty good—easy, actually. And right away, don't you know it, as all those young fellers were wont to do in those days, Hoffman's talkin' trash. "Boys, boys, boys, wouldja look at this, yettanother catfish. And a big 'un," he's saying, with a Howard Cosell canter and swagger in his voice. "Maybe the biggest old catfish to ever come from this or any stream of any size, anywhere in this here country. Just call me King Catfish—the Catfish Kid. Better yet, just call me Mister Catfish—the hottest, the most astute catfish angler of this or any age. Tell you what, if Bill Dance calls, he can just cool his jets; my agent will be in touch."

After a half hour of all that lip and me sweatin' and shootin' photos, well, that kind of uppity was uppity enough. So I say, "Hold it there, Spiffy. Take the camera and shoot me."

"But you don't have a rod," he says.

"Not a problem where I learned to fish, " I say.

So I pick up an old tree branch with an impressive bend. Cut myself 8 feet of line and tie it to the end of the branch. Add a hook. Catch a grasshopper. And in three minutes I'm swingin' a catfish bankside.

"Cost per catfish catch-ratio, four cents," I say. "Let me know when you can break 50 cents and you can be editor in chief." Trash in, trash out.

I have occasionally fished like that before—just picking up a bankside stick and making do. What you find if you do this a few times is that soon you go looking for just a little bit better stick—a little thinner and lighter and maybe longer than the one you have. No surprise then that we do the same thing as we bring today's rods and reels to bear on any fishing situation. We're always looking for a little bit better tool. And even when we've probably found it, we still keep searching and also get pleasure in debating our choices with other anglers who have chosen something different.

But this fishing is easy enough most of the time that just about any rod—reel or no reel—works just fine. Any old canepole works. Some streams have enough cover to require heavier line and a rod with backbone, but many streams in farm country don't have any timber cover at all.

Talk about fun, last year I fished with a Shakespeare Ugly Stik Crappie Pole. They make them 10 and 12 feet long and they break down into 3 or 4 pieces for easy storage. Not a lot of backbone in these sticks, but that's just fine in most cases. I used an 8-foot section of 12-pound line and no reel. Hand-to-hand combat. Little box of hooks in one pocket, a bag of split shot and maybe some cutbait in a plastic bag in my back pocket, just in case I couldn't catch grasshoppers from along the stream bank. Dipbaits work well this time of year, too. The meat from crayfish tails can be dynamite. Carry a wire fish basket with you as you go if you want to save a fish or two for dinner.

Dinner, indeed. The stream section I've been walking the last couple years runs through an old farmstead with a retired couple living in a mildly weathered, classic old three-story house. As of last year they were still doing a beautiful garden. Most days I can see the two of them sitting in the shade on the back porch when I round a bend in the stream. So I go up and sit for a spell, have a Kool Aid, and enjoy the summer breeze as it blows through the trees.

They drive a hard bargain. I skin them several small catfish and they insist that in return I take a few ears of sweet corn and a couple big fat ripe tomatoes. When I get home there will be deep-fried catfish fillets, sliced tomatoes with blue-cheese dressing drizzled on top, and freshly buttered sweet corn sprinkled with salt and cayenne pepper.

That's late summer in catfish country—simply as good as it can get.

{ Historic Perspectives

This book is scheduled for 50 chapters, but just before the press date there is a need for five pages at the end to fill what printers call a “signature.” This book primarily targets the period up to year 2000, but, as we mention before, Stange continues to write about catfish during later years, including the essay found here, which he pens in March 2010, for the June issue. Catfish as food fish continues as one of his favorite topics—and you find him herein taking another unique tactical approach to covering it.

And what about his favorite catfishing after all these years—or, to put it more pressingly, “When it comes down to it, you know it's your last trip, the real end of it all—where are you going and what are you fishing for?”

Stange: “Well, you know how I love to fish for flatheads. But even more I suppose I enjoy the kind of quiet, simple day on a small river, as depicted in the previous chapter.

“You know what? I'd like to do something I haven't done that much—that's always fun. I've caught some big blue cats, but during most of my life they were never that available to me. So give me a week on a body of water with giant blues and give me a chance to put a couple of monsters on the bank. A 150 would be just right. Wouldn't she be a beaut swimming in a big aquarium somewhere?

“But I'd stipulate she could only be on display for one year. Then she'd go back to where she came from. That would be good press on conserving big fish. We have come a fair piece down a long road in that regard. That makes me smile.”

Illustration by Larry Tople

CHAPTER 51

JUNE 2010

Honk If You Love Wild Catfish

A Deep Satisfaction In The Eating!

TO HEAR ZACKER TELL IT BACK IN THE DAY, that being the late 1980s when he was well into his eighth decade, the place to get a piece of perfectly fried catfish in the old days was in one of the river settlements along the Mississippi and Missouri rivers, or in one of the river towns spread across the South. Some of you might remember that Zacker was well traveled during his 20s and early 30s, those being his wild years as a bootlegger and part-time scoundrel of the Robin Hood sort.

He was a catfisherman since childhood, so he sampled his share of catfish meals; and, as you might also know, he spent most of his later years—40 of them—as a commercial fisherman in Nebraska and the Dakotas. Zacker skinned and steaked a million fish. He knew fresh catfish, prime on the fin, or fried perfectly in a pan—crunchy-crisp outside; moist and juicy, tender and tasty inside.

Zacker and I had in common being natural-born hunter-gatherers—and modest amateur cooks of all things hunted and gathered. Indeed, one passion, beyond the ambiance of the fishing, the exhilaration of the pursuit and the catching, has always been a deep satisfaction in the eating.

There must be a rogue fry-fish gene buried deep within many of us. Whenever the country Catholic church in Zacker's area needed a man for a fish fry—never mind that he never got a sliver from a church pew—he not only provided the fish, he oversaw the cooking. The biggest nights in his little town were always Friday night fish fries in the small pavilion in back of the local bar. Again, he put up the fish and oversaw these events where farmers, ranchers, and town-folk from the surrounding area might travel 20 miles to gather. Beer by the bucket flowed along with basket after basket of perfectly deep-fried fish. You brought your own bucket for the keg beer and a basket for the fish as well. The scene and the fresh fish couldn't be any better today than it was then.

I believe hunter-gatherers are hunter-gatherers by nature. Wild asparagus, ramps, fiddleheads, mushrooms of many sorts; elk, deer, and bear; squirrels and rabbits; pheasants, ducks, geese, and grouse—and every fish swimming—Zacker and I sampled just about everything that walks, crawls, or swims.

Anyway. We'd be sitting on the back porch of his little three-room cabin perched on the river bluff, looking out over the high prairie to the north, back down over a vast portion of what had become one of the Missouri River reservoirs to the south. It was a comfortable spot to have a cup of coffee and eat a cookie. No, he didn't bake cookies, but he always seemed to have neighbor ladies dropping by to look after him. Zacker always said that a cookie a day kept the doctor away and also kept one trim. I suspect it had more to do with his prodigious gaggle of girlfriends. He was an old rooster, that one.

Seems one of his favorite stories was about a place he spent time during the wild years. When the whiskey routes from Canada or from out West tightened up because of pressure from the government boys, he headed into the Deep South to tap into the moonshine trade. Zacker always said that Baptists made the best 'shine—and you didn't have to worry about them drinking up the profits.

Long story short, he met a girl and, "drama" being his middle name during those years, there was romance and there were fisticuffs and gunplay with another suitor over the girl—another story. Meanwhile, he on occasion took dinner with the girl and her family at their farm in Mississippi, but only after he had won her father's approval with his fishing—I doubt after all that any father with common sense and a shotgun would normally have let Zacker within many miles of his daughter. But, seems the farm was next to a river so he and the girl secretly stole away to go fishing, the two of them bringing home an impressive catch—a welcome addition to the family larder.

His first meal with the family was catfish fried in traditional southern fashion, which he said, aside from "the sides," really wasn't much different than the way folks cooked a mean meal of fried fish farther North. Zacker always said that if there are turnip greens in heaven, he didn't want to go. You can add chitlins to the list on my behalf.

What brings this all to mind and eventually to story here is that for another project I am Internet searching about eateries that serve catfish and straight-up-the-tracks from outer space comes mention of Taylor Grocery, Mississippi, USA. What the hay, I say, not having thought about it since Zacker passed on. Taylor's the little town that was his hideaway in the South.

So, ticka-ticka-ticka, I type *taylorgrocery.com* onto my Mac and I'm there, transfixed, looking at the old grocery store where Zacker must have bought his tobacco—maybe even looking at the very bench in front of the store where he sat with his sweetie. He always said the girl was as hellcat wild as he was—perish that thought—and they'd race horses bareback from the farm to town to sit on a bench in front of just such a grocery, drinking soda touched up with a toot from the tin flask he carried in his coat pocket. Two wildcats in love.

If you have a look-see the storefront and most of the store has been preserved so today it likely isn't so much different from Zacker's time, which I figure to have been around 1925. There was a giant flood in the region in 1927, and he lost touch with the girl, never again saw Mississippi, although he spent time in Memphis in the early 1930s.

Bringing the story full-circle—and Zacker would have loved this—is that today Taylor Grocery is a laidback restaurant that specializes in superb catfish. Seems the store was built around 1889, and was a dry-goods business, changing hands several times over the next 90 years, until in 1980, a local couple started cooking and serving catfish there.

By the late 1980s Taylor was being called the catfish capitol of a state that takes its catfish seriously. Taylor Grocery continues the tradition today, with bone-in catfish and fillets dusted in a special breading and deep-fried.

Taylor Grocery is a bona fide regional catfish joint. Not only is the food outstanding, the atmosphere completes the show. The place is friendly, the pace laid back, and the preservation of the building and the décor that was this old store connects one with the region the way it was and continues today. The Memphis Blues scene is right next door. If a plate of catfish somehow helps you discover Delta Blues artists like Olga Mathus, Jesse Mae Hemphill, and Memphis Minnie you're the better for it.

What gets lost in the history of the last 150 years is how important catfish was to many of the eateries of the times. We easily picture a cowboy riding off the range to get a steak at the Longhorn, but closer to the truth in many regions was the common working man walking into Momma Kate's for a catfish sandwich—or purchasing just enough fresh fish from a cooler wagon on a Friday or Saturday after work to fry it up at home.

Besides, cowboy longhorn in the heyday was high priced and most cuts were tough as leather. Even the grass-fed cows of Zacker's day were still relatively costly. But whether 1860 or 1930, catfish was cheap and universally as tender and flavorful then as it is today.

Taylor Grocery epitomizes the hundreds and hundreds of catfish restaurants across North America, especially across the South. A Catfish Fry Line of sorts starts at the Iowa-Missouri border and extends jaggedly across country. Well-cooked catfish is catfish wherever it swims in hot oil. But it's nice to have a little more original regional flair.

You couldn't do better than Middendorf's of Akers, Louisiana, just north of New Orleans. They do a plate of thin-stripped deep-fried catfish that looks incredibly delicious. The restaurant goes through 2 tons of catfish each week, shipped butcher fresh from Mississippi.

Texans are as serious about their catfish as they are about their barbeque. Floyd's Cajun Seafood is a hot spot in Houston. Catfish Mike's is in Katy, a Dallas suburb; Huck's is in Denison, just north of Dallas; and there are hundreds of other restaurants in towns large and small.

In the North, South, East, or West, the principle side dishes are hushpuppies and fries; other options vary from fried okra in Texas, to corn bread and pickled onions in Alabama. But the heart of catfish cooking remains pretty much the same—catfish dusted in a "secret" breading and panfried or deepfried. Or catfish dusted in seasoned flour, then dipped in an egg-milk wash before being dusted again in a crunchy exterior covering like corn meal or Panko breadcrumbs, before being fried up.

It is, however, a rare place that today serves wild catfish. One noteworthy exception is Joe Tess Place in Omaha, Nebraska. They're actually most famous for their deep-fried carp sandwich.

I was about to say that farm-raised fish are grain fed and therefore a predictable product to work with in restaurants. Zacker tasted farm-raised catfish and always said it didn't taste like "real" catfish. He considered it bland. It is mild but I think delicious.

Anglers who take home wild fish to eat have advantages over folks who depend on farm fish. Most importantly we know exactly how much time passes before they go into the pan. Fish doesn't age well, so it's best as fresh as possible and should be frozen if it's going to be stored for more than about three days. Fish in many grocery stores routinely sets for much longer than that—and some restaurants only get fish in once a week.

Wild fish—free-range catfish—are more distinctive tasting and folks like Zacker can tell the seasonal difference in the taste, as well as differences in fish from different bodies of water. It's no different than seasonal difference and regional difference in the taste of wild oysters, to use just one example.

We also have three different catfish species to choose from, while all farm-raised fish are channel catfish. I have almost never had bad channel catfish, but I have caught stream catfish that had mealy flesh. Those fish need to be discarded at the cleaning table. And I have caught fish from small streams that were old males that weighed only a couple pounds. Those fish have flesh that's coarsely marbled and tough.

Wild channel cats are delicious, but of the three primary catfish species they tend to become stronger and tougher faster than blue cats and flatheads. It's usually best to harvest channel cats that weight less than about 5 pounds.

THE GOOD TIMES
IN FISHING CONNECT
US ALL...

By comparison, flathead catfish are one of the finest of all fish on the table, and they are lean and tasty at all sizes, although I quit harvesting fish larger than about 10 pounds at least 20 years ago. The big fish deserve to get even bigger, remarkable sportfish that they are.

Blue cats seem to stay tender and delicious in sizes up to at least 15 pounds. I haven't eaten many fish larger than that, so I'm no expert on the bigger fish—although I think fish that big should also be released to sustain high-quality fishing.

Zacker was a stickler about trimming up his catfish fillets. He removed any yellowish flesh off the top of any fillet and trimmed the reddish lateral line flesh off the outside of the fillet. Then if the fillets are from fish bigger than about two pounds, he would score the top of the fillet on the side where the ribs were by making 4 or 5 two-inch-long diagonal cuts about a half-inch deep into the fillet or portions of the fillet if, say, the fillet was cut into three portions. He also scored smaller fish that were kept bone in by making two cuts down to the bone on each side of the fish. This adds a visual touch and also helps the fillet or piece of bone-in fish crisp up when it's fried. He also usually marinated fish in a little milk for a half hour before cooking.

As I sat to write I wondered how many of you are just like me—just like Zacker? We always fished better when we were out there with intent to harvest selectively—a meal of fresh catfish evermore on the mind. Surely over the years we've taught you enough about the actual fishing that you can allow me pause to tell a few stories to inspire you to get out fishing—instead of teaching you any more about how to fish? Zacker always approved of a good yarn. He'd read one of mine and give me a nod: "Good man," he'd say. "Embellish, but don't exaggerate."

After more than 50 years of catfishing, and at 60-mumble years of age, you sometimes find yourself daydreaming, whether writing an essay or walking along a river. You round a river bend, crows are raising a ruckus in the distance, probably harassing an owl; a farmer's working in a field nearby, and gives a friendly wave; the river's running quietly past a timber tangle you just know is going to hold catfish—and the mind tumbles from the present to times past. You've been here before and it was good and it will be again for those that follow. It's a life-long road we travel. The good times in fishing connect us all, and so does the privilege that goes with being able to harvest a meal of fish.

The bumper stickers on my truck read, "Honk If You Love Wild Catfish!" And, "What Would Zacker Do?"